# THE

# CONTENDER

# THE

# CONTENDER

*The Story of Marlon Brando*

## WILLIAM J. MANN

HARPER

*An Imprint of* HarperCollins*Publishers*

HarperCollins books may be purchased for educational, business, or sales promotional use. For information, please email the Special Markets Department at SPsales@harpercollins.com.

FIRST EDITION

Designed by Fritz Metsch

Frontispiece photograph by Philippe Halsman/Magnum Photos

Library of Congress Cataloging-in-Publication Data has been applied for.

ISBN 978-0-06-242764-9

19 20 21 22 23    LSC    10 9 8 7 6 5 4 3 2 1

FOR TIM, AS ALWAYS

# CONTENTS

# THE

# CONTENDER

# THE MAN ON THE WITNESS STAND

THE LARGE OLD man in the black turtleneck was asked to raise his hand and swear to God. "No," the man replied, "I will not swear on God, because I don't believe in the conventional sense and in this nonsense. What I will swear on is my children and my grand-children."

Unfazed, the judge told the clerk to read another oath. "Will you solemnly affirm," the clerk tried again, "that the testimony you are about to give will be the whole truth and nothing but the truth—"

"I do indeed," the man interrupted, impatient to get this done.

The courtroom hushed as the man turned and wedged himself onto the witness stand—no easy task, given that he weighed somewhere above three hundred pounds. Then he was asked to state his name.

"Marlon Brando," the man said—adding, half a second later, "Junior."

The cameras, as always, were on him.

THE STORY OF Marlon Brando Junior does not really begin here, in this sad, wretched courthouse in Santa Monica, California, on February 28, 1991. Brando's story might better be said to have orig-inated in the American Midwest, where he was born, or in New York, where he first rose to prominence. But Brando had been challenging false gods his entire life, refusing to swear by con-vention and calling out nonsense everywhere he went, from the

Hollywood Hills to the South Pacific to the arrondissements of Paris. So, while this moment in Santa Monica, with Brando sitting sideways on the witness stand (the only way he fit), is neither the beginning nor the end of our story, it is one way into it, as the camera draws in close on a sad, broken, yet ever-defiant old man.

Brando was testifying on the third day of a sentencing hearing for his thirty-two-year-old son, Christian, who had pled guilty to voluntary manslaughter. The man whom Christian had shot on the night of May 16, 1990, at his father's house high above Los Angeles on Mulholland Drive, had been Dag Drollet, the father of his sister Cheyenne's baby. Six months pregnant at the time, Cheyenne had told her brother that Drollet beat her. "I didn't mean to do it," Christian cried to his father, insisting he'd only been trying to scare the young man, that he'd thought the gun's safety catch was on. Brando tried to revive Drollet with mouth-to-mouth resuscitation. But paramedics pronounced Drollet dead.

Christian was initially charged with first-degree murder. For the next ten months, the case was a circus of lawyers and witnesses, one of the first big celebrity murder trials to receive cable news coverage and "one of the most publicized criminal cases in Los Angeles history," according to the *Los Angeles Times*. Cheyenne was revealed to be suffering from schizophrenia; her history of accidents and institutionalizations was bannered in the tabloids. The media coverage made the tragedy a thousand times worse for everyone involved. For years, Brando had railed against such "celebrity peephole publicity," as he called it. Now he watched helplessly as his family deteriorated around him. Cheyenne, emotionally fragile, was spirited out of the country, away from prosecutors who wanted to put her on the stand. Back in her native Tahiti, the twenty-year-old woman gave birth to a son, Tuki, then tried to kill herself. "Misery has come to my house," Brando said, his voice raspy, his eyes bloodshot, to the reporters who gathered on Mulholland Drive.

Eventually, Christian pled guilty to the lesser charge of man-slaughter. Still, his father feared he'd get twenty years. On the stand, Brando made one point clear: "This is the *Marlon* Brando case." If the defendant had not been the son of the man widely regarded as the greatest American actor of all time, but "black or Mexican or poor," the media "wouldn't be in this courtroom."

Black and Mexican and poor lives, Brando charged, mattered little to the media. For most of his career, he'd used his fame to draw attention to racism and injustice, decrying the media indifference when young men of color were imprisoned at rates higher than those for white men. Now Brando's celebrity had turned against him. Fame, Brando believed, was an amoral beast, one he'd been wrestling with for forty-four years without ever managing to weaken its hold. He hadn't wanted fame, and forever mourned the anonymity once so dear to him. "I can't convey how discomforting it is not to be able to be a normal person," Brando once lamented, a statement that goes a long way toward allowing us to understand him.

Brando was never like other celebrities, with their gazes forever outward. He was a thinker, an observer, an examiner of himself and the world, with the goal of figuring out both. For much of his time in the public eye, Brando had served as the nation's critic, pointing out society's injustices and failures. Now, trying to convince a judge to show mercy to his son, he was about to reveal some of his own.

"I led a wasted life," he said on the stand, a statement that surprised many. For, while Brando's life had often been controversial and contentious, few would have called it "wasted." This was the man who had revolutionized acting! Yet Brando was speaking personally, in a regretful tone rarely heard in previous interviews, where he'd usually been in control, needling or bamboozling his interviewers. To the court, Brando said he'd "chased a lot of women" and fought bitterly with Christian's mother, and failed to shield his son from their hostility. Shifting that enormous body,

Brando admitted, "Perhaps I failed as a father. There were things I could have done differently."

*Things I could have done differently.* Back through the years, that statement reverberated. So many things could have been different. Brando's first dream back in Illinois had been to be a drummer. He lived for rhythm, he said, and for a while, he'd also considered a career as a dancer. Brando came to despise acting. Many times, he wanted to quit and do something else, something he found more meaningful and fulfilling, such as political activism. He might have been happier if he had done so, more content; he also might have caroused less, committed himself more to his work and his family. But he hadn't. And it was too late to do things over now.

Never a man to indulge the vanity of regret for very long, here on the stand, Brando was, at last, forced to consider it. The pain on his face flashed intermittently, like a neon sign: sometimes visible and unbearable; other times blank and dark. He gripped the railing of the witness stand. "I did the best I could," he said. He was crying.

Some in the courtroom were moved by Brando's words. Others hardened against them. "He was giving to Christian the one thing he knew how to do best, his acting talent," said his friend George Englund, from whom he was later estranged. "But this wasn't the greatest actor of his time seizing everyone's imagination. This was a former champion, overweight, out of shape, sloppy with technique."

The family of Dag Drollet, whom Brando addressed next, also thought he was acting. "I cannot continue with the hate in your eyes," Brando said, turning to face them. "I'm sorry with my whole heart." He delivered a long apology in French, their primary language, his tears falling. Yet Drollet's father remained unmoved.

Was Brando acting on the stand? He liked to say that everyone acts. "We act every single day," he once said, "to bring about a certain outcome, to ensure something we care about comes true." So, if he loved his son—and he did, very much—Brando would of course try to give the very best performance he was capable of giving on the stand. Wasn't Dag Drollet's father trying to be equally persuasive when he stood to speak, hoping to convince the judge in the opposite direction, to sentence Christian to the harshest term possible? Two different intents, two identical strategies. Acting doesn't mean the emotions aren't real; that was always Brando's point. For fifty years, the best Marlon Brando performances were those that layered his own deeply felt experience onto his brilliant imagination. So why was Drollet called true and Brando false?

For much of his life and career, it had been this way. When, as a little boy, Brando wasn't able to sit still in school, his teachers decided he must have no interest in learning, when nothing could have been further from the truth. When he refused to dutifully pay homage to Hollywood's gossip columnists, the guardians of Screenland concluded he must be arrogant and difficult, when what he was attempting was to be genuine and honest. When he marched for civil rights, the media felt certain he must be doing so for the personal publicity. When he expressed creative concerns on a movie set, directors and producers figured he must be brokering for more money, when money was usually the very last thing Brando was interested in. Doubting Brando's sincerity on the stand was just one more chapter in the same old story.

In truth, he was devastated by the calamity that had engulfed his family, and torn up by fears that his own failures had contributed to it. In the privacy of his home, Brando uttered a cri de cœur into his tape recorder, which served as a sort of audio diary: "What a life. Why does it have to be this way?"

MARLON BRANDO CHANGED the way actors think about their craft. He made acting natural, honest, personal. There is near-universal agreement that he was the greatest. Brando's impact on the culture at large is nearly as significant, challenging and encoding our ideas of masculinity and sexuality. And at a time when it was de facto forbidden for celebrities to do so, Brando used the platform of his fame to confront some of the most crucial moral issues of the last century, daring to call out the deeply rooted racism in the American psyche.

He hadn't wanted to be an actor. It was never his dream. He'd been an aimless kid, sent to drama school upon the advice of his sister, because acting in student productions was the only thing (other than sports) that had ever brought him any praise. Almost immediately, he was acclaimed a genius by his drama teacher, the great Stella Adler. Her faith in him was justified first on the stage, where Brando played Stanley Kowalski in Tennessee Williams's *A Streetcar Named Desire*, and then in a series of film roles that inspired a generation of actors and raised the bar for what could be achieved on the screen. Brando was heralded as the American Hamlet, the one Yank who could dislodge the British grip on classical acting greatness. In one fell swoop, he relegated Olivier, Gielgud, and Richardson to the past.

But Brando wasn't interested in that sort of acclaim. The major conundrum any assessment of his life and career must face is this: the talent that others revered in him excited very little interest on his part. The acting historian Foster Hirsch called him "a genius who fought against his genius." Brando's real passion was reserved for his fights for social justice. Acting, he came to believe, was largely irrelevant to the pressing issues of his time: racism, war, civil rights, capital punishment. Moreover, he resented working in the puritanical, mercenary world of the American film industry. He was a gazelle penned up in the Hollywood zoo.

For about five years, from the end of the 1950s to the early 1960s, Brando tried to play the Hollywood game by its rules. That's a fact often forgotten or overlooked. Those five years are the exception that proves the rule of his rebellion. When he could take it no more—when the powers that were mutilated the one film

he directed, *One-Eyed Jacks*, into which he'd poured his lifeblood—
Brando bolted over the fence and, from then on, did things on his
own. If he made a movie, it was almost always for the money—
not out of any personal rapacity, but as a way to support his
self-sustaining, ecologically friendly home in Tahiti and his ever-
growing family, made up of children from various mothers and
the offspring of friends.

That Brando would work for the money and not for the role
troubled those who remembered him as the game-changer of *A
Streetcar Named Desire* and *On the Waterfront*—and as the single
American, up to that point, to master *Julius Caesar*. Yet, there he
was, in a brief cameo as Jor-El of Krypton in *Superman* (1978), wearing a big *S* on his chest. The film's star, Christopher Reeve, complained that Brando was indifferent about his scene. How sad it
was, the young actor said, to be as big as Brando "and not give a
damn." What Marlon gave a damn about was the three-million-
plus dollars he earned for two minutes of screen time. That would
go a long way toward keeping him solvent, and pay for another
generation of turtles to be released into the lagoon off Teti'aroa,
the atoll he owned in the South Pacific.

For those like Reeve who viewed the art of acting and the enterprise of filmmaking as sacred things, Brando was an apostate.
After *Last Tango in Paris* in 1972, he admitted he no longer challenged himself as an actor, while peers such as Paul Scofield and
Paul Newman still burned up stage and screen. Even Richard Burton, who also dabbled in his share of fluff, at least came back with
one mighty, late-career triumph in *Equus*. Brando, meanwhile, just
got fat.

"Brando is certainly regarded as the most widely known case
of a film star selling out," film critic and historian David Shipman
wrote soon after the tragedies of Brando's children had dominated the headlines. Full of indignation and censure, Shipman
wrote, "As a young man, Marlon Brando was renowned for his

acting. Conceivably he is better known now for the California trial in which Cheyenne's half brother Christian was sentenced for killing the young man whose child she was carrying." In his piece excoriating the star, Shipman tut-tutted over how many women Brando had gone through and how many children he had sired, as well as decrying "the ill-judged and self-indulgent performances of his later years." The difference between the early Brando and the later Brando, Shipman averred, was "indecent."

Brando admitted that he sometimes felt like "the Congressman with his hand in the till" when he took high-paying, undemanding roles in such films as *Superman* or *The Formula*. But what was he "selling out" exactly, and to whom? Almost from the start of Brando's career, some people seemed to believe they were owed something from him and that he was being stingy in paying it back. Because they'd held such high opinions of him, they were angry when he didn't meet, or share, their expectations. People such as Shipman bemoaned Brando's not taking seriously what, in their view, was more important than anything else: *acting*. But his priorities were different: Teti'aroa, his children's education, Martin Luther King Jr.'s Southern Christian Leadership Conference, the standoff at Wounded Knee.

What's significant is that, even though he was lauded, Brando had never been beloved. Even at the height of his box-office power, in the late 1950s, he was always a little edgy and dangerous; he was never Jimmy Stewart or Rock Hudson. Brando was a rebel, overturning the applecart of Hollywood expectations. Critics and the public liked that—so long as, in the process, he gave them *Guys and Dolls*, *Désirée*, and *Sayonara*. But when he stopped giving them those sorts of crowd-pleasing films, his rebel shtick got old. And the media jumped at the chance to tear him down.

For a brief moment, in the early 1970s, Brando came roaring back into favor, when *The Godfather* turned into the biggest movie of all time. But then he turned down the Academy Award for it—

how ungrateful could he be? Worse, he sent a Native American woman to the ceremony to refuse it for him, and she had the gall to insult Hollywood to its face, claiming that all those dead Indians in John Ford movies were somehow something to be ashamed of. From that moment on, for much of the media and the public, Marlon Brando became a grotesque, symbolized by how fat he got and the scandals of his children. His friendship with Michael Jackson made him tabloid-ready. Brando, the conventional wisdom went, was, for all his talent, eccentric, erratic, narcissistic, and hypocritical. For much of the 1990s, and even after his death in 2004, this was the image that predominated in articles and books, including the one major biography, by Peter Manso. Only a few people, such as Jack Nicholson and Martin Scorsese, spoke out to suggest otherwise.

TIMES HAVE CHANGED. It's a very different world now than it was a decade or more ago. We can see Brando in another way—as not just the great actor but also a whistleblower on the culture, a Cassandra warning us of what was to come.

In a world where everything is hyped and hawked, where every available space, even the risers of subway steps, is claimed for advertising, Brando's admonitions against the monetization of the culture, voiced frequently from the 1960s on, feel extremely prescient. Money drove him only so far as it could be useful. Brando often asked to be paid up front, when he could have made much more money waiting for the back end. He wanted only enough to pay his bills and keep the turtles breeding. "After you've got enough," he insisted, "money doesn't matter." He refused to be sold, he said, "like Kleenex or Dial soap."

He was speaking the obvious but also, for his time, the unmentionable: one was not supposed to tell the emperor (Hollywood, the media, American culture) that he had no clothes. When Brando appeared on Larry King's talk show after his memoir came out in 1994, he acknowledged that he was there to hustle, but that so, in fact, was the host. When King professed not to understand, Brando got impatient: "You know perfectly well what I mean." Every ten minutes or so, King cut to a commercial break; CNN had been touting the Brando interview for days, to build ratings. One can only wonder what Brando would have had to say about the ubiquitous clickbait of online news and advertising today.

Success as an artist, Brando lamented, was measured by money. "When I was young," he said, "I never understood that it was a matter of business. I believed that there was a measure of sincerity. But then I came to learn that everything today has a price tag. I don't think Van Gogh had a price tag. I think he painted because he had to paint." An artist is, of course, entitled to make money, and Brando didn't claim otherwise. What he struggled with was the conflation of art and commerce, a phenomenon he first observed in the 1960s and watched mushroom beyond all expectation into the twenty-first century. "I don't know if there are any artists left now," he said. "They are so degraded and so confused by the mercantile mind."

Of course, by speaking this way, he left himself open to charges of hypocrisy: he made many more *Supermans*, movies unworthy of his talent but that paid him big bucks. Yet here's the difference: Brando did not then climb aboard the bandwagon to market the product as if it were the greatest thing since frozen dinners. He'd always balked at playing the huckster, something he associated with his abusive, traveling salesman father. On the rare occasions he was roped into promoting a film he knew was inferior, such as *Morituri* (1965), he turned the publicity on its ear. When a reporter said she was eager to see the picture, Brando advised against it: "It might be an absolutely terrible film; you don't know."

What he was doing was upsetting a carefully ordered protocol, one designed to maximize profits and endow those who played by the rules with cultural influence and standing. Award shows,

Brando groused, weren't about honoring the best: "They're about making more money, and about Hollywood telling itself that it's important." He asked why optometrists didn't have awards for "creating inventive, arresting, admirable eyeglass frames." Every time he turned on the television, Brando marveled, there was another celebrity award show, and this was in 1979: by 2018–19, there were several hundred award presentations during the period of December to April, all designed to add more revenues to the film's or show's bottom line. "And while they're giving out these awards," Brando remarked, "they pat themselves on the back, calling each other geniuses, and they really believe it, too."

The most egregious form of hucksterism, however, from Brando's point of view, was the "peephole" kind—the more intimate and salacious, the bigger the return on the dollar. The smallest details of a celebrity's life became grist for the mill. "If you smoke the grime from your navel, that's big news," he quipped. "That's important." Twenty years later, he saw the full evolution of that prurient impulse when the media turned their glare on his family during Christian's arrest, sending the ratings for the new, round-the-clock cable news shows skyrocketing.

Brando charged the media with focusing on pop culture ephemera at the expense of issues of substance, thus allowing the public to avoid what was really going on—which, to his eyes, was "the rich getting richer, the poor poorer"; racism becoming "more deeply entrenched"; and a partisan news media "making a mockery of the fairness doctrine." He asked what happened when that sort of "bullshit is all that's written about, all that people care about?"

Even he would probably have been surprised by the answer.

THIS BOOK ATTEMPTS to see Brando's life, career, choices, and actions in a new light. In 1973, his refusal of an Oscar was perceived as the ultimate insult to the moviegoing public by an eccentric egotist. Yet, forty-five years later, during the #OscarsSoWhite controversy, Jada Pinkett Smith found affirmation for her own decision to boycott the Oscars by watching a clip of Sacheen Littlefeather refusing Brando's award. Today, calling out Hollywood's racism is no longer an extremist act. In the 1960s, Brando's protests against racial segregation and discrimination—he was arrested at least once—were condemned by some as needlessly provocative. Now, in the era of Black Lives Matter, they seem the very least someone in Brando's position could have done during that period of widespread injustice.

In reconsidering Marlon Brando, I've had to go back to the beginning, reviewing the ways the press and the public responded to him, and why they responded in those ways. The press was often hostile to Brando, but it could also be obsequious, especially in the later years, after he was lauded as the Greatest. Dick Cavett, usually a resourceful interviewer, appeared nervous sitting so close to the legend, actually stammering, "If at any time I get into things you don't want to talk about, give me a signal." There were times when Brando was allowed a pass when he appeared in inferior films just because he was Brando. But there were also times when he was treated more harshly than others because of his political activism. I realized quickly that cutting through the layers of other people's perceptions, which formed so much of Brando's narrative over the years, would take some work.

In truth, nearly everyone who's written about him has gotten him wrong. The exceptions have been very recent. Susan Mizruchi's *Brando's Smile* and Stevan Riley's documentary film *Listen to Me Marlon* are insightful explorations of his life and work. But nearly everything else has missed Brando's story in both the details and the bigger picture—a particularly regrettable situation for a man whom most agree was the supreme American actor. For example, there's the myth, endlessly repeated, that Brando was a Method actor, when in fact he loathed the very concept and found those who used the term pretentious. There's the legend that he walked away from *One-Eyed Jacks*, his sole directorial effort, when that wasn't the case at all; *Jacks*, a remarkable film, is finally given its due here. There's also been the suggestion that Brando was sexually conflicted, or a repressed, guilt-ridden homosexual, when in fact he was a man utterly at ease with his fluid sexuality, someone who blithely disregarded the binaries of love and gender decades before anyone could have described him as doing so.

Finally, Brando's acting, as great and as important as it remains, is not the most interesting thing about him, though previous chroniclers have often resisted that truth. After watching Brando's interview with Larry King, *New Yorker* columnist Harold Brodkey haughtily asserted that the screen clips of the actor's career King showed had "said more about him" than his rambling banter with the host. In 1973, *Time* magazine rued the fact that Brando always seemed to be looking for something "that is permanently true" for which he could "lay down his life," when, in fact, the magazine insisted, he'd already found it: "his art." Outside observers like these often presumed to know more, or better, than Brando himself.

It's time to see his story the way he did. Acting came easily to Brando; he never needed to work at it. Like Barbra Streisand, who just opened her mouth and sang without ever having a singing lesson, it was hard for Brando to view something that came so naturally to him as a great gift, let alone genius. Praised for his acting versatility, he recoiled: "You can say the same thing about a hula hoop." His statement that everybody acts wasn't just a philosophy; it was also an attenuation of his talent, which he was always eager to downplay. "Acting comes easily to everybody," he insisted. "All I've done is just simply learned how to be aware of the process."

Brando's disillusionment with the exploitation and mercantilism of the American film industry grew in direct proportion to his political awareness; once he got involved in political causes, acting became for him "a fundamentally childish thing." The boy who had been despaired of by his teachers and derided as a "ne'er-do-well" by his father wanted to matter in the world, not as an actor but as someone who made a difference, who helped right wrongs. Working on behalf of those with less privilege than he had seemed to be an antidote to the sense of alienation he'd experienced in his own life. "He felt very protective toward people who were denied a voice," said his friend and executor, Avra Douglas. "He just had such enormous empathy."

Working as an actor, to Brando's mind, when people were being refused fundamental rights or put at risk of death was shamefully self-indulgent; it was "quitting acting," he said, that would be "the mark of maturity." After his emotionally exhausting experience on *Last Tango in Paris*, Brando decided that he'd henceforth reserve his passion for political causes and make his performances demonstrations of technique, not true feeling. And technique, Brando insisted, wasn't art. "We have somehow substituted craft for art and cleverness for craft," he complained. With one interviewer, he tried to force an admission about what, to his mind, was plain: "In your heart of hearts," Brando insisted, "you know perfectly well that movie stars aren't artists."

On other occasions, however, he could be more conciliatory about the work he did: "I don't put acting down," he said. "I resent people who put it up." That seems closer to his true feelings. There were times (*A Streetcar Named Desire, On the Waterfront, The Godfather*, and others) when Brando was truly engaged and invigorated by the process of creating a character. And even in the worst of his films, there's always something worthwhile to discern from what he does on the screen, no matter if he derided it as "mere" technique. "Even though he mocked acting," Foster Hirsch observed, "he never gave an indifferent performance."

THERE WAS ANOTHER conundrum I needed to resolve in order to understand Marlon Brando. How could this man, so empathic and solicitous toward the underprivileged, have treated so many of the women in his life so callously? Rita Moreno's memoir reveals a decade-long affair of manipulation and deceit, and she is just one woman among many who could have told that story. Only by understanding Brando as a survivor of trauma could I put his behavior in perspective. Both his parents were alcoholics. His father was physically and emotionally abusive, and his mother was emotionally distant and neglectful. Brando grew up anxious, self-doubting, sometimes depersonalized, easily depressed, and even more easily provoked to anger. Survivors of trauma feel new traumas very intensely, doing whatever they can to protect themselves. Brando's depressions and rages can be fully understood only in this light; his inability to commit and to love, or to allow a woman into his life as an equal, grew out of his eternal desire to find his mother's love and then reject her for hurting him. His turbulent childhood left lasting damage.

Yet, while Marlon was, without question, a world-class heartbreaker, it's important to point out that there are no stories of unwanted sexual contact. None of Marlon's leading ladies ever made complaints of this kind, not even Maria Schneider, his *Last Tango in Paris* costar, who, when raising serious issues of sexual exploitation on the set, always defended Marlon. When, on rare occasions, a woman wasn't interested in him, Marlon withdrew his attentions. After his secretary Alice Marchak first came on board, he tried to sleep with her, but when she made clear that would never happen, Marlon backed off—and respected her more for it.

But here's something else that often gets overlooked or, even worse, derided: unlike so many others with his history, Brando proactively attempted to understand and overcome his trauma. Sometimes, in his darkest moments, he succumbed to victimhood. But for the most part, he resisted it, seeking help and transformation through psychotherapy, meditation, and other consciousness-raising practices. Journalists and biographers sometimes ridiculed his efforts, portraying him and his various therapists as eccentric or flaky. But how many never attempt to understand their problems at all?

Success, to Brando, meant "understanding yourself." Success, as it was defined by Hollywood, held no appeal to him. This was a man who was hailed as the greatest in his field, a two-time Oscar winner, a box-office champ, the first actor to get a million dollars a picture. He made it to the top of the heap—and when he got there, he found success didn't have "the fiber," as he told talk show host David Susskind. He spent his life searching for things that *did* have the fiber, those permanently true things for which he could lay down his life. He wanted to feel as if he were—to play on his famous line from *On the Waterfront*—a "contender," someone who mattered, someone who had fought the good fight. He wanted to feel as if he had made a difference, left a mark, and not just on acting. What he did *not* want to be was an "unthinker," the way he described those people who never examined themselves or their place in the world.

This is the man I have attempted to understand.

WHEN RANDOM HOUSE bought Brando's memoir for five million dollars in 1992, the publishing company promised that the truth behind the myth would finally be revealed. Because Brando wasn't disciplined enough to write his own book, he hired the respected journalist Robert Lindsey to interview him. Lindsey would then have the tapes transcribed and stitch something together. Those transcripts reveal the hell Lindsey went through in the process. Brando was constantly interrupting him, playing the contrarian, taking issue with his coauthor's questions and, in the process, evading the point of what Lindsey was asking. To wit:

"The common perception," Lindsey observed, "was that after your big hit—"

Brando cut him off. "You said the key word, 'common.' Whenever you use 'common knowledge,' or 'common perception,' it's not definitive."

Lindsey tried again. "It's been written that—"

"It's been written." Brando sighed. "God spare me."

Lindsey kept going: "—you made a lot of shitty movies in the sixties. And that *The Godfather* was a comeback. Is that true?"

"I don't know what that means," Brando replied. "I can't—it's so coarsely defined that I don't know how to respond to it."

It's a wonder Lindsey got anything at all. Brando was making a point, however: words matter. The stories about him had always been told a certain way, and he'd almost never agreed with the premises behind them. He certainly didn't want to see those old talking points (some used by movie studios to build him up and some by columnists to tear him down) regurgitated for his own memoir. Warning his coauthor against relying on the "morgue files," which were stuffed with clippings from newspapers and magazines, Brando declared, "They are almost always inaccurate, and they do a great injustice to the facts."

Facts matter. And that's why those unedited transcripts between Brando and Lindsey are far more revealing than the final published memoir, *Songs My Mother Taught Me*. In the transcripts, Brando often goes on for pages about something seemingly tangential to the conversation, yet embedded in that soliloquy are insights into the man and the way he saw the world. Lindsey did his best to clean up Brando's rambling syntax; he reordered many of his stories in an attempt to fit them into a cohesive whole, but in doing so, he lost a lot of his subject's irreverence and, often, the point he was trying to make. ("Whenever anyone would say to Marlon, 'I loved your book,'" Avra Douglas recalled, "he'd reply, 'I didn't write it.'") I've used these original transcripts to form my own, very different impression of my subject; as often as possible, I've used Brando's own, unedited words to tell his story.

Of course, the question arises: can we trust what he tells us?

"I only mean about forty percent of what I say," Brando once told
Truman Capote. Even as far back as 1948, he told Jessica Tandy, his
costar in the stage version of *A Streetcar Named Desire*, "Seldom do I
say what I mean and I say little because of it." Fifty years later, his
secretary, Alice Marchak, observed the same thing: "Marlon did
not tell the truth if a lie would suffice." So how could I trust what
he said?

The truth, as it turned out, was easy to discern. Brando lied
when it suited him, which was usually to get out of making small
talk with boring people or to extract himself from uncomfortable
situations. These were never big lies, only silly ones, such as blaming Western Union for his being late to a rehearsal with Tandy.
Other times, Brando might lie in order to end an interview, giving
the reporter what he or she wanted to hear. He also, sometimes,
lied to get a rise out of people. He appeared to be trying to shock
Robert Lindsey with the explicit details of his sexual adventures,
which seem at times at least slightly embellished.

Yet Brando never lied when he truly wanted to make a point,
or when he perceived the person he was speaking with as someone who honestly wanted to know what he thought. The interviews to stay away from, I learned, were those where Brando was
clearly uncomfortable and therefore more likely to dissemble or be
misquoted. I passed over much of the braggadocio in the original
transcripts with Lindsey, though I took note of the general theme.
Instead, I focused on those times when my subject was talking
about things that deeply mattered to him: personal integrity and
responsibility, civil rights and social justice, the search for love and
satisfaction, the siren call of success. Then I found him to be completely sincere.

I take a decidedly more sympathetic approach to Brando than
some earlier biographers, though I'm not an apologist: I catalog his
flaws and inconsistencies, and they are considerable. I just don't see
those flaws and inconsistencies as evidence of a persistent pattern

of malicious hypocrisy or unbridled narcissism, as other writers, from the 1950s to the 1990s, have done. Instead, I see a man who was trying to do his best, not always succeeding, but always, always trying. Enough time has passed by now that we can stand back and reassess this cultural icon. It's time to see and hear Brando the way he was trying to make himself seen and heard.

Perhaps, then, we can understand better that large old man on the witness stand—an actor, yes, but also a father, grieving for his children and the fact that he'd failed them, much as his own father had failed him. Waiting for the judge to pronounce Christian's sentence was undoubtedly excruciating for Brando. For now, this is where we will leave him, as we travel back to the true beginnings of his story.

In my telling of that tale, I don't repeat every anecdote of Brando's life, every bit of arcana of his career or his publicity, every single girlfriend or sexual tryst, simply for form's sake. That minutiae can be found elsewhere. Instead, I drop in at key moments of his life and get in as close as possible to understand him and his world, then fade out and drop in again, a few years down the road. That means the book doesn't always unfold strictly chronologically. (If you think I've missed something important, wait for it; it'll come around.) This also isn't a story of Brando's films. The important ones are all here, presented in new and revealing detail. But a book that focused on the films, every one of them, even the trifles, would be the exact wrong way to tell the story of Marlon Brando.

The correct way to recount his life is to take him, finally, at his word. Too many other chronicles of Brando's story have sought to prove him wrong: that no matter what he said, his acting mattered and that's the most important thing to talk about, case closed. Yet we don't need to prove Brando wrong to say that he changed film acting, or that *On the Waterfront* is a gigantic work of art, largely because of his contributions to it. We just need to hear him out. We need to respect what Brando had to say, and not refute it, or doubt it, or read ulterior motives into it. His story is far more interesting, valuable, and relevant that way.

NOTE: I HAVE not fictionalized anything in this book. All scenes described come from primary sources: letters, interviews, contemporary articles, production records, and other such material. Nothing has been created for drama's sake, and anything in quotes, including dialogue, comes from direct sources. Full citations can be found in the notes.

# AN

# IMAGINATIVE

# YOUNG

# MAN

**SUMMER 1943** / Our story begins on an upper floor of a building in Greenwich Village, where a young man hurls the Sunday newspaper through an open window, then sits back to watch, transfixed, as the pages flap over the neighborhood like a flock of gray birds.

The motion of the world fascinated Bud. The way it flowed, rippled, soared, crept, burst into pieces. Since arriving in New York a few months earlier, he'd observed every movement of the city, every flash of light, every spin of a revolving door, every turn of a wheel or a head. For hours, he would sit inside a telephone booth in Times Square monitoring people as they passed, "analyzing their personalities," he said, in just that one, fleeting moment. Watching "the way people behave" became a fixation for Bud. The human face, he pointed out, has forty-three muscles, and "the combination of those muscles can hide many things."

Bud knew about hiding things. He'd been hiding things all his life, and in those cases, it was best there be no movement at all. Sometimes Bud lost his fascination with the world. Sometimes the nineteen-year-old Midwestern boy found his interest dimming, and he turned surly. He might punch a wall, cracking the plaster. "Quick temper," Bud admitted, "quick to fight." Sometimes a guy would act a certain way, and Bud would threaten to punch him in the nose. His girlfriend, Celia, would have to hold him back. He'd slump down in a corner until his anger wore off.

Such moods could last days. But then, rousing himself, Bud might get a little drunk and do "insane things," he'd admit, like throwing himself (instead of a newspaper) out the window. Hiding on the cement ledge below, he'd let his friends think, at least for a moment, that he'd plunged to his death five stories below. Such pranks made Bud the king of practical jokes. He had a whole repertoire of them. He'd disguise his voice on the phone, put tacks on seats, remove hinges from doors. And after a prank, Bud's laughter would bubble up from deep down inside him, high pitched and slightly feminine, and those around him couldn't help but laugh along.

Then, laughed out, Bud would curl up on a sidewalk in Washington Square and just fall asleep, oblivious to everything and everyone around him. When he'd awake, he'd feel exhilarated, because in that whole time he'd been sleeping, no one had bothered him—no one had come along and made him go home, or go to school, or go milk the cow, or go find his mother, who'd wandered off again. This was what Bud loved most about New York. He didn't have to "go anyplace anymore."

He was already where he was supposed to be.

**OCTOBER 4** / The morning was cool, in the low fifties, with strong winds and the occasional spritz of rain, as Bud hoofed it up Sixth Avenue from Patchin Place, the little alleyway of row houses off Tenth Street where he'd been staying with his sister Frannie. That day, as on most weekdays, the city had a deserted feel. New

York in wartime was all Bud knew, a place where the women out-numbered the men, where the khaki of the City Patrol Corps had largely replaced the blue uniforms of the New York City police, where grocers rationed canned goods, where nary a burger could be found on "Meatless Tuesdays." The nights still came alive, especially on the weekends, but the days were quiet. What the city would look like after the war, Bud had no idea.

He was a handsome young man with blondish-brown hair and gray-blue eyes. His five-ten frame was solid but lean, without a lot of muscle. He was the rare nineteen-year-old on the street not wearing a uniform. Bud had been classified 4-F. But even if he *had* gone into the army, he thought, he wouldn't have been any good. "Somebody tells me what to do," he explained, "and I'm going to wonder why I should do it." He'd never been able to "'snap to' and salute."

Still, he'd done his duty, trooping down with the rest of the boys back in Libertyville, Illinois, to enlist when President Roosevelt declared war nearly two years earlier. For the recruiters, Bud was prime meat: young and strong, a former military school student, and "they were snapping kids up from military school pretty fast," Bud remembered. But when the doctor asked him if he'd ever had any injuries, he answered truthfully, "Well, my knee has bothered me a little bit." During one football scrimmage at school, he'd snapped his semilunar cartilage. The doctor grabbed his leg, pulled it in and out of joint, and announced, "Sorry, son, you're Four-F." Bud felt bad about that, since all the boys around him had been packed off to war.

But guilty? No, he didn't feel guilty. He just felt bad for the boys who went off to die—while he came here, to New York, to stroll up Sixth Avenue on a crisp, windy morning to start a new chapter in his life.

He knew little about the conflagration that was tearing up the rest of the world. Most of what he did know came from the Trans-Lux Modern Theatre on Forty-Seventh Street and Broadway, where he'd sit hunched down in the dark watching war movies, thrilling to "the beautiful, artful, extraordinary pyrotechnics, warfare in the sky." Just as artfully, he'd snake his arm around Celia—or maybe another of his girlfriends, depending on his mood. To Bud, the war meant "I can't get the kind of cigarettes I used to smoke, or the candy bars I used to eat." It meant sitting in crowded trains surrounded by men in uniform, who glared suspiciously at him in his civilian clothes.

When he reached Twelfth Street, Bud turned right. Up ahead, his new life awaited.

THE BUILDING THAT housed the New School for Social Research at 66 West Twelfth Street was built in 1931, designed by Joseph Urban, the pioneering Art Deco architect and illustrator. Defined by clean lines and stark geometric components, the building might have appeared crushingly plain to the eyes of a Romantic, but to a Modernist, with a gaze set firmly on the future, it seemed boldly prophetic. Even before Bud walked inside, the building itself announced the guiding principle of his new school: form and function have no distinction. They are the same thing. That would be the way of the world after the war, the New School assured its students.

A throng of young people milled about in the reception room. Bud had no friends here, no connections. That he was at the New School at all was surprising, given his life up to that point. A few weeks earlier, he'd been digging ditches back in Libertyville. From the looks of the other students, few had ever done much manual labor. The young men wore jackets and ties, the women plain dresses and low heels. They all seemed to know one another, or at least were eager to make acquaintances. According to the newspapers, registration had "boomed" at the New School that fall. A total of 2,128 students had signed up for the semester, a net gain of 33 percent over the previous year. Some 200 of them had enrolled along with Bud in the Dramatic Workshop. On that debut morning of October 4, hope and expectation crackled in the air, and ambition elbowed its way around the room.

Bud stood apart from the rest. He wasn't wearing a tie and didn't make small talk. He was there, he admitted, only "for want of something better to do." Acting school was at least preferable to digging irrigation ditches on the outskirts of Libertyville, the penance his father had exacted from him after he'd been expelled from military school. For much of the late spring and early summer, Bud had labored at the task, earning thirty-five dollars a week. Looking back on the experience, he'd say, "I did a little manual labor for a while. I *hated* that." And yet, in some ways, the work hadn't been all that bad. Beer tasted better, Bud thought, "when bought with my own paycheck." Still, every night when he went home, dirty and sweaty, mud crusting his eyelashes and caked under his fingernails, he saw "the hopelessness and disappointment" in his parents' eyes. He'd gotten used to that look over the years, but he couldn't take it forever. It was time, he realized, to go.

And so: this place, this school, this unlikely refuge for a boy like Bud.

His father had agreed to cover the tuition (five hundred dollars for the first year, paid in three installments), but only after much cajoling from Bud's older sister Jocelyn, the "propper-upper" in the family, the one who took care of things when things broke down, which happened rather frequently in their household. Even as a little girl, Jocelyn had had an "old-looking" face, prompting Bud to call her "Mrs. Tiddy," or "Tidd," for short. And so, after the disgrace of her brother's expulsion, Tidd had made the case to her father that a drama school was the best choice for Bud. He'd never shown much aptitude for anything other than sports, and his knee injury ruled out an athletic career, so why not take a chance on the one other thing he'd gotten some praise for: his performances in the school's Drama Club?

So impressed, in fact, had Bud's drama teacher been with his work that he'd invited Bud's mother out to the school to see him in one play, and she'd concurred that the boy was very good. Bud, however, thought the acclaim unwarranted. He "couldn't imagine" he'd done anything interesting, since Drama Club was just a lark for him, a welcome break from the rigid precision of his military school. Still, the praise he received from his teacher gave his parents something to cling to after the expulsion—the reasons for which no one ever spoke out loud, least of all Bud.

Tidd was pursuing an acting career herself; she'd just finished a year at the American Academy of Dramatic Arts. But for Bud, she recommended another program: the New School's Dramatic Workshop, presided over by Erwin Piscator, the great German émigré director. Given Bud's disinclination for traditional curricula, Tidd thought the Workshop would be the perfect fit. "Perform while you learn!" the ads read. "You can get professional training and a chance to perform before the critics and talent scouts." Unlike many acting schools, the Dramatic Workshop stressed performance over classroom lectures; Bud would be kept "very, very busy," Tidd told their father—which was what everyone agreed he needed. Upon completion of the two-year course, he would be awarded a certificate that was accepted by many accredited academic and professional institutions. And so, after deliberation, his father had finally agreed: "That's where Bud can go."

New York, however, was expensive. To earn spending money since coming to the city, Bud had worked several odd jobs: waiting tables, operating an elevator at the Best and Co. department store on Fifth Avenue, and other "stuff like that," he'd say. But he was luckier than many young transplants: his father sent him a regular allowance. For all the disappointment Bud had caused, he was not punished financially by his father. His punishment took other forms, weightier and more insidious. And even here, eight hundred and fifty miles away, he still felt the sting.

---

"NAME?"

Bud stood in front of the registration desk, hands shoved down into his pockets. "Marlon Brando," he mumbled.

A mimeographed copy of the first-term schedule was handed to him. The official number of course work hours per week at the Dramatic Workshop was twenty-seven, although students were expected to devote (at the very least) another ten to rehearsal and study. The first term at the Workshop focused on acting, voice, dance, theater history, and regular performances of the classics in the "March of Drama" series. The curriculum featured eight divisions: directing, acting, dramaturgy, musical stage, design, production, preparatory training, and community drama—with students exposed to some aspects of all of them. The second term would be more specialized to the students' particular interests. The dilemma for Bud was that he had no particular interests.

That first day, he attended lectures on the contemporary American drama: Anderson, Rice, Hellman, Odets. There were also readings from *Winterset*, *Street Scene*, and *The Little Foxes*. Most likely, Bud had never heard of them.

He was painfully aware of how different he was from the others. The faces of his classmates were flush with passion for theory and debate as they discussed the tension between contemporary American theater and Neo-Romantic French drama. Bud had no clue about any of that; nor, he admitted, was he in much of a hurry to learn. He'd agreed to attend the Workshop not for any love of acting but because he loved *New York*. On a visit the previous Christmas to see his second eldest sister, Frannie, who was studying art with the Expressionist painter Hans Hofmann, he'd decided New York was "the most fascinating town in the world" and the place he wanted to live "when I start living." Nineteen years he'd been on the planet, but Bud started counting only once he arrived in New York.

The problem was, now that he was a student at the Dramatic Workshop, he didn't give a fig about Rice or Odets when everybody else did. "A great feeling of inadequacy" rose within him. He was convinced that he didn't know enough to be there, that he was "dumb and uninformed," and he had little faith in his skills to catch up. A frequent inability to concentrate in his classes had plagued him in military school. Making matters worse, Bud also suffered from a form of dyslexia, which made reading difficult. Consequently, he'd flunked many of his classes. Deep within him, Bud carried a memory of a teacher once telling him in front of the entire class that his IQ test had shown he "wasn't very smart." Now he was fearful his teachers at the Workshop would discover the same thing.

He didn't even meet the most basic requirement for admission to the Workshop: "Students must have had at least a high school education," the course catalog read. Bud had, of course, been kicked out of his military high school before graduation. Proving himself at admissions, therefore, had been fraught with anxiety. Like all incoming students, Bud had been required to sit for an interview and perform an audition. "Since it is in the interest of both the students and of the Workshop to determine whether the applicant is suited to a career in the theatre," the school's *Bulletin* declared, "a careful sympathetic examination is given for evidence of talent in the selected field of specialization. In cases in which the decision is doubtful, the applicant will be allowed a probationary period of one month."

Just what Bud's audition had entailed, he never told anyone—or, if he did, no one would record it anywhere for posterity, and neither would he. But whatever his entrance interview had been like— whatever part he'd read, whatever his teachers' reactions—he had done well enough to be accepted into the school. And, critically, he was not on a probationary period. The school had been satisfied with his work. They'd found no reason to consider him inferior to the other students.

Bud's doubts about his abilities were entirely his own.

THE WORKSHOP STUDENTS were herded into an assembly hall. It was time to meet "the Director," as everyone reverentially called Piscator.

His nose and chin preceded him into the hall. Piscator was an austere, sharp-featured man of fifty with a heavy German accent and hair the color of iron. Before the war, he'd been an important figure in his native country, one of the first to propose the idea of an "epic theatre," one that emphasized sociopolitical intent over purely emotional characterization. Piscator's vision influenced Bertolt Brecht, who served as his dramaturge for a time. But Piscator's Communist sympathies had caused him to flee when the Nazis came to power, first to the Soviet Union and then to France; he immigrated to the United States in 1939. The next year, he founded the Dramatic Workshop at the urging of Alvin Johnson, the president of the New School.

Students regarded Piscator with awe but not much warmth. The Director was regal and aloof. Few knew him well. He set the vision for the Workshop but taught very few classes, understanding that his poor command of English created an insurmountable chasm between himself and his aspiring actors.

Still, he did his best to welcome them. His words outlined the Workshop's mission: "The Dramatic Workshop serves as a link between academic education and a professional career," he intoned. "It is, besides, a laboratory that provides opportunity for extensive experimentation." Piscator followed the vision of the larger New School for Social Research, which promised "a more interesting life in the world of tomorrow," a postwar utopia based on "humane culture" and learning. "The advent of the war," the New

School averred, "has shown the limitations of a world in which the premium has been upon mere technical competence. Without liberal enlightenment, no thoughtful citizen can understand or discharge his responsibilities to himself and to society."

*Humane culture. Liberal enlightenment. The duties of a thoughtful citizen discharging his responsibilities to society.* This was the message Bud heard his very first day at the Workshop, and every day that followed. He listened intently. The message resonated.

The teachers who moved through these halls, Bud came to believe, were paragons of integrity and intellect, and the institution that accommodated them, rare and august. "A haven for hounded foreign scholars," the *New York Times* called the New School. Within its stark, modern walls, the New School housed the "University in Exile," men and women like Piscator, whose voices and ideas had proved too dangerous to the forces of authoritarianism that had spread across Europe. Over the next decade, Hans Speier, Erich Fromm, Aron Gurwitsch, Max Wertheimer, Claude Lévi-Strauss, and Hannah Arendt would spend time at the school. The *Times* believed that "the New School's pioneering lead in bringing these prominent scholars to our shores" had made America "the intellectual and cultural center of the world." The postwar implications, the newspaper suggested, were "manifold."

They stood on "the cusp of a new world," Piscator told the assembled students. If circumstances had been different, many of them, Bud included, might have been trudging across the Continent with bayonets on their backs. But here at the New School, they had a chance to change the world without weapons. "This is not a war of nations, or races or classes," New School president Alvin Johnson wrote in his own welcoming message to students. "It is a war of barbarism against civilization. It is not a war that can be won alone on the battlefields. It must be won also in the minds and hearts of the men and women who take over when the firing ceases. We must be building our values now lest posterity say of the war for civilization we gave too little and came too late."

Up at the podium, Piscator, a blur of silver intensity, was calling the students to their destiny. What the Workshop would teach them, he declared, was "not art, but life." In his guttural German accent, he exhorted, "Let it be life! The here and now! Art is man's ambition to create beyond reality. Reality—the Sphinx of all Sphinxes, the riddle of all riddles. But every new beginning—is it not a riddle?"

On that first awkward, fearsome day at the Workshop, Bud was struck by a "clear sense" that he was in "a very important place" at "a very important time" and that everything "would change from this moment on."

AT FIRST, BUD remained a loner. Few took notice of him. "I remember only a shadow of a young man in those first few weeks, always with his hands in his pockets, looking down," one classmate recalled. Another classmate, Mae Cooper, found him "rather superficial . . . with no depth." From the others, Bud felt isolated. "I don't understand life," he wrote home around this time, "but I am living like mad anyhow." Later, he would look back and call himself "a naïve kid trying hard to understand the galaxy he had stumbled into and looking for a purpose in life."

After classes, he spent most of his time looking for a new place to live. Frannie already had a roommate, and her apartment was overstuffed with easels and canvases. She was really quite serious about her work, and brother and sister "argued a lot," Bud said. So, it would be best if he got a place of his own.

Until that time, however, he'd found a safe haven elsewhere.

At University Place, Bud slipped stealthily around the iron gates that cordoned off Washington Mews from traffic. Scurrying past the row of two-story brick town houses, he was spotted by a resident, who watched him suspiciously, as he'd later tell the story. At number 16, Bud rapped three times in succession. The door was quickly opened by a beautiful woman with dark, grateful eyes, who grabbed his arm and pulled him inside.

Much of his time these days was spent at Celia's, but each time he visited, he'd need to sneak in and out, enduring the hostile stares of her neighbors, because Celia was married, with a two-year-old son. Her husband, Thomas R. Webb, a lawyer at a prominent firm in the city, was currently serving in the Naval Reserve; he'd shipped off just a few months earlier. Neighbors gossiped about how often Ensign Webb's pretty war bride entertained the young drama student at their apartment, but Celia seemed incapable of discretion. She was head over heels in love with Bud—and he was quite fond of her as well. She had been his first friend after he arrived in New York, the first to offer him a refuge in the big city. When everything else seemed against him, or when he felt one of his black moods descending, Bud could retreat to Celia's arms, and be safe.

Almost twenty-five, Celia was an exotic older woman to the young boy from the Midwest. Her full name was Blanca Cecilia D'Artuniaga. Born in Bogota, Colombia, she'd been naturalized as a U.S. citizen only a few months before meeting Bud. "Olive-skinned, fetching, extremely artistic and a great cook," Bud described her. One night, she invited him to dinner at her place, with candlelight and wine, and that was that, Bud said: "I lost my virginity." Working as a window dresser at a department store, Celia had a flair for style, and wore colorful sashes, wide-brimmed hats, and long black satin gloves. She also had a temper, especially when someone called her Mexican. Her father, she declared, had been born on the border between France and Spain.

She'd come to the United States in 1924 with her mother, who taught Spanish at a Catholic school in Lower Manhattan run by the Convent of Jesus and Mary. For much of her youth, Celia had lived in the convent with her mother; when she graduated from

Cathedral High School in 1937, it was with Cardinal Patrick Hayes himself swinging the thurible. Friends speculated that Celia's adultery with Bud was a rebellion against her cloistered, religious upbringing—and against a husband who'd left her alone, after less than two years of marriage, with an infant child, to go off to war. For little Thomas E. Webb, just learning to walk, the man sitting beside his mother cheering him on wasn't his father, but Bud.

The attraction between Bud and Celia was intense. To his pals, Bud boasted about her sexual appetite, claiming he "screwed her dog-fashion while she was on the telephone." Another time, he said, they each brought the other to orgasm while at the ballet, their hands in each other's lap. Whether that was braggadocio or not—and Bud did an awful lot of bragging about sex—the lovers were clearly passionate about each other. Celia confided to friends that she was so in love with Bud that she planned to divorce her husband so she could marry him.

Bud, however, didn't see things quite that way.

Celia was his first, but she wasn't his only. If he couldn't stay at her place on a particular night, he would hook up with some random girl in order to have a place to crash, as his Dramatic Workshop classmate Darren Dublin would recall. Bud didn't hide his extracurricular activities from Celia, and, for the moment, she accepted that a teenage boy, fresh off the farm in the Midwest, would want to sow his oats during his first months in Manhattan. She hoped eventually things would change.

Yet Bud simply wasn't interested in "dating," he said, not in the way most people thought of it, the way it was done in the movies. "I didn't date anybody," he insisted later on, looking back on those years. "The concept of dating was . . ." His voice trailed off as he tried unsuccessfully to find the words. Dating was inconceivable to him. After growing up with the mother and father he had, with all the memories of his life with them, Bud couldn't be expected to believe in dating or romance or love. The women he met in

New York, the women he would attach himself to, were for sex, not love. He had no need of a girlfriend, or a wife, or a mother. A woman's love held no appeal for him. At least, that was what he believed.

THERE WAS ONE woman, however, who fascinated him.

One morning in October, she strode into the classroom, her dark blond hair swept up onto her head, a choker of pearls strung around her swan neck. Her legs were long and elegant, encased in silk stockings, and she wore ankle-strap shoes, like the ones Joan Crawford made fashionable on the screen.

Stella Adler was not just a teacher. She was theatrical royalty, the daughter of great stars of the Yiddish stage and already a legend herself, having performed in more than a dozen Broadway shows, many of them with the acclaimed Group Theatre. That fall, Stella was rehearsing the play *Manhattan Nocturne*, which would mark her directorial debut when it opened at the Forrest Theatre on October 26. That she found time to teach at the Dramatic Workshop was testament to her fierce work ethic. Divorced, the mother of a sixteen-year-old daughter, she had recently gotten remarried to Broadway director Harold Clurman, with whom she had worked at the Group. Forty-two years old, looking ten years younger, she was glamorous, showy, mannered, larger than life.

And when she entered a room, people *noticed*.

"She *presented* herself," one of her students, the actor Karl Malden, would remember. "It wasn't just, come in front of the class and talk. It was an *entrance*."

In the back of the room, slouched down in his chair, Bud took notice.

About twenty students comprised Stella's acting class; only three of them were male. Due to the war, girls slightly outnumbered boys at the Dramatic Workshop.

If Bud was drawn to Stella immediately, she took some time to spot him. Asked when her mother first noticed him, Ellen Adler said, "Not right away." If she perceived him at all in those first few weeks, it was because of the way he dressed. He wasn't sloppy; that was a later myth. There were no dirty tee shirts or greasy dungarees. His outfits consisted of casual open-collared shirts and khakis, and they were always clean, as were his sneakers and his two-tone shoes. What set Bud apart sartorially was the fact that he didn't wear a necktie, which gave him a certain bohemian reputation around the school.

That, and not much else, was what drew Stella's attention at first. "Who's the vagabond?" she asked colleagues after one early class.

She'd find out soon enough.

**OCTOBER 15** / The students rehearsing that night's presentation of Eugene O'Neill's *Strange Interlude* for the March of Drama series were running through their lines with John Gassner, the erudite head of the dramaturgy department. Voices echoed through the school's Art Deco auditorium. One student remembered Gassner coaching the actress playing Nina up on the stage while, in the back, another student experimented with the spotlight. Long, strange shadows zigzagged across the room.

Off to the side stood Bud, biting the nails of one hand. In his other he held his script, the first few pages rolled behind the others.

He didn't have much to do in the performance, but he was "listening closely," the student would recall, "absorbing everything, his eyes flitting back and forth between Gassner and the stage."

After his initial lack of enthusiasm, Bud was starting to take a real interest in his studies. Compared to digging ditches, acting was a piece of cake. "Acting didn't grate on me," he said. "It didn't bother me." That's hardly an enthusiastic embrace of the profession, yet he was nonetheless intrigued enough to stick to his new schedule. There was no more skipping classes, as he'd done over the last few months at military school. Each day, Bud was at the school by ten in the morning, and was often still in the building at midnight. Rehearsals for the March of Drama series took up the bulk of his time; they were held Tuesdays through Fridays, from two to six, in between morning and evening classes.

Bud liked Gassner, editor of the influential *Twenty Best Plays of the Modern American Theatre*, published in 1939, and head of the play-reading department at the prestigious Theatre Guild. The instructor had been able to evoke in Bud "a curiosity about the history of the theatre," Ellen Adler thought. The March of Drama productions were a unique opportunity for such learning. Working backward in time, they started with O'Neill, who was followed by Galsworthy, Barker, and Barrie. By the end of the term, they'd reach Strindberg; and by the end of the following semester the goal was to get all the way back to Euripides and Aeschylus. It wasn't the typical way things were taught, but this was not a typical school. In his classes back home, Bud had always been easily distracted, fidgety and confused. Not so here.

By 1943, the March of Drama had become quite the popular series among New York theater aficionados. Originally open only to students and their guests, since the previous spring the school had begun allowing the public to attend for a dollar apiece. "An audience of surprised playgoers discovered a wealth of theatre for the first time," Piscator's wife, Maria Ley-Piscator, remembered. "What had seemed merely further study became a sporting proposition, a serious, alive way of learning." The night began promptly at 8:40, with a lecture on the topic at hand from Gassner or his colleague, Paolo Milano, professor of Romance languages. On this night, the topic was O'Neill "and the awakening of the American theatre." After the lecture, the students would perform readings from various O'Neill plays. Sometimes the March of Drama performances were embellished with a few props and costumes, and occasionally, well-known guest actors took part. Sam Jaffe and Phillip Huston had shown up in the past.

And sometimes the Director himself paid a visit, both to rehearsals and the performances, to oversee what his instructors were teaching his students. That night, for the presentation of *Strange Interlude*, Piscator would be in attendance.

The Director was one of the few people at the school Bud didn't care for very much. He was "distant" and "prickly," Bud thought, and many of his classmates agreed. Mae Cooper was still furious that Piscator had refused to let her skip a class so she could attend her sister Elena's dance performance at Carnegie Hall. "An actress does not excuse herself to do something with her family," Piscator told her. "You must make a choice."

Tensions between Piscator and the rest of the school were particularly strained that fall. The Studio Theatre, the New School's well-equipped professional playhouse, for which the Director had great hopes, had been shut down over a union dispute; Actors' Equity claimed that waiving certain rules for the theater while holding other houses accountable was "unfair." Making matters worse, the school had denied the Workshop the twenty thousand dollars needed to bring the theater into union compliance. After such a turndown, Piscator questioned just how committed the school remained to his vision. He'd grown insecure in his position. In the early days of the Workshop, his epic theater was taught much more frequently, and his wife had been head of the acting department. That post was now held by Stella Adler, whom the school went out of its way, Piscator believed, to accommodate, and whose acting philosophy was radically different from his own.

In the conflict between Adler and Piscator, Bud definitely took sides. "He sort of absorbed Stella's disdain for Piscator and his self-conscious mentality," a classmate would remember.

The tensions over acting philosophies at the Dramatic Workshop came to a head that night with the presentation of *Strange Interlude*. According to official policy, the school's curriculum was indebted to "no particular theories." Yet most instructors were moving away from Piscator's emphasis on epic theater and the "objective acting" he espoused, which intended audiences to *think* rather than *feel*. The new consensus aimed for a more personal approach to acting—and for many, it was Stella Adler who personified that vision. Claiming she had the backing of the great acting teacher Konstantin Stanislavski himself, Adler emphasized the writer's text; the actor's only job, she said, was to bring the writer's words to life, through the power of their own imaginations.

Piscator, not surprisingly, opposed such a philosophy, arguing that Adler's approach produced only "sugared realism . . . the branch of the tree and not the tree itself." The debate at the Workshop grew more and more intense until, finally, on the night of October 15, it exploded in the school's auditorium.

While the cast was rehearsing *Strange Interlude*, voices rose in anger. The actress playing Nina began to cry. Gassner suggested that someone more committed to O'Neill's text should take over the part. Another instructor, anticipating Piscator's presence at the production, shot back that "anything that didn't make a comment on the state of the world was not worth putting on the stage."

Off to the side, Bud had stopped biting his nails. He shook his head derisively. Such discussions, he told a classmate, were "highfalutin."

For all his growing interest in his studies, he would often balk when he encountered something he didn't understand, that seemed beyond his grasp. He often didn't get the references that were made in class, the comparative analysis, the literary allusions. And so, he would withdraw, dismissing it all as "highfalutin."

His companion that night during the *Strange Interlude* rehearsal was a second-year student whom Gassner had selected as stage manager. The student was constantly being called on to mediate disagreements among the actors, who were either being "too Stanislavski" or not being "Stanislavski enough."

Listening to it all, Bud rolled his script up tight and stuffed it down into his back pocket. His eyes, the second-year student would remember, were "angry and hooded." He was growing impatient. He couldn't understand all the fuss.

Bud would never feel he belonged with these people. His future brother-in-law Richard Loving would say he had "an aversion to theater people," regarding them "as phonies, narcissistic." In those moments, Bud's "own involvement" in acting seemed to embarrass him. Sometimes he managed to laugh off his discomfort. Other times, he got angry. As ever, the rage came suddenly, unexpectedly, surging from zero to one hundred in the course of seconds.

Turning to the harried second-year student, Bud snarled, "Our lives are strange dark interludes"—a climactic line from the play. Then he pulled the script out of his pocket, threw it down on the floor, and stalked out of the auditorium.

"I WAS AN anomaly," he would say, looking back. Not only was he a "non-Jew in a Jewish milieu," he said, but he was a military school dropout learning from teachers who'd attended the best schools in Europe and who would go on to teach at Princeton and Yale. Bud felt like a fraud. He was just some light-eyed goy, after all, a corn-fed kid from the sticks trying to blend in with city sophisticates. Bud came to conflate being Jewish with being cultured; Jews, he believed, were naturally inclined to culture. Most of his classmates had grown up attending concerts, plays, art exhibits, and poetry readings. Beulah Roth, Rosalyn Weiss, and Mae Cooper (whose real name was Klein) all came from artistic families. Sara Farwell's father was a composer and head of the music department at UC

Berkeley. Farwell had grown up hearing conversations "about Isadora Duncan and Paderewski," she'd remember, while Bud had heard little more than grumbling about sales receipts from his traveling salesman father.

He couldn't escape the fact that he was an outsider at the Workshop. "I could hardly speak the language," he said. When one of his new friends gushed over the Bach double violin concerto, Bud remarked how "cultured" she was; he had absolutely no idea what she was talking about. To the second-year student observing him during the rehearsal for *Strange Interlude*, it was clear that Bud's occasional "angry or sullen outbursts" arose from his feeling "terribly self-conscious about his lack of culture."

He wasn't poor. His father sent him ninety dollars a month, a heftier sum than many students got. Still, his middle-class roots were obvious to his classmates at the Workshop. Joy Thomson was the daughter of a Montreal banker. Dorman Leonard was the son of a prominent Flatbush dentist; his grandfather had been a well-known manufacturer and inventor. Mae Cooper's father was a bookkeeper for a large retail company, and one of the first Jews in his upscale Brooklyn neighborhood. When she brought Bud to visit, she observed how he felt "out of place" in her family's well-appointed house. No surprise, then, that Bud chose as his closest friend Darren Dublin, the son of a Russian-Jewish immigrant and itinerant furrier who lived in a working-class section of Queens.

To mask his insecurity, Bud could sometimes seem condescending to his classmates. "He was laughing at all of us," remembered Elaine Stritch, who was an innocent eighteen-year-old when she enrolled at the Dramatic Workshop the same semester as Bud. "I have a memory of him laughing at everything and everybody."

Sometimes, however, the laughter stopped and he just brooded over being in the Workshop at all. Any fleeting interest he might take in acting was forgotten the moment he felt inadequate. If he'd had his way, Bud would have preferred to be working in a roadhouse, playing the drums. If he'd ever wanted to be anything, it was a drummer. "I could'a been a drummer," he'd say wistfully, years later—an unconscious rewrite of a movie line he would make famous. He'd wanted to be a musician ever since riding a train when he was twelve years old and falling under the spell of the rhythm: "I started banging on the doors and the walls with my hands," he remembered, "grooving to the beat of the train as if it were a jazz quartet." After that, he said, he was "a changed boy": he'd wanted nothing more than to be a drummer. But that dream, like so many dreams of his childhood, had been thoroughly and efficiently snuffed out.

IN THE LIVING room of the Brando farmhouse in Libertyville, on the Townline Road bordering Mundelein, sweat was flying off sixteen-year-old Bud as he played the drums, keeping beat with Gene Krupa and Buddy Rich on the radio. His parents had bought him a set of Slingerland drums, the kind Krupa used in his orchestra, and Bud had taught himself to play by listening to records. Jazz came naturally to him. He could feel it in his bones. Artie Shaw, Duke Ellington, Jimmy Lunsford—these were his heroes. "I would turn the radio up," he said, "and play my drums for about eight hours." Machine-gun drumming—that's what he called it, his hands moving so fast over the drums they were a pink blur. "A whole solo of rim shots" he mastered, singing along to "Drummin' Man" on the radio: *Drummin' man, he's a drummin' man.*

The sound of Bud's high-pitched voice, backed up by the steady *rap-rap-rap* of his drums, flew out the windows and across the farm, all the way down to the railroad tracks, where it was finally drowned out by the screech of a passing train.

"He'd just sit there pounding," remembered Frank Ward, a friend from back home, "with the radio or the phonograph turned up. He was totally inside himself."

Fired up by his dream, Bud formed an orchestra with some of

his pals. Someday, he said, they'd be known as "Keg Brando and His Kegliners"—an homage to the Keglined cans of beer they drank. One night, the orchestra played a gig at a Libertyville roadhouse. Bud's sisters went; Tidd thought her brother "was very good."

"Some people," Bud explained, "are drawn to tone, or color." He, by contrast, was drawn to rhythm. At night on the farm, he'd lie in bed listening to the donkey engine that powered the water pump. "I used to love to listen to that thing pulsate," he'd remember—an "eccentric" sort of sound, he said, like the chugging of a train, irregular expulsions of air. Keeping time with his foot, he'd eventually drift off to sleep to the sound. Even now, if asked, Bud could mimic that old donkey engine. *Foosh, foosh, foosh.* "It just had something to say to me," he said.

Soon after he had arrived in New York, the rhythm found him again, beckoning him up to the jazz clubs in Harlem. One night, with "about a third of a bag on"—not "falling down drunk," he said, just "a very pleasant buzz"—he rode the subway up to 125th Street. Swaggering up to the band in one club, he asked the guy playing the bongos if he could take over. "I pulled ten dollars out of my pocket," he said. There he was—the only white guy in the place—waving cash around in the air. The bongo player ignored him. Finally, one guy—"evidently the bouncer," Bud remembered, "with these ball-bearing eyes, who would put the fear of death into any tackle, linebacker or anybody else"—sauntered up to him.

"I'll take your money, boy," the bouncer said. "I'll see that you play the drums." Bud sensed that nothing of the sort would happen, that all he was about to get was a swift kick out onto the sidewalk, ten dollars short. For a change, he didn't get angry, didn't fight back. "I'll just listen," he said, unobtrusively taking a seat.

In those jazz clubs, Bud felt far more at home than he did at the Dramatic Workshop. "It's the rhythm," he explained. "Jazz is universal. Everybody speaks that language."

His love of music, he believed, came from his mother. And that made him cherish music all the more.

Dodie Brando loved all kinds of music. She would let Bud play his drums and sing his heart out without ever asking him to tone it down. Sometimes she'd even sing along. Whenever Bud wanted a happy memory of his childhood, all he had to do was close his eyes and think of his mother playing the piano—"one of the few times we had any family activity," he said. Seated at the piano, his mother taught Bud and his sisters "the lyrics and tune of almost every song ever written." For hours they'd sit there and warble all sorts of songs. Popular standards and religious hymns and Old World lullabies such as "Annie Laurie" and "Killarney." For the rest of his life, Bud would remember the words to all of them.

But then his father would return home from one of his sales trips, and the piano cover would be closed, the singing would come to an end, and a black silence would descend over the house. If Bud tried to play the drums when his father was home, he'd be told to pack it up, to "stop that infernal noise."

For all Bud's passion, a career in music was out of the question. His mother tried to defend his choice, calling him "musically gifted," but her husband cut her off short. A boy as easily distracted as Bud, Brando père believed, needed "far more structure" in his chosen career. And so, that was that. The dream of Keg Brando and His Kegliners was shattered. "I had some notion about [a career as a drummer]," Bud would say, looking back. "But it never worked out."

Father and son were separated by a wall as ironclad as it was invisible. They lived in the same house but existed on alternate planes. Only once would Bud ever recall any affection from his father. "I remember his putting his arm around my shoulder and playing with my earlobe at a movie," he said, but such a gesture was rare, alien. Marlon Brando Senior would give the children each a kiss when he returned from traveling, but such kisses were always perfunctory, devoid of any meaning. "Perhaps he didn't know how" to show affection, Bud said, "or was too proud or too frightened to do it."

Frannie would remember a Christmas when Bud was just a toddler. Sneaking downstairs before dawn, the little boy had found a mechanical car left for him by Santa Claus. "It was yellow and very spiffy looking," Frannie recalled. "It ran on pedal power, big enough to get into which made it seem powerful." Bud was thrilled. He hopped in and "instantly became a skillful driver," Frannie said. All around the room he drove, enjoying himself tremendously. Yet, while his mother and sisters applauded, Marlon Brando Sr. kept his distance. He did not play with his son. He did not praise him or encourage him. He remained silent and distant as he watched the child zip around the room in his little car. "He was very proud of his handsome son," Frannie believed, "but alas, too proud to show it."

Showing it, Marlon Senior believed, would be weak. He'd learned that from his own father, a penny-pinching clerk whose wife had abandoned him and their son after just seven years of marriage. The only way to raise a child, Bud's father believed, was stoically, with fortitude and not a trace of coddling. That was the reason he'd sent his son to his alma mater, the Shattuck Military Academy in Faribault, Minnesota. But Bud hadn't been up to the task and left there in humiliation. The boy was a hopeless case, his father believed. "A ne'er-do-well," he called his son, as Bud would always remember.

What sort of ambition, after all, was it to be a drummer? Dramatic school wasn't much better, but at least the boy was out of his sight. Marlon Senior believed he had done everything he could do for his son. He paid his tuition on time and made sure he received a regular allowance. It was Bud who had failed him, not the other way around.

---

"MR. BRANDO."

Bud looked up. Stella Adler was standing in front of the class. They were doing improvisation exercises that day with some of the second-year students. Adler believed it was the best way to get to the truth in a performance. "Make an actor improvise," she said. "And in the improvisation, the actor's guts, his life, his everything, starts to work."

Bud looked at her. He'd been surly for days, but he melted a bit under his teacher's gaze.

"You're a father," she told him, "cradling his newborn son."

The assignment made him self-conscious, a classmate thought. But Bud trusted Stella Adler; he thought she could do no wrong. In her ongoing battle with Piscator, as much as the arcana of their argument bored and eluded him, Bud passionately took Stella's side. Small wonder: he hadn't left Libertyville to escape one despot only to embrace another.

He got to his feet. Standing very still for a moment, he suddenly brought his arms together in front of him as if he were holding an invisible baby. "And then," the second-year student from *Strange Interlude*, now assisting Adler, observed, "he just stood there. He wasn't looking down at the baby, but across the room, out the window, over at me, anywhere but at the baby, as if he couldn't care less about what he was holding." Finally, as everyone watched, he turned to one of the women standing near him and handed the "baby" over to her.

"Stella—the whole class—was silent," the second-year student said, as Bud returned to his seat and slumped down in his chair. "Well, we thought, what a fine father *he'd* make!" Bud offered no explanation. His teacher let the performance go, perhaps storing it away in her mind for future reference.

Yet if his classmates had gained an impression of coldness and aloofness, a few nights later they had reason to reevaluate Bud.

A handful of students was smoking cigarettes at the end of the block when a little boy, maybe seven years old, came wandering up the street, barefoot and crying. The students could see that the child had Down syndrome, and his speech was nearly unintelligible. "So, Bud leapt into action," his classmate recalled. "He took the boy by the shoulders and spoke to him very tenderly. He was the only one among us who was able to understand what the boy was saying." Through fragments of words that tumbled from the child's mouth, Bud deduced that he was lost; he also figured out where the boy lived. How he did this, no one was sure. Bud might not speak the language of his teachers or his classmates, but the words of a frightened little boy he understood just fine.

Taking the child's hand, Bud led him a few blocks up Sixth Avenue, where the boy's sister recognized him and took him inside. "Bud stood there," his classmate remembered, "for the longest time, shouting up at the window, wanting to make sure the boy was safe." Not until the mother finally came to the window and held the child up so Bud could see him did he finally saunter off.

**NOVEMBER** / The days got cooler, and so did Bud. Soon after arriving in the city, he'd bought a used motorcycle, a four-cylinder Indian with eighteen-inch wheels, and he sometimes rode it to school. Less sleek than the newer models, the Indian was still pretty damn fast. Bud would ride all over the city, darting in and out of traffic, flipping the bird at taxi drivers who cursed at him for getting too close. At night he'd park his bike outside the apartment he'd found for himself at 39 West Twelfth Street—just across from the school—and in the morning it would still be there. "There wasn't much crime in the city then," Bud would remember.

After the last class of the day, the Workshop students spilled out onto the sidewalk, several of them asking Bud for rides on his bike. It was a cool night. Most of the leaves had dropped from the trees, and a hint of winter chilled the air. The students watched as Bud straddled the Indian, revving it a few times with his foot and then crooking his finger at one of the girls, who slipped on behind him. Off they blasted in a staccato roar, leaving behind smoke and the sweet aroma of gasoline. The other girls stared after them in awe. The boys watched in envy.

"Just before Thanksgiving," one classmate remembered, "everyone seemed to have a crush on Bud." When he strolled into class these days, he was often wearing a biker's cap and black boots that came up to the middle of his calves. "This was Marlon Brando *before* Marlon Brando," the classmate went on, "before James Dean, before the whole sexy motorcycle bad-boy image became such a part of the culture. In 1943, this was brand new, daring, and unexpected."

Little Elaine Stritch was madly in love with him: "I mean, who wouldn't be?" Those soft eyes, that perfectly carved nose, that smile. "Girls were faking faints in dramatic classes so that he'd pick them up." Many of the boys, too, Elaine said, both gay and straight, seemed besotted with Bud.

Finally, Bud was getting noticed. Not for his ideas, his intelligence, or his talent, but for his looks, and for the confident physicality he displayed. "I was a reasonably attractive young man," he'd understate, years later, "full of vim, vigor, and sexuality. I was an exotic person for them. I didn't follow any of their rules and they didn't follow any of mine. So they were fascinated with me."

And, he admitted, he was "fascinated with them," too. When he stopped feeling defensive, Bud wanted their friendship, their experience; he desired entry into their world of ideas. They, in turn, seemed to want his raw sensuality, something their more sheltered upbringings had failed to offer them. At last Bud discovered the makings of an exchange.

"This is how he got into things," Elaine Stritch said, "how he became a part of the clique, so to speak. First one person gets a crush on him, then another, and he knows it, and he feels more at ease, not so much of an outsider."

Still, Bud played it cool. His classmates could not know that he wanted anything from them. He made sure to appear as if he were the only one giving. Rarely in his life had Bud ever asked for anything, because if he asked, he usually didn't get. So now, Ellen Adler surmised, if his classmates knew he wanted what they were giving, he was "afraid they'd stop giving it." The lesson of Bud's childhood was that he had to *take*. And so, this elaborate charade with his friends.

"Do you know how I make a friend?" Bud would ask, a few years later. "Very gently. I circle around and around. Then gradually I come nearer. Then I reach out and touch them—ah, so gently. Then I draw back. Wait a while. Make them wonder. At just the right moment, I move in again. Touch them. Circle. They don't know what's happening. Before they realize it, they're all entangled. I have them."

He would stare at people, too, making them uncomfortable. "He would sort of look into your eyes and assess you," Sara Farwell said. He was making it clear that *he* would be the judge of others, not they of him. In this way he overcame his self-doubt, his sense of inadequacy—or at least, he found a method to obscure such feelings, to gain some mastery over them.

After Bud finished giving his classmates rides around the block, they lingered for a while in front of the school, Bud's best pal, Darren Dublin, among them. Everyone was smoking. Bud remained in the street, straddling his motorcycle, telling stories to his classmates—about his exploits with women up in Harlem, perhaps, or his practical jokes at military school. "He would regale us all," the second-year student remembered. "We all just stood around listening to him, not saying much, just letting him ramble." It was as if Bud were onstage, commanding his audience with far more power than he did during exercises in the classroom.

But he shared only so much. While his friends spoke freely of their childhoods, Bud was vague about his. He'd made it this far, after all. He'd won their friendships; he might even be gifted with some of their culture if he played his cards right. But if he shared too much, he feared, he might risk that. If his new friends learned the truth, he might no longer be so cool in their eyes. They couldn't know of the hardships, the anguish, the secrets he carried about his mother and his father. "We knew there was a lot he didn't say, that was hidden," said Elaine Stritch.

Reminiscing about his past, Bud believed, was just too fraught with danger.

To these "clean-fingernailed city people," as he called them, Bud chose his memories carefully. The memories he shared were idyllic: lazy summer days sitting on the railroad tracks until he felt "the vibration of the oncoming train" and staying in place until the moment he could see the train approaching. For the rest of his life, Bud would insist that memories of his past came to him only in little picturesque snatches like that. "The smell of hay, the smell of spring," he'd say, when asked to remember his youth. More memories would come as he cast his mind back: fragrances wafting in from the kitchen, his mother frying eggs and bacon on the old-fashioned woodstove in their Illinois farmhouse.

But that was where the memories got stuck—like a piece of sprocket film in an old movie projector, melting against the heat of the bulb.

The memory of that old woodstove, in fact, triggered something in Bud. Embarrassment. Shame. His family was often financially strapped and always eccentric. "I just remember," he said, "if I ever invited any friends over, I would always engage them and lock their eyes to not notice the stove."

That was the way memory worked for Bud. Starting out sunny and buoyant before turning dark and corroded.

BUD BRANDO WAS born April 3, 1924, in Omaha, Nebraska. As a very young boy, he played happily in his grandmother's big back-yard on Thirty-Second Street with its wisteria arbor—"fresh air all day," his sister Frannie would recall. Every morning, bread and milk came delivered by horse-drawn wagon. There were trees to climb, picnics to go on. But when Bud was six, the family moved to Evanston, Illinois, and the memories of his childhood lost their rosy glow.

They moved so they could be closer to Bud's father's new job as a traveling salesman for the Chicago-based Calcium Carbonate Corporation, a manufacturing concern that sold chemical prod-ucts for building and farming. Marlon Brando Sr. earned a thou-sand dollars a month plus commissions. He was very proud of his income, and the hustling he had to do on the road to make it. At the height of the Great Depression, he considered a good job like that a gift from heaven. In Evanston, they occupied a lovely new home with four bedrooms, a marble fireplace, and a grassy front lawn, on Judson Avenue, a quiet street lined with green and red maples and flowering crabapple trees.

But the idyll was an illusion. Bud's parents often fell into long, cold silences. Sobs broke the stillness of the night. Finally, when Bud was twelve, his mother packed up the children and left her husband, traveling all the way across the country to live with her mother in Santa Ana, California. Bud didn't understand exactly why his parents split—there was a lot he didn't understand about his parents—but he knew enough to grasp that any change was for the good. Like Poe's telltale heart beating under the floorboards, the unhappiness in that house in Evanston had pulsated round the clock. Bud had been glad to move to California. Here the memories were once again fleetingly happy. At school, he set the record for pushups: fifty-eight in a row without stopping.

But less than two years later, the Brandos were back in Illinois, all of them living together again, the family reunited. This was when they moved to Libertyville, to the farmhouse with the old woodstove that so embarrassed Bud. The problems that had severed the family had not been resolved however. Here in Libertyville began the mood swings that would define Bud's adult life.

Their farm actually belonged to other people; the Brandos only rented the house. Still, they had their own chickens and cows. Bud's mother named one of the cows Violet. Every morning, Bud would be sent out to milk Violet, and by the age of fourteen, he'd become very good at the task. When his father tried, Bud recalled, "he'd miss the bucket completely," getting the milk all over his sleeve. Sometimes Bud would be milking Violet, "and all the barn cats would line up and sit on their haunches," hoping for a drink. "Anybody could squirt if they knew how to milk," Bud boasted, and he proved it by squirting the milk eighteen feet across the barn into the faces of those cats. "It was a sight to see," he'd remember—and a story he liked to tell his friends at the Workshop, enjoying how they laughed.

But once again the memory darkened. Sometimes Violet would lift her leg and plop it smack down into the bucket of milk. "And [the bucket] would be full of manure," Bud said. Fear of his father's anger would rise in Bud's throat. Rather than risk a rebuke, he'd pour the manure and the milk through cheesecloth and bring the contaminated milk into the house. "Everybody would drink it," he said, before pausing in the memory. "I never told anybody," he admitted.

Bud took dark amusement from such duplicity. His sense of humor, sometimes farcical, sometimes black, helped him endure many of the less pleasant moments of his childhood. Because he despised school, he'd get through the day by shooting rubber bands over the heads of his classmates—sometimes, if he was lucky, pinging the ear of an instructor. Military school was even worse, so, one time, just to lighten things up (and delay classes) he removed the pins from the hinges of a door; when a teacher tried to enter, the door fell down in front of him.

Bud's "sense of absurd," as he called it, was his salvation and his refuge. And it came, appropriately enough, from his mother, who often needed salvation herself. Bud's father was humorless; his mother, in contrast, had a devilish streak. On their farm they had a goose named Mr. Levy, who would chase after anybody who came too close. "That goose would flap its wings and run right up to you and hiss and stick its neck out in menacing fashion," Bud remembered. One time, a snooty woman from town was bitten by Mr. Levy. Bud would never forget her "going round and round with this goose hanging on to her ass by its beak." One Christmas, Bud's mother decided to have some fun with Mr. Levy, dressing the goose as Santa Claus, with "a little red costume and beard." The sight of that demonic goose flapping around the yard, honking at trespassers dressed up like Santa Claus, was truly theater of the absurd. Best of all, to Bud, was the sight of his mother laughing. His mother, Bud believed, "had the most beautiful laugh in all the world."

Before she married Marlon Brando Sr., Bud's mother had been Dorothy Pennebaker. People called her Dodie. Growing up, her son saw her as the epitome of beauty: dark blonde hair, blue eyes, high cheekbones, elegant fingers. As a toddler, Bud followed her wherever she went. Dodie taught him to love nature: the swallows in the barn, the frogs and tadpoles in the creek, the way sunsets would stain the sky red and green. Dodie had a special fondness for the night sky: the dome of stars, the phases of the moon, "the magic of the universe," as she called it. To Bud, she imparted "a sense of closeness with nature," he recalled. It was a gift he treasured.

But there was so much about his mother Bud didn't know, or didn't understand. Just before he'd left for New York to join the Dramatic Workshop, he'd learned from Tidd that their mother had been an actress. "I didn't know that, ever," he'd say later, looking back. Tidd, being five years older than her brother, had seen their mother perform at the Omaha Community Playhouse. She was "very good," Tidd thought. But after the move to Evanston, Dodie had stopped acting. The light inside her, Tidd thought, had dimmed.

Bud thought his mother had "the soul of an artist." She sculpted and wrote poetry "and was just someone who saw the beauty in life," he said. He owned a photograph of his mother from when she was young. She wore a bolero jacket and a wide-brimmed hat. Her chin was high, and she gazed defiantly at the camera, holding a cigar between her fingers. "Quite a character," Tidd said of their mother in her younger years. "Very independent lady."

But then Bud's mother—his lovely, artistic mother, with her beautiful laughter and her love of nature—"broke apart like a piece of porcelain," he would remember, and his own life cracked, too, in a million different ways.

SNOW CAME EARLY that year. Nothing heavy, but sudden flurries that took people by surprise, spinning and spitting for an hour or so before disappearing. Forecasters predicted a rough winter. With the city's resources drained by war, the mayor was worried about manpower to remove snow from the streets and was calling for volunteers. Temperatures plunged. Upstate, ski resorts boomed.

And Bud Brando, his heart still heavy with his mother's disintegration, looked to women to give him solace and warmth.

A light snow was falling as little Elaine Stritch, not quite believing her luck, made her way through Greenwich Village, Bud at her side. Finally, her crush had asked her out, and the young actress had accepted Bud's invitation with a mix of excitement and terror. "He was so beautiful that he scared me," she said. When she told friends that she was going out with Bud, they understood exactly how she felt. His charm, they all agreed, was "devastating," enough to leave them flustered and tongue-tied. When Bud spoke, his eyes twinkled. Dimples dented his cheeks. And when he sat there on his motorcycle, telling his tales of squirting milk across the barn and last-minute escapes from oncoming trains, he made his listeners feel special, "as if he were talking directly to you," Stritch said, "and no one else."

Going out with him one on one, however, as Stritch discovered, was a different experience. They were taking a tour of the Village's churches—First Presbyterian, St. Luke in the Fields, St. Joseph's, United Methodist in Washington Square—and at each stop, Bud would comment on their architecture and stonework, "seeming as if he knew all about it," Stritch said. But the rest of the time, he spoke very little. This, too, was something his friends at the Workshop had noticed. When not "in control," telling his stories, Bud often lapsed into "awkward silences" after saying hello. Sitting on his motorcycle holding court, he could be garrulous and glib, but small talk was impossible. "I am by nature, and to a noticeable extent, self-conscious," he admitted. If he walked into a room where students were already deep in conversation, he'd either hang back or, if addressed, stammer out a reply that made little sense. "When I am confronted with [an uncomfortable social] situation," he explained later, "I am not surprised to find my mouth full of stories."

Just as the conversation started to lag with Stritch, he detoured from their church tour and took her to a strip club. "He had a sense of humor like that," Stritch said, "but it was also a world he was comfortable in." She, however, found the place "dirty," so Bud suggested they head back to his apartment.

The snow was still falling, so Bud built a fire in the tiny fireplace. Everything seemed very romantic until, without warning, he changed into his pajamas. The inexperienced eighteen-year-old

Stritch, who lived in a rooming house run by nuns, panicked. Certain that Bud meant to seduce her, she announced that she was going home. Bud shrugged and said okay. Stritch was miffed that he didn't get dressed and walk her down to the street and wait with her for the bus. For the rest of her life she'd remain convinced that Bud was angry with her for rejecting his sexual pass.

But that might not have been the case at all.

Many women would, in fact, tell stories like Stritch's. That same fall, Mae Cooper fixed Bud up with her sister, Elena Klein, the dancer from Carnegie Hall. Klein later revealed that they dated, on and off, for about a year, and not once did Bud put the moves on her. Instead, he accompanied her to museums and the theater, seeming to hope that some of the "culture" Klein had grown up with would rub off on him. Given Bud's reputation as a heartthrob, Klein thought "it was probably a relief for him to feel that I was somebody he didn't have to worry about impressing." Another woman Bud dated, Carmelita Pope, reported that their intimacies never went past necking. A third woman told friends, after several nights out with Bud, "All he wants to do is hold hands and cuddle."

Quite possibly, that's all he had wanted from Stritch that snowy night in front of the fire. Because of the tales he told—the bragging about sex with Celia and other conquests—Bud had gained a reputation as a womanizer. Men, he insisted, were "no different from mice. They're born to perform the same function. Procreate." So, to prove it, "he went out and fucked half the women in New York," Stritch believed.

But not women like Stritch, or Klein, or the others from the Workshop—cultured, artistic women searching for the beauty in life. For sex, Bud turned to women like Celia, dark and exotic, hardened by the world. At the Harlem jazz clubs, he'd sit in the smoky darkness, reveling in the raw sensuality he found there. One night, the sweet perfume of a woman intoxicated him: "It made me dizzy it was so good." So, he introduced himself. The women of the jazz clubs fell under his spell much as the women of the Workshop did: a smile, a wink, a flash of his eyes. Bud was always chivalrous with women, no matter where he met them: "I open the door for women," he said, "pull out their chairs when they're sitting." That was hardly the behavior most women in Harlem were used to from a white man. No surprise, then, that the woman with the sweet perfume invited Bud home.

At the New School, he bragged to one friend that he'd had as many white girls as he wanted; now he wanted only "Spanish, blacks, and Asians." Race was something Bud had discovered after he came to New York, a foreign cuisine they hadn't served back in Libertyville. "I'd never met any black people before in my life," Bud would remember, except for a couple of boys who'd turned up one day in his high school and with whom he'd become friendly. "I never had any sense of race at all," he said, until he came to New York and couldn't get enough of the dark-skinned, dark-eyed women who were so different from the women he'd grown up with.

So different, especially, from his mother.

He had needed to get away from her. He had needed to find a world where the women were not fragile blue-eyed blondes liable to shatter if he gripped them too hard. The women he desired were those who could survive in a world of wolves and brutes, women who were sturdy and strong and different from the others. Women who could take care of him, who could wrap their arms around him and hold him tight, chase away his doubts, and assure him that he was beautiful and worthwhile and that he would succeed, the way his mother had never held him, but the way he had always longed for her to do.

THE HOUSE WAS in disarray. Dishes cluttered the sink; newspapers were piled high on the couch; the trash was beginning to smell.

Bud's drums took up the entire floor of the living room. Dodie was spread out on her bed, surrounded by crossword puzzles, magazines, and cookie crumbs. It was Sunday. No one thought of church. The closest the Brandos had to religion was the Christian Science of Dodie's mother, but only Frannie had ever taken any catechism lessons, and then only because her friends did. Sundays were free of any schedule. Bud listened to records in his room. The girls ate chocolate on the front steps. Sundays were wonderful, lazy, and messy—at least when the man of the house was on the road hawking Calcium Carbonate.

The phone jangled, and word came that Pop was on his way home. Dodie immediately leapt out of bed. "Got to make a hole in the house!" she shouted to the children. In a fury, they burrowed through the clutter to make the place presentable.

The locals considered the Brandos "bohemians," with Bud's drums and Tidd's acting and Dodie's poetry and sculpting. Not many women in Libertyville took sculpting classes. She also volunteered with the League of Women Voters and the local children's theater. One of Bud's friends mused that had Dodie lived in a different era, "she probably would not have had a family. She probably would have been an artist of some sort. She had that sensitivity. She certainly didn't have the housekeeping component." The cookie crumbs in her bed and the newspapers covering the couch attested to that fact.

Yet the bohemianism of the Brandos wasn't merely aesthetic. They utterly rejected middle-class mores. Going to church was bourgeois; politics and sex were topics not off limits at the dinner table; and racial prejudices had no place in the Brando household. Dodie preached "tolerance of others and the courage to be yourself," one aunt remembered; she valued "an independent and inquiring mind, personal integrity and self-fulfillment." When Tidd began having sex before marriage, Dodie didn't disapprove; even Marlon Senior at one point suggested Tidd and her boyfriend ought to live together for a while before tying the knot.

Some thought the Brandos were wealthy, because Dodie, for a time, employed a live-in maid, a Danish girl named Irmeline Jensen, to help with the children, and after Irmy left, a series of additional maids came and went. But money was never flush in the Brando house. Marlon Senior blamed his wife's mismanagement of her weekly allowance; Dodie insisted the trouble was her husband's spendthrift ways on the road. Nonetheless, they managed to give the impression of a comfortable life. When Dodie roused herself and put away her crossword puzzles, she could put on quite the show. She sometimes employed a driver to escort her around town.

She could also curse like a sailor, a trait she shared with her husband. "Fuck this" and "fuck that" bounced around the house, with no one lifting an eyebrow.

The Brandos drank like sailors, too. While Prohibition was in force, they brewed their own beer at home; even after repeal, in 1933, they kept their fermentation bucket in use. The Brando kitchen often smelled of hops, malted barley, and brewer's yeast. Visitors on bottle-corking days would find Dodie and Marlon Senior, hands in long rubber gloves, covered in suds and more than a little tipsy. It was a sight few other children in town ever saw in their own homes.

"It used to bother me very much that they didn't act like other parents," Bud would admit. The Brandos required explanation. One aunt said they didn't believe in "behaving like everybody else, just because everybody else behaves that way." Their parents' bohemianism might have instilled in the Brando children a tolerance of others and the value of self-expression. But it also embarrassed the young, sensitive Bud.

The town whispered about the Brandos. Sometimes, after one of her art classes or political meetings, Dodie would head out with her friends for dinner and drinks. Not many mothers in Libertyville did that. If it was a week that her husband was on the road, she knew she could stay out past midnight, so she'd ring Tidd to say she'd be late; other times, she wouldn't ring at all. Tidd—loyal, stalwart Tidd—did what was expected of her. She made dinner, got her younger siblings to bed, and, in the morning, when her mother slept in, unwilling to get up "because she couldn't face the day," she got the children off to school. Sometimes Dodie would stay in bed for days at a time, her room reeking of whisky, until the ring of the telephone announced her husband's return and she'd force herself to rise.

That was the way things happened in the Brando household. That much wasn't bohemianism. That was alcoholism. But no one said a word about it. It was just the way things were.

The summer he was ten, however, Bud dared put the truth into words. He was riding his bike by a lake and came across a woman who was staggering, unable to walk. He tried to speak to her, but the woman was incoherent. So, he "took her home," he remembered. When he got there, holding the woman by the shoulders, his parents were on the front porch. "I think we should take care of her," Bud told them, "because she's sick." He would never forget the embarrassment on his parents' faces. "But I was quite sincere. I thought that she was ill, and that she needed help."

The woman, of course, was drunk. Irmy, the maid, phoned a local hotel and got her a room. "Bud had to be assured that she would be all right," Tidd remembered, so she and Irmy had to take him down to the hotel to see for himself, just as, some years later, Bud would need to make sure that the little boy with Down syndrome was okay before he left.

In his pleading for the woman, Bud had done more than just try to help someone in need. He had, unwittingly or not, exposed the unmentionable secret at the heart of the family, a secret that would eventually incapacitate them all. "I think we should take care of her," he said, "because she's sick."

It was his mother he was pleading for, his mother he wanted

to make whole and strong. Even as a young boy, Bud somehow seemed to know that her drinking, her nights out, her long, silent retreats in her bedroom, would lead to even worse things, and that someday she would just break apart. "I thought that she was ill, and that she needed help," he said about the woman, but he was speaking as much about his mother. It was Dodie he wanted to take care of, Dodie he wanted to save.

**NOVEMBER 12** / Another week, another rehearsal for the March of Drama. At last Piscator was having his day: he was the topic of the week. Gassner's Friday night lecture would be "The Epic Theatre of Brecht and Piscator," and to demonstrate it, the students were presenting a performance of *Power*, the 1937 Broadway hit by Arthur Arent, an adherent of epic theater, about the electrification of rural America. Gassner was presenting the lecture, but the Director himself would oversee the rehearsals.

Bud wasn't happy about that. By now he'd come to loathe Piscator, who likewise remained impervious to the young man's charms. By contrast, over the past couple of weeks, Gassner had taken some chances on Bud, allowing him to step up and play some meatier parts. In Shaw's *Saint Joan*, on October 29, for example, Bud had played Brother Martin Ladvenu, who testifies that Joan of Arc is not possessed by the devil. And in a brief excerpt from Synge's *Riders to the Sea*, on November 5, Bud had played Bartley, the last of a widow's sons to drown. In *Power*, however, he played no significant part, for which he probably blamed Piscator.

It might also have been, in truth, because he hadn't really distinguished himself much in the two roles he'd done. In *Saint Joan*, he'd been "very intense" but ultimately "less than adequate," according to the Broadway actor Norman Rose, who was part of the cast. Of all the student actors, Rose thought, Bud "showed the least promise, because he seemed to have less equipment than anyone else."

And so, during rehearsals for *Power*, Bud was once again on the sidelines, "surly and tight-lipped," the second-year student remembered.

*Saint Joan* and *Riders to the Sea* were tragedies of the human condition. *Power*, in contrast, was about the collective potential of humanity, not the struggle of one individual. "The Epic Theatre," Piscator taught the students, "demonstrates life. It pretends to be theater but in the highest sense is the representation of ideas, rather than private relationships." Although Bud mocked Piscator and his philosophy—classmates would remember him mimicking the Director's pigeon-toed walk through the corridors—it was mostly out of loyalty to Stella Adler rather than a rejection of the political imperative of epic theater. In fact, the second-year student thought, Bud seemed to respond to the underlying theme of *Power*, "the idea that the citizen has responsibilities in society."

This was the effect of just five weeks at the New School: Bud had fully embraced the liberal philosophy of citizen activism and collective responsibility. Decades later, he would denounce a disengaged citizenry: "We refuse to admit that we are our brother's keeper," he said. "If we are not . . . our brother's keeper, then we are just simply not socially responsible." It was a worldview preached by impassioned exiles from vanished European democracies and absorbed by an impressionable, searching young man—"a naïve kid," in his own words, "looking for a purpose in life."

He was getting closer to finding one. That night, during rehearsals for *Power*, cheers from a demonstration outside distracted the actors. Bud followed some of his fellow students out onto the sidewalk. There were placards and posters supporting labor, chants of "one for all, all for one," and calls for the removal of

Francisco Franco in Spain. Bud seemed delighted, the second-year student thought. All at once, lifting his fist in a show of power, Bud shouted, "Proletariat of the world, unite!"

Whether he was being funny or serious, or a mixture of both, was irrelevant. For the first time in his life, Bud was a part of something; for once, he and his classmates were of the same mind. "Everyone was feeling very political the night of *Power*," the second-year student said. Just days before, Soviet forces had liberated Kiev from Fascist control and were on the offensive elsewhere. In this country, American Communists felt "their time had come [and] that the Soviets were proving themselves as freedom fighters." In New York, two Communists, including an African American, Benjamin Davis Jr., had been elected to the City Council. "There was an energy in the air in late 1943," said the second-year student. "Socialism, or something like it, was coming to America." And to the students of the Dramatic Workshop, including Bud, that was a very good thing.

Dodie had been liberal in her politics, working with the League of Women Voters, and while politics back home had always been vague and inchoate, without any labels, Bud had absorbed a sense of civic responsibility. Writing home to his parents soon after arriving in New York, he'd lamented the "bitterness and fear and hate and untruths" he saw in the world, adding, "I want to do something about it." At the Workshop, politics became clarified for him. "There was a lot of political energy at the school," Elaine Stritch said. "People would get up on soapboxes."

That, in turn, could lead to other kinds of energy. "Talking about politics was a turn-on for some people," Stritch said. Bud discovered that sharing his fervent political beliefs to someone of like mind, getting all red in the face, his heart pounding a mile a second, could be a terrific aphrodisiac.

That night, during the production of *Power*, lots of students were fired up, "talking about revolution," the second-year student remembered. This sort of talk was not highfalutin to Bud. This was empowering. Sexy.

The one figure who seemed unaffected by the energy and ardor expressed during the rehearsal was the Director. For all his commitment to social change, Piscator remained coldly distant from the emotion of it all. Irked by the distraction of the demonstration, he clapped his hands and shook his bony finger at the students, telling them to get back inside. Bud didn't like to be told to quiet down. He didn't like to follow orders if they conflicted with his own impulses. That was why he would never have been any good in the army. Bud hated autocrats, and resisted their power as best he could.

Prime among them, of course, had been the autocrat for whom he was named.

Piscator's squelching of the students' spontaneous response to the demonstration may have triggered memories in Bud that he usually kept buried. Memories of being told to put away his drums or to go out and milk the cow. With such thoughts rushing back to Bud, it was perhaps inevitable that the evening ahead would turn out to be disastrous—because at the heart of his loathing for Erwin Piscator was one simple fact: the Director was simply Marlon Brando Sr. with an education and a German accent.

"MY FATHER," BUD said, "was a miser, and his miserliness was attached to [the] insecurity, instability, that prevailed [in] his psyche." Off on the road huckstering for Calcium Carbonite, Bud's father never left enough money behind to keep his wife and family afloat. That was hard enough. But, for Bud, his father's miserliness went even deeper than that. He was a miser in affection, compassion, and understanding.

"He was a card-carrying prick," Bud would say, looking back. "A frightening, silent, brooding, angry, hard-drinking man, a bully who loved to give orders and issue ultimatums. His blood consisted of compounds of alcohol, testosterone, adrenaline and anger."

At fourteen, Bud sat in the living room looking up at his father. Marlon Senior stood with his elbow on the mantel, giving the illusion that he was taller than his five-foot-nine frame. He was angry about his son's grades—Bud was pulling in mostly Ds—and his overall lack of ambition. The anger, however, went much deeper than that. Bud's father was unhappy with the loss of control over his household, the volatility of his wife, the disintegration of his family. Bud bore the brunt of that anger. When Bud was younger, he would just sit there and take whatever punishment his father gave him: cruel, demeaning words mostly, and arduous tasks around the house. But sometimes there was physical violence as well: a swat to the side of the head, a punch in the chest.

Now that Bud was older, however, he didn't just sit there and take it. He argued back, which infuriated his father more. Conflicts between father and son, said Don Hanmer, who was dating Tidd at the time, "would get louder and louder until there was a real fight." Blows were thrown. When Bud was too little to escape them, he'd suffered under his father's beatings. Now he dodged and darted, leaving his father breathless. That only made the older man more dangerous, because he sought revenge in other ways.

It came when Bud least expected it. Not long after one fight with his father, Bud was in his room dressing for a date. "All dressed up," his sister Frannie would describe him. An actual date, wearing nice clothes, was a rarity for Bud. He was taking the girl to a basketball game. Excited, he bounded down the stairs. But his father blocked his way. "You have to milk the cow," he told Bud.

The boy was crestfallen. "Would you please milk it for me?" he pleaded.

"No," his father replied. "Get your ass out there."

"So, I went out," Bud would tell the story. "I was in a hurry, didn't have time to change my shoes, so I had cow shit all over my shoes. All the way to the basketball game it smelled in the car." He paused, as he often did when dredging up his past. "I can't remember very many good things."

The cruelty of the incident stayed with the whole family. "This was the sort of thing that happened to Bud," Frannie said, "growing up in that lonely, friendless household." Their father's rage and his petty revenge defined their lives. They lived in fear. Tidd's son Gahan Hanmer would recall a photograph of his mother, aged five or six, "not smiling, eyes cast down slightly." Whenever he looked at that photo, it was obvious to him "that this little girl was terrified right down to her bones."

"I don't remember forgiveness," Frannie said. Instead, what stayed with her was "blame, shame and punishment that often had no relationship to the crime." Bud, Frannie said, "suffered this many more times" than either she or Tidd.

They were powerless to change things. Sometimes Dodie tried meekly to defend Bud against his father's tirades. But her husband was sole authority. If he said Bud was worthless, a "ne'er-do-well," then that was what Bud was. Dodie would withdraw, disappear. She had learned that opposing her husband was futile.

"Very extreme in his inaccessibility," Gahan Hanmer said. When Hanmer's father asked Marlon Senior for Tidd's hand in marriage, "Pop" said nothing. He "just sat in his chair and glared at him until my father gave up and left." His "inaccessibility as a father," Hanmer said, was "not just passive, which is bad enough, but threatening, which is ever so much worse."

The irony, Tidd said, was that "everybody outside the family loved [Marlon Senior], and thought he was so charming and marvelous and handsome and funny." But his children were "extensions of himself," Tidd said. "If we didn't toe the line, it reflected on him. Discipline somehow translated to love." Praise or affection was nonexistent. "Eat in the kitchen until your table manners are good enough to come to the [dining] table," he'd say. If the children didn't like something on their plates—rutabaga, for example—he'd fork up a double helping and stuff it into their mouths. He'd criticize the way Frannie dressed, complain about Tidd's cooking, tell strangers that Bud wasn't smart enough to pass his exams. Frannie said that his "black moods and thunderous silences" were in some ways more damaging to them than their mother's drinking.

And that, Bud believed, could be laid squarely at his father's feet as well.

Before her marriage, Dodie had been "a free spirit," Tidd said. Even in the first years of her marriage, when she'd acted in plays at the Omaha Community Playhouse, she still possessed "a certain joie de vivre." But things changed after they left Omaha for Evanston, a move Dodie had opposed but that Marlon Senior had insisted upon. Dodie had hated leaving her friends, family, and community, and she'd found the people of Evanston stuffy and pretentious. But her husband had argued that the money was good, even if he had to be on the road hustling most of the time to earn it. Bud grew to hate hearing his father bragging about his hucksterism, how he'd lure new clients for Calcium Carbonate through duplicity and crafty salesmanship. "You had to be a sneak to sell your product, a pusher," Bud would say derisively, years later.

What made it all worse, however, were the other activities his father was engaging in while traveling. "Whore fucker," Bud would call him. Word got back to Dodie that when Marlon Senior stayed at various hotels along the way to Rockland, Dubuque, or Waterloo, he wasn't always alone. "It was an era," Bud said, "when a traveling salesman slipped $5 to a bellboy, who would return with a pint of whisky and a hooker. Then the house detective got a dollar so that the woman could stay in the room. My Pop was such a man."

As the years went by, Marlon Senior tried less and less to hide his philandering. Lipstick and other stains covered the clothes he'd bring home for his wife to wash. "At least you could get your laundry done and I wouldn't have to see it," Bud heard his mother snap one night at his father. So, Dodie turned to the only consolation she could find in that cold and aloof community: the spirits she smuggled into the house after her trips into town.

They'd always been hearty drinkers, Dodie and Marlon Senior, though he was far better at holding his liquor than his wife. Still, when Dodie's drinking reached a critical point, Marlon attended a meeting of the newly formed Alcoholics Anonymous in Chicago—though it would still be several years before he gave up drinking himself. Dodie, however, refused to accompany him to the support group (at the time, AA membership was largely male, at least in Chicago), which allowed Marlon Senior to blame his wife for her ongoing problems.

Tidd, the eldest child, could see plainly what was happening with her parents. But little Frannie and Bud just heard the hushed, angry voices rising from downstairs, the occasional cry or the slam of a door. Mostly their parents fought out of view. Still, Bud said, "there was this grinding, unstated miasma of anger." The sensitive little boy possessed a child's sixth sense awareness of the problem. Once, while his parents were fighting, he gathered their empty bottles, carried them outside, and lined them up on the sidewalk in front of the house. It was almost as if he were explaining to the world the troubles within.

Dodie had tried running away to California with the children. But for whatever reasons, she'd agreed to give her marriage another try. In Libertyville, though, things had only gotten worse. Marlon Senior continued to stay away from home for as long as he could. Wandering around that old farmhouse like a lame mare penned up in a barn, Dodie went a little madder each day. If the rumors around town were true, she may have retaliated against her husband's infidelities with affairs of her own. Her letters reveal intimate relationships with male acquaintances, and she was often spotted with men in Libertyville cafés. Local busybodies thought

Marlon Senior's affairs were bad enough. An adulterous woman was judged even more harshly.

Dodie's drinking came in waves. She could be sober for weeks, even months, seemingly happy and gay—and then the children would suddenly come home to find her still in her housecoat, her hair a mess, slurring her words, and either manically playing the phonograph or despondently slumped in her chair. Right in front of the children she'd sip her whisky, telling them it was "Empirin" (liquid aspirin) for her headaches. "She'd put liquor in the bottle," Bud remembered, "and we would see her taking sips, and we all thought it was Empirin." They weren't fooled for long, however. "We would smell [the whisky] on her breath," Bud said.

He was terrified to bring friends home from school. When she was drunk, Dodie sometimes flirted with Bud's friends, using words their own mothers would have washed their mouths out with soap for using. That was why Bud brought few friends home—why, in fact, he had few friends.

Sometimes Dodie would get drunk and call the children in to listen to a phonograph of Stravinsky's *The Rite of Spring*, played at the highest volume. She'd sink back into a chair, savoring the emotion of it, Tidd recalled. "Isn't it beautiful?" she'd ask the children. "Isn't it beautiful?" And then she'd burst into tears.

Sometimes, when she didn't come home, Bud would go out in search of her. "I used to come home from school," he remembered. "There wouldn't be anybody home. Nothing in the icebox." Then the telephone would ring. "Somebody calling from some bar. 'We've got a lady down here. You better come get her.'" And Bud would go claim his mother, like a lost dog, bringing her home and carrying her up to bed. One time, however, as he'd confide to a friend, he found her drunk with a marine, and she refused Bud's pleas to come home, telling him to go away.

When the children were younger, they'd had Irmy, their maid, to tide them through their mother's truancy. Bud, especially, had loved Irmy a great deal. At three or four years of age, he would crawl into bed with her. Irmy was seventeen or eighteen, and always slept naked. She felt no shame about the human body, and Bud would fall asleep curled up beside her, her arm protectively around his slender shoulders. If he woke, he would caress and explore her body inquisitively. "She was all mine," he'd remember. "She belonged to me and to me alone." It was a feeling he never had with his mother.

To Bud, Irmy was as different from Dodie as possible. She was dark, he remembered, with "a touch of Indonesian blood" tinting her Danish heritage, and "a slightly dusky, smoky patina" to her skin. Later, he'd describe her as "black" to his friend George Englund. Yet, here again, it seems, was a moment when memory got twisted into something else, overlaid by later dreams and desires. If Irmy had Indonesian blood, it could only have been from many generations back, for census records reveal that both she and her parents had been born in Denmark and, moreover, that both sets of grandparents had been born there as well. Irmy's photograph in her high school yearbook reveals that she did indeed have dark hair but otherwise traditionally Scandinavian features. Yet it was vital that Bud remember her as fundamentally different from his mother. No way could Irmy be anything like Dodie. Irmy was constant and reliable. His mother was erratic and unsteady. Irmy gave Bud the stability his mother could not.

Yet Irmy, too, would abandon him. When Bud was eight, the housekeeper left the Brando household to get married; in Bud's memory, she never came to say good-bye to him. She just left. The little boy was heartbroken.

Other maids came and went; just before Bud had left for New York, the Brandos employed the sixty-six-year-old Scottish-born Margaret Pollock. There'd also been at least one African American maid. But none of the housekeepers had held the family together like Irmy when Dodie came undone. Some of the later help, in fact, would go out drinking with her at Libertyville saloons.

When Marlon Senior came home to find his wife missing, he seethed. On one occasion, with Dodie gone and Tidd making supper for the family, he furiously started packing his bags to go stay at his social club. At last, Tidd exploded. "You're just going to leave us here?" she shouted. "You're going to leave us here to cope with all these things?" Marlon Senior stayed that night, but only reluctantly. When Dodie at last came wandering home, her husband called a family meeting, shaming her in front of the children. "We can't survive if this continues," he shouted. Dodie dissolved into tears, vowing never to drink again. But it was a promise they all knew was impossible for her to keep.

For all the ache he felt, Bud rarely blamed his mother for her lapses. "Bud was upset by it," a friend said, but "more than anything he wondered why this was happening to his mother"—to his beautiful, sensitive, compassionate mother, who'd read him poetry, who'd taught him "the words to all the songs in the world." She had taught him to love nature, but "that was the most," Bud came to understand, "that she could do." Her problems were not her fault but his father's, Bud believed. His tormenter was also his mother's, and he'd never forgive him for it.

When she'd been a young nursing school student, Dodie got drunk one night just for the experience. She hadn't liked it. "I drank half a quart of whisky with ginger ale, smoked six cigarettes, drank port wine and more whisky," she wrote to Marlon Senior, who was then her boyfriend. "I've been sick ever since. I wanted to get stewed once to see what it was like." She would never do it once they were married, she promised her future husband. "Dearest, that's the one thing we'll never, never do is get stewed. I think it's horrible." Not long afterward, Dodie was expelled from school for climbing out her window in the middle of the night to meet Marlon Senior and their friends.

Dodie's tragedy was that she was smart, eloquent, and artistic, and she could see what was happening to her. She knew she was reaching bottom, but she was unable to reverse course. One night, alone in her room, she swallowed some pills. If Bud was home that night, the exact memory would apparently be too painful for him to keep or to speak out loud; all he'd retain of his mother's breakdown, he'd say, were fleeting images of her returning home from the hospital, shrunken and weak. But out in the yard, the stable hands were whispering that Mrs. Brando had needed to be pumped out. And it wasn't, apparently, the first time.

And so, as her son would heartbreakingly and accurately describe, Dodie Pennebaker Brando shattered like porcelain, her son helpless to save her. "My mother was everything to me," Bud said. "A whole world." And then that world had disintegrated around him.

ON THE NIGHT of the performance of *Power*, one Workshop student recalled, Piscator was growing ever more autocratic, insisting that students perform the piece his way, no questions asked. He seemed hyperconscious of this opportunity to demonstrate his epic theater philosophy, his chance to show Stella Adler and all those "sugared realists" what theater was really meant to do.

Meanwhile, backstage, his actors were passing around a bottle. Piscator, of course, was in the dark about it. He would have had convulsions had he known. Disguised in a small paper bag, the bottle went from mouth to mouth, and everyone started getting a little bit livelier. "Releasing inhibitions," the second-year student said. Whether Bud partook was unknown. But he was definitely flirting with one young woman who did; her identity was not recalled, but she was "dark, gypsy-like," the student said. And most likely her breath smelled of alcohol.

"I used to love the smell of women who had liquor on their breath," Bud said. "Some people drink and their breath becomes very, very sweet. It's a lovely fragrance. And some people drink and it's a caustic sensation to the nose. But I was always sexually aroused by that kind of smell. I don't know why."

In truth, he probably had some idea.

Children of alcoholics respond to the trauma in their families in different ways. Some hate the drunken parent; others love him or her too much. Some become "perfect children," highly motivated to escape their surroundings. Bud's sisters were like this. Tidd got out of the house by studying acting in New York; Frannie did the same, choosing art as her focus. The siblings had been through the fire together; their stories overlapped, intertwined. "Whose detail is whose when we are all crammed into a crowded match-box?" Frannie would ask. But eventually each of them had to save him- or herself. "We were all bruised and dismembered by the experience of growing up in that family," Bud said. "We all had to resuscitate ourselves the best way that we could."

Bud didn't have his sisters' ambition, however. After Irmy left when he was eight, he became "a delinquent," he said. He fought with other boys. He skipped classes. One of his teachers remembered, "He always put on a tough exterior. His face would be all tied up in a scowl, and it was as though getting into fights answered a need for him. It let him get something out, even though he couldn't or wouldn't talk about it."

At the age of twelve, Bud was described by his mother (with an offensive racist term common during the period) as "emotionally resembl[ing] a Fourth of July nigger chaser"—slang for an exploding firecracker. As he got older, Bud's explosions came faster and more furious. He tossed rocks at the glass insulators on telephone poles, considering it a "triumph" when he broke one. He threw paint all over the walls of a friend's house while it was being remodeled. He carried a knife and slashed tires. He shot his BB gun through the screens of his house from inside, one time hitting a man down the street in the neck. The real crimes began in high school. "I remember stealing money out of the neighbors' houses," he said. "Resentment was building up in me."

Very few who grow up with alcoholic parents can escape some measure of resentment. Some of the luckier ones find constructive means to get rid of it. Bud was not one of them. Without the aspirations of his sisters, with no apparent talents or skills, by the time he was fifteen he felt hopeless.

"I think that when things are extremely painful to you," Bud would say, "you don't want them in your consciousness and they are repressed naturally. And I suppose that there are memories that I have of incidents, things that fill me, even now, with a glint of shame and embarrassment and anger. It makes me very angry, and [made me] get in a lot of fights and things like that. See, when you fill a balloon up and you take a pin, the air rushes out at a tremendous rate of speed. So that's what happens when you're deeply angry at something. The air comes out from these little holes at tremendous force."

Asked, years later, where such rage comes from, Bud responded as if the answer were the most obvious thing in the world. "It always comes," he said, "from childhood." The trauma he experienced as a boy imprinted the rest of his life, and the post-traumatic stress he was left with was never fully exorcised. He lived in a constant state of fear. His father, Bud declared, "was the golem that stomped across the geography of my psyche." And never was his father more golem-like than one night when Bud was fifteen.

Dodie was drunk. Her husband had just brought her home from somewhere. Purple with rage, he took her up to bed. In terror, Bud sat downstairs. He could hear his mother stumbling, his father's harsh rebukes. Then, in a moment that would sear his consciousness for the rest of his life, he heard the sound of his mother being struck. He bolted upstairs.

Barging into his parents' room, he saw his mother collapsed on the bed. She was crying. His father stood over her. All at once, the teenager flew into a rage.

"If you touch her again," he seethed at his father, "I will kill you."

Marlon Senior saw the look on his son's face. "And whether it was a sense of shame," Bud mused, "or whether it was because he was out of adrenaline [and] I had the strength of four chimpanzees at that point," the older man backed down. Otherwise, Bud said, "I would have killed him. There's no question in my mind."

In that instant, the relationship between father and son shifted forever.

Everyone, Bud said, has "some measure of rage" inside them. People learn to repress their "natural instincts," however, so their rage usually goes unexpressed. But when provoked, it's right there, especially for those still recovering from trauma.

Which would describe Bud on the night of *Power*.

LESS THAN AN hour before the public was let into the auditorium, Piscator was running some lines with his actors. Everyone was bruised from rehearsals. Emotions were raw. Suddenly a scream from backstage caused the Director to jump. Out rushed a young man, his hand to face, his nose bloody. "He hit me!" the young man muttered, spitting blood as he spoke.

Piscator hurried backstage.

Bud stood there glowering. As he'd remember it later, a fellow actor, while attempting to get him to stand up straighter, had patted his crotch and asked him what he liked. "Planting my foot for leverage against a scenery board nailed to the floor," Bud said, "I unleashed a punch that sent him sailing across the room and to a hospital with a smashed face."

*Everyone has some measure of rage inside them.*

The man's hand on his crotch was the pin to Bud's balloon. His reaction surprised the other students; this wasn't how most people responded to sexual passes at the Workshop. "There wasn't usually any violence when a butt was pinched or a breast grabbed," said the second-year student. "Right or wrong, it was part of the culture. If everybody threw a punch after every pinch and every grab, there would have been fights every day." At the Workshop, a "sexual fluidity" prevailed, and same-sex flirtation was common. Bud had never previously expressed "any animosity toward the men who were seen as fairies," the student said. But the man's hand on his crotch—today it would be considered sexual assault—triggered something in Bud, and he had responded instinctively. His balloon was pricked, and the air came rushing out with a terrible, awful force.

"This is *not* how we handle things in the theater," Piscator reprimanded him. According to another student, he sent the brooding young actor home "to cool off." But once the rage was out, Bud always had a difficult time pulling it back in. Possibly he stormed around town, or rode his motorcycle at high speeds, or punched the plaster of his apartment until it crumbled all over the floor. Or maybe he showed up at Celia's and fucked her until he wasn't mad anymore. What was certain, however, was that he held on to some part of his rage, not at the guy who'd made the pass, but at Piscator, who'd thought he knew best, who'd embarrassed him in front of the others, who'd never seemed more like Marlon Brando Senior.

**LATE NOVEMBER** / The Dramatic Workshop closed from November 20 to December 4 for Thanksgiving. Those students with families in the city returned home for turkey and stuffing and cranberry sauce. Those who came from farther away celebrated with friends, if they were lucky enough to get an invitation, or else they "tended to disregard the holiday," one student remembered, "since holidays were bourgeois capitalist money-making schemes anyway."

If Bud went anywhere for Thanksgiving, it was probably to Darren Dublin's parents' house in Queens. The two young men had become inseparable. The day they met, Darren would remember, they'd stayed up all night jabbering in the basement of the New School, talking about New York and girls and sex and music and theater and everything else, until they eventually fell asleep on top of a pile of costumes in the wardrobe closet. Darren and Bud pulled pranks, took chances. Students would look up and spot them walking the narrow parapet of the school, six stories above the street. When Bud arrived for morning classes on his bike, Darren was often on the back. At night, they whistled at strippers in burlesque joints or swayed to the sound of trombones in jazz clubs.

"He was so exciting to be with," Darren said. "Whatever he proposed was more exciting than what my life had been." Darren had attended the Workshop a year earlier, before being drafted into the army. Discharged on "psychoneurotic grounds"—a term a psychiatrist would later use to diagnose Bud himself—Darren had returned to the Workshop this fall, but his studies were once again interrupted, this time by his new pal Bud. "They just weren't serious about school," said a classmate. "Darren might have been, but it was apparently more fun to goof off with the guy on the motorbike."

After a night of carousing, before the sun was up, Bud and Darren arrived at a friend's house in Brooklyn. Upstairs, they were still wired, unable to sleep. Lodging themselves at the window, they watched the sun come up and the army of workers that soon appeared, trudging toward the subway to start their day. "There but for the grace of God," Bud told his pal. "We were about ready to go to sleep," Darren said, "and these poor motherfuckers had to go to work." Such a daily grind was intolerable to Bud's mind: "That would be the worst thing in the world," he told Darren.

The two friends divided the world between the "interesting people"—among whom, of course, they counted themselves—and everyone else. "We felt superior to most people," Darren said, "like we were on the cutting edge."

They were preoccupied with girls, other classmates remembered. On Twelfth Street, the two young men would sit on the curb, ogling the females who walked by. They were fascinated to know which girls "put out" and which didn't. "They were always looking around to see who was going with whom," Mae Cooper said, "who's having an affair"—gossipy, really, she said, "like two girls would do." While the other students were discussing Irish drama and Greek tragedies, Bud and Darren "were imagining who was fucking who," said the second-year student.

And sometimes, they wondered about the boys as well.

"There were definitely homosexual couplings at the Workshop," recalled the second-year student. "People talked about it, gossiped about it, just like any other relationship." And that included Bud: "He was very interested, and not in the slightest way judgmental." Bud said that "many of the artists in the world" were homosexual, and that "it might even be found that artistic sensibility comes from or is present in the homosexual brain." Like Jews, it seemed, Bud saw homosexuals as a specially gifted species.

He was also aware, Elaine Stritch said, that some of the boys fancied him as much as the girls did. "How could he *not* know?" she asked. "You talk about a femme fatale—what's the similar expression for men?" Whatever it was, that was Bud. "The trait," she explained, "is feminine," even if "the man himself was a paragon of masculinity." And, she added insightfully, "those categories always threaten to touch at their extremities."

Indeed, they did: Bud's entreating eyes and his soft, slightly high-pitched voice made him a tantalizing mix of the masculine and feminine. For all his black leather motorcycle gear, he wasn't embarrassed to sit with Darren and gossip and giggle; neither was he threatened by "the fairies," as the second-year student called them, the male students who flirted with him in the corridors of the school.

So why had he thrown that punch?

The answer, as always, was buried deep in his past, a past that had the power to erupt at any time, upending everything in Bud's present.

ONLY ONE MAN had ever truly believed in Bud. Only one man had seen his potential to succeed. But like so many of those who mattered in Bud's life, that man had been deeply flawed, and had failed him when he needed him most.

His name was Earle M. Wagner. He was the head of the English department at the Shattuck Military Academy, and was known to everyone on campus as "Duke." At Shattuck, Duke was also the drama coach, and it had been he who first spotted some dramatic talent in Bud, inviting the boy's mother up to see him act.

Before Duke, no one had ever really championed Bud. Most of his teachers had despaired of him. The principal of his high school in Libertyville had called him "a bum . . . good for nothing" and predicted, "You'll never do anything but dig ditches"—a prediction that had, for a few terrible months anyway, come true. Bud said of his time in school, "I had never received accolades, or adulations, never even encouragement." Only once did an instructor give him anything resembling praise. His shop teacher at Julia Lathrop Junior High School in Santa Ana, California, had commended him for making a screwdriver. "I can't even remember his name," Bud would say. That was it: one moment of recognition in the course of a decade.

Duke, however, saw something others didn't. Forty-four when Bud met him, Duke was a pillar of the school, having been teaching there since three years before Bud was born. A native of Indiana, the son of German immigrants, Duke was a graduate of the

University of Chicago, a world traveler and a fiercely opinionated theatergoer. At one point he argued in print with *Chicago Tribune* critics over the merits of Shakespearean actor Richard Mansfield. (Duke felt he lacked any.) A bachelor, Duke lived on campus with his English bulldog in a suite decorated with Oriental rugs and antique lithographs, and sometimes he'd invite the cadets in for readings of poetry or Shakespeare. To the delight of the boys, Duke would pepper his literary readings with biting, sometimes risqué, asides. He was a character. "He wore his coat," Bud remembered, "without putting his arms in the sleeves, off the shoulders, fancying it was dashing and cape-like." And his "old battered hat," Bud added, was worn "at an improbable angle." His mustache was thin, in the style of movie star John Gilbert, and "he had kind of a slanted smile," Bud said, "with a lot of charm in it." When Duke directed the school's dramatic productions, he brought to the effort all the flair and flamboyance of a Broadway impresario.

The first time he watched cadet Bud Brando on the stage, his eyes lit up. Playing "a rather difficult role" in the one-act play *A Message from Khufu*, Bud stood out from the others, Duke thought. He wrote to the boy's father, "He seems to be taking hold fairly well." After seeing Bud perform and encouraged by Duke, Dodie took her son on a walk across the campus, telling him that if he wanted to be an actor he'd have to spend many years developing his craft—though, tellingly, she did not discuss her own work in the theater.

If, however, Bud considered the idea of an acting career at that moment, his father wasn't buying it. Brando Senior had attended Shattuck himself. He'd sent his son to the military academy to straighten him out, not to turn him into an actor. In the opinion of the elder Brando, the theater was no way to make a living. He might have allowed Tidd to study acting, but Tidd was a girl. Bud was a boy and a wayward one at that, one whose path needed to be clear and direct, and what Duke Wagner was suggesting was simply unthinkable.

Still, Bud's teacher urged Brando Senior to consider some new ideas to bring out the boy's abilities. A new program of study could "strike at the root of the boy's weakness and give him the work he is most qualified for," Duke wrote. To do this, however, meant dropping Bud back a grade in English and French, something Marlon Senior could not abide. Despite having already completed three years of high school in Libertyville, Bud had entered Shattuck as a sophomore. And now Wagner was suggesting they push him back even more? "I feel that he must be in college in the fall of 1943," Marlon Senior wrote to the school a month after Duke's letter. There was no room for further delay or deviation. The subject was dropped.

Stymied by the intransigence of Bud's father, Duke found other ways to mentor the boy. He understood that the rigid, authoritarian nature of the military school chafed against Bud's natural instincts. "The mind of the military," Bud would explain, "has one aim, and that's to be as mechanical as possible so they can rely on things. They want to have the same reliability in a man as they would a telephone or a starter in your car. And it is only through that order, through the successful excise of individuality, that they make a good soldier. They want you to act as a unit, not as an individual—no matter what kind of horseshit they tell you."

*The excise of individuality.* That was something Bud instinctively rebelled against, both at Shattuck and at the Dramatic Workshop under Erwin Piscator. Bud called it "indoctrination," and he thought Duke "seemed to get my point." Cannily, the drama coach suggested that Bud join the "Crack Squad," the school's drill team—a traditional military endeavor, but one in which a boy like Bud might be able to find some room to shine a little on his own. The Crack Squad was mostly show: "You had to be able to throw a rifle up in the air," Bud said. "All that stuff." He quickly mastered the moves, throwing the rifle, catching it, dismantling it, and putting it back together, all in a matter of seconds. Shattuck's Crack Squad was "quite famous," Bud learned, "and put on exhibitions everywhere." So, when he made the team, he knew the achievement would please his father, an old "Shad" himself.

Bud took the moment to pen an extraordinary letter home. Reading his words many years later, there seems to be a hope that his father might finally understand him. "All my life," Bud wrote, "I have been told that I could do it 'if I wanted to.' Ever since I was a little kid I can remember people telling me that. Ever since I can remember I've been riding along on my potentialities. Now if there is anything that I want to do it is to live up to your expectations of me. This probably sounds really disjointed and vague cause I'm in a funny mood. You see, they just made the announcement about who was on the Crack Squad. Well, I got on and it makes me realize more than ever how far from an honor it is to me. I don't give a damn for football teams, swimming teams, and crack squads. I am sorry to have been so weak for so many years but that doesn't help the situation much. I have set my goals and I am hard at them (as I have said so many times before) but this time is really it."

In other words, he was telling his father that he could do what was expected of him—make the Crack Squad, for instance—but that, ultimately, he hoped to live up to his father's expectations in another way. Just how, he wasn't entirely clear. But he seemed to be trying to leave behind old, destructive patterns. "I feel as though I were just getting over a terrible sickness," he wrote to his grandmother, Dodie's mother, in California. "As I look back on the four preceding years I can hardly believe it's me. I was absolutely intolerable. Even though I am a long way from the pinicle [sic] of success, I know that someday I'm going to quit this." Just what he meant by "quit this" is unclear, but apparently he was referring to his "intolerable" behavior. Bud had grown weary of being a disappointment to the family.

In his letter to his father, he seemed to suggest that the way forward for him was academic, or at least more cerebral than athletics or the military. Duke Wagner had helped him see that. Duke, Bud told his father, was an inspiration. Duke had shared stories of great poets and writers, men who "had gone against the grain to achieve greatness," Bud recalled. It seemed to be Duke's way of affirming those boys who were "different," the ones called "wayward" by their parents and teachers. For Bud, the affirmation worked. In his letter to his father, he expressed some insight about himself: "We have been studying men like Ben [*sic*, Samuel] Johnson, who at eighteen translated Pope's *Messiah* into Latin verse, and men like [novelist] Sam Richardson. A study of their lives has made me realize what excruciating mental work it takes to get to the point of development that they did and also it makes me realize how pitifully short I have fallen already."

He ended his note with a plea and a promise. "Keep writing and telling me to get at it. I won't let you down. Love, Bud."

The letter is heartbreaking in its sincerity and humility, two words not usually associated with Bud. At this point in his life, so unhappy at Shattuck, he was struggling to find a way forward for himself, one that might satisfy both him and his father, as impossible a task as that might have been. Years later, reading the letters he'd sent back home, Bud would see "an eager, lonely child who never had much of a childhood, who needed affection and assurance and lied to his parents in the hope that something he might say would make them want to love him."

Yet, for all his pleading with his parents, something had shifted for Bud. For the first time, as evidenced in his letter, he had hope. He'd been told for so long that he was worthless, but now he was hearing a different message from the first sympathetic mentor of his life. Suddenly, he had the faith and the courage to plead with his father: *Let me be me. I can make you proud in my own way.* His letter was a cri de cœur—perhaps the first genuine outreach either had ever made toward the other. Only Duke's influence, and his belief in Bud, could have made that happen.

Yet, if Marlon Senior ever wrote his son a note in reply, none would survive. Bud would never speak of any effort on his father's part to meet him halfway.

DESPITE HIS SHOWMANSHIP with the rifle, Bud was never going to fit in at Shattuck. The Crack Squad was really just theatrics—something he was always good at. Commitment to the cause, however, was another thing entirely.

"To see people regimented as they are, marching up and down, marching as one," he said, "is nauseating to me."

At one point, an army colonel came to campus to question the cadets. "Soldier," he said to Bud, "the battalion leader has been killed. What do you do?"

"Well," Bud replied. "I'd ask the company commander."

"He's been killed, too. What would you do then?"

Bud thought about it. "I'd ask the squad leader."

"He's been killed, too," the colonel said. "What would you do then?"

"Run like hell."

That was Bud's sense of humor, the sort of comeback that made his friends laugh. But no one was laughing at Shattuck. "They were really pissed off with that," Bud recalled. "So, they put me in my room. I was delighted. I didn't have to go out on an extended order drill."

But to drop out of the place meant failure; to drop out meant going back to his father's house, which was just as intolerable in its own way. Still, from his lonely perch in his Gothic granite dormitory, the miserable seventeen-year-old conjured up a home and family very different from reality. He addressed one envelope to "The Greatest

Family in the World, the Brandos, General Delivery, Libertyville, Illinois." So unhappy was Bud at Shattuck that he was feeling nostalgic for Libertyville. "This last week and a half has been terrible," he wrote. "I hurt my back in football so I haven't been playing at all. I'm getting awfully mean and moody and lonesome."

More and more, he turned to Duke. A devout Episcopalian, Duke was an unlikely mentor; Bud once offended him by taking Communion and removing the wafer from his mouth to inspect it. He called the concept of eating Christ's flesh "cannibalistic"; Duke told him he was "tempting the Devil."

Yet Duke could also be irreverent, with his double-entendre jokes and winking explanations of Shakespeare's puns on sex and genitalia. "He saw himself as rather rakish," Bud thought. Students whispered that Duke was "having an affair with the wife of the headmaster, who at the time was serving overseas as an army chaplain," Shattuck student William Peverill recalled. Those rumors may in fact have obscured a secret even more dangerous: Duke would eventually be accused of having sex with cadets. This was the memory of both Peverill ("Few were aware of [Duke's] sexual versatility") and Reginald Kramer, an assistant headmaster, who remembered Duke's being fired, five years after Bud left the school, for "sexual activity" with cadets. "During the night," Kramer said, "he had to pack up and get out." Peverill corroborated the story: "He was, after 26 years [sic, twenty-eight years], unceremoniously bounced from the campus for having sexual relations with one of the cadets." It was a humiliating fall for a man who had been honored with a dedication in the Shattuck yearbook just a few years before, praised for his "enthusiasm and loyalty" and contributions to school morale.

Just how much Bud knew about Duke's sexuality is unknowable. But at the same time that he was being mentored by Duke, Bud was quite open about a sexual fling he himself was having with another young man on campus. The relationship was nothing extraordinary; sexual play between cadets at military schools was not uncommon. "For me, sex is something you can't describe," Bud said later, acknowledging sexual experiences with men. "Let's say sex has no sex." In an environment where there were no women around, a "soft, sweet, moony" boy (as one cadet described Bud's friend) might have proven just as satisfying to him.

What's far more remarkable than Bud's relationship with the boy is the fact that he didn't try to hide it from his friends. This was the carefree, bohemian, nonjudgmental approach to sex with which he'd been raised. Of his "homosexual experiences," Marlon would later declare that he was "not ashamed." There was no guilt, no shame, no implication for one's self-identity. For Bud, sex was meant to be enjoyed. He was insecure about many things, but sex was not one of them.

Did Duke know about his protégé's sexual relationship with another student? Did Bud know about his mentor's sexual relationships with cadets? Was Bud Brando one of the cadets Duke had sex with? All unanswerable questions.

But something happened, in the first few months of 1943, to change Bud's relationship with Duke. Something so traumatizing that Bud could never bring himself to speak of it, leaving that to others. Whatever it was, the man who had once empowered him, who had taught him to believe in himself, suddenly turned on him, rejected him, failed him, just as everyone eventually did in Bud's life.

The answer to the question of why Bud threw that punch, some nine months later at the March of Drama, might lie somewhere here, in the sad, messy conclusion to his time at Shattuck. It was a time that ended with his being unceremoniously expelled from the school, and the promise he made to his father never to let him down exposed as the posturing of an immature, desperate boy.

**EARLY DECEMBER** / In a biting wind, Bud stood on the roof of the New School. He wore no coat, no sweater, only a button-down shirt and khakis. The temperature was near freezing, according to the second-year student, who stood on the street looking up. Bud's hands were thrust into his pockets, and he was staring straight ahead, looking at nothing. Spotting Bud Brando on the roof was not really all that uncommon, but usually Darren was with him, and they were daredevil-ing their way across the edge. But on this morning Bud stood alone, rock still. "For a second, I was worried," the second-year student said. "Was he going to jump? He looked as if he might."

Finally, as the student watched, Bud turned and disappeared from the roof. He reappeared inside the school, where he moved "like a ghost" through the day's classes. Over the past few weeks, a change had come over him. The second-year student wasn't the only one to detect a shift in his mood. Elaine Stritch remembered the "depression he got into" that winter, "when he wouldn't talk to any of us." Joy Thomson, a stage design student, thought Bud just "didn't seem dedicated" to his studies. Stritch heard talk that he was planning to drop out at the end of the term.

Given Bud's track record, no one would have been very surprised if he had.

Another student spotted him in the dance studio downstairs around this time. Once again, Bud was alone, sitting on the edge of a table, holding a lit candle in one hand and letting the wax drip onto the other. When the student asked what he was doing, Bud just looked at her without answering. Soon stories were spreading about him. Elaine Stritch heard that he was quitting school, but others believed he was facing probation. His friend Carmelita Pope, who'd recently moved to New York, found him very different from the boy who used to visit her in Chicago. Moody and withdrawn, Bud "hated anybody prying into his private life," Pope said, "and would get angry if you asked too many questions about why he was unhappy."

Bud had slowed down quite a bit by the late fall, to the point where several people described him as depressed. Retreating from his classmates, he grew quiet and querulous, and lost much of his energy in class. Survivors of trauma often experience these sorts of mood fluctuations. Bud also became extremely sensitive to noise, another common symptom. On the subway, he'd rip pieces of bread from his sandwich and stuff them down into his ears. He seemed a different young man. "A major swing from October to December," the second-year student recalled.

Bud himself acknowledged the change. He wrote to his former counselor at Shattuck about this period: "I came to New York. Went to drama school. Raised seventeen different kinds of hell, indulged in emotional experiences wantonly . . . [and] almost had a nervous breakdown from lack of security and direction."

*Lack of security and direction.* As always, that was the root of it. Nearing the end of his first term at the Workshop, he still carried with him the same "great feeling of inadequacy" he'd started with. He still considered himself "dumb and uninformed." He was an oil-and-water mixture of confidence and doubt; he had no doubt that he could walk the parapet of the New School, but the very act of risking it was to make up for what he believed he *couldn't* do in the classrooms below. That he'd been at the Workshop for only two months, that it took time to absorb all this new information, was irrelevant: Bud had never been a very patient young man. The difficult situation was compounded, of course, by his recurrent mood swings, and so, by the time winter set in, he was sulky and morose.

And possibly even worse than that. He had witnessed his mother's nervous breakdowns. Was it just hyperbole when he described himself as "almost" having one as well? What exactly did Bud go through that winter? Arguments? Tears? Fistfights? An alcoholic bender lasting several days? Or did his breakdown immobilize him, keeping him confined to his room? He would leave no record of what occurred, only that something did.

At the Workshop, he'd found some elements that he liked, some moments that sparked his interest. He'd found a fellowship of like-minded friends in terms of politics and civics. But he was no closer to caring about the art of theater than he had been when he first enrolled. He was still not like the others. Most significantly, he had done nothing to distinguish himself at the Workshop. It was Shattuck all over again: there might have been a few bright moments on the Crack Squad, but in the end, none of it mattered. He didn't belong.

Bud was ready to give up. He'd never succeeded at anything. Why should he have thought this time would be any different?

JUST WHY BUD was expelled from Shattuck in the spring of 1943 was never made clear. But from the very start he had been trouble, doing his "best," he said, "to tear the school apart and not get caught at it." Filling condoms with water, he tossed them out the window at people walking by. He dyed his hair (and that of his fellow cadets) green. He spread Vitalis, a hair tonic with alcohol in it, down the hall and up the stairs, then set a match to it. When he didn't want to go to class, he'd shove paper clips into the door locks to prevent the masters from using their keys. They'd have to call a locksmith, but by that time, the period for class had passed. "I screwed up a lot of locks," Bud boasted. "They knew who did it, but they never caught me."

The most legendary of his misdeeds concerned the school's bells. As always, sound had the power to unnerve him, and the bells, tolling every fifteen minutes from the Gothic clock tower in the center of campus, drove Bud mad. "I was always sensitive to certain kinds of sounds," he said, "especially sounds that had an authoritative ring." As he would tell the story, he slunk out of his dormitory in the middle of the night—grounds for "immediate dismissal from school," he knew, but he didn't care. Determined to put an end to those bells, he made his way stealthily up the stairs of the tower. He found the culprit. "A huge clapper," he said. "It must have weighed 150 pounds." Wrenching the clapper off the bells, he hoisted it onto his shoulder and hurried back down the stairs of the tower. On a remote part of the campus, he claimed, he buried the offensive object. And that, he said, ended the bells at Shattuck. As Bud told it, the clapper was never recovered, although "anybody with a metal finder," he insisted, could have found it.

The story of Bud and the bells would become part of his (and Shattuck's) lore. How true it was—fully, partly, not at all—no one was quite sure. Another version of the story had him simply cutting the ropes to the campus chimes. In fact, no official report was ever filed about damaged bells at Shattuck; if a bell stopped chiming, officials said, it would have been fixed as a matter of course. No one, as far as anyone knows, ever went hunting for Bud's buried clapper with a metal detector.

The story, like many of his stories, probably benefited from the retelling. Yet embellished or not, the anecdote did illustrate his rebellion and his deep unhappiness at the school. Bud's time at Shattuck was marked by the same ups and downs he would experience in New York, from manic highs to depressive lows.

And by the early spring of 1943, he was very low indeed. The one supporter he had, the one person who didn't view him as a delinquent, had turned against him.

In every account of Bud's expulsion from Shattuck—except, tellingly, his own—it was his cherished mentor Duke Wagner who was the instigator. Several cadets would recall Bud and Duke at odds in the weeks before the dismissal. Something had occurred to disrupt their friendship. Rehearsing Molière's *The Doctor in Spite of Himself*, in which Bud was set to play the lead, Sganarelle, director and student clashed repeatedly. At one point, in front of the whole cast, Bud called Duke "an asshole," which set off an explosion. "Nobody calls me an asshole!" Duke shouted. Bud stormed out of the theater, and the production descended into chaos.

A short time later, Bud was caught in town without a pass, and that was enough, apparently, to decide his fate. Today, the official line from Shattuck is that Bud's dismissal was "a case of the straw that broke the camel's back"—one violation too many. But another story circulated at the time: Duke had caught Bud smoking and recommended expulsion—Bud's one-time champion now his chief accuser. Until this point, Duke had seemed to take "a vicarious thrill" in Bud's imaginative pranks, according to Bud's own recollections. Now the drama coach evidently used them to get Bud kicked out of school.

On May 22, 1943, a letter was written to Marlon Senior that his son "didn't keep to the rules and broke probation" and so was being expelled.

"I was bored," Bud would say years later, when asked the reasons for his dismissal, "and I went downtown, and I got caught. I was off bounds." As much as he hated the place, the shame of being asked to leave was devastating. It was "another sense of failure," Bud said. Yet again, he "hadn't been able to 'skin the cat.'"

Bud never put any of the blame for his expulsion on Duke Wagner. But "something *did* happen" between him and Bud, insisted Charles Sweatt, a classmate, and "everyone knew it." Another cadet, Geordie Hormel, confirmed, "They were very close and then they were estranged."

Catching Bud smoking isn't believable as the reason for their estrangement. The "asshole" comment might have done it, but what had soured their relationship in the first place? "There was never an explanation," said a fourth cadet, Jim Leigh.

Whenever Bud spoke about his former teacher, which was rare, he always recalled him fondly. Many years later, he told a story of going to see Duke after the expulsion was announced, and in his memory, his mentor was gentle and kind. "He put his hands on my shoulders," Bud recalled. "I was crying. And Duke said, 'Don't worry, my boy. I've seen you. I know you. The world is going to hear from you.' And then I really cried. I put my head on his shoulder and sobbed."

The memory of Duke's arms around him left an impression. "It was the first time," Bud said, "that anybody had ever been so open. It was the first time that someone had faith in my ability to do something. He didn't say what it was. He just said, 'Don't be saddened. Be proud. And the world is going to hear from you.'"

Perhaps, at that moment, Duke regretted his actions and really did console Bud in this way. Or perhaps, for Bud, it was simply too difficult to remember Duke as anything other than supportive. For once, someone had believed in him. To lose that memory, on top of everything else, was perhaps too much to bear.

"Memories," Bud said, "get fuzzed over. You think that things happened this way, and then you're astounded [when] somebody says, 'No, that never happened.' Because you invent things in your mind. Think of stories that we tell, over and over again, to people. We make them true because we remember them in a certain way. And [maybe] they never happened that way at all."

For all Bud's silence on Duke's role in his expulsion, he did leave a clue that suggests things didn't end happily between them. One interviewer, many years later, would ask if the man who'd predicted great things for him had followed Bud's career. Did he ever see his belief in him vindicated? In reply to the question, Bud was terse. Duke, he said, died before he could witness the success he'd predicted for his young student.

But that wasn't true. After his own dismissal from Shattuck, Duke was hired by the U.S. Army for its training center in Kitzingen, Germany, where he supervised the education of black troops. He returned to the United States in June 1951; he didn't die until June 1966. That was plenty of time for him to see what had become of his protégé—plenty of time, in fact, for the two of them to reconnect. But according to Bud, he had no further contact with Duke, the first man who'd ever believed in him, the first who'd had faith in his ability to succeed.

Something kept them apart all those years. Whatever their conflict, it was undoubtedly very painful for Bud, and would still have been fresh in his mind a few months later in New York. If sex had had anything to do with their break, might the memory of it have been raw enough to trigger a violent response from Bud when a man patted his crotch backstage? No matter its details, the break with Duke—the loss of the first and, so far, only champion in his life—exacerbated the rage that Bud carried around with him, ensuring that it would continue, irregularly but reliably, to burst through the surface for some time to come.

AFTER HIS DISMISSAL from Shattuck, Bud was placed on a train back to Libertyville. He braced himself for his father's wrath. He'd promised his father he wouldn't fail, and yet he had. The cadets who accompanied him to the train station remembered Bud's solemnness, the way he just stared off into the distance. When he got home, his father was "mad as hell," Tidd remembered. He made his son feel like a "nogoodnik," Bud remembered. And so the young man had started digging ditches. It seemed all that he was good for.

Word that his fellow cadets had gone out on strike, calling the dismissal of their friend unfair, touched Bud deeply. But it didn't change his feelings of shame, which soon gave way to anger and resentment. When the cadets' strike caused the school to reconsider and ask the expelled student to return, Bud wrote a letter in response that he'd later call "adolescent [and] heroic." He told them that he'd reached a fork in the road and was going another way.

In fact, he was telling the school to go to hell.

In many ways, Bud's experience at the Dramatic Workshop

echoed his time at Shattuck. At both institutions, he did not share the commitment or the discipline of his classmates; he also didn't fully "buy in" to the underlying philosophy. Of course, the Workshop made more room for individuality, but it, too, was predicated on regimentation, and Piscator ran the place with an authoritarian hand. Once again, Bud was faced with the likelihood that he was about to fail. The Dramatic Workshop had turned out to be just one more cat he'd been unable to skin. And so, by the end of 1943, another train ride back to Libertyville loomed, this time from New York.

That winter, Bud was going through hell. The troughs of his mood swings were always especially difficult to get through. He cut himself off from everyone. "He would feel hopeless," said one friend. "Nothing was ever going to get better." The world closed in on him. He felt annihilated.

A similar desperate moment had occurred when he was in the seventh grade. "I had the fear that everyone had died," he remembered, "and that there was nothing behind me, and [the world] only appeared when I turned around and looked." People were only "pretending to be alive." Another time, at fourteen, his fear gave him a splitting headache, his eyes "all blurry on the sides." Everything went dark; he thought he was going blind. "I didn't know what it was," he said. "And nobody else knew, so I just endured it." He called such depersonalization (one of the more disturbing symptoms of post-traumatic stress) "the darkness."

That December, the darkness was back. Bud missed several classes, but one day, somehow, he managed to drag himself to school. Looking up from under hooded eyes, he saw John Gassner approaching him. The instructor had an offer to make him. He wanted Bud to play a part in that week's March of Drama production. In fact, a double role.

Bud didn't know it, but the darkness was about to lift. For a little while, at least.

**WINTER 1943/44** / Lit by a spotlight, Bud entered, stage right. In his arms he cradled the limp form of a young girl barely dressed in dirty rags. The girl's face was pressed against his throat, and her long hair cascaded everywhere. In contrast, Bud was dressed in the jacket and waistcoat of a professional; a fake beard was glued to his cheeks. Crossing the stage, he gently laid the girl down on a bed. Behind him, a group of actors dressed like paupers gathered to watch.

"Hot bricks, Seidel!" Bud shouted over his shoulder. "Quick!"

The girl's teeth were chattering.

"There, there," Bud assured her. "We'll soon put you right."

Out in the audience, some regular attendees of the March of Drama performances were intrigued by this actor who spoke so tenderly to the girl. They flipped open their mimeographed handouts to learn his name.

*Hannele's Way to Heaven* was presented on December 17, 1943, at the New School auditorium. The latest English-language adaptation of Gerhart Hauptmann's *Hanneles Himmelfahrt*, the play was described by its author as a "dream-poem," its two acts a strange mix of naturalism and fantasy, heavy on Christian theology. A teenaged girl, Hannele, abused by life, attempts suicide, but is fished out of the lake by a caring schoolteacher, Gottwald. By the end of the second act, Hannele gets her wish to go to heaven with an assist from a bevy of angels in full winged regalia and the timely arrival of Christ himself. Hauptmann wrote the play so that the actor who portrayed the schoolteacher would also play Christ. John Gassner, backed up probably by Stella Adler, thought Bud Brando just the right student to take on this extraordinary double part.

"There weren't a lot of male students to choose from," one classmate pointed out, "especially not ones strong enough to carry the girl across the stage, which [Bud] could do easily. But here's the other thing. He was *beautiful*. And they needed a young man who was really sort of angelically beautiful to play Jesus Christ. Beautiful in a no-mere-mortal kind of way."

Given the lack of impact that Bud's previous performances in the March of Drama had made on his teachers, it would seem that his physical appearance—his strength combined with his ethereal mix of femininity and masculinity—was the clincher in his casting in *Hannele*.

It was a rather hoary old play. Even when it was performed at the Lyceum Theatre in 1910, with Minnie Maddern Fiske in the title role, it had generated plenty of eyerolls from audiences and critics. During key melodramatic moments, theatergoers laughed and hooted; the *New York Times* opined that the final scene, in which Hannele ascends into heaven, "was almost rendered ridiculous." The story didn't fare much better in 1924, when Eva Le Gallienne took on the part at the Cort Theatre. "Stilted" and "quaintly grotesque" were the verdicts from the *Times*.

Still, *Hannele* provided Gassner's students an excellent example of the difference between naturalistic and allegorical theater, all in one production—which was no doubt why it was chosen to accompany the lecture on naturalism on December 17. The first scenes are models of naturalistic style, with the actors behaving realistically and speaking in true-to-life dialect. It is only with the entrance of the schoolteacher—Bud's entrance—that the play shifts, alternating back and forth between naturalism and allegory, until, by the end, it is all allegory. The play is far more complicated, structurally and stylistically, than it first appears. So, while Bud may have been chosen first for his looks, Gassner had to have been sufficiently confident in his ability to deliver more than just a pretty face.

From the memories of those who were there, Gassner's faith was justified.

"It gave you the chills," Mae Cooper said of Bud's performance.

"It was so good, so quiet, like the dawn of something great." She watched in amazement, unable to believe that this was their lackadaisical, motorcycle-riding classmate. "It was like suddenly you woke up and there's your idiot child playing Mozart."

"There was a surprising radiance to him," said the second-year student. "And it didn't all come from the spotlights."

In the part of Gottwald, Bud convincingly displayed tenderness, anger, fear, and grief toward the little waif Hannele, played by fourteen-year-old Priscilla Draghi. As the sandal-clad stranger who arrives in the second act, he conveyed mystery, compassion, authority, and, finally, when he was revealed as Christ, divinity. With the play already top heavy with symbolism and sentiment, Bud couldn't resort to "obvious theatrical tricks," the second-year student said, "like lifting his eyes and hands to heaven." Instead, he had to find ways to make the cloying dialogue sound natural. He did all that and more. Bud's successful performance was doubly impressive given the turmoil of the past few weeks.

The key to his success was simple. Unlike the other students, Bud had no preconceived notions of what "acting" was supposed to look like. He'd heard the arguments comparing Stanislavski and epic theater, he'd sat through the debates over realism, and he'd found it all, quite frankly, pretentious. Stella Adler had taught him a much more useful way of seeing things: she'd told her students that *everyone* acts, every day. The trick, she said, was just to be as open to the moment as possible, fully spontaneous and real, and to use the imagination. In fact, if Adler saw one of her students consciously trying to play a part, she'd shout, "Stop acting!"

So, when it came to technique, Bud didn't have any. Rather, he possessed an unspoiled naturalism—what Gassner understood *Hannele* needed. Bud's acting could have been overwrought and operatic. Instead, it was simple and sincere.

*Hannele* changed everything for him. From here on, Bud would be called "gifted," something that would have been inconceivable in any other chapter of his life so far.

At the climax of the piece, Bud intoned, "Thy shame I take from thee. I fill thine eyes with everlasting light. Let thine ears be opened to the music of the millions and millions of God's angels. Thus, I do loose thy stammering tongue and quicken it with the life of thine own soul and my soul, and the soul of God Almighty. With these thy tears, I cleanse thee from the dust and stain of earth. I will raise thee high above the stars of God."

He might have been performing a eulogy for the boy he had been.

HANNELE WAS SUCCESSFUL enough that Gassner decided to develop the play further, rehearsing his actors over the Christmas break for an encore presentation in January as replacement for another Hauptmann play, *The Weavers*. Meanwhile, Bud was also tapped to be part of *Bobino*, an original musical penned by the author (and later film critic) Stanley Kauffmann. The story of a boy who could speak the language of animals, *Bobino* was staged throughout the Christmas holiday by the American Theatre for Young Folks. Bud played a giraffe; Elaine Stritch doubled as a tiger and a cow. Mae Cooper dressed in drag as a prince.

Dark for much of the past year, the Studio Theatre was swept out and fixed up as the magical land of King Pampo, where the little boy (played by Priscilla Draghi) must discover "why the animals and the birds of the kingdom refuse to work." Exchanging Christ's robes and sandals for a costume of white and brown fur, Bud found his entire torso transformed into the giraffe's neck. Playwright Kauffmann described a typical performance of *Bobino*: "There are happy shouts [from the audience] when the hero steps out on stage. 'Hello, Bobino!' 'That's Bobino, mother!' There is the spot when Bobino's life is in danger because he cannot remember the magic verses, when the entire first row prompts him." At the end, one "hardened theatregoer of perhaps eight," Kauffmann wrote, turned to a friend and said, "That was the best play I ever saw in my life."

Bud was having just as much fun. His entire mood had changed. In other circumstances, he might have been lonely over the holidays, but with *Bobino*'s schedule, he didn't have time to be. Rehearsals took place the two weeks before Christmas, and the show opened on Christmas Day, playing straight through January 1. *Bobino* was so successful that it was continued on weekends through February. The entire company of twenty-five, a mix of children and adults, would come together for the big musical numbers ("Three Little Pigs," "The Horse and the Hen," and "The Fly"), choreographed by Eugene von Grona, a German émigré dancer and the founder of the First American Negro Ballet. With its singing animals and boisterous audiences, *Bobino* was quite the different theatrical experience from *Hannele*, and Bud loved the contrast.

Every day, his depression lifted a little bit more. *Hannele* was presented again on January 21, 1944. The auditorium was packed. Classmates recalled that Bud was even more accomplished this time. His performance would, in fact, become legendary at the Workshop. Two years later, when *Hannele* was revived, a new class of students was told that Bud's work in the play was something to live up to; it was "already part of the Brando myth," according to actress Judith Malina.

Something auspicious seemed in the air. After that January 21 show, Bud received a message backstage. Someone in the audience wanted to see him. They had an offer to make.

STELLA ADLER SAT on her red divan, a cigarette in her hand. She used the cigarette as a prop when she spoke, punctuating sentences, emphasizing points. Just whom she was regaling this particular night, the night of *Hannele*'s second performance, her daughter, Ellen, couldn't recall. But whoever it was, she held them in thrall, as usual. She was probably talking about theater, or politics, or both. Laughter and cigarette smoke filled the room.

Stella lived in a large, multilevel apartment on Fifty-Fourth Street at Seventh Avenue. One observer would call the place "part Venetian, part Madame Pompadour"; Stella's friends called it "shtotty"—Yiddish for "self-consciously elegant." Tassels dangled from lampshades. Sofas were upholstered in velvet. Satin and chintz draped the windows. On the walls hung paintings by Norman Raeben, the son of Sholem Aleichem, whose stories about Tevye the Milkman would inspire the musical *Fiddler on the Roof.* Everywhere one looked there were gilt-framed photographs of Stella's famous parents and her family's famous friends: Sarah Bernhardt, Ethel Barrymore, Rudolph Schildkraut. Scrapbooks bulged with newspaper clippings from sixty years of Adlers onstage. Books were everywhere, piled high on tables and crammed into bookcases that nearly reached the ceiling.

At some point that evening, a knock was heard on the door to the parlor, and Stella was informed that she had visitors: two of her students from the Workshop.

Bud Brando and Darren Dublin entered tentatively, anxious as well as titillated to be inside their teacher's home. Taking seats on antique chairs, they kept glancing around at the paintings and the photographs. Stella saw her previous visitor to the door, then took a seat opposite her students. The cigarette still dangled from between her fingers. "Now," she said. "What can I do for you?"

Darren spoke first. With trembling excitement, he explained that an agent, a Hollywood agent, had come up to Bud after the performance of *Hannele* and offered him a seven-year movie contract.

Stella turned her eyes to Bud. "Is this so?"

Bud nodded.

"Did you accept the offer?" she asked.

Bud replied that he'd told the agent he'd have to think about it.

Stella said nothing. She took a long drag off her cigarette, exhaling the smoke over the boys' heads. Darren filled the silence by explaining he'd advised Bud to come talk to her. "Stella will know what to do," Darren said.

The teacher was still looking at Bud. Clearly the young man was conflicted. Accepting the offer would mean dropping out of the Workshop just at the moment he'd finally accomplished something worthwhile. But in Hollywood, as Stella knew well, he could make a lot of money. She'd been out there herself. She knew the allure of the place. But in the Adler world, there was no love for Hollywood. Movies were utterly irrelevant to the Adlers, those great stars of the Yiddish and Broadway stage. They barely knew what movie stars were. "Hollywood was not a big deal in my family," Ellen Adler remembered. "That's not what [real actors] did. You didn't go to Hollywood. You stayed, and you became [Katharine] Cornell or Alfred Lunt, and that was the big glamour. People who went to Hollywood were *mourned*. Franchot Tone and Julie [John] Garfield were *mourned*."

Finally, Stella spoke. "If you came here looking for advice," she said, "here it is. *Don't do anything*." A seven-year contract, she insisted, was "slavery." She told Bud plainly, "If you ever go to Hollywood, you make them take you on your own terms."

Bud smiled. It seemed to be the answer he was hoping for. He had no desire to be famous, nor even any desire to make a lot of money. What he wanted he had found—with the Workshop, with Gassner, with Stella. For the first time, he'd done something well, something that people actually praised. He wasn't about to bolt now—not when he finally felt the first sensations of *belonging*.

He told Stella that he'd decline the agent's offer.

After the boys left, Stella stood at the window watching them go. Puffing on her cigarette, she was deep in contemplation. Her daughter, Ellen, would remember a change in her mother's attitude toward Bud after that visit. Later, the Brando legend would insist that Stella had latched on to him from day one, but in fact, according to Ellen, it wasn't until this moment, after *Hannele*, after Hollywood had come courting, that Stella decided to take her young student under her wing. Certainly, she'd always found "the little puppy" full of energy and instinct. But now she sensed something more in him, something potentially great. After *Hannele*, Stella told Ellen that Bud could be as great as "Papa," meaning her father, the renowned actor Jacob Adler. From that moment on, Stella made it her mission to make that happen.

**EARLY FEBRUARY** / The doors of the New School flew open, and out burst a band of students, laughing, hooting, many of them arm in arm. Bundled in jackets, they were in a celebratory mood, though just what they were celebrating, Sara Farwell couldn't remember half a century later. What remained clear in her mind, however, was the sheer exuberance with which they spilled out of the school. "It must have been a Sunday," she said, "because the street was clear." At the front of the group was Bud, and "he broke into a somersault, a complete somersault in the middle of the street—forward, over." The other students laughed and followed suit.

At the start of the Workshop's second term, on February 6, 1944, Bud was exuberantly happy. For the first time in his life, people believed in him—and even more important, he was living up to those beliefs. After writing to his Shattuck counselor about his close call with a nervous breakdown, he went on to itemize a few other, more positive developments: "Found that I had an unusual drama talent—utilized it [and] made a successful promising actor out of myself." He'd come to a conclusion: "My soul," he wrote, "is a part of a harmonious whole in which there is nothing ever to fear." (He was also reading Immanuel Kant, which came through in his letters.) Change was inevitable, Bud had come to believe, and the best thing to do was to give in to it "fully and willingly."

He'd moved from the back of Stella's classroom to sit in the front row, his eyes wide and his chin up, hanging on to his teacher's every word. Through the door, Stella would burst as if she were coming onto a stage—and in many ways, she was. Each class began with a grand pronouncement: "You must listen with your *blood!*" she might declare, or "It's either life or the theatre!" Then she'd launch into a dramatic soliloquy, her voice lifting high and then dropping low. With her hands, she gestured expressively, her many bracelets jangling. Her lips puckered as she spoke; she blew kisses; she called everyone "darling" or "sweetheart." Such larger-than-life style utterly entranced Bud. "He just loved the whole thing," Darren Dublin remembered: the exaggerated laugh, the fiery temper, the big rings on her fingers.

Bud enjoyed doing things to make his teacher applaud. His impersonation of a chicken would become part of the Brando mythos. It's wartime, and a nuclear bomb is on its way, Stella said. What would the chickens in a barnyard do? As the rest of the students ran around the room clucking and flapping their arms, Bud just sat there. "What are you doing?" Stella asked him. "Laying an egg," he supposedly replied. "What does a chicken know of bombs?" Pleased, Stella announced that Bud was the only one to get the assignment right.

Apocryphal or not, the story illustrated what Stella found so appealing in him: his naturalness, his common sense. Most important, as the second-year student said, she considered him "an imaginative young man." Imagination, to Stella, was supreme. How Bud reveled, for the first time in his life, in being the standout student in the class.

Stella didn't love everything Bud did. Sometimes she made

him reconsider his choices, and she called him out when he was grandstanding. "She got to know him very well," Ellen Adler said. "She knew when he was just trying to impress her." When she needed to be, Stella could be unsparing. She demanded full and complete immersion in the task at hand. "Stop coughing," she once barked at a student. "No actor coughs. They don't sneeze and they don't catch colds. They're not tired, they don't yawn, and they don't chew gum." She admitted, "I ask a lot. There is no kindness in my demand. We are in it together, and together we fight it out."

"When you were wrong," Bud remembered, "she would tell you. She'd tell you *why* you were wrong. If you hit a sour note, she'd say, 'No. Wait, wait, wait, wait. That is incorrect. You can't do that.'" All they had to do, she told her students, was remember that everybody acts. "You act all the time," Bud came to understand. "It's built in. Whenever you want something, whenever you don't feel something, or you want people to believe something, it's just acting. The difference is that [nonprofessionals] do it unconsciously and automatically." In her class, Stella was making her students "aware of the process," Bud said.

"In the course of one exercise," said the second-year student, who was assisting Stella, Bud would "suddenly stop what he was doing and do something else, like itch [*sic*] his upper arm, or react to a passing siren, always staying in character, always perfectly natural. Stella adored that. No one else did that. He wasn't acting in the usual sense. He was acting like we all do, every day."

In the first months of 1944, his classmates saw Bud in a new light. Sara Farwell sought him out when she needed a partner to rehearse scenes. "Let's do it again," Bud would tell her when her reading wasn't quite right, not unlike the way Stella would coach him. "I learned by watching him," Farwell said. "Something that would come from him would grab me, make me do a line or a scene differently." For once, Bud was the fast learner in class, no longer the dumb kid with the low IQ. Now he was actually helping the other students learn.

For all her grandiosity, Stella also impressed upon her students a deep humility about their craft. An actor's curtain call, she said, was not about the applause. "Actors bow to their audiences," she explained, "the way subjects bow to royalty." Her thinking was summed up in two words: "Actors *serve*." Her philosophy, as her grandson Tom Oppenheim would observe, "was always about uplifting humanity," a credo passed down from the Yiddish theater of her father. In her acting classes, Stella would show slides of Renaissance paintings or read the letters of Van Gogh "describing fifty different shades of one color," all in the hope that her students might expand their minds, their hearts, themselves. Actors, in her view, had to be "uplifted human beings," Oppenheim said. "The growth of an actor and the growth of a human being are synonymous." The job of the actor, Stella impressed upon her students, "was to lead society into a higher self."

Once restless, aimless, desultory, Bud now sat rapt in the front row, soaking up Stella's thoughts, words, and ideas like a long-dry sponge. They would define his outlook for the rest of his life.

WATCHING HER STUDENTS file out of class, Stella often let out a sigh, as the second-year student recalled. She unhooked her earrings and kicked off her shoes under the desk—the way she might after a performance onstage. It was a lot of work being Stella Adler.

She'd been in the public gaze since she was three years old, when she'd toddled out onto the stage of the Grand Theatre for one of her father's plays with the Yiddish Art Theatre. Taking his curtain call, Jacob Adler had brought his little girl along with him. "He lifted me up and showed me to the audience," Stella remembered. An offering, in a sense: *Here she is. She is yours.* Ever since, Stella had belonged to the theater. "I was simply brought up to be what I am," she said with a laugh. "Which I suppose is very theatrical."

The grand gestures, the bracelets, the highs and lows of her voice continued at home. "My mother is a queen," her daughter, Ellen, once told a friend. "I'm not sure of what, but she is a queen." Like most people in New York theater, Stella was theoretically in favor of socialism, but there was no way, she said, she could ever live in the Soviet Union unless she "could be its queen." Indeed, Stella liked to tell a story about herself and her airs. In Tiffany's one time, a clerk asked if she was English. "No," Stella replied. "Not English. Just affected."

For small talk or society niceties, she had no time or patience—something Bud would have related to very well. "I'm not a playgirl," Stella made clear. "I don't like to lunch. I don't like to chat." She tended to charm and flirt her way through conversations, something else she had in common with her young student. Her daughter said she didn't have many women friends, and none who was her intellectual equal. When Stella met Margaret Mead, Ellen recalled, "they didn't have anything to say to each other."

Stella could be vain. When she'd appeared in the Group Theatre production of *Awake and Sing!*, she'd hated wearing the old-age makeup that had left people thinking she was her brother and costar Luther's mother. "She had this image of herself as this great beautiful goddess," said the second-year student. "Her whole life had been spent in making this glamorous, elegant, powerful creation. And sometimes I think the creation was a little tiresome for her, a little lonesome."

The goal, early on, had been to make that glamorous creation a star. Stella had fully expected to become a great Broadway success, and so did everyone around her. Her father, after all, was Jacob Pavlovich Adler, one of the giants of the Russian stage before Yiddish theater was banned, and someone who, after he'd moved to New York, had reestablished himself as the predominant Yiddish star in America. Through Adler veins flowed greatness; acting was in every drop of blood. Three times Jacob married, and all his wives were actresses. All his children, too, went into the theater; Jacob's brood spent more time on the stage than they did in school.

Stella made sure she got an education, however. Even as a child, she believed that to be a great actor one needed to be fully knowledgeable in art and culture. So, while she waited backstage for her cue, she read great plays and classics of literature. At her family's house, she listened intently to the conversations of the scholars and playwrights who orbited her father. Her natural inquisitiveness matured her into a fine, intuitive actress. She made her adult debut at age eighteen in *Elisa Ben Avia* with her father's company in London. A few years later, she studied with Stanislavski's Moscow Art Theatre during its tenure in New York, an experience that proved transformative. "I saw the most subtle, the most truthful, the most theatrical kind of acting," Stella said. "I was stunned." Her future was now set. She would, she determined, become the greatest American actress.

In 1931, Stella was one of the founding members of the Group Theatre in New York, along with Harold Clurman, Cheryl Crawford, and Lee Strasberg. The Group was a noble experiment, committed to a disciplined, modern, naturalistic American theater. Its founders saw a connection between their goals and the traditions of Yiddish theater, Stella's grandson explained: "to uplift, to be a part of its times." For the next ten years, the Group was highly influential, producing works by such important playwrights as Clifford Odets and Irwin Shaw. The collective also included a wide array of esteemed directors and actors, such as Elia Kazan, John Garfield, Canada Lee, Franchot Tone, and Frances Farmer. Perhaps the Group's greatest success was *Golden Boy*, in 1938, which starred Stella's brother Luther Adler. Stella herself starred in a number of Broadway productions for the Group, but while she shared its political mission, she never felt at home there. Odets said, "An Adler could never be a part of any group," which was certainly true of Stella.

Believing she'd shine more brightly on her own, Stella went out to Hollywood, even if her family turned up their noses at the movies. For a brief, flickering moment, she seemed to have a hope, maybe even an expectation, that she'd become a bona fide movie star. In 1937 she costarred in *Love on Toast*, a B picture with John Payne; a few years later she took a supporting role in MGM's popular *Shadow of the Thin Man*, with William Powell and Myrna Loy. Neither effort brought Stella much acclaim. Hollywood was a humbling experience. For the privilege of acting on the screen, she had even let them change her name to Ardler: "If I can pronounce it," she quipped, "you can spell it any way you want." But she couldn't get away from the fact that it was merely an attempt to make her seem less Jewish, and the ruse troubled her. She left Hollywood feeling "a little bit dirty," her second-year assistant at the Dramatic Workshop thought.

Stella's whole life had been the theater, and her goal had been to reach the top. By 1944, she'd come close. She had the respect of her peers, but she wasn't the box-office power on Broadway she'd hoped to be. She'd been single-minded in her pursuit of greatness. For her, the theater was the one and only great passion in her life. Of romantic love affairs, she took a dim view, an attitude she'd inherited, she explained, from her mother, who'd spent time in a sanatorium after her husband left her for another woman. "If you like a man, that's fine," Stella would remember her mother counseling her. "But don't let it go down too far. That's dangerous." For the most part, Stella had sidestepped such romantic entanglements. Her brief marriage to Ellen's father, the British photographer Horace Eliascheff, had been a sort of "shidduch," or arranged marriage, lasting only long enough for Stella to get pregnant; after the divorce, Ellen always went by her mother's maiden name. Stella's second marriage, to her former Group Theatre colleague Harold Clurman, was more in line with what she thought a theatrical coupling ought to be: a union of equals with shared goals but different projects. To her students, Stella advised that passion be reserved for their work. Anything else, she said, distracted them as actors.

Some of her driving ambition had faded, but Stella still had plans, still had dreams. During that spring term, she was busy preparing for *Pretty Little Parlor*, an original drama in three acts by Claiborne Foster. She was set to play the lead, a glamorous nineteenth-century schemer along the lines of Regina Giddens in *The Little Foxes*. With Hollywood star Ralph Bellamy as director, there was every belief that the production would be a success. Stella needed a hit; she was determined to show producers and critics that she could still act and not just teach. On February 10, Stella turned forty-three. If she was going to become a star, the clock was ticking. *Pretty Little Parlor*, set to open at the National Theatre that coming April, was perhaps her last chance.

"She was, I think," Bud would say looking back, "deeply embittered that she was not a famous actress. She wanted to be." But, in fact, even as she learned her lines in Foster's play, Stella was shifting her focus away from herself and toward making someone else a star.

FOR MUCH OF the rest of that semester, Bud's time was taken up by *Bobino*: the children's play had turned out to be so successful that it was scheduled for an Easter run as well. Rehearsals for *Bobino* meant that Bud frequently missed class; sometimes he was excused, but more often his name was typed up as "absent" on a list submitted daily to Piscator. Bud had also been slated to appear in *Nathan the Wise*, Piscator's plea for tolerance in the wake of European Fascism and the inaugural play of his reopened Studio Theatre. To his parents, Bud wrote, "I am studying the part of the Templar in *Nathan the Wise* which is a very good part for me." Piscator didn't agree, however, as Bud was soon replaced in the role, even as other Workshop students, such as Darren Dublin and Jack

Bittner, remained. For Piscator, *Nathan* was just too important an endeavor for him to take any risks. Not content with his role at the Workshop, he hoped the play would realize his long-held dream of bringing the Studio Theatre on a par with Broadway.

For Stella, of course, a play such as *Nathan the Wise* would have held little interest. She found didactic theater (defined by ideology and message) utterly boring, even, in some ways, offensive. "That's not theatre," she quipped. "That's indoctrination." No doubt she preferred Bud stomping around the stage in his long-necked giraffe suit in *Bobino* to his standing still preaching platitudes.

Their time together continued to be electric. Coincidence—fate, divine providence—had brought Bud to the one acting teacher in New York whose methods allowed him to advance and not retreat. It was Stella's emphasis on imagination that made the difference, an approach that set her apart from most other drama coaches in the city, such as Lee Strasberg, who taught that great acting comes from "emotional memory." The way to discover emotions necessary for a performance, Strasberg taught, was to summon experiences from one's own life.

Of such technique, Stella was utterly contemptuous. "I didn't want to think about when I was moved by my sister when she vomited," she said. Rather, she wanted to meld "with the author and the author's characters" through the power of her own imagination. After spending time with Stanislavski in Europe in 1934, Stella had returned to New York with a statement signed by the Master himself declaring that "imagination and not emotional memory" was the key to successful acting. "He wanted to take the actor deeper into the play rather than into himself," Stella said. Stanislavski's statement caused controversy in acting schools throughout the country; Strasberg and many others simply hardened their views, and continued to rely on emotional memory. "A great disservice was done to American actors," Stella told her students, "when they were persuaded that they had to experience *themselves* on the stage instead of experiencing the *play.*" The answer wasn't in an actor's past, Stella argued, but in the writer's script. "Oh, sweetheart," she'd counsel a flailing actor, "we don't need your emotion. We need the text."

Not that memory played no role, however: "The actor," Stella said, "has in him the memory of everything he's ever touched or tasted. He is by nature gifted with memory."

If Bud had ended up with anyone else, he would, almost certainly, never have gone on to become an actor. Forced to depend on emotional memory, he would have spiraled down into one of his black, angry moods, stomped out of class, and never returned again. Asking him to summon all the pain and trauma of his past would have been too much for him to bear. "I think if he hadn't run into Stella," Ellen Adler mused, "nothing would have happened in his career. The only way he could have existed as an actor was with Stella, because she said, 'Don't use yourself. You're too small. Find it in your imagination.'" And Bud—the milk squirter, the door buster, the window jumper, the people watcher—had "more imagination than any human being" Ellen had ever known. "If he'd had to go inside," she said, "the way Strasberg would have insisted, he would have had a breakdown. It would have been chaos. *Chaos*, I tell you. And the world would never have known Marlon Brando, the great actor."

With Stella, Bud was doing things that he already did and already enjoyed: Read to find the author's intent. Experience the world. Use his imagination. "Your life is one-millionth of what you know," Stella taught. "Your *talent* is your *imagination.*" Everything else, she insisted, was "lice." True, she wanted to uplift her students and make them better human beings. But she had no patience for those who would use acting as a substitute for psychoanalysis. Standing in front of her students, eyes blazing, arms akimbo, Stella told them plainly that she had no desire to help them learn who they were. "It's much better to know what you can *do*," she said. "And then do it like Hercules."

For Bud, this was the license he'd been seeking his entire nineteen years. *Your life is one-millionth of what you know. Your talent is your imagination.* Better credos could not have been invented for him. All Bud's life he'd been reprimanded, shamed, and exiled for acting out his imagination. The only other mentor who'd ever encouraged him, Duke Wagner, had ultimately turned against him, and used Bud's shenanigans as an excuse. Now Stella was applauding the same sort of antics—indeed, the more spontaneous Bud was, the better. He had no fear that Stella would turn on him as Duke had done. For the very first time in his life, Bud felt safe and affirmed.

**LATE MARCH** / "This is the air," Bud intoned, "that is the glorious sun; This pearl she gave me, I do feel't and see't; And though 'tis wonder that enwraps me thus, Yet 'tis not madness."

Nine months earlier, the young man standing in the center of the New School auditorium rehearsing the part of Sebastian in *Twelfth Night* had been digging ditches in Illinois. Now the play's director, Chouteau Dyer, sat back in her chair and marveled over the actor's ease in the part. Sebastian was supposed to be beautiful, the double of his twin Viola, and Bud was certainly that; but "the way he moved," Dyer would recall, "possessed such grace [and] such unforced authenticity" that the nineteen-year-old seemed to her "far older, far wiser, than he really was."

Dyer had been chosen by Piscator to work with Gassner on three major Shakespearean productions for the March of Drama.

The Bryn Mawr graduate had started as a student at the Workshop but had so impressed Piscator with her "brilliant mind," one student remembered, that he made her an assistant director. Dyer's relative youth (thirty-one) set her apart from the other directors at the school, and her levelheaded demeanor endeared her to students. An expert on Shakespeare, Dyer "knew each scene" in *Twelfth Night*, the student remembered, and "understood the play in terms of its most concrete manifestations."

Significantly, this Shakespearean expert thought Bud the most perfect Sebastian she'd ever seen.

*Twelfth Night* was set to open on April 14, following *Othello* and *Macbeth* the previous week. For the first play, noted actor Canada Lee was set to play the title role. Most likely, Bud had small parts in these plays as well, or else he worked on the crew; Elaine Stritch said they all "worked on every March of Drama production in some shape or form." Bud's energies, however, were being reserved for Sebastian, a part that required him to be both sensual and noble, qualities he'd brought so memorably to *Hannele*.

By this point, Bud was "the talk of the school," said Stritch—though only part of the talk was about his talent. The rest was about how close he'd become to Stella. Bud came and went from his teacher's apartment pretty much at will, and the other students noticed. He chose books to read from her library; he met her famous guests, who might be Clifford Odets one evening and Oscar Levant the next. To her friends, Stella was wildly enthusiastic about her discovery. "Wait till you meet this kid," she gushed to the composer David Diamond. "This is a genius." Never before had Diamond heard Stella enthuse over a student in this way.

For all her enthusiasm over Bud, Stella had to be careful not to give the impression that he was receiving preferential treatment from her. New School rules clearly stated that students were "not permitted to ask or pay for private lessons from any member of the faculty or to enter any arrangement for instruction outside the Dramatic Workshop." Stella justified the attention she lavished on Bud, her daughter said, as "helping a lost young man."

Bud was struck, even humbled (a rare experience for him) by the attention. Stella, he would say, was "a very kind woman, full of insights, and she guided and helped me." His sister Tidd could see how the act of one person believing in him reset the parameters of Bud's life. Stella, Tidd said, "put Bud in touch with himself as he had not been before. She gave him permission to try himself out." Before, his instincts had been repressed or punished. "It was only Stella," Tidd said, "who cared enough to say, 'That's interesting, your reaction to that. Go ahead, do more.'"

Whatever personal conflicts had existed between Bud and his last mentor, Duke, were not present with Stella; there was just an intense, Pygmalion-like focus on developing Bud's possibilities. Gossip that Stella had romantic or sexual interest in Bud was nonsense; she was entirely focused, her daughter said, on "making him great." They flirted with each other, but that was the modus operandi of both of them. If anything, Stella was using the flirtation to motivate him. Her job as a teacher, she believed, was to give "the actor confidence in himself, a confidence which nothing can shatter." And her success, she added, could be measured only when that actor had "achieved a *self*."

Bud was her greatest challenge yet.

Still, their relationship went deeper than just teacher and student. David Diamond observed the look of "maternal love" on Stella's face whenever she watched Bud. Certainly, Bud felt a nurturance from her that he'd never experienced before. "She offered me a home," he said, "when I was suffering and disjointed and disoriented with life, going through times of shock, [when] I felt dismembered. She was always very loving towards me."

*Love* was not a word that had ever meant much to Bud, at least not with any consistency. Until now, love had usually come with conditions, with worry and with danger, and with the smell of whisky on its breath.

DOWNTOWN LIBERTYVILLE HAD been rebuilt entirely with brick after a fire in the nineteenth century destroyed most of the wood-frame buildings. The brick gave the downtown blocks along North Milwaukee Avenue a steady, permanent feel. From the doorframes flapped American flags; window boxes bloomed with flowers in spring; the sidewalks were busy with mothers and fathers strolling with their children. The Brandos did not come into town very often, partly because they lived so far out and partly because when they did, they were usually on missions like the one Bud undertook one day when he was about sixteen.

That morning, he'd gotten a call from the Libertyville Police. His mother had been out all night; she'd been arrested for vagrancy. Now it was Bud's job to take the truck down to Police Court and fetch her. His father was away. Bud's sisters couldn't bear the task of going into town for their mother, so Bud, as he told Ellen Adler years later, "just did it. He didn't think about it. He just went down there to get her out."

Steering the old truck south along Milwaukee Avenue, Bud passed Molidor Grocery, Lovell Drugs, and the Hanlon Motor Company before turning left onto West Cook Avenue. Up ahead, right beside the firehouse, was Libertyville Police Court. Bud parked the truck and made his way inside the small brick building. He gave his name to the officer at the desk. "You don't feel anything," he'd say of such moments. "You just do what you have to do." The officer escorted him to a holding cell in the back of the building. Dodie was slumped on a bench, asleep, a blanket wrapped around her. Under the blanket, she was naked. That was how the police had found her, although *where* she'd been found, Bud was never clear. Perhaps he didn't know. It was unlikely he would have asked.

He just gently walked his mother out to the truck and drove her home.

They never spoke of such things. They never spoke much of anything these days. If things had been different, they might have spoken of poetry or music, which they both loved, or ideas or hopes or dreams or desires. But silence descended over mother and son. The only sound was the old truck rattling over the dirt paths back to Townline Road.

STELLA SAT ACROSS from Bud, watching him as intently as she listened to him. The teenager was hunched down on her couch, hugging his knees to his chest, as words tumbled from his lips. For some time now, he'd been speaking nonstop, and Stella hadn't interrupted him once. She'd just let him ramble. She "sensed he had never said any of this to anyone before," her daughter said.

One night, perhaps a month into his mentorship, Bud opened up to his teacher. He told her about his past, about his mother and his father and his troubles in school—or at least enough of it so she'd understand where he was coming from. He trusted her, which was extraordinary. "He found some of me that was adamant and strong and with a definite point of view," Stella remembered, "and he felt secure." If he hadn't felt that way, if he hadn't trusted her completely, he would have given up "the whole thing," Stella said, by which she meant acting. But having discerned his talent, she was not about to let him give up. In the classroom, in after-school discussions about drama and literature, in passionate parleys with visiting playwrights such as Odets at her apartment, she convinced Bud of a once-unimaginable possibility: *he could be great.*

If Erwin Piscator was the distant, disapproving, authoritarian father Bud knew all too well, then Stella was the strong, nurturing, supportive mother he'd never known. "She was very helpful," Bud said, "in a troubled time in my life." Before he met her, he'd been "confused and restless," he said, but Stella discovered a "hidden sensitivity" within him. "She is a teacher not only of acting but of life itself," Bud explained. "She teaches people about themselves. I wouldn't want to say that it's psychotherapy, but it has very clear psychotherapeutic results." From Stella, he learned to make sense of all he'd been through; he learned "about the mechanism of feeling." His struggles, he discovered, need not define him; the abilities he possessed were stronger than his struggles. By validating his intellect and his imagination, Stella was teaching him to trust his own choices, something he'd never been able to do until now.

She offered him more than just a stable and supportive mother figure; she gave him an entire family. "Stella and Harold and Luther and the rest of the family," said Ellen Adler, "and actors from the Yiddish theater and the Group Theatre. They all became part of his family." An eclectic, colorful, spirited group of artists, activists, and bohemians: Odets; Levant; Paul Muni; Cheryl Crawford; Aaron Copland; Luther Adler's wife, Sylvia Sidney; and actors, writers, and directors from the latest Broadway shows—Stella's house, her daughter said, was "the epicenter of what was going on in Manhattan," and Bud was right there in the thick of it. His home back in Libertyville had been chaotic in a terribly damaging way. But the chaos at Stella's house was "creative," Ellen said, and it energized Bud. "So, he became embedded in this Adler world," Ellen said. "That was stability for him."

Stella's friends were charmed by the beautiful young goy with the blue eyes and the eager desire to learn. Sitting at the table, his chin in his hands, Bud would listen to the conversations around him, his eyes moving back and forth as if at a tennis match. Paul Muni would be challenging Luther Adler on some point; Sylvia Sidney would be telling tales about her days in Hollywood. "The jokes went around the Adler table like bullets," said Stella's grandson Tom Oppenheim. When the conversation turned to acting, Bud witnessed the deep respect these people had for their craft. "He came into that world," said Oppenheim, "where an actor was an aristocrat of the spirit, where theater had a higher purpose, and he absorbed that." Acting was not, and should never be, about the fame or the glory. Bud took it all in. Eventually he began to speak up, offering ideas and opinions. Bud found himself affirmed, respected.

And then, Ellen Adler said, "a pipe would get stuck and he'd get up and fix it." Bud could participate "in all these intellectual discussions" and then expertly take care of the most mechanical task. "The car would break down," Ellen said, "and he'd open the hood or slide under the car and fix whatever it was. He could do anything."

He became a fixture of the place. "We made him an honorary Jew," Ellen said, which Bud considered a profound honor. He'd never known people like the Adlers and their friends before. Jewish history became an obsession for him; he avidly learned Yiddish words and phrases, reading the *Forverts* (the Yiddish daily newspaper; *Forward* in English) until he understood the language. All night long he'd stay up, "asking questions, arguing, probing" with the Adlers and their friends. When Luther Adler substituted for Stella for a few classes, Bud wrote to his parents that his new teacher had "a Jewish smartness and perception that works wonders." Later Bud would observe, "I was never educated until I was exposed to Jews. I was introduced to a sense of culture that lasted me a lifetime. They gave me a sense of education [but] also of *value* for education. If anything, it's Talmudic, fundamentally Talmudic. It is the *regard* for learning." That ethic, he believed, explained "the extraordinary accomplishments of the Jews . . . the most accomplished people, per capita, that the world has ever produced."

The lost young man from Omaha, Nebraska, had finally found his tribe.

AS IT TURNED out, however, not everybody liked Bud. The one holdout in the Adler household was Stella's tiny, formidable, eighty-six-year-old mother, Sara Adler, once a great beauty and a star of the Yiddish stage. "She walked sideways," Ellen said of her grandmother. "Very, very slowly. I think it was because she was always walking the stage with the audience on the other side." A child prodigy back in her native Russia, winning a scholarship to the Odessa Conservatory to study voice, Sara was very discriminating when it came to those she considered worthy of her friendship. Bud was simply a little too American working class for her. "Omaha, Nebraska," Ellen said, "was always a big part of his presentation." He hadn't read the classics; he had no knowledge of Tolstoy or Ibsen; he shambled around the place and mumbled when he spoke. "She looked at him," Ellen remembered, "and said, 'He's a bum.'"

As if to prove her wrong, Bud embarked that spring on a mission of self-improvement. One day, Norman Rose spotted him buying books at a Greenwich Village bookstore. "I have to read," Bud told him. "I have to study. I have to learn things." Stella had awakened a curiosity in him. "She taught me to read," Bud said. "She taught me to look at art. She taught me to listen to music." Hunkered down on Stella's couch, he would underline phrases in the poetry of Aristotle and Euripides. "He felt badly about not having had a real education," Ellen said. "I think he felt that keenly and most of the time."

So he decided to educate himself. "His intellectual appetite was enormous," Ellen remembered. "He had a hunger for knowledge." Recently turned seventeen, Ellen would come home from school to see Bud, this handsome, intense, slightly older teenager, hunched over several opened books at the dining room table, with a pile of other books waiting at his elbow. "He read about science," Ellen said. "He read about race. He read about geography." What he didn't read, however, were novels. "He said he started *War and Peace* and got stuck with all the names," Ellen said. There was "no interest" in Hemingway or Faulkner. "But he read everything else.

He read a lot of poetry. A lot of Shakespeare. Very, very serious philosophy books. *Mechanical Digest*. Einstein." He read slowly, due to his dyslexia, sometimes running his finger along the lines of the book to make the words easier to follow.

Just as he made little effort with novels, so, too, did Bud disregard modern art. Renaissance paintings and sculptures from antiquity held great interest for him, because "the feelings were shown," he explained to Ellen. Picasso and other modern artists, however, left him cold, as did much of modern music. "It didn't give him access to those emotions," Ellen said—unlike the Liebestod, for example, from Wagner's *Tristan und Isolde*, which summoned great cathartic emotions in Bud. "That he experienced very profoundly," Ellen remembered.

He became fascinated by language. "If I said, 'That's incredible,'" Ellen remembered, "he'd say, 'Don't say incredible,' because it was too hackneyed. He was very, very interested in language, and that remained true all his life." Language, words, ideas—these were like buried treasures Bud was discovering, one by one.

Oftentimes, even when he was at the Adler house, Bud would be alone, off in a corner, reading or "just thinking," Ellen said. He could be alone like that, Ellen thought, "because he lived within himself so much . . . lived with his imagination." She could sit across from him and actually watch Bud thinking. "You could see the ideas moving through his mind." Being alone on a regular basis was something he apparently needed, almost as a way of digesting everything he had taken in.

Yet his mentor got the idea that spring that maybe Bud shouldn't be alone so much. Maybe, Stella thought, he needed some companionship. So, she began urging her daughter to spend more time with him, to engage him, to go for walks with him in the park. "A romance began," Ellen remembered. One of "the great relationships," in fact, of her life. One day, Bud looked up and there was Stella's daughter, no longer a girl but a woman who, in a wonderful change of pace for him, could be his intellectual peer. The relationship would be one of the great ones of his life, too.

"IT NEVER CROSSED my mind that he would look at me," Ellen said. Especially not with Susan Douglas, a stunning nineteen-year-old blonde actress, sitting in the same room. On a day in early April, Ellen came home from high school. She was wearing her usual bulky sweater, bobby socks, and saddle shoes. In her living room she found Bud—nothing unusual about that—but this day he had Darren Dublin with him, and the two were deep in conversation with a knockout woman wearing a black dress with a plunging neckline. She also wore high heels, Ellen said, "and stockings with a seam." Susan Douglas was "a grown-up," and next to her, Ellen felt like an adolescent.

Another of Stella's protégées, Douglas was a Czechoslovakian war refugee with acting ambitions; her well-connected mother had sent her to Adler. Douglas laughed easily, batted her eyelashes, and responded to the boys' questions with her musical Czech accent. Ellen kept mostly silent. At one point, Bud suggested they go to the movies, so the four of them headed out to a nearby theater. Just what they saw, Ellen didn't remember. What would never leave her mind, however, was the feeling of Bud's arm slipping around her in the dark. "So, he started to see me," Ellen said, the satisfaction in her voice still evident decades later, "and not Susan Douglas."

Bud turned twenty on April 3. Ellen was seventeen, and stunned by Bud's attention. She knew about Celia, and remarked that Bud had never before seemed to be interested in American girls. "But you're not American," he replied. "You're Jewish." In her bobby socks and saddle shoes, Ellen was about as American as a teenage girl could be in 1944, and for a moment she was taken aback. But then she saw herself from Bud's point of view. "I was a New Yorker. I was cultured. I was definitely not Midwest. So, I was exotic." She was also a brunette. "Bud had no interest in blondes,"

Ellen came to realize. So, she'd had the upper hand all along, over Susan Douglas and her blonde, blue-eyed kin.

With Stella's blessing, Bud and Ellen began dating, going to concerts, museums, the theater. As he had with Elena Klein and others, he seemed to enjoy the cultural education that Ellen could give him. But with those other girls, Bud had kept the relationships platonic. With Ellen, he'd admit, "one thing led to another"—though until she was eighteen, things led only so far. The romance dazzled the young woman. "What we had was special," Ellen said, looking back. Bud trusted her, but even more than that, he *admired* her. Ellen was the sort of girl, if circumstances had been different, he could have brought home to meet his mother. "I think he thought his mother would like me," Ellen said.

One day, he suggested that she buy a certain perfume. Ellen complied. Taking her in his arms, Bud pressed his face to her hair and inhaled the fragrance. "That was the perfume my mother always wore," he told her.

Still, he made clear that he was not giving up Celia. He continued to spend nights with her; sometimes they took off for the Jersey Shore on weekends. As always, Bud kept no secrets; the two women in his life knew about each other. Ellen instinctively understood that to demand anything from Bud would be to lose him. And while she did feel jealousy, she believed, in the end, that it didn't matter. "There is so much talk about all the girls and the gossip and the sex," she'd say, looking back. "I do feel that almost anyone meeting him couldn't help becoming aware of this really unique sensitivity that he had, which explains why he was so unusual." In other words, Bud was worth having even if it meant sharing him. She was only seventeen, but Ellen had a growing sense that he could never belong exclusively to her. No one, in fact, could ever be first in Bud's heart—except for maybe the woman whose perfume Ellen wore.

**APRIL 17** / The lights of the National Theatre dimmed, the curtain rose, and after a suitable buildup, there was Stella, looking gorgeous in her period costume, striding "all over the stage, harassed, moaning, vicious in turn," as one reviewer wrote. In the audience, Bud watched his teacher. Out-of-town critics hadn't been kind to the play or its leading lady. Bud had learned enough by now to distinguish between good theater and bad. (About one play, he wrote to his parents, "Stinks. Terrible acting, worse direction.") He knew how to spot flaws and determine who was to blame for them, and who was not—and in this case, it was the playwright's fault, he believed, not Stella's, when the show was panned by New York critics.

*Pretty Little Parlor* closed after just eight performances. When the curtain came down the last time, it marked the end of Stella Adler's hopes of a great acting career.

Sitting on his motorcycle outside the school, Bud defended his teacher to anyone who suggested she was in any way responsible for the disaster of *Pretty Little Parlor*. "She made it as good as it was," he said. "She was the only thing good in it." He would tolerate no criticism of Stella. It was the way he'd once felt about his mother. She could do no wrong in his eyes.

Stella felt the same way about him. The night after her own show ended, she sat in the audience of the Studio Theatre to watch Bud in *Twelfth Night*. She didn't often attend Dramatic Workshop productions, but she was there for Bud. So successful had the Shakespeare March of Drama plays been that *Twelfth Night* was being given the big-stage treatment, with full costumes and sets, for a two-night run, as part of the end-of-semester production schedule. Just as he had in the school's auditorium, Bud shone as Sebastian on the Studio Theatre stage, playing up the amalgam of masculine and feminine that so many of his classmates had observed in him, that powerful mix of virility and delicacy. "He'd come in from riding his motorcycle, kick off his boots, put on Sebastian's tights, and just become that fey little figure," said the second-year student. "Let's not forget Vivien Leigh once played Sebastian. There's tremendous androgyny there." From the one persona to the other, Bud moved easily. "That's what they talk about when they talk about having a craft," said Elaine Stritch. "Being able to do it and then go to dinner between shows and come back and do it again."

To the one person who'd ever consistently championed him, Bud was justifying her faith. After *Twelfth Night*, Stella encouraged him to try his hand at farce, promoting him for the lead in a show based on Molière's *The Doctor in Spite of Himself* (a role Bud had done at Shattuck for Duke). After that, he was set for another encore of *Hannele's Way to Heaven*. He'd also scored his Broadway debut. *Bobino*'s run of matinee performances had taken place at the Adelphi Theatre on Fifty-Fourth Street, produced by the American Theatre for Young Folks. During the day, Bud had lumbered about the stage in his giraffe suit and then hurried back downtown to play Sebastian at night. An inauspicious Broadway debut, but he'd managed it quite capably.

His attitude toward his craft, however, remained nonchalant, despite how good he'd gotten at it. Perhaps because he'd mastered acting so quickly and with such apparent ease, he failed to see any weight to what he was doing. From an intellectual standpoint, he understood the Adlers' reverence for acting; he just didn't feel it emotionally. To Bud, acting remained a lark, a game of pretense, an excuse to don a giraffe suit. Once, in response to an impersonation assignment, he came into class dressed as Judy Garland in *Meet Me in St. Louis*, lip-synching to a record of "The Trolley Song." Elaine Stritch called it "one of the funniest things" she'd ever seen in her life. That was acting to Bud: good for a laugh.

"He simply did not see acting as a way of life," Ellen said. The lesson he took most strongly from Stella was that *everyone acts—*

and if that was the case, what he and the others were doing at the Workshop (and on Broadway and in the Yiddish theatre and in the movies and everywhere else) was not all that special. "I think what happened was," Ellen said, "he wandered in there [with Stella and the Workshop] and he got stuck. This was what he could do, this was what got him affirmation, and so he stuck with it"—at least for a while. "He always thought there was something else coming, that this was just a moment in time."

And for the moment, he was having fun with it. Bud was intellectually stimulated, emotionally fulfilled, sexually satisfied, and personally affirmed. For someone who'd spent his first nineteen years in a state of despair and discontent, this was heaven; if this was being "stuck," he wasn't going to try to unstick himself.

Yet his new, hectic life meant going to the theater more often, and eating out at fancier restaurants, and needing better clothes. Bud hadn't needed to worry about money before, subsisting well enough on his allowance. But by May 1944, he was having trouble making ends meet. Darren Dublin remembered him saving money on laundry by wearing Celia's dungarees (and sometimes her underwear, too) to class. It was obvious Bud needed a raise in his allowance, but that, unfortunately, was one area where he was still under the control of his father. Gathering up the courage, Bud wrote home asking for a thirty-dollar increase. "I found I can't pay my own rent out of $90 and live too," he argued. The extra cash was needed, he added, "kind of pronto," because at the moment he was "dead broke."

Just what his father said in reply went unrecorded and unpreserved.

THE ELEVATOR OF the New School slid open and out popped Sir Toby Belch, in his ruffled collar and feathered hat, calling down the hall for Sir Andrew Aguecheek to come and rehearse with him. In the library, as Piscator's wife, Maria Ley-Piscator, remembered the scene, Malvolio was running his lines by himself, disturbing the silence, while "Feste and Maria made most unwelcome entrances and exits through the graduate faculty rooms." The last days of the spring semester were overrun with costumed characters turning up in the unlikeliest places, scurrying from wardrobe to dress rehearsals, much to the amusement and consternation of the non-theatrical students. *Twelfth Night* had been such a hit in its previous presentations that Piscator and Gassner had decreed it would be one of the final March of Drama productions of the school year, with the public and critics invited.

The pressure was on—because, in fact, they were rehearsing three plays at once. In addition to *Twelfth Night*, they were doing the Molière farce and *Hannele*, with only a night in between each performance. Bud was getting his lines mixed up, sometimes sounding Shakespearean in *Hannele* and sometimes sounding like Christ when he was doing Sebastian. "It was pandemonium," said Elaine Stritch, who played Feste in *Twelfth Night* and had small roles in the other two plays.

The Molière farce was the first presented, on the evening of May 20, under Maria Ley-Piscator's direction. The production combined *The Doctor in Spite of Himself* and *The Imaginary Invalid* into one comedy of manners called *Dr. Sganarelle*. At the last minute, Bud dislocated his shoulder, which forced him to surrender the lead to Jack Bittner; no one wanted to risk his being out of commission for *Hannele*. For *Dr. Sganarelle*, he took a less strenuous, smaller part. Still, George Freedley of the New York *Morning Telegraph* spotted him in the background and singled him out, along with Darren Dublin, as having done "well with two younger and slighter roles."

No other student in the March of Drama productions would get as much ink as Bud in any of Freedley's three reviews. The critic seemed very glad to see him front and center two nights later, in *Hannele*. "Easily the best acting of the evening," Freedley wrote in his review for the *Telegraph*, "was contributed by Marlon Brando, a personable young man and a fine actor. He has authority, smoothness, careful diction and an easy command of the stage to commend him." Indeed, when *Twelfth Night* was finally presented, on the night of May 24, Freedley reserved the most words for Bud: "Marlon Brando handled the tiny bit of Sebastian satisfactorily though it would have been interesting to have seen what he might have done with Feste or Orsino. His playing was naturally keyed to that of Viola."

Bud had surpassed his classmates. The acclaim he had earned was greater than any of theirs. Against all odds, the awkward loner of the previous fall, the boy with his eyes cast downward, his hands balled up in his pants pockets, had come out on top. He looked up now, instead of down. His first year at the Dramatic Workshop had ended far better than he, or anyone else, could have imagined.

As spring warmed into summer, Bud finally broke free of his past. With the Adlers and their friends, he'd found his moorings. "I was very lost," he said, "with no idea of where I was going, and after all I'd been through, how could I have possibly known what to do with myself?" He'd found a new family, however, one that supported him, believed in him; he could no longer imagine ever returning to the family he had left behind. "I would have been better off in an orphanage," he came to believe, "rather than [with] the parents I had." Only away from his parents, away from everything he once knew, could he chart a new life for himself.

That new life, he decided, demanded a new name.

"My name is Marlon," he told a new classmate around this time. "Bud belongs back home."

"He was Bud when we first met him," the second-year student remembered, "and then suddenly, late in the second semester, he became Marlon."

It was his father's name. When the family said "Marlon," they were referring to Senior. The son now took the name for himself, appropriating what had been the exclusive property of his father and making it his own. He would be a very different Marlon Brando. The world now belonged to him. He was free. Until he got a call, shortly after the end of the school year, informing him that his mother was moving to New York. She'd left his father, and she wanted her son to live with her.

**MID-JULY** / On the beach, several young people in Elizabethan dress were running around barefoot, taking orders from a man standing in the water with his pants rolled up. Off to the side, a reporter was jotting down observations in a notebook, while a photographer prowled back and forth along the sand, snapping pictures.

"We're radical," the man in the water shouted, pulling a young woman in ruffles and hoop skirt into the surf with him. "We drown Viola in real water."

The man was Erwin Piscator, and the young people in costume were his actors, rehearsing *Twelfth Night* on Sayville Beach, where they'd all decamped for the summer. The reporter and photographer were from *Collier's* magazine, sent out to Long Island to cover this latest endeavor of the New School's Dramatic Workshop.

At the foot of Candee Avenue stood an old white Colonial playhouse and an adjacent barn, surrounded by two acres of windswept seafront property. Piscator had brought his company of twenty-five out to this pristine setting for the summer, a last-minute decision made just as the semester was drawing to a close. Wanting to stay together, a number of students had asked the Director if he'd head up a summer company with them. The idea of his own summer stock company appealed to Piscator, so he agreed—on the condition that the students find the theater themselves. Sara Farwell, leading the charge, settled on the Sayville Playhouse, which for the past few years had presented a mix of new plays and revivals but was slated to go dark that summer. With money raised by the students themselves, Piscator leased the play-house from its owner, theatrical manager Edith Gordon, for a thousand dollars. Their season would run from July to September.

The company had arrived "loaded down with mops, luggage, dishes, pans, blankets and costumes," the writer from *Collier's* re-ported. That first day, the actors had gathered inside the playhouse, while Chouteau Dyer climbed up on a chair to address them. "All right, children," she shouted, "here are your instructions. You will sleep, eat, and work in this building. We want you here, so that we can keep an eye on you." Dyer told them to find a room or an alcove to claim as their own. The actors then scattered, no one wanting to end up in a closet.

Newcomer Freddie Stevens, feeling a bit awkward and alone, was grateful when one member of the company took him under his wing and suggested they bunk together. His new friend intro-duced himself as Marlon Brando. "He was carrying two leather bags that looked very expensive to me," Freddie remembered. "He was wearing a button-down Oxford shirt open at the neck, tan cot-ton slacks, and scuffed tennis shoes. He was the image of the ideal American youth—dark blond hair, blue-gray eyes, tawny complex-ion, a stride that was an easy athletic lope." This striking young man told Freddie that he'd found the perfect spot to sleep, one that no one else had thought of: the attic over the barn. Up a ladder and through a trap door, Freddie and Marlon hauled a mattress for them to share. "I realized with great relief," Freddie said, "that I felt no uneasiness in sharing a bed with someone who had been a total stranger until that morning. We were instant friends." That first night, exhausted from the day, Marlon snored deeply, Freddie recalled, "rumbling like thunder."

It wasn't surprising that Marlon cottoned to Freddie; like Darren, the new actor hailed from a more working-class background than others in the company. The son of Sicilian immigrants, he was born Carlo Fiore—though he'd always be Freddie to Marlon—and before joining the company, he'd worked as a steam presser in a garment factory. Freddie was also a character, and Marlon liked characters. He wore his hair in a pompadour with a duck-tail in back, and often sported zoot suits and blue suede shoes. To top it off, Freddie spoke what he described as "unmistakably Brooklynese," leading Elaine Stritch to ask if he was a gangster.

Among the other new actors that summer was Eugene von Grona, the German-born choreographer for *Bobino*. At thirty-six, he was considerably older than the other actors; he'd come to the Workshop on Piscator's invitation the previous spring, to help teach dance. He'd played Malvolio so flamboyantly in *Twelfth Night* that he was asked to spend the summer with them in Sayville. Von Grona's wife, Leni Bouvier, also joined the company.

For Marlon, however, the most interesting newcomer was a pretty nineteen-year-old named Blossom Plumb. The name was real—and she was every bit "as amusing, attractive and likable as the burlesque-queen name implies," one friend said. Another friend, the actress Ellen Burstyn, who knew Blossom when they were both modeling in New York, recalled that she "spoke in po-etic metaphor," and "not everyone could understand what she was saying." Burstyn would often find herself translating. Blossom, like Freddie, was a character, and so Marlon gravitated to her as well. Before long, they were sleeping together.

The affair irked Piscator, who had announced on their first day in Sayville that "everybody was to sleep in their own bed at night," according to Elaine Stritch. He had seen sexual shenanigans de-stroy other companies, breaking down order and morale, and he insisted that his actors comport themselves professionally at all times. He seemed to be aiming his decree personally at Marlon, whose closeness with Blossom had not gone unnoticed. The Director often checked on his actors after they'd turned in, just to make sure there was no hanky-panky—but he couldn't do that with Marlon, who regularly pulled the ladder up into the attic of the barn before shutting the trap door for the night. That left Piscator standing among the weeds of the barn floor, staring up at the ceiling and clenching his fists.

What made his pique even worse, some thought, was the obvious interest the Director had taken in Blossom himself. From day one, his eyes had followed her wherever she went. "He wanted her," said Joy Thomson. But he couldn't have her, of course: his wife was ever present, and besides, Marlon had already gotten her.

Among Marlon's girlfriends, Blossom was an exception. Blonde and petite, she was about as all-American as they came, and voted the best-looking girl in the senior class of her Westport, Connecticut, high school. When one aspiring actress, Maureen Stapleton, saw Blossom and Marlon together, "it was like looking at Mr. and Mrs. Perfect. He was gorgeous, she was gorgeous. You thought, 'Oh, that's the way it should be.'" Blossom's late father had been a New York real estate broker; her mother had recently been remarried, to the president of a Connecticut electrical company who sidelined as an investment broker. Dating delicate blonde beauties from wealthy WASP families had not been Marlon's habit in the past.

But by the summer of 1944, things had changed. Another delicate blonde beauty had resurfaced in his life, arriving in Manhattan just as Marlon was heading out. Now, sixty miles and two hours away, Marlon preferred to spend as much time as possible on the pristine white beaches of Sayville, Blossom on his arm, declining all offers from his friends to head back into the city on a night off. "What would I want to do that for," he would ask, "with all I've got here?"

"THEY LIVE ON stardust and sunshine," *Collier's* wrote of the Sayville players, and as they rehearsed on the beach in their bathing suits—the costumes had been for the magazine photographer's benefit—the summer really did feel idyllic to them. "Life was pleasant," Freddie remembered. "When we weren't rehearsing, we went swimming in the bay or walked through the meadows." Occasionally, Marlon borrowed a friend's convertible and took Freddie cruising along the old Route 27, toward Patchogue, stopping to eat at roadside stands. "He liked quick food, like a child," Freddie said. "Hamburgers, hot dogs, French fries, thick malteds."

The irony of their situation was not lost on Darren Dublin. "Here we are in the sun," he said, "young and healthy, and people are dying. We'd lie on the beach and think of all those poor motherfuckers in Europe, and we're going, 'Roll over. Am I tan on this side?' That's the hand that life gives you."

Fortune had indeed dealt them a very good hand. The war had exploded that summer. During Marlon's two terms at the Dramatic Workshop, more than 130,000 Americans had died. But in just the last two months, while he and his friends were packing their costumes and their bathing suits to move out to Long Island, the number of casualties had skyrocketed: 143,000 in June and July alone. The war was at a turning point. Rome fell to the Allies on June 4; Normandy was invaded two days later; and by the time the Sayville players mounted their first production, the Germans were in retreat across the Continent. Victory was at last in sight.

Lying on the sand after a show, staring up at the stars, Marlon and his friends wondered what the world would be like when the war was over. For many of them, wartime was all they'd known during their brief adult lives. As students, they'd done their part for the war effort, gathering paper and metal and buying war bonds. But what came next? What sort of civic responsibility awaited those who hadn't served? "We had to do something," Marlon would remember the group concluding—a lesson they'd heard since their very first day at the New School. Winning the war was just the beginning. New School president Johnson had spoken of the men and women who "must take over when the firing ceases." Marlon and his friends realized that *they* were those men and women. "We'd have to become citizens," Marlon said, "in the full meaning of the word."

For Piscator and many of his actors, that meant developing theater that made people think, that exposed injustice and intolerance, that offered society a better way forward. But for Marlon, trained under Stella to seek emotional truth from theater, rather than social or political truth, his way forward as a citizen was not quite as clear. How was what they were doing, out here on the beach in Sayville, dressed up in funny costumes and putty noses, making a difference in the world?

Their season had opened on July 1 with a presentation of *Claudia*, a lightweight romantic play in which Marlon played no significant part. The next week, however, he'd played the lead in *Dr. Sganarelle* (after giving it up in May due to his dislocated shoulder). The Molière farce about a phony doctor in seventeenth-century France is undeniably amusing, and Marlon, according to those who were there, delivered his comic monologues with great verve. But for all Molière's keen observations of society, what did *Dr. Sganarelle* have to say about postwar life in the twentieth century, with all those American soldiers coming home in coffins and, as many feared, a holocaust in Europe waiting to be discovered?

"I had a sense of not doing anything important, of wasting time," Marlon would say, looking back at this moment. This was how he was feeling even as, on July 14, he starred in his fourth production of *Hannele's Way to Heaven*. The cast was populated with local children and the audiences with their parents; the performances were more boisterous than they were reverent, with mothers calling out their toddlers' names and fathers climbing up onto chairs to take snapshots. After spending six months with the Adlers talking about art and culture and psychology and war and peace, Marlon had rarely felt more frivolous.

Freddie (Stevens) Fiore could see it in his work. After being apprised of his new friend's great talent, Freddie was struck by how indifferent Marlon was to it all. "He never knew his lines and often failed to pick up his cues," he said. "He kept the play script handy backstage so he wouldn't get totally lost." Marlon's lack of interest in his work, Freddie came to understand, was because he "hadn't really decided to be an actor" yet, and at any moment, he might just give it all up.

Freddie wasn't the only one getting that impression. Erwin Piscator was often present in Sayville as his actors rehearsed. *Twelfth Night* was the most prestigious of their productions so far, so he drilled down on his actors especially hard. He rarely complimented anyone, but was quick with the insults. "When I think I will go out of my mind from the bad acting," he told the *Collier's* reporter, "I can jump in the water quick. This helps."

Marlon especially grated on him. "I don't think Piscator believed that Marlon truly rated the kind of acclaim he got for those early performances," one student said. "He thought Marlon didn't take the work seriously, which maybe he didn't. But in Piscator's mind, if you didn't take the work seriously, you couldn't be good."

On the night of *Hannele*'s premiere, there was at least one member of the audience who was more reflective than the shouting, camera-toting parents. That was Maynard Morris, a well-respected and influential theatrical agent, who'd come over to Sayville from Fire Island to see the show. Morris, who'd helped propel the careers of Gregory Peck and Charlton Heston, had heard of Marlon through Stella. So, his expectations raised high, the agent made his way, probably by boat, to Sayville that weekend.

His expectations were exceeded. Not to him did Marlon seem indifferent. Instead, he seemed *incandescent* as the Christ-like

Stranger. None of the problems that Freddie had witnessed back-stage were evident to Morris. After the show, the reviewer made sure to give Marlon his card.

The Director probably fumed.

The possibility that Marlon, the least dedicated, the least serious of the company's actors, might be scooped up by a big Broadway agent, while Piscator himself toiled away thanklessly at the Workshop, underappreciated by the New School, tapped the deep sense of insecurity and inferiority plaguing the Director.

But he had a plan. After the disappointing reception for *Nathan the Wise*, Piscator had decided to bend his principles a bit in order to get back on Broadway. He would direct a melodrama called *Last Stop*, about a gaggle of old ladies in a retirement home who solve a murder. There was nothing political, nothing epic about the project at all—just a chance for some old-time actresses to get back up on the boards. Piscator was aiming high: he wanted Laurette Taylor and Maude Adams. He hoped for a big commercial success that would finally make him the theatrical powerhouse in America that he'd been in Germany before the war.

And so, halfway through rehearsals of *Twelfth Night*, Piscator took leave of the company to go into Manhattan for a few days to oversee casting, putting his Sayville actors in the hands of his wife, Maria Ley-Piscator. He fully expected the rules he'd laid down at the start of the season to be followed in his absence.

So far, the players had behaved themselves; even the romance between Marlon and Blossom had been relatively discreet. But with the Director gone, the young people let loose. "We bathed bare-assed in the bay at night," Freddie remembered, "held all-night bull sessions in the barn, read poetry, flirted and made love—all of this when we should have been thinking about our roles and memorizing our lines."

And—no doubt with some reservations given what waited for

him there—Marlon finally gave in to his buddies' entreaties that they sneak back into Manhattan for a couple of nights.

SUMMER SHOWERS HAD cooled off the sweltering city earlier that week, so when Marlon arrived at Penn Station, the air was clean and crisp. Sunshine was everywhere, cascading onto Seventh Avenue from between the buildings. Whenever he arrived back into the city, his first stop, Ellen Adler said, was always her house. So, he and Darren and Freddie rode the subway up to Fifty-Fourth Street—or maybe they hoofed the twenty-some blocks, loping along like a pack of wolves, howling like them, too, whenever a pretty girl passed. Marlon had left Blossom back on Long Island. He had other opportunities for feminine companionship in the city.

At Stella's, Ellen said, there was probably gossip to share about the Workshop and laughter to be had over Piscator's earnestness in Sayville. Probably Stella encouraged Marlon to follow up with Maynard Morris, and Marlon, probably, remained noncommittal. Perhaps there was also dinner and conversation, especially if Luther Adler or Harold Clurman was there. But at some point, Marlon had to depart from his chosen family. He could no longer tarry there indefinitely as he once had. His original family now expected him, another eighteen blocks uptown.

Upon her arrival in New York, Dodie had taken a spacious, ten-room apartment on West End Avenue at Seventy-Second Street. Her estranged husband was paying the rent as well as for the maid Dodie had insisted she needed. Now zealously attending AA, Marlon Senior had issued his wife an ultimatum: either join him and quit drinking or get out of the house. Dodie had chosen the latter option: whether she was drunk or sober, living with her cold, unfaithful husband had become intolerable. The Libertyville house was vacated, Marlon Senior moving to Chicago. Dodie came to

New York, she said, "to make a family with her children." She'd even brought along the family's old, failing Great Dane, "Dutchie."

Tidd and Frannie, who'd been finding it hard to make ends meet sharing an apartment on West Tenth, had gratefully moved in with their mother. Tidd was now married to Don Hanmer, who was off in the war, and she'd just given birth to a son. Marlon, however, while complying with his mother's wishes to move in with her, had not done so quite as gratefully. He'd given up his apartment on Twelfth Street but had spent only a few nights on West End Avenue with the family, preferring to stay at Celia's, before heading off to Sayville for the summer.

The apartment was sparsely furnished. Dodie had brought little with her from Libertyville besides Dutchie. Everything echoed through the large, empty rooms: people's footsteps, the dog's barking, the baby's cries at night. Frannie's boyfriend, Dick Loving, called the place "impersonal," especially compared to the house in Libertyville, which had been stuffed full with books, art, and the bric-a-brac of life. "There was nothing there," Loving said of the New York apartment.

But Marlon's friends thought that "Dodie's pad was really hip," according to one Workshop student. Compared to the tiny flats they were used to, the West End Avenue apartment "went on for miles." The hostess herself seemed pretty "hip," too. When his mother first arrived in New York, Marlon's friends had all loved her. "She was divine," said Joy Thomson, "absolutely foreign to any mother I'd ever seen." Darren thought of her as "one of the gang." She laughed at "off-color jokes and swore like a longshoreman," said another classmate. "She was a *broad*."

Ellen Adler, however, saw another side to Dodie. Despite the swear words and the raucous laughter, she could be soft and fragile, like the image on a lacy Victorian valentine. "She was very dainty," Ellen said, "in an old-fashioned way." She was also very conscious of her appearance. One evening, when Ellen observed that Dodie looked particularly pretty, the older woman replied, "Do you know why that is? Because I'm wearing pink, and pink becomes me." False modesty never did.

That night in July, as Marlon rode the elevator with Freddie and Darren to visit his mother for the first time in weeks, he reminded his companions that there was to be no talk of drinking. He didn't say why, but Ellen understood. She'd accompanied the young men uptown to West End Avenue, and she knew Dodie's secret. Ellen was, in some ways, Marlon's good-luck charm. He'd been right in thinking that his mother would like her. Certainly, she liked her far more than she liked Celia, whom she considered too old and too uneducated for her son. So, whenever he visited his mother, Marlon brought Ellen. Dodie was always on her best behavior when Ellen was around.

The door to the apartment opened, and there his mother stood, the mother whom Marlon had treasured, defended, longed for, and, finally, abandoned. She was glowing, as lovely as ever, her delicate hands and radiant smile welcoming them. Freddie would never forget the impression Dodie made on him. "She was a true beauty," he said, "tall, willowy, ash-blonde, with large wide-set eyes appearing constantly to change color, reflecting hazel or grey and sometimes green, depending on the light." She spoke softly, warmly, to Marlon and his friends.

Tidd thought her mother had been empowered by the separation from her husband. She ran the household ably, doing the grocery shopping, taking care of the baby when Tidd was off on auditions, supervising the maid. Marlon, too, was proud of his mother for finally leaving his father. "That took courage," he'd say, looking back. But he wasn't ready, Ellen said, "to just go back to living with her and worrying about her" again. That was why he had scurried off so quickly to Sayville and why he was so reluctant to return to Manhattan for visits.

That night, he watched his mother warily. She was warm and

witty. The place was filled with laughter. But there was a familiar "slur to her voice," Ellen said, indicating she'd had a nip or two ahead of their visit. Freddie and Darren didn't notice; Darren would claim he was in the dark about Dodie's drinking problem for the longest time. But Marlon had learned years ago how to spot the signs.

This was why he'd stayed away from her. His mother might have taken a leap and freed herself of an abusive husband, but she'd brought other demons with her. Dick Loving noticed her bribing people when she thought no one in the family was looking, asking visitors or even the maid to bring her a bottle. When she got it, she'd hide it in the flour bin. Everyone pretended they didn't know it was there.

Most embarrassingly for Marlon, the Adlers had noticed, too. Dodie made a great show of thanking Stella "for what she had done for Marlon," Ellen said. Stella "had given her back her son," Dodie insisted, "freed him from all his troubles." But in her effusive thanks, she had slurred her words just enough to leave Marlon mortified. For old Sara Adler, meeting Dodie only confirmed her opinion of Marlon. "He's a bum, and his mother's a drunk," Ellen remembered her grandmother saying.

At long last, Marlon had found a place for himself in the world. But his mother had barged into that world, threatening to ruin it all.

BACK IN SAYVILLE a day or so later, Marlon and the company prepared for the first public presentation of *Twelfth Night*, on July 21. A stagehand projected illustrated settings onto a backdrop—castles, doors, trees—"a la Walt Disney," as one local newspaper wrote. But the cast wasn't as memorable, missing cues and forgetting lines. Their lack of focus during rehearsals had caught up with them. The show "bombed," Freddie Fiore recalled plainly.

Piscator's wrath was nothing compared to what Marlon got

from his mother, who'd been in the audience. "Dodie sailed into me," he later told Freddie. She harangued him about his performance and "a thousand other things." Only recently had Marlon learned of his mother's own acting background, and that seemed to give her the authority to criticize his work. But this was more than a critique. Dodie was furious with him, in a way Marlon wasn't used to seeing, almost as if the cork had finally popped off the bottle of her unfulfilled dreams. She told her son that he needed "to take acting seriously" or—and this was what surely stung—"go into business with Pop." Not until he had "grown up," Dodie added, did she want to see him again.

Marlon was stunned. *Go into business with Pop.* The man she had just left. The man who had abused them all. Dodie knew very well that working with his father was the one fate that Marlon could never have abided. And yet she had said those words. She had said them knowing just how much they would hurt her son.

If Marlon had thought he'd freed himself from the binds that kept him tethered to his mother, he was about to learn differently. A week or so later, Piscator announced that Dodie was joining their company.

**EARLY AUGUST, 1944** / On the beach, the women of the company were rehearsing *Cry Havoc*, the play by Allan Kenward about army nurses tending wounded soldiers in Bataan. Described in Sayville press releases as a "heroic story of valiant women," the play was a novelty for the company: the cast was almost exclusively female. Sara Farwell was the strong-minded leader of the group; Elaine Stritch was the wisecracking chorus girl; and Blossom Plumb took on the "fiery, swaggering Irish girl." In the small part of "Doc," the nurses' commanding officer, a new member of the company was getting ready to shine: Dorothy Brando, eager, enthusiastic, her hair clipped short, making her look, Joy Thomson thought, "Katharine Hepburn-ish."

As Chouteau Dyer put the women through their paces, the men in the company mostly sat cross-legged in the sand, watching and cheering them on. Marlon's eyes followed his mother intensely. Part of him, Ellen Adler thought, would have been "very proud" of her. Her speech was clear, never slurred; she reported on time to rehearsals; she stayed up late working with actors twenty years her junior and never complained. But another part of him would have felt that Dodie was encroaching on his world, claiming what was his and making everything about her—just as she had done when he was growing up. At night, she regaled the company with stories of her time at the Omaha Community Playhouse, revealing that she had encouraged a young Henry Fonda to take his first part with the company—implying that, without her, Fonda might never have become a success. Marlon had never heard these stories growing up. The woman who captivated his fellow actors as they sat around a campfire at night was not the same woman he had known in Libertyville: hunched, hungover, shivering naked under a blanket in a jail cell.

There were certain proprieties a woman of her age insisted upon, however. Dodie didn't live with the company, but instead took a hotel room in town. One night, soon after her arrival, she invited Marlon and Freddie out to dinner. Not knowing Dodie's history, Freddie ordered a martini. "I'm sorry about your having to drink alone," he remembered Dodie telling him. "I'd like to join you, but I can't. I'm an alcoholic. You know—one drink is too many, one thousand not enough."

Embarrassed, Freddie offered to cancel his drink. Dodie refused to hear of it. "I get vicarious pleasure watching friends enjoy their drinks," she said.

Marlon sat watching and listening to all this, uncomfortably silent. As the dinner went on, it became clear that his mother was flirting with his friend. When the band struck up "Blue Moon," Dodie turned to Freddie and asked him to dance. "My pleasure," the young man replied, leading her out onto the dance floor. With Dodie pressing against him, Freddie wanted "nothing more in the world than to make love to Marlon's beautiful mother." The sexual energy was obvious. Glancing back at Marlon, Freddie saw his friend with "elbows on the table, chin cupped in his hands, staring at me with unblinking, blank eyes."

Later that night, as the two young men walked back to the playhouse, Marlon asked bluntly, "Would you go to bed with my mother?"

Freddie acknowledged that he was attracted to her, but insisted he would never go to bed with her because Marlon was his friend. "I wouldn't hurt your feelings like that," Freddie said. The answer seemed satisfactory, at least for the moment, and they walked on. But as they neared the barn, Marlon suddenly challenged Freddie to a race. Freddie demurred. Marlon kept challenging him, until Freddie, exasperated, shouted, "I said no and I mean no!"

Whereupon Marlon hauled off and punched him square in the stomach, knocking the wind out of him and almost doubling him up.

The rage had returned. Dormant these past eight months, ever since Stella had taken Marlon under her wing, his fury had begun to erupt periodically after Dodie's arrival in New York. If someone was late to an appointment, he'd explode in anger; if he didn't like a stage direction, he'd gripe and curse about it. His anger was unpredictable, and sometimes violent. It unnerved his friends, especially Ellen, who until this point had known only a calm and sensitive boy. "You're like Rumpelstiltskin," she told him. "One day you're just going to go up in a big puff of air and there won't be anything left."

To her amusement, Marlon didn't get the analogy. He thought she meant Rin Tin Tin, the canine star of the movies. She had to explain to him the old German fairy tale of the imp who got so angry so often that finally he exploded. "I suppose that kind of anger was to be expected after all his family problems," Ellen said. Marlon's rage was in fact his desperation to keep those problems from returning.

CRY HAVOC OPENED on August 11. The local press found it "moving and thought-provoking" and called Dodie "warm and sympathetic." After the show, Marlon lured Blossom away from the cast party to celebrate in private up in his loft.

Piscator may have hoped that the presence of Marlon's mother in the company would inhibit his carousing, but it seemed to have had the opposite effect. Marlon made no attempt to hide his sexual escapades from Dodie; pursuing women with even greater vigor than before, he was letting his mother know, consciously or not, that other women were now priorities in his life. When a pretty young drifter began hanging around with the company, Marlon brought her up to the attic to "share" with Freddie. The woman slipped into bed with the two of them. "While [Marlon] was humping away silently in the dark," Freddie remembered, he reached over to stroke Freddie's face, apparently so he wouldn't feel left out.

"There was a lot of fucking going on," Marlon admitted, looking back years later, "and I was in the thick of it." And that infuriated Piscator.

The Director wasn't having an easy time at the moment. *Last Stop* was already tagged as a "melodrama" and it hadn't even premiered yet; the description no doubt rankled Piscator. His dream of a top-notch cast had fallen through, and after rehearsing the play for its Boston tryout, Piscator was no doubt fretting about his shot at Broadway's big time.

During the week of August 14, he stormed about the playhouse. The actors were rehearsing their next production, *The Petrified Forest*. An announcement ran in the local paper that Marlon would play a part in it, as would Blossom and Darren.

At some point midweek, Piscator's preoccupation with the peccadillos of the company got the better of him. Just what set him off, other than his own personal frustrations, was not clear. Perhaps he'd had words with Marlon, or had observed something that displeased him. In any event, prowling around the property at three in the morning, he made his way out to the barn. As always, the trap door was shut, the ladder pulled safely inside. This time, however, Piscator would not be deterred. Hauling another ladder into the barn, he placed it against a beam and started climbing up toward the trap door.

Inside, blissfully unaware, Marlon and Blossom lay on the mattress. As Freddie would tell it, nothing indecent was going on. The couple was merely going over their lines from *The Petrified Forest*. Blossom had the female lead; the part Marlon was set to play would never be known for sure, but it may well have been Duke Mantee, the gangster who holds the family hostage. Suddenly, without warning, the trap door sprang open, and "this face appeared," Marlon would remember, "with the white hair glistening like Toscanini with the moonlight behind him." Piscator seemed rapturous by his discovery. "So, Mr. Brando!" he exclaimed, eyes blazing.

Marlon would admit to being "fucking scared" by the sudden intrusion into his space. "If only I'd had enough presence of mind," he'd say later, "I could have just shoved the ladder and he would have gone over backward. That would have been the end of it." But in the moment, all Marlon and Blossom could do was sit there in stunned silence. Piscator told them he wanted them both gone in the morning.

By sunrise, Marlon had reclaimed his wits. He sought out Chouteau Dyer. "You can't fire me," he said. "I'm in the next show.

You can't fire Blossom either, because she has the lead." Dyer was unmoved. She had her orders straight from Piscator. Both of them were to pack their bags and go.

The company was thunderstruck, and also angry, seeing the expulsion as terribly unfair. A couple of the actors revealed to Marlon that Piscator himself was no angel, that he'd been taking one woman from the company back to his room regularly all season. The great arbiter of morality, as it turned out, had been fooling around himself behind his wife's back. "This lady," Marlon would say, still bitter about the incident nearly fifty years later, "was servicing Erwin Piscator all that summer, and giving him sexual favors, and that always tickled me to death."

When Stella learned what had happened, she attempted to intervene with Piscator. Getting him on the phone, she argued that nothing improper had been taking place, and therefore the Director should reinstate Marlon and Blossom. Piscator remained implacable. Stella would tell a friend that he told her quite plainly, "in very *deutsche* fashion, that he found Marlon troublesome and did not want him back." Here, then, was the real truth behind Marlon's dismissal: Piscator didn't like him, didn't appreciate his independence, and was almost certainly envious of him. He'd gone looking for a reason to get rid of him, and he'd found it.

It was the hypocrisy that rankled Marlon more than anything else. Despite Stella's protestations that he was innocent, Marlon admitted that he'd broken the rules many other times that summer, but that wasn't the point. "It wasn't so much that I was innocent with her or with half a dozen other girls," he would say. "It was that the Director was just as guilty. What an act of hypocrisy that was."

The company gathered to say good-bye to Marlon. "We all felt shock because he was our big star," Sara Farwell said. "Up until then, it had been a wonderful summer." After helping his friend pack, Freddie remained inside their attic loft, watching from a window. "I saw him toss his bags into a waiting cab and wave good-bye to the company," Freddie said.

A short time later, Dodie arrived from her hotel. "What's this I hear?" she asked Chouteau Dyer, who told her that Piscator had dismissed Marlon and Blossom for defiance of the rules. "You're dead right," Dodie replied, offering no defense of her son. "It's too bad. I'm sorry." With that, she headed off for rehearsals.

Struck by the injustice of it all, Darren packed his own bags and left the company that day. But the rest of the actors regrouped; the show had to go on. *The Petrified Forest* opened on schedule, with the parts hastily recast.

Soon after Marlon's dismissal, Paris was liberated; the war in Europe turned decisively toward its conclusion. Marlon would tell friends that he felt similarly liberated, finally free of Piscator's dictatorship. "I just blew with the wind," he said. "Like a newspaper in a strong wind." It was an image he took pleasure in for himself: just like those newspapers he tossed out of windows, he could now spread his wings and go where the currents took him.

Yet the expulsion from Sayville was merely Shattuck redux— he'd been exiled from a community of people he cared about for being too spontaneous, too independent. Marlon had been a success at the Dramatic Workshop, but only so long as Stella championed him. Without her, who would tolerate his iconoclasm? If he'd been considering a second year at the New School (and most of his friends believed he was), it wouldn't happen now, with Piscator blacklisting him. But if he felt any heartache or regret, he masked it. He was done with acting, he told Ellen. He'd never wanted to be an actor anyway. It was time for something new. Maybe this time he'd finally find a cat he could skin.

A few days later, Piscator was savaged by the critics when *Last Stop* opened in Boston. The *Globe* called the play "an also-ran," complaining that Piscator's direction "goes in for whirligig motion." Worse came when the show opened in New York and Lewis

Nichols of the *Times* declared it a "little horror" and "badly directed." *Last Stop* closed a couple of weeks later, Piscator's final try for Broadway success.

In his gloom, however, he might have taken some consolation that he, and the theater, had apparently seen the last of Marlon Brando.

And so, once more, Marlon was wandering the streets of Greenwich Village, observing the motion of the world around him, listening to buskers playing jazz, keeping time with the music with his hands and feet. For now, that's where we'll leave him, as happy as he will ever be.

# THE

# HOODLUM

# ARISTOCRAT

**AUGUST 18, 1947** / Heat and humidity choked the city, with temperatures averaging in the low nineties. Youngsters pried open fire hydrants to cool off. At the Liebling-Wood Agency at 551 Fifth Avenue, between Forty-Fifth and Forty-Sixth Streets, things were just as hot. Giant electric fans rattled in the windows. Agent Bill Liebling sat with rolled-up sleeves as he made phone call after phone call. He'd finish one only to hang up and start making another.

The agency was abuzz that morning. Word had come in that John Garfield, the big Hollywood movie star, had dropped out of the upcoming Tennessee Williams play being produced by Irene Selznick, and the hunt was on for his replacement. Since Liebling's wife, Audrey Wood, represented Williams, agents from all over the city were dropping off headshots of their clients. The part of Stanley Kowalski, rumor had it, was daring, sexy, radical—the one everyone would be talking about next awards season. Yet Liebling wasn't bothering to look through the headshots coming in. He already had an actor for Stanley in mind—if only he could find him.

"I'm trying to get in touch with Marlon Brando," he barked into the phone for the eighth or ninth time that morning. Once again, he had no luck. Marlon Brando, apparently, didn't want to be found.

Three years after he was kicked out of Sayville, a great deal had happened in Marlon's life and career. He'd been in several shows on Broadway; he was now known to many of the top producers. Yet, for all that, the late summer of 1947 was really not so different from the late summer of 1944. Marlon had climbed high only to be knocked down once more. This time, instead of the autocratic Piscator, it had been the flamboyant actress Tallulah Bankhead who'd been his adversary. In tryouts for her play *Eagle Rampant*, Bankhead had disdained Marlon for his idiosyncratic style and vindictively fired him in front of the company. When he walked away from Bankhead's play, he was also, he believed, walking away from the entire enterprise of the theater. No one had seen him for months. His agents, Maynard Morris and Edie Van Cleve, had no idea how to reach him.

Liebling wasn't giving up. He felt certain Marlon was the one to play Stanley Kowalski. Both he and Wood had seen the young actor in a play called *Truckline Café* a year and a half earlier, and both had agreed he possessed the intensity and rawness Williams had in mind for the character. Stanley had been conceived as older than Marlon's twenty-three years; Garfield, who'd been Irene Selznick's first choice, was thirty-four. But there was something about Marlon—and the way he'd let out a bloodcurdling cry toward the end of *Truckline*—that convinced Liebling he was ideal for the part.

So, he put the call out on "the grapevine," as Audrey Wood remembered. Liebling didn't just work the phones. He stopped everyone he knew; he asked people to spread the word. The hope was that some agent would tell some producer who would tell some audition manager who would tell some actor who would tell some bartender who would tell one of Marlon's pals who would tell one of Marlon's girls who would finally tell Marlon himself. And the message being passed from ear to ear: "Come to the offices of Liebling-Wood."

In the old days before the war, it had been simpler to send a message along the grapevine. Now the city teemed with returning GIs looking for work, and fewer people knew one another; New York was quickly becoming a city of strangers. Tens of thousands of GIs swelled the factories, offices, bars, and nightclubs. Whether the economy could absorb them all was still a matter in question. Some predicted an economic boom bolstered by consumer spending on new manufactures; others warned that the war had merely interrupted the death throes of capitalism, and at any moment the nation would revert to the economic breakdown of the 1930s.

Yet, in the midst of this collision of hope and anxiety, the American theater was experiencing a creative renaissance. Tennessee Williams and Arthur Miller were the vanguard of a postwar generation of young playwrights exploring the human condition in ways far deeper (and often darker) than ever before. Williams's *The Glass Menagerie*, opening in late 1944, had revolutionized Broadway by mining the interior landscape of memory and emotion. Until that moment, the American theater, overrun with musicals and melodramas, had seemed to some critics disconnected from the real world, which was racked by war and intolerance. *The Glass Menagerie* helped change all that. Melodramas were now passé; so were the ubiquitous "social message" plays of the 1930s. Now the trend was for psychological depth, with actors relying on the text for serious insight. Journeymen playwrights were out; poets were in. It was just the sort of theater Stella Adler had been pining for.

No wonder Liebling thought her star pupil was perfect for it.

AT THE PARK Savoy Hotel on West Fifty-Eighth Street, the pay phone in the first-floor hallway was jangling. When someone picked it up, they heard Bill Liebling ask if Marlon Brando still lived there. No, Liebling was told, Marlon had left the hotel some time ago, leaving no forwarding address. But the bohemians who still lived there remembered him fondly. There was talk that he'd gone "on the road"—not with a show, but with a carload of activists fighting for a political cause.

From the window of a speeding passenger train, Marlon stared out at the rapidly changing landscapes of Pennsylvania and western New York. Everywhere, it seemed, new housing was going up, guaranteed by federal programs for qualified returning veterans, complete with the latest appliances and the requisite picket fence. Now twenty-three years old, Marlon was fascinated by how the world was rebuilding itself—a task he was attempting for himself as well. After three unrewarding years in the theater, disillusioned and personally drained, he had needed something to believe in, something weightier and more meaningful than the superficiality of the theater. And so, for much of the spring and summer of 1947, he'd been crisscrossing the country with the American League for a Free Palestine, advocating for a Jewish state in the Middle East.

"I am now an active and integral part of a political organization," he wrote home proudly. "My job is to travel about the country and lecture to sympathetic groups in order to solicit money and to organize groups that will support us." A three-week training program had left him thoroughly familiar with and committed to the ALFP's mission. After the horrors endured by Jews during the war, Marlon believed the only moral restitution was an independent Jewish state. The Western powers had "trampled" on the Jews, he said, and it was time for the British occupiers of Palestine to return to the Jews their ancient homeland. To his family he wrote, "You wouldn't believe the injustices and cruelties that the British Colonial Office is capable of." He assured them he was "not being rash" in his judgment, and sent home some literature to prove what he said was true.

Marlon's attraction to the ALFP was not surprising. Both Stella and Luther Adler were on the organization's board. The mission of the group was the mission of Marlon's family, his emotional family, and so, quite naturally, it also became his.

At Beth Hillel Temple in Kenosha, Wisconsin, Marlon walked up to the podium, a little nervous and awkward. To the audience he seemed even younger than he was. In New York, he'd developed a reputation among Broadway aficionados as the powerhouse who'd let out that heartbreaking howl in *Truckline Café*, but here in the land of lakes and cheese, even that minimal recognition was denied to him. In Kenosha, Marlon was just a good-looking, slightly gangly young man in an ill-fitting beige suit. He made these tours with other young, largely unknown New York actors who supported the cause of the ALFP; joining him in Kenosha was Jerry Solars, who'd appeared at the Barbizon-Plaza Theatre in the comedy *We Will Dream Again* in April 1947. They were billed grandly as "actors from the New York stage," even if no one west of the Hudson River knew who they were.

Yet when Marlon began to speak, the people in the audience sat up. "The British Colonial administration of Palestine," he declared, his voice rising an octave, "is guilty of violating human rights at the very moment European Jews are most in need of sanctuary." His blue-gray eyes flashing, he demanded that the United States pressure Britain into granting "Hebrew national citizenship" to all Jews in Palestine, Europe, and North Africa who wanted to be part of a new Jewish state.

The audience, mostly middle-aged Jewish immigrants from Russia and Poland who had come to the United States well before the war, burst into applause. Some had been unconvinced of the necessity of a Jewish state, but after hearing Marlon and the other speakers from the ALFP, many were now on board. The applause from that Kenosha synagogue "meant far more to Marlon," Ellen Adler thought, than any he had been given by any Broadway audience.

He'd found a way to address what he'd once described to his parents as "the bitterness, fear, hate and untruths" of the world, a condition he'd vowed "to do something about" soon after arriving in New York. The instinctive leftist politics he'd grown up with were finally given voice. "The work that we'll be doing," he told his parents after joining the ALFP, "won't be easy by any matter of means. It is a tougher and vastly more responsible job than anything the theatre could offer. I'm going to try to do my best to add my little bit."

His "little bit" quickly became the center of his life. With Stella and Luther and others, Marlon debated tactics about the best way to achieve their goals. He tended to be more radical than some in the ALFP; he sided with the militants, for example, who argued that "terrorism and military action were necessary to wear down British resistance and lead to the early creation of Israel." After seeing the harrowing newsreels of concentration camps, Marlon had come to believe that the Jews "had to do whatever was necessary" to acquire their own state.

This was the sort of thing that fired him up. This was the sort of dialogue that kept Marlon alert and engaged: justice and freedom and human rights. The conversations of his actor friends, analyzing the move away from didacticism and toward psychological exploration in the American theater, bored him to death. The war, he believed, had imposed a greater urgency for civic responsibility. "I had a sense that though the world had gone through a cataclysm, little had changed," he would recall. "Black people were still being treated as less than human, there was still rampant poverty and anti-Semitism, and there seemed to be as much injustice as before." Only whites, for example, could apply for most of those new housing tracts being built for returning veterans. A persistent voice in Marlon's head was telling him that "acting was not an important vocation in life when the world was still facing so many problems."

The young man who had been denied access and expression for much of his life, who'd been kept back and discouraged, who'd been told repeatedly that he didn't matter, felt far more drawn to social advocacy than he did to acting or the theater. For others, success in the theater might provide a sense of personal affirmation; the applause might fill up some empty part inside them. But not for Marlon. He desired "more concrete results" than that, Ellen Adler said; he wanted "a change in the entire world, not just *his* world." Away from the theater, "working for something he believed in," Ellen said, "Marlon was much happier." To his parents, he declared that working for the ALFP left him "stimulated more than [he'd] ever been."

Perhaps, then, this was his calling. Perhaps, Marlon thought, political advocacy or social justice work was what he ought to pursue. During a visit to Washington, DC, with the ALFP, he witnessed firsthand the racial segregation in the nation's capital, and it left him furious. "I felt I had a responsibility to do something about it," he said. All his life, injustice had followed him—a different sort of injustice, certainly, than that faced by Negroes or Jews, but injustice nonetheless. Marlon seemed to feel that he could make up for what he called "the captivity" of his youth by working for the freedom of others. "I knew what it was like to feel hopeless," he'd say. "So that was the sort of work I should've been doing. Not acting."

Stella, still convinced of her protégé's potential to be great, argued that he could combine his political passion with the theater. And for a few months at the end of 1946, Marlon had done just that, costarring in *A Flag Is Born*, a play produced by the ALFP to advance the cause of a Jewish state. The British navy's seizure of a Jewish refugee ship headed for Palestine in March 1947 had convinced the ALFP of the need for a high-profile response. "To see the British soldiers taking people off the ship forcibly," Marlon said, "with guns pointed at them, and putting them behind barbed wire in Cypress [*sic*, Cyprus], seemed to me to put the world topsy-turvy, because what in the world had we fought for if not liberty and the right for people to be protected?" *A Flag Is Born* was the ALFP's strongest salvo yet against British hostility and American inaction. Written by famed screenwriter Ben Hecht, the play was directed by Luther Adler, whose elder sister, Celia, starred alongside Oscar-winning Hollywood actor Paul Muni. Marlon was the only non-Jew in the cast. He played a concentration camp survivor headed to the promised land of Palestine. Opening on September 4, 1946, for a limited run at the Alvin Theatre, *A Flag Is Born* was successful enough to be given an extended run at the Adelphi, where Marlon had made his Broadway debut, in *Bobino*, two years earlier, in a giraffe costume.

Marlon, who rarely idolized anyone, was awestruck by Muni. "The best acting I ever saw in my life," he said. That was because, he felt, Muni's acting was in service to something greater than the play; the performance mattered well beyond the proscenium arch. "Art for art's sake" was abhorrent to Marlon. In the months before signing on to *Flag*, he'd read Eugene O'Neill's *The Iceman Cometh* and thought very little of it, declining to pursue what would become O'Neill's latter-day masterpiece. *Iceman* wasn't about anything Marlon considered "timely"; there was nothing in it, he thought, that mattered to "the practical here and now." *A Flag Is Born*, by contrast, was about as "now" as one could find in the theater.

The play was, in fact, Piscator-style pedagogic theater: "an obvious bit of propaganda," *Variety* called it, with "the defects of all propaganda." Yet Marlon, and the Adlers, overlooked those defects, because the play filled an urgent need. Reviewers tended to agree with them, turning blind eyes to the play's gimmicks and moralizing; its "stirring message," *Variety* concluded, "demands attention."

To Marlon, his work in *A Flag Is Born* was the most important acting he'd ever done. This *mattered*; most everything that had come before had not. As payment, he accepted only the Actors' Equity minimum; any money the play made, Marlon agreed, should go toward the ALFP's efforts to establish the state of Israel. *Variety* praised his "emotional intensity" in the part, but it was offstage where Marlon's zeal really came alive. When he left the play in late November 1946, replaced by Sidney Lumet, he was ready and eager to start touring with the ALFP.

But before he could do that, he needed one other thing: money. Since he'd made next to nothing during his two months in *Flag*, he was now broke.

That was how he had ended up with Tallulah Bankhead in a play that meant nothing to him. *Eagle Rampant* was an English translation of a Jean Cocteau play. Bankhead was a friend of Marlon's agent Edie Van Cleve, which was how he'd gotten the role. After feeling empowered during *A Flag Is Born*, part of a constructive and vital movement, he chafed at being involved in what was essentially a vanity project for an aging actress. With Bankhead "constantly drinking and sloshed most of the time," Marlon came to think of her as "a Duesenberg [automobile] that's been hit by four trains." Bankhead played a fictional European queen, Marlon the assassin hired to kill her. The antagonism backstage was nearly as lethal.

The play opened in Wilmington on November 28, 1946, then moved on to Washington, Boston, Hartford, and New Haven, where, on January 2, 1947, Marlon was abruptly fired and replaced by Helmut Dantine. As much as Marlon had disliked the play, he admitted to being "vaguely depressed" boarding the train for New York. The expulsion undoubtedly summoned a barrage of old memories, from Shattuck to Sayville. For the rest of his life, he would badmouth Bankhead, claiming she'd put the make on him ("plunging her cold tongue into my mouth like an eel"). While certainly not out of character for the bawdy Tallulah, Marlon's claim that he was fired because he wouldn't sleep with her is dubious, given the stack of bad reviews he'd accumulated since the play's premiere. In Wilmington, *Variety* wrote that he failed "to impress as a revolutionary poet"; the *Boston Globe* concluded that he was "not equal to his role"; and the *Hartford Courant* called him "ineffectual as assassin and poetic inspiration." With notices like that, it was a wonder he lasted as long as he did.

To Marlon, *Eagle Rampant* was the worst kind of theater, empty and artificial. He was there only for the cash he could make. But even that came to naught when, on the train back to New York, someone stole two thousand dollars out of his bag, leaving him with nothing to show for all his aggravation. "I arrived in New York with holes in my socks and holes in my mind," he said. As far as Marlon was concerned, he was done with acting. He happily embarked on his seven months of travel for the ALFP.

He didn't return to New York until the late summer of 1947, just as Bill Liebling set out looking for him. Once again, Marlon was broke; working for a nonprofit never made anyone rich. He didn't care about being rich, of course, just about having enough money to pay the rent at his new apartment at 37 West Fifty-Second Street. He also wanted to take dance and flute lessons, plus he was saddled with doctor's bills for Celia, who'd had some bad times.

Marlon was dependent, yet again, on his father for a regular allowance. Dodie had left New York and returned to her husband, and so the old family charade had resumed. As long as his mother was estranged from her husband, Marlon could be free of him as well. But once his parents reconciled, Marlon once again became the little boy trying to make his father proud. "I must learn how to handle money myself," he wrote home. "You're damn swell to offer your dummy son help." Marlon Senior had recently gone into business for himself and was having difficulty setting up sales accounts; hoping to make some money on *Eagle Rampant*, Marlon Junior had told his father, "It won't be long until I can give you the world." That plan had gone bust. It seemed he might be doomed to being the "dummy son" forever.

That late summer of 1947, Marlon was in the position he usually was in when an acting offer came his way: broke and without any other options. When the grapevine finally caught up with him,

Marlon learned that Bill Liebling was looking for him. And so, on a hot, humid August day, he hiked over to Fifth Avenue to see what all the urgency was about.

**AUGUST 20** / Bill Liebling kept grabbing on to Marlon's arm as they walked, almost as if he were afraid he might lose him again. They were on their way to Henry Miller's Theatre, on Forty-Third Street, to meet with Irene Selznick and Elia Kazan, the producer and director of *A Streetcar Named Desire*. Excited to show off his discovery, Liebling began to hum. Marlon, feeling playful, asked him if he sang.

He did indeed. Marlon asked what songs he knew. Liebling rattled off a number of titles, and Marlon settled on "Dear Old Girl," a very old standard that Dodie had taught him at the piano back in Libertyville. Walking along Fifth Avenue, Liebling and Marlon harmonized together: "'Twas a sunny day in June / And the birds were all in tune / And the songs they sang all seemed to be for you . . ."

At the theater, the harmony continued. The moment Marlon walked into the building, Elia Kazan knew they'd found their Stanley. A little more than a year earlier, Kazan had produced *Truckline Café*, the production that had brought Marlon his first real attention from New York theater critics. The show had lasted less than two weeks, but the glowing reviews Marlon had received landed him roles in *Candida* and *Antigone* with Katharine Cornell, *A Flag Is Born*, and finally the disastrous *Eagle Rampant*. But after that, Marlon had dropped out of sight—and, apparently, out of mind. On Broadway, one was only as current as one's last show, and it had now been nearly a year since he trod the boards of the Great White

Way. It took seeing him again, in that sweaty tee shirt and with that unself-conscious swagger, to convince Kazan that he could play Stanley Kowalski.

Still, the director said little as Marlon read for the part. He just observed. So intently did he listen and observe that "a white line" formed under his eyes, Bill Liebling recalled. The agent took that line as evidence that Kazan was sold.

Kazan was among the shrewdest directors then working on stage and screen, the ideal helmsman to bring to life the words written by a new generation of psychologically driven playwrights. He'd directed Arthur Miller's *All My Sons*, still running on Broadway, a harrowing story of moral consequences; and he'd just gotten back from Hollywood, where he'd directed *Gentleman's Agreement*, an indictment of anti-Semitism. The film would be released in a few months' time. Thirty-seven years old, born in Turkey to Greek Orthodox parents, the Marxist Kazan was profoundly interested in the complexities and contradictions of the human character. As he listened to Marlon read, he was thinking about a letter he'd received from Tennessee Williams. "There are no 'good' or 'bad' people," the playwright had explained. "Some are a little better or a little worse but all are activated more by misunderstanding than malice . . . Nobody sees anybody truly but all through the flaws of their own egos. Vanity, fear, desire, competition—all such distortions within our own egos—condition our vision of those in relation to us."

*Vanity, fear, desire, competition.* Even from their short collaboration on *Truckline*, Kazan knew that each of those motivators had played its part in propelling Marlon through his twenty-three years of life. They were also the forces that drove Stanley Kowalski in *A Streetcar Named Desire*.

If Kazan was immediately sold on the casting, Irene Selznick took a bit longer to come around. "She was especially unenthusiastic about me," Marlon recalled. To Selznick, Marlon was just too young. Jessica Tandy, the actress playing Blanche DuBois (Stanley's adversary, with whom he shares a dangerous sexual tension), was thirty-eight, and Selznick worried about the chemistry between the two leads. She had a great deal riding on this play. Forty years old, Selznick was the daughter of Louis B. Mayer, the head of Metro-Goldwyn-Mayer film studios, and the estranged wife of film producer David O. Selznick. With *Streetcar*, she was attempting to carve out a career for herself away from Hollywood and the men in her life. To Kazan, she was a dilettante. They were frequently at loggerheads—and no more so than that day in Henry Miller's Theatre, when the producer remained frustratingly ambivalent about Marlon even as Kazan did his best to persuade her.

Selznick had wanted John Garfield for the part because of his box-office appeal. Marlon, for all the critical praise he'd gotten for *Truckline*, was still largely unknown, and Selznick believed they'd be taking a risk if they went with him, a risk she was resistant to take. So, it was decided to turn the matter over to the playwright. At the moment, Williams was in Provincetown, the arts colony and summer resort at the very tip of Cape Cod, where, thirty years earlier, Eugene O'Neill had written and performed his early plays. Now it was Williams's artistic retreat as well; he'd penned much of *Streetcar* there, in a ramshackle little cottage perched at the end of a wharf. Kazan and Selznick told Marlon that he needed to get up to Provincetown as soon as possible. Everything would now be dependent on Tennessee.

Marlon was game, but there was a practical problem, he said: he didn't have bus fare. While that was true, it was also, almost certainly, a delaying tactic. Did he really want to sign on to a potentially long-running play after all he'd been through, one that would potentially keep him away from his activism, no matter how much he needed the money?

Kazan wouldn't be deterred, however. Digging into his pocket, he handed Marlon twenty bucks. The investment, he was convinced, would be worth it.

HEADING OUT OF the theater twenty dollars richer, Marlon didn't purchase a bus ticket. He used the money to buy food, which he brought back to the West Fifty-Second Street apartment of his pals, the actresses Maureen Stapleton and Janice Mars, and pretty soon they were having a party. That's the way things happened at 37 West Fifty-Second. "A few people would get together to share a meal in the late afternoon," the actress and singer Kaye Ballard recalled, "and before you knew it, more people showed up and suddenly a party is underway and it would go on like that until the wee hours of the morning."

Marlon was loath to give up this life and start learning lines again. "I never liked the idea of going to work," he said, looking back. "I would have much preferred to stay and have fun and only pay the bills when I absolutely had to." So, while Kazan and Williams waited, Marlon partied.

The ambivalence over accepting *Streetcar* was not so much rooted in any insecurity on Marlon's part about his abilities, as some later accounts would suggest, though he'd always harbor some nagging doubts about himself. Rather, at that particular moment, his equivocation grew out of the unhappy memories he held of most of the previous plays he'd been involved in—"soul-crushing" experiences, as he called them. Three years earlier, when he'd fled Sayville and Piscator's dictatorship, he'd had great expectations of finding a new life, a new way of making a living, anything but acting—but his freedom had lasted only a few days. His sister Tidd had hauled him over to the offices of Maynard Morris, the agent who'd been so smitten with him in his Dramatic Workshop appearances, and in no time, Morris had secured Marlon an audition for John Van Druten's play *I Remember Mama*. Without much effort or enthusiasm, Marlon had won the small role of the teenaged Nels. When his casting was announced on September 2, 1944, only two weeks had passed since he bid the company good-bye in Sayville. "So I just stepped on one lily pad and then another," he recalled. "I lived a charmed life."

Not that he found much charm in it. *Mama* was the first soul-crusher that led to all the rest. Marlon had been blindsided by his sister's and his agent's enthusiasm. "I was swept up in acting," he said, "before I knew what I wanted to do with myself." If he'd had his way, he might have taken a longer hiatus from the stage—perhaps a permanent one. He might have pursued other things, such as dancing or music. The problem, as always, was nothing else was being offered to him at the moment, and he needed the money.

So, off he went into *I Remember Mama*—and hated every moment of it. His ordeal dragged out for more than fifteen months as the play turned into a gigantic hit. As the sweet, rather boring Nels, Marlon was barely in it; the stars were Mady Christians, as the mother of the close-knit Norwegian clan, and Oscar Homolka, as the comical Uncle Chris. Most of Marlon's time was spent backstage, reading books between his appearances. He was miserable. He despised the producer, the legendary composer Richard Rodgers. At the audition, Rodgers had been "very nasty" and "pissed off at everything," Marlon said. "What have you done?" he barked at the young actor. Marlon replied he'd been in summer stock and played in *Twelfth Night*. "Come on," the producer said, "what have you *done*?" Marlon told him, "Nothing."

The drudgery of doing the same thing every night (and twice on Wednesdays and Saturdays) was, for Marlon, like living in "a torture chamber." Rarely was there any time off; nothing was ever different; and the money he made was about as little as it was possible to earn on Broadway, just sixty-five dollars a week. Instinctively resistant to the idea of "going nine to five," Marlon was living out his worst nightmare during *Mama*. Not long before, he and Darren Dublin had watched those weary morning commuters heading for the train, thanking God they weren't among them. Now he was one of those "poor motherfuckers" himself.

Partying with his friends, his bus ticket to Provincetown unbought, Marlon would think long and hard before agreeing to any new Broadway commitment. He was leaning toward staying right where he was.

PLAYING THE BONGOS, sweat flying off his face, Marlon moved his hands so fast they were only a blur. Alongside him was some guy playing a trumpet, and every once in a while, twenty-one-year-old chanteuse Kaye Ballard would belt into song. A cloud of blue cigarette smoke hung over the heads of the people sitting cross-legged on the floor listening and swaying to this impromptu band. The music ended only when hostess Maureen Stapleton announced that the stew was ready, and the hungry young actors, artists, and musicians all made haste for their bowls.

"Maureen Stapleton had what they call a salon," the actor Eli Wallach remembered. "Where the actors would go and gather." All the cool cats hoping to make it big on Broadway (or in the art world, or the literary scene) came by Stapleton's apartment on Fifty-Second Street, which she shared with the actress Janice Mars. "We'd make a big pot of stew," Kaye Ballard remembered, "because nobody had any money to go out to eat." After the stew came chocolate pudding with whipped cream, and in between the courses came entertainment. Someone might practice a scene for an upcoming show; someone else might play a piece on a piccolo; lots of people read poems. They also drank bourbon and gin and smoked a ton of cigarettes, and sometimes someone brought a little weed.

All were up-and-comers. Stapleton had recently completed a tour in summer stock in Tennessee Williams's *The Glass Menag-*

*erie*; Mars had been on Broadway that past spring in *Message for Margaret*. Eli Wallach had done a number of plays that year; he and Maureen would soon start rehearsals for *Antony and Cleopatra*, with Katharine Cornell. Kaye Ballard had just finished touring with *Three to Make Ready*; at Maureen's salon, she'd often try out songs. "I fell into such an exciting world," Ballard recalled. "Everybody so committed."

There were dozens of other regulars. From the Dramatic Workshop came Harry Belafonte and Beatrice Arthur; Marlon also brought Freddie Fiore into the circle. Billy Redfield had been an actor on the stage since he was a kid; Sam Gilman was a comic book artist (*Iron Skull* and *Vapo-Man*) with acting ambitions; and James Baldwin was a writer of essays and poems (mostly unpublished at that point) who possessed, according to Marlon, "the most artistic soul."

The twenty-three-year-old Baldwin was just as impressed. "I had never met any white man like Marlon," said Baldwin. "Totally unconventional and independent, a beautiful cat. Race truly meant nothing to him—he was contemptuous of anyone who discriminated in any way." Marlon loved the story of Baldwin tossing a glass of water in the face of a waitress who refused to serve him. What connected the two young men, Marlon believed, was a shared history of not belonging. Baldwin, Marlon said, "was dominated by his father who was not such a wonderful man." Still, Baldwin "had the capacity to deal with life."

That capacity was what bonded the young people at Fifty-Second Street. They were survivors and rebels. "A family of waifs," Janice Mars called them. "Flouting all the conventions, orphans in rebellion against everything." Lacking what Mars called "emotionally secure family backgrounds," the friends had formed a new family to make up for it. This sort of nurturance was exactly what Marlon needed after all the ups and downs of the past three years.

He was such a regular at Stapleton's gatherings that when he got back from traveling the country with the ALFP in the summer of 1947, he took an apartment in the same building.

"Bud was a charter member of the 37 West 52nd Street Regulars," Stapleton wrote, revealing her closeness to him by using his childhood nickname. They'd first met while Marlon was still at the Dramatic Workshop, and Maureen and Janice were taking evening classes there with Herbert Berghof. Initially, both women had been smitten with Marlon, flipping a coin to decide who would "commit the act of aggression" against him. Nothing came of it. (Neither, with their northern European backgrounds, was Marlon's type.) They were better off as buddies, free of any sexual tension. Mars encouraged Marlon's love of poetry; together they read "lots of Yeats," she remembered, especially Marlon's favorite, "The Lake Isle of Innisfree," about finding contentment beyond the daily grind of life.

Marlon did cast a more suggestive eye at Ballard, who was dark, fiery, and Italian. "Our affair never got serious," Ballard said. "He couldn't conquer me as he did other women. I was this tough Italian Catholic. But we stayed good friends."

Ballard was Marlon's entrée to other salons, such as the gatherings at the loft of Maggie Eversol. A freelance artist with connections everywhere, Eversol introduced Marlon to Eartha Kitt and the choreographer Katherine Dunham, with whom he began studying dance at her school on West Forty-Third Street. His dream now was to become one of the few white dancers to join Dunham's company.

With his mother now making only periodic visits to the city, and his sisters married and relocated, Marlon had assembled a new family for himself. One face at Stapleton's salons, however, did go back to his childhood. Marlon had known Wally Cox, a designer and aspiring actor, since they were both nine-year-old boys in Evanston. They'd run into each other again, quite by chance, on Sixth

Avenue. "Hello, Bud," Wally had said, and instantly the old friends had reconnected. Marlon had been pushing a shopping cart, Wally had hopped in for a ride, and off they went, laughing and careening down the street as if no time had passed. Like Marlon, Wally rode a motorcycle, and the two of them often tore around town together.

"Wally Cox wasn't really my friend," Marlon would say years later. "He was my brother." Physically, they were opposites. Marlon wasn't tall, but his broad shoulders gave the illusion of height to his five-nine frame. Meanwhile, Wally was barely five six and as slender as a whisper, with small bones and features; he also wore glasses. Even as boyhood friends, their physical difference had been apparent. "Marlon was kind of a rough little boy," Wally's sister would remember. "He tied Wally to a tree one afternoon and then left him. I'm surprised they remained friends, but they did." Yet Wally was strong enough. Throughout their life, the two men would wrestle, and more often than not, Wally would come out on top, pinning Marlon down and thumping his skinny chest. "Wally actually had a very strong body," said Kaye Ballard. "It was the skinny neck that fooled people."

Wally made up for his lack of heft with a muscular intelligence. Few people could keep up with Marlon when he talked science or philosophy, but Wally read the same books and asked the same probing questions. "They were both intellectuals," Wally's sister said, "and had lofty conversations on unusual subjects." Wally, Marlon mused, "came closer than anyone I've ever known to being a genius."

When he reconnected with Marlon in New York, Wally had no showbiz dreams. He'd studied botany at City College, and was trying to make a living as a silversmith, crafting and selling jewelry. He'd show up to Maureen's salons with pillowcases full of his creations, but his sales pitch was so comic that everyone encouraged him to put together a stand-up act. His humor was droll, very dry, and very observant. "Marlon was fascinated with how funny

Wally was," Wally's sister said. "The same things amused them."
They pulled pranks and imitated people. Cox could yodel, which
always broke Marlon up. "You should be a performer," everyone
told him. Before long, Wally was studying with Stella.

Like all of them, Wally had survived a damaged childhood. His
alcoholic mother had constantly denigrated him. "He didn't feel
worthy," Marlon learned after many conversations with his friend
about their childhoods. Marlon rarely spoke of his own childhood
misery to others, but Wally could understand. They had no secrets. Once, Marlon found some magazines among Wally's things
that featured men and women in bondage. At first Wally denied
they were his, but finally Marlon got him to admit that sadomas-
ochism turned him on. Open-minded about all things sexual, Marlon asked Wally if he'd ever tried S/M. When Wally replied that
he had not, Marlon encouraged him to do so. "Get it out in the
open," he said. "People like all sorts of things." Eventually, Wally
erected a trapeze in front of a mirror in his apartment. "He'd dress
up in boots and have girls whip him," Marlon remembered. "They
would make him grovel, and it made him sexually happy." And
that, in Marlon's view, was all that mattered.

That late summer of 1947, the parties at 37 West Fifty-Second
Street reached their peak. Marlon banged away at his drums as if
he hadn't a care in the world. Not for several days did he tell anyone about his audition for Elia Kazan.

When his friends finally learned of it, they were thrilled. "Go
for it," Kaye Ballard said. "But he just didn't care. All the rest of us
wanted to make it big. But Marlon just acted to survive."

Why give up this world of adventure and experimentation and
ideas and fun to get trapped in another play, especially one with no
political cause behind it? Marlon much preferred to hang around
the city, where nothing was more urgent than making sure a sax
player was on hand to accompany him on the drums. "He had a
wild-kid kind of fun," one friend remembered of those days. That

wildness was expressed by having a pet raccoon named Russell, a gift from his mother, which had free rein of his apartment. It also came through in the way he would drop plastic bags filled with water from the roof of his building onto "the stiffs" below. On the wall of his apartment, he'd pasted a sign that summed up his philosophy of life: "You Ain't Livin' If You Don't Know It."

For Marlon, living was making music and talking philosophy and pulling pranks with your friends. Living was fighting for things that mattered, for causes you believed in. Living was having sex with whom you wanted, when you wanted. What *wasn't* living was learning lines, traipsing through preview towns, greasing up your face, and parading yourself across a stage every night. He'd done that in *I Remember Mama*, and it had nearly killed him.

The end of *I Remember Mama* had, in fact, coincided with the worst period of Marlon's life so far, a time his friends knew never to speak of. He had gone to a very dark place then, and he was very reluctant to do anything that might take him back there again. This time, Marlon feared, he might not survive.

ACROSS TOWN, ELIA KAZAN was ringing Tennessee Williams in Provincetown. Almost a week had passed since he'd given Marlon the twenty bucks for bus fare. He was eager to know what the playwright thought of the young actor he considered ideal for Stanley Kowalski. Kazan had let Williams know that Marlon was coming, singing the young actor's praises. Williams had been unsure about going with an unknown. Was the director certain they couldn't lure John Garfield back?

Still, Williams had agreed to see the young man. He'd written to Audrey Wood that he was "very anxious to see [Brando] and hear him as soon as I can." At the time, he'd expected Marlon any day. That was on August 25. Kazan placed his phone call either that day or the day after.

When Williams picked up, his voice was crackly. The reception on outer Cape Cod wasn't very good. Kazan asked if Marlon had shown up. Williams said no.

Kazan was crestfallen. The rascal had disappeared again. "I figured I'd lost twenty bucks," he said. He began to look elsewhere for his Stanley Kowalski.

THE LAST WEEK OF AUGUST / Somewhere east of Manhattan, along the Merritt Parkway, Marlon stuck out his thumb and faced the oncoming cars. Most whizzed past him. An experienced hitchhiker, he knew someone would eventually stop for him. He might get a lift that lasted only a few miles, but he might also get lucky and ride for a couple of hours. Either way, he'd be that much closer to his destination.

Marlon was heading to Provincetown to meet Tennessee Williams. After a week of doubt, he'd decided to give the part of Stanley Kowalski a chance. As always, of course, the need for money had finally outweighed his concerns.

The summer heat wave continued. Marlon probably wasn't the only one with his thumb out along the parkway that summer day. Hitchhikers were a common sight on the nation's roads after the war. For Marlon, hitchhiking meant freedom. The only better way to travel, he told friends, was by motorcycle. But he couldn't afford to pay for the gas up to Cape Cod.

At last a car pulled over, and Marlon hopped in. Friends thought he probably gave the driver a story about the reason he was traveling—"something very imaginative," said Ellen Adler, or "something terribly amusing," said Kaye Ballard. Perhaps he'd just gotten in from Malaysia, another friend speculated, and he was "heading up to Cape Cod to see a dying aunt"—proving Stella's adage that the best acting was ad-libbed. Marlon likely had to repeat this scenario several times, as he needed to hop from car to car on the long trip, eventually leaving the parkway for the coastal road. But then, after the first few bits of excited conversation, he would have had plenty of time to think as he gazed out at the marshy shoreline of Connecticut, Rhode Island, and southeastern Massachusetts.

That day heading to Cape Cod, Marlon almost certainly was thinking about his parents. They were the real reason he was going after the part in *Streetcar*. His father would be pleased with the money, and if his father was happy, Marlon reasoned, his mother was less likely to start drinking again. She'd gone back to the old man after she fell off the wagon in New York. As much as he'd initially resented his mother's intrusion into his life, having his mother nearby had been better, Marlon believed, than having her go back to his father. No matter how angry he got with her, he couldn't turn his back on her. "She wasn't to blame for what she did," Ellen explained. "The blame was his father's."

"I don't want her to go," Marlon had told Freddie when Dodie announced her decision. "I want her here. With me." She'd started attending Alcoholics Anonymous, with Ellen going with her as support. She could have gotten better in New York, Marlon believed. He could have helped her, and they could have been together.

But she'd left to continue her work with AA in Chicago. To Dodie's credit, she did get sober, though Marlon remained wary about what came next. He shared with his mother only things that would make her happy, and the audition for *Streetcar* had made her ecstatic. In fact, her enthusiasm had played a large part in Marlon's decision to head to Provincetown. If his mother could live out her own theatrical dreams through his work, then maybe she wouldn't shatter into a thousand pieces again. Maybe Marlon could keep her safe and whole that way. Maybe, by taking the part in *Streetcar*, he could keep both his parents happy, and by doing so, he could keep the darkness from overtaking him again as it had three years earlier, right after his mother had left him to return to his father.

That had been a bad period. Once again, Marlon had faced the terrible sensation of nothing being behind him, of the world appearing only when he turned around to look. Indeed, that last breakdown had been perhaps his worst ever, which was why he never spoke of it to his friends. To avoid a return of the darkness, Marlon would do just about anything—even make another long-term commitment to a play.

THE SUN WAS setting over the sand dunes when Marlon arrived in Provincetown. He loved the bohemian spirit of the place. He'd first visited not long after he was kicked out of Sayville. He and Darren Dublin had made the trip, bumming around and sleeping with girls until Marlon needed to report back for *I Remember Mama*—or, as he called it to Darren, "some shit Broadway show." The following summer, during a hiatus from *Mama*, the two friends had made the trek up to "P'town" again. They'd befriended Clayton Snow, twenty-four, the son of a local baker and a bartender at the New Central House. Snow let the two washashores crash at his cottage. While he continued chasing girls, Marlon also slept with Snow, an undisguised and unapologetic gay man. His new friend's personal integrity impressed Marlon. "He liked that Clayton was his own man and played by his own rules," said one Provincetown old-timer. In the easygoing artists' colony, gender and sexuality were rather fluid things, nothing to attach permanent labels to and certainly nothing to get worked up over. Marlon felt right at home.

During his third sojourn to Provincetown in the summer of 1946, Marlon was arrested for playing his drums late at night and disturbing the peace. He gave a demonstration for the judge. The local paper reported: "Town Hall reverberated to the beat of a Cuban voodoo drum in a command demonstration by Marlon Brando of New York City." As Marlon banged away, Clayton Snow wrapped himself in a sheet and sashayed around the courtroom, performing the Dance of the Seven Veils. "The spectators were convulsed with laughter," longtime Provincetown resident Beata Cook remembered. The spirited rendition, however, failed to mollify Judge Robert Welsh, who sentenced Marlon and Clayton to six months in jail, a sentence the judge suspended, though he kept them on probation until October 28. It was therefore with a record that Marlon returned to New York. "He thought it was a hoot," said one old resident of Provincetown, where the story became legend.

Now Marlon had once again returned to the seaside resort town, a little older, not much wiser, but possibly on the brink of a new chapter of his life.

As soon as he got to town, he found Ellen Adler, who was visiting the Cape herself. Marlon may have known Ellen would be there; possibly the knowledge that he'd have a friend and ally in town had helped crystalize his decision to come. They were no longer dating, but the friendship with her was rooted deep; as Stella's daughter, Ellen was family. Now twenty years old, she was a student at Bard College, in upstate New York, and dating others. The relationship with Marlon had been intense; neither liked to speak about how it had ended, during the period of Marlon's breakdown. Nonetheless, when Marlon asked her if she'd accompany him to see Tennessee Williams, explaining she'd make him less nervous, Ellen agreed.

Together they set off down Commercial Street, to the playwright's cottage in the far East End, almost to the border of Truro. It was late in the afternoon. Williams's waterfront bungalow stood out from the others on the beach. The playwright and his Mexican-born lover, Pancho Rodriguez y Gonzalez, had painted it green, white, and red, the colors of the Mexican flag, "to counteract the grey weather," Williams had written to Kazan. He called the place Rancho Pancho. The day Marlon arrived, Tennessee and Pancho had two houseguests, the director Margo Jones, who'd helped helm *The Glass Menagerie* on Broadway, and her friend Joanna Albus. After his guests arrived, "there was considerable consumption of firewater," Tennessee would remember. So, when a knock came at the door and the visitor was revealed to be Kazan's missing discovery, everyone was a bit rambunctious. They let out a cheer.

"I had stopped expecting him," Tennessee wrote in his memoirs, "when he arrived one evening with a young girl, the kind you would call a chick nowadays." (Williams evidently didn't know this was the great Stella Adler's daughter.) The bungalow was dark; the playwright explained that they must have blown a fuse, and they didn't know what to do. Marlon "immediately fixed that for us," Williams recalled, by inserting a penny into the light fuse. The toilet was also out of order—"we had to go out in the bushes," Williams admitted—but Marlon was able to get that working as well. The playwright couldn't take his eyes off the mostly silent visitor as he fiddled with the fuses and bent over the commode. "He was just about the best-looking young man I've ever seen," Williams recalled.

Just why Marlon had been nervous about meeting Williams wasn't clear. Ellen didn't think it had anything to do with auditioning: "that never bothered Marlon," she said. His anxiety seemed to be personal, a fear that Williams might make a pass at him, Ellen thought. Possibly Marlon wondered if the playwright, a Provincetown regular, had heard of his friendship with Clayton Snow. So, when he finally sat down to talk with Williams, Marlon placed Ellen on his lap. "That way," Ellen said, "he didn't have to look Tennessee straight in the eye. I was always just enough in the way."

Eventually, however, prompted by Williams, Marlon moved Ellen off his lap and, cued by the playwright, began speaking Stanley Kowalski's lines.

His reading of the part, Williams would remember, was just as he'd later play it onstage. "A new value came out of Brando's reading," the playwright observed. "He seemed to have already created a dimensional character, of the sort the war has produced among young veterans." This was remarkable, since Marlon had spent the war largely bumming around New York.

Ten minutes was all it took to convince everyone in the room that Marlon was Stanley. Margo Jones leapt from her seat and shouted, "Get Kazan on the phone right away! This is the greatest reading I've ever heard!" At least, that would be how Williams remembered it. He looked over at the young actor in the corner. "Brando maybe smiled a little," he said, but there was no elation, the playwright noted—nothing like the rest of them were feeling at that moment.

Of course not: Marlon knew his life was no longer his own.

Williams insisted he stay there at Rancho Pancho overnight, in one of the double-decker bunks on either side of the main room, so they could go over the part again in the morning. Marlon bid good-bye to Ellen, who trekked back into town on her own. She was certain he would rather have gone back with her. "He wasn't happy in that world," she said, "that theater world."

The next morning, despite all the alcohol consumed the day before, Williams was astir early, still ecstatic over the "Godsend" of the young man who'd snored the night away on a twin cot beside Margo Jones. "I believe they behaved themselves," Williams wrote to Audrey Wood, "the fools!"

Once awake, Marlon seemed to want some alone time with the playwright, insisting they take a walk on the beach. "And so we did," Williams recounted to Wood. If he'd been expecting his Stanley to pepper him with questions about character, or the playwriting process, or artistic vision, however, he was surprised. Marlon said nothing as they walked. It was a twenty-minute hike to the end of the beach, where the piers of the town interrupt the way, and all that time, the two men walked in silence, stepping over seaweed and the carcasses of horseshoe crabs.

Williams, and most everyone he told the story to, interpreted Marlon's silence as evidence of his genius. Yet, if Marlon was thinking anything at all during that walk, other than about the science of tides or the feeding habits of terns, it was probably to reassure himself that his decision to take the part in *Streetcar* was a sound one. "Pop," he would write when he got back to New York, "I want the money I make to help in a large part to take the load you've been handling. I'm not counting my eggs, but I want it known that I would like to have my money be of use." He wasn't thinking about Stanley as he walked with Williams; he was thinking about his father, his mother, his bills, his dance lessons—and probably how he might survive a year on the stage better than he had the last time.

When they reached the end of the beach, actor and playwright turned around. "And then we walked back," Williams wrote, once again "in silence."

**THE FIRST WEEK OF SEPTEMBER** / When he got back to New York, Marlon hid out. None of his friends saw him to congratulate him about landing the part in *Streetcar*, which was announced on September 3. Alone in his apartment, Marlon rued the fact that he'd had to commit for two years—his contract stated he was stuck in the show through the 1948–1949 season—but his agents did get Irene Selznick to agree to a two-week vacation (unpaid) beginning on June 28, 1948. That was an awfully long time away.

Marlon brooded. "He wasn't happy," Kaye Ballard said about his accepting the part in *Streetcar*. He was terrified of another breakdown. Rather than excitement on the eve of his big break, he knew nothing but fear.

The roots of his distress went back three years, during the period he was feeling increasingly trapped in *I Remember Mama*. At that point, he was still living in the West End Avenue apartment; it was right before his mother's departure. Marlon was juggling three girlfriends (Ellen, Celia, and Blossom), a precarious balance that worked—until it didn't anymore.

For a while, "all three women had a place" in his life, Ellen remembered. "I lived in a lovely home with Stella and Harold. I went to college. I was the good girl." She and Marlon would have dinner with Stella and Harold and others from their circle, then they'd go out to see a play or a film, and finally they'd head back to Marlon's, where they'd listen to Rachmaninoff's Piano Concerto No. 2. "As long as we lived," Ellen said, "that was our piece." Nearly every weekend, she came home from Bard to be with Marlon. Celia and Blossom knew not to come around on weekends. The weekends belonged to Ellen.

Weeknights, however, Marlon led a different sort of life—"a very, very wild life," Ellen thought, with Maureen, Janice, Wally, and "all those kids making their way in the theater." To these gatherings it was usually Blossom who accompanied him, because she was an actress and "fit in with the crowd," Kaye Ballard said.

Celia was the one who increasingly felt left out. She'd been Marlon's first, and he'd been besotted with her as many teenage boys might be with their first love. "She was very important to me then," Marlon would remember, "but after her there were many other women." Celia wasn't an actress; she wasn't an educated college girl like Ellen; just what she brought to Marlon's life, especially now that he was having sex with so many other women, was increasingly unclear. Janice Mars thought Marlon had been "looking for a substitute mother" when he took up with Celia; he'd go to her, Janice remembered, when he got sick, so she could take care of him. But more than once, when Celia came looking for Marlon after he'd been "a bad boy," he would hide from her in a closet in Janice and Maureen's apartment.

As the distance between them grew, Celia became more posses-sive, talking about divorcing her husband and marrying Marlon. But Stella was hinting broadly that if Marlon married anyone, it ought to be Ellen. "She was worried that I wouldn't ever get mar-ried," Ellen recalled. College girls, Stella argued, often didn't find husbands. "Marriage was a big deal for my mother," Ellen said. "She wanted me married and stable." So, Stella started in on Mar-lon: "You have to marry Ellen." In his other ear, Dodie was echo-ing the same message. She adored Ellen, and loved the connection with the Adlers, so she began applying her own pressure.

Marlon, of course, didn't want to marry anyone. The pressure, the arguments with Celia, the worry over his mother, and the torment of the play all combined to leave him surly and quick-tempered. By late 1944, the rage was once again taking over. During this period, Marlon punched walls; he broke windows; he bloodied noses. To Ellen, he was once again Rumpelstiltskin, always this close to disappearing in a cloud of smoke and anger.

It was at this moment that Celia told Marlon she was pregnant.

The news left him dumbstruck. As a friend recalled, it was "a big shock, a big moment, for Marlon, really shattering." Filled with a sudden sense of honor, he announced he would marry her. To his friend, he said he couldn't allow a child to come into the world without a name, without a father. He bore the scars from a bad father; he did not want the past repeating itself. Celia, of course, was already married; the plan was to divorce Thomas Webb, who was still off in the war, and marry Marlon. Filing for divorce in New York, however, would take far too long; the baby would be born before the divorce was final.

So, Celia and Marlon came up with a plan. In December 1944, four months pregnant, Celia took the train to Reno. Under Nevada law, she needed to reside in the state for only six weeks before be-

ing eligible to file for divorce. That would give her just enough
time to shed Webb and marry Marlon before the baby came. Arriving in the glitzy gambling town, she took a room at the Parkway
Hotel, a resort that catered to out-of-state ladies looking to shake
their husbands. This would be Celia's home for the next month
and a half.

Back in New York, Marlon steeled himself to break the news
to Ellen. Still a teenager, she was very much in love with him.
Around this time she had a recurring nightmare in which Marlon
left her to become a big star. She'd be walking down Fifty-Fourth
Street pushing a baby carriage, "and he would come along," Ellen
said, describing the dream, "and look in and say, 'That's a lovely
baby,' and I would go off with this baby that I didn't love that
I'd had with a man that I didn't love." So, when Marlon came to
her during the holidays of 1944/45 and told her, very seriously, that
he needed to speak with her, she hoped he might be getting ready
to propose. If he had, Ellen would likely have said yes before he
finished the question.

But his news was very different.

"I never wanted to hurt you," he said, and right away Ellen
knew "something unbelievable was coming down." He told her
that Celia was pregnant and that they had to get married. "I was
devastated," Ellen said. When Stella found out, she was furious.
So was Dodie, who came to Stella in tears, and probably drunk,
wailing over the "terrible irony" of Marlon, for whom Stella had
done so much, hurting Stella's child. Dodie couldn't bear it. Neither could Marlon. The three most important women in his life
were in tears and angry at him.

But, as it turned out, the copious tears shed over Marlon's marriage were for naught. Something happened in early January 1945
that kept the union from ever occurring, and presaged Marlon's
breakdown not long after.

On Tuesday, January 16, Celia was admitted to Washoe General

Hospital outside Reno with severe bleeding. Doctors determined she was pregnant and possibly miscarrying. At eleven o'clock that night, she delivered a stillborn female fetus. Doctors determined the cause was a placental abruption or, as they wrote on the certificate, a "detached placenta." The next day, the fetus was buried at Mater Dolorosa, a Catholic cemetery. A brokenhearted Celia gave her address as the Parkway Hotel and the name of the father as Thomas Webb.

Placental abruptions occur on their own in about 1 percent of pregnancies; almost always they result in stillbirths. The causes are not entirely understood, but among them are heavy smoking, hypertension, or trauma to the abdomen or vagina. In the years before abortion was legal, self-induced abortions sometimes caused the placenta to detach. Severe bleeding could occur, often fatal to the mother.

Ellen would understand that Celia had an abortion; Kaye Ballard heard the same. "Marlon didn't really want to marry her," said one friend. "And Celia knew that. They fought all the time about it. Did he back out of his promise? Did Celia decide, after one fight, to end the pregnancy herself?" Whether the loss of the baby was deliberate or accidental, it was unquestionably devastating for everyone involved. "Marlon was crushed when he got the news," said the friend.

Celia went through with the divorce, gaining her freedom from Webb just eight days later, on January 24, at the Washoe County Second Judicial District Court. The grounds were "extreme cruelty of a mental nature." Webb didn't contest his wife's action and agreed to pay seventy-five dollars a month for the support of their son.

Celia checked out of the Parkway Hotel and returned to New York. Marlon was there waiting for her, and over the next few months, as she battled depression and complications from her labor, which required seeing several doctors, he did his best to help pay her bills. But he was never going to marry her now. That was clear. All the Sturm und Drang of the past two months had been for nothing.

Except to hasten the worst darkness of Marlon's life so far.

FOR ELIA KAZAN, the deciding factor that made him choose Marlon for the part of Stanley Kowalski was the climactic scene from *Truckline Café*, when Marlon had let out that howl. "Volcanic, explosive," Marlon himself described the scene. Near the end of the play, his character burst forth with such primal pain, grief, and rage that audiences were left shaken both physically and emotionally. "It electrified everybody," Marlon acknowledged. How he'd done it—how he'd managed to summon such inner power—was a mystery to Kazan. Indeed, even during *Truckline's* short run, critics had wondered the same thing, how such a young actor—Marlon was only twenty-one when he appeared in *Truckline*—could convey such profound, fully experienced emotion. That was because they didn't know what he had been through in the twelve months leading up to that moment.

Almost exactly one year before *Truckline Café*, Marlon had let out a similar cry from the heart, this time not onstage, but in the large echoing rooms of his mother's apartment on West End Avenue. She was gone now, and Marlon was alone. "I had kind of a nervous breakdown," he'd admit many years later, one of the few comments he'd ever make about this difficult period. In the weeks after the tragedy of Celia and the baby, everything fell apart for him. Trapped in *I Remember Mama*, a play he despised, the twenty-year-old had watched helplessly as his mother's drinking threatened to spiral out of control once more, as it had back in Libertyville. Moreover, he had lost Ellen, whose grounding presence in his life he'd taken for granted. Finally, when his mother left him all alone in that big empty flat to return to his father, Marlon had disintegrated.

"I was there, fending for myself in the special anonymity of

New York City, and it was tough," he said. "Things seemed to make less and less sense." He couldn't stand to hear people argue. When he did, "I felt as if I were being consumed by insects," he said. Loud noises once again had the power to set him off. "Even the slamming of a door sent me into a panic," he said. To quiet his mind, he'd retreat to a nearby Christian Science reading room, but the effort did little good. "I thought I was going nuts," he recalled. "If I was offended in the slightest, I wanted to punch somebody." Finally, he got out of that cavernous West End Avenue apartment, with all its memories of his mother, and took a smaller place, at 158 West Fifty-Eighth Street, where he holed up for weeks. He emerged only for performances of *I Remember Mama*, which he dreaded, but which he needed to continue, if he was going to pay his bills.

Marlon described the breakdown of 1945 as "severe for several months." He lost ten pounds. Still so young, he had no plan for the future, no role modeling, no guide. "I was in emotional disarray," he remembered. "Depressed and vulnerable." As he'd done before, he turned compulsively to sex, "bringing home a new girl almost every night," he said. His charm and good looks made getting girls easy. "There would be thirty girls—I'm not exaggerating—at a party all trying to get Marlon for themselves," Kaye Ballard remembered. "I called them a ship of fools."

Sometimes Marlon would grab a script girl or wardrobe assistant in between his scenes in *I Remember Mama*. "For him, sex was like eating or going to the bathroom," said Herbert Kenwith, a young actor in the cast. Freddie Fiore was Marlon's most frequent cohort in sexual adventures. One night, Freddie showed up with a couple of women in a Cadillac and told Marlon he could have his pick. "What the hell," Marlon thought; it was a way to escape his funk for a little while. The women in the Cadillac were black, and smelling of the sweet perfume that was always such an aphrodisiac for him. Back at the women's apartment, they paired off and, after sex, played cards. At length, the woman Marlon was with announced that her "daddy" was on his way up the stairs. "I had never heard the phrase," Marlon said, "that women referred to boyfriends as their daddies." As he'd tell the story, he and Freddie flew down the fire escape, barely dodging a beating.

His stories, repeated many times over the years, were always full of such lightheartedness and braggadocio. But the jaunty tone masked the pain of this period. None of the dozens of women who passed through his life in these years, Marlon admitted, ever assuaged his loneliness. If women stayed around too long, in fact, they became irritants. "You had a perverse need to humiliate," Janice Mars told him, "to see how far a female would go to indulge you. Your attitude to women was very ambivalent." To those who knew him, the psychology was plain: "He was acting out his history with his mother," said Ellen Adler. He'd make his women indulge him in ways that his mother never did, and then punish them for doing so by rejecting them. During the long months of Marlon's depression, this pattern nearly destroyed him, not to mention the damage it inflicted on the women unfortunate enough to be ensnared in his web. "I was killing myself," Marlon said, "and nearly killing everybody around me."

His recovery came about gradually, he said, after he found solace, as usual, at Stella's. The Adlers forgave him for breaking Ellen's heart, and with the young woman off at college, Marlon was welcome to sit with Stella, Harold, Luther, and the others and share in their laughter and conversation. Eventually, Ellen forgave him, too, and resumed their friendship, though she did her best to keep any romantic feelings under control. The salient fact was this: they remained together, Marlon and the Adlers. That was something new for him, the idea that families might stick together through adversity. From this dynamic, creative, colorful clan, he learned about loyalty, support, encouragement, trust—things his own family had never taught him. And so, once again, the family

Marlon had found to replace the defective one of his birth proved to be his salvation.

"They were very wise people," he said of the Adlers, "who didn't allow setbacks to keep them from living." Writing to his parents several months after his breakdown, he seemed to be consciously attempting to emulate the Adlers' self-discipline, while also appearing embarrassed by his own recent emotional weakness. "Hysteria," he said, "is as infectious as flu or dysentery. Half of the world is running crazily and fearfully toward the other half [while] the other half . . . is running just as fast and just as scared." When the two halves met, he said, the whole world was left in "the blue funks of blue funks." His goal now was to avoid those blue funks, and to find a way to take care of himself "and live and work and be happy."

Harold Clurman gave him that chance. Planning to direct the new Maxwell Anderson drama *Truckline Café*, Clurman cast him as a returning GI. Marlon jumped at the offer, not so much because he wanted the part but because it got him out of *I Remember Mama*, in which he'd been laboring now for more than a year. His last performance in *Mama* was on February 7, 1946. There was no time to relax, however, as he went directly into rehearsals for *Truckline*. His part was far more complicated than sweet Nels in *Mama*. "If not for Harold," Ellen said, "I think Marlon would have played teenagers like Nels for the next five years."

*Truckline Café* was about the psychological fallout of World War II on veterans, their families, and the nation at large. Elia Kazan, Clurman's comrade from the Group Theatre, was producing. Set in a diner on the Pacific Coast Highway, the play was expected to be timely, relevant, and successful. Marlon would be playing Sage McRae, a vet who murders his wife after discovering she cheated on him during the war. Cornered by police toward the end of the play, Sage cracks and admits his guilt, letting out a scream that Clurman wanted to shake the rafters. Marlon, often a mumbler

onstage, was unsure he could do it. "I don't know how I'm going to cry," he fretted. "It embarrasses me." So, Harold devised a
plan. During rehearsals, he kept going farther back into the theater; no matter what Marlon did onstage, he would shout, "I can't
hear you!" Each time, Marlon would have to raise his voice louder.
Finally, perched up on the highest balcony, Clurman shouted, "I
can't hear you!" And at last Marlon achieved the volume the director wanted, the veins popping on his forehead as he let out his
thundering scream.

*Truckline Café* opened in Schenectady, New York, on February
16 (just nine days after Marlon's last performance in *Mama*) and
then moved on to Baltimore and Newark for a week in each city.
"The show looks good," Marlon wrote to his parents. "My part is a
sensational role that takes plenty of sweat." He was "working like a
truck," he assured them. He was earnestly hoping for a success, he
said, because he'd "love a little rest and some time and money for
piano and dancing lessons." He was pleased with the money he was
making: after agency fees and taxes, he'd net $154 a week. "This
will enable me to save," he told his parents, "and at the same time
allow me to cover any additional expenses I might have." Those
additional expenses weren't just dancing lessons. Marlon had also
started paying Celia's doctor bills.

But *Truckline Café* was a bomb. "Anderson has written the worst
play I have seen since I have been in the reviewing business,"
declared John Chapman in the *Daily News* after the show's New
York premiere at the Belasco Theatre on February 27. The only
standouts in the cast were Karl Malden, a Group Theatre alumnus
just back from the war, who scored with a running gag about a
sailor with too many girls, and Marlon, whom critics unanimously
praised. "Rarely in the theatre have we heard such applause," the
critic H. I. Phillips noted, "as marked an interlude when Brando,
confessing the murder of his wife, yields himself to the police."

The moment became the stuff of Broadway legend. Having

killed his wife, Sage slunk into the diner and confessed his crime to the waitress, played by Virginia Gilmore. And suddenly he just came apart. The howl took everyone by surprise, rushing up from deep inside him and echoing through the theater even louder than Clurman had dreamed. Marlon fell from his stool to the floor of the stage, writhing and keening, an explosion of raw fury and grief. There was nothing melodramatic about it; if there had been, the critics would have said so. Instead, it was seen as devastatingly real. "Oh God, oh God," Sage cried. "I wish I had her back!" So powerful was the moment, the first time Marlon did it, that Gilmore jumped involuntarily, as if something truly had happened to her costar. Later, she told Ellen Adler that she'd "never been onstage with this kind of thing before." It was all Gilmore could do to hold her place and stay in character.

Out in the audience, the actress Anne Jackson was rattled. She would never forget Marlon "curling up in an almost infantile position" after he let out that scream. "He curled his feet up and his whole body almost like a fetus," Jackson said. "He started to sob. Of course the audience sobbed with him. It went beyond tears. You were shaken by what he did. He had that power."

But how, critics wanted to know, had Marlon done it? "Where," one asked, "does such power come from in such a young, inexperienced actor?"

Stella had taught Marlon that an actor's power comes from his own imagination in relationship to the writer's words. So, he'd done as he was bidden: he'd imagined himself as a soldier by the name of Sage McRae, a flesh-and-blood human being responding to the news that his wife had been unfaithful to him while he was off risking his life defending his country. But Stella had also taught that sometimes there were aspects of one's life that might give the imagination an assist. She wasn't preaching emotional memory, of course—memories dredged up simply to be transposed onto roles produced artificial emotion, she believed, contrived and insincere—but she *did* assign memory an important role in acting. The basic, existential memory that all human beings carry with them, she taught, was what actors needed to summon: *The actor has in him the memory of everything he's ever touched or tasted. He is by nature gifted with memory.*

It was that intrinsic memory, consciously or unconsciously invoked, that allowed Marlon to imbue the climactic scene in *Truckline* with such unforgettable feeling. For, in fact, his imagination did not have to search all that far. The parallel to his life was unavoidable, with one significant difference: he wasn't Sage McRae. He was the other man, the one who had cheated with Sage's wife. Sage McRae, in fact, was Ensign Thomas Webb, and his wife's name wasn't Tory, but Celia, and she was dark and exotic, not blonde and fair like Ann Shepherd, who played Tory in the play. But the anguish that burst forth onstage during *Truckline* was Marlon's own, the explosion of a powder keg that had been building up for some time. That primal scream, grabbing the attention of the critics and making the young actor the "find of the year," was the detonation of all the worst torments of what Marlon called his "fuck you" years—Celia, the baby, his mother, his father, his isolation, his self-doubt. Rarely could he speak of such grief, guilt, rage, or fear. All he could do was scream.

To the critic from the Associated Press, Marlon's cathartic scene was "the single memorable bit of the entire play." That one moment, the critic said, didn't quite make *Truckline Café* worth seeing, but he was glad to have it nonetheless, "particularly as it came very near the finish, as it took away a little of the hopeless boredom." The actor who did the scene, the critic reported, was named Marlon Brando—a name he predicted would "be remembered for quite a while."

*Truckline* closed on March 9, 1946, after only thirteen performances at the Belasco Theatre, taking a devastating (for the times) sixty-thousand-dollar loss. But Marlon, everyone agreed, was another story entirely. He was phenomenal.

For his performance, Marlon was named the best supporting actor of the year, as well as most promising male newcomer, in the annual poll of New York drama critics conducted by *Variety*. *Truckline* won him another, unexpected fan as well: eighty-seven-year-old Sara Adler had been mesmerized in her seat during his performance. "She saw him in *Truckline*, and that was the end," her granddaughter Ellen recalled. "She saw the genius." To Marlon, the old woman who had once disparaged him, who'd called him a bum, now said, "You can change your name to Adler"—the highest compliment she could bestow.

A year and a half later, as he hid out in his apartment, Marlon understood that by accepting the part in *A Streetcar Named Desire*, he had the chance to prove that genius again. Would he deliver? And if so, would he destroy himself in the process?

**EARLY OCTOBER** / Truman Capote was a little elf of a man, twenty-three, blonde, delicate, and a darling of New York's literary set. His story "The Headless Hawk" had just been included in *The Best American Short Stories 1947*, from Houghton Mifflin, and galleys were already being prepared for his first novel, *Other Voices, Other Rooms*, to be published by Random House in January 1948. Many were predicting a major career ahead for the vivacious young writer with the lilting Louisiana accent. On this October day, when the air had suddenly turned chill, Capote was at Henry Miller's Theatre to watch a rehearsal of Tennessee Williams's forthcoming *A Streetcar Named Desire*. The play's leading man,

Marlon Brando, was also being touted as on the brink of a major career. He and Capote were almost exactly the same age.

The writer peered into the empty theater. He was early, and the only other person in the auditorium was "a brawny young man stretched out atop a table on the stage under the gloomy glare of work lights, solidly asleep." Capote took him to be a loafing stagehand "because he was wearing a white tee shirt and denim trousers," and because of "his squat gymnasium physique." Curiously, however, a copy of *The Basic Writings of Sigmund Freud* was resting on the young man's chest, as if he'd been reading some psychology before falling asleep.

Capote looked closer. "It was as if a stranger's head had been attached to the brawny body, as in certain counterfeit photographs," he said. "For this face was so very untough, superimposing, as it did, an almost angelic refinement and gentleness upon hard-jawed good looks: taut skin, a broad, high forehead, wide apart eyes, an aquiline nose, full lips with a relaxed, sensual expression." He realized this was Brando himself. Capote prepared himself, rather skeptically, to see how this creature might transform himself into "Williams' unpoetic Kowalski."

Marlon was the linchpin of the play; everything turned on what his character said and did. But the star of the show remained its Blanche, the fragile flower Stanley destroys. Blanche was being played by the English actress Jessica Tandy, who hoped the part might establish her as a bona fide Broadway draw. Her contract stated that her name would accompany every advertisement of the play; Marlon's name, however, would appear only in those ads in which the names of the actors playing the secondary parts of Stella and Mitch were also included. It was a way of keeping Marlon in his place, of preventing him from getting a swelled head. But Marlon didn't care about such things. What mattered was the $550 salary he was getting, more than enough to pay his rent, help Celia with her bills, and send some home to Pop. Five hundred and fifty smackers a week was more than Marlon Senior often made on the road, a fact in which his son no doubt took some pleasure.

Rehearsals began on Monday, October 6. It was exactly four years and two days since Marlon had started at the Dramatic Workshop. So much had changed in his life since then, but so much had also remained the same. In Kazan's contact list, the other players were all comfortably ensconced at hotels or in friends' upscale apartments. Tandy was staying at the Hotel Adams, on East Eighty-Sixth Street; Kim Hunter, who was playing Stella, was at the Algonquin; and Karl Malden, another carryover from *Truckline*, who was playing Mitch, was staying at the well-appointed apartment of the playwright Edith Sommer, on West Fifty-Fifth Street. All had telephone numbers inscribed beside their names on Kazan's list; only Marlon, in a cold-water flat on Tenth Avenue, had no phone. So, if Kazan or Selznick didn't get him while he was at the theater, they would have to wait until the next time he showed up.

What had changed most in the past four years was Marlon's appearance. Capote was right in observing "his squat gymnasium physique." Marlon had been working out at local gyms for some time now, lifting weights and boxing. He'd also been to dancing school, which had firmed his legs and torso. Now, in anticipation of playing the coarse, carnal Kowalski, he'd stepped up his game, breaking his own personal best on push-ups and sit-ups. The lean musculature of his late teens had filled out considerably. When Sara Adler got a look at him, she recoiled. "You're so ugly, what you did," she groaned in her Yiddish accent. "You will never play a poet, you will never play a prince." With his newly buff physique, Marlon would be typecast as a ruffian, she feared, when he should be playing Hamlet.

Yet, whether the eighty-nine-year-old Sara Adler could see it or not, *A Streetcar Named Desire* was the way forward, part of a new direction for American theater. Galvanized by their failure with *Truckline Café*, Kazan and Clurman had moved full speed ahead with Arthur Miller's *All My Sons*, which had won the New York Drama Critics' Circle Award and a best director prize for Kazan at the very first Tony Awards, in April 1947. Kazan was now the person to go to in order to make compelling, relevant theater— "the favorite director of such distinguished younger playwrights as Arthur Miller, Tennessee Williams, Arnaud d'Usseau and James Gow," according to the *New York Times* (the last two were the authors of *Deep Are the Roots*, a play about racism Kazan had directed in 1945). Miller claimed Kazan's great insights allowed him to "hit the audience in the belly, because he knows all people are alike in the belly no matter what their social position or education."

By the time rehearsals for *Streetcar* officially got under way, Marlon was ready to roll. A few weeks earlier, he'd been adrift, unsure of his path. Now his spirits soared as he got down to work. He liked the project, something he hadn't felt since *A Flag Is Born*, though *Streetcar* was, of course, a very different enterprise. "It's a strong, violent, sincere play," he wrote to his father, with "emotional rather than intellectual impact."

For his collaborators, he had only the highest respect. Tennessee Williams, Marlon thought, was "an extraordinary writer . . . truly a poet." He was "a man with no skin, defenseless, vulnerable to everything." Marlon recognized the playwright's "very deep-seated neurosis" that stretched back to an unhappy childhood, during which he'd been bullied by a violent, alcoholic father. Marlon empathized; he knew how it felt to be skinless. But Williams, unlike Marlon, had never hardened himself. Marlon had toughened his hide, built up his muscles, taken refuge in an armor of anger and provocation whenever he felt backed into a corner. Williams, on the other hand, remained exposed, unarmed. "He was a very, very, dear, sensitive man," Marlon said, always protective of the playwright. "He never, never lied. He never said anything nasty about anybody. I liked him very, very much."

Kazan, however, was Marlon's hero. As rehearsals wore on,

Marlon came to view the director with the sort of regard he'd reserved so far only for Stella. "He was smart enough to give the actors freedom," Marlon said. "It wasn't a question of whose ego was in charge. He had enough sense to remove his ego from the conversation. If you convinced him that you were right, he'd let you do whatever you wanted to do." It was very much Stella's approach, all about the actor's imagination and spontaneity, and always in service to the text.

Marlon not only respected Kazan; he liked him as well. That didn't often happen. "For Marlon to really like you," said his old classmate Elaine Stritch, "you had to be both smart and unpretentious." Not an iota of pretension could be found in Kazan. According to one observer, he was "adept at striking up conversations with bus drivers, grocers, barbers, newsstand dealers and absolute strangers," a quality Marlon both admired and shared. Moreover, as the same observer noted, the director's speech was "usually slangy, charged with the pointless profanity of the barracks." Kazan's friends called him "Gadge," a nickname from his college days. Marlon often added a *t* to make it "Gadget."

Kazan was also whip smart, and like Marlon, a bookworm. They could sit around and banter about Jung, or parse the meaning of Nietzsche's Übermensch. But there were differences between them, too. Kazan was well educated, having graduated cum laude from Williams College; he'd then gone on to the Yale School of Drama, although he did not finish the degree. He possessed the sort of ambition and drive that Marlon lacked, and was motivated to prove himself to all those who had doubted him throughout his life. Marlon had faced his share of doubters, too, but he felt less compelled to prove them wrong; just getting away from them was usually enough. Kazan had also settled down when he was not much older than Marlon. He and his wife, the playwright Molly Day Thacher, had four children. That was something Marlon seemed utterly incapable of doing, at least so far.

What connected the two men most, though, was their tough-ness. Kazan would not be destroyed by life the way Marlon feared Williams would be. No one pushed Gadge around, which Marlon respected. Yet neither did Kazan browbeat anyone himself. Had he been dictatorial like Piscator (or Richard Rodgers or Tallulah Bankhead), Marlon would never have worked with him so well. Authority, for Marlon, always required the balance of humility.

The rehearsals, therefore, that the young Mr. Capote was priv-ileged to observe at Henry Miller's Theatre were something quite special indeed. Marlon was always at his best when he felt "in the moment," Ellen said, when he was thinking no further than his next line or next improv, when he had nothing to prove, sur-rounded by those he liked and trusted. That was when his artistry came through, whether in Stella's class pretending to be a chicken, or playing Jesus in *Hannele*, or letting out that scream in *Truckline*. For Marlon, the thrill was always *now*. His eye was never on the future, or on becoming "great," or on making Stanley Kowalski an archetype of the American theater. If that happened, so be it; it was not his intention.

Such dispassion set him apart from the entirely self-conscious, calculating, ambitious young man whom Kazan permitted to watch from a seat in the center of the auditorium. Truman Capote and Marlon Brando would make their bows on the public stage within weeks of each other. They were the same age; both were the darlings of critics. But that's where their similarities ended. Their paths would cross again some years hence, and their differ-ences would never be starker.

STANLEY KOWALSKI WAS born from chaos. But it was the chaos of creativity and imagination. The first week of rehearsals, Kazan declared, would simply be spent sitting around the stage, read-ing from their scripts, and asking questions of one another and their director. Given that they had just three weeks of rehearsal, spending a third of that time not moving around was risky. Yet Kazan had found this to work in the past, and his actors didn't protest. The *New York Times* called this his "scientific approach to the theatre." Kazan broke the production down into all its parts, and then built it from the floor back up.

The key was to make his cast and crew feel like partners in the enterprise. When Murray Schumach, a reporter from the *Times*, came to observe rehearsals, he turned Goethe's critical description of Stendhal into praise for Kazan: "This man knows how to use others with skill and make their ideas his own."

Kazan took Marlon aside. "Now, listen," he said. "You go off and work on the scene and bring something back here." It was almost like being back at the Dramatic Workshop. "So we'd go over and we'd rehearse a scene," Marlon said, "improvise anything, go to the prop man and say, 'I need some spaghetti,' or 'Have you got a fly swatter?' Or whatever we needed. And we'd work it out and come back and [Kazan would] say, 'That's good. I like that,' [or] 'No, that isn't good at all. You've got the wrong attack in the scene.'" Having been an actor himself, Kazan "would inspire you," Marlon said, "just by the fact that he was there. He understood."

Schumach observed the director's strategy firsthand. "Kazan will not tell an actor at which word he must wave his forefinger or take a step," he wrote in his report for the *Times*. "He feels that an actor who understands his role will do those things naturally." Kazan, from the same Stanislavski-inspired background as Stella Adler, believed that it was impossible for an actor to "go up" on his lines if he thoroughly understood the character he was playing. "He may forget the exact words," Schumach reported, "but his knowledge of the character will furnish him with words that convey the right meaning." Marlon took this to heart.

As ideas ricocheted all around the auditorium, Kazan was constantly scribbling into or reading from his spiral-bound notebooks. In one of them, he described himself as "the fellow who doesn't waste a minute. Always has a little book with him and in lapses of conversation, or if things fail to interest him, he disappears and is to be found in a corner with his notebook." If an idea came to him, he didn't want to lose it; writing it down preserved it. It also preserved a remarkable record of the creation of the play. In fact, Kazan had been jotting down ideas, characterizations, and stage directions since he'd first signed on, inscribing Williams's advice upfront on an early bound script: "As you know, no villains. All do some bad things, even Stella. All do some very nice things, even Stanley. Begin easy. Look for real motives, as you would understand the complexity of people in life." Kazan made sure to read that admonition to his cast on day one.

That first week of rehearsal, Tandy and Hunter perched on stools on the stage, Malden sat with his legs dangling into the orchestra pit, and Marlon paced around in back. They all listened as Kazan set forth his vision. Considerable attention was paid to all the characters, of course, but if his notebooks are evidence, Kazan spent the most time on Stanley, finding all the nuances necessary to bring this man to life. Stanley, after all, was the one who could most easily slip into parody. On the one hand, he is Stella's "day and night," as Kazan wrote in his notebook and then reiterated to his cast: "Her entire attention is to make herself pretty and attractive for Stanley. In a way, she is actually narcotized all day. She is buried alive in her flesh. She is half asleep." That is, until her sister shows up, Kazan pointed out. "Blanche makes her consider Stanley, judge Stanley and find him wanting for the first time. But it is too late. In the end, she returns to Stanley."

Creating Stanley was a layered process. When John Garfield was still attached to the project, Kazan had advised "the performance should have a thickness." The casting of Marlon, however, brought out fine distinctions Kazan hadn't fully considered before. Stanley was still "physical, sensory, tactile," Kazan wrote, but he no longer simply enjoyed his cigars for their sense of hedonism.

He smoked them, Kazan explained to Marlon, "because he can't suck a tit."

Stanley had "it all figured out," Kazan said, "what fits, what doesn't. He has all the confidence of resurgent flesh." Stanley acted with "a kind of naiveté, even slowness," Kazan told his cast. "He means no harm. He wants to knock no one down. He only doesn't want to be taken advantage of. His code is simple and simple-minded. He is adjusted now. Later, as the power of his penis dies, so will he. The trouble will come later, the 'problems.'"

Marlon had not yet, as far as anyone knew, suffered from the sort of sexual impotence Kazan suggested for Stanley. But he could most definitely relate to someone who meant no harm, who wanted only to be left alone—but who might lash out if taken advantage of. Marlon would later say that he did not know Stanley Kowalski: "I never met Kowalski. I never met that guy who was antithetical to everything." Kowalski, he insisted, was certainly not him. His performance, he said, was "a compendium of imagination. I just sort of created him. When you have a good play like that, you don't have to do anything. You just have to get out of the way and let the part play itself. Some parts you have to make up."

But, as was true with *Truckline*, sometimes lived experience could aid the imagination in making a part memorable. Proof of this could be found in something Marlon had done earlier that year, in between his work for the ALFP. He'd taken on one acting assignment, and it was terrible: a screen test for Warner Bros. using a script for an abandoned film project called *Rebel Without a Cause*. (The 1955 film would be made from a different script.) Pressured by his agents to do the test and desperate for money, Marlon proved awkward and uncomfortable in the five-minute clip, which survives; his acting is forced, which it almost never was. That was because he had practically nothing in common with the young man he was playing. There was nothing to draw upon, nothing to relate to. No amount of imagination could make the role feel real.

Once again, some aspect of himself seemed necessary to make his acting come alive. Imagination, on its own, no matter how much Marlon declared otherwise, was insufficient. As Stella had taught, an actor's instinctual memory, even if not fully recalled, was a vital ingredient to the best performances. Kazan agreed. "The only way to understand any character," he wrote in his notebooks and advised his cast, "is through yourself. Everyone is much more alike than they willingly admit—*if you will dig and be honest about what you see*" (emphasis Kazan's).

There was more of Stanley in Marlon than he knew, or wanted to admit. Kazan's notes on how Stanley related to women could have been written, almost to a word, about Marlon. "He's got a great girl, with just enough hidden neuroticism for him to awaken and make interesting," Kazan wrote, which described Marlon's relationship with Celia quite well. Marlon had often used Celia's fear of losing him to get what he wanted; although less true with Ellen, he'd done the same with her. Kazan also wrote that to win his wife, Stella, Stanley had "conquered" her; that, too, was Marlon's strategy with women, especially now that he'd lost both Celia and Ellen. To the women in his life, even the most transient among them, Marlon was lord and master; women played by his rules. Likewise, Stanley had Stella exactly where he wanted her: "Their relationship is right," Kazan wrote. "She waits up for him." Marlon's friends would recall many a woman sitting on the doorstep of his apartment building, waiting for him to come home.

The similarities didn't end there. By keeping Stella dependent and docile, Stanley avoided conflict, which he, like Marlon, loathed. He didn't go around wanting to "knock [someone] down"; when that happened, he was usually pushed into it, and his inner monster would awake. Better to keep "the things the way he wants them," Kazan wrote about Stanley, and if some "phony, destructive" person came along, threatening to destroy things, he would feel justified in taking whatever action he deemed necessary to safeguard his way of life. Stanley was, as Marlon could be in his angriest moments, filled with a sense of being "right." In the play, Stanley rapes Blanche "because he has tried and tried to keep her down to his level . . . to make her shit like him, in every other way, and failed." Marlon had never, as far as anyone knew, treated any woman, any *person*, quite so brutally, but his dark moods had resulted in many a fistfight and driven away many of those he loved.

The rage of Stanley and the rage of Marlon were the same—always there, under the surface, waiting for something to prick the skin of its balloon.

And after the explosion, both Stanley and Marlon would revert, predictably, to the terrified little boys they were underneath. "As a character," Kazan wrote, "Stanley is most interesting in his contradictions, his 'soft' moments, his sudden, pathetic, little-tough-boy tenderness towards Stella." In one scene, after hitting his wife, Stanley was scripted to cry and then to utter what would become his iconic wail: "Stella!" Although Marlon was rarely physically abusive with women, his girlfriends would tell similar stories of his creeping back to them after a vicious argument with a hangdog look on his face. "How can I keep taking him back?" one of his later lovers asked herself. But she always did.

What could keep Stanley's explosions at bay, Kazan wrote, were "the physical, immediate pleasures, if they come on steady enough." To placate himself, Stanley took refuge in somatic pastimes. "He's desperately trying to drug his senses," Kazan said, "overwhelming them so that he will feel nothing else. Usually his frustration comes out in eating a lot, drinking a lot, gambling a lot, fucking a lot. He's desperately trying to squeeze out happiness by living by ball and jowl"—by which Kazan meant sex, food, and drink. And yet "it really doesn't work," the director added, "because it simply stores up violence."

Marlon did not gamble, smoke, or drink like Stanley did, but he did fuck like Stanley. "There is nothing bigger than his penis,"

Kazan wrote about Stanley, but once again, he could have been describing Marlon, who found power and satisfaction, at least temporarily, when he "had a woman" (the way he described the sex act to friends). Marlon also *ate* like Stanley: eating was a sensual experience for both of them, even if both were still young enough to keep themselves fit. But not forever, Kazan predicted: "He's going to get very fat later," the director wrote about Stanley, but he could have been writing about Marlon as well.

Between the two, there were some significant diversions, however, enough that Marlon could, quite sincerely, argue that he was nothing like the character he played, that he had simply "imagined" Stanley into being. Marlon cared about books, poetry, psychology, ideas; Stanley cared about cigars and poker. Stanley was deeply cynical; Marlon, through his activism, believed he could help change the world for the better. Marlon was also not nearly as resentful or as greedy as Stanley. One of Stanley's most salient traits, Kazan wrote, was that he was satisfied with his lot only *"as long as no one gets more"* (emphasis Kazan's). Stanley, Kazan explained, "thinks he stinks," and the only way to explain why he stinks was "that everyone else stinks." People who had more than he did, Stanley believed, should be "taken down." This, finally, was the biggest polarity between Marlon and Stanley. Marlon didn't waste time comparing himself to others. "Let them have what they have and think what they think," one friend remembers him saying about people he considered snooty. "Why should I care? I just don't let them into my life."

Pacing back and forth on the stage, Marlon absorbed all Kazan's insights on the character. He "listened experientially," Kazan recalled. "It was as if you were playing on something. He didn't look at you. And he hardly acknowledged what you were saying." But he was definitely listening, Kazan understood, though the process was more "emotional" than "intellectual or mental."

When, during the second week of rehearsals, the director

finally had his actors start blocking their entrances and exits, Marlon gradually brought Stanley Kowalski to life. Kazan observed the process with astonishment. Marlon's face fascinated him, "the brooding sadness in it, the poetry." Sometimes he made Kazan think of a cat. "Ever notice when you watch a lion in the zoo," he asked a reporter, "the way slowly he'll turn his head and look straight at you without blinking? You're uneasy. The lion isn't. Brando will look at you that way."

Imagination, memory, instinct—all went into molding the character Kazan called the "hoodlum aristocrat," a term that, in fact, described Marlon better than it did Stanley. Marlon broke rules, did things his way, defied fashion and convention. He might be insecure deep down, but once he got going creating a character, he was utterly, supremely confident. Like a true aristocrat, Marlon needed no approval from anyone once he started to act.

NOT EVERYONE SAW the magic. One afternoon, Jessica Tandy sat stewing in the empty theater as the company waited several hours for Marlon to show up for rehearsal. This wasn't the first time their leading man had been late. For Tandy, it was impossible to imagine John Gielgud, opposite whose Hamlet she'd played Ophelia, or even the young, studio-trained Tom Drake, with whom she'd co-starred in the film *The Green Years*, being so unprofessional. Finally, the doors opened, letting in a swirl of crisp autumn air and a wind-blown, red-cheeked Marlon, who shrugged off his tardiness by blaming it on Western Union. He'd sent a telegram, he explained; it wasn't his fault that it wasn't delivered. After that, Tandy turned to ice whenever he approached her.

Kazan, no doubt, was behind the note of apology that Marlon penned after this incident, in which he called his flippancy a cover for his "social intuitions"—he seems to have meant "inhibitions"—and accepted full blame for "the rehearsal upset." Tandy wasn't mollified. Marlon, she'd later insist, was "an impossible, psychopathic bastard." Waiting several weeks, Tandy responded with a note of her own, a three-page typewritten missive cataloging all that she found wrong with the young man and his performance. "Perhaps you are not conscious of your faults," she wrote. "The ones that seem to me to be the most damaging are (a) your inability to say the lines as they are written and (b) the indistinctness of your speech. Do you have a stammer? Or is it just something that happens to you on stage? I wish you would try to cure it."

Classically trained on the British stage, Tandy expected a certain formality during line readings. But Marlon frequently changed his delivery, depending on how he felt that particular day. Stella had taught him never to just recite lines; they'd sound memorized that way. So, instead, he might pause, scratch his nose, look in a different direction than he had before. This sometimes threw off the timing of his costars, Tandy most of all. "You must realize," she admonished in her letter, "that an author of the caliber of Williams considers the speech of each of his characters most carefully . . . The lines have a decided rhythm. Yours are direct, forceful. Mine are more flamboyant and flowery." By inserting words like "look here" or "listen," Tandy believed, Marlon was "destroying the author's intention." He simply had "no right," she scolded, "to impose his personality and style" on the roles he played. If he did not desist in doing so, she said, he'd never be successful in "plays by Shakespeare, Sheridan, Goldoni or Euripides." Instead, his range would be limited to those few characters "that have the same characteristics as Marlon Brando."

"And now I think I have meddled enough," she ended her note, though not before adding that she thought Marlon had tremendous talent and that no one could play Stanley "a quarter as well" as he did. "I do hope," she said finally, "you will take this in the spirit in which it was written."

No doubt Marlon did exactly that: he took the letter as yet another "highfalutin know-it-all" (one of his favorite expressions) explaining to the "dumb kid" how he'd "fucked up yet again," said one friend. About his range, Marlon had no worries; he possessed no burning desire to play Euripides. "What the hell was this stuck-up lady even talking about?" a friend imagined him saying in response to his costar. "He never liked schoolmarms," Kaye Ballard added. Tandy's letter surely irritated and alienated him. Certainly, it had no effect on how he portrayed Stanley, and may actually have hardened his resolve to do it his own way. But, Ellen thought, such criticism always stung. "Those self-doubts went so deep," she said.

Tandy's attempt to mold Marlon more to her liking may have been prompted by deeper motives on her part. *Streetcar's* leading lady likely had begun to recognize the fact—too late—that this naturalistic, charismatic actor might actually have the power to pull the audience away from her. After one run-through of the play, a select group of friends and supporters were astonished by how good Marlon was. He'd been inspired, perhaps, by the presence of Stella Adler in the audience. While everyone raved, Tandy's husband, the actor Hume Cronyn, took Kazan aside and asked him to keep coaching Jessica until opening night: she "could do better," he said, than she'd done this night. "Perhaps Hume meant," Kazan said, looking back, "that by contrast with Marlon, whose every word seemed not something memorized but the spontaneous expression of an intense inner experience—which is the level of work all actors try to reach—Jessie was what? Expert? Professional? Hers seemed to be a performance. Marlon was living on stage."

Any real-life antagonism between the two leads may, in fact, have helped their characterizations. Tandy's letter is just the sort of thing Blanche might have tried with Stanley: "Perhaps you are not conscious of your faults." The two are adversaries, after all, miles apart in style and temperament; both fear one might destroy the other. Real life was imitating the drama, and vice versa.

Ultimately, Tandy's complaints about Marlon concerned procedure: he threw her timing off, or he slammed down the phone in the middle of her key line. Marlon's gripes about Tandy, on the other hand, were about art: he didn't think Tandy was "believable" in the part, that she was "too shrill." Moreover, she lacked a sense of humor, he thought, something Marlon could never abide. When rehearsal audiences would laugh at Stanley's antics, Tandy resented it, fearing that sympathy was slipping away from Blanche. She was right.

Marlon may have fervently believed he'd never met Stanley Kowalski, but it seems impossible that he didn't recognize Blanche DuBois. Even subconsciously, the sight of a delicate, once-dignified, literate, cultured woman hiding her drinking and clinging to an increasingly tenuous sanity must have resonated for him. "Now don't get worried," Blanche says to Stella at one point, waiting for a drink, "your sister hasn't turned into a drunkard, she's just all shaken up and hot and tired and dirty!" It was the same sort of line Dodie might have used, trying to reassure her family that she had her drinking under control. Stanley's response to Blanche was likely informed, at least in part, by Marlon's to Dodie, in the same way his memories, even subconsciously, had intensified his onstage breakdown in *Truckline Café*.

"Blanche, at the beginning should be a heavy," Kazan instructed his actors. Dodie, at times, had certainly been a heavy in Marlon's life, most recently when she'd come to New York and insinuated herself into his life, competing for his friends. Blanche, like Dodie, could also disempower those around her. Blanche's arrival returns her sister, Stella, to "infantilism," Kazan wrote. Marlon understood infantilization. He'd felt like a child again himself after Dodie started drinking in their West End Avenue apartment, reduced once more to the boy who lived in constant fear and worry, and who'd fallen to pieces once she was gone.

Kazan also instructed his actors that eventually "the audience should begin to feel that [Blanche] is a complex, sensitive woman, out of her environment, really rather helpless *and in real difficulty*" (emphasis Kazan's). Once again, the director's words could have been describing the way Marlon saw Dodie. "A democracy of pain and need," Kazan wrote, "basic human tragedy, begins to show, and slowly the audience should begin to feel sorry for her and admire her." The commentary was uncannily similar to how Marlon would always describe his mother.

Blanche was simply too close to Dodie not to evoke some flicker of recognition in Marlon. One critic who saw a preview of *Streetcar* called Blanche a "lady of culture, breeding and education, whose early tragedy in love has sent her spinning on a downward path." Even Blanche's final line—"I have always depended on the kindness of strangers"—conjured Dodie, whom Marlon found in the arms of strangers several times in the bars of Libertyville.

Imagination was the key to Marlon's art. Yet, subliminally or not, Stanley's response to Blanche—anger, resentment, fear, desire—was deeply rooted in Marlon's life experience, as all of the best Brando performances would be.

**OCTOBER 30** / Occasional light showers fell over New Haven, Connecticut, as temperatures dropped into the low forties, on the night of the first preview of *A Streetcar Named Desire* at the Shubert Theatre. The last time Marlon had been in that theater he was fired by Tallulah Bankhead after stacking up a pile of bad reviews. Everyone expected things to be very different this time. But no one knew for sure until the ink of the local newspapers was dry the morning after their first night.

Along with New Haven theater enthusiasts, curious New Yorkers had taken the train up from the city, hurrying to the Shubert under their umbrellas. From backstage, Irene Selznick kept a sharp eye on the crowd. The auditorium was filling up. Jessica Tandy was sequestered in her dressing room. Marlon was reading a book.

Their New Haven run was to be brief: Thursday, October 30, through Saturday, November 1. After New Haven they'd head to Boston and then Philadelphia, before finally rolling into New York in December. Selznick, who'd funded a quarter of the $100,000 production herself, was grateful for the long tryouts. This way, they could build up hype and interest and get the actors polished— especially Marlon, she hoped. She still didn't fully share Kazan's and Williams's faith in him.

*Streetcar*, in its first tryouts, was a longer play than it would become later, perhaps by as much as fifteen minutes. Audiences sat through well over two hours of some of the most graphic drama many of them had ever seen. Williams's reputation as a fearless explorer of human depths was well known. Yet *The Glass Menagerie*, his best-known previous work, for all its psychological and emotional complexity, contained nothing approaching the scandal of *A Streetcar Named Desire*: Blanche's history as a prostitute; the suicide of her homosexual husband; Stanley's brutishness; the climactic rape. The language was raw, and sex hung in the steamy New Orleans air whenever Blanche or Stanley was onstage, which was practically all the time. Twenty years earlier, plays much tamer than this had been shut down by local vice squads, their actors hauled off to jail. Irene Selznick could only hold her breath and hope for the best.

At the end of the play, the audience applauded heartily. Congratulations came from friends and supporters. But the reviewers slunk off to write their copy without giving any clue as to what they might say. A few warning signals left some people nervous. The young playwright Robert Anderson, a friend of Kazan's, admitted he was "not 'taken'" with *Streetcar* the way he'd been with *The Glass Menagerie*, which he'd considered "a small gem."

Shedding their costumes, the cast headed over to a postshow gathering at the home of another playwright, Thornton Wilder, then in residence at his alma mater, Yale, just around the corner. Williams immediately clashed with the older playwright. He described the visit as being like "a papal audience," with Wilder receiving his guests grandly and generally behaving snobbishly. He wasted no time trashing the play: *Streetcar*, he declared, "was based upon a fatally mistaken premise." Williams was all ears. "No female," Wilder insisted, "who had ever been a lady [he was referring to Stella] could possibly marry a vulgarian like Stanley." Williams saw right through Wilder's affectation. "This character," he thought to himself, "has never had a good lay."

For *Streetcar* to be a hit, it would need the support of those willing to see the world as it really was, and not how the theater had long tried to pretend it was. When dawn broke and Kazan sent his assistants out for the local newspapers, it seemed New Haven was somewhere in the middle. The *Hartford Courant* acknowledged that the play was "richer" than *The Glass Menagerie*, but otherwise offered no real superlatives. *Variety*, which had, as per tradition, sent a reviewer to the first preview, called *Streetcar* "a mixture of seduction, sordid revelations and incidental perversion," but predicted it was one "trolley that should ring up plenty of fares on Broadway." That was encouraging, but overall, as Audrey Wood recalled, the reviews in New Haven were good but not "great."

Kazan wasn't satisfied. Something still wasn't quite right. These early reviews suggested a couple of things that stuck in the director's mind. First, the play was long, possibly too long. So, he and Williams got to work streamlining the scenes. The second observation was that Blanche was clearly the focal point of the play; appropriate and intended, certainly, but not if she completely eclipsed Stanley, as she seemed to be doing in these first performances. The reviews always mentioned Tandy first, and often; Marlon came second, sometimes third, and not nearly as often. The *New Ha-*

*ven Register,* after the first performance, called him "shrewd" and "properly resentful" in his performance. But Tandy, the reviewer declared, was "electrifying"; she brought "sheer poetry" to her lines.

On the way to Boston, Williams took pencil to script, looking at places to bring Stanley out more. They had quite the rare find in Marlon Brando, the playwright believed. It would be an injustice to waste him.

IN BOSTON, THE puritans were waiting to pounce. *Streetcar* was scheduled to run for two weeks at the Wilbur Theatre on Tremont Street, from Monday, November 3, to Saturday, November 15. The Boston censors were not happy about that. Advance word on the play's profanity and sexual situations had reached the Hub, and local regulations against obscenity were being used to pressure Selznick into making changes. But at the last minute, the Massachusetts Civil Liberties Union stepped in and reached a compromise: the essence of the play could remain the same, so long as "the attack scene," as the censors called Stanley's rape of Blanche, was muted. Kazan found a way to do this by staging the action behind a screen. Scenic designer Jo Mielziner had, quite ingeniously for the time, created a set with transparent walls, so the audience would be able to view action that took place outside the apartment. Mielziner's "wizardry with lighting," as one review called it, also no doubt assured that the rape was presented modestly enough for the censors' approval while also artistically enough to align with Kazan's standards.

Shrewdly, Selznick capitalized on the play's "salacious" reputation. She admitted to one Boston reporter that *Streetcar* was "very violent [with] a smidge of rowdiness." The puritans wouldn't see it no matter how many changes were made, but the promise of a little sex and violence would surely lure in others. Still, Williams was nervous about what audiences would think. He was reassured by a carpenter backstage, who "knew several people" who'd seen the show. They might not have found it "very amusing," he said, but "they liked it."

Just as in New Haven, *Streetcar* played to packed houses and satisfied audiences. "The remarkably responsive first-nighters appeared to be entirely uncritical and completely absorbed by this latest Williams play," wrote the reviewer for the *Evening American*. In the audience, Kazan turned to Williams and said, "This smells like a hit." *Boston Globe* critic Cyrus Durgin, while somewhat ambivalent about the production, nonetheless defended it from the bluenoses. "Last week I heard it called 'just a dirty play,'" Durgin wrote. "That I think is unfair."

Blanche, however, still commanded the reviewers' attention, often to the detriment of Stanley. "There seem no words adequate to describe the remarkable performance by Jessica Tandy as the tragic Blanche," Elinor Hughes wrote in the *Boston Herald*. "The play is largely hers." Marlon was dispatched far more succinctly: he "fulfills his earlier promise with a mature and thoughtful performance." Durgin, meanwhile, sang accolades to Tandy in the *Globe*, writing that her performance could "only be described as magnificent . . . [and should] make her a Broadway star." Brando, Durgin observed less effusively, but perhaps more tellingly, "contributes realistic acting of 200 proof strength."

These were fantastic reviews; Selznick was ecstatic. Still, Kazan pushed Williams to find ways to bring Stanley out more. Certainly, he was pleased that critics liked Tandy; even if he had come to dislike her himself, he wasn't trying to take her down by lifting Marlon. He just knew that for *Streetcar* to be truly great, Stanley had to be as compelling a character as Blanche. Most critics got Blanche's pathos; not as many got Stanley's.

There were a few, however, who were a bit more attuned to the changes in American theater, slightly more sympathetic to the idea of the "antihero." Elliot Norton, from the *Boston Post*, departed from the other critics by observing that while Tandy was good, she wasn't great. If only she could have added "one cubit to her professional stature," Norton judged, she might have lifted her performance into greatness. For Marlon, however, he had only unreserved praise: "Marlon Brando plays the man Stanley as a bull and a bully, big, burly, slow of wit, devoid of humor, fired into anger by an underlying pride and vanity, terrifying in his moods of rage. A wonderful performance." Norton was the only critic so far to single Marlon out like this.

Norton was considered a "play doctor," particularly by younger writers and directors. Joshua Logan thought Norton had "an absolute dead eye for a play"; after just one viewing, he could "form an opinion that struck at the very core." He had helped shape a number of productions on their way to Broadway, notably the musical that became *Oklahoma!* Now he seemed to take solicitous interest in *Streetcar.* Seeing the play for a second time, he found that Tandy's weaknesses hadn't changed, but Stanley remained perfectly realized. Alone among critics, Norton seemed to fathom the complexity of the character that Williams had created and Marlon was inhabiting, and why Stanley was critical to the long-term success of the play. "Colossally proud and vain" Stanley might be, Norton wrote, but "somewhere hidden, a small voice must suggest at times that other men, or women, see things more clearly, or do them more adeptly. But he roars in rage at such a hit."

Williams's finessing of the play was paying off. Stanley—and therefore Marlon—was emerging from the background. Needing to run briefly to New York to attend the opening of *Gentleman's Agreement,* Kazan instructed his leading man "to talk to Tennessee himself" to keep polishing up certain lines.

"THIS WAY! COME ON! Follow me," Marlon shouted at his pal Kaye Ballard, whom he'd invited up to Boston for the tryouts and to keep him company for a few days. "He was in great spirits," Ballard recalled. He practically shoved her onto the trolley in their tours of the city. As he did most visitors, Marlon wore Ballard out. But he knew just the restaurant to liven her up. "A little out-of-the-way place he'd discovered," she said. "My first Greek restaurant. It was the first time I ever had baklava." Over wine and dessert, they laughed well into the night.

During *Streetcar*'s tryout period, Marlon was having a ball. His sister Tidd, the one who'd wanted to be an actor from a young age and who'd dragged her indifferent brother into the profession, wrote to her parents saying she was glad Bud was now "settled and pleased" with his life. Despite marriage and motherhood, she had recently returned to New York to resume her acting career. Marlon's success had inspired her to try again.

For Marlon, the reason the previews were so much fun, and so creatively stimulating, was the constant variety: different theaters, different cities, frequently different lines and stage directions. New pages came regularly from Tennessee. If something wasn't fully working one night, they'd switch it up the next. For Marlon, it was almost like being back in Stella's class. Yet he'd been through all this before. He knew eventually they'd have to freeze the show. Then the monotony would set in.

Almost as a reminder, when the company rolled into Philadelphia to start its run there, another play was being advertised down the street: the roadshow tour of *I Remember Mama*. Two plays more opposite than *Streetcar* and *Mama* could not be imagined, "the former almost insupportably haunting and harrowing in its mental and emotional tragedy," according to the *Philadelphia Inquirer*, and "the latter heart-warming and wholesome in its gentle and genial humor and homespun humanity." In *Mama*, Marlon had been little more than background; now he was front and center, the beating heart and rage of the play.

Marlon's earliest memories were halcyon: sunshine and happiness at his grandmother's home in Omaha. After that, things darkened. *Reproduced by permission of Brando Enterprises, LP*

Dorothy "Dodie" Pennebaker Brando outside the farmhouse in Libertyville, Illinois. *Reproduced by permission of Brando Enterprises, LP*

The complicated emotions Marlon held for his parents—to make them proud, to keep his mother safe, to upstage his father—were at the bottom of everything he did.

Marlon Brando Senior, either in Evanston or Libertyville. *Reproduced by permission of Brando Enterprises, LP*

Although he looked good in the uniform, Marlon was a bad fit for the Shattuck Military Academy: he was never able to "'snap to' and salute," he said. *Author's collection*

The one parental figure who never failed him and saw his magic when no one else did: legendary acting teacher Stella Adler. *Reproduced by permission of Brando Enterprises, LP*

Stella's daughter, Ellen Adler, was the one woman Marlon could never overpower—and never forget. They remained friends for life. *Reproduced by permission of Brando Enterprises, LP*

As a student, before all the fame, Marlon had a ball acting. Here he is with Blossom Plumb rehearsing *Twelfth Night* on the beach in Sayville, Long Island, during the summer of 1944. *Author's collection*

As a professional, however, he loathed acting, especially here, in his thankless role as Nels in the long-running Broadway hit *I Remember Mama* (1944–1946). *Billy Rose Theatre Division, the New York Public Library for the Performing Arts, Astor, Lennox and Tilden Foundations*

Marlon's howl of grief and pain in *Truckline Café* (1946) brought him acclaim and attention, though the play, by Maxwell Anderson, closed after just thirteen performances. *Billy Rose Theatre Division, the New York Public Library for the Performing Arts, Astor, Lennox and Tilden Foundations*

In the 1947 stage version of *A Streetcar Named Desire*, Tennessee Williams, Elia Kazan, and Marlon helped revolutionize the American theater. Jessica Tandy, as Blanche DuBois, failed to fully appreciate what Marlon was doing with Stanley Kowalski.

*Author's collection*

Marlon preferred Vivien Leigh as Blanche in the film version of *Streetcar* in 1951. "Perfect casting," he said. "Very much Tennessee's wounded butterfly." *Author's collection*

Marlon spent the 1950s reinventing masculinity, blurring sexuality, and challenging gender expectations. He unnerved the powers-that-were, who often banned his film *The Wild One* (1953). *Author's collection*

With Kazan and *On the Waterfront*, Marlon lifted the bar for what could be achieved on the screen. There have been few actor-director partnerships more influential in the history of film. *Author's collection*

Marlon with Rod Steiger in the iconic taxi scene. *Author's collection*

*Streetcar* opened at the Walnut Street Theatre, at the corner of Walnut and Ninth Streets, on Monday, November 17. This was the sleek, streamlined, sharply focused production that had taken shape in the past three weeks. Not a scene, not a moment, not a word, was extraneous, and the cast was as expert as they would ever be. The Philadelphia critics agreed. "*Streetcar* travels from the gutter to the stars and tells us with tenderness and bitterness how close the two can be," Edwin Schloss declared in the *Inquirer*. And for the first time, Blanche and Stanley were treated as equals in a review: the "inspired company of actors," wrote R. E. P. Sensenderfer in the *Evening Bulletin*, was "headed by Jessica Tandy and Marlon Brando." Tandy, the critic adjudged, was "infinitely skillful" though "at times uneven." Marlon, meanwhile, was simply "superb."

Philadelphia was where it all came together, where they all realized it would be a success. While in the City of Brotherly Love, Williams went out and bought an expensive tweed coat "on the strength of the favorable notices there."

Now, at last, it was on to New York.

Marlon knew his parents would be there. It wouldn't be the first time they'd been in the audience for one of their son's plays. They'd been present for his turn in *Candida* a year and a half earlier; his father had even complimented him afterward on his performance as Marchbanks. Dodie was very excited about *Streetcar*; having read the play, she recognized its potential. But just what Marlon Senior would think of all the deviance and dissipation was anyone's guess.

As for Junior, he was noticeably glummer than the rest of the company, who were buoyed by the reviews as they arrived back in New York. For *Streetcar*, the adventure was just beginning. For Marlon, it had come to an end.

**DECEMBER 3** / Opening night of *Streetcar* was the event of the season on Broadway. The Ethel Barrymore Theatre, on Forty-Seventh Street, had sold out so quickly that Irene Selznick had needed to buy up a block of seats in order to get all the newspaper reporters she wanted there. At the Adler house, Stella was getting ready to head to the theater, exuberantly confident that her steadfast belief in the vagabond who'd sauntered into her class four years earlier was about to be vindicated by the top critics of New York. Her daughter, Ellen, home from Bard, was down the hall, getting ready herself. Ellen might no longer be Marlon's girl, but she was planning on attending the premiere with her mother and stepfather regardless.

A couple of hours from show time, the telephone rang.

"Marlon called me the night of the opening," Ellen remembered, "and asked me to go out with him afterward. He always did that at the last minute."

She stewed. She hadn't heard from him since Provincetown, and she already had plans for the night: she was taking Leonard Bernstein as her date. Ellen admitted she was hoping Marlon would "die of jealousy" when he saw them together. Bernstein was Marlon's "equal . . . young and unbelievably charming, and also a genius." As conductor of the New York City Symphony and composer of ballets (*Fancy Free*) and Broadway musicals (*On the Town*), Bernstein, just twenty-nine, was certainly a force to be reckoned with. So, it was with some satisfaction that Ellen told Marlon she couldn't possibly go out with him after the show. She already had an after-show date.

"Who with?" Marlon demanded to know.

"I'm not going to tell you," she replied. "You're mysterious, I can be mysterious." She did agree, however, to meet him backstage and wait with him until the curtain.

The crowd outside the theater was enormous. The night was mild, in the high fifties, and an electric sense of expectation crackled in the air. Inside the auditorium, Tennessee Williams was looking over his shoulder to see who was there. "Packed house," he described it the next day to a friend, poet and New Directions founder James Laughlin, with "the usual first-night decorations"— by which he meant Cecil Beaton, Dorothy Parker, the fashion designer Valentina, and other famous New Yorkers. People filed into their rows, draping mink stoles and white gloves over their seats.

Backstage, Irene Selznick was a bundle of nerves. But, as Ellen discovered, Marlon was calm, almost indifferent. He'd already done this show a couple of dozen times, he said; he had no reason to feel nervous. "He did not prepare," Ellen said. "He just went on." She was, of course, familiar with his attitude toward his craft, but still, this night she was surprised. She'd grown up among Group Theatre types—before every performance, an actor always "took a minute." Marlon just strode into the wings to await his cue. Ellen slipped out into the audience, sitting beside Stella and Harold. Marlon's parents, she recalled, sat in front of her.

For Williams, that long-ago tryout in New Haven was now just "a reading of the play," as he told James Laughlin. This night, at the Barrymore Theatre, his work came alive. "The second act sent the audience zowing to new heights," said Williams, "and the final one left them—and me—wilted, gasping, weak, befoozled, drained." The four principals received "many curtains," the playwright reported, and then Tandy took a bow alone, as the audience got to its feet and whistled and cheered. Finally, Williams himself got up onstage, as cries of "Author! Author!" filled the theater.

Marlon, meantime, headed backstage, preparing to face his parents.

"MARLON'S FATHER HAD this little half-smile," Ellen remembered. "It was as if he was never really fully satisfied." Backstage, after the applause finally died down, she watched as Marlon Senior approached his son, the new Broadway star. The usual half-smile remained affixed to his face. While Dodie embraced Marlon and congratulated him, her husband hung back, Ellen said, "very, very distant." He'd always believed "Marlon was hopeless, and nothing seemed to change that."

Marlon wasn't expecting anything different from his father. "I was always a ne'er-do-well to him," he said. "No matter what."

Still, he was determined to show his parents a good time. The cast party was being held at Sardi's, the legendary showbiz restaurant on Forty-Fourth Street. "You can't imagine two more attractive people," one Broadway regular told Truman Capote after meeting Marlon's parents. "Tall, handsome, charming as they could be." What impressed everyone, the source told Capote, was how solicitous and attentive Marlon was to them. "In their presence, he wasn't the lad we knew. He was a model son. Reticent, respectful, very polite, considerate in every way."

Perhaps that was why he held his tongue when he greeted Ellen at her table. She was seated beside Bernstein, who, not knowing the history between them, introduced Ellen to Marlon. "She is the most beautiful woman in New York and I plan to marry her if she'll take me," Bernstein said. Marlon's face froze. "He was green with jealousy," Ellen said, loving every minute. "It was the only way you could make him feel something, because otherwise he was always protecting himself."

Marlon did his best to protect himself for the rest of the night. The whole place was swarming around him, clapping him on the back, shaking his hand, telling him how marvelous he was, how talented—except his father, of course, who sat at the table acting like a refined gentleman, not the raving, unpredictable skinflint Marlon knew him to be. How Marlon despised events such as this. "Everybody being phony," he would describe such ordeals later.

"Everybody pretending to like each other and praising each other for being a genius but full of resentment deep down."

Yet he couldn't escape it. Not now. There was no way out of his two-year contract. And *Streetcar* was a hit. No chance this one would fold like *Truckline*. So, from this moment on, gone were Marlon's spontaneous parties at Maureen's, his anonymous sojourns to the jazz clubs of Harlem, his lazy summers in Provincetown. His life, as he knew it, was over.

Although Brooks Atkinson, in the *New York Times*, would reserve most of his acclaim for Tandy and Williams, he called Marlon "high quality" and praised his "insight." And as the weeks rolled on, it became increasingly obvious that the main draw was Marlon—"the unforgettable find," as one fan magazine called him, who "pulls no punches," according to *Variety*, and who "has the ladies coming back for repeat performances," as one columnist observed. The raw power that the young actor brought to the stage was something entirely new and different for Broadway.

That first night, Ellen lost him among the crowd at Sardi's. Bernstein brought her home, and Ellen went to bed. At three in the morning, however, she was awakened by Marlon calling to her from the hallway outside her room.

"The door was never locked at our apartment," Ellen said, "and Marlon knew it." So, after whatever unpleasantness he'd had to endure—meeting *Streetcar*'s investors and playing nice with newspaper reporters—he'd snuck away from everyone and come to the one house where he'd ever truly felt at home. Old Sara Adler heard him come in and met him in the dark. Marlon was wearing a long-sleeved black tee shirt with a turtleneck, then all the rage, Ellen remembered; his muscles seemed to burst through the seams. Once more Sara upbraided him for turning himself into a brute. Then, softening, she left him alone to go see Ellen.

"And I must say," Ellen recalled, "I knew from his stride [that] his life had changed." He sauntered into her room, no longer really a part of their world, yet here he was, one last time. Sitting with Ellen, he didn't talk about the play or his career. "He never talked about that," Ellen said. Instead, as usual, they discussed art, philosophy, music. Pointedly, Lenny Bernstein's name never came up.

From the clamor of *Streetcar*, Marlon had taken refuge in the house where he'd first learned to accept himself, and with a woman who knew him, and loved him, for himself. But for how long could he remain? Ellen wasn't kidding herself. She knew Marlon was inexorably moving away from all of them. His destiny couldn't be stopped. He belonged now to the world.

**MAY 1948** / Marlon was feeling desperate. Arriving at the theater as close to curtain as he could manage, he headed backstage to change into his costume. He was moody, impatient, and counting the days until his three-week summer vacation. For six straight months he'd been speaking the same damn words every night. To friends, he'd grouse, "I have to go to the theatre and rape Jessica Tandy again." Just as he had with *I Remember Mama*, he hated every minute of it.

True to form, he found ways to mix things up when he could. The show might have been frozen in Philadelphia, and its actors instructed by Kazan to perform exactly the same way every time, but such conformity was congenitally impossible for Marlon. He'd shorten a line, move to a different spot on the stage, pause for emphasis where he'd never paused before. Sometimes, according to stage manager Robert Downing, "he seemed to shrug away entire scenes, or substitute grimaces and gestures to cover his temporary

loss of concentration." His leading lady was infuriated, but returning playgoers liked spotting something new.

"It is difficult to talk about Brando's stage performances," wrote
the *New Yorker* essayist Harold Brodkey, some years later, "because
they varied from night to night, and nobody saw every one of them.
One can easily guess he was interruptible—that his performances
were infinitely fragile. They were like translations in progress."

Marlon was different from anything veteran theatergoers had
ever seen. Brodkey would recall conversations about how Marlon
could be "tricky or erratic" onstage, yet one's eye would never leave
him: he was "a scene-stealer," Brodkey said, "and strong-willed and
ruthless beyond belief." From Marlon's perspective, he had to be.
Only by acting this way could he keep from being bored out of his
mind.

In his dressing room, Irene Selznick was waiting for him. It
seemed Marlon had won some sort of award.

By a large margin, the New York Drama Critics' Circle had
voted him the Most Promising Young Actor of the 1947–1948 season.
Marlon won with a total of five votes, with runners-up James
Whitmore, John Sylvester, David Wayne, and Robert Lenn taking
just one vote apiece. Selznick was thrilled, but Marlon couldn't
have been more indifferent, recalled Wright King, who'd taken
over the part of the young Collector. "He was very restless," King
said. "Always complaining about having to say the same lines
every night." To deal with his restlessness, Marlon often boxed in
the basement of the theater in between acts. His sparring partner
was Nick Dennis, who had another small part in the play.

Marlon firmly believed that none of what they were doing
mattered. Tennessee's words might have been lovely, poetic, and
brilliant, but they had no relevance to the problems of the world.
What the audience was applauding every night, what the critics
were raving about, had no value in the world, Marlon argued—or
at least, not the sort of value that such groups as the New York

Drama Critics' Circle assigned to it. Marlon was now twenty-four years old. Increasingly, he felt as if he were wasting his life.

"This is child's play," he grumbled to Karl Malden in the dressing room they shared. "What the hell are we doing? This isn't man's work. This isn't the right thing. What are we doing here?"

He was expected to be grateful for his success and for the praise he'd been given. He was expected to appreciate his talent as much as everyone else appreciated it. But he simply could not do so. "This huge crown was put on his head," Ellen Adler said, "this four-thousand-pound crown, as the greatest actor that ever lived. He resented that. He couldn't live with that."

And so we will leave him here for now, striding out onstage as surly and belligerent as the character he plays, his shoulders slumped under the weight of that crown.

# THE

# AMERICAN

# HAMLET

**JUST AFTER THE NEW YEAR, 1954** / No one could quite remember a winter this cold. A few hardy souls were shooting a movie at the Hoboken piers, shivering under multiple layers of clothing. "Everybody looked ten pounds [heavier] than they were," said Karl Malden, one of the film's stars. When he spoke his lines, his breath was visible in front of his face. Up and down the waterfront, salamander heaters stood like sentinels to ward off the chill. Back in November, when the company had started shooting, the warmth of an Indian summer had prevailed. But ever since, temperatures had remained stubbornly below freezing. "The coldest movie I ever did in my life," Malden said.

The cold was a "hardship," the picture's director admitted. But it was also, he insisted, an unexpected blessing: "The bite of the wind and the temperature did a great thing for the actors' faces. It made them look like people, not actors."

Elia Kazan had always been interested in making films about people. The picture—working title, *Waterfront*—was about the struggles of working-class longshoremen caught between poverty and the Mob, based on an original script by Budd Schulberg. As was his custom, Kazan had assembled a cast of actors he knew well. Malden was a *Streetcar* alumnus; so was the picture's leading man, Marlon Brando, now twenty-nine and one of the most famous actors in the world.

On a bitterly cold Friday night, Marlon hurried along the pier, hunched down in his red-and-black buffalo-check jacket, his hands stuffed in his pockets, making a beeline for assistant director Charlie Maguire. Kazan had kept them working late that night, and Marlon, as was his habit on weekends, was eager to return to Manhattan. But he didn't have subway fare. He rarely did, Maguire recalled. Pulling off the putty strips he wore on his upper eyelids to give his character swollen "fighter's eyes," Marlon asked Maguire, "You got fifteen cents?" As usual, the assistant director obliged. Then the heartthrob of millions of young people scampered down the subway steps and caught a late-night train, his head lowered, his chin against his chest, hoping against the odds that he wouldn't be recognized.

Marlon hated living like this.

Once, he had watched his fellow train passengers intently, observing every movement they made. Now the situation "was reversed," said Ellen Adler, "and people were looking at him." To throw them off, Marlon had gotten used to hiding behind newspapers, sunglasses, the brim of a hat. Sometimes, however, the effort was just too much, so he didn't go out at all—which broke his wanderer's heart. The film version of *A Streetcar Named Desire* in 1951 had turned Marlon into a movie star; his subsequent films, while not as immensely successful, had nonetheless burnished his public image. No one quite like Marlon Brando had ever come around before, this beautiful man-child uncomfortable with his fame.

But he was no longer the boy of six years earlier. He was harder now, warier, and even more volatile than he'd been. Toward the end of *Streetcar*'s Broadway run, he'd broken his nose in one of his backstage sparring matches with Nick Dennis; the slightly uneven result had turned his boyish beauty into something almost feral.

There was danger now in Marlon Brando's appeal, a sort of menace that hadn't existed on the screen before, even with rogues such as Clark Gable or James Cagney, whose defiance was always subdued by the picture's finish. Marlon, by contrast, resisted any harness. *Photoplay* writer Gladys Hall thought he possessed "the brooding quality of a jungle animal just about to spring." And now his latest picture, *The Wild One*, in which he played a version of his leather-jacketed, motorcycle-riding self, had just gone into wide release, certain to stir libidos everywhere. At the Hollywood studios, Marlon's fan mail overflowed.

His life had been fundamentally and permanently altered. "Nobody ever acted normally around him again," Ellen Adler said, "only the people who had known him before." That was why Marlon craved getting away from movie sets, returning as often as possible to Manhattan and his friends: the Adlers, Wally, Maureen, others.

Still, he was trapped. *Waterfront* might be scheduled to finish in a matter of days, but then he was obliged to head to Los Angeles soon afterward to start work on *The Egyptian*, a gaudy, big-budget CinemaScope epic in which he'd play the noble physician of an ambitious pharaoh. Marlon wasn't happy about it. At least *Waterfront* was a serious project, with a heavyweight director like Kazan. But Marlon had made a pact with the devil, and there was no way out.

The boy he'd been might have run off, or gotten himself fired for breaking the rules. But no longer. The reasons for Marlon's newfound perseverance were waiting for him when he got back to Manhattan. His parents were in town, preparing to embark on a trip to Mexico. They'd come out to Hoboken to visit him on the set as well, on a particularly cold, drizzly day, as Freddie Fiore, hired as Marlon's stand-in, recalled. The last time Freddie had seen Dodie, she'd seemed rather frumpy, so unlike the sassy woman he remembered. Marlon preferred his mother that way, he told Freddie: a little plump and grandmotherly. But on the *Waterfront* set, she was once again "slim and chic," according to Freddie; they huddled together under a lean-to smoking cigarettes. Marlon introduced his parents to the cast and crew, posing for photos. Then the elder Brandos were off for their Mexican adventure.

That they could afford the trip was thanks, in large part, to their son and the money he now made. Marlon still sent much of his income to his father to invest and manage, and he wasn't averse to his parents using some of it for themselves. His money had bought them a ranch in Nebraska, where Marlon Senior managed a thousand-head cattle operation, which was, in truth, a shelter for his son's rapidly increasing earnings. The $550 a week Marlon had made on *Streetcar* had grown from project to project, and now he had "more money than [he] needed," he said, or could even keep track of. The irony of sending it home to "Pop" wasn't lost on him. His father, Marlon said, "couldn't understand how this ne'er-do-well son of his could [succeed]. He measured everything by money [and] was dumbfounded that I was making more in six months than he made in ten years."

The same forces that had compelled Marlon to accept the role in *A Streetcar Named Desire* now kept him moving forward in his early Hollywood career. The complicated, conflicting emotions he held for his parents—to make them proud, to keep his mother safe, to upstage his father—were always at "the bottom of everything" he did, said Ellen Adler. Seeing them off on their Mexican holiday, Marlon took some satisfaction, his friends thought, in his success, an achievement he'd managed despite all his father's pessimistic predictions.

Yet something else had been unleashed within him these past six years: his own personal ambition. With the phenomenal success of *Streetcar*—first the play and then the film, also directed by Kazan and starring Vivien Leigh as Blanche—Marlon had discovered that the world could be his if he wanted it. He hadn't thought he wanted it, but that was when the world was still out of his reach. Now producers were willing to pay him any amount of money he asked just to get him to be in their play or movie. Now Marlon set the terms. He no longer needed to haggle to get a couple of weeks of vacation, as he'd done with Irene Selznick, and if he wasn't ready to start a project on a certain date, the producers were glad to wait until he was.

Marlon hadn't gone in search of the world. But since the world was being handed to him on a platter, he would have been a fool not to take it.

The Brando legend would remember only the prickly, taciturn, reluctant actor, resentful of fame. Yet, in the early part of the 1950s, Marlon chased after the perks, the money, the accolades. "He was burning for it," Ellen said—a sharp turn from the career indifference he'd demonstrated in the late 1940s. Competition had always galvanized him. "I had a strong sense of competition in sports and games," he admitted, "and I liked to win. I felt at one time in my life that I *had* to win." His brother-in-law Dick Loving said Marlon's competitive nature "could take virtually any form. Like how your shoelaces were tied, or guessing the number of hairs on the back of your hand . . . anything, everything could get turned into a challenge or contest." Acting might have been thrust upon Marlon, but if that was the game he was now playing, he intended to prevail just as he had in sports and sex. He was being measured against the legendary titans of the theater, Olivier, Gielgud, and thrust into competition with another rising, iconoclastic, critically acclaimed young actor, Montgomery Clift. That was enough to fuel Marlon's instinctive hunger to come out on top.

"Do you take inspiration from Monty Clift?" columnist Ed Sullivan asked him during one break in shooting on *Waterfront*.

"I think you might want to inquire of him if he takes inspiration from me," Marlon replied. And so, the game was on.

Marlon had met Clift a few years earlier, during the Broadway run of *Streetcar*. Clift had made a splash in movies by that time, first in *The Search* and then *Red River*, and was being groomed to play the male lead in *The Heiress*. "Marlon wanted Monty's career," said Ellen Adler. Clift's rise was one of the reasons Marlon was "burning" for success himself; Monty's career was evidence that quality work could be done in Hollywood. The two young men had liked each other well enough; their camaraderie is documented by home movie footage shot by another actor, Kevin McCarthy, one of Marlon's costars from *Truckline Café*. In the silent, sixteen-millimeter film, Marlon and Monty horse around, trying on disguises, making funny faces at each other; at one point, they don women's hats, and Marlon stuffs his shirt to give himself breasts. The two actors coo and flirt, Monty playfully tapping Marlon's face. Clift, who was gay, is frisky in response to Marlon's own sexual fluidity—though stories of any intimacies beyond these home movie flirtations seem rooted solely in wishful imaginations.

Once both actors were in Hollywood, however, the playfulness subsided; they were pitted against each other, and Marlon, especially, wanted to come out on top. He'd made three films between *Streetcar* and *Waterfront*, one of them *Julius Caesar*, an attempt to establish him as a great classical actor. This was the moment for the first big Brando-Clift showdown, at least from the point of view of the press. Many columnists, including Ed Sullivan, declared Clift's effort in that same year's *From Here to Eternity* superior to Marlon's Shakespearean turn. Clift, Sullivan wrote, had to create a unique characterization from scratch; Marlon's performance, while "expert," was "pretty much formula."

Marlon did have his own champions. What set Marlon apart, the essayist Harold Brodkey thought, was, once again, that sense of danger: "The morality of Clift's characters was never in doubt. Brando's questionable morality and the questionable morality of his art, its graffiti quality . . . all this was new." Clift was the first actor of his generation to bring such naturalness to the screen. But

Marlon brought more than just naturalism. He brought a sense of revolution.

Yet, for all his instinct for competition, Marlon had been unprepared for the rules of the game. How much was he willing to endure in order to come out on top? Hiding his face on subways, fidgeting through interviews with moronic columnists, fending off hordes of autograph seekers—it was all taking its toll. He might have been burning for it, but how much, really, was he willing to be scorched?

HOPPING OFF THE subway in Manhattan, Marlon was spotted by a couple of young women, who squealed when they recognized him. They were pretty, too, just Marlon's type: dark, possibly Puerto Rican. "But I couldn't always stop and talk to these women," he said, looking back. "Sometimes I just smiled and blew a kiss."

Sometimes success could be fun. "I think," Marlon said, "I was enjoying the fact that I'd never done anything in life, except sports, that anybody ever said I was good at." The little boy who'd been shamed by his teacher for a low-scoring IQ test was having his moment. "Suddenly, to be there, and to have money . . ." His voice trailed off, as he remembered how prosperity had, without warning, taken over his life, a tidal wave of wealth.

Half a million dollars a year. That was what Marlon estimated he brought home in the early 1950s. In today's dollars, that would be about six and a half million annually or more. His success hadn't happened overnight of course, but it had nonetheless been fast. In 1947, he'd taken the part in *Streetcar* in the hopes of paying his bills; just a few years later, he was bragging to Ellen that he had more money than he knew what to do with. He was, Ellen said, "a bit full of himself" in these years. Visiting her in Paris, Marlon had quickly grown bored when she kept talking about someone else: a composer Stella had told her was "brilliant," and who charged a hundred francs a lesson. Marlon scoffed. "I just made forty thousand dollars for a few weeks of work in a movie," he said, referring to his first picture, *The Men*. When Ellen repeated the anecdote to Harold Clurman, he lamented, "It's over. He's corrupt." Bragging about money was déclassé, bourgeois, capitalistic—all the things the Adlers loathed, and which they had thought Marlon loathed, too.

But money was very real, very tangible, especially to a young man who'd never had any. "I became an actor," Marlon told the fan magazine writer Gladys Hall, "because it's the easiest way I know to earn big money." That was around the time of the movie version of *Streetcar*, but it was a sentiment Marlon would repeat many times during his career. Four decades later, he was still saying, "There isn't anything that pays you as much money as acting while you are deciding what the hell you're going to do with yourself." Even after becoming a movie star, he still held on to the idea that all this was temporary, that he'd make some money, put it in the bank, and then find more fulfilling work. But, for the moment, why not live as large as people were letting him?

The past six years had been a whirlwind. He'd been to Paris three times, where he "was like a child romping around," Ellen said—jazz clubs, swanky parties, leisurely boat rides along the Seine. He was quickly fluent. "I always had a good ear for languages," Marlon remembered. Ellen was now living in Paris, and though she was seeing someone else, she spent time with Marlon as a friend. She introduced him to the French actor Christian Marquand, and the two became tight. They shared a love of sex and its free, fluid expression. Marquand was "able to speak to any girl," remembered Hervé Mille, editor of *Paris Match*, "and bring Brando that girl if he wanted her"—and he usually did. At some point, Marlon and Marquand became lovers as well. According to the publicist Dick Clayton, who was immersed in Hollywood's gay subculture, Marlon and Marquand would "share a girl between them and afterward keep going themselves." The description fits the flexible, open-minded, no-label sexual outlook by which Marlon always lived his life.

In August 1953, he'd branched out from Paris, traveling to Venice, with Ellen, Wally Cox, and Billy Redfield in tow. There, the actor Farley Granger was waiting to pay homage; the star of Alfred Hitchcock's *Rope* and *Strangers on a Train* was desperate to impress the man the critics were hailing as a game-changer for American actors. "Poor Farley," Ellen remembered. "He was telling Marlon how he wanted to leave the movies. He was going to give his life over to being a good [stage] actor." All the while Granger spoke, however, Marlon "was making faces" behind his back, mocking his earnestness and cracking the others up. "In other words," Ellen said, "he got us to laugh at Farley." She wasn't happy with herself. "It was pretty rotten," she said.

Not long afterward, Marlon granted another audience, this time to the groundbreaking Italian director Roberto Rossellini. For the entire visit, Marlon remained stretched out on his bed at the Grand Hotel. "He was in his undershorts," Ellen remembered with horror. "He didn't move for this older man." Rossellini remarked that his wife, Ingrid Bergman, "would give anything to work" with Marlon. No response came from the man on the bed. "Marlon was really, really awful," Ellen said. After the meeting was over, she stormed out of the room and remained angry with Marlon for some time over his "impossible behavior."

Yet, when she thought about it, Ellen realized that his rudeness, however inexcusable, made some kind of regrettable sense. "He hated this position he had been put in," Ellen said. "He enjoyed the perks—why not? But that didn't mean he thought he deserved them. If people were going to be crazy enough to pay him all this money and attention, fine. But they were still crazy." Marlon believed the only reason people came flocking to see him was because some critics "in their ivory towers" back in New York had declared him to be a "great actor." Granger's earnestness was absurd to Marlon. Being earnest in support of a cause—civil rights or ending poverty—would have been admirable. But giving one's life over to being a great actor? How was that praiseworthy? And when an old pro like Rossellini "made a fuss" over him, Marlon could feel only contempt. "That reduced Rossellini in Marlon's mind," Ellen said.

If Marlon enjoyed the benefits of his fame, it was compensation for putting up with all the foolishness. He was aware that he sometimes came across as a boor: looking back, he told Ellen he regretted being cruel to Farley Granger. He didn't take any pride in being a jerk. It was just that sometimes "he found it so difficult," his good pal Maureen Stapleton observed, "to put up with all the phoniness," especially when he "believed, in his heart of hearts, that he should really be doing something that mattered more than acting, like fighting for the underprivileged." How could he truly respect another actor's career when he didn't respect his own?

On a cold New York Monday, Marlon headed back out to Hoboken to finish making *Waterfront*. Maureen Stapleton had seen him not long before. He was contemplating how much more of "the bullshit" he could endure, she said. "I think he constantly told himself, 'This one will be the last. This is the last movie or the last play I will ever take on, and after that, I'm out of here.'" But such a break was difficult, when people kept offering him projects with lots of dollars attached, and his mother kept getting so excited about those projects, and people kept saying he was neck and neck with Clift in the acting race—and predicting someday, maybe, he'd surpass Olivier. "It was like a drug," publicist Dick Clayton explained, that fired up that old competitive drive. Every new role, every new review, made him feel he had something else to prove, something else to win.

THE PHONE WAS ringing in Marlon's high-rise studio apartment on Fifty-Seventh Street. It seemed always to be ringing. "In the

old days," one friend recalled, "Marlon never had a phone. I think
he probably regretted installing one." On the other end of the line
was his agent, Jay Kanter, calling from Los Angeles. Kanter was a
young man whose star had risen along with Marlon's. He'd been
an assistant at MCA when Marlon had come west to make *The
Men*. Marlon had liked Kanter enough to insist that he be the one
to represent him, instead of others higher up the MCA ladder. For
the past four years, Kanter had kept his client's career running,
even when Marlon was antsy and irritable about it and might have
preferred to walk away.

Now Kanter was calling to report that Darryl F. Zanuck expected Marlon to start work on *The Egyptian* immediately after
*Waterfront* was completed. There would be no break between
films, as the exhausted star had hoped. When Marlon had made
*Viva Zapata!* at Fox in 1951, he'd agreed to a multiple-picture deal.
Now Zanuck, the crafty head of the studio, was calling in his
chits.

Marlon stewed. The big salaries, the competitive urge, the desire to impress his mother—as justifications for the madness, all
were wearing very thin, especially when he'd read reports about
*The Egyptian* in the newspapers. Gossip maven Hedda Hopper was
crowing over the fact that Victor Mature would have "one of the
best roles" in the picture because he got to "kill a lion." Hopper
added, "If Marlon Brando steps out, as he's threatened to do, the
top part goes to Kirk Douglas." This was clearly a movie-star vehicle, a typical Hollywood spectacle, nothing Marlon could be proud
of—nothing, he rued, Monty Clift would be caught dead in. And
for this, he'd be leaving New York and trekking across the country
to Los Angeles, a place he loathed. "This was not a project," said
one pal, "that was calling Marlon's name."

Yet, there was no way out, Kanter explained to Marlon. He'd
signed the contract with Zanuck.

In blood, it would seem.

**THE FIRST WEEK OF JANUARY 1954** / At the corner of Broadway and Forty-Seventh Street, a group of teenaged girls in ponytails, poodle skirts, and fur-trimmed boots—the weather was only a few degrees above freezing—waited impatiently outside the Palace Theatre. "This is the fifth time we've seen it," one of them told a reporter, referring to the film that was emblazoned up on the marquee: *The Wild One*, starring Marlon Brando. "We'll probably see it five more times." Brando, they said, was their "favorite movie star."

Three thousand miles away, in Los Angeles, film producers were keeping close tabs on how *The Wild One* performed at the Palace. Everybody was talking about Marlon Brando, about how new and different and exciting he was, and everybody wanted Marlon Brando in their pictures—but whether Marlon Brando was good box office, nobody had quite figured out yet. Despite his notoriety and critical acclaim, he was not, in early 1954, a big Hollywood moneymaker. "I don't know why all the fuss about him," Hedda Hopper sniped in her column. "Few of his pictures have made money." Only the film version of *A Streetcar Named Desire* had risen to the top-ten box-office list, racking up $4.2 million, or fifth place, in 1951. All Marlon's other films had come up short. And now, *The Wild One*, despite the enthusiasm of those teenaged girls, was not held over at the Palace after a week's run. Not a good sign.

Those girls, however, were representative of Marlon's devoted young fan base. The trouble was, in 1954, the teenage audience was not yet a target demographic for movie producers or, in fact, for many businesses or brands. One advertising analyst complained that most companies devoted "too little promotional activities toward the youth market, and advertising agencies are afraid to suggest remedying the situation." In the early 1950s, parents still controlled how their children spent their money, and only the most audacious industries found ways to circumvent parental authority and appeal directly to the kids. Hollywood, at the start of the Eisenhower era, was definitely not among the daring. Although the Production Code (that repressive system of self-censorship that had controlled the movie business since 1934) was gradually breaking down, producers were still willing to go only so far in marketing a picture, especially one as provocative as *The Wild One*, about a motorcycle gang that terrorizes a small town.

Still, if they could find Brando's audience, Hollywood expected big things from him. The cachet of his name alone was worth any risk. When Hedda Hopper asked Darryl Zanuck how Marlon compared to other actors, the Fox chief replied, "He stands so much alone." No one, Zanuck said, had been able to get Brando under contract except for him. "I am the only one," the producer boasted, "who has an option on his services."

Up in his studio apartment, Marlon cursed the day he ever agreed to Zanuck's demands. When he first went out to Hollywood, in 1949, to make *The Men*, he'd gone willingly, even enthusiastically. Movies, Marlon believed, were preferable to the theater, for which he'd lost all enthusiasm. In Hollywood, Marlon said, "you had to work maybe three months" at a time, and then "could do as you please." Gone was the monotony he'd endured on the stage. The last year of *Streetcar* had been a nightmare for him, much as *I Remember Mama* had been: "You can imagine," Marlon grumbled, "having to go someplace every night at 8:30, and then go through all that stuff, and get yourself upset and yell and scream and cry and kick the furniture—do that and try to be as convincing as you could. It was taxing."

He tried television—"theater in a jar," he called it—the new electronic phenomenon that could put a couple hundred smackers in an actor's pocket for a single night's work. All over New York, fledgling television stations were producing dramas for the home market. The weekly anthology drama *Actors Studio*, affiliated with

Kazan's school, was broadcast live from WJZ on Sunday nights at 8:30. On January 9, 1949, Marlon played a doctor forced at gunpoint to perform an operation on a gangster in the episode titled "I'm No Hero." *Variety* thought he was "competent" in the role, "but imparted no special edge." That edge came the following year, on April 18, when he played a boxer in *Come Out Fighting*, a live pilot for a series starring Hollywood actor Lee Tracy. In the half-hour drama, Marlon's sparring partner was real-life pugilist Johnny Britenbruck, with whom he struck up a friendship. He based his character on the middleweight champ Rocky Graziano, a pal from a local gym. When Graziano saw the show, he felt as if he were "looking in the mirror," he said. "Every gesture, every word, even the way he fights, it's me." Yet *Come Out Fighting* wasn't picked up; it wasn't even reviewed in the trades. And so ended any chance of a TV career for Marlon.

Hollywood, of course, was where the real money was. After making four pictures, Marlon was now collecting $150,000 for *Waterfront*, for just over one month of work. The theater, by contrast, had been "three hours of blood, sweat and tears every night," Marlon said. Yet, by not staying on the stage and doing Shakespeare or Shaw, he knew he had disappointed the Adlers, his mentors. In the end, however, Stella gave her former protégé at least her tacit blessing. "Most who were successful on Broadway," she admitted, eventually "went to the movies."

When he first went west, Marlon hoped that he could have the best of both worlds: he could rake in the big Hollywood cash while making only serious films with something to say. Montgomery Clift was doing it; so could he. Movies, Marlon insisted, had "a greater potential" than the stage; they could be "a factor for good, for moral development." Or, "at least some can—the kind of movies I want to do."

His first film, he believed, fit those criteria. *The Men*, like *A Flag Is Born*, was a piece of didacticism dressed up as melodrama. Pro-

ducer Stanley Kramer wanted to make a film exploring the struggles of paraplegic veterans, hoping to increase public awareness
and government support. Marlon prepared for the part the way
he'd prepared for *Flag*: by immersing himself in the culture he was
portraying. He liked the challenge of "working out of a wheelchair," Kramer recalled, and not being able to use his legs in his
performance. Upon arrival in Los Angeles, he was given a tour
of a VA hospital to observe the physical therapy of the paralyzed
vets. Shaken by the men's injuries, Marlon had to retreat to the
restroom to compose himself, as one vet remembered.

After that, he met the challenge head-on. He was intent on getting the part right, which meant he often came across as "quiet and
distant . . . a little bit lost," according to his costar Richard Erdman.
He spent a couple of days at the hospital in a wheelchair, with his
legs encased in steel braces, to get a sense of what paraplegics went
through. The film's publicists would later inflate his stay to several
weeks living at the VA hospital day and night. But Marlon had been
taught that a good actor didn't need that much time. He quickly
became familiar with the men's lives, imprinting the experience
on his mind.

On the surface, his approach would seem beholden to "the
Method" school of acting that was then being taught by Lee Strasberg at the Actors Studio—the philosophy of memory that was diametrically opposed to Stella's emphasis on the imagination. But
Stella had always recognized the benefits of real-life experience,
too, and spending time with the injured veterans had merely been
the start of Marlon's process, the catalyst for his imagination. "I
went through all these things," he recalled, "and I was depressed,
and I cried. I was rehearsing in the dressing room. And I got all of
these emotions out of me. I really reached down into the depths of
myself."

The misidentification of Marlon as a Method actor would persist for decades, and the label infuriated him. He had never been

taught the Method; he'd never been a student at the Actors Studio. During the early run of *Streetcar*, he'd occasionally wander over on a Saturday afternoon to the Studio at Broadway and Fifty-Third Street—"a place to go [and] monkey around," he said, and meet "a lot of girls." Founded by Kazan and other Group Theatre alumni in the fall of 1947, the Studio was a natural hangout for Marlon; not surprisingly, he sometimes, though unofficially, took part in a class. Anthony Quinn remembered him participating in a few sessions. "He managed to mock the process and still do provocative work," Quinn said. Told to freeze at the clap of the instructor's hands, the students were then instructed to "do a bit" based on their frozen postures. Marlon, as Quinn recalled, had been caught in a headstand. For his improv, he blithely remarked: "I have a stomachache and I'm standing on my head hoping I can pass it out of my mouth."

As usual, Marlon wasn't taking the process very seriously. He became even more dismissive of the Method once Lee Strasberg, Stella's nemesis, took over as chief faculty at the Studio. Part of Marlon's antipathy toward the Method grew out of loyalty to Stella, but a great deal came from feeling exploited himself by Strasberg. As canny a salesman as he was a teacher, Strasberg used Marlon's presence at a few sessions to claim him, retroactively, as a member of the Studio. In membership lists published in newspapers during this period, Marlon's name was usually included, often at the very top. "They did such PR," Ellen said. "Lee claimed that Marlon had studied with him. But Marlon was in *A Streetcar Named Desire* before the Studio opened. He *despised* Lee. He went to the Studio because *Gadge* was in the Studio." Marlon said the same thing. Strasberg, he declared, "took credit for everything. He was a tasteless man. I didn't like him very much at all. Some people are worshipful about him, but I didn't really get along with him. I didn't go there to study, and he never taught me acting. Stella did. And Kazan."

At every opportunity, Marlon would make clear that he was

not a Method actor. The actors he admired were all non-Method: "Spencer Tracy is the kind of actor I like to watch," he said. "The way he holds back, then darts to make his point, darts back." Tracy, Paul Muni, Cary Grant, these were the figures he liked—movie stars for the most part, not stage actors. Still, in many ways, Marlon did epitomize the work of the Actors Studio, its "style of luminous American realism," as the critic and historian Foster Hirsch would describe it. To act like Marlon Brando, to bring forth his "charged psychological realism," would be the goal for countless Actors Studio members over the decades.

When *The Men* was released in July 1950, critics were mixed in their reactions to the film but nearly unanimous in praising Marlon. "So vividly real, dynamic and sensitive that his illusion is complete," Bosley Crowther wrote in the *New York Times*. Yet Marlon thought he'd "dried up completely" after summoning all that emotion. The truth lay somewhere in the middle. It's easy to see how Crowther would have been so impressed: Marlon's performance stands out as the most natural in the film, and it's an obvious break from traditional screen acting. The actors he meshed best with were the nonprofessionals, especially Arthur Jurado, a real paraplegic hired by director Fred Zinnemann for verisimilitude.

Yet sometimes in his performance, Marlon still seems hesitant, as if he's second-guessing himself, especially in scenes when the writing deteriorates: the fight between him and Teresa Wright after their characters' marriage, for example, feels contrived and forced, and the actors can't rise above it. Marlon was keen enough to pick up on moments like this: "There was a good deal to be learned," he admitted, "about acting in front of a camera."

Still, the camera loved him. His eyes, his smile, his dimples, the way he moved his body from the wheelchair, the sheer power of his arms: he's sexy not in spite of his disability, but in large part because of it. He's a very different sort of movie hero from those who had come before: vulnerable and combustible. As always, his performances seemed to come most alive when he channeled some part of himself. The angry outbursts of his character were very much like the "Rumpelstiltskin" rages Ellen identified in real life. Intentionally or not, there's considerable autobiography in *The Men*: Marlon's character is named Ken, but he's called Bud; he's originally from the Midwest; his girlfriend's name is Ellen. He's also got the same chip on his shoulder Marlon carried: "You try and you try," Bud says at one point, "and you're still behind the eight ball." Of course, the major biographical departure was that Marlon had been 4-F during the war.

*The Men* did only moderate business at the box office, but it launched Marlon Brando as a movie star. Stanley Kramer believed he was "the world's greatest actor." Before long, everyone thought the same thing—except, of course, Marlon himself.

IN A CRAMPED, makeshift New York studio, Elia Kazan sat watching the rushes of what they'd shot so far on *Waterfront*. Spools of celluloid unwound before his bloodshot eyes, the tail of the film flapping against the projector when he reached the end of the reel. Kazan was exhausted, but he was determined to get this film finished and released before summer. *Waterfront* was very important to him—the most important film he'd yet made, he believed, and for very personal reasons. More than any of his previous films, he needed *Waterfront* to be acclaimed by the critics. And everything depended on Marlon's performance.

The world had finally caught up with Kazan's assessment of Marlon Brando. The director had championed him to a doubting Irene Selznick, sent him unbidden to Tennessee Williams, and, when it had come time to make the film, had insisted to Warner Bros. that only Marlon could bring Stanley to life on the screen. (There'd been talk of John Garfield again.) Now Kazan's faith in the young actor was shared by everyone who mattered. Rare was the review of a Brando film that didn't hail his power and talent, even when the film itself left something to be desired.

And yet, for Kazan, something had shifted. He no longer looked at Marlon the same way he had even just a couple of years earlier. Something had changed between them. Something personal and, for both of them, traumatic.

At first, Kazan hadn't wanted Marlon to play Terry Malloy, the working-class hero of *Waterfront*. He'd write in his memoir that he'd always "preferred Brando to anybody," but that was not, in fact, the case. His private letters reveal that he wanted Paul Newman or, failing that, Frank Sinatra. "In my opinion, he [Brando] is quite wrong," Kazan wrote to Budd Schulberg before casting was final. Terry Malloy must "be hungry and anxious," and "the power to be that disappears with your picture on an ad." In other words, Marlon's fame would bleed through into Terry's character. Newman was "just as good looking as Brando," Kazan thought, "and his masculinity is also more actual." Marlon's masculinity, then, was *less* than actual in Kazan's mind. So much for the idea that Marlon Brando could do anything. Kazan, who'd discovered him, apparently no longer believed this was the case.

Part of his initial opposition to Marlon was just what Kazan insisted it was. He took great care with his films, and he needed exactly the right actors, or else everything would fall apart. Maybe Marlon's newfound fame did unnerve him, but something else lurked beneath Kazan's resistance. When he finally gave in to producer Sam Spiegel's demand that they send a script to Marlon, who was on his way to Europe, Kazan had snarled to Schulberg that they couldn't wait for "his majesty to get comfy in Paris and send us an answer when he feels like it." His hostility to Marlon was clearly personal.

And it went both ways. Marlon had accepted the part only after getting past his own reluctance to work with Kazan again. Once each other's greatest admirer, both men were ambivalent about making another picture together. Marlon's misgivings, like Kazan's, were also personal. They weren't about the script or the character. They were about Kazan himself, a fact of which Kazan was all too aware.

This tension between actor and director had persisted throughout the shoot. More than once Marlon had made a point of telling Kazan he was "unenthusiastic" about the film. The once-vaunted partnership of Kazan and Brando was now painfully strained, and Kazan worried about the effect it would have on the film. *Waterfront* would be either hailed as a classic or used as an excuse for the industry to turn on the director, which—ever since that day in April 1952, when Kazan sat in front of the House Un-American Activities Committee and provided the names of former Communist Party members when others had gone to jail for refusing to do so—many had been itching to do.

And, Kazan suspected, Marlon was one of those with that itch.

**THE SECOND WEEK OF JANUARY** / Shooting a picture on a swaying, bobbing soundstage was no easy task. But the *Waterfront* company, set up on "the slightly rolling deck" of the 333-foot Dominican freighter *Rhadames*, had adjusted to it these last couple of months. Cinematographer Boris Kaufman had learned how to keep his camera steady, and costume designer Anna Johnstone had gotten used to fitting leading lady Eva Marie Saint without sticking her with pins. The crew of the *Rhadames* treated the filmmakers like family, so no one complained when Kazan, after a week of interior filming in a New York studio, called for some final shots on the Hoboken piers.

The working-class New Jersey city had become as much a character in the film as any being played by the actors. "I like Hobo-ken," Kazan told a visiting reporter. "All that wonderful red brick background. And the feeling and sight of New York's skyline over here in the distance." Off to the east, the spires of Manhattan rose behind a scrim of smoke and wintry haze. At first Kazan had been disappointed that the skyline would not be vivid and distinct in the film, but after a few days of shooting, he'd come to consider it a metaphor for the story he was telling: a community trapped by the circumstances of their lives, economically and culturally op-pressed, unable to envision a clear future for themselves.

*Waterfront* was not a typical Hollywood crime picture. Screen-writer Schulberg called the film "a character study more than any-thing else." The posters might promise action and romance, but at its heart, *Waterfront* was about the human spirit. And in particular, the spirit of one lost human named Terry Malloy, a former pugilist now working as a longshoreman, who regularly informs on his workmates to the Mob that controls the pier.

"Why am I doing this part?" Marlon mused to a reporter, who'd just asked him the question. Repeating a reporter's inquiry was a habit he had acquired, probably to give himself more time to pon-der the answer. "I liked the script," he said at last. "It's worthwhile, it has pertinence and the drama is appealing." As Marlon spoke, Kazan sat off to the side, "nodding to himself," the reporter noted, "with a speculative half-smile." Perhaps the director was anxious about what his unpredictable star might say. After all, Marlon knew the real reasons Kazan was making this film, and they had much more to do with simply exposing the rampant corruption at the nation's ports.

For the past several years the newspapers had been filled with stories of graft, fraud, and investigations into the activities of long-shoremen. Schulberg had interviewed many of those involved in these scandals; their accounts formed the background of the script. Yet the film had more personal resonance for its creators.

Schulberg, like Kazan, had also given Congress names of people with whom he'd shared a membership in the Communist Party two decades earlier. At its heart, *Waterfront* wasn't about long-shoremen. It was about Kazan and Schulberg, and what they had done. It was their response to the critics and former friends who'd called them stool pigeons, cowards, and worse.

Kazan would admit in his memoirs that in the film the Mob stands in for the Communist Party. When Terry Malloy eventually names the names of Mob members, the director said, it is a heroic act—exactly the way he and Schulberg envisioned their own testimonies. They'd given those names to Congress, both men claimed, for the greater good, to stop the "Reds" from undermining America, just as Terry turns on his friends and even his brother to stop the corruption of the Mob.

Unlike Kazan, Schulberg would always deny any overt connection between his script and his testimony. "To see the film as a metaphor for McCarthyism," he said, "is to trivialize [the] courage" of the men he'd interviewed on the docks. But Kazan freely admitted that Terry's turning "canary" in the film was parallel to his own decision to testify before Congress in April 1952. The two actions, Kazan believed, were morally equivalent. "When Brando at the end yells, 'I'm glad what I done!'" the director wrote in his memoir, "that was me saying, with identical heat, that I was glad I'd testified as I had." And when the other longshoremen turn their backs on Terry, even after his "squealing" has freed them from the Mob, "that, too," Kazan wrote, "was my story, now told to the world."

Everyone on the set was aware of the film's subtext. Kazan "was going to tell his side of the story," said Karl Malden, who played the heroic priest, "or he wasn't going to do the picture."

Much of Hollywood considered Kazan a "rat" at this point. In his first interview with the House committee, Kazan had refused, on principle, to name anyone other than himself. But at his second appearance, pressure from California senator Richard Nixon, among others, had caused him to reconsider. He named eight people with whom he'd shared Communist Party membership in the 1930s: the writer Clifford Odets and actors Lewis Leverett, Art Smith, Phoebe Brand, Morris Carnovsky, Tony Kraber, J. Edward Bromberg, and Paula Miller (Lee Strasberg's wife). The committee already knew their names; Kazan was merely being asked to confirm them, which was partly how he justified his action to himself. Yet others had refused to do even that; writers Ring Lardner, Dalton Trumbo, and other members of the so-called Hollywood Ten served time in prison for their silence.

Under such a threat, Kazan's testimony is not entirely incomprehensible. Yet there's no doubt that by doing so, he made other peoples' lives more difficult. Of the eight he named, Odets provided friendly testimony himself and therefore survived. But the others, less prominent, were cast into various degrees of professional exile. Kraber was fired from his job at CBS; Smith and Leverett saw job opportunities disappear; Carnovsky lost work and was generally shunned. He called his time on the blacklist "revolting, injurious, hurtful."

Among Kazan's friends, there was horror at what he had done. Many had lived through the atrocities of the Holocaust; discretion, confidentiality, and the protection of one's peers were principles they lived by. When Ellen went off to college, Stella had advised her to overlook any indiscretions by her classmates: "As long as you live," she counseled her daughter, "never, never report anybody." This was their doctrine, and they thought it was one Kazan shared.

As a result, many in his circle turned on him. "I'd been snubbed by friends each and every day for many months," Kazan said, recalling the period leading up to *Waterfront*. Several members of the Actors Studio, including Maureen Stapleton, resigned in protest. "I'd not forgotten," Kazan said, unrepentant even decades later, "nor would I forgive the old friends . . . who'd snubbed me."

And one of those who'd snubbed him—not to his face, but in reports Kazan was hearing—was Marlon.

That was why Kazan had been so resistant about approaching him for the role of Terry, and part of the reason he'd argued so forcefully for Paul Newman. When, pressured by Spiegel, Kazan had finally drafted a letter asking Marlon to consider the part, he wrote, "I can't pretend that it's easy or simple to write you. Ultimately, in our little world, everyone hears everything. I will always feel most warmly and devotedly for you, but this does not blot out the things unsaid between us. I will for the time leave them unsaid. I will write you here professionally, and you can behave as you wish from whatever criteria you wish to act from."

The reports Kazan had been hearing about Marlon were true. He was indeed repulsed by his mentor's congressional testimony. He'd learned of it while reading the newspaper in a café on the Champs-Élysées in Paris with Ellen on an April morning in 1952. He was so upset he couldn't finish reading the story; he handed the paper over to Ellen so she could finish reading it to him. Marlon knew some of the people Kazan named; he'd worked with Bromberg on *Come Out Fighting*. Making matters worse, Kazan was completely defiant about what he'd done, taking out an ad in the *New York Times* to run on the same day the news broke, insisting that the American Communist Party took "its orders from the Kremlin" and declaring that the American people needed "the facts about communism." But even if what Kazan said was true, what sort of useful "facts about Communism," Marlon asked Ellen, did the public gain by learning that a few small-time actors had been sympathetic to the cause two decades earlier?

"I can never work with him again," Marlon had said, utterly distraught, when Ellen finished reading him the article. In fact, he didn't think he could ever make another movie. "I don't know how to act for anyone but Gadge," he told Ellen. Kazan had been a god to him, and now his god—like Duke at Shattuck—was revealed to be a fraud. "He squealed on a lot of his friends," Marlon said plainly. That was simply unacceptable. "Squealing" was something Marlon had always instinctively reacted against—as a boy, as a military cadet, but even more so since being taken under the wing of the Adlers. This was abominable.

Shortly after learning the news, Marlon sailed back to America. He did not contact Kazan upon his return. The director took his former protégé's silence for what it was: agreement with the prevailing consensus that Kazan was a rat.

During the making of *Julius Caesar* in the summer of 1952, Marlon continued to struggle with his grief and disillusionment. "What do I do when I see him?" he'd asked the film's director, Joseph Mankiewicz. "Do I bust him in the nose or what?" Attempts by Mankiewicz to console him, or to get him to see things from Kazan's perspective, proved impossible. "What do you say to somebody whose father has just died?" Mankiewicz asked. Marlon had not been lucky with fathers.

So, when Kazan finally approached him about *Waterfront*, Marlon had a tough decision to make. If he wanted to continue doing quality films, then Kazan was his best bet. But he almost certainly knew the director's motives in making the film. In a draft of a letter Kazan may or may not have sent to Marlon before his casting, the director was quite upfront about his intentions: "The moral problem [the film] treats—the social responsibility of a citizen as it comes into conflict with his personal allegiances—is one of the oldest and most universal of all problems a man can face. Make no mistake about it, there is a parallel inference to be drawn to the inquiries into Communist activities." He added, however, that "[t]his parallelism is not the main value of the script. This is a story of a human in torment, and in danger."

Much later, Marlon would insist he'd made the film unaware of the equivalence Kazan was drawing to his own life. "What I didn't realize," he said, "was that *Waterfront* was really a rationale. [Kazan] and Budd Schulberg had both squealed on their pals, named names, and so they got together and [made] this film which symbolized and justified their course of action. I didn't realize that until it was over. [Terry Malloy] squealed on the Mob. The Mob represented the Communists, and I represented the spirit of Kazan." Marlon insisted that the director had never directly admitted this to him, however, as an actor, he had "just perceived it, later."

Yet, even if Kazan had never sent the letter to Marlon in which he explicitly outlined the parallels to his testimony, he was crystal clear about his intent in his notes for the character, notes he routinely shared with his actors. "He hates the gang," Kazan wrote about Terry. "He can't take it. Relate to the testifying. His dignity can only come when he tells what he saw!" Kazan positioned Terry's informing on his pals as a way of reclaiming his manhood: "This is about Terry. A boy becomes a citizen! A man finds his dignity again!" It's hard not to see the analogy he was making to his own life. "The biggest loyalty a man has is to all the people, which in a democracy, is the state," Kazan wrote in his notebook. "The biggest obligation a man has is to be a citizen."

Marlon was sharp: he couldn't have missed this. No matter his later disavowals, he must have understood at least some of what Kazan was doing. He saw how extremely personal and urgent this film was to the director. "What I am especially anxious to show," Kazan wrote to Schulberg, "is that [Terry's] act of sacrifice (both the testifying and the fight) *has a value*. It does benefit the men there because it takes the fear out of their hearts. Terry accomplishes one thing: the men are no longer afraid and to an extent they have even committed themselves to taking sides." That was the outcome Kazan was hoping to bring about for himself: his detractors would see the value of his testimony and, indeed, take his side.

Yet the two situations were *not* parallel, despite Kazan's attempts to make them so; therefore, the film he made was never going to sway many people. Terry witnesses a murder. His ratting on murderous Mob bosses was not at all like snitching on rank-and-file actors whose only "crime" was membership in a political party. If there was any equivalency at all to be made, it's Leverett, Kraber, and Bromberg as the dockworkers being abused by the Mob. If *Waterfront* were a true parallel of Kazan's situation, then Terry would have snitched to the Mob, not to the good guys.

Just why, after his initial moral outrage, Marlon agreed to work with Kazan again remains unclear. The role of Terry was undoubtedly an extraordinary one, and the film, as directed by Kazan, was sure to be quality. But such things were rarely strong motivators for Marlon. Ellen thought his decision had more to do with the psychoanalysis he was undergoing at the time, in which "he was working through his anger, his rage," and "letting go" of grudges. Marlon himself explained, "It's so easy to judge other people, to castigate them for what they did." To condemn Kazan forever, to avoid him and reject him, was not "constructive," as his psychiatrist, Bela Mittelman, explained to him. Mittelman had also been Kazan's analyst, so possibly there was influence there as well. Most influential of all, however, were Stella and Harold, who, offended as they were by Kazan, had decided to forgive their old friend. "They let it be," Ellen said. And so, Marlon did, too, though the relationship with his mentor would never be the same again.

SEAGULLS SWUNG OVER the waterfront. A cold mist rose from the Hudson. On the pier, the director was preparing one more take before the sun was entirely gone. But his star was already peeling off his putty eyelids and calling it quits. In frustration, Rod Steiger, who played the brother of Terry Malloy, swore under his breath. Marlon was getting preferential treatment, he believed. Just days away from finishing the picture, when every second counted, Kazan said nothing as his star headed off the set. This was the agreement they had, however. Every Wednesday at 4:00, no matter what else was needed, Marlon was allowed to leave and see Dr. Mittel-man. A car would take him from Hoboken into Manhattan.

Karl Malden thought Kazan could have insisted that Marlon see Mittelman on the weekend. But the star, Malden believed, was demonstrating who was "in charge." By being a bit of a "heavy" on the set, Malden speculated, Marlon could keep "people who hated what [had] happened" (Kazan's testifying) from thinking he'd "gone over" to the director's side.

In the face of Marlon's belligerence, Kazan bit his tongue. The picture was too important to him to risk alienating his lead actor. But inwardly, the resentment built. "I remember on *Waterfront*," Kazan wrote to Marlon years later, "where you told me repeatedly while we were shooting the picture that you weren't enthusiastic about it and were only making the picture 'because your psycho-analyst was in New York' and that you wanted to make enough to pay his bills while still remaining in that city." When rumors of Marlon's discontent turned up in the papers, Kazan was hurt. "I differ from more rational men," he wrote to Marlon in 1967, "in that I always believe the columns." But at the time, he said nothing.

It was a sad reunion of two artists who had done so much for each other. Few actor-director teams have ever been so potent or influential. Together, Brando and Kazan had changed the American theater. How very different their relationship was now, in 1954, from three years earlier, when they'd made the film version of *Streetcar* for Warner Bros., and set about transforming the American screen.

Reconfiguring the play for film had restored Marlon's enthusiasm for the story, which meant he could bring entirely new dimensions to Stanley. The intimacy of the camera had stimulated him. "In movies," Kazan explained, "much more than on the stage, you are dealing not with words and actions but what's going on in the hearts and feelings of the characters." The camera, he believed, could "photograph thoughts and feelings." That's true in the film of *A Streetcar Named Desire*. Even more so than in *The Men*, Marlon's face comes alive on the screen: at times he is wistful and vulnerable; at other times he's threatening and desperate.

The stage version of *Streetcar* had been Blanche's story. But the film has no choice but to make the photogenic, intense Stanley, as played by Marlon, an equal point of focus. This is apparent even in the movie's poster, where Stanley looms large over Blanche, essentially snatching top billing away from her. Had Jessica Tandy reprised the role, the character of Blanche might have been completely overshadowed. Fortunately, however, alone among the main cast members, Tandy was replaced by a more established movie name, Vivien Leigh, whose Blanche convincingly wrestles Stanley for domination of the screen.

To Marlon, Leigh was far preferable as Blanche, in large part because she held her own against him. "I've always thought it was perfect casting," he said. "In many ways, she *was* Blanche . . . very much Tennessee's wounded butterfly." Yet, underneath her fragility, there's a fire burning in Leigh's Blanche, which makes her eventual extinguishment by Stanley all the more tragic. Like Tandy, however, another stage-trained British actress, Leigh had some trouble in the beginning adjusting to Marlon's unpredictability. She complained to Kazan that she never knew "what he's going to do next, where he's going or what he's going to say." Eventually, however, "she got over it," the director said, and acknowledged the powerful performance her costar was giving.

Released in September 1951, *A Streetcar Named Desire* was a box-office smash. The picture "throbs with passion and poignancy," wrote Bosley Crowther, who judged it "as fine [as], if not finer, than the play" (even though, much as Kazan fought it, the Production Code eliminated the more graphic moments and lines). Leigh "has created a new Blanche du Bois on the screen," Crowther observed, "a woman of even greater fullness, torment and tragedy." Marlon was "no less brilliant." Now that "we're so much closer to him," the critic observed, "he seems that much more highly charged, his despairs seem that much more pathetic and his comic moments that much more slyly enjoyed." The following March—just a month before Kazan's HUAC testimony—Leigh, Karl Malden, and Kim Hunter all won Oscars for their roles. Only Marlon and Kazan were left empty-handed. Fitting, perhaps, because in that halcyon period, they still thought of themselves as a team.

After *Streetcar*, Marlon could have had his pick of scripts and directors, but he didn't want to work with anyone other than Gadge. He was idle for nearly five months, rebuffing offers to return to Broadway as Romeo to Olivia de Havilland's Juliet and to star opposite Montgomery Clift in the Howard Hawks Western *The Big Sky*, for RKO Pictures. Only Kazan could get Marlon back to work, and by the late spring of 1951, he was sweating through ninety-degree heat with his mentor on the rocky mesas of Texas and Colorado playing Mexican revolutionary Emiliano Zapata.

*Viva Zapata!* was another political treatise close to Kazan's heart. Made before his congressional testimony, the film comes close to celebrating communism. Scripted by John Steinbeck, whose pro-Soviet sympathies were well known, the film valorizes Zapata, a socialist hero. "The theme of this movie," Kazan scrawled in his notebooks, "is 'No strong man—a strong people!,'" a slogan that unnerved the front offices of Twentieth Century–Fox, the studio releasing the picture. It suggested revolution. There were other concerns as well. "Here again we mention the word 'peace,'" Darryl Zanuck wrote to Kazan. "This is the word the Soviets have adopted as their own. The very use of it today for some strange, peculiar reason makes the user sound like a Red." To placate his boss, Kazan argued that by walking away from power, Zapata reveals he is no Communist, as "no Communist has ever done it, nor ever will." Yet he was making a picture about a revolutionary who overthrows the state; Kazan's allegiance to the state, so earnestly articulated some years later in *Waterfront*, is nowhere to be found here.

When *Viva Zapata!* was released in February 1952, some called it "pro-Red." After Kazan found himself in the crosshairs of Congress, he eagerly pointed out that the Socialists had had troubles with *Zapata!*, too: "The gist of the thing is," he said, "we were attacked in Mexico by the left, who thought we were not making our hero an undeviating enough character. In New York, we were attacked by the extreme right, who say the picture is class angled." In a folder marked "HUAC" in his personal files, Kazan kept a clipping from the *Daily Worker*, the official American Communist Party organ, which complained that the film pulled too many punches. Kazan had "falsified" the Mexican Revolution by being too vague about its politics: "Truth has become anti-American in Hollywood," the *Worker* charged, "permanently blacklisted, not to be brought before the American people." Kazan may have kept the clipping as evidence that he was no "Red."

The real problem of the film, however, is in its simplistic, almost naïve rationale for democracy and the often heavy-handed dialogue and exaggerated acting used to make its arguments. Anthony Quinn would win an Oscar for playing Zapata's doomed, hotheaded brother, but his outsize performance lacks the subtlety of Marlon's, though they play off each other well. (Quinn, who'd been Stanley Kowalski in the touring company of *Streetcar*, had desperately wanted the starring part in *Zapata*; his bitterness caused him to spurn Marlon's attempts at friendship, according to Rita Moreno, who dated both men.) There's also the racism so typical of films of the period, which the *Daily Worker*, alone, commented upon: all the major actors (with the exception of Quinn, who was Mexican) were played by Anglos slathered in brown pancake makeup. The writer of the *Worker* piece, Harry Wyllis, observed sarcastically, "Didn't Marlon Brando show in his lumpenproletarian role in *A Streetcar Named Desire* that he can act the part of a scowling, impulsive, inarticulate half-savage? And the publicity blurbs boast that Brando wore plugs in his nostrils to flare them out and make him look more like the real Zapata. What more could a Mexican want?"

Indeed, at times, Marlon is unrecognizable in the makeup and nose prosthetics. In New York, producer Cheryl Crawford saw some prerelease stills and observed to Kazan that Marlon looked "very sinister or noble," she couldn't "quite tell which." And whatever accent Marlon attempted in the film, it wasn't Mexican. (The Mexicans, of course, speak English throughout the movie.) Yet he remains compelling, from the very first glimpse we get of him, emerging from a group of farmers demanding justice. His natural gestures, expressions, and tone stand out from those of the more theatrical day players around him. When he's being led to execution, a rope over his neck, he's almost disturbingly sexy, striding confidently in his tight pants, a knowing smirk on his face.

Once again, Marlon owns the camera; audiences can't take their eyes off him, even when the script, for the most part competent, veers into triteness, notably the contrived courtship scenes with Jean Peters, who plays Zapata's wife. After the sexual realism of *Streetcar*, these moments, played for humor, seem lifted from another era. They don't serve the story, and are there for only one reason: the producer believed audiences would want a romance amid all the gunfighting. "We want to turn on the juice whenever we get a chance between Josefa and Zapata," Zanuck wrote to Kazan. "By juice I mean sex. If we don't actually see it, we must smell it and know it is there. Marlon Brando is playing the role and if he doesn't make love to her, somebody is going to throw a brick at us."

Marlon was an unlikely choice to play Zapata, but Kazan still believed at that point that his leading man could play anything. In this immediate post-*Streetcar* period, both men remained each other's greatest champion. As usual, Marlon devoured Kazan's notes in his development of the character. No wonder he couldn't imagine working with another director, for who else took such care? "It is about a man who has leadership forced upon him," Kazan instructed him about Zapata. "It is about a man who was *half* a leader and knew it!" In this, Marlon could relate very well: greatness had been forced upon him, too, and he believed on some level that he was "only half as good as people said he was," as Maureen Stapleton observed.

*Zapata* received positive reviews, though a few singled out its tendency to romanticize and to mix "the realities of revolution . . . with abstract ideas." The *Chicago Tribune* thought its "occasional lapses into symbolism" were "overdone." But, as was so often the case, even those critics who had quibbles with the film loved Marlon. He was "sensitive, cruelly honest, provocatively passionate"; he was "violent and smoldering by turns, courageous and baffled, but ever interesting"; he made the film into "something besides a lively political treatise."

Yet the consensus was also that the film was too dark to make much money. The early 1950s viewed rebellion as unpatriotic, something that needed to be stifled; as a result, the film underperformed. The *Hartford Courant* opined that *Viva Zapata!* would add to Marlon's "artistic stature, but not to his box-office draw."

Marlon didn't care. Once a project was done, Ellen Adler said, whether it made money or not was immaterial to him. (He'd already been paid, after all, and this was before actors made anything on the back end.) For Marlon, when a film was over, he could go back to his "real life," Ellen said, to the things that mattered. He was still caught in a battle that pitted fame and success on one side and himself on the other; he might have been "burning for it," as Ellen observed, but he also hated himself for the fire.

There'd been one other line that Gadge had given him about Zapata that almost certainly resonated for Marlon beyond the character he was playing. "It's too late now to get what he really wants," Kazan wrote about the Mexican rebel. "He gives up hope of life . . . in fact, he feels *he has not lived his life but someone else's.*" That was precisely what Marlon often said to his friends: "Some other guy would love this chance to be a great actor," he told Jack Larson, an actor he'd met when he first went to Los Angeles. "But I'm not some other guy."

ON A NIGHT during the third weekend of January 1954, a party spilled out from an apartment on the eighth floor of one of the towers above Carnegie Hall, and instead of complaining, neighbors opened their doors and joined in. In the warren of studios that rose atop the fabled concert hall, artists, actors, and musicians made their homes and practiced their crafts. Over the past sixty years, Agnes de Mille, George Balanchine, Isadora Duncan, and Marilyn Monroe had lived or studied there. Enrico Caruso had made his first recording there. Currently, Leonard Bernstein was a resident; neighbors often heard his piano tinkling late into the night. Acclaimed violinists practiced in the halls; avant-garde photographers asked neighbors to critique their prints. The Carnegie towers housed a fraternity of fame.

So, on this night, when Marlon Brando, in Suite 801, threw a party to celebrate completing his film *Waterfront*, the whole building turned out. People packed the small flat, standing shoulder to shoulder throughout the living room as well as the alcove he used as a workout space, equipped with barbells. Half a dozen guests squeezed onto his couch, which still bore chew marks from Russell, his pet raccoon. A couple of rowdy friends banged his bongos, which Marlon kept in a corner.

"It was such a magical moment in time," said Kaye Ballard, who was there for the party, along with many of the old "37 West Fifty-Second Street Regulars." The band of friends, once poverty-stricken, had done quite well for themselves. "Everybody was following their hearts and their dreams," Ballard remembered. At the moment, she was rehearsing for a much-anticipated Off-Broadway musical, *The Golden Apple*. Maureen Stapleton, also present at the party that night, had just finished a run on Broadway as Lady Anne in *Richard III*, opposite José Ferrer. Wally Cox, seated on the arm of Marlon's chair, had hit it big in television, starring in his own comedy show, *Mister Peepers*. Marlon's sister Jocelyn ("Tidd"), passing out hors d'oeuvres, had returned to New York and resumed her career; over the past few years, she'd landed a series of standout roles on Broadway, notably in *Mister Roberts*.

Less successful old friends showed up as well. Freddie Fiore was there, mixing drinks for everybody. After his stint as Marlon's stand-in on *Waterfront*, during which he'd frequently snuck off the set to score some heroin, Marlon wanted to keep his old friend close; he was determined to help him kick the habit. "Marlon was incredibly loyal," Ballard said. "He didn't forget someone just because they hadn't made it big themselves." He seemed to take responsibility for them, as if he felt guilty they hadn't received the same breaks he had. He'd arranged for Darren Dublin to play bits in *Julius Caesar* and *The Wild One*, and for Carmelita Pope to understudy Kim Hunter on *Streetcar*. After Hunter left to make the film version, Pope took over the part of Stella, staying with the show through August 1949.

Of course, Marlon also had a girlfriend at the party. That was simply de rigueur. But no one could quite remember which one. At the time, he was ending a relationship with the Mexican actress Movita (born Maria Luisa Castaneda), the star of such 1930s movies as *Flying Down to Rio* and *Mutiny on the Bounty*, and eight years Marlon's senior. He was also starting one with Josanne Mariani, a French au pair eleven years his junior. "It was probably Josanne" who was there, one friend said, "because she started living at the Carnegie Hall studio around this time." But Movita, the friend said, "was still in Marlon's orbit." Indeed, one columnist had recently reported how Movita had helped Marlon "make his 57th Street apartment prettier," a redecoration he'd resented for its assumption of domesticity.

One figure, however, was notable by his absence. Elia Kazan

was nowhere in sight. For Kazan, the film hadn't wrapped; he still had another week or so of shooting to complete. Marlon had finished his scenes early, by agreement, so he could get out to Los Angeles and start *The Egyptian*. Yet several others from the cast and crew of *Waterfront* were present, Marlon's friend remembered: it was clear that "Marlon didn't want [Kazan] there," the friend said. "There was distance. It hadn't been a happy shoot."

When Marlon left the set earlier that week, it had been an anticlimactic ending to seven years of an extraordinary partnership. At the last minute, as Freddie Fiore recalled, Kazan had called after his star, offering Marlon one final bit of directorial advice: "Don't forget to wet your lips when the camera starts to roll!"

But, in fact, Marlon wasn't looking to Kazan for advice anymore.

Once, he'd thought Kazan was the only director he could work with. Now he was returning to Hollywood to labor under Michael Curtiz, who was known for swashbucklers and musicals and wartime spy dramas. After that, who knew? In any event, there was no talk of future work with Kazan.

As for *Waterfront*, Marlon remained ambivalent. It had been an arduous shoot, and he was exhausted. As significant as the role had been, he hadn't relished playing Terry Malloy. When a fellow actor assumed he took joy in playing such meaty characters, Marlon replied, "Actually, no. If you're playing a heavy, serious part, you really can't get too far away from your part, and the mood, and it's tedious work." On *Waterfront*, he said, "I was never more miserable in my life."

At his party, someone offered a toast to the picture's success. "Marlon just shrugged," Ballard said, "as if he truly did not care." Part of his reaction was his usual indifference to his profession; part of it was probably lingering disillusionment with Kazan. But part of it was also, most likely, an act. Making *Waterfront* may have been agony, and it may have been tedious to sustain the "heavy, serious mood," just as it had been on *Streetcar*, but as always, "after the thing is over," Marlon admitted, came "satisfaction—if I've accomplished what I wanted to." And he had to know that *Waterfront* was an extraordinary film.

If he had learned anything in the five years he'd been making movies, it was how to recognize quality. He'd been part of some excellent productions and some not-so-excellent ones, and he could tell the difference. For all his dismay over Kazan, he knew their work together was valuable. "I am indebted to him for all that I learned," he would say late in life. So, surely he knew that *Waterfront*—its script, its direction, its cinematography, its design, and its acting—was first-rate. Perhaps the finest project he had ever been a part of, or might ever be.

Yet his friend was right: it hadn't been a happy shoot. There'd been none of those inspired tête-à-têtes with Kazan as there had been on earlier projects, those "very creative fights" that had so invigorated actor and director, where Marlon would take something, work on it, and then bring it back to Kazan. Perhaps such exertion was no longer necessary. Working together for so long, Kazan and Marlon had become sympatico; few words were needed between them. "It comes alive better," Marlon would say, describing the process of working with a director whose vision he implicitly trusted, "if the director knows exactly what I'm trying to do, and I know what he's trying to do, and we achieve it together." As a man and as a citizen, Kazan may have been diminished in Marlon's eyes. But as an artist, the director had few peers, and Marlon knew that all too well.

As always, he'd read Kazan's notes about the character closely. He'd listened carefully to his thoughts on motive, plot, and action. And together, just as they had created Stanley Kowalski, they had created Terry Malloy.

IN THE BEGINNING, Kazan wrote, Terry was a "regular, nice guy, a good fellow. He runs with the pack. He is a medium-sized hero in the pack and he'd rather give up everything and anything including his dignity and self-worth rather [*sic*] than lose his position in the gang." Where Stanley Kowalski was the center of his gang, "Terry is lonely, by himself," Kazan wrote in notes specific for Marlon. Stanley was essentially "un-self-questioning, un-self-doubting, unaware," whereas Terry "is all three." Stanley's "growing self-awareness makes him confused, defensive and mean," while "Terry's growing self-confidence makes him stronger, a more direct and honest man."

Marlon had specifically requested these character comparisons from the director. They would prove essential for his performance. "As a kid," Kazan wrote about Terry, "he felt homeless, unwanted, even scorned, inferior to the rest of mankind. Fighting was his move for recognition. It was his bid for a place in the sun against a world from which he had been shut out from birth. When he fought, he was 'someone.'" Terry was also lonely, Kazan told Marlon, a "fundamental" quality that was needed to understand him. "Consider he lives alone in one small room. Consider he has no girl." His only sustenance, Kazan pointed out, was his gang.

Once again, Marlon could harness considerable autobiography in his creation of a character: Kazan's description fit him to a *T*. Marlon could relate to Terry's loneliness, his bursts of rage, his sense of isolation and unworthiness. Except for the brief time with his mother on West End Avenue, Marlon had lived only in tiny studios since coming to New York. And while he had many girls, they were largely transient, even marginal to his life, with no one but Ellen ever really penetrating the armor. Only with his band of friends—mostly male, except for nonsexual buddies like Maureen, Janice, and Kaye—did Marlon, like Terry, ever find any approximation of home. Working with Kazan, Marlon created Terry Malloy out of broken fragments of his life, tied together by the ribbons of his imagination.

Marlon might dismiss such an extraordinary achievement, try

to trivialize it, and push back against the idea that it had anything to do with art. But others on the set, watching Terry come to life, responded to Marlon's efforts with awe. For Karl Malden, it was Marlon's work with the pigeons on a Hoboken roof that made his genius so clear. "There was something Marlon did with those pigeons that I don't think any other actor could do," Malden said. "He loved them. You knew that he loved them. He was just beautiful with that." It was easy for an actor to connect with a dog, "but pigeons!" Malden exclaimed. "That was something."

Malden had no patience when Marlon would start belittling his own work. When Marlon would call acting "a survival mechanism" or dismiss it as "a social lubricant," Malden would steam. Marlon clung to his assertion that *everybody acts*: "We act to save our lives every day by not saying something that [we] think or . . . don't think." But Malden had a decidedly different view. "[Marlon's] whole idea was: we're acting every day, there is no difference" between what everyday people do and what professional actors do. "In that case," Malden said, "let's hire a kid. Go do it, kid." He laughed at the insanity of it. "A professional knows where to take the script and peak it, or how to give it some interesting things for the audience to take it through. That's a *talent*. It's *not* just acting every day."

Consider, Malden argued, the scene where Terry breaks into the flat of his girlfriend, played by Eva Marie Saint, who's just discovered his connection to the Mob (and to her brother's death). "That scene was all Marlon," said Malden. "I think [Eva] was a little frightened of him." In the scene, Terry is very aggressive, insisting his girlfriend face him and what he did. They kiss passionately, and according to Malden, Saint was terrified: Marlon's reputation as a womanizer preceded him. "But he was so good," Malden said, "that she gave in [and] really went with it." Saint corroborated his account. "I was so nervous, I cried a little," she said. But the scene, largely improvised, turned out "beautiful," she said, and Marlon "was a dear."

His most powerful moment in the film, however, was one that would slip into legend, and it wouldn't have happened if Marlon had done what actors were supposed to do: follow the script.

IN THE BACKSEAT of a taxi, Terry's Mob-controlled brother, Charley, played by Rod Steiger, pulls a gun on him. This is the moment in the script when Terry realizes just how low they've fallen, and how different his life might have been, if only Charley had looked out for him, if only they'd been able to escape the prisons of their disadvantaged lives. To convey this, Schulberg had written some powerful dialogue for Terry to deliver when he realizes his brother's betrayal—words that melt Charley's heart and cause him to let Terry go.

Yet just how that pivotal scene would play out in the final film, and whether it was writer, director, or actor who shaped it most, would become a matter of some dispute.

As drafts of the script reveal, the scene went through several rewrites. In the earliest versions, Terry says nothing at all to prompt Charley's change of heart; Charley backs down out of his own guilt. By the time Marlon got the script, however, the scene had been rewritten as Terry's cri de cœur. When Charley pulls the gun, he says he's sorry it's come to this. He wishes the guy who'd managed Terry's prizefighting career had done a better job—implying that if he had, they wouldn't have sunk so low. But Terry replies, "It was *you*, Charley!" Schulberg's script directions at that point read: "Years of abuse" come "crying out" of Terry. The fights Charley made him throw for the "short-end money" had gotten him only "a one-way ticket to Palookaville," he laments. Charley counters that he always placed a bet for Terry, which makes his brother explode: "You don't understand! I could have had class. I could have been a contender. I could have been somebody. Instead of a bum. Which is what I am, let's face it." Then he delivers the knockout punch: "It was you, Charley." Broken, his brother lets him escape from the taxi.

This was the dialogue Marlon would have read when the script was sent to him that previous summer, dialogue he would have been very familiar with by the time shooting began. But in the days leading up to the scene, he'd started to grumble about the script to anyone who would listen. Schulberg didn't know what his exact objections were, but he'd had enough of his bellyaching, so he got Kazan to call a meeting between the three of them.

In later years, Marlon would remember his objection to the scene in this way. The audience, he said, would not believe that Terry's brother, his protector for so long, was going to shoot him in the backseat of a cab. "That's absolutely absurd," Marlon recalled for his memoir. To fix the absurdity, he claimed he'd had to change "the scene around completely." He and Steiger, he alleged, were forced to rewrite much of it. "Gadge let me do it that way. I convinced him."

When Schulberg read this, nearly forty years after the film was made, he blew his top. He remembered Marlon's objections to the taxi scene very differently. What troubled Marlon at the time, Schulberg argued, wasn't the idea that Terry's brother might pull a gun on him (the script had clearly prepared the audience for that), but that Terry would, in response, deliver that great, impassioned "I could've been a contender" monologue with a revolver stuck between his ribs. (In the original script, Charley doesn't lower the gun until after Terry has finished speaking.) "Nobody," Schulberg remembered Marlon insisting at the meeting Kazan called between the three of them, "would go on talking if a gun is aimed at you." Both screenwriter and director agreed that the objection was reasonable, so Kazan suggested that Steiger lower the gun before Marlon starts to speak. In red pen, he scrawled, "Charlie [sic] lowers the pistol" after Terry reacts in disbelief at what is happening and murmurs his brother's name. That small red notation would seem to prove that Schulberg's memory was correct and that Marlon, as was sometimes his habit, was remembering events the way he wanted them to be.

In fact, it's more complex than that. Marlon *did* rewrite that scene in small yet significant ways, even if the dialogue remained largely as Schulberg composed it. Since Marlon never rigidly memorized his lines, he'd often move a phrase from one part of a sentence to another, or omit a couple of words, or add an interjection, allowing for a more natural flow. This was something Kazan had always encouraged. "If you're just waiting to say your line, it's not real," Marlon explained. He didn't learn lines so much as learn the emotion: "You have an idea of it," he said, "and you're saying it [even if] you can't remember what the hell it is." The only exception to this practice, he said, was Shakespeare, "where the language has value."

Budd Schulberg's language, apparently, was not valued so highly. The "contender" speech, for example, reads this way in the final bound shooting script: "I could've been a contender. I could've had class and been somebody. Real class! Instead of a bum, let's face it, which is what I am." But in the film, Marlon delivers the lines as: "I could've had class. I could've been a contender. I could've been somebody. Instead of a bum. Which is what I am, let's face it." Marlon was speaking the lines as if they'd just come to him, rather than as memorized dialogue. The cadence is both more poetic and more real.

So, Marlon's memory that he had changed the scene around and that Gadge had let him do it isn't entirely off base. When the cameras started rolling, Marlon didn't wait for Steiger to lower the gun, as Kazan had indicated with his red pen. Instead, the action seemed more natural, more in character, for Terry to do it himself. In a subtle, almost unnoticed gesture at the bottom of the frame, Marlon lowers Steiger's gun, then goes on to deliver

the speech that history would record as one of the greatest moments in film.

They weren't sitting in a real taxi during the scene, but rather,
in "an old beaten-up prop from a TV studio," Steiger recalled. For
all their obvious chemistry, the two actors weren't fond of each
other. The taxi scene took seven takes to shoot because Steiger,
immersed in his character, couldn't stop crying. "He's one of those
actors who loves to cry," Marlon recalled. "We kept doing it over
and over." Frustrated, Marlon bolted as soon as all his scenes were
complete, which meant that Steiger was left to shoot his close-ups
without his scene partner, a courtesy most actors gave to each
other. Steiger had been there for Marlon's close-ups, feeding him
reaction lines. "Acting is basically reacting," Steiger remembered,
"so it all depends on who's off-camera to help you." With Marlon
gone, he had to settle for the stage manager, whom he called terrible. "That son of a gun," Steiger said of Marlon. "It was like a
wounding. I couldn't believe that a man of his talent would walk
out." Steiger would carry a grudge over Marlon's snub for the rest
of his life. Whenever he'd see Eva Marie Saint, he'd bring it up,
until she finally told him to get over it.

Steiger might not have been a fan, but Karl Malden, watching
Marlon's performance with fascinated eyes, certainly was, and his
admiration only increased as he watched Marlon during production. "If I knew what made him tick," Malden said, "I would have
stolen it from him and used it. But I'll be damned if I could figure
out what he did, because you never knew what the hell he was
going to do."

As a case in point, he cited a tiny, telling moment in the taxi
scene that wasn't in any version of the script. It comes right after
Terry lowers the gun and Charley sits back. Terry looks away, his
left hand coming to his face, and mutters, "Wow." Just a simple
little sound, hardly more than a whisper, made in disbelief that
his brother would betray him. "This is where his genius comes

through," Malden said. "You know exactly what he's thinking . . . He put himself in the situation." Marlon wasn't reciting dialogue; he was inhabiting Terry Malloy, and Terry him, and that's how you act, not through any method or memorization.

Schulberg, whose script Marlon was using as a springboard, was generally very proprietary and protective of his words. But even he acknowledged, when Malden pointed it out to him, how Marlon's little ad-lib was perfect, how it contained everything these two brothers had been through. "It was a very pregnant 'wow,'" Schulberg admitted. And it could only have come from the mouth of the actor playing the part, not the typewriter of the dramatist writing it. Marlon, Schulberg conceded, "hears it more than he sees it." That simple "wow"—so small, so human, so formidable—exemplifies everything that made Marlon Brando the actor great.

**FEBRUARY 4** / Marlon pulled the blinds down in his apartment and crawled into bed. Cookie crumbs littered his sheets. Empty Coca-Cola bottles lay on the floor. He hadn't left the place in days. He told friends he was withdrawing from the world.

The telephone rang, but he didn't answer. It was probably Jay Kanter calling, telling him that Darryl Zanuck was demanding he show up for work on *The Egyptian*. But Marlon wasn't going back out there. He'd made a quick trip to Hollywood on January 17, participating in a cast reading of the script, but a week later, on January 24, he'd returned to New York, where, ever since, he'd hidden behind closed blinds. He could no longer play the Hollywood game.

*The Egyptian* was scheduled to start shooting that very morning.

Instead, Marlon pulled the sheets over his head, letting the phone ring off the hook.

The trauma had come back. Once again, the darkness threatened to overtake him. For the past few years, amid all the hustle and bustle of moviemaking, Marlon had managed to keep the "intervals of anxiety and depression," as he called them, under control. But lately he would sometimes panic and fall to the floor, frozen in fear until he gradually started breathing normally again. "My life [was] a mess," he said a few years later, describing these terrible weeks of early 1954.

After *Streetcar*, he'd been "burning" for success, but "once success happened," Ellen Adler said, "I think he was really horrified." Maureen Stapleton said "the bullshit" simply wore him down: the lack of anonymity; the constant pawing at him; and the different, inauthentic way he was treated now that he was famous. "That was the worst thing," Stapleton said. For someone who had no tolerance for phonies, not being treated "like a normal person" was "soul-killing."

Had he lived in France, Ellen speculated, he might have handled the fame better. "The French have no celebrity," Ellen said. The actor Gérard Philipe "could just wander through the streets, and they let him go. No big fuss." By contrast, Marlon would walk into a restaurant in New York—or worse, Los Angeles—and the whole place would explode in an uproar. "He would be so annoyed," Ellen remembered. He'd witnessed the more casual approach to celebrity in Europe and couldn't understand why America had to be so different. "Travel made him more worldly, more sophisticated," Maureen Stapleton pointed out. "He wanted the country to be more intelligent. He wasn't the naïve kid from Nebraska anymore."

Yet, in those moments when he was lying on the floor, unable to move, he might as well have been.

Marlon's psychiatrist, Dr. Mittelman, had cabled Zanuck on

February 2 and described his patient as very ill, unable "to work for a period of at least ten weeks." Zanuck had offered to fly Mittelman to Hollywood so he could be on hand for Marlon as he made the picture, but the offer was declined. Zanuck was enraged. Accommodating Marlon's whims had become standard practice in Hollywood, but a ten-week delay, with the film ready to roll, would cripple the production.

Finally Marlon's telephone stopped ringing. Late that afternoon, Twentieth Century–Fox released a statement to the press that they were suing the actor to recover the amount that would be lost due to "the delay he has caused to the production." This was the first time, Zanuck told a reporter, he'd ever agreed with "instituting a suit against a film player."

The studio chief was convinced there was nothing physically or mentally wrong with Marlon. Yet Zanuck also categorically refused to concede that this could be, as some columnists were alleging, a matter of Marlon turning down inferior material. In a letter to Elia Kazan, Zanuck claimed that Marlon hadn't objected to the script when he'd done the read-through. Rather, he'd had a problem "working with another man who was assigned to the production," a man Zanuck did not identify, a claim that is impossible to sustain. Of course, it was highly unlikely that the studio chief would admit to Kazan, against whom he bore a grudge over *Waterfront*, that there could possibly be any question about the quality of the script or the picture.

Had *The Egyptian* been another *Waterfront*—or *Julius Caesar*—perhaps Marlon would have found a way, despite his depression, to soldier through it. No doubt the picture's lack of caliber had contributed to his decision to break his contract. Just a couple of months earlier, in fact, he had written to cinematographer James Wong Howe about a book that had "entranced" him, *Fifth Chinese Daughter*, by Jade Snow Wong, suggesting the story could make "an absorbing and warming film." Marlon added, "Perhaps we could do it together." So, just a short time earlier, he had not been averse to making movies if he deemed the material worthy.

Yet, that cold, damp February of 1954, with icy rain beating against his windows, Marlon's illness was real. Zanuck was wrong. The star's breakdown was genuine and severe. Even Zanuck had noted "his exhaustion and nervous condition" at the read-through. When he got back to New York, Marlon had collapsed. Fame had left him "isolated and a little alone," he'd remember, and there was no one currently in his life he could turn to for comfort.

As in past breakdowns, the final crisis that broke him was once more a very personal one. The burdens of success were terrible enough to bear, but it was, once again, as Marlon would acknowledge, "woman troubles" that had brought him down. In one fan magazine, gossip maven Louella Parsons named Movita as the woman whose departure had left Marlon "emotionally upset." Parsons was wrong. In fact, it was the same two women as before, Celia and Ellen—the ones who went back the farthest with him, who meant the most to him, who shared so much history with him—who had left Marlon prostrate on the floor.

WHEN MARLON HAD first gone out to Hollywood, columnists took note of the striking, stylish brunette who was always at his side. Down on her luck, Celia had accepted a job as his secretary, and almost immediately, rumors of a romance took off. "Marlon Brando will wed Celia Webb (a non-pro) in the summer," one columnist forecast in March 1948. Two years later, the items were still turning up, though some scribes were getting wiser: "People here would have you believe," a jaded Hedda Hopper wrote in May 1950, "that Marlon Brando is still proposing to Celia Webb, and she's still turning him down." Celia would have married Marlon in a heartbeat—she was still in love with him, and the loss of their child bound him to her, friends thought—but she'd become a little jaded herself, observing the parade in and out of Marlon's bedroom of "in-between love affairs, friendly lovers," as one of those who came and went, Shelley Winters, described the situation.

Marlon had always preferred inconsequential sex, and now that he could have, almost literally, any woman he wanted, he took advantage of it: one more of fame's gift horses he was not about to look in the mouth. Most of the women he slept with understood this wasn't about love or romance. "I really couldn't compete with all his sexual commitments," Winters recalled; "nor did I want to." But for Celia, with her particular history, watching the parade eventually became too much. In April 1951, she left Marlon's employ, and his inner circle, moving to Paris, where her ex-husband now lived, sometimes with their son. Gossip columnists, of course, jumped all over the separation. "The romance twixt Marlon Brando and Celia Webb has iced," one reported, "and she's off to Europe to forget." Dorothy Kilgallen, queen of the New York tattlers, predicted Marlon would "pop the $64 question" to Celia, "the object of his affections," on his next trip abroad.

That was nonsense, of course. But Celia's loss nonetheless stung. She was a link to his past, to the days before fame. Marlon would continue to feel responsible for her welfare, sending her money and making a place for her whenever she came back to the States. "It wasn't that he couldn't love," said Kaye Ballard. "He loved some of [his women] very much. He just couldn't show it very well." For all his sexual adventuring, what Marlon craved most, many friends averred, was affection, nurturance, and constancy; Celia's departure left a real void. And the cycle persisted. To console himself, Marlon continued the compulsive sexual activity that had driven her away in the first place.

Ellen thought the role of "great lothario" was as wearing on Marlon as the role of "great actor." To be sure, he loved sex, but after a while, the merry-go-round overwhelmed even him. "He was mythologized for the great acting, but also as this sex symbol," Ellen said. "He would walk through Grand Central Station and women would open their shirts. I think that destroyed him. He was completely unprepared for that." Deep down, Ellen believed, he had a longing for something else, something more lasting and substantial.

Her belief was confirmed during the summer of 1953.

This was the period just before Marlon started on *Waterfront*. Ellen was home from Paris for a few months, and they'd started seeing each other again. For Marlon, being with Ellen was effortless. No other woman except for Celia went as far back with him; no other woman knew him as well, or remembered what he had been like before the monstrosity of fame. Ellen wasn't a friendly sexual tryst like Shelley Winters; nor was she a slap-on-the-back buddy like Maureen Stapleton. She also wasn't an exotic, publicity-ready romance like Movita. With Ellen, Marlon could talk about his dreams and his anxieties. He could read poetry and debate politics. With Ellen, he could admit that he didn't know something and not feel inferior; he didn't feel threatened when she challenged him or told him he was being foolish. So, when it came time for her to head back to Paris, and Marlon took her to the plane, their good-bye was wrenching.

Then and there, they made a decision: "We would try something," Ellen said, "try to be together." She flew off to Paris believing the great love of her teenage years had come back to her. Indeed, they had a lovely, if brief, reconnection when Marlon visited that summer. Ellen made plans to return to the States after he had finished *Waterfront*, so they could pick up where they left off.

And so, on February 3, 1954—just a day before Twentieth Century–Fox filed its lawsuit—Ellen stepped off the *Île de France* and onto the pier at West Forty-Eighth Street. She rang Marlon immediately. But he didn't answer his phone. She tried again, and then again. He never picked up.

Lying in bed, his shades drawn, Marlon knew the caller on the other end of the line was either his agent or Ellen. And he couldn't bear to speak to either one.

Because, as it turned out, he wasn't alone in that apartment above Carnegie Hall. Josanne Mariani was there, doing her best to take care of him, to coax him out of his depression. Josanne, however, knew only the movie star Marlon. Unlike Ellen, she didn't know what to say to cheer him, or what the root causes of his anxiety were. She was very young, barely eighteen years old, and the world of celebrity was new and alien to her. Just a couple of years earlier, Josanne, the stepdaughter of a fisherman, had been an artist's model in Bandol, a tiny commune on the southeastern coast of France. One day, she was swept up by an admiring tourist, New York psychiatrist Daniel Schneider, who insisted that the petite, olive-skinned, dark-haired gamine return with him to the United States as an au pair for his children. A theater aficionado, Schneider was the author of the book *The Psychoanalyst and the Artist* and a lecturer at the American Theatre Wing. No surprise, then, that he would encourage his protégée to study acting. And, Schneider decided, only the very best teacher in New York would do: Stella Adler.

At a party Stella hosted in December 1953, Josanne had stood bashfully in a corner. Marlon had spotted her, and asked her to dance. "I recognized him," Josanne recalled, six decades later, "but knew nothing about him—including his previous love affairs." Over the next few days, Marlon wooed Josanne with Chinese restaurants and Harlem jazz clubs and his irresistible dimples. Learning of her arrangement with Schneider, he set up a meeting with the psychiatrist. As Josanne sat by passively, the two men discussed her fate, like tribal chieftains bartering for a bride. At the end of their discussion, Schneider informed her that Marlon "would be taking care of her from then on." Dutifully, Josanne packed her bags. "I've never been inclined to ask questions," she said, looking back.

Just days later, Dorothy Kilgallen, who had spies everywhere, reported that Marlon was "in a trance over a French girl" who'd been "brought to this side of the Atlantic recently by a psychoanalyst and his wife." From Marlon's point of view, he wasn't cheating on Ellen. The two women couldn't have been more different. He couldn't discuss classical music or modern art with Josanne. But he could *teach* her those things. For the first time, Marlon could be the mentor and someone else the protégé.

"I'm eleven years older than you," he told Josanne, promising to be a good example for her. He seemed excited about this new role. Celia had taught him about sex; Ellen had taught him about culture. The much-older Movita had inculcated in him a deep respect for spirituality, teaching that everything, even inanimate objects, possessed a spirit. Now Marlon saw himself as playing the older, wiser, more sophisticated lover to Josanne.

Yet, for all his justification, rationalization, and compartmentalization, when Ellen called to let him know she was back, he couldn't pick up the phone.

Through friends, Ellen learned that he was living with Josanne. The irony, of course, was that he'd met this latest girlfriend through Stella. Ellen wasn't surprised by Marlon's unfaithfulness. How many times had this happened before? But she was angry at his refusal to see her. Finally, after many attempts, she got him to come downstairs to face her. In no uncertain terms, she laid down the law: "Don't have anything to do with me," she told him, "until I'm married to somebody else." None of Marlon's other women had ever had the strength to issue such an ultimatum—and stick to it. Not for several years would Marlon see Ellen again.

"Nobody," Ellen realized at last, "could be married to him." Marlon might accept a woman as his equal, if she was a pal. But the moment any sort of romance arose, the moment things became "eroticized," she said, "everything changed." A decade after coming to New York, Marlon was still unable to forge a serious adult relationship with a woman. As much as he longed for intimacy, a part of him didn't want to try: relationships, he believed, were doomed. His parents had loved each other once, after all, but marriage had killed that love. It had broken them both, made them want to hurt each other. On the edge of his thirtieth birthday, Marlon was still powerless to stop reenacting the old dramas of his family. He still demanded that his women adore him, serve him, and love him extravagantly—all to make up for what he'd never gotten from Dodie. And then he'd lose respect for them, much as he'd lost respect for her.

Fame had left him lonelier than ever, and losing both Celia and Ellen in the course of a few years left him devastated by the start of 1954. The only way to assuage the loneliness was to keep his women in constant rotation. Josanne filled part of that vacuum. But other times, he would call another girlfriend, even someone he'd just met, and keep her on the phone for hours at a time. One woman who'd soon be added to his mix remembered the "long periods of silence" during phone calls with Marlon, with only the soft sound of his breathing and his "busy mind ticking like a clock" in her ear. On the other end of the line, a silent Marlon took some fragile comfort in the connection, like a little boy afraid to be home alone.

He was smart enough to know what he didn't have, and what he'd lost by letting Ellen go. In his memoir, he disguised Ellen as "Caroline Burke" and reflected, "She was not only physically beautiful, but bursting with elegance, charm, taste and appreciation for beautiful things." Nearing the twilight of his life, he admitted, "I always regretted not making a more permanent investment" in her.

Yet, even if they'd tried, how much success they might have had is debatable, given how much remained unresolved for him with the woman who had first given him cause to doubt and to fear.

**MID-FEBRUARY** / The psychiatrist's home office at 130 East Sixty-Seventh Street was spare and spartan, as quiet as a tomb, overlooking a courtyard just as barren. Yet the place was Marlon's refuge from the rest of the world. During those cold, unhappy weeks of early 1954, the only times Marlon left his apartment was to keep his appointments with Dr. Mittelman. Stretched out on the couch, his hands crossed over his chest, Marlon spilled his thoughts about his work, his fame, his parents, his women. Seated across from him in a chair, Mittelman, fifty-four, a small, blue-eyed, Hungarian-Jewish immigrant with a thick accent, mostly just listened. A follower of Freud, Mittelman only occasionally offered insight or advice; rarely was there any encouragement or praise. "Colder than ice," Marlon would describe him.

But, for several years now, he'd been seeing Mittelman regularly, sometimes twice a week, ever since Kazan had recommended him. For Kazan, Mittelman had proven insufficiently challenging, so he'd sought out another analyst. For Marlon, however, Mittelman's approach was ideal. "I think Marlon found Mittelman uncritical enough so he could talk to him," Kazan said. "That would mean a lot, to lie back on the sofa without feeling he was going to be judged."

Sometimes the psychiatrist allowed Marlon to bring friends with him to his sessions, a not-uncommon practice if the practitioner feels it might be therapeutic for the patient. Darren Dublin accompanied Marlon a number of times, and thought Mittelman's less aggressive style was a smart move. "He probably realized Marlon couldn't have handled any other kind of therapy," Darren said, "and probably would have walked out."

To outside observers, Mittelman's work with Marlon could seem unorthodox. Occasionally he'd accept theater tickets from his famous patient, a practice usually frowned upon and often cited as evidence of Mittelman's lack of ethics. Yet the first thing a good therapist must do is determine what works best for an individual client, and sometimes rules can be broken. By accepting gifts from Marlon, Mittelman may have been attempting to provide his patient with a sense of balance, allowing him to believe he could be as helpful to his therapist as his therapist was to him. Such a perspective, according to Marlon's friend Jack Larson, would have been "very important to somebody like Marlon, who liked to appear so self-reliant."

In those early months of 1954, Mittelman could do no wrong in Marlon's eyes. "When something would come up," recalled one of Marlon's girlfriends, the actress Sondra Lee, "he'd say, 'I have to talk to Mittelman.'" He'd pepper his statements with "I talked to Mittelman" or "Mittelman says." Friends, columnists, fellow actors, and biographers would view this attitude as eccentric; indeed, Marlon's embrace of psychotherapy would often be presented condescendingly, as an amusing example of just how offbeat he was. But the truth is something else entirely. Unlike other conflicted artists who wrestled with emotional and mental illness, Marlon did not run from his problems; nor did he take to the bottle or drugs. He knew, given his family history, that he had a predisposition for addiction, and "so he rarely drank," Ellen Adler said. Jack Larson corroborated this: "I don't think he ever imbibed. He went to a shrink instead. Wiser choice." Unlike so many of his peers, Marlon took the lead in trying to conquer his demons. That should be applauded, not ridiculed.

Psychotherapy, of course, was not as understood or as accepted in the 1950s as it would be later. "I was afraid of it at first," Marlon admitted. Going into therapy, he feared, might blunt his creativity. After all, "a sensitive person," as he considered himself, "receives fifty impressions where somebody else might only get seven." Would analysis smooth out his sensitive edges too much? The danger for sensitive people, Marlon believed, was that, out of fear of losing their creativity, they would never confront their conflicts and therefore "never evolve." But did he want to go through life never feeling anything because sometimes he "felt too much"?

So, he'd taken the leap and started seeing Mittelman, and thereby began the process of lassoing and subduing his troubles. His childhood, as he'd already figured out, was to blame for the "emotional disorders and psychological disarray" of his life. But he needed to learn how "to refrain from doing certain things" that were destructive toward himself and others. Analysis, Marlon said, was "a constant state of revolution, of throwing over the old." Whether he ever truly and fully succeeded in his efforts is arguable. But at least, unlike so many, he tried.

Even with his most recent breakdown, Marlon believed that he'd made some progress. The rage came less often by early 1954, he said, because, with therapy, he'd "acknowledged the pain." The problem was that he still didn't entirely understand it. "I knew I had to find out *why* I was angry," he said years later, describing his process in psychoanalysis. "I believe that unless we look inward we will not ever be able to clearly see outward." Most of his therapy, as Marlon described it, focused on his parents and the dark memories of his childhood. But he also dealt with a pervasive sense of "not mattering in the world."

For children of alcoholic parents, that's not an uncommon belief to internalize. Marlon's profession only made that feeling worse, he said: "What difference does an actor really make in the scheme of things?" He was a hugely successful actor, yet he felt "utterly useless and extraneous" in the world, an existential frustration that haunted him. It could leave him feeling physically sick on film sets, or crippled for days with a headache, unable to learn his lines.

Despite his low-key approach, Mittelman turned out to be an ideal guide for Marlon through this process. In the 1930s, Mittelman had led a study into psychosomatic illnesses, concluding that the mind has the power to influence the body: such things as heartburn and stomach disorders, the psychiatrist declared, were directly linked to stress and emotional strain. Eighty years later, this is a fundamental tenet in health care, but at the time, the claim was considered radical. Mittelman also lectured around the country urging parents to provide "understanding support" in response to the individual needs of their children, instead of raising them as carbon copies of themselves. In short, he was completely aligned with the issues that plagued Marlon, and far from the comical fraud other accounts have portrayed him as being. Marlon may have wished Mittelman were warmer and more expressive during their sessions, but in terms of psychotherapy, he was in very good hands.

Mittelman diagnosed Marlon as "psychoneurotic." It was a term used frequently in the 1950s—Darren Dublin had received the same diagnosis—for chronic anxiety that stopped short of delusions or hallucinations. Psychoneurotics could usually function day to day, but in stressful conditions they could manifest exactly what Marlon described: panic attacks, depression, paranoia. The diagnosis was viewed as serious enough during the Korean conflict to keep him out of uniform once again. Summoned before the draft board, Marlon discovered his 4-F classification had been changed to 1-A, indicating he was "available." Yet an army psychiatrist, who knew Mittelman, quickly scrawled "not suited for military service" across Marlon's form when he learned he was psychoneurotic.

At this distance, it is, of course, impossible to diagnose Marlon. The best way to understand him, however, remains as a survivor of trauma; the post-traumatic stress of his youth could produce all the symptoms he described to the draft board. No matter his diagnosis, he was in very real distress that cold winter of 1954. He was not exaggerating when he said he was in hell.

Some would try to argue that without that constantly roiling inner turmoil, he might not have become such a great actor. To such arguments, Marlon grew impatient. "What you're saying," he replied, "is that unless you irritate an oyster with a sand grain, he will not make the necessary compensations for the purposes of that sand grain, and will [therefore] never create the pearl." He made a sound of contempt. "Who gives a damn about the pearl?"

SOMETIMES, WHEN HE left Mittelman's, disguised in a fake mustache and sunglasses, Marlon would return home to find police cars on his block, with sheriffs waiting to serve him the summons from Twentieth Century–Fox. So, he'd head to Janice Mars's apartment, or Wally's, or the tiny Murray Hill studio of his sister Jocelyn's friend Barbara Baxley. Josanne got used to his not coming home, taking it "in stride, no questions asked." Other times, Marlon stayed at out-of-the-way hotels, registering under an alias. Baxley recalled him describing the whole situation as "sick-making" and declaring he "couldn't cope with any more shit." Just starting out as an actress, Baxley was struck by how difficult Marlon found his fame. "What was apparent," she said, "was that he was really in fear of being destroyed."

At last, Marlon could stand it no more. Managing to slip by the phalanx of policemen, he made it back upstairs to Josanne, out of breath and letting fly a string of curses. "It was really frightening," Ellen described the situation, having delivered her ultimatum to him in the midst of similar chaos, "because they had the cops and everything downstairs to subpoena him." And so, at last, on February 16, nearly two weeks after the standoff began, Marlon faced a U.S. marshal outside his building and accepted the subpoena. His attitude appeared to be: *Go ahead and sue me.*

They did. The two-million-dollar claim for damages filed in a Manhattan federal court charged that Marlon had refused "to perform under his current contract" and that his truancy was causing the studio to lose ten thousand dollars a day. Marlon's reps had no comment. Most likely, they couldn't reach him, either.

Josanne did her best to console him. "The poor thing," said a friend. "She was trying to get him out of bed and cook for him, but he just turned off the world." As often happened, depression eventually morphed into anger, and Marlon began to rage against Zanuck and Fox and what he called the "unfairness of a business that treats people like chattel." On February 27 came word that he'd been officially replaced on *The Egyptian* by the British actor Edmund Purdom.

In the midst of this, he was nominated for an Academy Award for Best Actor for *Julius Caesar*. He had been nominated twice before (for *Streetcar* and *Zapata*), and both times he'd paid very little attention to all the fuss, not attending the ceremonies nor commenting on his losses. But this nod was different, even if he was loath to admit it publicly. This was for doing Shakespeare, and he was pitted against Montgomery Clift. This one, Ellen thought, he wanted to win. Yet Marlon's struggle with the acclaim was twofold: on the one hand, he didn't think acting was anything to be proud of, but on the other hand, he didn't want to be proven a fraud. One way to solve both dilemmas was to do the classics: if any acting could be considered worthwhile, it was Shakespeare, and if Marlon could master the Bard, then maybe he'd be worthy of that ponderous four-thousand-pound crown.

The Adlers—especially the tempestuous Sara, who'd recently passed away at the age of ninety-four—had always wanted Marlon to play Shakespeare. The last time he'd done so had been back in Sayville, in *Twelfth Night*, when he was just twenty years old. In the summer of 1952 he'd finally accepted the challenge to do so again when he took the role of Mark Antony in *Julius Caesar*, directed by Joseph Mankiewicz for MGM. Of course, he gave the impression of indifference, but underneath, "he was terrified," said Jack Larson. Without Kazan to guide him, could he do this?

On the set, Marlon's swagger disappeared. John Gielgud, playing Cassius, found the young star "self-conscious and modest." Marlon arrived wearing "his fine, tomato-colored toga," Gielgud recalled, "his hair cropped in a straight fringe, and would look around nervously, expecting to find someone making fun of his appearance." Then he took out a cigarette and stuck it behind his ear. He turned to Gielgud for advice. In his dressing room, Marlon was listening to tapes of Maurice Evans and John Barrymore in the role—"to improve his diction," he told Gielgud. He pumped the older actor for tips on Mark Antony's speeches, thanking him "very politely" for his assistance. "The next morning, when we shot the scene," Gielgud recalled, "I found that he had taken note of everything I had said and spoke the lines exactly as I had suggested."

Whatever Marlon's strategy, it worked. He is a revelation in *Julius Caesar*. If he worried about his diction, he needn't have; his speech is not only flawless but also inspired. He makes Shakespeare's words sound natural, as they were intended; poetry, yes, but also conversation. He's a match for such Shakespearean veterans as Gielgud, James Mason, and Louis Calhern. Wisely, Mankiewicz directed with the camera in mind. There are no grand, center-stage orations; instead, when Marlon delivers Antony's famous speech ("Friends, Romans, countrymen, lend me your ears"), he speaks it not as a soliloquy but as a real address to the Roman public. When he grieves over Caesar's body, there's fire in his eyes, a sparkle caught by the camera that would have been lost on the stage. For an actor who had trouble memorizing his lines, Marlon is perfection here, never missing a beat and leaving viewers stunned by his power: "And Caesar's spirit, ranging for revenge, / With Atë by his side come hot from hell, / Shall in these confines with a monarch's voice / Cry 'Havoc,' and let slip the dogs of war."

Bosley Crowther called Marlon "the delight and surprise of the film," proving he could do more than bluster as Stanley and Zapata: "A major talent has emerged." After *Julius Caesar*, Marlon became, in the words of his friend Billy Redfield, "the only American actor to be seriously thought of as Hamlet," the great hope of

American theater enthusiasts to finally measure up against the English. "We who saw him in his first, shocking days," said Redfield, "believed in him not only as an actor, but also as an artistic, spiritual and specifically American leader. We flung him at the English as though we owned him and we all but shouted, 'He does without your damned elocution lessons, your fruity voices, your artificial changings of pitch and stress, your bleeding love of words, words, words, and your high-toned, fustian, bombace technique. He throws away your books and burns your academies. He does it from within. And he is better than all of you!'"

The problem was Marlon didn't want to be flung at the English—or anyone. He'd been hearing the comparisons to Olivier and Gielgud since his early days with Stella, yet such comparisons meant little to him, except as pressure to keep acting. What had propelled him forward these past few years had been the desire to succeed, to win—not to be the American Hamlet. Marlon did not share Redfield's reverence for the noble calling of the actor. He had no desire to be great. If others held expectations for him, they held them without his consent. Redfield was on point when he said that he and others urged Marlon forward "as though they owned him." They did so at their peril, however. Marlon Brando would never be owned.

For all the accolades he received for *Julius Caesar*, Marlon was in no hurry to repeat the experience. Throughout the spring of 1953, John Huston pursued him for a 3-D film of *Richard III*. Repeatedly, Marlon told Huston no. "Cannot fathom Brando's not wishing to do this great role unless he has no high opinion of me as the director," Huston cabled his agent. His inability to fathom Marlon's opposition was because he assumed him to be like other actors he knew: ambitious and self-admiring. In truth, Marlon's lack of high opinion wasn't for Huston as a director, but for himself as an actor. "In spite of the fact that I received a good deal of the back-pounding and hand-grabbing for *Julius Caesar*," he finally wrote to Huston, "I think my performance was wanting for reasons too numerous to relate here." He'd read *Richard*, Marlon told Huston, "and it's too big a chaw for me at this stage in the game." He seemed to be reasoning that he'd gotten through *Caesar* unscathed. Why press his luck?

Huston, however, would not be deterred. Though Jay Kanter told him that any further back-and-forth "would only prove embarrassing" for the both of them, the director penned a long, heartfelt letter, vowing that if Marlon didn't do the picture, he'd abandon the project. "I think you would make the best Richard alive," Huston wrote, "and it's getting a little late for me to be interested in second bests." Such glib words might have worked with another actor, but with Marlon, they had the opposite effect; truly, Huston had no idea as to how Marlon thought. Talking about who was the "best" in terms of acting only hardened his resolve. Not only did Marlon struggle with his own sense of self-worth, but he also wrestled with whether the very enterprise of acting had any intrinsic worth. He gave no response to Huston's last appeal, and the director, true to his word, never made *Richard III*.

INSTEAD OF SHAKESPEARE, Marlon's next project after *Julius Caesar* was *The Wild One*, his paean to rebels and male camaraderie, made for Stanley Kramer, the producer of *The Men*. The picture was directed by Laslo Benedek, who'd previously helmed the film version of Arthur Miller's *Death of a Salesman*. Kramer gave all sorts of noble reasons for wanting to produce the film—the fear of "juvenile delinquency" was all over the news, with the U.S. Senate planning hearings on the matter—but really, the project was green-lit because it provided an opportunity to get Marlon on a motorcycle, in a leather jacket, and hell-bent on kidnapping a girl.

The film certainly had potential. The underlying conflict in the script, by John Paxton, was one Marlon knew well himself:

the struggles faced by young people who don't live up to societal expectations. When someone asks his character, Johnny Strabler, what he's rebelling against, there's a great deal of Marlon in his famous response: "Whad'dya got?"

But the film never really addresses that struggle with any depth or intelligence. It's contrived, disjointed, and exploitative; at one point, Benedek reportedly broke down into tears at the mess he had on his hands. The film, an original screenplay, is stagy in a way that *Streetcar*, adapted from the stage, is not, with matte shots of motorcyclists on the road diluting any sense of cinema verité Benedek may have been striving for. Yet, as always, Marlon manages to rise above the wreckage, at least in a few scenes: when Johnny runs away and hides, we see the scared little boy he is deep down, and which Marlon could still be himself. Bosley Crowther wrote that while *The Wild One* "falls short" of its goals, Marlon, when allowed to by the script, offers an "incisive and picturesque" performance.

He might have turned down Shakespeare for the less challenging *Wild One*, but he did attempt Shaw soon thereafter. Despite saying he had no desire to return to the stage, Marlon's next project during the summer of 1953 was a tour of George Bernard Shaw's *Arms and the Man*, an undertaking intended to put some cash into the pockets of his out-of-work friends, including Billy Redfield, Freddie Fiore, Janice Mars, and Sam Gilman. It was a noble gesture on Marlon's part, and absolutely characteristic, though he seemed also to be trying to recapture those carefree early days at Sayville, the last time he'd truly had fun as an actor. He seemed to be wondering if he could truly enjoy acting again. Could this profession actually be enjoyable—and therefore, sustainable?

He established the company himself, persuading Edie Van Cleve to find a manager and funding. Maybe, in this way, he could satisfy the calls from people such as Redfield to fulfill his destiny as the American Hamlet. It was what Stella and others had always envisioned for him: if it hadn't been for the movies, Ellen Adler told him once, "You would have had a repertory company. You would have traveled all over the country. You would have had a nice life, doing what comes naturally"—reinterpreting worthy plays and giving the British some competition in the classics. And he might have made something of it, too, Ellen believed, if "he'd been more serious about it, more of a businessman."

But for Marlon, *Arms and the Man* was a lark. He intended it to be good—Redfield and the others wouldn't have signed up if that hadn't been the aim—but he also aspired to have fun. Giving the lead to Redfield, Marlon took the secondary part (the pompous Sergius) and played it with a heavy dose of camp and slapstick. According to one person involved with the show's staging at the Falmouth Theatre on Cape Cod, this was an attempt to make the production "more relatable" to audiences, as Shaw could "sometimes be inaccessible." Several years earlier, Laurence Olivier had played Sergius much the same way at the Old Vic. If it was good enough for the old Olivier, Marlon seemed to reason, it ought to serve the new just as well.

How successful Marlon was in the effort is unclear. Billy Redfield recalled he was "brilliant once or twice a week," but the remainder of his performances he "threw away." But Redfield was bitter by that point, disappointed that Marlon had refused to take his role as the American Hamlet more seriously. A legend would arise, in part due to Redfield's memory of it, that *Arms and the Man* was an unmitigated disaster, but the contemporary evidence does not bear that out. Remembering the experience, Janice Mars wrote to Marlon that he'd been successful in enlarging the part of Sergius "to the size of a blown-up cartoon." A few times Marlon blew his lines, Mars admitted, though he "would improvise with double talk that was completely convincing and [then] exit with a flourish." Once, when the sounds of sirens from outside drowned out the dialogue, Marlon walked around Mars "as if to locate the source" of the sound, making the best of a momentarily bad situation.

The *Hartford Courant*, reviewing the show at the Ivoryton Playhouse, called the production "a tour de force." Marlon seemed "to enjoy the performance as much as the audience," the reviewer noted, and while the cast was "uniformly excellent," it was this new, "fiery Brando" who would keep the audiences coming. That hardly sounds like a disaster. Likewise, Marjory Adams, reviewing a Falmouth Theatre performance for the *Boston Globe*, thought the show was good fun and, like the *Courant*, noted how much the audience enjoyed themselves. "Brando was handsome," Adams wrote, "he was funny, he gave the women a thrill. What more could a July summer theatre audience, in best bib and tucker, require of a star?" She admitted, however, "If Brando brings the show to Broadway, as he hopes, there's a lot more for him to do before he masters Sergius."

It was left to Elliot Norton, who'd been the first to spot just what made Marlon's Stanley so special in the previews of *Streetcar*, to seal the show's legacy. After attending the premiere at Framingham's Summer Theater, Norton wrote in the *Boston Post*, "Marlon Brando opened here tonight and made a fool of himself." That was Norton's lead, and it got worse. "In recent years, no major star, no actor with anything like Brando's reputation, has ever given such a completely ridiculous performance." Norton compared Marlon to one of the Ritz Brothers (which Marlon, a lover of Laurel and Hardy and the Three Stooges, probably wouldn't have minded) and summed him up as "a ham actor who just doesn't know how to play comedy." Norton was a kingmaker; he could make or break a show. With a review like that, there was no way *Arms and the Man* would ever make it to Broadway.

Norton's review infuriated Marlon. This was exactly what he despised about the business he was in: the power of critics and the tyranny of the box office. He'd also, in the course of the tour, encountered firsthand the behemoth his fame had become. Although he'd deliberately not taken the lead, and instructed the press releases for the show to focus on Billy Redfield and Nydia Westman, the two stars, his photograph was routinely slapped on top of the piece when it ran in local newspapers. Audiences were coming to see him, not the two unknowns. When Marlon came striding out onstage in the middle of the second act, in his skintight gold-and-white uniform, "the audience lost interest for the moment in anyone else," Marjory Adams reported. No matter what Marlon did to democratize the situation, the company was fated to rise or fall on his reviews, not theirs.

With *Arms and the Man*, Marlon tried to find the joy in acting again. Rehearsing and performing that summer, Freddie Fiore remembered, had been "pure fun," as they'd traveled, gypsy-like, from playhouse to playhouse through Connecticut, Rhode Island, Cape Cod, and central Massachusetts. Marlon often followed the company on his motorcycle. Sometimes the actors slept under the stars and cooked out on a grill. Other times they cracked lobsters on picnic tables along the shoreline. Their audiences were having fun, too, which, Marlon wrote his parents, "is the measure of importance worth considering." He was worlds away from the stifling confines of studio commissaries and backlots. He'd be criticized for not acting professionally enough in the production, for telling Redfield, "Man, don't you get it? This is summer stock!" Yet that was exactly the atmosphere Marlon wanted, laid-back and unpressured; anything more serious he had no interest in.

With the failure of *Arms and the Man*, Marlon abandoned the idea of a company of his own. He also vowed never again to act on the stage, and he never did. No matter how he tried to fix things, acting for Marlon always equaled anxiety, agitation, and admonishment. He was aware of the expectations people had for him, and he resented them. After *Arms and the Man*, Marlon took off, traveled, ignored his agents' calls, and did not act again until Kazan corralled him for *Waterfront*. For those months he had been utterly free.

Now here he was, a prisoner in his apartment, slapped with a summons to appear in court, miserable and depressed, unable to pick himself up off the floor. This was his reward for acting. This was what people like Billy Redfield demanded he endure for the privilege of possessing his great gift, which he was expected to share with the world without complaint. No wonder Marlon kept his blinds drawn against the world. "I hated with every fiber," he said, "what my life had become."

**MARCH 25** / In the audience at the RKO Pantages Theatre sat Hedda Hopper, reigning queen of the Hollywood columnists. She was listening to Shirley Booth, via live hookup from Philadelphia, read the names of the Best Actor nominees. More than rooting for any one actor to win, Hopper was rooting for one to lose. For four years, she'd done everything she could to bring down Marlon Brando. He was a hypocrite: "He scoffs at our films," Hopper wrote in her column, "but he never overlooks our money. He cries to high heaven that each picture is his last, but nobody believes him, and he always comes back for more." He was a philistine: "He reminds me of a fellow who'd been reared sixty miles back in the hills, having acquired neither the taint nor the culture of an urbane civilization." When Marlon sailed for Paris, Hopper sniped, "Can you picture Brando on his visit to one of the most beautiful cities in the world? He probably arrived wearing a pair of blue jeans with a ham sandwich stickin' out of his hip pocket." And he might even be a Communist. In her files, Hopper kept information about Marlon's political associations in case they ever proved useful.

Hopper's vendetta against Marlon was deeply personal. Four years earlier, on the set of *The Men*, Hopper had arrived as she always did, in a flurry of chatter and air kisses, expecting Marlon, her latest interviewee, to bow and scrape, as newcomers were obliged to do. But he greeted her "with a grunt," Hopper recalled, and paid no more attention to her than he did any reporter. For her efforts at promoting a new actor, Hopper expected gratitude, as well as scoops about whom they were romancing and glamorous outfits she could gush over in her columns—not to mention flowers delivered regularly to her house. Marlon offered none of these things. Hopper steamed. This was not how the game was played.

Marlon Brando represented everything that was wrong with this new crop of actors and directors taking over the business; Hopper was similarly disdainful of Montgomery Clift, who was also in the running for Best Actor. But "Brando was her bête noire," said Hopper's longtime legman Robert Shaw. So, it was with considerable pleasure that the columnist applauded when William Holden was named the winner for *Stalag 17* and came bounding up to the stage to collect his award. That was what was expected of Hollywood stars, Hopper believed, to show up and say thank you. The older generation knew this; these kids, most of them from New York or Europe, seemed to take delight in doing things their way.

Meanwhile, in New York, Marlon may have felt some flicker of disappointment that he didn't win, some friends thought. But he could not have cared an iota less about how the Hollywood game was played or whether Hedda Hopper liked him. She was, he told friends, a "nincompoop." Once, speaking candidly with a reporter, he called her, in a slip of the tongue, "Hedda Hawker." It broke him up. "That's a good mistake!" Marlon said, laughing.

On a cool spring evening, wearing sunglasses and a floppy hat, Marlon perched on the stoop of a friend's apartment, shooting the breeze with Jack Larson, visiting from Los Angeles. The lawsuit loomed, Larson recalled, and Marlon could speak of nothing except "getting out of the business." Maybe he'd make pictures in Europe, he mused; maybe he'd do something else entirely. He was beyond fed up with "the protocol of the movie star," Larson remembered, "all the dictates and decrees of Hollywood." He did not consider it unreasonable, Marlon declared, to refuse to "speak with people who write gossip columns, who . . . chastise and generally exploit people" whose only "crime" was saying, "I don't want to talk to you." Whatever he said, he complained, was routinely turned "into some kind of digestible slop for the people." Hopper wasn't the only culprit; there were also Louella Parsons, Dorothy Kilgallen, Mike Connolly, Ed Sullivan, Sheilah Graham, and a dozen or so more. Marlon did his best to avoid what he called "people with pencils," autograph hounds as well as interviewers. Yet, by doing so, he was committing "a cardinal sin," he acknowledged. "If you do that, you are a renegade."

So, he wanted out. Larson truly thought that was the end of Marlon Brando's movie career. Sitting there on the stoop that spring evening in New York, Larson believed Marlon's commitment was sincere. "He intended to give it all up and do something else," Larson said. He was interested in the racial desegregation issue, Marlon said, particularly around education. Maybe he could make a difference there.

Indeed, many of Marlon's friends from the American League for a Free Palestine were now involved in the struggle for African American civil rights. Marlon felt similarly drawn. "I needed to feel I was doing something that really mattered," he would say, "because otherwise I was just occupying space and using up oxygen." He'd felt this way ever since first arriving in New York, well before all this business of acting and fame had started, when he'd written to his parents deploring the "bitterness and fear and hate and untruths" he saw in the world and wanting "to do something about it." Maybe now, finally, was the time.

Marlon wanted, in fact, the very same thing Hedda Hopper wanted: his exile from Hollywood. "He really hated the fame," Budd Schulberg said. "I mean, he hated it, he wasn't just uncomfortable [with it]. He resented it. It made him angry." He lamented the discomfort of not being "a normal person."

As a teenager, Marlon had once spotted jazz musician Gene Krupa, his idol, driving down a street. He'd taken off after him, breathlessly reaching Krupa's car when it stopped for a red light and asking him for his autograph. The great drummer "just scribbled something," Marlon remembered, "looking agitated." All these years later, Marlon could finally understand his hero's attitude. Krupa had just been living his life, and suddenly there's this kid, whom he doesn't know, getting in his face and asking him to sign a piece of paper. And for what possible, logical reason? "I think that people after a certain age should know better than to ask for an autograph," Marlon griped. "Utterly idiotic."

He was "contemptuous" of fame, Ellen Adler said, and "contemptuous of people who fawned over fame." Few got "the reasons behind" his position, she added. "They just got the contempt."

Only his competitive urge, his need to win, had gotten Marlon this far, and by the winter of 1954, even that engine was losing steam. His old life, while not easy (and while certainly not insulated from breakdowns) had at least allowed him to ride the subway in peace, and no one was serving him with subpoenas to appear in court.

Marlon wanted that life back. Tennessee Williams, with whom he felt a strong kinship, had once expressed very similar feelings. *The Glass Menagerie*, he wrote, had "terminated one part" of his life and begun "another about as different in all external circumstances as could well be imagined." After his success, the playwright felt "a spiritual dislocation," a longing for a time when he had had to struggle. Marlon, too, missed the struggle. Of his old friends, only Wally Cox could comprehend what he was going through. By now, Wally's television show, *Mister Peepers*, was in its third season on NBC. The sitcom and its star had been nominated for a slew of Emmy Awards. Wally didn't enjoy the notoriety any more than

Marlon did. "They had similar attitudes toward fame and publicity," Wally's sister recalled. "They were among the first generation of actors who fled from the press and hid from the public." Yet there was a difference: Wally wasn't a romantic movie idol whose face was splashed on the covers of fan magazines. That meant he could slip out of town and not have a posse of rabid reporters on his heels. And so, Marlon remained a prisoner in his New York apartment.

From the depths of his spiritual dislocation, Tennessee Williams had fought his way back. Salvation from "the vacuity of life without struggle" was found, he said, by returning to work: "It is only in his work," Williams wrote, "that an artist can find reality and satisfaction." But what if the work itself was not the artist's choice? What if the work gave him no such satisfaction as Williams's writing gave him? What if he had not been born wanting the work as Williams had been born wanting to write, but had instead stumbled upon the work, been proclaimed a genius for it, and been forced to continue producing it?

That was Marlon's dilemma those miserable first few months of 1954.

DARRYL ZANUCK DECLARED Marlon "half beast and half human"—as rare, apparently, as a centaur, minotaur, or triton—which was why the producer was fighting in court to keep him. Beasts, of course, were tracked, hunted, turned into prey. In Hollywood, Marlon was both all-powerful and powerless at the same time.

Even as Marlon vented to Larson and others of his desire to escape, it may have already been too late. He had tapped a nerve in the culture. He'd become a symbol, something more than just an actor, and with the upcoming release of *Waterfront*, that public perception would only grow stronger. The culture was not about to let him go. A new generation was rising for whom the staid, suburban, nuclear family, postwar conformity was restricting and repugnant. They were rebels, bohemians, beatniks—and Marlon, in the words of the critic Lyall Bush, embodied "the Beat preference for the raw over the cooked."

By 1954, Marlon was leading (willingly or not, consciously or not) the transition away from the likes of Cary Grant and David Niven, actors who were defined by their charm and grace, to the "stew-fed and unschooled Nixon and Eisenhower loners," Bush wrote, "dirty cowboys in white T-shirts and baby smiles: Warren Beatty, Jack Nicholson, Robert De Niro . . . every one of them Brando-ized." Pauline Kael wrote that Marlon offered "a reaction against the postwar mania for security." His films were dangerous. *The Wild One* had been banned in several places throughout the United States, Canada, and the United Kingdom. During the hearings of the U.S. Senate Subcommittee on Juvenile Delinquency, William Mooring, editor of a Catholic magazine, testified he'd seen young men "dressed like Brando in leather jackets" at several screenings of *The Wild One*. "It was clear they identified with the arrogant character he played in the film," Mooring said. "They put on his swagger, and some of them went off recklessly on their motorcycles, just like the gang in the picture."

Marlon—and, a little later, Elvis Presley and James Dean and, still later, Beatty, Nicholson, and others—pushed against the safe sexual boundaries of the culture, at the precise moment when men and women throughout the Western world were rethinking the parameters of gender and sex. That was why Marlon resonated so strongly with the public; even as he broke rules and offended old cultural warhorses such as Hedda Hopper, he was being embraced by a world that was changing a little bit more every year. Marlon was, in the words of the writer Jack Kerouac, "a free soul." That was why the public was not about to let him go.

The problem for Marlon, of course, was that he didn't feel like a free soul. He felt like a prisoner. A new generation might be projecting themselves and their dreams and desires onto him, but he hadn't asked them to do it. In fact, he resented their need of him, their presumption of ownership, their interference with his own journey. "The public Somebody you are," Tennessee Williams wrote, "is a fiction created with mirrors." That was Marlon's struggle. "The only somebody worth being," Williams wrote, "is the solitary and unseen you that existed from your first breath." Marlon had only begun to discover his authentic self in the few short years before his rise to fame. How was he ever going to find him again now?

OVER THE TELEPHONE, all the music had evaporated from his mother's voice. Marlon knew she hadn't been well since they'd returned from Mexico. She and his father had forgone a cold, damp Nebraska winter to spend some time with her sister in Pasadena. There Dodie had suffered a seizure and was taken to the hospital, where doctors diagnosed her with encephalopathy, a dysfunction of the brain due to hypertension. For years, the family had been worried about her blood pressure; her own mother had died from the condition. Doctors were confident Dodie would improve through medication and diet, so she was released.

Yet what made her feel considerably worse than the encephalopathy, Dodie told her son over the phone, was the scuttlebutt she was hearing about how he was walking out on his contract, how he was risking the livelihoods of everyone involved—right down to the property men and electricians, many of whom had families to support. Dodie's embarrassment over her son's behavior was personal: she was a friend of Bess Meredyth, the wife of Michael Curtiz, the director of *The Egyptian*. So, she told Marlon to settle the lawsuit and go back to work.

Weeks might go by without Marlon hearing from his mother, but a phone call like that could transport him right back to his childhood, leaving him desperate to please her and guilt-ridden for causing her distress. Accordingly, sometime in the middle part of March, Marlon told his lawyers that maybe, under the right terms, he might consider going back to work—a startling reversal from his recalcitrance of just a few weeks earlier, when he'd sat on the stoop and insisted to Jack Larson that he was through with the movies. When Ellen Adler asked him later why he'd surrendered, Marlon replied simply, "My mother didn't like the fact that there was all this scandal."

The brooding, masculine heavyweight of the screen, the iconoclast who defied gender and sex and was upending the very power structure of the culture, was behaving like an obedient boy, doing what his mother told him to do.

Of course, more than filial duty accounted for Marlon's willingness to settle the case. His lawyers surely told him he couldn't win; his contract was plain and would be held up in court. Still, in the end, Ellen Adler believed it was Dodie's distress more than anything else that brought him to the bargaining table. Dodie enjoyed being the mother of a movie star, basking in the entrée it gave her into Hollywood circles. Over each new script, Dodie gushed far more than her son ever did. Was he truly going to walk away from this world that had given his mother so much pleasure, after all the pain they'd been through together?

*The Egyptian*, of course, had already been recast, so that ship, thankfully, had sailed. But might there be something else to fulfill his contract? Darryl Zanuck suggested all might be forgiven if Marlon returned to play Napoleon Bonaparte in a film of Annemarie Selinko's novel *Désirée*. The project would be every bit as gloriously junky as *The Egyptian*, but if Marlon agreed to go back, he couldn't exactly be picky; he'd have to take what the studio gave him.

For a tantalizing moment, Marlon stood on a precipice, trying to decide which way to jump. One way meant freedom. The other meant more sacrifice of integrity and self. Marlon held his future in his hands. If he chose not to go back, he would have to fight—and would almost certainly lose—in court, and probably pay a huge sum of money to Fox, money he didn't have except by liquidating his investments in his father's Nebraska cattle business. Yet he would be free. He would never act in Hollywood again, that was for sure, but that was fine with him.

In that fraught, fleeting moment in the spring of 1954, Marlon might very well have decided to go that route, and so Brando, the great screen star, would have reached his apex in Elia Kazan's *Waterfront*, and then disappeared, either to become someone else: a politician, a social justice activist, a musician—or a recluse, like Greta Garbo or J. D. Salinger, living off what he'd earned for as long as he could and resting defiantly on his laurels. He could have done so. *Streetcar*, *Zapata*, and *Waterfront*—even *The Wild One*, with all its cultural potency—would have been enough to guarantee his legend.

But then the call came in from his father. His mother was dying. And Marlon's decision was made for him.

**MARCH  31**  /  At just past midnight, the corridors of Huntington Memorial Hospital in Pasadena were largely quiet and still. Occasionally, a soft blue light would flash at the desk and a nurse in rubber-soled shoes would silently pad down the hall to a patient's room. A couple of times a night, some bedraggled soul, sitting up with a family member, would find a nook by the windows and have a smoke.

Marlon and Jocelyn took their places at their mother's bedside. They'd relieved their father and Frannie for the night, letting them head back to Dodie's sister's house to rest. Ever since the doctors had told them that Dodie's death was imminent, someone was always present. The frail fifty-seven-year-old woman had stopped speaking. She hovered in that twilight between sleep and wakefulness. Marlon himself hadn't slept more than a few hours since flying in from New York. He kept grasping his mother's hand, staring at her face.

So, this was how it ended. After all the agonies, it finished here, quietly, in the blue darkness of a hospital room, with Marlon and Jocelyn—Bud and Tidd—on either side of her, watching her breathe.

The encephalopathy had gotten worse. Dodie's eyesight had begun to fail, and then she lost control of her bodily functions. Rushing her to the hospital, her husband had been informed she was suffering from malignant nephrosclerosis, or kidney disease. The condition was brought on by chronic high blood pressure, but it was nonetheless very rare; most hypertension patients did not lose kidney function. Unstated, but no doubt understood by Dodie's family, was the fact that alcohol abuse can agitate high blood pressure, and can also be a predictor of kidney disease. Sober for a decade, Dodie was paying the price for her past. Doctors estimated she'd been suffering from the nephrosclerosis for thirty years. They told Marlon Senior to gather the family.

For more than a week now they'd been holding their vigil. Every day, Dodie was a little less alive. All the indignities of her past were gone now. Jocelyn thought she managed her death "beautifully, very calmly." In dying, she seemed to have found the grace that had so eluded her in life. At one point, she whispered to her family that she wasn't scared, and neither should they be.

Marlon rarely took his eyes off her. As the night wore on, the pauses between breaths became longer, Jocelyn remembered.

Gripping his mother's hand, Marlon urged her to let go—the hardest thing, surely, he had ever done. In those quiet, fraught hours in the middle of the night, he was once again the little boy who wanted to take care of his mother, to find a way to fix her. His mother should not be dying at the age of fifty-seven. Marlon hated the alcohol that had compromised her, despairing of the "family curse," as he called it. It wasn't just his parents who'd been drunks; there were uncles and grandparents on both sides of the family who drank. Both Marlon's sisters were already drinking too much, but Marlon stayed dry, taking only "the merest courtesy sip" when he had to, an interviewer observed.

Morning approached. Marlon watched his mother, so small, so frail, tremble toward death. For all his conflict with his parents, they still exerted such a hold over him. He still signed his letters to them, "your little boy, Bud." He was always writing, "I love you both." When his mother had left him in New York to return to his father, Marlon had felt deeply abandoned and betrayed. "There was a time," he told his friend, the actress Maila Nurmi, "when I had so little feeling for her that she could have dropped dead and I would have stepped over her and gone for an ice cream cone." Now, however, she was once more the angel of his childhood, the woman who taught him to sing, who introduced him to nature, whose affection he yearned for. The moment he'd gotten word that Dodie was near death, Marlon had dropped everything—lawsuit, be damned—and flown across the country to be by her side. He sat there stroking her hand, giving her the tenderness and care and solicitude he'd never received from her.

Although the intensity of the feelings between Marlon and his parents had not diminished these past ten years, the drama had. His father had stopped drinking as well, with he and Dodie attending AA meetings together. Their violent fights were things of the past. On the Nebraska ranch, Dodie had seemed to find some solace, and she liked very much the travel and Hollywood access that Marlon's stardom afforded her. "She had a happy time," Marlon thought, "the last ten years of her life." Whether his father gave up "the whoremongering that had brought so much sadness" to his wife, Marlon wasn't sure. "But the two of them shared a life of sorts," he acknowledged, taking "the shards of their broken lives" and fitting them together. Unwilling ever to admit that his parents might have truly loved each other, this was the most that Marlon seemed willing to give them.

When he arrived earlier in the week, Marlon had found, much to his relief, his mother conscious and communicative. Dodie had beckoned to him. Not long before, she'd confided to friends that she was worried about Bud, who she felt was "on dangerous ground, half out of control, pushed by his own intensity, his demons." That he'd been slapped with a lawsuit was part of his self-destructive nature, she believed. Why did he want to turn his back on a life that she herself, in the days of the Omaha Playhouse, would have loved? From her hospital bed, Dodie told Marlon, "Be sensible with your life. Think about tomorrow."

Those were among the very last words his mother ever said to him. Marlon nodded; at that point, his heart breaking, he would have agreed to anything.

He was still holding her hand when Dodie died at 5:20 a.m.

Marlon bent over his mother's body. Carefully, he snipped off a lock of her hair. Then he took her pillow and removed an aquamarine ring from her finger. Clutching these talismans, he made his way outside, where the sun was just coming up. "I felt instantly that she had been transformed into everything that was reflective of nature," he said. Birds, plants, animals, little children—they were all Dodie. Standing there outside the hospital, in the crisp morning air, Marlon suddenly had a vision ("I actually saw it," he insisted) of a great bird "floating up and down the face of a cliff."

This was his mother, he believed, rising to the sky. The bird made its ascent to the strains of Ferde Grofé's "Mississippi Suite," a stirring orchestral piece Ellen had introduced Marlon to, and which he often found himself humming.

The day passed in a haze. As his father and sisters made arrangements for a private funeral, Marlon sat staring into space. "Demolished," Fran described him to a friend. That night, despite having been awake for more than twenty-four hours, Marlon still couldn't sleep, so he drove to the house Darren Dublin was renting in Los Angeles. When Darren's mother had died, Marlon took his pal to a club. But Marlon didn't want to go out on the town this night. He just wanted to sit with someone from his old life. "He didn't say much," Darren remembered. "He was broken up."

His grief went even deeper than his mother's death. With that loss had come another. That afternoon, Marlon's lawyers had told Twentieth Century–Fox that he would agree to the studio's terms. He would pay half the costs caused by his absence from *The Egyptian* and would start work on *Désirée* on June 7. "It was half a victory," Marlon said, looking back. A protracted court case would have nearly wiped him out. But by giving in and going back, he stood to lose a whole lot more, Marlon believed: his integrity, his sense of self. And yet, trying to make his mother happy—the old, familiar, thankless enterprise of his childhood—he had agreed to resume the grind he hated. "She made him promise," Maila Nurmi said.

Dodie was cremated after a private service at the Lamb Funeral Home on Orange Grove Boulevard in Pasadena. Two days later, Marlon turned thirty. If there had been a moment when he might have found something else, something for himself, something that gave him joy—or at least *tried* to find something of the sort—it was now gone. Keeping his promise to his mother would set the course for the rest of Marlon's life.

**JULY 28** / In the orchestra of the elegant old Astor Theatre, A. H. "Doc" Weiler of the *New York Times* watched the screen intently. Elia Kazan was a filmmaker of the first rank, and had produced some great films in the past. But *On the Waterfront*—two words had been added to its prerelease title to locate its setting more exactly—was something else entirely. This film, Weiler believed, would change everything.

After the final reel had unwound, and Terry Malloy, played by Marlon Brando, had stumbled, barely alive, across the pier, the audience at the Astor had leapt to its feet, shouting and cheering and whistling. Weiler made for the exit. On the sidewalk, filmgoers were gathering, excitedly tossing around such adjectives as "phenomenal" and "unbelievable." Over the years, the Astor had given many classic films their New York premieres: *The Big Parade, Grand Hotel, Gone With the Wind*. But *On the Waterfront* heralded a new era. Up on the screen had been the Production Code Administration's seal of approval, and yet Brando had still uttered the line "go to hell" for everyone to hear. This wasn't a glossy studio product. This was the real world, about real human experience. This was about people like Doc Weiler, who'd grown up on the Lower East Side of New York, whose father had been a clothes presser, and who made it a point among his colleagues to deride culture that got too "highfalutin"—the same word Marlon often used. Weiler had been reviewing pictures for nearly twenty years. At last an American film was speaking to people like him.

Back at Weiler's office, his words flew. "A small but obviously dedicated group of realists has forged artistry, anger and some horrible truths into *On the Waterfront*," he wrote, "as violent and as indelible a film record of man's inhumanity to man as has come to light." The film's greatness, the critic believed, was due largely to the "shatteringly poignant portrait" that Marlon had created of Terry Malloy—"a beautiful and moving portrayal." So highly did Weiler think of the film and Marlon's performance that he wrote a second review a few days later, expanding upon his first: "It is Brando's portrayal of the inarticulate but colorful hero which is the film's outstanding attribute. The grasping for words, the pugilist's walk and language, the inner torment of this young man in a vicious world he can't quite understand, are made pitifully clear when he agonizingly says to his brother, 'I could have been a contender instead of a bum.'"

Three days after the film opened, the line was already ascending into legend.

Weiler was hardly alone in his praise. *Variety's* reviewer declared, "Marlon Brando puts on a spectacular show, giving a fascinating, multi-faceted performance." Jane Corby of the *Brooklyn Daily Eagle* marveled at "the fascinating spectacle" Marlon was able to create "of a nearly lost soul in the throes of evolution." Attending a matinee screening of the film, Corby was stunned by the way Marlon's performance "hypnotized his audience, literally immobilized it."

*On the Waterfront* has strengths beyond its star, of course. All the actors are superb. Kazan's direction kept the story "moving with the speed and shocking effect of a sudden left hook," Weiler judged. The stark gray cinematography of Boris Kaufman, so much of it exteriors, gives the film a European feel, akin to Italian neorealist cinema. The score was composed by Leonard Bernstein, Ellen Adler's one-time beau, the only time the maestro ever wrote specifically for the screen. The film opens with a single French horn, breaking convention in a period when movies tended to kick off with an entire orchestra. Throughout, Bernstein's score elegantly and precisely accompanies the script to convey the story. *Waterfront* was a game-changer in American film, in both content and form. Less than two weeks after its premiere, Bob Thomas of the Associated Press reported that the film was "being hailed as the best picture of the year."

Yet, unquestionably, the wellspring of the film's power is Marlon. "If there is a better performance by a man in the history of films in America," Kazan wrote, "I don't know what it is." Critics shared his assessment, and for six decades, that opinion has not wavered. Foster Hirsch, the historian of the Actors Studio, called Marlon's portrayal of Terry Malloy "the finest performance in American films." Hirsch noted that for Marlon's portrayal of Stanley Kowalski, the most important thing had been "his body and the way he talks." But what was important about Terry Malloy was "how he thinks." For all its exterior shots, the real drama of *On the Waterfront* is interior. Marlon allowed the audience to see that.

From this moment on, Marlon's acting became the benchmark for everything and everyone else; the declarations of virtuosity bandied about since *Streetcar* were now seen as justified. Profiling Marlon for the *New York Times*, Cecelia Ager stopped herself when she referred to her interviewee's "talent" and wrote, "Okay, we'll say it out loud—genius." Marlon Brando was no flash in the pan; he was, in fact, the master. Nearly overnight, all his contemporaries were left in the dust, and Olivier was dethroned. As wonderful as the British actor could be, his performances, according to the critic Harold Brodkey, were really "glorified readings." Marlon, on the other hand, made what he did seem so real. "He doesn't think about it," Kazan said, trying to explain his star's talent to a befuddled press. "Nobody can make him be phony; he holds on to his sense of the truth."

For the man himself, of course, all the talk about genius and truth made him distinctly uncomfortable. *Streetcar*, he believed, remained the better film, because of his "great respect for Tennessee's play." Marlon wasn't as impressed as everyone else by his performance in *Waterfront*. After seeing a rough cut of the film, he'd described his efforts to Karl Malden as "in and out," meaning sometimes he was good, sometimes he wasn't. "I took a look at the film," Marlon remembered. "I thought, 'It can't be that it's come to this.' I walked out. I couldn't even say anything to Gadge." Even the moment that had everyone talking left Marlon ambivalent. The taxi scene, he said, was "actor proof." He downplayed his contribution to it (and, by extension, Steiger's, Kazan's, and Schulberg's). "Everybody feels like he could have been a contender, he could have been somebody," he said. "So that was what touched people. It wasn't the scene itself." Marlon wasn't trying to be modest; he was expressing his continued discomfort with the idea that acting was some sort of achievement for which one should be exalted.

Yet the drumbeat went on. An Oscar nomination was a forgone conclusion, especially since *Waterfront* wasn't just a critical success, but also an enormous box-office hit, Marlon's first since *Streetcar*. The film went "roaring along" all summer, according to *Variety*, overwhelming theaters too small to accommodate the number of people who wanted to see the film. At Oscar time, box-office success always helps, and it wasn't long before the betting games started: would Marlon attend the ceremony the following spring? He hadn't shown up any of the times he'd been nominated previously.

But Marlon was a changed man, people were noticing. He was—dare they say it?—a Hollywood player now. Even as *On the Waterfront* made its triumphant debut in New York, Marlon wasn't there to hear the acclaim. He'd abandoned the city that he loved so much. In the past, when he shot films in Los Angeles, he'd shared places with other actors or stayed in hotels. This time, however, he'd secured a house.

THE REPORTER WAITING in the living room of the Spanish Mission–style house in the hills above Hollywood was taken by surprise when Marlon Brando suddenly appeared before her, "immaculate in pale blue denim pants and white Basque shirt with blue stripes"—which, the reporter noted, marked "the exceptional breadth of his shoulders." Marlon smiled and gestured to the buffet lunch laid out by the studio publicity department in the dining room of his house. "He stands easy and relaxed," the reporter observed, and "the astonishing delicacy and sensitivity" of his face was "at odds with his strong athlete's torso." The lady was definitely charmed.

Since arriving in Los Angeles, Marlon had been entertaining members of the press regularly at his home. This was what movie stars did, after all. They wooed reporters, provided them with scoops, radiated charm and graciousness to press and public alike. Marlon knew how to be charming, especially with women (though he still kept his distance from Hedda Hopper). Another reporter who got the buffet lunch treatment called him "a new man, in attitude and behavior," and dated his newfound bonhomie to the previous April.

Dodie, of course, had died on March 31. Marlon was plain about the reasons he was now playing the Hollywood game: "I promised my mother that things would be okay," he told *Modern Screen*. Dodie had wanted him to stop fighting with people, he explained; she'd wanted him to be cooperative. Admitting that he hadn't been "too diplomatic" when he first came to Hollywood, Marlon said he wanted to revamp his image. From here on in, he was taking his career seriously. "Up until a while ago," he told another reporter, "I regarded acting not as my career, but as a way to make a living. I really didn't know what I wanted to do. Eventually, a man's got to channel his energy into something, and for me it's acting."

Marlon's change of heart was, of course, great news to the studio. Now that they had a cooperative accomplice, the public-relations machinery kicked into high gear. *Streetcar* stage manager Robert Downing was recruited to write a piece for *Screenland*. He cast the star as a regular Joe: "Throughout the many months that Marlon played Stanley, he did not change toward any member of the company. Neither the sensational personal reviews or the fantastic attention [he] drew from magazines and the general public altered Brando's relationships with his colleagues." Downing, who'd also played a bit in *Waterfront*, complained that writers rarely mentioned Marlon's "humility, his affectionate attitude toward his coworkers, his loyalty to friends, his quick defense of the underdog." While his actions in turning down *The Egyptian* might have seemed arrogant and selfish, Downing posited, "I have a notion that whatever lies behind Marlon's . . . decisions, there is to be found a very special kind of personal courage."

A coordinated rebranding effort was taking place. Downing's *Screenland* article was hyped in advance in *Variety*. An article in *Modern Screen* continued the same theme of Marlon as a man of the people, revealing how he had defended the day players on *Waterfront* when Sam Spiegel was late with their pay. "Where do you come off with that stuff?" Marlon had supposedly bellowed at the producer, making him sound an awful lot like Terry Malloy. Alice Hoffman wrote in *Modern Screen* that Marlon never turned down a fan, signing autographs "until his fingers were numb." That much was simply balderdash, but necessary for the rebranded Brando.

MARLON BRANDO REFORMS, blared the cover lines of one fan magazine. "It's a brand-new Brando," the article inside revealed. Publicists made sure that reporters noticed how Marlon refused to be photographed in a tee shirt on the set of *Désirée*. "I've got suits," he said. "I've got shirts. I know how to knot a tie. I want to destroy the impression that I'm constantly bumming around." Alice Hoffman triumphantly declared, "The T-shirted terror is tame at last."

As proof of that, one needed only to look at his latest projects. Marlon no longer occupied himself with all those grimy, edgy, dangerous pictures that had gotten churches and Senate subcommittees so worked up. Instead, here he was, in his ruffles and red velvet, playing Napoleon. Gossip columnist Mike Connolly poked fun at the idea, imagining "Marlon wearing a spit curl, with his hand stuck in the front of his waistcoat, strutting like a peacock." But Marlon wasn't fooling around. For a while, he also considered starring in a film version of the Rodgers and Hart musical *Pal Joey*. Director George Cukor was surprised by how personable the young actor was; he'd heard horror stories. "I had a very satisfactory talk with Brando yesterday," Cukor wrote to Columbia Pictures chief Harry Cohn. "He seemed to me to be genuinely interested in playing the part. He was forthright, friendly and simple. He is coming to see me tomorrow for several hours to talk about it further."

Marlon never did sign on for *Pal Joey*. But the fact that he was considering a musical film after the lightweight *Désirée* is evidence that his eye was now on the box office instead of the script. Kazan had called him "only the greatest [and] getting better all the time," but during the summer of 1954, it was hard to find evidence of that, based on the projects Marlon was considering. During these weeks, he was a frequent guest at the home of independent producer Samuel Goldwyn, "which can only mean one thing," Hedda Hopper reported: Marlon was being offered the lead role in the Tony-winning Frank Loesser musical *Guys and Dolls*. A year earlier, Marlon would never have entertained the idea of becoming a song-and-dance man, let alone allowing himself to be wooed by the bourgeois Goldwyn in this way. But this was a new Marlon.

Over elaborate dinners in a dining room dripping with crystal chandeliers, the malaprop-prone Goldwyn insisted that Marlon could play the part of the suave gambler who stops the show with the song "Luck Be a Lady." A smiling Marlon sat there soaking up all the fawning sycophancy. He'd always considered himself merely "a bathtub singer," he told reporters, but if Goldwyn insisted he "could sing and dance, why not take the chance?" On August 4, Hedda Hopper announced, "Marlon Brando gets the plum role of the season, Sky Masterson, in *Guys and Dolls*." For his efforts, Marlon would earn more than two hundred grand, almost double his salary for *Waterfront*.

Playing the game had paid off. No doubt Dodie would have been pleased.

IN THE MAKEUP room on the Twentieth Century–Fox lot, Rita Moreno, a pretty, petite, dark-eyed actress, was getting pancaked and rouged for her bit part in the Napoleonic melodrama *Désirée*. She'd get no credit for her appearance in the film, but she was nonetheless a starlet on the rise: her face had adorned the cover of *Life* magazine the previous March. Born in Puerto Rico, the daughter of a seamstress, Moreno was trained as a dancer and possessed extraordinary drive. She was determined to play more than "the stereotypical Latina roles," she said, "the Conchitas and Lolitas in Westerns" where she "was always barefoot." Although her part in *Désirée* was only as a dancer, she had every hope it would lead to bigger things. Nothing was going to get in Moreno's way of achieving major stardom.

Then she met Marlon Brando.

He strolled into the makeup room wearing a white cotton tee shirt and white cotton trousers. As he'd done every day since shooting on *Désirée* began in the spring of 1954, Marlon hoisted himself up onto a high stool to be transformed into the legendary emperor of France. Hedda Hopper had spotted him up there once, "chewing gum enthusiastically, with his hair combed over his forehead à la Audrey Hepburn, a ponytail behind, and a new nose [being] built up by the make-up experts." Marlon sat on the stool beating out "a bop rhythm on his chest."

Hopper found him absurd. Rita Moreno, however, had a very different reaction. She was struck first by Marlon's scent—"fresh, clean and natural," she said—which she learned later was Vent Vert by Balmain, a woman's perfume. As she watched Marlon being transformed into Napoleon, Moreno was mesmerized. He was "swaggeringly irresistible," she said, with his "muscular physique, hooded eyes, full lips, and quick mind." When she was introduced to him, she responded with a deep, "full-body blush," as though she had been "dropped into a very hot bath."

Marlon wasn't immune to the chemical combustion. His eyes had already found Moreno before they met; he remembered her from the *Life* cover. She was exactly his type: dark, vibrant, earthy, sensual. The attraction between them was palpable in the makeup room. "It was the sort of rush that inspires poetry and songs, novels and Wagnerian operas," Moreno recalled. "From the moment we met, I felt that a web had been spun between us, drawing me to Marlon." And she believed he felt the same way toward her, as he "made no secret" of his attraction to her.

Not long afterward, they became lovers. For more than half a century, Moreno would retain a visceral memory of Marlon's "smooth, polished skin and [the] taste of his sweet breath." In her memoir, her words still reverberated with the emotion she felt back then. "To say that he was a great lover," Moreno wrote, "sensual, generous, delightfully inventive—would be gravely understating what he did not only to my body, but for my soul."

It wasn't just sex: Marlon gave her books on history and philosophy, which Moreno read avidly, hoping to please him. "He introduced me to many ideas and really educated me about the world," she said. He awakened her political conscience, passing on his passion for civil rights and making it hers as well. "There was a lot going on in the world that I'd never thought about," Moreno said. Until that time, she admitted, "I was mostly absorbed in 'me.'" But so were most actors; their narcissism was what made Marlon so uneasy about his profession. Moreno knew the best way to ensure that he kept coming back to her was to embrace his interests—and to never, ever, talk about acting. "I knew he didn't like to talk about it," she said, "and bemoaned people who made it the topic when they were with him."

And so, one more woman fell head over heels in love with the charismatic, enigmatic Marlon, that "sensitive soul" who shielded himself with a "self-protective armor," as Moreno described him. "Marlon's arms embraced me in a way I had never known," she wrote. "It wasn't just his muscles holding me, loving me, but his very being. Even though we never said the words, 'I love you,' as much as Marlon could love any woman, I knew he loved me."

*As much as Marlon could love any woman.*

Sitting on the set, watching Moreno and Marlon rehearse an "intricate" dance routine, Josanne Mariani, visiting from New York, was impressed with their professionalism and intense concentration on each other. "How wonderful!" she thought. Remembering the moment sixty years later, an older, wiser Josanne would call her younger self "very naïve." In some circles, the pretty French girl was known as Marlon's girlfriend, but he didn't introduce her that way, certainly not to Moreno, who seemed oblivious to her presence. For Marlon, juggling two (and sometimes more) women at the same time was a skill he'd mastered long ago.

*Désirée* wrapped that summer. *The Egyptian*, the film that had caused Marlon to try to escape, to find something beyond this world of acting make-believe, had turned into a box-office bonanza. If Marlon cared about such things, he might have hoped *Désirée* would do even better. But he had little love for the picture. He'd enjoyed working with his leading lady, Jean Simmons, whom he'd found "charming, beautiful and experienced," but the film itself was "superficial and dismal," he thought, especially following *Waterfront*. The director, Henry Koster, was pedestrian after Kazan. Marlon's performance has moments of interest, especially when he's playing Napoleon not unlike himself, tender and charming if a bit manipulative with his ladylove. But mostly he's just reciting the overblown dialogue that was so common to epics of the period, at one point melodramatically knocking over a chair as he does so: "Can it be that you have forgotten the battlefields on which you fought and the armies which you led?"

Unintentionally campy as he scowls and poses, Marlon strides across the CinemaScope screen in his epaulets and skintight satin breeches, revealing a wider seat and thicker waist than in the past. This was just the sort of nonsense he'd known he'd have to put up with when he decided to return to moviemaking. *Désirée* had been forced upon him. But at least he could content himself that his next project, while hardly Shakespeare or Shaw, would have the wit of Abe Burrows, whose book for *Guys and Dolls* would've won the Pulitzer if Burrows hadn't been blacklisted by the House Un-American Activities Committee. Enduring these ups and downs would be Marlon's lot now that he had decided to ride the Hollywood carousel.

THE NIGHT WAS warm and the sky flecked with red neon. Marlon made his way down Hollywood Boulevard, past the bars and the poolrooms, the souvenir shops and the strip clubs. He was wearing a ragged hat, eyeglasses, and a fake mustache, a disguise prepared for him by his friend Phil Rhodes, a makeup man, specifically to enable excursions like this. Back in New York, before he was famous, Marlon had loved to watch people while he himself remained unobserved. Appearing like a shaggy hobo was the only way he could accomplish this now. From behind the thick spectacles, he watched the colorful parade of pedestrians.

In many ways, Marlon was alone in Los Angeles. The friends who'd anchored him in the past were mostly back east, or out of his life completely by now. He'd made very few intimates in the film capital, eschewing the social scene of the Brown Derby and Mocambo. He had Moreno, of course, but that relationship was still very new and mostly clandestine. Louella Parsons observed how Marlon tended to shield himself with "his own pals—his makeup man, his secretary and his stand-in . . . his private life is so completely his own." Phil Rhodes had been a friend since the 1940s; Phil's wife, Marie, was Marlon's stand-in for lighting and camera angles. The Rhodeses were the last remaining intimates Marlon had on the West Coast; Celia Webb, who had briefly resumed secretarial duties, had once again departed for Europe. Even Josanne had left his side temporarily, returning to visit her parents in France.

Meanwhile, Maureen, Janice, Kaye, and Wally were all busy in New York, and while Marlon had started off in Hollywood by securing old friends extra work on his films, that had come to an end. Sam Gilman had played a bit in *Désirée*, but had returned to New York to work in television. Freddie Fiore, after several jobs on Marlon's sets, was now back on heroin, and no one knew where he was. And, sadly, there'd been a quarrel with Darren Dublin. On the set of *Désirée*, Darren had reportedly made a pass at Josanne, perhaps in retaliation for Marlon's coming on to Darren's wife, Florence, who played the small part of Napoleon's sister. The two old friends nearly came to blows, and they never spoke again. "I was very hurt," Darren said, "even though I had seen that Marlon had been changing. They forced him into doing the film and he was bitter."

Even with Stella, there was distance. Never in her life would she breathe a word of criticism of Marlon in public; even in private, she remained guarded about him. "I don't think she was hurt," Ellen would say, when asked if Marlon's frequent disparagement of the acting profession bothered her mother. Yet, Stella had harbored grand hopes for Marlon. She'd thought he could be as great as her "Papa," Jacob Adler, playing Shakespeare, Schiller, Lessing, Chekhov, Gorky, Ibsen, Shaw, Strindberg. Watching him strut through such fluff as *Désirée* must have given her some pangs. She'd accepted that Marlon, like so many theater actors before him, would go to Hollywood; but when he stayed there, taking on trifles while abandoning the stage, surely she was disheartened. And on some level, Marlon must have known that he had disappointed Stella, one of the few people in his life who had never disappointed him.

They rarely saw each other now. So much of what had grounded Marlon in the past had disappeared. Significantly, he was also no longer seeing Dr. Mittelman; their sporadic sessions since his relocation had proved insufficient to keep Marlon moored. As a result, he lashed out at his therapist, the man whose every word he'd once hung on. Twelve months earlier, he'd revealed in a letter to his parents that Mittelman had told him he probably needed only another year of analysis. When that year was up, however, and all his issues weren't resolved (Dodie had died in the meantime), Marlon felt cheated. "I came to him seeking empathy, insight and guidance," he griped, "but all I got was ice." Once again, he felt abandoned by a father figure. "I was still on my own," Marlon realized, left to deal with the trauma by himself.

If he'd hoped that wandering in disguise through the streets of Hollywood would have been a tonic, he was disappointed. This wasn't New York, where adventure, mystery, culture, and music awaited at the end of every alleyway. "It's a daytime town," Marlon said of Los Angeles. In some ways, the film colony existed only for sunshine and palm trees and swimming pools, and its streets were as much façades as those on the studio backlots. "All artificial emotion," Marlon said, "and insincere fellowship." Jack Larson put it plainly: "He hated it out here." And when Marlon felt off course, alienated, unsupported, and purposeless, danger lay ahead: the darkness could come back at any moment and annihilate him.

OCTOBER 29 / "Ils sont là!" shouted one of the journalists on the white sand beach of the Île des Embiez, off the Côte d'Azur of France in the Mediterranean Sea. He pointed over to the man and woman meandering along the marina. "There they are! Monsieur Brando et Mademoiselle Josanne!"

The late-afternoon sun shone in a cloudless blue sky, reflecting across a sparkling turquoise sea. The day was warm, in the low seventies Fahrenheit, and the beach Marlon and Josanne were strolling along was an isolated one, with few tourists. If it hadn't been for the pack of reporters rushing toward them across the sand, they would have gone unnoticed, just one more pair of lovers on the Riviera, wearing similar blue-striped Basque shirts.

"Is it true?" one of the newsmen shouted. "Are you really getting married?"

Suddenly, as if they'd planned it, Marlon and Josanne dropped hands and bolted, kicking up sand as they made a dash for the trees. For fifteen minutes, they played "hide and seek," in the words of one journalist, making a great show of not wanting to be caught. They'd been evading reporters all day long, ever since a two-line notice had appeared in a morning newspaper of the nearby town of Toulon, placed by Josanne's parents announcing her engagement to Marlon. When reporters showed up outside the family's modest home in the village of Bandol, the couple had quickly hopped onto a motor scooter and, with great gales of laughter, zoomed off along the coast road. Josanne clung to Marlon's waist, her head scarf trailing in the wind. In hot pursuit, the newsmen followed. When they'd get too close, Marlon would zig this way and that, shaking them off. Returning to Bandol, he'd commandeered one of Josanne's stepfather's boats and taken the chase across the Gulf of Lion to Embiez. It was there where they finally surrendered. After their spirited pas de deux among the trees, the couple emerged from the woods.

The newsmen wanted to know: Were they really tying the knot?

"This is no gag or publicity stunt as some reporters have had the disgustingly bad taste to imply," Marlon insisted. Yes, they were getting married, he said, as Josanne stood meekly by his side. He'd arrived in France during the second week of October and had spent some time in Paris, before taking the train down to Bandol on the twenty-seventh. There, as Josanne would recall many years later, Marlon took her aside and slipped a ring on her finger—"a beautiful silver Native American ring with a turquoise oval stone"—and said to her, "We're engaged." He didn't ask her, he told her, and sealed the deal with a kiss. "He wasn't the kind of person who would get down on his knee and propose," Josanne said. "That just wasn't his style."

Although some reporters suggested Josanne's parents had pressured Marlon to make her an "honest woman," their daughter insisted that wasn't true. Nor was the engagement a publicity stunt, she said—or, if it was, she wasn't wise to it. The day was "entirely joyous," Josanne remembered nearly six decades later. "That night we celebrated at dinner with my stepfather's freshly caught lobsters."

On the beach at Embiez, reporters noted how frequently Josanne looked up at Marlon with "stars in her eyes." When her fiancé told her to pose with him for the cameras, she happily complied. Marlon smiled broadly into the flashcubes, though Josanne's expression was more discreet. Then, as one journalist recounted, "Brando cut short the performance when he took Josanne by the arm and led her back to the boat they were using." Off they went, back across the gulf to Bandol, as the sun began to sink in the west, staining the water red and pink.

What was going on here? Had the notoriously footloose Marlon Brando really decided to settle down with a wide-eyed ingénue who possessed neither the sophistication of Ellen Adler nor the street smarts of Celia Webb?

Early the next morning, the affianced couple faced reporters again, this time with Josanne's parents. "I want to get to know my future parents-in-law," Marlon told the gathered news corps, explaining he'd be spending some time in Bandol. "Very nice people." They were, in fact, people Marlon would like: unpretentious, indifferent to fame, dedicated to their simple way of life. "I cried at first," Josanne's mother said, in a statement translated by the United Press, "when my daughter told me she would marry an actor and become an American citizen. But I know she will be happy because Marlon will do everything in his power to make her happy."

At last, Josanne herself spoke, saying she hoped Marlon's holiday in her little village would give him "the peace of mind and soul he is seeking."

"I love Josie," Marlon told the newsmen, doing his best to erase any doubt. "We are going to be very happy."

THE NEWS OF Marlon Brando's engagement hurtled across the globe in a matter of hours. In the United States, people picked up their newspapers on the morning of October 30 to see the story confirmed in stark black and white: Brando—heartthrob of millions, defiant Hollywood maverick—was getting married.

His friends were dumbstruck. Tennessee Williams, aware of Marlon's fluid, unorthodox sexuality, told Elia Kazan that their protégé was "smoldering with something, [but] I don't think it's Josanne." This was not how Marlon lived in the world. "At first I didn't believe it," Rita Moreno told Aline Mosby of the United Press. "Once on a date he said that society wants to tie a person down. He wanted to find some island and live there and do what he wanted." She admitted, however, that Marlon could be "a lost soul, looking for a niche." Her heartbreak was obvious. "Apparently," she said, "he's found it."

Movita, older and shrewder, wasn't buying any of it. "It is difficult for me to believe," she said. "He is such a free soul. He never wanted to be tied down. We shall see. There is a big difference between being engaged and getting married."

Indeed, there was, for later on the same day that Marlon had posed so warmly with his in-laws-to-be, he "cut short his idyll" in Bandol, wire reports revealed, and left Josanne "weeping at the window as he drove off down the coastal road." To reporters, he insisted that he and his fiancée would reunite in a few weeks in New York; he was leaving now, he explained, only because of the "persecution" of the press. For the rest of his European holiday, Marlon told a Reuters scribe he had no definite plans; he would head from Bandol to Cannes and "might tour Italy." Then, darkly, he reportedly confided to another writer, "I put no stock in engagements."

Whether he actually said those words didn't matter, as the quote ricocheted around the world. In Los Angeles, Louella Parsons called it "the year's low in taste." No one seemed to believe that Marlon was really going to marry Josanne—except, apparently, Josanne.

WHEN HE'D ARRIVED in New York on October 6 to depart on his European voyage, Marlon's taxi had driven him straight through a picket line of baggage handlers on Pier 88, members of the International Longshoremen's Association, who were striking for better wages. The *New York Times* made mention of the irony: Terry Malloy crossing a picket line of longshoremen. "The movie star meekly joined his 533 fellow passengers in shepherding their own luggage," the *Times* reported, until office employees of the *Île de France* took over, trundling the bags onto an elevator to get them onto the ship. Marlon made no statement about the strike. If he was going to Europe with the intention of asking Josanne to marry him, he didn't want to launch his journey with the wrong kind of headlines.

For the past seven months, Marlon had been complicit in a public-relations campaign to remake his image. It's impossible to see the announcement of his engagement to Josanne outside that context. The stunned girlfriends were correct: Marlon *did* believe that marriage was society's way of tying a person down. He really *was* a free soul. Marriage to him was "bourgeois," as he once told Maureen Stapleton. Certainly, he saw few positive images of the institution in his own life.

But if Brando were truly to be rebranded, he would need a wife.

Since the beginning of the movies, marriage had been the protocol of the film colony, offering real cachet to those who participated. In a community that prized middle-class respectability (and which made selling the same to the nation its primary business), marriage served its members well, providing them with a veneer of social standing and clout. How preferable it was to be invited to an industry function (and to be written up in the columns) as "the Marlon Brandos" rather than as "Marlon Brando and date du jour," which only served to remind the public of one's outsider status. In this light, divorce wasn't seen so much as the antithesis of marriage, but rather, a tolerable consequence of it. In Hollywood, after all, marriage wasn't meant to be forever, just for the amount of time it was useful.

Marlon cared about Josanne. No doubt he intended to treat her well. But he wasn't marrying her because he loved her. He was marrying her because she was the ideal choice. Kaye Ballard said if Marlon were ever to get married, "He would need a very tolerant wife." The nineteen-year-old Josanne was submissive, deferential, and unencumbered with her own ambition. Unlike Movita or Rita Moreno or any of Marlon's other women, Josanne would remain in the background. Most important, her naïveté would allow her husband to continue the relationships with other women—stronger, sultrier other women—that he needed, frankly, to survive.

Because it was only in the arms of strong, passionate women that Marlon had ever been able to find refuge from his childhood trauma, and that was never truer than now, in the middle part of the 1950s, when he was still grieving his mother and trying so hard to make a go of his career. Josanne was for show; she was far too acquiescent to truly excite him. His women needed to be strong—strong enough not to break the way his mother had, but also, significantly, not stronger than he was. That was the clincher. "He needed to have control so as not to get wounded," Ellen Adler said. "He had been so wounded as a child."

Yet, at the start of a relationship, Kaye Ballard added, Marlon never intended to be malicious or heartless: "He never wanted to hurt someone he cared about." It was simply beyond his control that so many of them—Josanne and Rita Moreno being merely the latest—fell in love with him in a way that he could not return.

Marlon's "womanizing," as various friends called it, became more compulsive after Dodie's death. Ballard said he often needed to have "every woman in the room, if not that night then soon." When he'd reminisce for his memoirs forty years later, he would spend more time talking about his sexual conquests than about almost anything else in his life. "I had a lot of affairs," he admitted. "Far too many to describe me as a perfectly normal, reasonable, intelligent person." The history of his sexual life, he told his collaborator, was essentially Richard von Krafft-Ebing's pioneering nineteenth-century study *Psychopathia Sexualis*, documenting hundreds of case histories of human sexual behavior.

Stories abound that Marlon had a sexual fling with Marilyn Monroe around this time. Blonde and fragile, Monroe was hardly Marlon's type, but she had an earthy sense of humor that he would have liked, so it's possible that he did go there, once or maybe twice. Mostly, however, he went after less-famous women. Even the wives of his friends weren't off limits; he admitted that married women were more exciting to pursue. During the fall of 1954, there were reports that he was having an affair with the actress Roberta Haynes, who was married to his agent, Jay Kanter. The couple split, but Kanter continued representing Marlon. Phil Rhodes accepted the fact that, at some point, Marlon would make a pass at his (dark and Italian) wife, Marie. "That was part of his background," Rhodes said.

Marlon admitted that his sexual adventures were in direct response to his feelings about his parents. "I went after women to make up for what my mother failed to give me and to spite my father," he said, reflecting back later in life.

For some women, his wounded nature acted like a magnet. Rita Moreno was unable to let him go, even with the announcement of his engagement to Josanne. Marlon was very aware that Moreno was falling in love with him, yet he hadn't forewarned her about his plans. To an outsider, it would appear he'd used her and then disposed of her, but Moreno saw things differently. "I don't believe he ever meant to be deliberately cruel," she said. "Marlon was in the throes of his own compulsion, which left him with insatiable sexual needs. He could seduce any woman he wanted, and that made him a walking A-bomb . . . unable to control his own desires." Only many years later was Moreno able to understand that pathology, of course; at the time, she was confused, miserable, and heartbroken. Yet, even though she came to understand Marlon, she never excused him: "Whatever damage was done to Marlon in his childhood was compounded by the hurt he inflicted on others."

From Marlon's point of view, at least during the 1950s, he wasn't behaving boorishly toward his girlfriends. In fact, he prided himself on always treating women with respect. "I lived with value systems that were taught to me when I was very young," he said. "I get up when a woman comes into the room. I open the door for women." Yet, beyond those superficial, outdated courtesies, he took no responsibility for what women might expect of him; they were being "hysterical," he told Jack Larson once, when they claimed he had "led them on." The strength Marlon was seeking in women was in fact an illusion if he always had to be stronger. "Marlon could perceive very quickly whether [women] had any dominance in them," said Phil Rhodes, "and if they did, you wouldn't see that [woman] in his company anymore." Only Ellen had possessed such strength, and after Ellen, Marlon never again pursued a serious relationship with a woman who led a life completely independent from, and equal to, his.

"I think, essentially, men fear women," Marlon said. "It comes from a sense of dependence on women. Because men are brought up by women, they're dependent on them. Men's egos are frightened by women." His generalized statement would perhaps be truer if it had been spoken personally. Not until much later would Marlon realize how his fear had motivated his own relationships, how it had caused him to steer clear of truly strong women. Not since Vivien Leigh had Marlon been cast opposite an actress with authority comparable to his. "He avoided having to measure up to women who were in any way his equal," observed the critic Molly Haskell. He was intimidated, for example, by the formidable actress Anna Magnani, resisting Tennessee Williams's attempts to costar them for years.

And so: Josanne. Sweet, docile Josanne, who made him feel like a man. They would marry soon after they returned to the United States, Marlon told the press. It would be the crowning achievement of his new life as a cooperative, bankable Hollywood star.

"We shall see," said Movita.

"WHO'S THE BLONDE?" the reporters shouted at him as Marlon arrived in Rome on the morning train from Nice, a day after he'd left his fiancée behind in Bandol. How fast news traveled. Late the day before, when the train had stopped in Genoa, Marlon had been spotted having coffee in the station café with a young blonde Italian woman wearing a tight-fitting yellow sweater and green skirt. Confronted with it now, Marlon tried to shrug off the incident. "She recognized me and sat down to talk," he said. "A little bobbysoxer type. I can't even remember her name."

But conductors were reporting that the woman, after boarding at San Remo, had made her way to Marlon's compartment; when a porter asked her to leave, she'd begged to stay, and there was no apparent objection from Marlon. At Genoa, when a photographer snapped a shot of them at the café, Marlon asked for a copy to be sent to his address in Paris. Only when more reporters descended did he realize that he might be causing problems for himself. To the reporters in Rome, he insisted that he'd told the girl "to take it on the lam, but she just wouldn't go away." Every time a photographer snapped a picture, Marlon griped, the girl was "there mugging it." He declared that there was nothing to the story; conductors backed him up by assuring the press the girl had spent the night in her third-class coach while Marlon remained alone in his first-class sleeper.

"Spittoon rubbish," Marlon called the story. "I love Josie." Yet, when pressed as to when the marriage would take place, he now hedged his bets. Contradicting his statement from the day before, he said the marriage would not take place right away. "It wouldn't be fair to her," he explained. "She has a lot of growing up to do yet. It's not fair to grab her away from her life before it is hardly begun."

In those twenty hours on the train, had Marlon found some time to think? Had he realized what he was asking of Josanne? He seemed genuinely concerned about her, about this Hollywood marriage he had planned for her. Less than forty-eight hours after announcing their engagement, he seemed to be wondering if he could really put her through such an ordeal.

"I'm worried that she might be upset," he told the newsmen hounding him, "especially about that blonde on the train." He turned to deliver a warning to the gathered reporters. Josanne was "a very shy girl," he told them, "and can be hurt easily." He advised them to be careful with her. "The French don't like their affairs pried into," he said. "I told Josanne to stay cool and not flip her lid."

If he was feeling concerned, perhaps even a little guilty, about grabbing her away from her life, he was also, surely, thinking of his own. This was how it would be if he got married. Every girl on every train, every girl he ever flirted with, would be suspect. Marlon understood he'd never make it as a top Hollywood star if he remained the unmarried lothario. But as a *married* lothario, he'd fare even worse. He'd forfeited a lot when he decided to play by Hollywood's rules; how much more was he willing to give up?

He'd come to Italy to attend the premiere of *On the Waterfront* in Rome, something he never would have done a year earlier, but this was all part of his new, accommodating role as industry player. When it was learned that he would go to Italy, *Variety* wrote, "The Motion Picture Export Association will naturally make use of him." Making use of Marlon Brando was not something the film industry was accustomed to. Yet what also drew him, certainly, was the chance to meet up with Christian Marquand; Marlon admitted to reporters he was planning to see his good friend. The invisibility of gay relationships in the press meant at least there'd be no scuttlebutt about spending time with Marquand, and so, for more than a week, news of Marlon dried up; whatever activities he and Marquand got up to, they kept them strictly below the radar. This would be his life if he got married, Marlon had to realize: to do what he wanted to do, he'd have to hide and sneak around.

When he reemerged on November 9, appearing at the Cinema Fiamma in Rome, hundreds of enthusiastic Italian moviegoers turned out. "A ruffled but grinning Marlon Brando had to shoulder his way through a crowd of shouting, applauding fans" to get inside the cinema, newspapers reported. After the screening of *Waterfront*, he was given a gold cup by an association of Italian critics. *Waterfront* had taken a second-place Silver Lion Award (behind the Italian-made *Romeo and Juliet*) at the recent Venice International Film Festival, and many critics felt Marlon had been overlooked for the top acting honor. This award was in some ways a consolation prize, and despite his antipathy to acting competitions, Marlon accepted the gold cup warmly. "Grazie, grazie," he said as the audience cheered. Rarely, one Italian reviewer said, was any American actor so "humble and accommodating."

ON NOVEMBER 26, Marlon steamed back into New York aboard the SS *United States*, posing for the newsreel cameras on the deck looking dapper in his dark overcoat and hat. At the pier, he gave a short interview to the newsreel reporters, who asked if he still planned to marry Josanne. Marlon was composed and deliberate in his reply. "Yes, I think sometime in the summer," he said. Josanne, as it turned out, was waiting for him in the city, where they posed for more pictures together. Asked again for a wedding date, Marlon now said "next month." Josanne, wearing a beret and scarf, said nothing, just smiled an enigmatic grin.

She'd been in the States for two weeks. Before leaving France, she had been caught by newspaper photographers at an artist's studio in Paris, where she'd once worked as a model. Asked to pose beside a nude painting of herself, she refused. "In France, it is different," the painter explained. "In the United States, they might not understand." More photographers were waiting when her plane touched down in New York. Her hair clipped in a short pixie style, she did not suffer the newsmen gladly, just as Marlon had warned. No, she snapped, she would not smile, because she was "too tired." Only after much coaxing did she hold up a photo they gave her of Marlon. When one reporter asked, "Is there any truth to the talk—" Josanne interrupted: "No!" The reporter finished his question: "—that it's just publicity?" Josanne replied irritably, "No, there is not."

A few days later she'd composed herself enough to appear on NBC's *Colgate Comedy Hour* with its "singing host" Gordon MacRae. She was billed as "Marlon Brando's girl—direct from France," with ads announcing her appearance running in major newspapers. "She did little more than say hello," reported the AP's Aline

Mosby, "but the ratings leaped." Not even Eddie Fisher and Debbie Reynolds, sometimes dubbed "America's Sweethearts," who'd just announced their own marriage plans, had generated this kind of interest.

If Marlon's goal had been to secure a new image, he'd achieved it by the end of 1954. "Four months ago," Steve Cronin wrote in *Modern Screen*, "we told you Marlon had been tamed. Now it seems the wild one has been domesticated as well!" Josanne had worked, at least in term of public relations.

Whether Marlon was pleased with his success remains an open question.

Before heading back to Los Angeles, he made a point to visit Stella. He had moved far away from the world over which she presided, the world that had first given him a sense of himself and of things that truly mattered. For the short time of his visit, sitting around the table in her dining room, he was transported back to that world. As always, the conversation soared. Stella was now the doyenne of acting teachers in New York. The fall term of her academy at 50 Central Park West had recently gotten under way; among the students she coached in the mid- to late 1950s were James Coburn, Peter Bogdanovich, Sydney Pollack, and Warren Beatty. Meanwhile, her husband, Harold Clurman, had recently directed Jean Arthur in *St. Joan* and was preparing to start William Inge's *Bus Stop*. Stella's brother Luther Adler had just finished a revival of Chekhov's *Three Sisters*, directed by none other than Lee Strasberg. So, there was plenty of art, culture, and literature to talk about, and lots of lively theater gossip, just like the old days. "Whenever he'd come back," Ellen Adler said, "they'd pick up as if there had been no time lost."

There were also, almost certainly, political discussions about *Brown v. Board of Education* and school desegregation. For all her high-minded love of art and theater, Stella prided herself as living in the real world. She once told the playwright and novelist

Irwin Shaw, "I spend my time experiencing the things you only write about." This was what Marlon had given up when he decided to accept the terms and conditions of movie stardom, and this was what he still craved: real, raw, messy, tricky, complicated life.

In Stella's apartment, there was no phoniness, no small talk, no idiotic questions about whether he considered himself a genius. But there *was* talk about civil rights and the arms race and creeping commercialism: just a few weeks earlier, Clurman had penned a piece for the *New York Times* deploring the pressure put on artists by producers to appeal to the lowest common denominator in order to maximize profits. How did Marlon feel, hearing such talk? How much, if anything, did he share about his own most recent project, in which he'd spent his time strutting around in Napoleonic breeches and mouthing insipid dialogue?

Whether he brought his fiancée to meet his old friends is unknown. Ellen didn't think he did—or would—but couldn't say for absolute certain. Josanne was, after all, a living, breathing example of how Marlon had sold out the ideals he'd learned from the Adlers in what now seemed like another world.

A year earlier, Marlon had brought Stella a gift: a rare Lhasa Apso he'd found for her in Venice. Was the dog an attempt, even an unconscious one, to win back any favor he feared he'd lost with her? Ellen couldn't say one way or the other. But Stella was, after all, the mother figure who had never disappointed him, and Marlon the son who, on some level, must have believed he'd let her down. "He certainly wasn't pursuing the sort of career she'd once imagined for him," Ellen said, though she stressed that her mother never offered any criticism of her protégé's choices. Yet even her silence on the topic might have communicated plenty.

That fall, shortly before Marlon's visit, the prized pooch had run off, and Stella feared the worst. Clurman took to a local television station to make an appeal to find the dog. A few days later, the

Lhasa Apso was returned safely to the Adlers. Marlon, however, would not be as easily brought back into the fold.

**MID-FEBRUARY 1955** / On the set of *Guys and Dolls*, Marlon was hunkered in a corner with choreographer Michael Kidd, his head lowered but the tops of his eyes visible, as one reporter noticed, "keeping a watchful gaze on the room." The moment his costar appeared on the set, surrounded by an entourage of friends and assistants, Marlon's eyes narrowed, and he exchanged "whispered confidences" with Kidd. Usually Marlon got along with his costars: Jessica Tandy and Anthony Quinn had been exceptions, though with them, he'd always kept things professional. On this film, however, Marlon openly disliked Frank Sinatra, and the feeling was mutual.

On day one, Sinatra's cavalier dismissal of Marlon's offer to run lines ("I don't go in for that Method crap") had surely irked his costar in more ways than one: Marlon didn't "go in" for the Method, either, and resented people who assumed he did. The bad blood between the two men stretched back to the casting of *On the Waterfront*; Kazan had courted Sinatra for the part of Terry Malloy during the period he was reluctant to work with Marlon again. Sinatra had also wanted Marlon's part in *Guys and Dolls*, believing (most observers thought correctly) that he was better suited to play the slick, singing gambler Sky Masterson. He'd taken the secondary, comedic part of Nathan Detroit hoping to make it into something more. That wasn't what the script called for, however. In his rendition of "Sue Me," he gave the song all the smooth jazz of a Sinatra standard, even as his duet partner, Vivian Blaine, was milking it for laughs. Watching from the sidelines. Marlon was furious. "He's supposed to sing with a Bronx accent, to clown it up," he complained to the director, Joseph Mankiewicz. "We can't have two romantic leads."

This, apparently, was something Marlon now cared about—the same Marlon who, just a year earlier, had happily handed over the lead in the summer tour of *Arms and the Man* to his pal Billy Redfield and taken the supporting, comic part for himself. But now he was worried about being overshadowed in *Guys and Dolls*. Mankiewicz, whom he trusted after their successful partnership on *Julius Caesar*, reassured him. Nathan Detroit, the director said, "offers nothing but variations on one joke. Fear him not, Antony. Let thy name be pricked with mine and let's kill the people."

Sinatra, however, was a force not easily contained in a supporting part. On-screen, his charisma matched Marlon's, although his was suaver and more elegant than his puckish costar's—further evidence that their roles might have been better served if they had been switched. But by early 1955, Brando was the bigger star, so he got to play the lead, something unimaginable just a year earlier.

He was also, as the studio was aware, likely to win an Oscar in a few weeks. For the first time, the nominations were announced live, on the night of February 12, during a ninety-minute variety special on NBC hosted by Jack Webb. When the names for Best Actor were read, no one was surprised that Marlon's, for *Waterfront*, was among them. Pundits declared that the race was now between him and Bing Crosby, nominated for *The Country Girl*. "The contest fixes to be close," observed the *Motion Picture Daily*; the trade paper placed its bets on Crosby because of his popularity in the film capital. Another bookmaker gave the odds to Marlon, but only by a whisker, 6–5, noting, "dislikes Hollywood turf, may hurt."

Yet Marlon was a player now: he was giving every impression of liking the turf just fine. When he got back from Europe, he'd done his part to promote *Désirée*, which opened with a gala "command performance" at New York's Roxy Theatre on November 17,

with twenty-four princes, twenty-three princesses, and an assort-
ment of archdukes, counts, and countesses from the royal houses
of France and Sweden in attendance. Just before the launch of the
film, there was a big hullabaloo about the discovery in Sweden
of a supposedly unknown cache of Napoleon's letters. "Whether
this break was coincidence," the editors of the *Film Bulletin* wrote,
"or just some fancy flacking by [Fox chief] Charles Einfeld's box-
officers, the result is the same: aroused public interest and crowded
theatres."

This was just the sort of hucksterism Marlon usually avoided,
yet while he didn't go quite as far as Fox had once hoped—they'd
wanted him to show up at the *Désirée* premiere wearing the "stylish knee pants of the Napoleonic period"—he did agree to many
of the PR department's requests. On his train trip across the country, he'd stopped off in Chicago to attend a press breakfast at the
Ambassador West Hotel. He was set to grace the covers of *Look*
and *Redbook*. He'd also agreed to promote *Guys and Dolls* when the
time came. "Marlon had never done publicity like this before," Joe
Mankiewicz recalled. "But maybe he said to himself, 'I've made
myself pretty fucking unliked because I pissed on all this stuff.
Maybe I want to go through a cure. Maybe I'll be a nice guy and
see how it works out.'"

On one level, the cure was working out quite well. Marlon was
now in the top ten of box-office stars, and while *Waterfront* had gotten him there, *Désirée* ensured he'd remain for some time to come.
In just its first week of release, the film had rocketed to second
place among the highest-grossing pictures in the country, reaching
number one not long after. By the end of the year, *Désirée* would
surpass *Waterfront* in profits, leaving Marlon astonished. "No one
ever lost money underestimating the taste of the American public," he quipped, paraphrasing H. L. Mencken.

The two films were as different as could be imagined: one the
product of a serious, independent auteur, the other a confection of

studio fluff. A "ponderous panorama," Bosley Crowther called *Dé-sirée*, with its stars "acting strangely barren roles." Marlon, Crowther judged, offered just "a fancy façade," and only rarely, as when he described his humiliating retreat from Moscow, did "the glint of a human being appear." To Hollywood bean counters, of course, such distinctions didn't matter. Both films were moneymakers: ergo, they were the same. Marlon's "leap from commercial nowhere to drawing-power rank," as one trade paper observed, would also serve him well at Oscar time. The Academy frequently rewarded not only the best but also the most bankable—and while Marlon was rising in the box-office Top Ten, Bing Crosby was sliding down.

But would Marlon go to the Oscars? That was the question everyone was asking. He had never attended the ceremony before, finding the whole idea of actors competing against one another "ridiculous [and] nonsensical," and decrying the amount of money the studios poured into the effort. "Marlon was sounding off in Hollywood about how meaningless the Oscars were, how all awards were just self-congratulatory nonsense," Budd Schulberg remembered. But if *Waterfront* won some Oscars, Schulberg and Kazan believed, producers might be more willing to make other serious, risky films. Marlon's attitude could doom the effort. Hedda Hopper and Louella Parsons, "those formidable dragons" at Hollywood's gate, as Schulberg called them, had heard Marlon's rants. The screenwriter recalled their reaction: "If that's how Brando felt, they huffed, no Academy members should vote for him or our picture."

Something had to be done. Given the lingering friction with Kazan, Schulberg was the one designated to fly out to Los Angeles to make the case for Oscar to the reluctant star. He didn't think his odds of success were very high—until he came up with a sure-fire idea that couldn't lose.

MARLON SAT IN the Goldwyn commissary, garbed in Sky Masterson's black suit and white tie, his hair slicked back with grease. He looked up from his lunch to see Budd Schulberg striding into the room, and with him was a burly young man. Recognizing Schulberg's companion, Marlon's face lit up. "Roger!" he called out.

The man was Roger Donoghue, the middleweight champ who'd taught him prizefighting moves for *Waterfront*. "Roger was a very appealing guy," Schulberg said. "Funny and extremely articulate." Marlon was very glad to see him. After much backslapping and joking around, Schulberg steered the conversation to the Oscars. They sat back down at the table, and then Donoghue took over.

"Marlon," the pugilist said, "we're still the underdog. The longshoremen are really hoping this film will help them get rid of the shakeups there."

Listening to Donoghue's words, Marlon grew quiet. "Only one thing to do," he said after his friend had finished his spiel. *Waterfront*, he declared, needed to win the Best Picture Oscar—and as many other awards as it could. Schulberg asked if that meant Marlon would show up for the ceremony.

Marlon gave him his dimples. "Okay, fine," he said. "I'll come."

He'd been convinced because Donoghue had made the contest about something bigger than Hollywood. For once, Marlon could play the public-relations game and not feel entirely like a huckster. Not long after that meeting, he accompanied Schulberg to the Golden Globe Awards and "charmed those European birds out of the trees," Schulberg recalled. He accepted the Best Actor award "with grace and a million-dollar smile." This was indeed a new Marlon Brando.

The one thing he wouldn't do, however, was place personal calls to Hedda and Louella. "Screw that," he said. "I'm not going that far."

IN THE *GUYS AND DOLLS* recording studio, Frank Sinatra couldn't hide his amusement. He'd been waiting for this moment. A star for more than a decade, not just in movies but on records and radio, he'd had to put up with this guy—"Mr. Mumbles," Sinatra called him—getting top billing and privileged treatment for the past several weeks. Everyone gushed over the Oscar that Marlon was surely going to win, while no one seemed to remember that Sinatra had won an Oscar himself the previous season, for his performance in *From Here to Eternity*. It had been a supporting Oscar, however—not a Best Actor award, like the one Marlon was surely going to get. It was just one more mark, much to Sinatra's chagrin, that Brando was his superior.

But not in everything. Certainly not here, in the recording studio. The light went on. Sinatra grinned. Marlon faced the music and opened his mouth to sing.

"They tried to record my singing," Marlon remembered, "and I can't sing any better than a kangaroo. So, what they had to do was, I'd sing one phrase and then they'd cut, because I'd be off key. And so, they had to put the whole thing together in tiny little segments." When they looked back at what they'd assembled, Marlon recalled, "They found I hadn't taken one breath during the whole song."

Marlon's talk-singing, especially in the duets with his leading lady (once again Jean Simmons), could never compete with the smooth, full-throated, velvet crooning of Sinatra. "He had no bravado," Ellen Adler said. "He was so soft. He had all this emotion inside, but he couldn't project"—at least not with music: the powerhouse who'd stopped the show with a single cry in *Truckline Café* and bellowed "Stella!" so memorably in *Streetcar* simply could not roar if the words were set to music. "He just couldn't sustain the force and intensity that long," Ellen said—which might be a comment about his life as well. A burst of power was inevitably followed by withdrawal and a period of quietude.

Years later, Sinatra was still steamed over the miscast. "Masterson didn't fit him and he knew it," he grumbled about Marlon. On the set, however, his was the lone voice of dissent. Marlon was shielded from criticism by Mankiewicz and by Simmons, who took his side in the rivalry with Sinatra. The Goldwyn front office wasn't concerned about any deficiencies in his singing, either. When the suggestion was made that Marlon be dubbed, Goldwyn nixed it. He wanted BRANDO SINGS! on the nation's marquees no matter how bad the star sounded. After the surprising success of *Désirée*, *Guys and Dolls* was expected to be a monster hit. The film was budgeted at five million dollars—a colossal sum for 1955—and MGM agreed to distribute it and go all out to promote it. Marlon, once again, promised to do his part.

On the set one day, Walter Pidgeon, the former banker who'd made a career playing courtly upper-class types, approached Marlon for an interview, as part of MGM's promotional campaign. Pidgeon was the sort of studio leading man Marlon had little respect for, and his conservative, antilabor, antisocialist political activism would have been, in any other situation, unpalatable. But here Marlon was gracious. He welcomed Pidgeon to his dressing room and even bought him lunch. During their conversation, Marlon offered the usual banal talking points ("It's not so important to be able to sing well as it is to be able to perform the song"), but he was also irreverent enough to interrupt Pidgeon's long-winded questions to ask for a match to light his cigarette. An obviously flustered Pidgeon complied.

There was also a moment of insight during the interview. Marlon had taken *Guys and Dolls*, he explained, because he'd needed a holiday from "heavy, serious parts" where he had to constantly keep himself "enshrouded in the mood." Indeed, how much more difficult would this experiment in movie stardom have been if Marlon had been playing repeats of Stanley Kowalski and Terry Malloy? That way led to madness, as Marlon so painfully knew. Now, despite Sinatra's perpetual glowering, he found it "pleasant to come to the set and make a joke or two" and not "bat anybody across the face with a dead mackerel." He told Pidgeon truthfully, "I've never been happier working than I am now."

It was when he was not working that things became unbearable. Reporters regularly badgered him about Josanne, whom Marlon had left behind in New York. How often did he see her? Were they still getting married? When was the wedding date? What about reports that he was seeing Rita Moreno again? He was ready to explode. "Marlon could get very angry at those sorts of questions," said Jack Larson. "I saw him punch a hole through a door once when some reporter called him at home and asked him some utterly foolish question."

Yet he put up with such frustrations because he was making two hundred thousand dollars for *Guys and Dolls*. "Two hundred fucking grand," he told Larson. That would go a long way toward offsetting the penalty he'd had to pay Fox for *The Egyptian*. If he was going to make this movie business work, then it had to be "fun and lucrative," he told publicist Dick Clayton, to compensate for "all the bullshit" that threatened to put him in "the nut house," a place he felt he'd come "dangerously close to entering" many times before.

THE TOWN WAS abuzz with Oscar talk. Given Marlon's new, obliging attitude, the industry coalesced around him in support. Columbia, which had distributed *Waterfront* for Sam Spiegel, took out full-page ads in *Variety* to boost Marlon's chances among Academy voters. Publicists collected testimonials from an array of big names—Kirk Douglas, Julie Harris, Shelley Winters, Mervyn LeRoy, Sam Goldwyn—claiming Marlon's was the performance of the year. None carried as much weight as Humphrey Bogart's, however, since he was nominated for Best Actor along with Marlon, for his role in *The Caine Mutiny*. "Wrap up all the Oscars, including mine," Bogie proclaimed, "and send them over to Brando."

Marlon had also been winning most of the awards leading up to the Oscars. He'd nabbed the New York Film Critics' Circle award (he'd skipped the ceremony, sending Eva Marie Saint to pick it up for him); the Best Foreign Actor award from the British Film Academy; and the Canadian critics' award. Even Hedda Hopper, despite not receiving a personal call, was now rooting for him. In her column, she reported that a clothing company was manufacturing a line of tuxedos all in different colors for Marlon: "Wouldn't it be fascinating," Hopper wrote, "if he showed up at the Academy Awards show wearing a strawberry colored tux?"

Marlon was being hailed from every corner. But at night, once the makeup came off and Sky Masterson's tap shoes were put away, he'd sit on the terrace of his Hollywood home overlooking the valley, "especially on warm nights," he said, "when the desert wind comes up over the hills." For hours at a time, he wouldn't say a word, even if a visitor came by to see him. "Sometimes," said Dick Clayton, who worked with James Dean and became friendly with Marlon around this time, "after a couple of hours of this, I'd just let myself out and leave him sitting there in the dark, thinking whatever it was that he was thinking about."

**EARLY MARCH 1955** / Marlon's house was ablaze with light. His quiet, contemplative mood had expired, and as was his pattern, he was on an upswing of frenetic activity. This night, he was throwing a costume gala. The bar was stocked, the records were spinning, the bongo drums were out. Marlon's parties, whether at Maureen Stapleton's Fifty-Second Street apartment or the Carnegie Hall tower or here in the Hollywood Hills, were always the same: loud music, drumming, madcap antics. Guests arrived dressed as Martians, marshmallows, and Mouseketeers. Wally Cox came as a roll of Saran Wrap.

For his own costume, Marlon wore just a tee shirt and boxer shorts, from which dangled "a thick, red-rubber schlong," his friend Jeff Brown remembered, "perhaps ten inches long and safety-pinned to the fly." With Brown was his nearsighted wife, known as Schwestie, who "never wore her glasses to a party." After being effusively greeted by Marlon, Schwestie pulled her husband aside and whispered, "Please tell Marlon that he's hanging out of his shorts, ever since we got here, for heaven's sake!"

Marlon's sense of humor had the power to liberate him from despondency. When he felt adrift or backed into corners, frustrated by his career or forlorn over relationships, he'd unleash his manic side. One friend would remember going to dinner with him, and he'd distract her by telling her to look across the room; when she'd look back, whatever had been on her plate was gone. Humor didn't always keep the darkness at bay, but it did save him several times. In Hollywood, humor was often his lifeboat. The stultification he felt in this land of philistines, the small capitulations he needed to make almost every day, could be offset by laughter.

Marlon's pranks could be bizarre. One time, he announced to his guests that he'd be riding a unicycle around the room covered in shaving cream, and the first person to laugh would have to come up with something to top it. Everyone prepared to keep stony-faced, but then Marlon showed up covered in lather, but on foot, asking, "Who stole my bike?" With puffs of cream dropping from Marlon's body to the floor, Rita Moreno let out a howl, and immediately everyone was laughing.

Marlon's parties were never going to be the sort of swanky, high-toned affairs to which the social arbiters of the film colony, people like George Cukor, were invited. "They were utter bohemians, the Brandos," said Ellen Adler, "and he more than the others." When he moved out west, Marlon was given a list of things from his agents that an actor should do if he wanted to be accepted. But while he agreed to toss out his tee shirts and put on a tie, he could not play the society game: as Ellen described it, he could not say, "I'm going to get a swell house, have dinner parties, and then get a wife, and she'll have dinner parties." Such a world was incomprehensible to him. "He had absolutely no grid on which to hang all of this," Ellen said.

That was why, as the months wore on, he saw less and less of Josanne. He'd installed her in an apartment on Havenhurst Drive and insisted to reporters that their wedding was still on. But he rarely saw her. By now, Josanne was fed up with the situation. She accused Marlon of having affairs with both Christian Marquand and the eighteen-year-old, newly signed Paramount contract player Ursula Andress. Yet still she "pined for him," said her friend, the cabaret singer André Philippe. Every night, Josanne waited for Marlon at her house. When he didn't show, she'd start smashing wineglasses, crying, "That son of a beetch!" It went on that way, in fact, for a couple of years, until Josanne finally packed up and went home. Marlon had treated her abominably, but at least he hadn't married her. That would have been much worse.

"I'VE REVERSED MY views on a lot of subjects," Marlon told a reporter for *Modern Screen* early that spring. "I used to feel that Hollywood producers weren't being artistic enough, that they were just a bunch of money-grabbing hucksters. Now I realize they have a financial responsibility, that a picture has to make money."

If that sounded very much like his father talking, it probably wasn't a coincidence. In the weeks leading up to the Oscar ceremony, Marlon Senior arrived in Hollywood. His son had likely summoned him. The Nebraska cattle operation had gone bust, and with Marlon's investment portfolio dominated by it, the elder Brando had lost his son a great deal of money. Wally Cox, who'd been roped in as an investor, also lost his shirt. "Like most misers,"

Marlon griped about his father, "he was a poor businessman." Yet, here he was, bringing his old man out to Los Angeles to start yet another business—one in which he intended to be a partner.

Sometime in March, Marlon and his father put together Pennebaker Inc., an independent film production company named in honor of Dodie—appropriately enough, since she'd been the one to send her son back to moviemaking. Working for himself meant that Marlon would henceforth be free from demands from the likes of Darryl Zanuck and Samuel Goldwyn. Yet the idea wasn't his. Most likely it had come from MCA; the agency had arranged similar companies for Charlton Heston, Kirk Douglas, and others. "I don't remember why [Pennebaker] was set up," Marlon recalled. "Probably for tax reasons. It wasn't my idea." He had no desire, he explained, to be "an executor in the film world." He had no interest in personally managing all the details of filmmaking that were traditionally left to the studio. So, he'd brought his father out to Hollywood to oversee that tedium.

Not because he had a high opinion of his father's executive management skills. But, for years, the elder Brando had been finding tax breaks for his son; now, with Pennebaker Inc., there was the promise that Marlon, as a corporate entity instead of an individual, would pay even less in taxes. His father pointed out that if Marlon's personal income was six hundred thousand dollars, he got to keep only sixty thousand of it. If, however, Pennebaker took in six hundred thousand, then Marlon got to keep three hundred thousand. Whether the old man's math was right or not, he'd convinced his son.

But in some ways, it wasn't even for tax purposes that Marlon had hired his father. The real reason he'd brought Brando Senior into the company was his ability to keep a secret—a secret that concerned much more than lower taxes.

The deal was this: his father would provide him with fifty thousand dollars a year to live on while investing everything else—not in cattle, but in gold mines. On the advice of a friend, "my father bought tailings in gold mines," Marlon said, "which had a considerable value because gold [always] went up in price." This time, his son believed, Brando Senior had made a wise investment; Marlon called it a "happy accident." Accident or not, it might do them both well in the end. After five years, Marlon calculated, he'd have enough money "to quit making movies." Five years was long enough to keep his promise to his mother. Just five more years, and he could finally realize his dream to do something else.

Now that he was among the top moneymakers in the business, Marlon could start counting the days until he was free. He had a plan; a cloud lifted. All this puffery and nonsense had an expiration date. "As soon as I could imagine a life for myself away from the indignities of moviemaking," Marlon said, "I was happier." His father was key. For all their antagonism, Marlon could trust his father to keep his secret. He needed the public to believe his commitment to the movies was sincere; it wouldn't do for his escape plan to leak to the press.

Still, where Marlon didn't trust his father was in the day-to-day management of the business. For that, he recruited George Englund, a young actor and would-be producer, and the husband of the actress Cloris Leachman. Marlon met Englund at a party given by Burgess Meredith, with Marlon arriving late, wearing a black leather jacket and escorting Reiko Sato, a Japanese dancer. A few days later, the Englunds accompanied Marlon, this time with Rita Moreno, to the beach. Not long after that, Englund was tapped to run Pennebaker. He had no previous business experience. His sole qualification was that he'd be Marlon Junior's man and keep Marlon Senior in check.

Pennebaker promised freedom to Marlon. But it wasn't without its risks, financial and emotional. Regular interaction with his father could be explosive. And now Hollywood would be watching to see how Marlon, long a critic of the way the established moguls did business, fared in their arena.

That summer, Pennebaker signed an agreement with Paramount to be its distributor. The company was given offices on the Paramount lot, on the second floor of the executive building, right next to the "biggest shots on the lot, Y. Frank Freeman and Hal Wallis," as story analyst Robert Dorff recalled. On the day they moved in, Marlon, in a blue suit, wandered through the suite. "He went to the window which overlooked the courtyard and stared out of it for a very long time," Dorff said. "As I watched him, I wondered what the hell he was thinking." It was reasonable to wonder.

Pennebaker's first film would be "a cowboy picture." The property was *To Tame a Land*, based on the novel by Louis L'Amour. The company also took an option on the baseball novel *Man on Spikes*, written by Jocelyn's new husband, Eliot Asinof. Taking his new position very seriously, Marlon Senior set about securing rights and permissions and kept detailed files on forthcoming productions. He was now sixty years old, and reminded his son of "a British officer in the Bengal Lancers, perhaps a Victor McLaglen with more refinement." Englund thought the elder Brando "spoke in a hypnotic monotone," and was "plodding" where his son was kinetic.

"Appointing his father head of his company, like so much about Marlon," Englund mused, "was a complex matter. Ostensibly he was sharing his success, giving his father a perch in the business world that he had never enjoyed, or earned." But Englund thought it also "provided a way to make war," where Marlon "could select a battle site and retaliate for abuses done in the long ago of his childhood."

One such battle erupted when Marlon Senior wanted to fire Englund, whom he resented. Marlon exploded at the suggestion. "This is my company, you hear me," he told his father, looming over him the way he'd once been loomed over. "You work for me.

You don't hire or fire. You don't leave this fucking office unless I say so."

The "long ago of his childhood" had been turned upside down. Now it was Marlon who made the rules, Marlon who was unyielding in his demands. His father grumbled and cursed, and wrote miles of memorandums critical of his son's decisions, but he stuck around, like "an ox who bore the yoke and beating from his master," in Englund's description. If he had left, he would have had nowhere else to go—at least nowhere as flourishing as this. Marlon, the "worthless" son of whom he had once despaired, had given him status of a kind he'd never known before. He'd once sold chemicals on the road. Now Brando Senior got to meet with movie producers and flirt with movie starlets, all because of his "ne'er-do-well" son. No doubt that was also a reason Marlon had hired him. Success was his best revenge.

**MARCH 30, 1955** / Heading into the RKO Pantages Theatre, on the corner of Hollywood and Vine, Marlon, dapper in his black (not strawberry) tuxedo, had to use the restroom. Leaving behind his entourage (Jay Kanter, his father, and his aunt), he realized, too late, that he had forgotten his security pass at home. A guard stopped him. Marlon had to tell him who he was. So much for fame.

The auditorium of the twenty-five-year-old theater glittered with guests decked out in diamonds and tiaras. A live hookup connected them to NBC's Century Theatre in New York, where those nominees who couldn't make it to Los Angeles awaited the results. Hosted by the efficient Bob Hope, the ceremony moved quickly and seamlessly. Reviewers thought the show was "easy going" but also "glamorous," with appearances by Dorothy Dandridge and Grace Kelly, and songs from Rosemary Clooney ("The Man That Got Away") and Dean Martin ("Three Coins in a Fountain"). Early in the night, *On the Waterfront* started its sweep of the top awards, with a win for Boris Kaufman's cinematography. When a pregnant Eva Marie Saint, in New York, heard her name called for Best Supporting Actress, she hurried up to the stage and announced, "I might have the baby right here."

While the cameras weren't looking, Marlon slipped out of his aisle seat and headed backstage. He'd been asked to present the Best Director award. Looking confident and extraordinarily handsome, he strode across the stage in his well-fitting tux to enthusiastic applause. For many in attendance, this was the first time they'd seen Marlon Brando in the flesh. He didn't rub shoulders with them at their favorite nightspots or sit among them at every awards gala. Shaking Marlon's hand warmly, Hope turned the podium over to him. To speed things along, the Academy this year had dispensed with the reading of the nominees' names, and the card handed to Marlon revealed only the winner. "For direction," Marlon said, his eyebrows lifting and a small smile playing with his lips as he saw what was written, "in New York, the winner is, *On the Waterfront*, Elia Kazan."

The broadcast immediately switched to New York, where Kazan accepted the award, and applause from both coasts, with a look of great satisfaction. He'd been hoping for some kind of redemption; the statuette in his hands seemed to be it. He thanked the "whole lot of people" who had made the picture with him, and ended his seven-second acceptance by saying, "Thank you, Marlon," presumably for being the one to announce his name. But he could thank Marlon for much more than that, of course; *Waterfront* would not have had the same impact without him.

Back in Hollywood, Bob Hope wasn't about to let this rare sighting of Marlon end that quickly. "How do you feel about Elia

Kazan winning that Oscar?" the emcee asked. Marlon replied, "I'm tickled to death, Bob," adding, "He looked pretty nervous." This was what Marlon chose to say about Kazan's award; not "he deserved it" or "what a great film we made" or anything of the kind. *He looked pretty nervous.*

Bob Hope, meanwhile, was trying to get something personal from Marlon. "How do *you* feel?" he asked, presumably about his own chances. Marlon hesitated for half a second, then repeated what he'd just said: "I'm tickled to death, Bob. He looked pretty nervous"—which got a big laugh from the host and the audience.

"Well, I want to tell you," Hope said, still not wanting to let Marlon go, conscious of the TV ratings his appearance guaranteed, "it's a great thrill having you." None of the other stars who walked across the stage that night was told what a thrill it was to have them. "I think this is your first Academy Award show, isn't it?" Hope asked. Marlon agreed that it was. "First time," Hope said, stroking Marlon's lapel. "We never could get together on the money." That brought another big laugh, but in some ways, it was true, metaphorically anyway. They were reading from cue cards now, delivering a prepared routine. "Your success is well deserved," Hope said. "You're young. You're handsome. You're vigorous. You're talented. Let me see, there was another reason why I hated you."

"Well, Bob," Marlon said, glancing down at the cue cards to follow along. "I've been very lucky. I've had good directors, and good stories. Why don't you do what I did and get Tennessee Williams to write you a movie?" That gave Hope the chance to quip that he'd be lucky to get Tennessee Ernie Ford, the comic country-western singer.

The utterly bizarre nature of this moment should be appreciated: Marlon Brando, the iconoclast, the truth-speaker, playing straight man to the corny jokes of Hollywood's favorite status quo comedian. A year earlier, it would have been unimaginable. Hollywood was riveted by the spectacle.

Back in his seat, Marlon awaited the Best Actor award. He was putting on a good front, smiling and laughing and dutifully saying his lines. But in his mind, as he'd reveal later, he was reliving this night from one year ago, when he'd sat at his mother's hospital bedside, waiting for her to die. He was here tonight because of Dodie. She'd always wanted him to win an Oscar, and had been disappointed when he hadn't gone to previous ceremonies. If Marlon hoped to hear his name called from the stage, one large reason was because he knew it would have pleased his mother.

Yet, there were other reasons, too. When Bette Davis, wearing a pointed turban to cover the part of her scalp that had been shaved for the film *Elizabeth the Queen*, swept out onto the stage to announce the Best Actor award, Marlon visibly tensed. Sitting behind him was the columnist Sidney Skolsky, who noticed how he "slumped in his seat" when Davis was handed the card bearing the name of the winner. "He was chewing gum faster than he rode his motorcycle," Skolsky remembered.

"The winner is," Davis announced, "Marlon Brando for *On the Waterfront*."

The audience erupted. All night, the applause had been generous, but now the theater thundered with it. Marlon ran down the aisle. Watching that sprint six decades later, it's impossible to miss the sheer joy in his movements. Unlike the earlier banter with Hope, there's nothing artificial about his smile. Bursting with pride was Karl Malden, who'd lost his Best Supporting Actor race but who, nonetheless, took great satisfaction in Marlon's win. Malden believed that Marlon was genuinely pleased by his achievement: "He felt, boy, this is mine."

Bounding up onto the stage, he accepted the award and a kiss from Davis: "You're just *great!*" she gushed. Muttering some thanks, Marlon turned to the audience. "It's much heavier than I imagined," he said, cradling the Oscar in both hands. "Gosh, I had something to say, and I can't remember what I was going to say for

the life of me. I don't think that ever in my life have so many people been so directly responsible for my being so very, very glad. It's
a wonderful moment, and a rare one, and I am certainly indebted.
Thank you."

As he strode off the stage, some in the audience rose to their
feet. For more than half a minute the crowd cheered, an eternity
in the fast-moving awards show. "It was a big deal that night,"
Skolsky wrote. "As if society had accepted Marlon Brando, and he
had accepted society." The one-time terror had been gracious and
charming and humble, not what any of them had expected.

Backstage, all the conflicting emotions caught up with him.
He posed for pictures with Grace Kelly, the Best Actress winner
(for *The Country Girl*) and Sam Spiegel, who'd accepted the Best
Picture trophy for *Waterfront*. Everyone was heading to parties
at Romanoff's or Chasen's, but Marlon begged off. On this anniversary of his mother's death, he told Skolsky, "I don't feel too
much like celebrating." Instead, he went to Jay Kanter's house for
a mugful of champagne and fell asleep on the couch.

The night had been overwhelming, the culmination of a year
of compliance, acquiescence, deference, and duty. The little boy rejected by his father and scorned by his teachers had been celebrated
and lionized in front of them and the entire world. But in receiving
such praise, he'd also given up parts of himself, and given in to an
ideology he'd once decried. "An error in judgment," he later called
his accepting of the Oscar. "I've done a lot of silly things in my day.
That was one of them." But at the time, the little gold man was his
reward for all his efforts over the past year. He was both honored
and horrified by it.

Heavier than he imagined, indeed.


"NOT MUCH IS left of the 'bop' Brando," the fan magazine *Screenland*
observed soon after the Oscar show. "The old lingo and moody
reticence" were gone. The new Brando, groomed and genteel, was

"here to stay," the magazine declared. The old Brando had, in fact, been "a triumph of sleight of hand," a persona "foisted on the public," a "myth." What was real, *Screenland* averred, was this "clean-shaven and extraordinary young man." Ed Sullivan declared Marlon "a likeable, decent, normal guy" after a sit-down with the suit-and-tied actor. How much Hollywood actually believed their topsy-turvy sales pitch is unknown. Perhaps all of it. Perhaps none.

In any event, the guardians of Hollywood's image had found a new target to scold: James Dean, the moody, defiant, twenty-four-year-old actor whose film with Elia Kazan, *East of Eden*, had just been released. Dean was taking a page from the original Brando playbook, refusing interviews, showing up at industry events in a tee shirt and dungarees. Marlon didn't know him well, but they'd met a few times. At Kazan's invitation, Marlon had visited the set of *East of Eden*, less to see his onetime mentor than to check out the kid people were calling the new Marlon Brando, just as Marlon had once been called the new Montgomery Clift.

"Brando was Dean's hero," Kazan recalled. "He dropped his voice to a cathedral hush when he talked about Marlon." On the *East of Eden* set, Marlon was "very gracious" to the younger man, Kazan said. In return, Dean visited the set of *Désirée*. A photo was snapped of him clowning around with the cast, leaning over the side of a cart, with Marlon's leg, encased in his Napoleonic tights, positioned at his shoulder. Some people suspected there was a sexual tryst between the two around this time; the actress Arlene Martel, a friend to both men, believed this to be true. Yet Dean's admiration eventually irked Marlon: just as with Farley Granger, he couldn't respect someone who hero-worshipped his acting talent. Dean, Marlon said, wasn't patterning his life on him but "on the person he thought I was after seeing *The Wild One*." Consequently, he rebuffed Dean's attempts at friendship. After the release of *East of Eden*, Marlon reportedly commented, "Mr. Dean appears to be wearing my last year's wardrobe and using my last year's talent." And last year was something Marlon was doing his best to put behind him.

*

TWO DAYS AFTER his Oscar win, Marlon opened his doors, dressed smartly in a suit and tie, and welcomed a news crew from Edward R. Murrow's popular *Person to Person* television program. Airing at 10:30 p.m. on the East Coast, the program was live; it was planned out in detail but not scripted. As Marlon stepped aside, a crew rolled six cameras into his living room and affixed bright lamps to his ceiling. Other technicians set up a microwave link that would send the television signals back to the CBS studios in New York, where Murrow waited to open the show. A sound engineer slipped a wireless microphone under Marlon's jacket so he could lead television viewers on a tour of his house. He was the man of the moment: the youngest Best Actor winner in Academy history and the current box-office champ.

Shortly after 7:30 Pacific time, the red On Air sign lit up. Murrow, famed for his challenge to Senator Joseph McCarthy, appeared on a monitor seated in his armchair in New York. "Good evening," he said. "I'm Ed Murrow. And the name of the program is *Person to Person*." Marlon waited, seated awkwardly on a low stone bench in his back garden, his hands clasped and hanging between his legs. "Marlon Brando," Murrow went on, "is an actor of very considerable talent, highly regarded by the industry he works in, the fans he works for, and those he works with." Then the scene shifted to Los Angeles.

With the camera on him, Marlon strolled across the terrace to give viewers a glimpse of the movie capital glittering far below in the valley. "It's really quite lovely in the night," he said. "It's awfully nice to come out here in the evening and have dinner, especially on warm nights when the desert wind comes up over the hills." He was gracious and charming, playing the game to the hilt, but there was an edginess to him, too, like a little boy squirming in his seat trying to behave until recess. Throughout the broadcast, he wrung his hands; he rarely smiled. For such a practical joker, he came across stiff and humorless; his attempt to tell a joke (slightly racist, about a "Chinaman") fell utterly flat. Showing off his Oscar, calling it "my friend," he did his best to appear lighthearted, but his anxiety was apparent.

He'd brought to life Stanley Kowalski, Terry Malloy, Mark Antony, and even, despite his singing, Sky Masterson, but this was one character Marlon couldn't make real.

"Up til last year," Marlon told Murrow, "I sort of regarded acting as a means of making a living and not much more. I was interested in other things. But I've taken a pretty active interest in it . . . I might as well put all my energies into being as good an actor as I can." Over the mantel hung Dodie's portrait; fitting, as this whole performance was for her.

No surprise, first chance he got, Marlon beat it out of the living room to play his bongos for the television audience, taking out his frustrations with every slap of his palms against the leather.

"On the whole," Murrow asked him when he was done, "would you say the movie people are doing a good job?"

"Yes," Marlon replied—and back in New York, his friends all fell over, one by one. "I used to feel that perhaps they weren't being as responsible to artistic considerations as they might be—but after all, you have to consider the fact that a movie can cost a million dollars. It is a legitimate investment, and it has to be protected with some commercial aspects. It is an industry . . . [that] has been awfully good to me and I've been appreciative of the things that have come my way."

Here was Junior, sounding like Senior, mouthing the sort of huckster talk that had so offended him in the past. Appropriately enough, Marlon's father was on the show that night, too. Before he came out, the younger Brando seemed to take some pleasure in divulging that the old man was in the other room "quaking with fear, never having been on television." There was a new power differential between them, and Marlon wanted the world to see it.

Once father and son were together, the tension crackled. When Murrow asked Marlon Senior if he was proud of his son, the older Brando stammered, "Well, as an actor, not too proud, but as a man, why, quite proud." If things had ended at that point, the tension might have subsided. But then Murrow asked if Marlon had been "hard to handle" as a child. "I think he had the usual childhood traits," Marlon Senior replied. "I think he had probably a little more trouble with his parents than most children do."

What did he mean exactly? "Trouble with his parents" because they had been alcoholic and neglectful and abusive? That was certainly one way to interpret Marlon Senior's words. But it is more likely that the old man's anxiety had left him imprecise with his prepositions. Certainly that was how his son discerned his intent: the younger Brando had been more trouble *for* his parents than most children. Hearing this, Marlon simmered with one of his Rumpelstiltskin rages, right there on national television—though by now he'd learned to control his actions and his expressions. But the fury was nevertheless there, obvious to anyone who knew him, pulsating beneath the surface, in the twitch of his smile, the quaver of his hands, the intensity of his eyes.

When Marlon scowled, Murrow asked if he wanted to defend himself. "I really don't feel I need to defend myself," Marlon said tightly. "I can lick this guy with one hand, so . . ." He shrugged. "Let it go," he said, apparently speaking to himself, patting his father's foot.

*Let it go.* Marlon had been letting it go for a year now. How long could he really keep doing it? How long could he keep up this charade, this bluff? Five years, he'd given himself. Five years, and then he'd have enough money from Pennebaker, from his father's investments, to escape this madness and do something else. But could he hold out that long? Sitting there, in front of the television cameras, Marlon seemed on the verge of cracking, as if at any moment he'd jump to his feet, punch his father, knock over the cameras, pull down the lighting, yank off his tie, tell the viewers to fuck off, and toss his Oscar straight over the cliff. But he held himself together. Here is where we will leave him this time, fidgeting in his chair, fixing his socks, twisting at the end of his rope.

# THE

# RABBLE-ROUSER

MAY 1, 1960 / The prison sat at the tip of Point San Quentin, on the edge of San Francisco Bay. Its cream-colored façade could be glimpsed intermittently through the haze. Crossing the five-and-a-half-mile Richmond–San Rafael Bridge, Marlon kept his eyes riveted on the place. Since leaving Sacramento, he'd said little to his new friend, University of California professor Eugene "Bud" Burdick, who was driving the car. They'd had a disheartening day, and the unbroken dome of clouds overhead, turning the late afternoon dark and cold, only made things worse.

They could hear the crowds before they saw them. Outside the prison's East Gate, a loudspeaker was projecting the voices of protesters ("lawyers, housewives, artists and teenagers," according to a newspaper report) into the surrounding foothills. On the other side of the prison, at Tiburon Point, a quieter demonstration was under way, with a small group of Quakers staging a round-the-clock prayer vigil. But here, at the East Gate, the two hundred people were making lots of noise, and they vowed to be there all night. A group of students had marched the eighteen miles from San Francisco across the Golden Gate Bridge to add their voices and bodies to the protest.

Burdick stopped the car. He and Marlon made their way to the crowd. It was a circus. Hot dog stands and candy concessions had sprung up, and there was music and laughter and singing. When the crowd spotted the two men approaching, they let out a roar of approval. Placards suddenly appeared reading, THANK YOU MARLON, alongside others proclaiming, CAPITAL PUNISHMENT INVOLVES US ALL IN MURDER and THE WORLD IS WATCHING US. "Speak, speak!" the crowd urged, passing over the microphone to Marlon. Burdick stepped in, insisting they wait until the TV cameras had arrived— a "cheap and meretricious" decision, he admitted, but necessary if their message was to get out.

Marlon was used to crowds. For a decade now, he'd been assaulted and abused by crowds at train stations, airports, and film premieres, and he hated them. But he didn't hate this crowd. He didn't resent the demands, the adulation, the presumed intimacy from these people. They were all in this together, Marlon believed, part of the same purpose, the same struggle. Today's hoopla was about something much bigger than a movie or whether he'd given his latest girlfriend a diamond ring. Standing outside San Quentin Prison, Marlon could look back on five years of his own, voluntary imprisonment, during which he'd been a willing, if begrudging, operator of the Hollywood machine. Exhausted by five years' worth of compromise, capitulation, superficiality, and exploitation, he was finally breaking free, going against tradition and the advice of his managers, taking a controversial public stand about something that truly mattered. The columnists and fan magazines, if they had a problem with that, could go to hell.

The television cameras arrived. Burdick disclosed that he and Marlon had been to see California governor Edmund G. Brown, and that their appeal to him had failed. Brown wouldn't stop the execution of the man for whom this rally was being held. Tomorrow, at 10:00 a.m., Caryl Chessman, a thirty-eight-year-old convicted rapist, would die in the gas chamber. When Marlon took the mike, his face was as gray as the sky. He told the crowd and the gathered reporters that he intended to use the power of his position to make a film about Chessman, a film that would expose

the abuses taking place inside this prison. It would be his most
personal, most important project yet. All profits from the film, as
well as his own salary, he vowed, would be used "in the fight to
abolish capital punishment." The crowd cheered as the cameras
snapped away.

As a protagonist for Marlon's magnum opus, Chessman was
an unlikely figure. He'd been convicted in 1948 as the "Red Light
Bandit," the perpetrator of at least two crimes in which he'd
fooled couples in parked cars into thinking he was a policeman by
using a red light on his dashboard. The state alleged that Chessman
had robbed the men and forced the women out of their cars, after
which he'd forced them to perform oral sex. Confessing under
coercion, Chessman later recanted. But prosecutors were able to
persuade a jury to convict him not only of robbery and rape but
also, based on the fact that the women had been forced out
of the cars, of kidnapping. That meant, since kidnapping was a
capital offense in California, that Chessman was given the death
penalty—one of the very few times a nonlethal conviction had
landed an American on death row since the nineteenth century.
Even if Chessman really was the Red Light Bandit, many argued
that the punishment did not fit the crime.

Still, the courts had upheld the sentence. Twelve years had passed
since Chessman's conviction, a record for time spent on death
row. Chessman and his lawyers had used every means possible to
appeal. Nine times his execution had been scheduled; seven times
the courts had granted reprieves to permit new appeals, and once,
Governor Brown, who was personally opposed to capital punishment, had issued a stay. But this time he'd turned down the request
made to him in person by Marlon and Burdick, as well as by
actress Shirley MacLaine, television personality Steve Allen, and
Burdick's colleague from UC Berkeley, Richard Drinnon. Their
voices were echoed by pleas from no less than Albert Schweitzer
and Pope John XXIII. But it did no good. "I am powerless to act,"

Brown told the press after turning Marlon and the others down. "As distasteful as capital punishment is to me, so long as it is on the statutes it will be enforced."

Chessman had one last chance. The California Supreme Court planned to meet the next day, two hours before his scheduled execution, to consider his latest petition for a stay. But time was running out. Even as Marlon urged the crowd outside the prison not to give up, within the concrete walls of San Quentin the prisoner was being moved to a cell next to the gas chamber. The countdown had begun.

THE MARLON WHO posed for photographs in front of the sign at the gate of the prison was still a very handsome man, dressed neatly in a dark suit, his overcoat draped over his arm, but his eyes seemed smaller than they used to be, set deeper in his face. His forehead was also higher than it was five years earlier, and he was definitely fleshier. At thirty-six, after spending half a decade as a pampered prince in Hollywood, he was putting on weight. When he'd made the film *Sayonara* in Japan three years earlier, he'd asked the director, Josh Logan, to shoot him only from the back whenever a scene called for him to be shirtless. "He was embarrassed about the bulges that were beginning to show in his stomach," Logan said. His love of Japanese food hadn't helped matters. Logan recalled how heartily Marlon ate; at one point, the director suggested maybe he ate too much.

It wasn't just Japanese food Marlon loved. He enjoyed many cuisines, and with his money, his connections, and his staff, he could enjoy anything he wanted at any time. "Food was always a friend," he'd say. When he was a boy, coming home from school to find his mother gone, there was always the apple pie in the icebox calling to him, saying, "Come on, Mar, take me out, and bring Charlie Cheese with you." Food was comfort, and many times over the past five years, he had needed comfort.

Putting on weight might also have been, Karl Malden suspected, an act of rebellion: "Everybody, male and female, saying how beautiful he is, how gorgeous, how perfect a human being he is. I wonder if he wasn't saying, 'You think I'm so great? I'll show you. I'll get as fat as a pig and then see if you love me.'"

Marlon wasn't fat, but he was bulkier than in the past, and aging quickly, showing far less concern about it than many other stars. Despite his embarrassment with Logan, he didn't attempt to maintain himself in the way, for example, Cary Grant did, or Frank Sinatra. Men didn't face the same pressures about their appearance that women did, of course, but Marlon wasn't just any man. He'd been a sex god, a generational game-changer. He'd dominated the box office for several years, until a very recent (and very precipitous) slide. But here, speaking to the crowd at San Quentin, looks, fame, and success didn't matter. Commitment, principles, ideals did.

This was what Marlon had been searching for since those early, aimless days in New York, when he wrote to his parents about the injustice he'd seen in the world and vowed "to do something about it." For the past five years, he'd been a loyal soldier in the Hollywood trenches, largely playing by the rules, but he'd been planning his escape all along. That his father had failed him yet again, thwarting his desertion, wasn't surprising; whether deliberately or through more mismanagement, the money Brando Senior had made in the gold mine investments remained inaccessible, at least to his son. He thought he'd be free by now, but here he was, still stuck. Marlon remained determined to find some way out of the movie biz, and sooner rather than later. His political activism around capital punishment galvanized that conviction.

Marlon had reached a crossroads. He "was in a profession he hated," his new secretary, Alice Marchak, quickly realized. Marchak saw how much he despised "making faces in front of a camera." To Elia Kazan, Marlon complained that he was "balding

[and] middle-aged," felt "like a fraud" when he acted, and desired to do something else. He'd made five films since *Guys and Dolls*, the last of them not yet released. Some of them were good, some not so good. He'd gotten married, had a child, separated from his wife, fucked a lot of women—and "none of it means anything," he told Kazan, if this was going to be the course of his life.

His passion was at San Quentin, and in the meetings he had with activists and organizers. "With so much prejudice, racial discrimination, injustice, hatred, poverty, starvation and suffering in the world," he said, "making movies seemed increasingly silly and irrelevant, and I felt I had to do what I could to make things better." Marlon's political convictions were something new and unusual for a Hollywood star. Producers, publicists, and columnists didn't quite know what to make of him. Indeed, many would attempt, then and later, to dismiss his convictions as the woolgathering of a dilletante, as if true commitment were something impossible for them to conceptualize. Cynics were convinced that Marlon was stealthily working for his own self-interests; there had to be a money deal somewhere behind all this Chessman nonsense, they believed.

Marlon abhorred cynics. "I have encountered many people over the years," he said at one point, "who have believed that self-interest is the thing always at work, underneath everything." These people dismissed "the idea of true belief." Marlon had one response: "I feel sorry for them."

He described the internal conflict that drove this period of his life as a "philosophical quandary." Despite what the Hollywood cynics said, this was no layman's hobby, no subterfuge for publicity. For Marlon, this was existentially *real*—the next step, in fact, in his recovery from his childhood trauma, in what just might become a lasting triumph over the darkness. Fixing himself meant fixing the world, too. "If I am not my brother's keeper," Marlon wrote, "then who am I?"

It was, of course, a fundamental Christian teaching, and although he worked with many Christian activists in the Chessman campaign, his own internal struggle had nothing to do with religion or doing "God's work." Marlon hadn't been brought up to believe in God; given his history, he had no patience for the "idea of a divine father who would care for him," as George Englund observed. Rather, this was about Marlon's conscience, his internal sense of what was right, decent, and just. It was the same impulse that had led him to bring home a drunken, disoriented woman when he was ten, wanting to help her; the same sense of duty that had kept him standing outside a New York apartment to make sure a little boy was safe; the same responsibility he'd felt for Celia and Freddie and other unfortunates among his friends. The child who'd been left to fend for himself by his parents, and despaired of by his teachers, had responded to his ordeal not by becoming bitter, or by pushing the world away, or by greedily taking whatever he could because he'd been so long deprived. Rather, he responded by trying to take care of the world the way he himself had never been cared for.

That didn't mean he couldn't be selfish; Rita Moreno's story alone shows how selfish Marlon could be, especially when he felt trapped and especially with women who claimed to love him. But selfishness doesn't preclude altruism. Marlon possessed a zeal for making the world better. He was a man driven by his passions: fun, excitement, music, sex. Acting was never on that list, no matter how much that disappointed, and still disappoints, some of his admirers. But activism was. Politics excited him. The last time he had felt truly engaged, inspired, *relevant* ("active and integral," he'd called himself) was when he'd been traipsing around the country making speeches for the American League for a Free Palestine. Back then, the misfit, the loser, the dropout had found a community with whom he belonged. Now, at last, he'd found one again.

---

"WHY DON'T YOU run for governor?" a young woman asked him, somewhat flirtatiously, at the San Quentin rally. Marlon simply smiled and flashed a *V* for victory sign.

Had he been younger, he mused years later, maybe he would have gone into politics at this point, so intense were his feelings about capital punishment. Certainly, as a career, politics would have ignited more passion for him than acting ever did. Josh Logan remembered how charged up Marlon would get talking about politics on the set of *Sayonara*, in a way he never did about film-making. "To devote one's life to the advance of humanity is certainly the noblest and most worthwhile of careers," Marlon wrote. He admired people such as Senator John F. Kennedy, who'd recently announced his candidacy for president. Certainly, Marlon could have brought as much charm and charisma to the campaign trail as Kennedy.

Yet electoral politics require the same sort of compromises that movie stardom does; the worlds of Hollywood and Washington are really not all that different. Both depend on illusion and the selling of dreams; both often bring forth a terrible tension between public and private lives. Ultimately, no doubt, Marlon would have chafed as much against politics as he did acting.

But what if he had been allowed to remain outside the fray? A couple of years earlier, he'd had an exchange with Edward Murrow, with whom he'd stayed in touch after their *Person to Person* inter-view. Marlon sent Murrow a thank-you note for presenting a show on opera singer Marian Anderson and her fight against racial seg-regation. "I often get terribly discouraged," Marlon wrote, "when I think that with all the extensive techniques we have at hand to communicate with each other, so remarkably little is accomplished." He feared the problem was not with the technology, but rather, the fact "that the only thing most of us want to communicate is hatred and distruction [*sic*]." Murrow's program gave him hope, Marlon said. "God knows it's hard enough to communicate with one's self, much less anybody else," but at least Murrow was making an effort. The broadcaster responded by asking Marlon to guest-host his show while he was away. Scheduling conflicts meant that Marlon couldn't accept his offer, but he hoped Murrow would ask him again. He couldn't think of anything, he wrote, that he'd "enjoy doing more."

What if Marlon had found a career, a vocation, for himself, in which his job was to prompt conversation and challenge assumptions? Hosting a show like Murrow's, perhaps, or speaking at lectures or symposiums, as he had for the ALFP, or drafting social-justice legislation, or lobbying for national organizations.

But actors weren't supposed to have opinions—or at least, that had been the conventional wisdom up until now. Times were changing. Marlon wasn't alone in speaking out. Shirley MacLaine and Steve Allen had been at his side when he'd gone to see Governor Brown, and an increasing number of actors were making their opinions known on topics ranging from race to war. The *New York Times* declared "thinking" actors "in vogue" that year: Jeff Chandler, Sammy Davis Jr., Kirk Douglas, and others (including Marlon and MacLaine) had formed a Hollywood branch of SANE (Stop All Nuclear Explosions). The change, the newspaper speculated, was due in part to a revulsion against the "McCarthyism" of the previous decade, and to the rise of television, which had brought to Hollywood many New York actors, "who are accustomed to intellectual stimuli."

Yet, even among this new breed, Marlon stood out. It wasn't enough that he took actions himself. He also publicly challenged those who did not, both his famous colleagues and his ordinary fans in the real world. "I think people who are looking at me right now," he said during one filmed interview, "and you who are [behind] the camera, you all have an obligation. We are all responsible."

What was clear for him, after the Chessman protests, was that he could no longer simply go on as before. Hollywood culture was corrosive. He'd been unable to make good on his escape, and his captivity threatened to make him fat, content, dull. Nearly everyone Marlon had worked with in the world of theater or film had ultimately let him down, exposing their greed and self-centeredness. Truman Capote epitomized the narcissism of the business. Marlon had trusted the writer, revealed things to him in an interview during the making of *Sayonara* that he'd never thought he would print, things about his mother and his own self-doubt. And then he'd opened *The New Yorker*, and there it all was—and the whole country was talking about it. Capote, that smirking little imp, had gotten Marlon to drink a little, something rare and dangerous, and had told lurid, exaggerated stories of his own family to get the star to open up about his. "That's how I trapped Marlon," Capote later admitted, gleefully.

Marlon had walked right into it. Of his mother, he said: "I thought if she loved me enough, then we can be together . . . we'll live together and I'll take care of her. But my love wasn't enough." Until this point, the world hadn't known of the long, troubled, complex history between Marlon and his parents. That was nobody's business, Marlon believed, and he raged to Josh Logan that he wanted to kill Capote. To the writer, Marlon's reaction was unfathomable. They were both famous, after all; they were both in the business of selling themselves. "To be an actor," Capote said, "you have to have absolutely no pride. You have to be a thing, an object."

Yet that was precisely what Marlon recoiled from. Capote lived and breathed fame. He'd chased it down and lassoed it, and when he finally lost it, it was as if he'd lost oxygen: he withered away and died. The publication of his *New Yorker* article, which he called "The Duke in His Domain," left Marlon with inescapable evidence of the terrible costs he had incurred by selling his soul.

Marlon had no friends in the industry. Those around him thought and behaved very differently than he did. Another star would have been thrilled by the sort of turnout that had greeted him at the New

York premiere of *Guys and Dolls*. When his limousine pulled up in Times Square, more than one thousand screaming people had surrounded him. Marlon panicked. "It required fifty policemen and two mounted police to push back the throng," the *New York Times* reported. "Brando proceeded into the theatre looking pale and drawn."

A Rock Hudson or Elizabeth Taylor would have taken such tumult in stride, pacified by the perks and goody bags that came with it. Not Marlon. He felt fundamentally different from the people in the entertainment business. Not with any of his directors in the past five years had he found any sort of affinity or camaraderie— not Logan, not Daniel Mann (*The Teahouse of the August Moon*), not Edward Dmytryk (*The Young Lions*), not Sidney Lumet (*The Fugitive Kind*). He was continually fighting with his partners at Pennebaker, including his father, because all they cared about was the bottom line. "He was extremely vigilant about anyone trying to blow smoke up his ass," his nephew, Gahan Hanmer, said after a visit to Marlon around this time. "He was horribly disillusioned by the people he was moving with in Hollywood."

The whole point of the entertainment industry is, of course, to make money: that has been its raison d'être ever since P. T. Barnum first put on a show. And Marlon had tried to rack up as much money as he could, too; it was supposed to help him get free of the business. Yet he'd been completely unprepared for the banality of the past five years. During that time, he'd acquired a deep antipathy for the growing culture of celebrity. In a country that had "the highest crime rate in the [Western] world, the highest delinquency rate, the most alcoholics, [where] two billion dollars' worth of tranquilizers were sold last year and half the hospital beds are occupied by mental patients," he asked, why did the media waste so much time on celebrity news? It was "madness," Marlon concluded. But "anyone who objects," he groused, "is considered to be idiosyncratic, bizarre, uncooperative, dishonest." He let out a cry. "I can't win."

In 1960, Marlon finally and definitively turned his back on what so many considered his destiny. It would be some time before he could actually break away; he was contracted to do *Mutiny on the Bounty* for MGM, and there were other looming commitments involving Pennebaker. But this was the point, when he stood outside San Quentin Prison and tried to save a man's life, at which he began seriously to reprioritize his life. It would take a little longer than the five years he'd imagined to break out of his own personal jail, but he'd get free eventually.

"This business of being a successful actor," Marlon had mused to Capote in that fateful article. "What's the point, if it doesn't evolve into anything? All right, you're a success. At last you're accepted, you're welcome everywhere. But that's it, that's all there is to it, it doesn't lead anywhere." Other actors would say it led to future challenges: Shaw, Chekhov, *King Lear*. But that sort of ambition was alien to Marlon. People such as Billy Redfield grew more disappointed every year, lamenting that Marlon didn't care about what they cared about. "To try may be to die," Redfield wrote, "but not to care is to never be born." Yet where were so many of Marlon's critics when Caryl Chessman was fighting for his life, when the marches for civil rights burned a hole in the nation's conscience, when a chance arrived to change the culture instead of simply going along with it, when a time came to make a difference in real people's lives instead of just winning the applause of a privileged few? To accuse Marlon of not caring, of never having been born, as Redfield did, was nearsighted in the extreme.

AFTER HIS APPEARANCE at San Quentin, Marlon returned with Bud Burdick to his home across the bay. They spent some time talking about Chessman. There was a paradox to their cause. The man they were fighting for was a cruel, arrogant man. Even many of Chessman's supporters disbelieved his protestations of innocence. His victims had suffered terrible trauma; one woman had been committed to a mental institution after the attack and, according to news reports, was still there.

Yet to take Chessman's life, Marlon and millions of others believed, devalued *all* human life. Chessman had written several books while in prison, with one (*Cell 2455, Death Row*) becoming a bestseller and drawing international attention to his case. The official Vatican organ insisted that spending more than a decade waiting for the gas chamber had "expiated his guilt, no matter how grave." Some people were arguing not just to spare Chessman's life, but to set him free.

Marlon was undecided on that. The words of Clinton Duffy, the former warden of San Quentin and an ardent opponent of capital punishment, were telling. He believed that while Chessman should live, he belonged in jail for the rest of his life. "He had an incurably psychopathic criminal mind," Duffy wrote, "and most likely could never have adjusted himself to the society he hated so intensely."

Marlon shared Chessman's disdain for society. Where they differed, of course, was that Marlon believed society could be fixed, and he wanted to help in the fixing. Chessman despised the world, expressing little concern for his victims, or for the other men on death row. He was motivated solely by his own case. Still, there were other identifications Marlon shared with the convict. They were close in age. They were both Midwesterners. Chessman's father had beaten him, too, and called him "no good." His mother was frail and needed to be cared for, especially after a car accident left her paralyzed. Chessman started stealing food when he was very young because his parents failed to provide for him. He was very smart, but school had been a bad fit for him, and he was largely self-educated. While in prison, he'd become a voracious reader of books on law, history, and philosophy.

"I could have been him," Marlon told his friend Jack Larson.

But not really. "Caryl Chessman had brains," Duffy wrote. "But

no wisdom." Marlon had wisdom. Even more important, he had a
conscience and a heart.

THE ANNOUNCEMENT CRACKLED from the radio with chilling de-
tachment: the California Supreme Court had rejected Chessman's
last appeal. The prisoner had been taken to the gas chamber and
strapped into the chair. The cyanide tablets had been dropped.
Caryl Chessman died at 10:12 a.m. on May 2, 1960.

Marlon was distraught. The execution, he wrote to Bud Burdick, had been "an act of vengeance" against a man "suffering from
an emotional disease." In the days that followed, he felt bereft. He
missed the regular interactions he'd had with Bud and others in
the anti-capital punishment crusade. "There is no one here who
understands," he told Burdick.

He longed for the fellowship of people who thought as he did,
who prioritized things the way he did, who saw the world the
same. Within the circle of activists, Marlon was beloved, a very
different experience from what he'd known in Hollywood. "Your
visit here did a hell of a lot of people a hell of a lot of good," Burdick wrote to him. "There was a fearful sense of being isolated
and eccentric. You . . . did a lot to evaporate that feeling." Burton
H. Wolfe, publisher of the *California Liberal*, also wrote to thank
Marlon for his efforts: "Those of us outside the prison that night
were pleased to have you there, lending your prestige." Another
demonstrator described the despair they all experienced at getting
the news. "None of us felt like talking on the way to the airport,"
he told Marlon. "I just want to write this note to thank you for your
great help. Your strength and dignity under most trying circumstances helped us all inestimably to keep going."

These had become Marlon's people. Not since his days sitting
with the Adlers around their table had he ever felt quite so much
that he *belonged*.

Cynics tended to dismiss them all, Marlon included, as bleeding hearts at best and crass opportunists at worst. No surprise, Marlon's détente with Hollywood columnists, carefully constructed during the past five years, came undone over the Chessman case. Hedda Hopper, as usual, led the charge. "It would take a derrick to get Shirley MacLaine, Steve Allen or Marlon Brando on the road to sell their pictures," Hopper complained, "yet they took time to go to Sacramento to plead for Caryl Chessman's life. It was nauseating." Hopper wasn't the only Tinseltown talking head feeling queasy: Lucius Beebe, writing in the *San Francisco Chronicle*, declared that Marlon was just seeking publicity in his appearance with the governor.

That became the new line of attack for Hollywood scribes, who seemed fundamentally incapable of perceiving sincerity in anyone. The fact that Marlon wanted to make a film about Chessman's life proved that this was all about money. "*Now* it comes out," Hopper crowed. "I understand both Shirley MacLaine and Steve Allen will be in the Chessman picture when and if Marlon Brando ever makes it. So it was business, not sentiment, after all." No basis to that claim exists; Hopper simply made it up. But to Hollywood journalists, that was the only way to make sense of Marlon's activism.

Outside of entertainment reporting, however, there was more sympathy. Herb Caen, who'd made clear his anti-capital punishment views in his widely read, influential column, reported that in the weeks after Chessman's execution, Marlon had visited the state capital twice on legislative matters without "publicity or fanfare." Caen directly refuted Beebe's charge that Marlon was in this for the notoriety.

America was embarking on a decade-long crisis of faith, principles, and identity. Long-cherished notions of what was right and what was wrong were being challenged. Ideas about family, race, patriotism, even God—all were up for reconsideration. Not surprisingly, Marlon was in the midst of it. Just as he had personified the cultural moment of the 1950s, when views of masculinity,

gender, power, and sexuality were in flux, now he was at the fore-
front of a movement asking Americans to reconsider their moral
priorities. The country was split. Although polls showed a slim
majority opposing capital punishment, the minority opinion was
loud and emphatic, and it let Marlon know how it felt.

"What is your interest in defending criminals?" one man wrote.
"Are you planning on murdering someone? Or are you just another of the ignorant Communists, like your friend Chessman?"
Another asked, "Why waste your time on having a picture made
of a sex pervert and expect people to waste their money to look at
him?" Still another called Marlon a "dupe" for the "antagonistic
Communist front against the state." Hate mail continued piling up
for weeks, the letters numbering into the many hundreds; Marlon
kept many of them. The outrage in the letters was genuine—but
also irrational, facile, and unmindful of any of the deeper issues
that Chessman's sentence had raised. "You use guns in pictures,"
one correspondent wrote. "Get one and kill that terrible young girl
who caused the death of your sweet pal Chessman."

There was no response to be made to such people, Marlon
realized, except to get to work. He met with Burdick frequently
on the best way to approach the California legislature to abolish
the death penalty, lending his name to lobbying efforts. He also
worked with the Quakers' Friends Committee on National Legislation, planning a symposium on the issue and offering to speak.
During the height of the Chessman controversy, he accepted an
invitation to read a passage from Walt Whitman's *Leaves of Grass*
at the Democratic National Convention in July.

But politics, as much as he might've been drawn to it, was not
Marlon's métier. In a different world, he might have been happier
leading a political crusade, like César Chávez or Bayard Rustin or
Ralph Nader. But that wasn't his lot in this life. Circumstance or
fate had brought him to this point instead. So, what he *could* do to

make a difference, as he had told the crowd at San Quentin, was make movies.

THE TEMPERATURE INSIDE the Pennebaker conference room was even hotter than it was outside in the parking lot, with the sun baking the asphalt. Marlon's partners grew angry as he steadfastly refused to meet their demands. What the company needed, George Glass and Walter Seltzer told him, was a "big, profitable, Hollywood film." Without such a film, as a report from Marlon's father had made clear, there was doubt about Pennebaker's "continued existence." In a company memo written sometime before, Marlon Senior had claimed it was his son who thwarted this goal. "In the past," he wrote, "important attempts to activate the company have been negated by Brando Junior by his simple action of refusing to okay a script."

Marlon seethed. His father had convinced him that Pennebaker would make him a fortune. But it had turned out to be a dead weight around his neck. Certainly, Marlon had made a lot of money over the past five years. A million and a half was the "conservative estimate" of his take from *Sayonara* (both salary and back end), and a few years later, he'd been the first actor to demand, and get, $1 million as salary (*The Fugitive Kind*). All his pictures had, in fact, done very well. *Guys and Dolls* had been the top-grossing picture of 1956; *The Teahouse of the August Moon* and *Sayonara* had placed in the top ten for 1957 and 1958; and *The Young Lions*, while making it to only eleventh place, still pulled in an impressive $5 million. The problem was, as a producer, Marlon had to keep putting his money back into the company, and Pennebaker Inc. required a lot of cash to sustain itself. It was also sharing profits with its joint-venture partners: producer William Goetz, for example, had taken a huge chunk of *Sayonara*'s revenues. Making all this worse was the fact that, at the start of the year, Pennebaker owed $255,190.48 in back taxes to the IRS, and that wasn't counting what would be owed for 1960. So much for his father's promise that the company would bring down his taxes.

What his partners wanted from Marlon was another *Guys and Dolls*, a big box-office hit. But he just couldn't go that route anymore. He still had a couple of films in the pipeline: *The Fugitive Kind*, based on Tennessee Williams's *Orpheus Descending*, had yet to be released, and *One-Eyed Jacks*, Marlon's first directorial effort, his "baby," as he called it, over which he'd labored for many months, was still being edited. He was also committed to make *Mutiny on the Bounty*. But after that he refused to make any more pictures unless the pictures had something to say—against the death penalty, perhaps, or racial discrimination. Marlon's Pennebaker partners worried such projects wouldn't be big moneymakers. Marlon blew his stack. They were simply mouthing his father's words at him— and he was long past listening to what his father had to say.

It wasn't just the disappointment with the gold mines. Soon after Pennebaker was founded, the old man's blunderings had dragged both of them into court, when the cattle operation finally collapsed under the weight of "conspiracy, mismanagement and fraud." Both Brandos were sued by creditors and stockholders. Settling that case had meant more money out of their coffers. Brando Senior was correct in arguing that what Pennebaker needed to survive was a "big, profitable Hollywood film." But after the fraud case, Marlon shut his ears whenever his father talked business.

From here on, he would only make pictures that meant something, contributed to the national conversation, and attempted to undo the damage of the past and build something new. An audacious dream, to be sure, but "it was the only way," Marlon said, "to keep me interested in movies." He assured Glass and Seltzer that he could make a profitable movie about Caryl Chessman's execution.

As angry as he was with his partners, however, Marlon couldn't just walk away. Pennebaker provided his income, and he had too many expenses by now to upset that. His ledgers reveal that, since the late 1950s, he'd been subsidizing friends and family members, including Janice Mars and his sister Fran. Now, on top of that, he had a hefty lease on a 4,363-square-foot house high in the Hollywood Hills, 12900 Mulholland Drive, and an increasingly costly, and volatile, custody battle with his former wife over their son, Christian, a serious, thoughtful, dark-eyed boy of two.

So, if Marlon couldn't give up the movies, he'd make only ones that inspired him. Maybe such pictures wouldn't be the colossal hits he'd turned out for the past five years; maybe, in this post-Chessman world, he'd be forfeiting his standing as a top box-office star. But so long as he could make a living, his drawing power "didn't matter to Marlon," said Dick Clayton, the publicist. "He couldn't have made a movie at that point that didn't have some bigger, redeeming message."

He got to work planning the Chessman film. That spring and summer, he read dozens of books and articles on the case. He read John Laurence's classic text, *A History of Capital Punishment*, which was reissued that year. He heavily marked up Elizabeth Hardwick's article on Chessman in *Partisan Review*, in which Chessman was described as "a cultural sacrifice." In the margins of Sidney Hook's *Political Power and Personal Freedom*, Marlon scrawled, "Reason is ever subjugated to the contagion of emotion" and, "There is an incessant belief that men will listen to reason." He also underlined Hook's observation that humanity needed to "agree on a certain number of fundamental positions—on what is good or evil, true or false—in order not to massacre each other."

His secretary, Alice Marchak, clipped everything she could find on capital punishment. Files began piling up on Marlon's desk: studies on the nature of false confessions; reports on murder statistics in states without the death penalty (they dropped); summaries of various prison reforms. This was what drove Marlon's passion. It is safe to say that his associates on the top-box-office list (Rock

Hudson, Jerry Lewis, Jimmy Stewart, John Wayne) were not thinking about such things. Marlon was a different animal entirely.

His handwritten notes about the Chessman project would eventually fill several legal pads. At first Marlon imagined that he'd play
Chessman, from the trial to the execution, omitting the crimes;
then he wasn't sure. Maybe it should be another actor; maybe he
should just direct. Maybe it should be a two-part film, half drama
and half documentary, or maybe he should mix the genres up.
Each new idea he had for the story was set off by the pound sign, a
habit of his. And in his musings on Chessman, he was also musing
on himself.

"# He was in mortal combat with his soul. His was a fight for
survival, his identity. People will die for that."

"# He wasn't caught by police. He was caught by his own mind."

"# His need to have an external enemy is clearly documented."

"# Question: why don't we kill all criminals? Cheaper, safer,
easier. Answer: because some can be remolded. Someone did this
to him. No one is born bad."

There were other ideas taking up space on his desk, too. He
wanted to make a film of his pal Bud Burdick's bestselling and
controversial novel, *The Ugly American*, about the racism and co-
lonialism of the American diplomatic corps in Southeast Asia. Another idea had come in from Kazan, who wanted to make a picture
based on "a piece of reportage" by William Bradford Huie about
racial discrimination in the South. The story appealed to Marlon,
but his goal, once *Mutiny on the Bounty* was finished, was to find
projects he could direct himself. He'd written a 312-page treatment
for a script that he called *A Burst of Vermillion*—a Western, but "not
just cowboys-and-Indians stuff," he'd insisted to Truman Capote
during that traumatic *New Yorker* interview. "It's about this Mexican
boy—hatred and discrimination. What happens to a community
when those things exist." After three years, *Vermillion* was still
unmade, however; George Englund, not only an employee but an

investor with Pennebaker, had called it "underwritten in terms of character and story structure," and he'd threatened to quit if *Vermillion* was their next project.

For Marlon, remaining focused was an ongoing problem. "I get excited about something," he had admitted to Capote, "but it never lasts more than seven minutes. Seven minutes exactly." He was being flippant, because ideas such as the Chessman film stuck around for a long time. Whether he got to realize all his ideas wasn't the point. In doing things his way, choosing his own projects, Marlon was renouncing the unholy bargain with fame he'd made after his mother's death. "Shakespeare says that it's an ill wind that blows nobody good," he said of this moment, slightly mangling the Bard's meaning. But Marlon's interpretation was clear: "You split yourself down the middle," he said, when you go against principle for material gain. He determined to make up for that now.

ALICE MARCHAK, MARLON'S secretary, worked out of a bare-bones office that had once been the maid's room in the house on Mulholland Drive. In the three years she'd been at the job, Alice had gotten used to last-minute decisions and frequent changes of plans from her unpredictable boss. Very little surprised the efficient secretary. So, one afternoon, about a month after Chessman's execution, she took things in stride when Marlon popped his head into her office and said, "Alice, I want you to go to Mexico with me tomorrow." She asked why.

His reply stunned even her. He told her that he was planning to marry his old flame Movita, and he wanted Alice there. "She just had a baby," Marlon added, "and she said it was mine." Alice was flabbergasted. "He turned and walked away," the secretary remembered, "leaving me staring at his retreating back."

It must be a prank, Alice thought. Marlon was famous for them. He'd call friends on the phone, disguising his voice, pretending to be a bill collector or an agent for a foreign government. But this,

Alice soon realized, was no joke. The next day, she arrived at work ready to go to Mexico. But Marlon told her that Movita didn't want anyone but the two of them. And so, off he went.

He had never mentioned Movita to Alice before. She was, in many ways, a relic from Marlon's past, predating *Waterfront*, Josanne, his mother's death, his time at the top of the Hollywood heap. Yet Movita had continued to show up in Marlon's life periodically. One of those times was during the middle part of 1959, just as Marlon and his wife, Anna Kashfi, were finalizing their divorce. On this occasion, he and Movita were, apparently, intimate. "She'd never given up on him," said one friend who'd been around since the early 1950s, when the romance between the hot young Broadway actor and the older Mexican beauty was in all the fan magazines. Forty-six now, Movita was still an attractive woman. Given her age, her pregnancy was surprising; more surprising still was the fact that she wanted Marlon to marry her, to give the baby, a little boy she was calling Sergio, a home, a name, a father.

Movita was aware—everyone was aware, due to the very public custody case—that when Anna Kashfi had gotten pregnant, Marlon married her. That, of course, had turned into a spectacular disaster. How could Marlon possibly consider such a thing again? Yet, more than a decade earlier, when Celia got pregnant, Marlon *hadn't* married her, and that hadn't turned out so well, either. Now he was torn over the right thing to do.

Certainly, he didn't want to marry again. That he had ever married at all still bewildered him and his friends. But one cold fact was unavoidable: there would now be two little boys out there, two little boys who might grow up just as Marlon had, without a father's love, without a family, without a sense of who they were or who they might become. How had he ever let this happen? That question "gnawed at him," his friend said, "after everything he'd been through with his own father." Every time Marlon returned his son, Christian, to his mother's house after a visit, it was as if "someone took a pickaxe" to his heart, as he him-self would describe it. He observed the way Christian, as young as he was, would wince when Anna started shouting about Marlon's unfitness as a father.

*How had he ever let this happen?*

During his involvement in the Chessman case, Marlon often spoke of honor, decency, and humanity. He placed a great emphasis on responsibility—the state's responsibility to its citizens and citizens' responsibility to one another. To be responsible, Marlon said, was to be human. "We refuse to admit that we are our brother's keeper," he said. "But if we are not our brother's keeper, then we are simply not socially responsible. He becomes our enemy, and we spend the rest of our lives enjoying what we enjoy and staring down the barrel of a gun from him." It was up to all people, he said, to be responsible in all aspects of their lives.

One morning in June, under the most intense secrecy, Marlon and Movita slipped down to Xochimilco, just outside Mexico City. There they were married on June 4, 1960. Later, when everything started to unravel, Marlon would tell a judge that he had married Movita because he "felt responsible for her condition."

**JULY 10, 1960** / Marlon didn't know what time or what day it was as he was hustled through the airport toward the Mex-icana Airlines counter. Just four days earlier, he'd landed in Los Angeles from Paris. He was still jetlagged from that trip, sleeping through the day, waking at midnight. Now, his eyes blurry and his hair badly combed, he was being told that it might be best if he started thinking it was a day later, because in Mexico City he'd be boarding a plane for Tahiti, where it was already July 11.

Marlon was off to inspect the South Seas locations where they'd be shooting *Mutiny on the Bounty*. He'd meet with director Carol Reed, producer Aaron Rosenberg, and cinematographer Robert Surtees. The plan was to return to Los Angeles in a month for final script conferences, then fly back to Tahiti in the fall to start shooting. Marlon wasn't happy that the film, a remake of the Clark Gable–Charles Laughton 1935 classic, would consume so much of the rest of his year. It meant he had to miss the Democratic National Convention in July and delay any further work on the Chessman picture until 1961.

He was pleased, however, that he'd be able to see Bud Burdick, who was building a house on Mo'orea, an island near Tahiti. But instead of working with Burdick on the pictures they wanted to do (not just Chessman but also *The Ugly American*), Marlon would have to spend his time being fitted for the foppish waistcoats and many-buttoned jackets Fletcher Christian wore on board the *Bounty*. Shades of *Désirée*.

As much as he was ready to break away from this sort of superficial moviemaking, his life was still ruled by the same realities that had dogged him since *Streetcar*: Marlon needed money. *Mutiny on the Bounty* would ease some of his (and Pennebaker's) financial pressures: industry experts were predicting he'd see about two million from the picture in the end. So, exhausted, disoriented, embittered to still be on "the Hollywood hamster wheel," as he called it, Marlon strapped himself into the airplane seat and took off into the southern skies.

Back at his house on Mulholland Drive, Alice Marchak was feeling exhausted, too. The past month hadn't been an easy one. The custody fights with Anna Kashfi had worn her out. Kashfi had been calling nearly every day, demanding to speak to Marlon. But Alice had her instructions: Marlon would not "take her call because it would result in a war of words and ruin his day," as Alice remembered. That meant Alice was the punching bag for Anna's verbal abuse. "She called Marlon everything but a human being and included me in the diatribe," Alice said. Marlon told his secretary she didn't have to take such abuse and should just hang up. But Alice feared provoking Anna further. "Hanging up on her would only add fuel to the fire," she feared, and Anna was capable of anything. Not long before, she'd shown up at the house and banged on the door, screaming to be let inside.

Under no circumstances could Anna learn that Marlon had gotten married again. Alice had her orders: *no one* was to know about Movita. She and the boy had to be kept an absolute secret. After returning from the wedding, Marlon had resumed his life as if nothing had occurred. Movita had taken little Sergio back to her own house. (Marlon eventually secured a place in Coldwater Canyon for her and the boy.) There was never any plan for cohabitation. Soon after the wedding, Marlon had left for Paris, and now he was off to Tahiti. The newlyweds and their little son had hardly had a chance to spend any time together at all.

Alice knew how to keep secrets. She was the guardian and gatekeeper of Marlon's career and life. For the past few years, she'd brought some order to his chaotic existence. "Everybody loved Alice," Ellen Adler said, "because you could get through to her and she'd say he's here or he's not. She was how you could reach Marlon." Before that, messages to him were lost in the ether; weeks or months might pass before any sort of connection was made with the slippery star. "She knew who we all were," Ellen said—in other words, whom Marlon wanted to hear from and whom he did not.

When Alice had first been brought over from Pennebaker to serve as Marlon's personal assistant, she was told that his two previous secretaries had had nervous breakdowns. Daunted but undeterred, she agreed to give the job a try. A native of Minooka, Pennsylvania, the daughter of a Czechoslovakian-born cigar salesman, she'd arrived in California in her early twenties after a bout of walking pneumonia sent her in search of warmer climes.

A secretarial job at Paramount had led to the position at Penne-baker, where Marlon Senior spotted her unflappable manner and thought she might be able to bring some order to his son's anarchic affairs. And so, at the age of thirty-seven, Alice took on the challenge of a lifetime.

"Where are your files?" she asked Marlon on her first day of work. He didn't have any, he explained. He threw everything out, and instructed Alice to continue doing the same. "He didn't want to keep anything that had to do with his movie career. When he was finished with a picture, he was finished." Wisely, Alice disregarded the order and set up Marlon's first official filing system, in a small three-drawer cabinet. Since there was hardly any money in the budget to pay for an office, she made do with the cabinet, a makeshift desk, and a swivel chair. Toilet tissue she brought in from home; otherwise, there wouldn't have been any.

Almost immediately, Alice realized just how much Marlon's personal habits bled into his professional life. She also discovered her boss's volatility. Finding that a note from Rita Moreno had been opened and resealed, Marlon accused his new secretary of reading his private mail. When she denied it, he called her a liar. In one of his Rumpelstiltskin furies, he punched the bannister of a staircase, sending pieces of wood flying in all directions. Fearful she'd be the next target of his fist, Alice fled, intending never to return. When Marlon learned that Moreno herself had opened and resealed the letter, he tried to woo Alice back with flowers and effusive apologies. She agreed—so long as he never called her a liar again and he held his temper around her. Marlon promised. He made good on the first, at least.

Alice brought order to Marlon's professional life. The personal she had no control over. By the time Alice signed on to work for him, his personal life had spiraled out of control and was erupting all around him: wives, girlfriends, children, custody battles, divorce settlements, showdowns with his father. After a relatively placid half decade, during which, despite his aggrieved playing of the Hollywood game, Marlon had largely maintained his equilibrium, the rage had returned. And when the rage was back, darkness and despair were never far behind.

ALL EYES WERE on the dark, shapely woman seated in the witness booth of the Santa Monica courtroom, who was taking her time replying to a question posed to her by Judge Allen T. Lynch. Why, the judge wanted to know, shouldn't he grant permission to her ex-husband, Marlon Brando, to make up thirteen visits with his son that he had been forced to miss because of business?

Just days after Caryl Chessman was put to death, Marlon had endured an excruciating ordeal in Los Angeles County Superior Court. Anna Kashfi commanded the room far more masterfully than she'd ever commanded a motion picture screen. Her black eyes flashed. "I feel Brando is an immoral man," she finally said, in answer to the judge's question. In her lilting Hindi accent, she said, "I don't want my child to grow up in this environment." The courtroom tittered. Marlon, seated with his attorneys in front of her, shook his head in frustration.

*Immoral* is a powerful yet subjective word. What did Kashfi mean by it? Certainly, Marlon's abandonment of her soon after their wedding, for which he had offered no explanation, might quite reasonably be considered immoral. His lack of honesty with her before their marriage, when he failed to disclose that he never intended to be entirely faithful to her, could also be considered immoral. But in her testimony that day in Judge Lynch's courtroom, Kashfi meant something very specific. What she meant was: Marlon was having sex with lots of women—and, as she made sure to point out, occasionally some men—and she was profoundly offended by it. No matter that they were divorced. Marlon had no right, Kashfi seemed to believe, to a sexual life without her.

A conservative young woman, and just twenty-three when she

married Marlon three years earlier, Kashfi had been raised by a British couple in Calcutta, India, the product of an "unregistered alliance," as she called it, between her Indian parents. Educated in a Roman Catholic convent, Kashfi was affronted by the sexual freedom she found first as a model in London and then as an actress in Hollywood. With only "a week's acclimatization to American customs," she'd viewed life on the studio lot as a scene out of Dante. The frequency with which American women had sex outside marriage was "shocking" to her. When she appeared in the film *Battle Hymn*, she expressed repugnance over star Rock Hudson's "peculiar infidelities" (he was gay) and sympathized with the "personal crisis" his wife must be going through. (The wife, as it later turned out, was also gay.)

So, it wasn't just heartbreak that fueled Anna's crusade against Marlon after their marriage ended; it was a deep, visceral moral umbrage over his lifestyle. Toward the end of their time together, Marlon hadn't hidden his affairs from her; Anna saw evidence to link several women to her husband. She also believed, as Josanne had, that the friendship with Christian Marquand was sexual; their affection, Anna remarked, overreached "the usual expressions of friendship." When Marlon named their son after his Parisian friend, Anna had retaliated by calling the boy Devi, which had been her Indian father's name.

The root of Marlon's unfitness as a husband, father, and human being, Anna believed, was the fluid, unapologetic sexual liberty that defined his life. She used this as her line of attack against him. Certainly, in some parts of the country, the headline MARLON IMMORAL, EX-WIFE STATES was read with sanctimonious agreement. Yet, while there's no question Marlon had done wrong by Anna, her focus on his sexual promiscuity was an attempt to sway public opinion and the courts against him, because, otherwise, she hadn't produced an iota of evidence that Marlon was an unfit parent, except for his absences during location shootings. In court, her attorney asked her if Marlon's immorality was the only reason she objected to his visiting their child. "Of course," Anna replied; otherwise, she added, "I'd still be married to him."

How different their story had been just a few years earlier, and yet, at least for Marlon, how very much the same. He'd spotted the lovely, dark-eyed young woman in the Paramount commissary while making *Guys and Dolls*, and quickly made his move. "She was a revelation out of Marlon's dream book," said George Englund, who was there. "Brown skin, lustrous eyes, fatal smile, and over the commissary commotion, tinkling fragments of her English-Hindi accent." Marlon wrangled an introduction. Anna had no idea who he was; she hadn't seen any of his pictures. Marlon liked that. "In those moments," Englund recalled, "Marlon is a lightfoot lad and gives some of his most charming performances. Struck by Anna, he turned it on: a little urbanity, a little shy guy, a touch of European inflection, a soupçon of British good manners, no vulgarity, no Wild One." He said he'd call her. "The ancient Noh play was about to be performed again," Englund mused.

They had an affair. When Anna was hospitalized for tuberculosis, Marlon was attentive and considerate. He'd rush to the City of Hope Hospital from the studio, still dressed in costume from *The Teahouse of the August Moon*, his eyes, as Anna described them, "Orientalized." He'd make her laugh by speaking in an exaggerated Japanese accent. As Anna recovered, they talked about poetry and Indian history, and debated traditional Buddhism versus Zen Buddhism, the latter of which Marlon preferred. Another time, discussing Krishnamurti, Anna wrote to him, "It is far more creative to set our own standards and way of living, mental and spiritual. The degree to which we apply ourselves will show what kind of human beings we are." This was exactly the sort of dialogue Marlon craved, and which acted as an aphrodisiac for him. To

Janice Mars, he praised Anna as an "incredibly beautiful East Indian girl with the soul of a poet [who] could see beauty in rain water standing on garbage cans."

But then, par for the course, his interests turned elsewhere. Anna, like so many others, was confused, but didn't try to get him back. That may have guaranteed her a second act. In Japan to make *Sayonara*, Marlon grew a bit lonely and homesick. To George Englund he wrote, "I'm experiencing loneliness, distrust, whistling hate, love impulses, soaring esteem for courage, the need for simplicity." He was reading Erich Fromm's bestseller *The Art of Loving*, about the challenges in relationships, and told Englund he found his "own shocking image on every other page." In this frame of mind, Marlon picked up his pen to write to Anna. "He wrote lengthy, rambling letters that were curiously childlike and mature at once," she recalled. When he got home, Marlon's renewed interest in Anna perplexed Alice Marchak, who'd just started working for him. "Little did I know this was a pattern of Marlon's," Alice said. "He would drop someone and then pick them up, only to drop them again. Like a child with a toy."

Anna was well aware that even though he was calling her again, he was still seeing Rita Moreno, so she tried to break things off with him—until she discovered she was pregnant. More than a decade after Celia, Marlon was still resistant to any sort of birth control, courting danger so blatantly that it seemed as if, subconsciously, he wanted to be caught. Maybe, during that period of Hollywood deference, he did; maybe Anna would work as a wife where Josanne had not. Marlon's agreement to marry Anna was both his attempt to do the right thing—much as it had been, initially, with Celia—*and* his ultimate capitulation to Hollywood protocol, to the rules he'd accepted when he'd gone all in for fame. By taking a bride, Marlon would be giving the fan magazines what they'd been demanding ever since he came out to California: a wholesome family, a wife and a child.

Yet, perhaps, there was a little bit of romance in it, too. Anna charmed him; her mind was as enchanting as her curvaceous body. "Do you know what love is, Anna?" Marlon had asked her at one point, quoting the German poet Heinrich Heine: "Has no one fathomed its nature? Has no one solved the riddle?" Always, deep down, there was a desire, Ellen Adler believed, "to find someone to love," even if he was absolutely unable to follow through and make it work.

When Marlon announced he was getting married, a stunned Alice Marchak asked, "Who'd have you?" She quickly discovered her boss hadn't changed. As the bridegroom was getting dressed on the morning of the wedding ceremony, Alice spied a woman upstairs in his bed with whom he'd just spent the night.

Even as Marlon said "I do," in a ceremony at his aunt's home on October 11, 1957, he must have known he was agreeing to promises he could never keep. Pointedly, he'd failed to invite such close friends as Freddie Fiore and Sam Gilman; he also vetoed his father's attendance. Jocelyn was there, but the only friends present were relatively new ones: Peter Berneis, a German writer, who served as Marlon's best man (and his wife as Anna's matron of honor); and Louis L'Amour, who told Anna an hour before the ceremony, "You can still back out." She didn't.

The news that Marlon Brando had finally taken a bride was a bombshell. In the glare of publicity, Marlon seemed to freeze, as if realizing the full extent of what he had just done. On their honeymoon, spent with the L'Amours at their house in Palm Desert, Marlon was gloomy and distant; at breakfast, Anna recalled, "he entertained us by extinguishing cigarettes on the back of his hand." When reporters began calling Anna's ethnicity into question, insisting she wasn't Indian at all, Marlon bolted from her side, reportedly hiring his own detectives to find out the truth. Anna had always been forthright about her mixed-race heritage. But Marlon, never a trusting soul, now thought she'd lied to him.

Spotting an opportunity to go after Marlon again, Hedda Hopper swooped in as Anna's champion, writing several columns and magazine pieces on Marlon's boorish treatment of his wife. "Most people here shrug off his behavior with, 'Oh, well, you know he's crazy,'" Hopper wrote to Jack Podell of *Motion Picture* magazine. "I think he's crazy like a fox and his bad behavior covers up his ill manners, inadequacy and belief every woman in the world would drop dead for him. Of course he chose such a perfect time to misbehave. [*Sayonara* was being released.] But he cares no more for a producer's investment than he does for his wife's feelings." Still, Hopper tried not to "hit him too hard in case there might be a reconciliation." Every woman, she told Podell, has that hope her man might return to her, "even though he may be a bastard."

Marlon did return, around the time the baby was born, on May 11, 1958. Christian, a beautiful mix of both parents, charmed his father, and Marlon agreed to stick around. But he couldn't (or wouldn't) hide his extramarital adventures. "He hadn't given up his bachelorhood," as Alice put it.

When Anna finally filed for divorce, Hedda Hopper quoted her as saying, "To me he's always played more at being a character than a human being. I never have understood him. Nor do I believe his talent is as great as he thinks it is. He loves the adulation of a mob sitting at his feet drooling over him . . . which feeds his ego[,] and after that, going home to a family must seem too humdrum." Much of that diatribe was, surely, Hopper's own editorializing; the columnist's notes from her interview with Anna show portions inserted in her own handwriting.

Although Hopper didn't want her readers to think so, there were two sides, as always, to this story. The "very sweet little girl [who] does not deserve such lousy treatment," as Hopper called Anna, was in fact drinking too much and neglecting her son. Perhaps, as some argued in her defense, Anna started drinking only after Marlon abandoned her. But any sympathy ends when she placed her child in harm's way. Friends reported finding Christian, before he was one year old, crawling outside by himself, at the edge of the swimming pool, while Anna was passed out in her own vomit inside. When Marlon hired a nurse to come in and take care of Christian, Anna threw a fit; she discerned (correctly) that the nurse was there to watch her as much as the baby. Her own doctor would be compelled to testify that Anna had "a wide, swinging personality, episodes of deep depression to normal elations, all with hysterical overtones." Marlon had witnessed his wife's instability long before they separated.

When they divorced, Anna got a $65,000 house in Beverly Hills, $5,000 per month in living expenses, and an additional $1,000 a month earmarked as child support. She also got an automobile. One hundred thousand dollars was put in trust for Christian until he was twenty-one. The court allowed Marlon to see Christian at Anna's house on Wednesdays and every second weekend. Holidays were shared.

His son fascinated him. Marlon marveled as Christian learned to say words and take his first steps. "I can teach him so much," he gushed to George Englund. "We have so much we can do together." Here, at last, was Marlon's chance to do parenting right, to undo his father's mistakes. "It was a real love affair," Englund said. "Marlon always wanted to feel inside himself that he was being a proper father." But then Anna would suddenly get angry, such as the Christmas morning when Marlon showed up at her house with not only an armful of gifts, but also the young actress BarBara Luna. Anna slammed the door in their faces. Telling the court of the incident, Marlon contended that his ex-wife was "emotionally disturbed." Hearing this, Anna retorted, "If I [was] emotionally disturbed, it was over the thought of sharing my child with one of Marlon's 'companions' on Christmas Day."

And so it went, back and forth, for the next two years. During periods when they were fighting, there was no visitation at all, and it was left to their lawyers to come up with a new plan. Each time, there would be dueling versions of what had happened between them. Did Anna grab Christian away from Marlon while he was holding him, or did Marlon push her to the ground and take the child? Did Marlon show up at Anna's house at midnight to harass her, or did she go to his house, drunk, break in, and bite him three times while he slept? Anna would admit that "a few drinks" could spur her into violence against Marlon. She hit him; she tried to stab him; and once, he lashed back by taking her over his knee and spanking her.

They were both violent, both at fault. They provoked each other. They brought out the very worst in each other and themselves. Meanwhile, Christian, now two, no longer smiled as much as he used to, and cried more than he should. "He felt the energy between his parents," said George Englund. Marlon was shattered by what this was doing to his son, but he felt helpless to stop it. "The sins of the father," he said to one of his friends, and that was all that he needed to say; his friend got his meaning exactly. *How had he ever let this happen?*

No matter. The fact was he had.

AS HIS PLANE touched down in Papeete, the capital of French Polynesia, Marlon was near to coming unglued. "What I brought to Tahiti," he said, "was a mind full of anxiety, disappointment and false expectations." The past couple of years had seen the awakening of his political consciousness; his eyes had been fully opened to the injustices in society. But not yet had he turned his gaze inward. So many of the disasters currently roiling his personal life were of his own making. Anna might be vindictive and spiteful in her court appearances, but if Marlon had taken some responsibility when they were dating, she'd never have gotten pregnant; and, if it was true that he'd *wanted* her to get pregnant so he could play Hollywood husband and father, knowing he could never truly make that commitment, then he was as much the author of those courtroom debacles as she.

Marlon's indifferent, sometimes exploitative, treatment of women exposes the corrosive underbelly of his progressive social activism: he didn't always practice at home what he preached in public. George Englund pinned the problem on "the ancient score" Marlon was always trying to settle through women. Rita Moreno knew that score, too—how Marlon had made her "love him the way his mother never had, and then punished [her] for doing so." He was simply unable at this point to make the connections between his public positions and his private life.

Moreno was still around. Josanne hadn't deterred her; neither had Anna. Shortly before her wedding day, Anna had found Moreno's wig hanging from Marlon's bedpost, "like an obscene trophy," she called it. Moreno's obsession with Marlon had taken over her life. When they'd break up, she couldn't stay away. Like Anna, Moreno got pregnant, but this time Marlon arranged an abortion instead of a marriage. "The sorrow over losing the baby," Moreno wrote, "and the humiliation of knowing what I had done with Marlon—and kept doing, over and over—was destroying me." For women such as Moreno, Englund pointed out, the memory that their lives "once had another purpose, to be a dancer or a writer," would recede and blur. Even after winning the role of Anita in the film version of the Broadway smash *West Side Story*, Moreno still snuck away whenever possible to see her unfaithful lover.

Marlon was maddeningly slow to understand the suffering he caused so many of the women in his life. After another relationship ended, he expressed astonishment to Alice Marchak: "Can you believe she really thought I loved her?" His secretary replied yes, she could believe it, because in the moment, Marlon made his women feel that way and allowed them to plan their lives around him.

An ancient score indeed: Marlon was in some ways as powerless as his women to break the cycle. He actually used the term *sex addict* decades before it became commonplace, to describe himself when Alice took the job as his secretary. "When I awake in the morning," he explained, "the first thing I think about is, 'Who am I going to fuck today?'"—even if a woman from the night before was still sleeping beside him. Moreno believed Marlon was as caught in his own compulsion as she was in hers. "It's collusion," she insisted, looking back, years later. "You collude. I'll be your little girl and your little maid and your little geisha and you be my daddy and you take care of me. It's a deal. No one ever says things like that out loud. But you know a deal has been sealed."

Not all Marlon's girlfriends, significantly, felt hurt or exploited by him. Many of these women were married, not exactly unhappily, but Marlon filled some empty place in their lives without threatening their marriages. With one such woman, the wife of a doctor, Marlon enjoyed a thirteen-year affair. He'd park his car around the corner from her house in Beverly Hills, scale a fence, and sneak in the back way. Marlon thought the woman's husband knew about the affair. "Those Beverly Hills ladies," he said. "They were as free and easy with sex as any man."

Sometimes, however, husbands weren't quite as understanding. On the set of *One-Eyed Jacks*, Marlon had taken up with a married bit player, and one night invited her back to his house. According to Alice, he also phoned the woman's husband and told him to drop by. He considered it a prank, though Alice was astounded by the cruelty of it. The man arrived, threw a tantrum, and the couple later divorced. The episode was, apparently, one more example of Marlon's need to provoke men with "a certain kind of masculinity," arrogant men like his father, by "fucking their wives."

Yet there was also something else possibly going on by this point. "I think Marlon had become very aware of how alone he was," Ellen Adler observed. Loneliness had been his curse for a very long time, and the motivation for much of his bad behavior. For all his love of sleeping around, for all his abhorrence of traditional marriage and commitment, Marlon was aware of what he was missing in his life. Marital bliss had eluded most of those around him, including his sisters, but a lucky few at least seemed happy: Phil and Marie Rhodes, the Louis L'Amours, the Elia Kazans. At times, Marlon seemed to resent his friends' happiness. He wasn't gracious when Wally found a new love, Millie Tirado, after the failure of his first marriage. "He comes in," Tirado would say of her first meeting with Marlon, "and he doesn't say a word. He was kind of sulky and very rude and I sensed, absolutely, that he was like a brother being jealous of an intruder." It was Marlon, however, who was the intruder, in a world he could never achieve for himself, and perhaps that's why he took some perverse pleasure in playing the homewrecker. He was lonely, and envious of those who weren't.

A few years earlier, in Paris, he'd reconnected with Ellen, after so many years apart. "I'd heard that he'd gotten married," Ellen said, "and I was glad, because I had just gotten married." She'd wed David Oppenheim, a clarinetist and a producer for Igor Stravinsky. They had a baby son. When Ellen was hospitalized for a minor illness, Marlon visited her. Once, many years earlier, she'd feared this very scenario: being married to someone else, having a baby, and Marlon coming along, completely detached from her. She'd imagined herself distraught and heartbroken, and Marlon tranquil. But the reality was very much the opposite. Ellen was "very, very happy and deeply in love," as she described herself, while Marlon was separated from and quarreling with his wife. At the hospital, Ellen and Marlon had a happy reconnection. Just as in the old days, he made her laugh. They talked about friends, and plays, and books, and reminisced about New York. Then, out of the blue, Marlon asked if he could lie down on the bed beside her. "You can't do that!" Ellen said, laughing. "You can't lie down on the bed next to me in a hospital." Marlon didn't press his request.

When he left that day, he promised to come to see her again—

every day, in fact, that she was in the hospital. But the next day, he didn't come, nor the next. One morning, Ellen looked up at the television and saw Marlon walking up the steps of an airplane. He turned around and waved his hat. The announcer said, "Marlon Brando on his way back to Los Angeles." Ellen could only smile.

SO, IT WAS a lonely, dispirited man who wandered the pristine beaches of Tahiti, Bud Burdick at his side. Burdick had discovered these islands during the war and had been coming back ever since. "Each particle of water is neutral," he wrote in his book about the South Seas, *The Blue of Capricorn*, "but between the great depths and the violence of the sun the water is made to look blue [and] close to perfect."

For Marlon, Tahiti was a revelation. From his first moments, when he and the *Mutiny* principals were given a traditional welcome in Matavai Bay, complete with dancing girls and leis, he'd fallen in love with the place. He and Aaron Rosenberg had spent less time scouting locations than they had sightseeing for their own pleasure. He'd turned down the posh house MGM had found for his accommodation and instead bunked in a small, traditional thatched-roof hut.

Marlon had been fascinated by the South Seas ever since he was a boy, poring over issues of *National Geographic*. "I love it down here," he told an assistant director who'd accompanied Carol Reed. "I can go around barefoot, stripped to the waist, and nobody pays attention. Here one is judged by local standards"—in other words, not the arbitrary, narrow-minded standards of Hollywood and America. Here, the people lived elementally, fishing for food, sharing what they caught, loving whom they wanted, when they wanted, without rules or judgment. "Love in these islands," Burdick quoted a Parisian transplant in his book, has "a simplicity, a spontaneity, a kindness we Europeans have lost. Here a man can live the life he is supposed to live: the life of the body, the life of the mind, the life of the heart." Sex in the islands, to Marlon's great delight, was just as elemental. "To the Westerner," Burdick wrote, "sex is a dramatic, committing, involving, often frightening thing. For the Polynesian, it is a simple matter, as simple as eating or swimming or a prayer or an argument. It need not have consequences."

Burdick's descriptions were, perhaps, oversimplified, an idealistic outsider's view of the place. But, for the moment, Marlon was enchanted by what he found in Tahiti. "There are more laughing faces per linear meter in Tahiti than in any place that I've ever seen," he said. "True happiness. We don't know how to produce that. We can produce anything, but we can't make people happy." Instead, he said, "We make people very angry."

On Tahiti, Marlon's rage and resentments melted away. Stepping into a double-hulled canoe, or outrigger, he paddled out into a 360-degree panorama of blue, white, and green. The air was so clean and pure, unlike Los Angeles with all its automobiles. Out onto the vast, omniscient Pacific he rowed, along with Burdick and a few Tahitian natives. Wearing nothing but a colorful cotton pareu wrapped around his waist, Marlon spent his time in Tahiti in a state of wonder that such places existed in the world, where how much money you made, or how famous you were, or how many different women you liked to fuck simply did not matter.

Then, on August 27, he had to put on a shirt and tie and fly back home.

HARSH REALITY STRUCK him almost immediately. On his way from the airport, he was caught in a traffic jam. At home, Alice had left a stack of telephone messages for him to go through, from Anna, from Movita, from his father, from MGM asking about *Mutiny*, from Universal asking about *The Ugly American*, from the electric company threatening to cut off power unless the bill was paid.

Marlon understood that unless he made some money, he would

be trapped like this forever. *Mutiny* would bring in some needed cash, but what about after that? What could get him solvent and keep him that way?

He'd been entertaining the idea of starring in *Lawrence of Arabia* for director David Lean. It wasn't what he wanted to do—what he wanted to do was the Chessman film and *The Ugly American* with Bud Burdick—but the money would be very good, more than a million up front, and every indication was that the picture would be a giant hit. That was the reason he'd gone to Paris before heading to Tahiti, to meet with Lean and attend his wedding to Leila Matkar. But when Lean estimated the picture would take six months to make, Marlon reconsidered. "Lean was a very good director," he wrote, "but he took so long to make a movie that I would have dried up in the desert like a puddle of water." He wasn't about to forfeit another half year of his life to a project that wasn't his idea.

Unable to find his way forward on the Chessman script, Marlon determined to direct *The Ugly American* once *Mutiny* was completed. Universal was already hyping his involvement, and it was really his best chance at the moment to make a direct political comment on American society. His partners at Pennebaker, however, weren't certain this would be the big blockbuster they needed to get out of debt. *That*, they all hoped, would come from *One-Eyed Jacks*, Marlon's directorial debut.

Marlon had once hoped so, too. He'd brought everything he had to that film, living with it day and night for many months. *Jacks*, Marlon once imagined, would be his ticket to financial and creative freedom; if a picture he'd directed himself was a hit, then he'd have carte blanche going forward, getting all the financing he needed to make the films that mattered to him. But despite having finished principal photography on *Jacks* the previous spring, Marlon was still haggling with Paramount over the ending, and no one was sure when, or if, the film would be released.

Pennebaker was now in desperate need of cash, spending far more than it was bringing in. Over the past year, the company had developed a number of projects without Marlon's direct involvement and with other actors, including *Paris Blues*, directed by Martin Ritt and starring Paul Newman, and *First Train to Babylon*, slated for Gary Cooper. Marlon's commitment to the company was clearly fading. "Marlon had no interest in corporate matters," said George Englund. "He had no urge to persevere through the arduous process of developing films. So when he received offers from other studios where all he had to do was act, he took them."

Pennebaker was supposed to have been his lifesaver; in fact, it nearly sank him. Alice was aware that he had "lost interest in moviemaking," but Marlon's partners (Englund, Glass, Seltzer) seemed to be in denial. Marlon Senior, however, could see what was happening. One of the few times his son came into the office during that fall of 1960 was to pitch two ideas, one listed on the company books as "American Indians" and the other as "Tahiti," two broad topics from which Marlon believed he could chisel out stories for successful films. The elder Brando wasn't convinced. A pessimist by nature but also a realist, he still argued that the company's dire financial straits required a big commercial hit. The top box-office films of the past year had been *Auntie Mame*, *Imitation of Life*, and *The Shaggy Dog*. At the moment, *Ben-Hur*, which even one of its screenwriters, Gore Vidal, dismissed as junk, and *Psycho*, Hitchcock's brilliantly produced and marketed story of a cross-dressing man who stabs naked girls in the shower, were the ones raking in the cash. This was what Pennebaker needed.

Marlon could have given them that. He could have made a big crowd-pleaser, pumped up the company's coffers, and then had the luxury of making films about Chessman, or American Indians, or Tahiti. Then again, he could have run his repertory company back in 1953 as a more conventional business, too, choosing a commercial vehicle, maybe *Romeo and Juliet*, instead of *Arms and the Man*, and playing the lead to bring in audiences, instead of the comic support. But he hadn't had the tolerance then, and he didn't have it now. Because, in fact, it probably would have taken *two* crowd-pleasers to sufficiently satiate Pennebaker's coffers, and maybe three or four—Marlon knew how that went. He'd spent nearly two years of his life on *One-Eyed Jacks*, and for all his efforts, all his painstaking labor, the studio was telling him how to cut it, how to sell it, and what sort of ending he should give it. He just couldn't play the same old game anymore.

"Life is short," he told an interviewer around this time. Life was precious, too, something he'd learned all too well during the Chessman ordeal. It was perhaps true that a wise investment, arduous and tedious at the time, might have produced dividends later. But Marlon had just spent five years doing arduous and tedious things as a loyal Hollywood foot soldier. He was *done*. How could he believe that this time, unlike all the other times, the investment would pay off?

He had to break away. Almost thirty-seven years old, he was still under his father's thumb. He'd thought that by making the old man his employee, he'd get to call the shots, but that wasn't how it had worked out. His father still controlled the purse strings, as he had all Marlon's life. From his desk at Pennebaker, Marlon Senior sent his son two hundred dollars a month to live on, compared to the five thousand dollars a month Anna was getting. And his allowance couldn't be raised, not now, because the money he brought in was also supporting Movita and her child. That meant the final notices on electricity, gas, and telephone were piling up on Alice's desk. Whenever his secretary told Marlon he might have his utilities shut off, he'd go through the roof. "Shades of New York," she remembered him saying, as if he were back in those coldwater flats instead of a sprawling house in the Hollywood Hills.

Since he refused to speak to his father, Alice had to intercede. Usually Marlon Senior would come through with the money. His son would rage after getting the check, telling Alice "how much he hated his father," how it was his father's fault that he was broke. "The more he talked," Alice said, "the angrier he became."

He was, thankfully, back in analysis. His psychiatrist was Gerald Aronson, a young, Brooklyn-born Cornell graduate and the son of Russian Jewish immigrants. They saw each other every week; when Marlon was traveling, they conducted phone sessions, even from Tahiti. No doubt Aronson helped Marlon make a critical decision about his father in the fall of 1960.

For some time, Marlon had been using the investment services of Guy Gadbois, who ran a financial management company in Beverly Hills. But now the time had finally come, he decided, to take all his personal finances away from his father and give them to Gadbois to manage. No longer would he have to beg his father for enough cash to pay his phone bill. Now, if he had to beg, he could beg Gadbois, and avoid dredging up three decades of conflict. In truth, the move was a fatal blow to Pennebaker, because now Marlon was free from his father's pressure to invest much of his money back into the company. He was also free to spend it all, if he chose, on message pictures or whatever else he wanted. A hut in Tahiti, maybe.

What mattered most to Marlon, however, was that he was finally free from his father's long shadow—or so he told himself. If only overcoming his father's legacy was as easy as changing accountants.

DECEMBER 1960 / Against a bright cerulean sky overlaid gently with white clouds, the *Bounty*, in full, majestic sail, glided slowly into Matavai Bay. The blue horizon of water was barely distinguishable from the sky. The air was warm, fragrant with flowers, and spiced with sea salt. A hushed, expectant silence hung over the harbor. Suddenly, in the water and in the bushes on shore, there was movement. Hundreds of Tahitians, paddling out in canoes and bursting onto the beaches, hurried to greet the ship. They wore full traditional costume, colorful pareaus, flowers in their hair, spears in their hands. Clapping, waving, they shouted and threw flowers—causing director Carol Reed, shaking his fist behind the bank of cameras filming the spectacle, to call "Cut!" in exasperation. They would have to do it all over again.

One of the film's publicists, Morgan Hudgins, explained to Hedda Hopper: "Things are moving along slowly, but well." Those five thousand native Tahitians welcoming the *Bounty*, Hudgins said, had been instructed to play the scene "enigmatically." The film's audience isn't supposed to know right away whether the natives are friendly or hostile. But "enigmatic" wasn't something that translated easily into Tahitian. The culture of the islands tended to be open, honest, forthright, with very little guile. Instinctively, the natives wanted to give the *Bounty* "a royal welcome," Hudgins wrote to Hopper, so they smiled and threw their arms wide. It was difficult getting them to understand direction. Finally, however, Reed was successful, and the extras, Hudgins reported, performed "magnificently."

All five thousand of them were paid ten dollars a day—twenty if they had a canoe. MGM was certainly pumping cash into the local Tahitian economy, and the residents were thrilled to be a part of the enterprise.

There'd been no penny-pinching on this film. The full-scale replica of the eighteenth-century ship was the first vessel ever built from the keel up specifically for a motion picture (or so the film's ad campaign promised). The *Bounty* was 110 feet long and 30 feet wide and flew 11,000 feet of sails. Built in Nova Scotia from blueprints of the original at a cost of $600,000, the ship had sailed down the

East Coast of the United States and along Mexico, crossed through the Panama Canal, and then made its way to San Francisco, before setting off on its thirty-seven-day journey to Polynesia. Reed and his cameras, and five thousand Tahitians, were there to record its arrival.

Marlon enjoyed the spectacle. He enjoyed himself even more when, climbing up onto the vessel, he was met by a horde of teen-aged Tahitian girls, all of them laughing and flirting, supremely comfortable and unashamed of their sexuality. They stripped him and some of the other men of their clothes and tossed them into the warm waters of the bay. This was the sort of moviemaking experience Marlon could live with.

He spent Christmas eating taro root and raw fish marinated in coconut milk, as well as a pig slow-roasted over a firepit. He sat among local Tahitians listening to their stories and their music, keeping time with their drums, his old instinct for rhythm playing out on the table in front of him. In his hut, he read everything he could about Polynesian history and culture. "The Tahitians have withstood fifteen different kinds of missionaries," Marlon said. "They withstood the English and the French and American tourists and New Zealand tourists and all kinds of exploitation. And they still stand up. They are flat-footed, and remain with their unassailable identities."

He could relate: he'd survived his own encounters with some very different sorts of missionaries, who'd tried to change him, too. "It's the most democratic society I've ever been in," Marlon went on. "They don't care who you are. They don't care what you do or what you represent, as long as you're decent and courteous and generally kind and interested in dancing and the things they're interested in."

The kindness especially impressed him. One day, while he was standing on a beach, looking out at the sea, a group of fishermen suddenly gave him a basket of fish—"for no reason at all," Marlon said. They had no idea who he was. Another time, late at night, he had a flat tire. With no jack in the car, he resigned himself to looking up at the stars for a while. But then a man came along. "Didn't say anything to me, not one word," Marlon remembered. He just "fixed the tire and went on."

The natives weren't saints. "They love gossiping," Marlon discovered. "They love telling lies for no reason at all." Little lies, not malicious ones. "You're talking to somebody," he explained, "and you say, 'Where's Mutua?' And they say, 'Oh, I saw him down at the dock this morning.' And they *didn't* see him. It's just to say something pleasant." So many times Marlon had done the same thing, concocting a story to smooth over some small talk, or just for the sheer fun of making something up. The Tahitians were tricksters, just as he was. He had rarely felt more at home.

They had something else in common. Sexual definitions, restrictions, proprieties were unknown or ignored. "You don't have any wife or husband," Marlon said of the natives he met. The sacrosanct Western nuclear family was a strange, alien concept. "They pass children around like Easter eggs," he said of the Tahitians. Family was spread out, diverse, communal. "If a child comes from an uncle who lives over on Bora Bora," Marlon said, "and he's living now with the aunt or somebody's friend," they were all still family. A sense of kinship defined entire villages. "There's no stigma of illegitimacy," Marlon added. "They love all children regardless of who they are or where they came from."

That much certainly resonated for him, as he was no doubt thinking of his two boys back home. The Tahitians' indifference to the tenets of Judeo-Christianity and the Western world in general had been advantageous to them, Marlon believed.

Of course, the rose-colored impressions that he and the other white men in his circle took from Tahitian culture were idealistic and sometimes patronizing, examples of outsiders peering into so-called primitive cultures and seeing what they wanted to see. Only later would Marlon see the Tahitians' full humanity, warts and all, and understand that no culture is ideal. Still, the initial joy and affirmation he felt from some aspects of Tahitian life were honest and genuine. He'd always been drawn to places that defied traditional values around sex, sexuality, gender, and family. New York had been that way for him in the beginning; Provincetown had served a similar purpose. But for the longest time, he'd been a prisoner of Hollywood convention, twisting and turning on a rack of rules and constraints. He'd longed to find a place where he could escape from all that. Now he had.

Certainly, the sexual freedom was particularly attractive. Phil Rhodes, whom Marlon had also brought along for the shoot, remembered Marlon feeling as if he'd fallen into a sexual "Shangri-la." He took full advantage of the opportunities that presented themselves. Here he could have different girlfriends for different days of the week, finally replicating that elusive arrangement he'd once had with Celia, Ellen, and Blossom all those years earlier. But it was also the spiritual pull of the islands that drew him. Alec Ata, the director of island tourism, became friendly with Marlon. "He was really floating," Ata recalled. "In the middle of breakfast or lunch, or even while they were filming, he might leave and go out to the reef, alone in a canoe, maybe with a ten-pound box of ice cream." Alone at sea, "he would talk to the birds and sometimes not come back until sunset." Ata sensed that Marlon was "desperately trying to discover something, as if he had a great uncertainty. It was in his eyes."

The change in Marlon's priorities that began with Chessman continued here, in the South Pacific. He seemed to be transforming into something new as he finally worked up the courage to play drums with the Tahitians on the beach. Pounding away, his eyes intent, sweat dripping from his forehead, he kept up with the native drummers and won their respect. The Marlon Brando who would emerge from this tropical chrysalis would be very different from the one who came before.

SITTING IN THE sand, his bare feet buried up to his ankles, Marlon read the latest version of the script. He was surrounded by his "people," as others in the company called them: Englund; Rhodes, and his wife, Marie; and Bob Hoskins, an old friend (not the British actor) from Libertyville who'd come along as Marlon's "dialogue director." That meant Hoskins, as well as the others, would help him rewrite the script, which Marlon felt was in very bad shape.

He was right. There'd never been consensus on what this film should be: a deeply psychological profile, primarily of Captain Bligh, played by Trevor Howard (which was Carol Reed's view), or a commentary on the current-day fixation on rules, protocol, and authority (which was Marlon's idea). The original script was an earnest attempt to do both, written by Eric Ambler, best known for his spy novels and the screenplay for *A Night to Remember*, about the sinking of the *Titanic*. But it went nowhere. Charles Lederer was brought in to rewrite much of Ambler's original, though his forte was comedy (*The Front Page*) and lighthearted adventure (*Ocean's Eleven*). He was at his typewriter constantly during the shoot.

Lederer found Marlon "always completely sincere" in his desire to turn the mutiny of Captain Bligh's crew, some one hundred seventy years earlier, into a clash of contemporary cultures, exposing "the idiocy of protocol and our unnatural formality and our lies." Ultimately, however, Lederer came to believe that the goal to make *Mutiny* "relevant" was "hopeless." It simply couldn't be done—or possibly, he just couldn't do it. Banging out page after page of rewrites, Lederer would hand them over to Marlon, who'd take them, plop himself down under a palm tree in the sand, and read them as he polished off his breakfast of coconut bread and hot tea. The pages he liked went into a pile, the ones he didn't like he'd tear up.

Marlon excised most of the curses that came from Christian's mouth, believing the man didn't speak that way. He'd done his own research on the historical character, and found Christian to be a cultured member of the gentry. He loathed Clark Gable's rough-hewn portrayal in the original, 1935 version, complaining that the legendary star "hadn't even bothered to speak with an English accent." Gable, Marlon griped, always just played Gable. Soon after production began, Gable had a heart attack and died (on November 16). Some called it a bad omen.

With his rewriting, Marlon was certainly working for his two million. At one point, the script, with all its additions and memos, swelled to more than a thousand pages, with Marlon's notes scrawled over almost half. Those drafts would remain in his archives, carefully preserved. His penmanship is tight and small, as if he had so many ideas he was trying to fit them all in. Some of the dialogue he translated into Tahitian, which, with his usual ear for language, he'd picked up quickly. A well-thumbed French–Tahitian dictionary was always in his pocket.

Of course, the greater problem for Lederer was discerning from whom he was supposed to be taking orders. There was a director on this picture, after all. "There seemed to be some question about who was captain," the journalist Murray Schumach observed. "While Mr. Lederer . . . was supposed to be working on the script, he was receiving unsolicited assistance from other quarters."

Carol Reed was aware of the competition coming from those other quarters. Mostly, the director had remained cordial with his star, who said he "admired" Reed. Reed had directed some fine films: *Odd Man Out, The Fallen Idol, The Third Man*. But he was too reserved for Marlon's taste. When Reed did give direction, he'd say, "Do this, do that," without any discussion beforehand about motive or situation. That was never going to work with Marlon. "An actor always needs a director," Marlon said. "And sometimes it's a very lonely world there in front of the camera with a director who is inept, or cannot articulate what is needed."

The problem with Carol Reed was the problem Marlon had found in every other director for the past half decade: he wasn't Elia Kazan. On the four films he made after *Guys and Dolls*, Marlon had learned what he considered a very valuable lesson: if the director wasn't up to snuff, he had to take charge.

ANOTHER SCENE IN another foreign land, another cast overflowing with extras. Surrounded by five hundred excited day players in Nara, Japan, Marlon had looked at the camera and placed his hands together in front of him, a traditional Japanese gesture. Behind him, the actor Glenn Ford was taking his own place in the scene. It was April 1956, and they were making *The Teahouse of the August Moon*, directed by Daniel Mann. Marlon had handpicked Mann to helm John Patrick's Broadway Pulitzer winner, expecting him to have the strength and the control to guide the picture over any trouble spots—such as what happened that day in Nara.

Marlon, nearly unrecognizable in blackened hair and eye prosthetics, was playing Sakini, the classic wise fool and interpreter to Ford's upstanding, by-the-book American, Captain Fisby. Right from the start, the two men had clashed. Ford was conservative politically; he resented Marlon's not-very-flattering comparisons of American versus Asian culture. Mann called the conflict between his stars a "pissing match," with each trying to upstage the other. Shooting with the five hundred extras, Ford kept cutting Marlon off from the camera, and finally the even-tempered, on-screen Sakini became the hot-headed, offscreen Brando and blew his top. "Do you see where I am?" Marlon bellowed. Ford was unmoved.

*Teahouse* was Marlon's first film after *Guys and Dolls*, and on that film, too, he'd been disappointed by his director failing to constrain his costar, Sinatra. He'd hoped Mann would be different because he'd worked with Kazan at the Actors Studio and was a longtime friend of Stella's. Mann had also directed other successful film versions of Broadway plays, notably *Come Back Little Sheba* and Tennessee Williams's *The Rose Tattoo*. But not only was Mann unable to control his two stars, he'd also allowed the trenchant social commentary of the Patrick play to be diluted by the comedy, most of which is predictable and puerile. The film was a hit—anything Marlon made in these years seemed to be a hit—bringing in almost six million dollars, which made it the sixth-highest-grossing film of the year. But Bosley Crowther thought Marlon's Sakini lacked "the warmth and candor called for in the role." His attempt at Japanese-accented, broken English sounded to Crowther as if he had "a wad of chewing gum clenched between his teeth." He was simply "too elaborate, too consciously cute." (Today the racially stereotyped performance borders on the offensive.) The reviews for *Teahouse* were the most negative notices Marlon had received in his film career.

Kazan would never have let him get away with it. To start with, Kazan would have met with his actors a couple of weeks ahead of shooting. They would have gone over all their parts. They would have received Kazan's highly detailed notes on their characters; he would have encouraged discussion and spontaneity. Rivalries would have been blunted as he told his actors, "Go off and work on the scene and bring something back here for us to work on."

Marlon's entrance into filmmaking had been nurtured by a remarkable and unique filmmaker; there were very few like Kazan. Despite his disappointment in his mentor's political failings, Marlon knew that this was the case. "Acting is such a tenuous thing," he'd told Capote. "A fragile, shy thing that a sensitive director can help lure out of you. Gadge can usually do it." But so far no one else could. Marlon, said Karl Malden, "felt he couldn't trust anybody" except Kazan.

The question arises: had Marlon found another director to replace Kazan, or to at least come close, would his filmmaking experience have been different? Would it have felt less tedious, less degrading, less irrelevant? If Kazan had never testified before Congress, and he and Marlon had made further films together, would Marlon have been more satisfied and respectful of his profession?

As it was, he spent his time in front of the camera—from 1956 to 1960, from Japan to Tahiti—unhappy and discontent, fighting with directors, writers, and producers, trying unsuccessfully to turn the experience into what he had known with Kazan. He developed his own strategies to cope. "Most of the time," he said, "you come like a journeyman plumber and you gotta have your own bag of stuff, ready to go." He'd wear the director out, Marlon said, by giving him "nine bad takes." Then, when he finally gave him "the one take" in which he really tried, the director would be so happy that he'd print that one. "So you don't give him a choice," Marlon said. "You have to play those games with dumb directors."

Mann wasn't dumb; he was, in fact, quite good most of the time. So were the other directors Marlon worked with in this period. But they weren't Kazan; they didn't bring his preparation, his style, his commitment to the process. In their defense, they also weren't directing the young, impressionable Brando whom Kazan had known. They were directing Brando the star—who believed he knew better than they did how to make pictures. The truth was, by this time, Marlon usually did. He could be cocky and arrogant about it, so it wasn't always easy for a director to admit it, but his instincts were almost always on target. He thought *Teahouse* should have caught "the magic of the play" better than it did, and that magic, he said, came from the "observation that Americans overvalue success and ambition." The film is mostly comedy, but the play is all about Fisby's realization that sometimes one can find a better life by taking a step backward. Kazan would have articulated that message on day one of rehearsals and reflected it in every scene.

On *Sayonara*, Marlon's second film made in Japan, he'd considered director Josh Logan to be "stricken with depression," a lifelong condition of his, and "not able to function properly." In response, Marlon rewrote and improvised on his own. Playing an American air force major who falls in love with a Japanese woman, Marlon pretty much did things his way. Logan sensed his star's discontent: "He simply didn't trust me as having as good taste as he had." Yet never did Logan confront his leading man; he was determined to get through the picture with minimal problems. He seemed, in fact, in awe of Brando, whom he called "the greatest actor of his time." All he did, Logan said, was "set up a big color camera, put Marlon in front of it and Japan in back of him, and then got out of the way."

Logan's awe manifested as deference and, possibly, fear—which was in some ways a worse experience for Marlon than confrontation. He might have gotten through *Sayonara* with very little stress (which gave him time to grow lonely and pen love letters to Anna Kashfi), but he also didn't emerge with any respect for Logan. It had been Marlon who'd seen the wisdom of changing the ending to a happy one, so that, for one of the first times in the history of American film, a mixed-race couple could be "thought of to be a natural thing, not an unnatural one." That ending, thanks to Marlon's foresight, guaranteed the film's number-one box-office success.

At one point while making the film, frustrated by Logan's ineffectiveness, Marlon decided to try an "experiment." He did everything wrong, he remembered. "Grimaced and rolled my eyes, put in all kinds of gestures and expressions that had no relation to the part." And what did Logan say to these antics? "He just said, 'It's wonderful. Print it.'"

Marlon's experiment merely confirmed to him what he believed deep down: that everything he did in Hollywood was a lie, that his so-called genius was a mass delusion, that he was simply the emperor without any clothes. But when his account appeared in print

(Capote again), he regretted the pain and embarrassment it caused Logan. "Josh was a sitting duck," he lamented. "He was suffering. You have to have some kind of care." Still feeling remorse, Marlon penned a short note to the director after the film's release: "I have received a lot of mail about *Sayonara*, among them many letters that have concerned themselves with people's revelation about the nature of their own prejudices, and I think that's a most rewarding thing. I'm happy about the results of the picture and really glad you talked me into it."

For all the discontent and hurt feelings, *Sayonara* is a good film. Essentially directing himself, Marlon creates a believable character of Major Gruver, moving convincingly from adolescent braggadocio to maturity. He also sustains a credible Southern accent, no easy task. In fact, his decision to make Gruver Southern, against Logan's opposition, turned out to be essential to deepening the character's transformation. The reviews for *Sayonara* made up for those of *Teahouse*. The *Chicago Tribune* declared that Marlon "dominates" the picture, correctly observing that Logan seemed "to have retreated and left him to his own devices." The results, the paper concluded, were "magnetic." Bosley Crowther thought that, unlike in *Teahouse*, this time Marlon got his "eccentricity" exactly right. "His offbeat acting of what could be a conventional role," the *Times* critic observed, "spins what could be a routine romance into a lively and tense dramatic show."

For his next film, Marlon conjured up another unexpected reconsideration of his character. In *The Young Lions*, he plays a German military officer; once again, the changes he desired for his character were to make him more three-dimensional. Set during World War II, the film tells the stories of three very different "lions": a Jewish store clerk, a Broadway singer, and the German officer. Lt. Christian Diestl originally volunteers for war service because he believes Hitler will bring positive change to Germany. Once he sees what is happening, however, he is horrified. In the original script, by Edward Anhalt, based on Irwin Shaw's novel, "all the Germans were bad," Marlon complained. Instead, he wanted to portray his character as "misled," just as he thought many Americans had been misled to believe "they were the righteous owners of the land" and the Indians were "savages."

Once again, however, he had only tepid support from his director, Edward Dmytryk, whom Marlon considered another "weakling." Like Kazan, Dmytryk had given names of suspected Communists to Congress. The director admitted he'd been "scared to death" of working with Brando, and the star had smelled that fear much the way a real lion might. There were conflicts with original novelist Shaw as well. Meeting with the author in Paris, Marlon justified his interpretation of the character by insisting that some Nazis must have wrestled with their consciences. Shaw refused to acknowledge this, insisting, "It's my character." Marlon reportedly replied, "I play the role; now he exists. He is *my* creation."

*The Young Lions* was notable as the first and only time Marlon costarred with Montgomery Clift. They share no scenes, however, save for the ending, when Marlon lies facedown in a river, dead, as Clift and their third costar, Dean Martin, stand over him. Dmytryk would recall some grandstanding between the two rivals, such as the time, at a restaurant, they seemed to be in competition over who could speak the best French. But, in fact, the two men got along well.

Jack Larson thought the basis for that camaraderie stemmed from a visit Marlon had made to Clift about a year earlier. Clift had just had a serious automobile accident, badly damaging his face. Depressed, self-conscious, and worried he'd lost his appeal as a leading man, he had started drinking heavily. "Marlon felt terrible," Larson said. "They were supposed to be rivals but he always liked Monty, and he came by to tell him so. He told Monty that he'd always admired him, that he'd actually been jealous of him in some ways, because Monty was so good-looking, so effortless in his acting. Monty was, in fact, the bar by which he measured himself." That was an extraordinary statement from Marlon, who rarely complimented actors. But his impulse for empathy was stronger than his disdain for acting. Worried about Clift's drinking, Marlon also offered to accompany him to AA. "The group had helped his mother," Larson recalled Marlon saying. Although Clift didn't take him up on his offer, he was deeply moved by the visit. "There were tears in his eyes afterward," said Larson. "He said Marlon's words had meant the world to him."

Despite Marlon's frustrations with his work during this period, his sense of humor, as always, was his salvation. On *Sayonara*, Logan found him "ridiculously determined to upset any note of sobriety." One day, Marlon showed up on the set with his arm in a sling, sending assistants scurrying to reschedule shooting. All of a sudden, Marlon removed the sling with a laugh and pounded his fist to show he wasn't hurt. Filming his last scene in *The Young Lions*, he stayed facedown in the water for almost a minute after Dmytryk called, "Cut," worrying the company that maybe he'd really drowned. Then up he came, dripping wet, a big smile on his face. "I could always hold my breath longer than any other kid on the block," he said.

*The Young Lions* did well at the box office, and Marlon's prescience about his character paid off. Film critic Andrew Sarris would call Marlon "positively uncanny" in his portrayal of the conflicted Nazi, a fully realized human being where previous portrayals had been cardboard cutouts. Marlon had the authority to do it, too, since he was well known as an ardent supporter of Israel.

This was also the first film on which Marlon used earphones as prompters. In a process that dated back to Stella's classroom, he believed that by slightly rewriting his lines to make them more personal to him, he could project more "spontaneity." In the past, he'd sometimes scrawled these new lines on plates or props. Memorizing them, Marlon insisted, defeated the exercise; what he wanted was naturalism. On *The Young Lions*, he found "a much better way to do it," he recalled. "And that was to put radio mics in my ear. That way, someone would be a hundred yards away reading the lines to me. It would save me a lot of time, because you would spend three hours, maybe four hours, studying the fucking lines, or you'd be working on them all day long as actors do. They go around muttering, learning their lines, and I had things much better to do than learn lines." Having his lines relayed to him also allowed him one final chance to speak the dialogue as it seemed most natural. Rarely, Marlon said, did he just repeat the line that was read to him. He was rewriting, in effect, up to the very second he mouthed the words.

For his final film of the 1950s, *The Fugitive Kind*, he had his best luck with a director, though even this collaboration was less than ideal. Sidney Lumet, who, a lifetime before, had taken over from Marlon as the lead in *A Flag Is Born*, had brilliantly played with form and structure in his first film, *12 Angry Men*, to convey the tense, claustrophobic experience of a jury room. Yet, like Logan, he seemed intimidated by his star, treating Marlon with "sort of kid gloves," observed Maureen Stapleton, who had a small part in the film (after playing the lead in the Broadway version). Despite his sharp work on *12 Angry Men*, Lumet was unsuccessful in shaping *Fugitive* into a compelling whole. Marlon was well aware of this, and it frustrated him. But unlike with other films, he didn't feel quite as free to blithely rewrite his lines, as the screenplay was based on *Orpheus Descending*, by Tennessee Williams.

At last the playwright had snared Marlon into playing his wandering hero, Valentine Xavier, as he'd wanted for some time. (Onstage, the role had been played by Cliff Robertson.) Williams also got the actress he'd originally wanted, too, Anna Magnani, convinced that her pairing with Marlon would be dynamite.

For once, Williams was wrong. Marlon had agreed to do the

film only because, yet again, he needed the money. He had his doubts about the film, even if he'd been impressed with the play when Williams first wrote it. Two versions of *Orpheus* had flopped on Broadway, but everyone hoped the film, with the expected chemistry between its two magnetic stars, would take off. "Lightning will strike," the ads for the picture promised, "when Magnani meets Brando."

If lightning struck, however, nothing caught fire. Magnani was hostile to her leading man, resenting his polite, courteous approach to her, when, according to several people on the set, what she wanted was to sleep with him. "She's like a vacuum cleaner," Marlon griped to Sam Gilman. "She's sucking me dry." His leading ladies had rarely been this powerful; he didn't know how to respond. The stars' hostility comes through on-screen: it's simply not believable that each is supposed to see the other as their last chance for happiness. Their physical attraction is unconvincing. Under these circumstances, one might argue that Lumet was powerless. Yet Kazan had conjured chemistry between Marlon and Jessica Tandy despite (or by using) their mutual antipathy. He'd swayed Vivien Leigh to Marlon's side and thereby set off fireworks. He'd even managed to make Marlon's scenes with Anthony Quinn, who disliked him, among the best parts of *Viva Zapata!* It's fascinating to speculate what he might have achieved had he been directing *The Fugitive Kind*.

Marlon is best in the very beginning of the film, all by himself, before the titles have even come up. In one take, he delivers his lines to an unseen judge—real, honest, natural. Whether he had his earphones in during that scene is unknown, but he achieves his goal of appearing to speak extemporaneously. From there, however, the rest of the film goes downhill. A more experienced director, a director less deferential to his stars, might have made a difference. Reviews were mixed. *Motion Picture Daily* called the film "soaring poetry," and opined that "Brando especially is effective."

The *Chicago Tribune*, however, thought "the film as a whole" lacked "the taut force" of other Williams adaptations. Calling it "weird," columnist Herb Lyon reported, *"The Fugitive Kind* is a flop at the box office, even with M. Brando's voltage." It was Marlon's first commercial disaster.

He had one film left in the can to release: his own, *One-Eyed Jacks*. Marlon had learned a great deal making that film, so he knew what he was talking about when he tried to fix the intrinsic problems with *Mutiny on the Bounty*. Until now, however, his directors had rarely listened to him. Would Reed?

ON FEBRUARY 19, 1961, Marlon stepped off the flight from Guadalajara at Los Angeles International Airport wearing an all-white suit, which set off his deep bronze tan. The *Mutiny* crew was taking a break from the rainy season in Tahiti to shoot interiors on the MGM backlot, where no fewer than three partial *Bountys* had been erected. They had left behind the majestic full-scale replica in the South Seas to await their return later in the year. About one-third of the picture had been shot.

The MGM publicity department kept the picture in the news by promoting a new addition to the cast. Arriving into Los Angeles on a separate airplane was Tarita Teriipaia, a twenty-year-old Polynesian native who'd been chosen, out of dozens of local women, as the love interest in the film. A hotel dishwasher, Tarita had been one of the hula-dancing girls in the big scene welcoming the *Bounty* to the island. Marlon had spotted her and asked that she be moved up to the front row. Tarita had something unique, he thought, something the camera would pick up. After that, he took the young woman under his wing, coaching her and then courting her. He wooed her with flowers and little gifts.

But the one thing he didn't do, much to the amazement of the crew, was sleep with her. He'd done enough of that in Tahiti. Tarita, Marlon declared, was different, special. He was deferential around her. "He would sleep on the floor and she'd sleep in the bed," said *Mutiny* assistant director Nick Rutgers. "They'd hold hands, that sort of thing." Everyone was surprised by his gallantry. "It was almost as if," one friend said, "he wanted to take things slow this time, so that nobody got hurt." No one could quite remember Marlon Brando ever behaving this way before.

**LATE FEBRUARY 1961** / Passing through the white-columned front entrance of the MCA headquarters in Beverly Hills, Marlon enthusiastically greeted his old friend Karl Malden. On one of Marlon's arms was Tarita, the Tahitian discovery he intended to make a star in *Mutiny on the Bounty,* and on the other was Rita Moreno, whom Malden had met before. They'd all come to MCA to see Paramount's long-awaited final cut of Marlon's *One-Eyed Jacks,* in which Malden had played the second lead.

They went back a long way together—all the way to *Truckline Café,* in fact, which had opened on Broadway almost exactly fifteen years earlier. Shown Paramount's advertising layouts for *Jacks,* with their names printed in big black letters, Malden observed to Marlon: "We've gone pretty far since then." Marlon smiled. "Yes," he agreed, "at least five inches."

For all his levity, Marlon was feeling uneasy. Before departing for Tahiti the previous fall, he'd placed the film, his baby, in the care of the studio. His emotions about the film went up and down. At one point it had meant everything to him; later, he despaired of it, hating the happy ending Paramount had insisted he tack onto it. But then he came to believe that if the studio had respected everything else he'd done on the film, his baby might still turn out okay.

They were ushered into a screening room. The lights went down.

*One-Eyed Jacks* had taken two years of Marlon's life, far longer than anyone had ever imagined when he started on it back in 1958. At every turn, there'd been an obstacle to completion. During the first two years, Marlon had spent eight weeks in Carmel and Monterey, two weeks in Death Valley, and another two weeks at Big Sur, each time being frustrated by weather. "We'd leave one place for another only to find the weather didn't match up to previous scenes," Malden recalled. "Once we worked in Death Valley during a terrific wind for several days. But then there was no wind for just as many days and we had to send all the way to Hollywood for a big wind machine. Weather was the one thing Brando was unable to control."

He'd tried to control everything else. By late 1959, many were starting to call *One-Eyed Jacks* "Brando's Folly." A year stretched into two and then three. More scenes needed to be shot, Marlon felt. Retakes were ordered. Then came the long, arduous process of editing. At first, Marlon had insisted on cutting the film himself. Once he was done, he invited Malden for a screening. "Come early and bring your wife," he'd said. With great excitement the Maldens had arrived. The lights dimmed; the projector was switched on; the film began to roll. Up on the screen, there were Brando and Malden, together again, riding their horses against a backdrop of the Pacific Ocean. But "after two hours," Malden remembered, "the picture suddenly stopped. Brando signaled for lights, and then he told us we still had two hours and a half to go. He ordered sandwiches and drinks before we went back to the showing."

The film was clearly too long. Marlon trimmed it from four hours to two hours and forty minutes. Under pressure from the studio and against his better judgment, he shot a new, happier ending in Monterey. He might have gone on tinkering with the film after that, but Paramount at last called it in. Still, even with its happy ending, Marlon was pleased with what he gave the studio. The photographer Sam Shaw got a look at Marlon's final cut and called it "a masterpiece." Karl Malden agreed. "It's as brilliant as Marlon can be brilliant when he's brilliant," he told Hedda Hopper at the time. Now, as the titles came up on the screen, they all waited to see what Paramount had done with it.

Marlon no longer wielded the power in Hollywood he once had. This was the first year since 1955 that he hadn't made the list of top box-office stars; his only film released in 1960 had been the disastrous *Fugitive Kind*. So, there was a great deal riding on *One-Eyed Jacks*. Not just Marlon's box-office reliability; not even just Pennebaker's financial viability—what hung in the balance was Marlon's very future in movies. Since he'd decided he was done making pictures the studio way (signing a contract, hoping to get lucky with a director), *One-Eyed Jacks* was intended to change that formula. If the picture was a success, he'd be seen as bankable. Studios would release his films; investors would back him; he'd get to make pictures that meant something to him. No more watching as incompetent directors blew everything to bits right in front of him. In this way, Marlon could make a go of this business he loathed by using its power to say something about issues he cared about.

"This was going to be his statement," his Pennebaker partner Walter Seltzer said of *One-Eyed Jacks*. "It was going to prove that he could produce, direct and star in a movie that was superior, correct and ethically mature."

The first scenes of the film unspooled on the screen in front of him. They were just as Marlon had shot them; no doubt he breathed an initial sigh of relief. He'd made plenty of concessions to the studio over the course of two years, but he believed that what he'd finally given them was solid. Every frame that could have been cut had been cut, in Marlon's opinion. Nothing was extraneous.

The final decision, however, rested with the Paramount editors. That had been their agreement with him. And the editors had been very sensitive to the task at hand, very solicitous of Marlon's opinion. He'd given them his trust. Stories would arise that Marlon had "walked away from" the picture. Nothing could have been further from the truth. As their correspondence proves, the studio assured him they understood his artistic vision.

But now columnist Leonard Lyons was joking that Adolph Zukor, the eighty-eight-year-old founder and president emeritus of Paramount, who'd been making movies since 1912, had taken a look at Marlon's production log and observed, in his whispery, terrifying voice, "It took the same amount of time to make this movie as it took our pioneers to settle eight Western states." That couldn't be a good sign.

With trepidation, Marlon watched as the rest of the film played out on the screen.

SITTING BESIDE HIM, Tarita was feeling dazzled. She'd never seen a theater as large as this one before. Ever since her plane had landed in Los Angeles, she'd felt as if she'd "arrived on another world." All she'd ever known were the islands of the South Seas. She'd never seen so many cars, so many tall buildings. She had never witnessed "people walking so fast," she said, "or talking so loud."

Yet, for all her awe of Tinseltown, Tarita was no wide-eyed babe in the woods, as the press made her out to be. She was smart and worldly enough to know what she wanted. Getting the part in *Mutiny on the Bounty* was a huge break for her and her family. Tarita may have been brought up on an island, but she'd worked in the tourist town of Papeete, where she'd danced in clubs and seen plenty of Americans, Europeans, and Australians throwing their money around. Marlon promised her more than money: he promised security. After experiencing all of this, Tarita was determined never to go back to washing dishes.

She appreciated how courtly Marlon was to her, how respectful, but she knew eventually he'd change his ways, as all men eventually did. "He attracted me and at the same time he scared me," she said. Eventually, she knew, he would want more from her.

She was prepared for that. Tarita had learned enough about Marlon from the *Mutiny* crew, and seen enough on this trip—such as the way Rita Moreno clung to his arm—to know that when that time came, when Marlon decided he wanted her, she'd have to handle it very carefully, or else her good luck might disappear very quickly. Tarita was sharper than anyone knew.

But a clever South Seas maiden was not what MGM wanted to promote. They'd just signed Tarita to "a longterm contract," and they wanted an innocent, nubile nymph in a sarong. Soon after her arrival in Los Angeles, she was turned over to the Hollywood press corps. "I've been very impressed by television, which I never saw before," she was quoted as saying. Drive-in restaurants amazed her, freeways frightened her. *Mutiny* cameraman Robert Surtees and his wife took her to a Polynesian restaurant in Pacific Palisades, a troop of reporters tagging along. Dutifully, Tarita put on a grass skirt and performed a native dance for the customers. A few weeks later, she made another appearance at a different Polynesian restaurant in Torrance.

Spies for Louella Parsons followed her into Ohrbach's department store and carefully observed her purchases. "Tahiti is going to see the latest thing in cotton prints," Parsons reported afterward. "Tarita practically bought out the store for a new wardrobe for her and her sister."

Some columnists, such as Leonard Lyons, saw through MGM's "exploitation purposes" in bringing Tarita to town, but went on to exploit her anyway. "She's never worn shoes," Lyons told the readers of his column, "and she arrived barefoot. Her first stop was MGM's wardrobe department. She was fitted for a gown and coat, but they had no shoes to fit her." Later, ensconced at the Beverly

Hills Hotel, Tarita was supposedly kicked out for using the pool. "There's nothing wrong with that," an MGM official reportedly insisted to the hotel. "But," the hotel manager reportedly countered, "she's got no suit on." Such were the Tales of Tarita.

Associated Press reporter Bob Thomas, a rare reporter whom Marlon actually liked, got to spend some face-to-face time with her. "An interview with Tarita does not produce a freshet of quotes," Thomas wrote. "Fact is, she doesn't know what an interview is. Nor does she know what Hollywood is all about." But she did know Marlon Brando, Thomas reported: "He is a very kind man," he quoted Tarita as saying, "and he is very helpful in teaching me how to act." She described going to dinner with him at the Hotel Tahiti before they'd left the South Seas. Thomas inquired whether she would go out with him again. "The answer required five minutes," he wrote, "during which she blushed, covered her mouth to hide her smiling, and finally came up with the diplomatic answer: 'If he asks me.'"

The little island girl knew exactly what she was doing. She wasn't about to be pushed aside after the movie was finished and Marlon started casting his eyes elsewhere. She knew what she was up against. Meanwhile, the woman on Marlon's other arm, Rita Moreno, also knew exactly what was going on, and she, too, was thinking about what came next. But for her, the choice was far more dire.

WHEN MARLON RETURNED from Tahiti and began showing Tarita around Los Angeles, Moreno had been deeply suspicious. Although he was always decorous around Tarita, Marlon was clearly "smitten" with the "exotically beautiful" young woman, Moreno observed. She'd been around long enough to predict what was coming: Tarita would be Marlon's next conquest. And unlike Tarita, Moreno had no game plan for survival. She was exhausted. Tarita's arrival was the last straw. "That," Moreno said, "along with the sheer number of his infidelities and the depth of his involvements, marriages, and babies, drove me to my limit."

During Marlon's sojourn in Tahiti, Moreno had sent him several letters. In one, she issued an ultimatum, one last chance for him to commit to her. No more affairs, Moreno demanded. She wanted something permanent. She wanted children. In his response, Marlon ignored her ultimatum and callously described his attempts to seduce a Tahitian woman. Moreno had found the letter so cold, she wrote back, that she could only take it as a total rejection of her.

Yet, there she was, on his arm just a few months later, at the *One-Eyed Jacks* screening. "He was my drug," Moreno said. "I was addicted to him." She was miserable when she should have been on top of the world. *West Side Story* had completed filming; everyone was predicting it would be a smash and that Moreno would be its breakout star. But all she could think about was Marlon. In the past, she'd been able to pretend everything was fine between them when they were together. That wasn't possible anymore with Tarita on his other arm.

The two women Marlon had brought with him to the screening of *One-Eyed Jacks* both had their secrets. Both had suspicions and grievances concerning him. Yet, caught up in his own problems, Marlon didn't give either of them, or their personal feelings, much thought. He had no idea that both were about to crack.

LEAVING THE SCREENING room, Marlon made little comment. But his face, Malden thought, betrayed his feelings. What he had seen on the screen did not match the film he carried in his mind. "He was deeply hurt," his costar and friend observed. He'd placed his trust in the studio editors. They had let him down.

The bowdlerization of his baby might have been expected to cause one of those "explosive" rages of which Alice Marchak was forever wary. But instead, from all accounts, Marlon reacted with sadness. He retreated. He said nothing.

The studio, however, seemed quite pleased with their cut. "Paramount is banking heavily on Marlon Brando's *One-Eyed Jacks* to bolster its profits during 1961," the exhibitor trade magazine *Film Bulletin* reported. A studio official predicted to the *Wall Street Journal* that the film could do as well as *Psycho*, then nearing a ten-million-dollar domestic gross. Marlon, meanwhile, kept out of the public eye.

The enterprise of *One-Eyed Jacks* had started out so promising. Back in 1958, Frank Rosenberg, a producer at Paramount, had sent Marlon the script, by Sam Peckinpah, then a young television writer of Westerns (*Gunsmoke, The Rifleman*). Peckinpah had based his script on Charles Neider's book, *The Authentic Death of Hendry Jones*, a fictionalized reimagining of Billy the Kid. Rosenberg thought the project might make an interesting coproduction for Paramount and Pennebaker. He didn't expect to hear back from Marlon right away. "Waiting for Brando to read a script and give you even a negative answer," Rosenberg said, "will age a man faster than trying to explain to Premier Khrushchev why he can't go to Disneyland." But within forty-eight hours, Marlon had responded. He loved it.

Marlon's interest in *One-Eyed Jacks* grew out of his earlier desire to film Louis L'Amour's *To Tame a Land*. "I want to make a frontal assault on the temple of clichés that have permeated the usual Hollywood Western," he'd told the press about *To Tame a Land*. One of his goals was to show that the white man was not "good or brave one hundred percent of the time."

Then began the long months of revision that everyone agreed the script needed. The whole point of the original novel was that Hendry, like Billy the Kid, gets killed. It opens with the line "Nowadays, I understand, the tourists come for miles to see Hendry Jones' grave out on the Punta del Diablo and to debate whether his bones are there or not." This was how Peckinpah had opened his screenplay, too. But at some point, Marlon decided to fictionalize the story even further. Not only did Hendry survive the experience, but his name was changed to Johnny Rio. His adversary, however, remained what Neider had called him: Dad Longworth. A villain named Dad seemed to appeal to Marlon.

Changing the basic storyline meant firing Peckinpah, which devastated the young writer. (He would bounce back just fine, of course, revitalizing the Western genre later with *The Wild Bunch*.) The new writer was Calder Willingham, who'd made a name for himself on Kirk Douglas's *Paths of Glory*; the director from that film, Stanley Kubrick, was also tapped to helm *One-Eyed Jacks*. Marlon now had his team. He kept his Pennebaker partners isolated from creative discussions. He was making it very clear that *One-Eyed Jacks* was his baby, nobody else's.

Although Willingham was the writer, Marlon's fingerprints were all over the script right from the start. Karl Malden later said there was only one writer on *One-Eyed Jacks*, and that was Marlon Brando. Several drafts were produced throughout 1958, but by the summer, they had finally arrived at one they liked, and they sent it off to Frank Rosenberg. "The new forty pages," Rosenberg wrote to Marlon, "are a vast improvement and begin to promise a picture of quality and excitement." But at more than a hundred fifty pages, the script was too long. Rosenberg had several cuts in mind, starting with the prologue before the main credits, which he feared might run a "full reel on the screen." Marlon and Willingham agreed to shorten it.

Of bigger concern to Rosenberg, however, were the liberties the script took with words and scenes that would put the Production Code Administration "on the defensive." No doubt Marlon recalled the hassles Kazan had faced with the censors during *Streetcar*. Still, he carried on without heed as he and Willingham wrote the script, almost as if he were jonesing for a fight with the PCA. After all, he'd gotten away with saying "go to hell" in *Waterfront*. But he'd never get away with explicit references to "whores" and "whorehouses," Rosenberg warned, and words like *greaserita*, used to describe Mexican women, would only "irritate" the censors and make them less likely to approve other things. Marlon countered that he wasn't using the word to be offensive; it was how the white cowboys would talk.

The one scene that really divided Marlon and Rosenberg was the conversation between the Mexican mother and daughter, which in the script was spoken in Spanish. Rosenberg called it "a little fancy." At the time, American producers were sensitive to the perceived "artiness" of European films, where English subtitles were the norm. Marlon wouldn't hear of changing it, however; this gave the picture a realism it needed. Eventually Rosenberg conceded that he was wrong, and the Spanish dialogue remained in the picture.

Since Marlon was, in essence, writing the script, it wasn't long before he was acting as director as well. He'd meet with Kubrick, Willingham, and Rosenberg at his home on Mulholland. "Everyone was calm and reasonable," Rosenberg recalled, "and in stocking feet—a requirement of the highly polished teakwood floors of Brando's oriental modern home." Marlon sat cross-legged on the floor with them, holding a Chinese gong that had come with the house. "When the discussions became too wildly emotional and nerves began to fray," Rosenberg said, "Marlon would hold up the gong and strike it twice." The reverberating sound filled the room, which was "a signal for everyone, including himself, to return to a neutral corner."

Kubrick remembered other sessions with Marlon holding a stopwatch. "We never got the story straight," he said, years later. "We never got anything straight." Finally, Kubrick said, "Marlon decided to get decisive . . . He got everybody in and we had to sit round the table. He put this stopwatch on the table." Everybody had three minutes to tell him what they thought the next steps on the film should be. Rosenberg spoke, Willingham spoke, and both were cut off by the stopwatch. When he got to Kubrick, Marlon said, "You've got three minutes." Kubrick wasn't having it. "Come on, Marlon," he said, "this is a stupid way to do things." Marlon eyed him icily: "Now you've got two minutes fifty." So, Kubrick started in; he got through a few pages of script when the stopwatch beeped. "That's it," Marlon said. "You've had your three minutes." To which Kubrick responded, "Marlon, why don't you go fuck yourself?"

Soon after that, Kubrick was fired. Marlon's behavior seemed despotic, but his eccentric style was actually his way of trying to make some progress on a project that had already been languishing for almost a year. The script was too long, there were too many unresolved story points, and Kubrick had never really presented a vision for the film that Marlon felt truly worthwhile. He wasn't interested in making a typical Western or thriller. The film needed to say something of importance.

For a moment, Marlon considered asking Kazan to take over. Then he decided to direct it himself. At first, those around him didn't think that was a very good idea. Rosenberg expressed reservations and remained nervous about it even after the decision was made public. A November 28, 1958, item announcing Marlon's debut as a film director was clipped out of a newspaper by the screenwriter Daniel Taradash, who was visiting New York, and sent to Rosenberg with an attached note of sympathy: "Omigod, what next? Home soon to hold hand."

Later, Marlon would try to downplay the huge challenge he faced as director. "You direct yourself in most films, anyway," he said—or at least, *he* did. But now his responsibilities had increased tenfold. "It was [an] ass-breaker," he said, looking back, remembering his experience as a director. "You work yourself to death. You're the first one up in the morning . . . I mean, we shot that thing on the run, you know. You make up the dialogue the scene before, improvising, and your brain is going crazy." So much for the myth that Marlon couldn't keep his interest in anything for very long. He didn't give up on *One-Eyed Jacks* for two years. For all his complaining, he loved the experience. He told a reporter from *Life* that directing gave him "deep personal satisfaction."

One of his first priorities was casting. He made some wise decisions, such as Katy Jurado to play Dad's strong, grounded wife, and some that were perhaps not so wise: Slim Pickens, as the sheriff's deputy, had never been known as an actor with much finesse, and this film wouldn't change that reputation. For Rio's young love interest, Louisa, a search was undertaken in Mexico to find the right unknown. *One-Eyed Jacks*, Marlon believed, could make the right girl a star.

His smartest move, however, was casting Karl Malden as Dad. Malden remembered Marlon calling him: "Karl, I've got a film I'm going to produce. I'm going to direct it, I'm going to act in it. I've got a part for you. Will you be in it?" Without a moment's hesitation, his longtime costar replied, "You got me."

Most urgently, they needed to get the script right. Guy Trosper, who'd written the screenplay for Elvis Presley's hit *Jailhouse Rock*, was brought in for rewrites. But yet again it was Marlon overseeing what words went down on paper. He needed to figure this story out for himself, much as Kazan would do. He photocopied forty-three pages from Neider's original novel, underlining the particularly vivid scenes. He was trying to prepare for the film the way Kazan prepared, by making copious notes. On yellow legal pads, Marlon broke down the action by beats, summarizing core ideas. Sometimes he did so by using snips of dialogue, employing his ubiquitous pound sign:

"# What do you do for fun in this town."

"# You're a funny kind of girl, like me—an outsider always looking in."

"# Let's see how strong you are."

It was as if he were inside the characters' heads—a contrast to the third-person omniscience Kazan employed in his notes. It was the way an actor might see his way into a story. Other times, Marlon would jot down quick notes to himself alongside a scene— "staring provocatively," he noted at one point, and "tells her what he sees," at another juncture—again, the way an actor might make notes in the margins of a script.

Marlon did attempt one notebook in a more typical Kazan style, though he never filled it. He didn't have Kazan's systematic methodology, being far too spontaneous and easily distracted. He got through only about a third of it. Nonetheless, in those pages he arrived at some important conclusions. Certain fundamentals needed to be established in the relationship between Johnny Rio and Dad. Marlon wrote, "When Johnny and Dad toss a coin for the only horse and for their lives, let Johnny win the toss. Dad cannot face death, heads or tails, win or lose, and seizes the opportunity to jump on the horse to leave Johnny to face the posse."

This little moment, right at the beginning of the film, sets the course for everything that is to come, and Marlon was astute enough to realize this. Two American bandits are on the run from the law in Mexico for robbing banks. They're finally cornered by a posse of lawmen on a mountaintop, with only one horse to use as a getaway. They flip a coin to see who takes the horse and the gold. Rio wins, but he hides that fact from Dad, allowing his friend to make the break. Dad promises he'll ride into town and return with another horse for Rio. Whether Rio believes him or not is immaterial. He assumes they're both dead men. But he has given Dad a slim chance for survival. This tells us, right away, that Rio possesses some core decency.

Later, when Rio is caught and sent to prison, he discovers that Dad made it through as well, but made no attempt to help him. From this point on, he burns with the desire for revenge. We meet up with him again a few years later, after he's escaped from prison and makes it back across the California border. He locates Dad, who's now the upstanding sheriff of a small coastal town, with a wife and a stepdaughter. Dad is terrified by Rio's arrival, fearing his revenge. But Rio seems to melt, even forgive, when he sees the happy family Dad has established, and the goodwill the townsfolk feel for him.

Or does he? This is the brilliant setup of *One-Eyed Jacks*. Who is the villain and who is the hero? Rio seems to be our hero when he secretly and unselfishly gives Dad the chance at life. But as we begin to see him brooding and seething with revenge, we find ourselves rooting for Dad, who's charming and fun, who dances merrily at the fiesta, and whose wife and daughter are endearing.

This fluctuating pull of loyalties drives the film. Who's bad? Who's good? It's what makes *Jacks* so compelling. Marlon realized this essential truth right at the very start, when they were still trying to figure out where to go with the story. Such a critical insight didn't come from the screenwriter. It came from Marlon. And without it, the entire story of *One-Eyed Jacks* would have crumbled.

Location shooting began on December 2, 1958, in Monterey. Much of the cast and crew stayed at the Tickle Pink Inn. After five days of shooting, Rosenberg arrived and informed Marlon that they were "two weeks behind schedule—a mathematical incredibility," he admitted, "that took its place among the legends but failed to impress Marlon." The director-star was, by now, "totally absorbed in getting the utmost quality on every inch of Technicolor film."

Sometimes the actor Brando did things the director Brando might have frowned on. He resisted using stunt doubles, preferring to do as much of the fights and the rolling down of mountains himself. Once Marlon's face got cut up so severely that he needed stitches. For several days they could shoot only one side of his face.

With all his actors, he worked very well; every one of them would speak highly of the experience. They also remained loyal as the two-month shooting schedule stretched into three and then into four. Pina Pellicer, the twenty-four-year-old actress chosen to play Louisa, Dad's stepdaughter, with whom Rio falls in love, had made only one movie before this, in her native Mexico. She'd been selected over dozens of candidates, including her sister Pilar, who had more experience. Pellicer felt guilty about that; she arrived on set anxious and very shy. She was also in the midst of a relationship crisis, Alice remembered, "fervently in love with a girl who constantly phoned." Eventually, Pellicer's girlfriend visited the set, but they quarreled; the girlfriend returned to Mexico, leaving Pellicer disconsolate. Marlon was very tender with her, lending "a broad shoulder," Alice said, and he urged the rest of the company "to try to cheer her up." Still, Pellicer's inherent sadness worked for her character, who seems somehow doomed right from the start.

The extras also enjoyed working with Marlon. At one point, he appeared to mock the idea of Method acting with his company. Ahead of the scene where Rio is flogged by Dad in the town square, Marlon told the day players who'd be posing as the townspeople, "Think of the horrible things in your own true lives and the camera will photograph the horror in your faces." He paused. "And besides, there is a $300 bonus for the man who manages to look most horrified."

The flogging scene had caused problems for the PCA when they read it in the script. "Too prolonged and too savage," the censors decreed. They wanted it shortened and shot more discreetly, insisting that the "shocking brutality of crushing Rio's hand with a shotgun" be removed. Marlon largely ignored their request. Both scenes remained in the picture; the flogging goes on for nearly a minute. And while he did not show the butt of the gun actually crushing the hand, the moment is still horrifying.

Four months lengthened into five. Shooting continued on location and on the Paramount backlot. The weather delayed them— but so did what some called Marlon's perfectionism. Rosenberg recalled a day when they needed an establishing shot of the Pacific

Ocean. Two hours later, the camera was still positioned in the same spot; Marlon said he was waiting for the perfect wave. What some called perfectionism others called madness, but still others called it simply the pursuit of excellence. *One-Eyed Jacks* was the last picture shot in VistaVision, Paramount's widescreen, higher-resolution format; Marlon knew the colors and depths of the film would be incredibly detailed and vivid. So, he was very aware of every shot of sky, mountain, desert, and sea, often peering through the camera of cinematographer Charles Lang. Such apparent indulgence would be defended decades later by Martin Scorsese. "That's what you do," Scorsese said. "You wait for the waves."

Marlon's vision for the film was constantly expanding. At one point he decided they needed a set for a Chinese fishing village. This meant scrapping the Mexican fishing village that art director J. McMillan Johnson had already built into a cove at Big Sur. McMillan had done "a magnificent job," Alice Marchak thought, "with all the adobe buildings, Mexican artifacts and jars, Mexican male extras with serapes and sombreros and Mexican women with bright colored skirts and shawls." But Marlon now wanted a Chinese village. McMillan didn't utter any protest. The next day, there was a Chinese encampment in place of the Mexican one, complete with wooden fish traps and extras in straw hats. Marlon was amazed.

The set was important because he'd added an encounter between Rio and a young Chinese woman, Mei-Mei, played by Lisa Lu. In a scene largely written by Marlon, Rio attempts to have sex with her; when she resists, he tries to rape her. Rio is acting out, angry at himself for having had sex with Louisa as a means of getting back at Dad, and breaking her heart in the process. He loathes himself so he decides to act loathsome. "You been wantin' me for a long time and you know it," he says, to which Mei-Mei responds, "You really want this way? Why you act like animal?" The PCA had strenuously objected to this scene and wanted it cut, but

Marlon held firm: it was an important insight into Rio's conscience and his conflict over right and wrong. Once again, Marlon defied the censor's wishes and filmed the scene.

Summer approached, and still they weren't finished shooting. Rosenberg took to standing behind Charles Lang and watching the film feed steadily into his camera, foot by foot. He'd mutter, "Half a buck, half a buck, half a buck," as each foot of film cost fifty cents to print.

The film ended with Louisa being killed by stray gunfire during the climactic shootout between Rio and Dad. Her death is bleak; she and her mother are the only two characters in the film who are unreservedly good. Both Rio and Dad have been turned into monsters by their own compulsions; both lose the little bit of love and happiness they have found, and both are punished for their sins. Louisa dies in Rio's arms, in a shot Marlon instructed Lang to hold for an unusually long time before "The End" appeared on the screen.

On June 2, 1959, Marlon called what he believed was his final "Cut."

It had taken six months to film the picture. By all accounts, Marlon had enjoyed the process thoroughly, and was very pleased with what they'd accomplished. "Wildly enthusiastic," he would call himself during the shooting, looking back on the film five years later. Yet, even as he said it, he laughed, as if he were mocking his own naïveté. He had no idea, that warm June day when cast and crew celebrated with champagne and cake, what lay ahead.

MANY MYTHS WOULD emerge about *One-Eyed Jacks*. One of them was that Paramount never saw any footage from the film until, many months later, the studio had to physically take the four-hour film away from Marlon. That's not true. Marlon and film editor Archie Marshek had a rough cut ready by the fall, and Paramount screened it in early November. While the studio felt it was "over length," there was no mention of four hours; if the film had really been that long at that point, there would undoubtedly have been more comment from the studio about its length.

The version Marlon showed Karl Malden, therefore, with the break for dinner at the two-hour mark, must have come sometime between June and November. This was the period during which Marlon cut the film nearly in half. It was an agonizing process. "He shot so many takes that choosing one was getting to him," said Alice Marchak. Never a man who made decisions easily, now he had to make dozens of important decisions every night while he was editing. Looking at images for hours on a Moviola left him rattled. "One of the most awful places in the world is the cutting room," he said. "You sit all day long in a dark place filled with cigarette smoke." At one point, Alice asked if he was afraid of making a mistake. Marlon glared at her. She'd touched a sore spot. "No, but you just did," he answered and stormed out of the room.

More than 1 million feet of film had been exposed. Of that, 250,000 feet were printed. Most films at the time exposed about 150,000 feet of film and printed about 40,000. If 250,000 feet of film were viewed continuously, it would run for *two days*. So, even assembling a four-hour, forty-minute picture, as Rosenberg recalled the film's original length, was a considerable achievement. It was actually thrifty, Rosenberg joked, when one remembered that the silent film classic *Greed* was eight hours long when director Erich von Stroheim thought "he had cut it to the bone."

Further cutting with Archie Marshek shortened the film still more; by how much is not known, but this was the version that was turned in to Paramount in November. The studio felt it was still too long. Jacob Karp, a Paramount vice president, offered thirty-four suggestions for cuts. Most of Karp's suggestions were about trimming existing scenes: "While the scene of the drunk and the girl at the bar must be sufficiently long to irritate Rio (and the audience), it might achieve its purpose in less footage." Asking a first-time director to pick up the tempo wasn't unusual, but the studio also wanted almost all the Chinese village scenes removed, especially Rio's attempted rape of Mei-Mei, because of the "serious censorship trouble" it would undoubtedly face. The request infuriated Marlon. He railed over Paramount's timidity; after all, more and more films were defying the PCA by 1960 and were still receiving seals of approval. Yet what Marlon most objected to was the call for a different ending. First, Karp thought he'd held the shot for too long: "You, of course, do not plan to retain the shot of Rio with the dying Louisa in its present length." In fact, Marlon did. But the studio also wanted a more "classic" ending: Rio should die, not Louisa, "with the implication that his child, product of his tempestuous life, will live in his place."

On both counts, Marlon held firm. In fact, he was less interested in cutting material out of the film than in adding more. On January 27, 1960, he shot additional scenes at the Warner Bros. ranch featuring himself, Malden, and Hank Worden (Doc), on both the cantina set and the porch of Dad's house. On February 12, additional shots were taken of Malden on Paramount's Stage 1. Not long after this, Paramount called the film in; fifteen months had now elapsed since Marlon started production, and it was time at last to get the film into release. Yet the stories that would arise of the studio moving in, snatching the picture away against Marlon's will, are untrue. Marlon himself perpetuated the myth: "I kept fiddling round and fiddling round with it, stalling," he said, "so they went and cut the film." In fact, when the studio demanded it, he and Archie Marshek cut a final version of the picture they were satisfied with and turned it in.

Even at this point, Marlon insisted on working with the new assigned studio editor, D. A. Doran, on any further cuts. Paramount agreed, and the two men headed to the cutting room together. To everyone's surprise, they got along well. Doran seemed to share the director's view of the picture.

But then, suddenly, Marlon couldn't bear it anymore. He just couldn't sit in the dark again, with all that cigarette smoke, tediously looking, frame by frame, for a second or two to cut. A more committed artist, who'd made film directing his life's work, would have stayed in place, reviewing every frame. But this was also, significantly, the moment when the campaign to save Caryl Chessman had intensified. Marlon's epiphany was at hand. Sitting in a dark room hunched over celluloid suddenly seemed "silly and irrelevant." He wrote to Karp, "You must understand that *One-Eyed Jacks* . . . isn't going to change the face or circumstance for anybody in this world." He decided to leave the final cut to Doran.

It wasn't an easy decision, and it left him downhearted. "I sat in the projection room that day for the first half," Marlon wrote to Karp, "and then realized the fact probably two and a half years of my life were dedicated to that project—two and a half years of worry, anxiety, striving, discouragement, hopes, and work, work, work. One of the sizable efforts of my life was in front of me and near the moment of fruition." Given the studio's constant demands for changes, Marlon had concluded that the film was a failure—"an agonizing failure," he wrote, and he had to "find a way to forget it." That old self-doubt was never all that far from the surface. As much as Doran wanted his involvement, Marlon couldn't give it. "It would just kill me to have to see it," he said. "I'll see it one day when my fires are banked and youthful fervor slightly bent."

If there was any moment when Marlon "walked away from" *Jacks*, this was it—yet even here, he left trusting that Doran shared his vision and could make it right. To Doran, Marlon wrote, "I have every reason to believe that any decision you might make will be intelligent, sensible and artistically valid." It's really not all that unusual for a director to place a picture in an editor's hands, especially if they share an overall artistic vision. Marlon felt he'd done as much on the film as he could, and had apparently bought (at least for the moment) the studio line that his best hadn't been good enough. As he took his leave of the project, his head hung uncharacteristically low: "I wish in the face of your good faith," he told Karp, "I had perhaps done a little better."

It was in this frame of mind that he'd agreed to shoot a new ending. Pina Pellicer was brought up from Mexico, nearly two years older now than at the start of the film. On October 14, 1960, she, Marlon, and a crew trekked back up to the Monterey sand dunes. Marlon had compromised with the studio: Louisa would live, but so would Rio, although he would need to flee for killing Dad. "The original ending had Marlon weeping for the first time, I believe, on the screen," Sheilah Graham wrote in her column. "With the new version, the tears are gone." *One-Eyed Jacks* was finally scheduled to be released in the spring.

"I think it might be okay," Marlon said, his only comment on the picture before heading back to Tahiti. Yet, while his hopes for his baby might have improved, he still had major reservations about the new ending. In the revised pages he used for the final retake in Monterey, he humorously included an epilogue after Rio rides off on his horse. "The audience storms the box office and, in a screaming rage, to a man demands their money back at the pain of death. The manager refuses and the theatre is razed to the ground. The End."

THE VERSION OF *One-Eyed Jacks* that Marlon saw that day at the MCA Building in February 1961 might have seemed, to the casual eye, not all that different from the print left with D. A. Doran in the early spring of 1960. Yet, to its creator, it was a different film entirely. The version Marlon had turned in, with the new, happy ending, ran two hours and forty minutes. The print that Paramount was preparing to release was two hours and twenty-one minutes. The loss of those nineteen minutes made all the difference.

Just as the studio had demanded, most of the Chinese fishing village scene had been removed. The near-rape of Mei-Mei was entirely gone. "In slimming the picture down to its present shape," Rosenberg assured the readers of the New York Times, "we lost none of its main storyline or sacrificed any scene that might have contributed to the delineation of character." He called the scene between Marlon and the Chinese woman "an ancillary and transient love story." Marlon, of course, thought differently. He'd been prepared to swallow the new ending, but he had not expected this. Just enough had been chiseled away from several scenes to strip the nuance from the characters, he believed. "In my film, everybody lied, even the girl," Marlon told Bob Thomas. He believed the character of Dad, especially, had been coarsened. "The only one who told the truth was the Karl Malden character. Paramount made him out to be a heavy, a liar." Dad might have been a hypocrite, Marlon conceded, but "hypocrisy is not necessarily evil." As the story progressed, Dad became more and more villainous. "Now the characters in the film are black and white," Marlon lamented, "not gray and human as I planned them."

Even before Marlon made his opinion known, rumors in the industry were blaming the studio's cuts for blunting the film's power. "The scissoring reportedly left some wide gaps in the continuity of the western plot," Film Bulletin, the trade paper for the nation's exhibitors, revealed. Marlon told columnist Erskine Johnson, "It's a potboiler now, but most movies are potboilers, aren't they? The movie business is just a business—a good picture is just one that makes money." One-Eyed Jacks might in fact make money for Paramount, Marlon conceded to Bob Thomas: "It's a good picture for them, but it's not the picture I made." To Newsweek, he called Jacks "quite conventional," which was about the worst thing Marlon Brando could say about a film, especially one he himself had made.

His sadness went very deep. This was one of the "sizable efforts" of his life, as he called it. "I took a long time on [One-Eyed Jacks]," he remembered. "After a while, I got an attachment to it." The abduction of his baby was significant. "Marlon had so much energy on the film," Phil Rhodes reflected. "He was into everything—the cameras, the lighting, the wardrobe, the makeup. He was working on the script. He was even going to rushes, which he had never done before." So, when Paramount cut the film against the vision he had for it, "Marlon was hurt." His interest in moviemaking, Rhodes said, "never appeared again in that force."

IT'S TEMPTING TO speculate how things might have been different if *One-Eyed Jacks* had been released as Marlon intended. His hope had been to direct more films. If *Jacks* had gone out as he'd planned, and been a hit, or at least a critical success, he might have spent the next decade as a director, transitioning to a new career the way such other actors as Clint Eastwood and Robert Redford managed to do. What sorts of films might Marlon have made— about capital punishment, or civil rights, or social injustice, or the myriad personal journeys humans take? Would his opinion of the movie business have improved? Might he, even grudgingly, have come to consider filmmaking an art?

Despite his disappointment in it, *One-Eyed Jacks* remains a remarkable film. Marlon was right that the Malden character becomes almost stereotypically evil in the second half of the film, which was clearly not the director's intent. The happy ending is trite and unbelievable; the death of either Louisa or Rio would have made more thematic sense. But those are not Marlon's mistakes. What the studio couldn't take away from him was the majestic sweep of the film and the sense that every detail is precisely in place: he really did get exactly the right waves. He also elicited pitch-perfect performances from Malden, Pellicer, Jurado, and, significantly, himself. Most important, for a man so guarded about his own emotions, Marlon was able to craft a compelling parable of human nature that holds the viewer spellbound, at least until the end, when the studio's tinkering becomes clear. Up until that point, one is never quite sure which way to look or whom to believe. *One-Eyed Jacks* is a film about the very thin line between right and wrong, good and evil.

Marlon tuned out the reviews, he said, which was unfortunate, because most were good. The trades loved the picture. "Marlon Brando's first try at film directing emerges as a first-rate film that should do very well at the box office," opined *The Hollywood Reporter*, "and might even take off to do better than just very well." *Variety* liked it, too: "There's a lot of jack (reportedly five to six million) at stake in the pot, but thanks to the one-eyed jacks that Brando has dealt into Paramount's hand, the studio has itself a happy full-house prospect for its gamble."

Once the film was officially released on March 30, 1961, the raves kept coming. Bosley Crowther compared Marlon to Alexander the Great, seeking "more worlds to conquer in the universe of films." He praised the film's dichotomy between realism and romance. Even some reviewers who were predisposed against Marlon ended up praising the film. Jim Henaghan of *The Hollywood Reporter* went in expecting to watch the star fail in his attempt to direct. He didn't like Marlon, Henaghan admitted, thinking him "a self-centered, willful hedonist." But he was blown away by *Jacks*. "I think it might be the best western ever made," he wrote. "It has taken the bones of clichéd drama and superbly enhanced them with daring innovation. Brando must indeed be honored as the father of this achievement."

The accolades were not unanimous. *Film Bulletin* called it a "two-hour-and-twenty-minute ode to an actor's ego," and claimed that, at the end, when Marlon rides off on his horse promising to return, "many moviegoers may end up hoping that if he does, he will stay on his proper side of the camera." *Film Bulletin*'s real beef with the picture, however, was that it had "cost a fortune." Many in the industry were biased against the film simply because of how much money had been spent. Budgeted at $2.3 million, *One-Eyed Jacks* had ended up costing $5,657,069.11, with $46,500 of that spent in the final few weeks for the revised ending.

Box office was quite good for *Jacks* in the beginning. Then, the sorts of films that Marlon Senior had said Pennebaker needed to make began to overtake it: *The Absent-Minded Professor, The Parent Trap, Swiss Family Robinson, Exodus*. In the end, *One-Eyed Jacks* pulled in $4.5 million, making it the fourteenth most successful film of the year. But $4.5 million meant a $1.1 million deficit, and both Paramount and Pennebaker (in the short run) lost money on it.

Marlon didn't tune everything out: he was aware of the way executives at both companies, including his father, were watching the film's box-office performance. What had once been his baby, his dream of becoming Kazan, was now just a line in a budget underscored in red. By making the film, Marlon realized, he'd played into the hands of the Hollywood moneymaking machine. "I'm a captain of industry," he said sarcastically during an interview with *Newsweek*. "Any pretension I've sometimes had of being artistic is now just a long, chilly hope. *One-Eyed Jacks* is a product, just like a news item." If he had needed any further convincing that the film business was not for him and that he should get out, he had it now. "Movies," he said bitterly, "are not art."

Utterly depressed and disillusioned that spring of 1961, Marlon figured his life in Hollywood couldn't get any worse. He was wrong.

ON THE MORNING of April 19, Marlon awoke early, got dressed, and headed over to the MGM studios. *Mutiny on the Bounty* had resumed shooting after its break. In the interim, Carol Reed had been fired. Marlon hadn't been all that sorry to see him go, but he remained unsure if his replacement, Lewis Milestone, would be any better. He'd find out soon enough: in a month or so, it would be time to return to Tahiti.

All smiles here between Junior and Senior after their appearance on Edward R. Murrow's *Person to Person* (1955), but earlier Marlon had seemed ready to slug his father. *Author's collection*

*Some of Marlon's women*

Briefly playing by Hollywood's rules, Marlon promised to marry Josanne Mariani, but didn't. *Author's collection*

Rita Moreno loved him far too much. *Author's collection*

He married Movita in 1960 when she showed up at his door with his son. *Reproduced by permission of Brando Enterprises, LP*

The wedding of Marlon and his first wife, Anna Kashfi, took place on October 11, 1957, with only a handful of guests, including Mrs. Louis L'Amour and Mrs. Peter Berneis, pictured here. Behind them is the portrait of Marlon's mother that he always hung prominently wherever he lived. *Reproduced by permission of Brando Enterprises, LP*

Marlon adored his son Christian, but the boy's laughter, like his own, faded as he got older and his parents' troubles overcame him. *Reproduced by permission of Brando Enterprises, LP*

Had Marlon not watched in despair as Paramount chopped up his one directorial effort, *One-Eyed Jacks* (1961), might he have made more films, respected his profession more, maybe even seen what he did as art? *Jacks* is still a very good picture, with both Marlon and Karl Malden turning in first-rate performances. *Author's collection*

A rare glimpse of the Chinese village scene that was cut from the film, which Marlon thought was essential. Lisa Lu's entire part was left on the editor's floor. *Margaret Herrick Library, Academy of Motion Picture Arts and Sciences*

Marlon's epiphany: protesting outside San Quentin Prison against capital punishment on May 2, 1960, in the days leading up to Caryl Chessman's execution. His friend Eugene Burdick wears the hat at right. *Fang Family San Francisco Examiner Photograph Archive, BANC PIC 2006.029:133284D-05-03-NEG.* © *The Regents of the University of California, The Bancroft Library, University of California, Berkeley*

In social and political activism, Marlon found his true passion. He was filled with hope for the world at the 1963 March on Washington, here with Charlton Heston, Harry Belafonte, his old pal James Baldwin, and a few hundred thousand others.
*Reproduced by permission of Brando Enterprises, LP*

The long ordeal of *Mutiny on the Bounty* (1962) ended any hope that Marlon could work within the Hollywood studio system. It did, however, introduce him to Tarita Teriipaia, who became the mother of two of his children.
*Author's collection*

Marlon's star was reborn with *The Godfather* (1972), and for the first time in nearly twenty years, he was enlivened by the creative challenge of a role. His powerful death scene was the first time he ever acted opposite a child. *Author's collection*

The emotionally draining *Last Tango in Paris* (1972), with Maria Schneider, led Marlon to declare that henceforth all he'd give on film were demonstrations of technique. *Tango* was the final showcase for the full power of Marlon Brando. *Author's collection*

By the 1970s, Marlon was in love with Jill Banner, and thought he was finally ready for a full, equal, mature relationship with a woman. But it wasn't to be. *Reproduced by permission of Brando Enterprises, LP*

"For my money," said Jack Nicholson, "nothing has ever gotten near him."
*Author's collection*

Marlon was glad about that. Nothing seemed to go right when he stayed too long in Los Angeles. Tarita was becoming cold and distant to him, resisting even his friendly gestures. What had happened? Dorothy Kilgallen reported in her column that Tarita was "terribly unhappy" in California and wanted to go back to the South Seas as soon as possible. Marlon was puzzled. It was as if Tarita had seen something about him, and his life here, that had turned her off. What that could be, Marlon had no idea.

Behind him, Rita Moreno lay sleeping in his bed.

After he was gone, Moreno stood and, without appearing to give it much thought, walked directly to the medicine cabinet in the bathroom. Withdrawing the bottle of Marlon's sleeping pills, she shook a handful into her left hand. Staring down at the pills, Moreno knew if she took them, she would surely die.

After a final moment of hesitation, she swallowed the pills with water. It was her way, she said, "to end the humiliation and pain."

**DECEMBER 28, 1961** / Stinging mad, in full public view, Anna Kashfi ambushed her ex-husband in the hallway of the courthouse and slapped him across the face.

"The sound of the blow was like a pistol shot in the corridor," a witness reported, and a photographer sprinted to catch Marlon ducking to protect himself. Anna kept coming at him; she had to be pulled away by her attorney. Turning to the photographer, she bellowed, "Don't ever say I didn't give you a good picture!"

Marlon hurried out of the courthouse without saying a word.

What had gotten Anna into such a fury was the ruling, moments earlier, that Marlon could spend more time with Christian. Anna had bitterly opposed the idea, once again calling Marlon immoral and charging that he lived "contrary to present established society." She offered to provide details "in the privacy of the court chambers"; when Judge Benjamin Landis declined her offer, Anna started reciting a litany of Marlon's sins, evidently describing his girlfriends and possibly even alluding to Christian Marquand. Her descriptions of Marlon's lifestyle became so obscene that the judge finally ordered them stricken from the court record.

Marlon had taken the stand in his own defense. He'd pressed for this hearing, he said, because he was "tired of always playing the heavy." The "nurses" that Anna sent with Christian on visits to his father were acting as spies, Marlon said. "The newest nurse brought her teenage sister along," he testified, "and the sister told me it was her obligation to repeat every conversation she overheard to Miss Kashfi." He made a direct appeal to the court: "Christian Devi senses the feeling of tension between myself and Miss Kashfi and blames himself for it."

Judge Landis granted Marlon's request that he could have his son at his home every third weekend in addition to the twice-weekly visits currently permitted. He also added summer visiting rights, during which Marlon could have Christian for up to two weeks. When he began to detail Marlon's rights to Thanksgiving and Christmas visits, Anna could take it no more and leaped from her seat, shouting at the judge, "What do you want to do, eliminate motherhood from America?"

"Five hundred dollars for contempt of court!" Judge Landis thundered at her.

He then went on to remove the requirement that a nurse supplied by Anna must accompany the boy to his father's home on each visit. Anna had argued that this was necessary because of "numerous other people" being present in Marlon's house. She was trying to imply that undesirable women, with whom Marlon was carrying on affairs, might damage the boy's morals by their sheer proximity.

Yet Marlon had craftily defused that charge. With him in court that day was Movita. Anna herself had exposed Marlon's secret marriage to the court. Now he used it to his advantage, presenting himself to the judge as a happily married man, reformed of his carousing ways. Movita had accompanied him to his last custody hearing as well, during which she and Anna had made faces at each other.

Judge Landis didn't know, of course, that Marlon's declaration of a joint household with Movita was untrue. Nor was he aware that Marlon was dating Marie Cui, a Filipino ballet dancer. Still, Marlon wasn't completely snookering the court. There *had* been a change in him, friends thought. "That was a period when he seemed to get more serious about home and family," said Jack Larson. Even if Marlon had no plans to live with Movita, he'd brought her and their son into public view, embracing them and establishing a family for himself.

"I think Marlon got more serious about relationships," said another friend, who'd known him since the early days in New York. "He didn't stop juggling girlfriends, but he did try to settle down with his children." And the reason for that, his New York friend said, was "what happened with Rita Moreno." That incident had shaken him to his core, Jack Larson said: "How could it not have?"

Anna had considered using Moreno's tragedy in her affidavit against Marlon as the perfect illustration of his immorality. But then she'd decided against it. Mentioning Moreno, she said, would have been "gratuitously cruel."

Eight months earlier, the sirens and flashing lights of an ambulance and several police cars had cut through the cool morning air outside Marlon's house on Mulholland Drive. Inside, Moreno lay unresponsive on the floor. Discovering her, Alice Marchak had called a doctor and then Marlon at the studio. He'd rushed home to stand helplessly by as the doctor tried to find a reflex on the comatose woman. Eventually Moreno began to respond with great bursts of sobbing. "Keening," she'd call it later.

There was no way to keep the story from the press. Alice contained it as best she could, lying to a reporter that she'd found Moreno at her own home and then brought her over to Marlon's, where she'd collapsed. The press was already gathering as Moreno was wheeled out of Marlon's house on a stretcher. Watching the ambulance drive off, Marlon was devastated.

On some deep level, he understood how damaging he was to the women in his life. In *One-Eyed Jacks*, he created Rio very much like himself. Rio gives Louisa what he claims to be his mother's necklace, when in fact he's just bought it at the fiesta. Many of Marlon's girlfriends received similar pieces of Dodie's jewelry. Were they authentic, or was Marlon revealing his modus operandi on the screen? Throughout the film, we see Rio acting duplicitously with women, the disregard he has for their feelings. We also see his chivalrous side, which Marlon had, too, defending a woman against physical violence. But in his cruel seduction of Louisa, Rio is loathsome, using her as revenge against Dad. As director, Marlon wanted his audience to identify with Louisa, and to condemn Rio for his deplorable actions. On some level, Marlon was also condemning himself. By his own account, he'd acted similarly in real life, sleeping with women to take revenge on their husbands. He clearly knew that what he was doing was wrong. With Moreno's suicide attempt, he finally had direct evidence of the devastating impact of his behavior.

In the early 1960s, Marlon experienced a political awakening that reset his personal and professional priorities. Yet, for all his desire to work toward justice in the world, it took a while longer for him to translate that commitment to the women in his life. Moreno's suicide attempt got him to look at what he was doing, friends believed. He made an attempt to understand his pattern in relationships, a process that would not be completed in any short order. One girlfriend recorded in her diary around this time the difficulties Marlon was enduring in his therapy, expressing his anger against his father and his guilt over his mother, and how he was becoming aware of how this played out in his own relationships.

He didn't reform overnight; trauma takes a very long time to heal, if ever. Still, Marlon did what he could. He established a routine with Movita and allowed her to visit with their son, who was now called Miko. At one point, he brought both mothers and sons together. Anna became furious when Marlon, attempting some family unity, asked his five-year-old son to give his two-year-old son a kiss. Movita demanded that Anna be thrown out of the house, and Anna fired back "a few choice epithets" at Movita. That was the last time Marlon tried that.

His main concern was what the custody wars were doing to Christian. He often used the phrase "Give me a child until he is seven and I will show you the man." He had just two years left, Marlon believed, to settle the turmoil that defined his son's life, or he'd grow up needing a therapist to resolve his trauma, too.

What Marlon himself needed, he remained convinced, was to get out of the movie business. But until he had enough money saved and invested, that couldn't happen. So, it was back to *Mutiny on the Bounty*, yet again. It was the film that would not end. But it was also the film, Marlon believed, with all the money it promised, that would give him his freedom.

ON ONE OF the last days of shooting, Marlon was feeling pretty cross when Bob Thomas of the Associated Press entered his dressing room. "I was here at nine and we got the first shot at three," he griped. But wasn't that the way this picture had gone since it began almost exactly one year earlier? "I know some people will crab," Marlon went on, anticipating Thomas's next question, "'What's he got to bleed about? He's getting well paid.'" Ever since the film went over schedule some months earlier, Marlon, as per his contract, had been making $5,000 a day. "But after you've got enough," he insisted, "money doesn't matter."

Finally, at least for the moment, Marlon had enough money. *Mutiny* had seen to that. His contract gave him half a million dollars up front as an advance against 10 percent of the picture's gross. But it was the guaranteed overtime pay that really filled his coffers: by early 1962, he would accumulate $1.2 million from that alone. Still, *Mutiny* had also been the most difficult movie-making experience he'd ever endured, and he vowed he'd never put himself through anything like it again, no matter how much money he was paid. Adding insult to injury, from his point of view, was that the press was making him out to be the cause of the film's long delays. But he'd come to expect as much.

*Mutiny* had, however, given him Tahiti. For that much at least, Marlon would always be grateful. He told reporters that as soon as he could, he would be moving to the islands. To hell with Hollywood, with America, with everybody. He would take his children there if their mothers let him.

Marlon had returned to the South Pacific the previous spring to finish the picture. As director, Lewis Milestone had turned out to be far worse than Carol Reed, in Marlon's opinion. Milestone personified the weak, indecisive director Marlon had been carping about for years. A studio-trained veteran, Milestone, called "Milly" by his friends, had some long-ingrained habits. His usual practice was to set up the camera, give the actors some instruction, and then simply call, "Action!" But Marlon was not an actor who could just be told what to do; Milestone should have known and pre-pared for that. When Marlon asked why Milestone wanted him to do a certain bit of business, the director would decline to answer, feeling that his authority was being questioned. So, Marlon would refuse to perform.

Screenwriter Lederer saw the problem and took Milestone aside. He was working too fast, Lederer said. "Of course, I'm working fast," the efficient Milestone replied. "Don't you think enough time has already been wasted on this picture?"

From Marlon's point of view, *Mutiny*'s new director didn't care about the picture and was speeding things up because he wanted "to get it over with as soon as possible." He was wrong about the first point but right about the second. Both men, in their own ways, thought they had the best interests of the picture in mind. Yet, because of the stubbornness of both, they could never come to terms.

"Milly is so exhausted at night he can hardly keep his eyes open," his wife wrote to a friend. "They are out on the boat from seven in the morning until sundown. It's terribly hot and the work is discouragingly slow. With Brando you are lucky to get two scenes a day. It's demoralizing to the whole troupe. When he finishes this one, I guess [Milly] can cope with anything!"

Eventually, Marlon maneuvered Milestone out of much of the decision making, bringing in producer Aaron Rosenberg to overrule him. Milestone continued to direct other members of the cast, but Marlon was left on his own. "He was directing himself," Milestone said. Which he knew, quite well, how to do.

Marlon had convinced MGM that the film should conclude on Pitcairn Island, where the mutineers set up a colony. When it came time to shoot those scenes, however, no one was satisfied with what Lederer had written. Marlon, always looking to make a relevant social comment, suggested they compare the starvation and tribal warfare the mutineers faced on Pitcairn to "what is going on in Africa today." Producer Rosenberg agreed to let Marlon take a shot at rewriting those pages. Ultimately, they scrapped Marlon's rewrite and stuck with the original ending. Marlon wasn't happy and showed it in his less-than-inspired acting. "This is what you want," he told Rosenberg. "This is what you'll get."

Milestone had directed some excellent films in his day: *All Quiet on the Western Front, The Front Page, Of Mice and Men*. But on *Bounty*, he failed in the director's first job, which is to build trust in his company. Marlon behaved poorly as well. Instead of boarding the *Bounty* on the dock with everyone else, he insisted that a private speedboat take him out to the ship. Wanting to experience what it felt like to really live on Tahiti, he took over an old villa about fifty kilometers away from the set and charged $6,000 to the studio to fix it up. Waiting for the waves and adding to the expense of an already overbudget film when you're the director is one thing. When you're an actor, it's quite another. Marlon, apparently, didn't see any difference.

What Marlon was doing, once again, was lashing out at male authority figures who were trying to manage him. The reason he "was really out of control" during the last weeks of *Mutiny*, his later director, Arthur Penn, speculated, was that "the studio had the father image for him at that point." He resented "the whole pressure—MGM and the money and [the fact that] he was taking the rap for the schedule." That pressure turned him, Penn believed, "wild and retaliatory."

By the time they returned to Los Angeles, however, Marlon had calmed down and, to his credit, did his best to make amends. Knowing they could never go out with the ending he had shot so halfheartedly, he agreed to redo his scenes on the MGM backlot for no further pay. Rosenberg was grateful, but Milestone petulantly refused to go anywhere near the camera while Brando was in front of it. So, as the last shots were filmed on a picture that had once seemed never to end, the director remained in his dressing room, reading a magazine. Watching the actors go through the motions without anyone to guide them was "eerie," Rosenberg said, "like seeing a ghost ship with no one at the helm."

By early 1962, *Mutiny on the Bounty* had cost MGM about $20 million. Estimates were that the studio would spend another $7 million before it was done. Only *Cleopatra*, the scandal-plagued Fox extravaganza starring Elizabeth Taylor in near-concurrent production, had cost more. By the final week of shooting, Marlon had constant indigestion. "I was snapping at aspirin like a Christmas goose pecking corn," he told Bob Thomas. Then, finally, it was all over. Marlon put away his tricorn hats for the last time and waited to see what the reviewers would have to say.

But if he thought he was through with *Mutiny on the Bounty*, he was wrong.

IN MANY WAYS, the conclusion of the *Bounty* shoot marked the end of Marlon's Hollywood bondage. The yoke he'd willingly slipped around his neck after his mother died, and from which he'd been struggling to free himself ever since, had finally been lifted. His next film was *The Ugly American*, a project he'd found and to which he owned the rights, and which would allow him at last to make some commentary on the problems of the world. This time, he wouldn't be thwarted by higher-ups as he had been with *One-Eyed Jacks*. This time, Marlon was working with friends: George Englund was directing from Bud Burdick's novel, and Pennebaker was the main production company. Universal would coproduce and distribute.

Marlon liked the fact that *The Ugly American* unnerved some people in Washington. Sen. William Fulbright of Arkansas had asked the State Department not to cooperate with the filmmakers, whose intention, in his opinion, was to make U.S. diplomats look bad with their "rotten film." One of the few voices of support came from Sen. Hubert Humphrey of Minnesota, who believed Marlon and his associates were "attempting to do an honest and responsible job" of outlining the challenges faced by the State Department in Southeast Asia. To Marlon, that meant looking at the institutionalized racism of American foreign policy.

He remained concerned with racism closer to home as well. Soon after *Mutiny* wrapped, at a gathering of the National Association for the Advancement of Colored People at its regional office in downtown Los Angeles, a man arrived late and took a seat in back.

He was noticed by C. A. Carter, a young volunteer for the organization. Carter had helped organize this discussion about police brutality and the random targeting of young black men by Los Angeles police officers. Many activists and businesspeople had shown up; several youths spoke about being stopped and frisked without cause. Some even revealed they'd been beaten.

While NAACP chapter president Edward Warren listened to all this testimony, C.A. Carter made a count of those in the room. Most of those in attendance were black, Carter remembered. But the man at the back of the room, who'd arrived late, was white. He wore a hat and heavy glasses. Carter also thought he might have had a mustache. "He never said a word," Carter said. "But he struck me as someone who believed strongly in what we were talking about, racial justice and equality, because he was always nodding his head and clapping his hands."

Once the meeting was over and everyone had dispersed, an excited young woman rushed up to Carter and asked him if he'd recognized the man in the back row. He had not. She claimed he was Marlon Brando.

In the days that followed, the more Carter thought about it, the more he believed his friend was right. He must have been wrong about the mustache. But when he learned, fifty-six years later, that Marlon's friend, makeup man Phil Rhodes, sometimes made him a disguise of a mustache and glasses, he was more certain than ever that the man he'd seen in the conference room was the famous movie star.

Whether chapter president Warren knew he was there, Carter had no idea. But Marlon's name had already been associated with the chapter. In November 1961, Warren had obtained Marlon's support for a declaration calling on the film and television industries to show more racial balance and equality on the screen. "Anytime they have a crap game, they show plenty of Negroes," Warren's report read. "But when do you see a Negro doctor or lawyer?" He also called on the craft unions to hire more Negro electricians, carpenters, designers, and other workers. Marlon's name was on the report when it was sent out to the press.

A year before, Marlon had also been one of the few white celebrities to sign a demand calling for police protection of Dr. Martin Luther King Jr. and the student protest movement when they went into Alabama. The demand led to the Alabama secretary of state calling for Marlon and the other cosigners to be arrested for libel.

"Racism is as much a part of American culture as Wonder Bread," Marlon believed. So, no one would have been surprised if he really was the man C. A. Carter saw at that discussion group, passionately listening to and learning from the speakers. Even if not, it's fairly certain he was following the story. When the Los Angeles chapter of the NAACP published its twelve-page report on police brutality in February 1962, there were no movie star names attached to this effort. Just the troubling facts: "Negroes in Los Angeles," Warren wrote, "never know where or at what hour may come blows from the guardians of the law who are supposed to protect them." The Los Angeles Police Commission denied the charges, calling them "libelous and provocative." One can only imagine the outrage the man in the mustache and glasses sitting in the back row felt after reading that.

SPRING 1962 / As the fishing boat drew closer, Marlon kept his eyes on the "slender pencil of land" on the horizon growing larger with each passing minute. This was the coral atoll known as Teti'aroa. He'd first spotted it while making *Mutiny*, from the top of one of the island's tallest mountains. The atoll was owned by an elderly American woman, Marlon learned, whose father had

received it from the last Tahitian king, Pōmare V. The place was
so remote that it might exist in another dimension. Tahiti was the
height of urban civilization compared to Teti'aroa.

Because there was no landing strip on the atoll, Marlon had to
hire a fishing boat to get there. As they drew closer, he realized
that Teti'aroa was not one but more than a dozen islands, spreading out over the blue of the Pacific for about fifteen hundred acres.
The place was far more gorgeous than Marlon had ever imagined.

"A dozen varieties of birds watched as we waded ashore," he remembered. "Thick stands of cocoanut [sic] trees stood in the sand
like brigades of sentinels adorned with feathery crowns. Everywhere broad sandy beaches stretched in front of us." What most
intrigued him was the wide, crescent-shaped lagoon embraced by
the largest of the islands. About five miles across at its widest point,
the lagoon sparkled with more shades of blue than Marlon thought
possible.

Deep within the palm jungle, Marlon found the old American
owner of the atoll. Nearly blind, she'd strung wire among the trees
to guide her movements around the island. She had only one human
companion, but a menagerie of dogs and cats. Her only connection
to the outside world was a radio. Marlon was in awe. This was exactly the sort of retreat from the world he longed for, the sanctuary
he needed to survive. He told the old woman that when she was
ready to sell, he was ready to buy. She told him she would keep
him in mind.

For the time being, Marlon had to settle for Mulholland Drive.

He was back there by the spring of 1961, and despite his longing
for Tahiti, Alice thought Marlon was more serene than he'd been
in a while. He was always happiest when he wasn't making a film.
*The Ugly American* had been completed; after *One-Eyed Jacks* and
*Mutiny on the Bounty*, wrapping a picture in just a few months was
quite liberating. It was mostly an uneventful shoot. As a change
from his usual period costumes, he got to wear suits in this one; he

even grew a mustache. He also secured his sister Jocelyn the small part of a nurse.

It didn't turn out to be the film Marlon had once hoped for, however; his clarion call for social change turned out rather bland and equivocal, in his opinion. He was disappointed with George Englund's direction, but had stopped trying to persuade him to do things differently halfway through the shoot. Marlon was done with fighting. Only at the very end does the film clearly deliver the message he had wanted to send. In his role as the American ambassador, Marlon gives a speech that sounds very much like something he would have said in real life: "We can't hope to win the Cold War unless we remember what we're for as well as what we're against. I'm not blaming my country. I'm blaming the indifference that some of us show to its promises." The film ends with an average American who's watching him on television switching him off mid-sentence.

"I don't suppose anyone is ever really satisfied with something they create," Marlon said about *The Ugly American*, "but I think it's an interesting picture." He seemed to be damning it with faint praise. "Many liberals won't like it because we don't jump on American foreign policy as athletically as they might want us to."

Mostly, he was just glad it was over. After three years of straight work, he could relax. Best of all, for once in his life, he faced no financial pressures. He had his wish: he had enough money to support his various families and himself. Alice said he was seeing Dr. Aronson regularly and seemed "content." Once again, he became the prankster, the short sheeter, the ketchup squirter, the crank caller. He phoned one friend and told him he was in the midst of entertaining and realized he was out of food. Would he send over a ham and some pineapple right away? The friend did, just as Marlon predicted. His laughter, as it had ever since he was young, bubbled up from way down deep inside him and made everyone else laugh, too. "There was no evidence of the angry young man," Alice said.

At least, not until June. Marlon, it seemed, couldn't go more than a few months entirely at peace.

ON JUNE 16, *The Saturday Evening Post* published a cover story about Marlon and *Mutiny on the Bounty*. "Six Million Dollars Down the Drain," the article was titled. "The Mutiny of Marlon Brando." The author was Bill Davidson, a bureau chief of *Collier's* magazine and currently a cowriter with President Kennedy on a book about past American chief executives. Marlon didn't have to read very far into the article before the fight came rushing back to him stronger than ever. As Alice remembered, "Marlon hit a high C in his tirade."

Davidson correctly pointed a finger at some of Marlon's extravagances, such as taking the speedboat to the *Bounty*. Yet everything, from shooting delays to script problems, was unfairly presented as being his fault. Davidson's main source was Lewis Milestone; the whole piece was seen through his bitter and offended eyes. Marlon was portrayed as the spoiled movie star who threw tantrums. "Did you ever hear of an actor," Milestone was quoted as asking, "who put plugs in his ears so he couldn't listen to the director or the other actors?" Apparently, Milestone didn't know that those "plugs" were earphones to feed Marlon his lines, a practice he'd been using for years. Most journalists knew all about Marlon's earphones. Yet Davidson didn't call Milestone on it.

Instead, he allowed him to grind his axe, disregarding one of the first rules of journalism. "The movie industry deserves what it gets," Milestone complained, "when they give a ham actor, a petulant child, complete control of an expensive picture." Milestone was now on record as calling Marlon Brando, of *On the Waterfront*, *A Streetcar Named Desire*, and *Julius Caesar*, a "ham actor."

Davidson itemized Marlon's flaws all the way back to Libertyville. He even got a quote from Marlon's high school principal calling the former student "rather irresponsible." There was also some nonsense about the actor's "regressive personality" being "ameliorated" by Bela Mittelman, whatever that meant. Yet what seemed to irk Marlon the most was the charge that he, and he alone, was responsible for the costly rewrite of the film's ending. Davidson portrayed Marlon as being the only one dissatisfied with the Pitcairn Island scenes, when in fact *no one* had liked them; Aaron Rosenberg had agreed that Marlon should try a rewrite. Stopping at that point *did* delay the film, but Marlon had only undertaken the rewrite with Rosenberg's agreement.

Davidson's article riveted Hollywood. Such a high-profile attack on an actor's behavior on a set was unprecedented. What was going on here was something deeper than just a clash of personalities. It was actually an assault in the war between "new" Hollywood and "old" Hollywood. Milestone was sixty-seven when he took over the picture; he'd been in the business since 1918. Moviemaking, to Milestone's generation, should be a well-oiled craft, one in which the studio chose the property, attached writers and actors from those they had under contract, and assigned a director who worked on a six- to eight-week schedule to get it done. In this way, thousands of films had rolled off the assembly lines of the various studios over the past forty years. Now, however, the actors were calling themselves artists and demanding all sorts of accommodation, including astronomical salaries. This, old Hollywood believed, was destroying the American film industry.

This generational divide comes through in Milestone's complaints. Marlon, he told Davidson, "rallied to his side every punk extra who claimed he was a Method actor." Marlon, of course, loathed the term *Method actor*, and considered the very idea that there was a "method" to acting to be pretentious. But that didn't stop Milestone from drawing conclusions and casting blame: "It got so bad," the director said, "that one eighteen-year-old punk walked off the set when I refused to reshoot an entire scene in which he 'emotionally felt' his performance was not quite right."

In Hollywood, the old guard was angry at the punks. The aging studio chiefs, veteran directors such as Milestone and columnists such as Hedda Hopper, felt nothing but contempt for these new, "artistically inclined" actors and directors. Their multimillion-dollar productions were bankrupting Hollywood, but the deeper problem was their egos. *Cleopatra* had them up in arms at Fox, not only because of the cost but because of the way Elizabeth Taylor carried on with Richard Burton. Marlon was even worse: he was now guilty of *two* overbudgeted, massively delayed pictures.

"I think the *Mutiny on the Bounty* problems with Brando," Robert Wise, another studio stalwart, told Davidson, "plus the problems with Elizabeth Taylor in *Cleopatra*, might well mark the end of the star system as it exists in Hollywood today." His advice: "To hell with the star. I'll make little black and white pictures with good scripts and unknown actors. We must do that to survive."

Marlon did not give one single damn about old Hollywood versus new; he had contempt for both. He also had absolutely zero interest in the debate over whether the studio way of making pictures was better than the independent way. What infuriated him was quite simple: he was being cast as the villain in this saga, blamed for every problem *Mutiny* had endured on its two-year road to completion. "The *Mutiny on the Bounty* problems with Brando" was the line that really set him off. He wasn't going to stand for it. He decided to do something that no actor had ever done before, no matter how angry he or she might have gotten at the press.

He decided to sue.

THREE EVENTS IN the early 1960s propelled Marlon onto the very different course he took for the rest of the decade and beyond. The first was Caryl Chessman's execution. The second was Paramount's mutilation of *One-Eyed Jacks*. The third was Bill Davidson's article in *The Saturday Evening Post*.

For years now, Marlon had been taking the abuse of columnists and fan magazine writers. The rage would build up inside him, like that balloon he once used as a metaphor, until some unfortunate lackey blundered by and pricked the balloon's skin, and out would come Marlon's rage "at a tremendous rate of speed." In the past, that rage was usually followed by a plunge into despair. That was because Marlon had felt powerless. Yet, in the wake of the *Saturday Evening Post* piece, he realized he was no longer powerless. He had, in fact, considerable power, and he was going to use it.

There was nothing to lose by suing. He'd already abdicated any sense of cooperation with the power structure of Hollywood, and Pennebaker was, he surely realized by now, on its last legs. *Mutiny* had made him a fortune; for some time to come, he didn't have to worry about money. So, he truly had nothing to lose, except for his name. "I have kids growing up now," Marlon explained. "I have to protect my children against the vulgarity that has been written about me." For him, Davidson's sanctimonious piece was "the point of no return."

His crusade, however, was more than just a personal vendetta. What troubled him, Marlon said, was the direction of the media away from important issues (capital punishment, civil rights) and increasingly toward "ephemera," as he called it (celebrities, movies, television, scandal). While tabloid journalism dated back to the nineteenth century, and movie fan magazines had been around since the days of the nickelodeons, the barrier between news and entertainment was increasingly being blurred, Marlon believed. *Time* magazine, he pointed out, was supposed to be "a serious purveyor of news and facts," but some editor there had decided to ramp up the importance of its "People and Places" section by publishing "silly little gossip." Those little nuggets of news were rarely accurate, Marlon said, something he claimed to know from personal experience. But because this was *Time* magazine, people believed they were true.

The rise of television made the situation even worse, bringing a glut of celebrities to "inane talk shows," Marlon said, where they "babble on about nothing." Meanwhile, in Mississippi, he pointed out, "state troopers were keeping James Meredith," a black student, from "his constitutional right" of attending his classes at Ole Miss. Was this really the sort of media Americans wanted?

Perhaps it was, Marlon realized to his horror. The reason television airtime wasn't filled with more Shakespeare or more honest political debate was "because the American people don't want to see it," he said. The public greedily consumed gossip about the private lives of celebrities while stories of black teenagers being arrested on the streets of Los Angeles went untold. Marlon called it a "peephole impulse," and concluded that it came from the public's "naïveté." Through "immersion in nonsense" fed to them by the media, people were content to live in blissful ignorance of "the painful truths of the world."

By the early 1960s, Marlon made it his mission to open people's eyes. "I've decided," he told one reporter, "I finally want to speak out against slop-oriented journalism and the conversational scavengers who exploit for profit and libel for entertainment." That was essential, he said, in any effort to "change the way the public saw the world." People got their impressions of the world through the media—so the media, in Marlon's view, needed to be changed. The 141-year-old *Saturday Evening Post*, though hardly the worst offender (except, perhaps, in Marlon's eyes), would be his first target.

If he were going to wage war, however, he would need to do so strategically. He would bide his time on filing his lawsuit. To prevail against the *Post*, he would need to demonstrate first just how wrong they were about him. When Aaron Rosenberg, with great apology, told him that August that they needed to shoot just a few more takes on the film, Marlon graciously agreed to come into the studio, providing he didn't have to work with Milestone. So, MGM brought in George Seaton instead, the picture's third director. The great screenwriter Billy Wilder had come up with what they all hoped was a better ending, with Fletcher Christian deciding to sail back to England to face trial for mutiny, which leads to his own crew rebelling against him. During that final week of shooting, Marlon was professional and courteous and, some thought, did his very best work in the film. When Rosenberg tentatively raised the subject of the film's release that fall, Marlon stunned him by saying he'd be back to attend both the New York and Los Angeles premieres.

*Mutiny on the Bounty* opened on November 8, 1962, at Loew's State Theatre in New York City. Marlon was there, smiling and shaking hands. Many columnists were surprised, given what they'd read in *The Saturday Evening Post*. Why had he chosen to attend this premiere, when he'd missed so many others? Marlon replied that he very much wanted the picture to do well. "If I didn't," he said, "I would be standing alone in the Gobi desert." In other words, he wanted what the producers and everyone else involved with the film wanted. He was a team player.

The reviews of the film that came out the next day, and then over the next several weeks, were not often kind. The best thing about it, almost everyone agreed, was the South Seas cinematography. Marlon's decision to play Christian as a dandy was not a popular choice. Pauline Kael thought it was like "a Dead End Kid playing Congreve." One New York critic called the performance "a trifle too arch for comfort," with Marlon rolling his eyes at the native women "until you think he's playing a game of marbles."

Most cutting of all, however, was Bosley Crowther, who'd usually been a stalwart supporter. But Crowther, too, was put off by "Christian's oddly foppish frame." His lofty airs persisted throughout the film, "to the point where one feels the performance is intended as a travesty or a lark." The final result, Crowther said, was "extremely disconcerting."

Marlon prided himself on finding the truth of a character. It's what made his roles, even in such less successful efforts as *The Young Lions* or *The Fugitive Kind*, so compelling. This time, however, he'd missed the mark. He'd discovered Christian's well-cultured background and made a choice to play him that way. But his arrogance and upper-classism does not serve the story. Crowther put his finger on the problem: why would a fellow of Christian's haughty nature be in any way "charitably moved by the suffering of the sailors?" Nothing follows logically; relationships with other characters feel forced. All because Marlon was determined not to play Christian as Clark Gable had played him.

Crowther did like Marlon at one point; the "blanching reaction" he gets when he realizes what he's done and "senses his fall from duty"; then, and only then, is Marlon "thoroughly reasoned and mature." Otherwise, the ending they'd all worked so hard on, for which Billy Wilder had supposedly provided the magic solution, falls emotionally flat. Yet there's no denying the power Marlon brings to Christian's death scene. Knowing that severe burns make the air feel cold, he lay on a bed of ice for maximum realism. In the shot, he visibly shivers as death approaches. "And he dies," said Tom Oppenheim, Ellen Adler's son, "with his eyes open, something that's very difficult to make believable." Marlon's best moment comes two hours and fifty-six minutes into the two-hour-fifty-eight-minute film.

Yet, despite its reviews, *Mutiny* performed decently at the box office; it was the sixth-highest-grossing film of 1963, bringing in $7.7 million. But against the nearly $30 million that had gone into it, that meant a staggering loss for MGM.

Not for Marlon, however. He might lose out on the back end like everybody else, but he'd made plenty of money up front. His eyes were already looking far past the debacle of *Mutiny on the Bounty*, anticipating the lawsuit he was fully prepared to bring against *The Saturday Evening Post* at the opportune moment. His cooperation in shooting the final scenes of the picture and his magnanimous involvement in its publicity would go a long way toward refuting the *Post*'s depiction of him as selfish and recalcitrant. No one could have guessed what Marlon was planning as he stood there shaking hands so gallantly outside Loew's State Theatre the night of the premiere.

AT MARLON'S SIDE throughout the *Mutiny* premiere was Tarita. There was no indication that the lovely Tahitian, dressed in a sleek designer gown, was anything more than Marlon's costar. Many gossip writers had stopped speculating about them.

In fact, a few months earlier, their long, unofficial courtship had finally become intimate. They were especially close during the last week of shooting in August. For so long, Tarita had been wary of Marlon, having seen and heard about his many other women. But she'd also grown quite fond of him, and felt sad that their time together was ending. She remained determined that she would not be forgotten once the film was complete.

They were together again at the gala Tokyo premiere, which Marlon had also agreed to attend, much to everyone's surprise. ("Look who's turned traveling salesman," Bob Thomas of the Associated Press joked to his readers.) Together, Marlon and Tarita made a gracious pair, bowing onstage to the Japanese emperor and empress. Tarita accepted a bouquet of flowers as Marlon looked on and smiled.

But underneath that smile, he was reeling. In Tokyo, Tarita had given him some very surprising news. She was pregnant.

He simply couldn't have another child, Marlon believed. What would Movita do when she found out? They were ostensibly still married, even if he no longer kept up any pretense of living with her. Even more worrisome: how might Anna try to use it against him? He pleaded with Tarita to get an abortion, but she refused. She was going to have his baby.

Yet Tarita wasn't like Movita. She hadn't come to Marlon looking for marriage; she didn't live by the American rule book of propriety. She had no desire to live in Los Angeles and complicate

Marlon's life. "I didn't want to live where I knew I'd be unhappy," she said, looking back. "I'd seen perfectly well what was happening before I became pregnant, all the women who came and went[,] and I didn't want to see that again." All Tarita wanted was a special, ongoing connection with Marlon and his world—and yes, the support and benefits that came with that. After all this time, she wasn't going back to working in a hotel kitchen.

At first, Marlon fretted over how the news media would react. But then, gradually, he stopped worrying. When the time came, he admitted to having a child with Tarita. What of it? If he was going to confront the way the news media reported on him, then he might as well quit making apologies for his life.

ON JANUARY 9, 1963, Marlon's attorneys sued Curtis Publishing Company, the owner of *The Saturday Evening Post*, in Los Angeles Superior Court. Marlon was asking four million dollars in general and special damages and one million in punitive damages. Statements in the Bill Davidson article, he alleged, were "false and libelous, designed to defame him as a movie actor and had succeeded in doing so." He specifically itemized eight false charges, including flubbing his lines, fomenting an insurrection among the cast, and forcing the company to shut down as he rewrote the ending. None of this was true, and could easily be disproven. Never before had a movie star taken the press to court in this way.

And so began a new attitude of defiance that Marlon brought to every public appearance thereafter. To him, this was a noble cause, not so different from the one Fletcher Christian stands up for when he tells his fellow mutineers toward the end of the film that the time has come to stand up and fight for what is right. "We all may be hanged," he says, "but decency is worth fighting for." That speech uncannily heralded Marlon's new determination. "I did not know until this moment," Christian says, "what the rightful cause to pursue was. But I know it now."

Marlon was primed for the fight, one that had been coming for many years, not just against the *Post* or the media in general but the entire structure of Hollywood and American popular culture. Longtime Hollywood publicist Jack Hirshberg observed that if Marlon lacked respect for the star system, "he must have even less respect for the men who created it, operate it, and who are in turn miserably frightened by and in awe of the very monsters they have sired."

This monster wasn't turning back. "I'm going after the magazine with whip and spur," Marlon vowed, "and whenever the time comes I shall be ready to face them." He was putting the world on notice: after *The Saturday Evening Post*, everybody was fair game.

**APRIL 21, 1963** / The television lights went on and the erudite host, seated in front of a round table in an unpretentious, spare studio, greeted the audience tuning in for tonight's show. "Good evening and welcome to *Open End*," he said. "My name is David Susskind." His guests that night were Marlon, George Englund, and Eugene Burdick, on a four-week media tour to promote *The Ugly American*. Waiting for his introduction, Marlon sat politely, almost demurely, dressed smartly in a suit and tie. For a fleeting moment it might have appeared as if he were taking part in another congenial, cooperative television interview to market himself and his movies, much as he had back in 1955. But his encounter with David Susskind would bear little resemblance to his appearance with Edward R. Murrow. The *Open End* broadcast is an extraordinary window into Marlon's mind and heart in the early 1960s.

Marlon was on a mission. In the past few weeks, he'd dialogued with Hugh Downs on *Today*, discoursed with Johnny Carson on

*The Tonight Show,* and even dallied with the humorist Art Buchwald for his nationally syndicated column. But it was Susskind who offered the sort of forum Marlon was looking for. *Open End,* broadcast by WNTA-TV, Channel 13 (the predecessor to WNET), offered serious, thoughtful conversation. Marlon was assured that he, Englund, and Burdick could discuss more than just the movie they'd made. What Marlon really wanted to talk about was the rise of irresponsible, tabloid-style, celebrity-focused journalism, a trend he believed was cheapening American culture—irrevocably, he felt, unless something were done about it now.

Marlon's lawsuit against *The Saturday Evening Post* had ignited considerable debate. Were his objections warranted or was he just a crybaby? During the program, Marlon attempted to put the suit in perspective. "I have withstood raps, justified and unjustified," he said. "But there comes a time when you have to pick up a tin can and turn around and fling it with a will." He had "two children growing up in this community," he said, and he believed they deserved "protection as [did] their mothers." It may have been the only time on record that Marlon had spoken charitably of Anna in public since their separation.

His appearance on *Open End,* Marlon insisted, was not just an opportunity to vent his own personal grievances. There was, he said, something pervasive going on that was changing the tone and character of the national discourse. An obsession with celebrity, epitomized by paparazzi chasing down stars such as Elizabeth Taylor and Richard Burton, was becoming ubiquitous. Magazines and newspapers that "purport to be responsible organs" were making "these pompous and condescending decisions about lives, about facts and situations." Where did that lead? As Marlon explained later, "I was concerned that the freedoms enshrined by the First Amendment were being misused to create a press that faced no consequences for diminishing the intelligence of the nation."

Today, Marlon charged, the goal of the press was too often "sensationalism." With magazines such as *Liberty* and *Collier's* folding over the past decade, those still struggling to survive would do "everything to keep them[selves] afloat." He'd been the first movie star *The Saturday Evening Post* had put on its cover in years, and its newsstand sales had skyrocketed. Gossip and celebrity reporting, Marlon claimed, was a "multimillion dollar industrial complex," and the "star scoop" had become the holy grail, often seen as more valuable than snaring a politician or world leader.

No matter how his case against *The Saturday Evening Post* turned out—"a jury of twelve Americans will decide that," he said—he hoped his fight would force Americans to look at other issues that "deserve some kind of attention."

For most of the program's two hours, Marlon kept up his condemnation of the status quo. Instead of the playacting he'd demonstrated with Murrow, where he'd been in fact complicit with the system, here Marlon was calling out the media for its increasing focus on trivia and trumpery and its single-minded preoccupation with the bottom line. Money—profits—drove everything. Where did it end? Where was America heading? Finally, with only a few minutes left of airtime, Marlon turned the tables and began to question Susskind.

"I want to ask *you* something, David," he said. "I'm interested to know what your position is in relation to your sponsors. Now, cigarettes cause cancer, by most medical researchers' findings—"

The host quickly cut in, laughing, apparently talking to his program manager outside camera range. "No, no," Susskind said, "he only means we are getting near a commercial." The host tried to find humor in the awkward situation. "Probably with my luck it will be a cigarette."

But Marlon wouldn't let him go. "It's something that absorbs me very much," he said, "because everything is sold to the American

public. News items . . . political concepts . . ." The idea of huckstering still troubled him, making him feel like his father on the road
pushing Calcium Carbonate. He leaned in closer to the host. "How
do you feel, David, when you know that you're on a program and
that you've got to go along with a hard sell that shames people into
buying a product?"

Susskind wasn't easily rattled. "I think this program is worthwhile
enough to live with the compromises it entails," he said. "You must
have made *Désirée* in the hope of getting to *One-Eyed Jacks*."

Marlon didn't deny it, but now he was asking a bigger question. Why had it become so important in the second half of the
twentieth century not just to succeed, but to succeed beyond all
expectations? How much did one need? What constituted success? Marlon was sincerely trying to understand. "What is your
attitude about success," he asked Susskind, "now that you've
achieved it? Does it mean to you what you thought it was going
to mean, when you were, you know, rousting yourself, trying
to get ahead?"

If he was hoping to get an answer to this most existential of
questions, one with which he had been wrestling these past few
years, Marlon would have to wait, ironically, for the commercial
break. "Let's get to that right after this message," Susskind said,
"probably from some cigarette company."

The host never got around to answering the question. Instead,
he made the observation that Marlon seemed "miserable" with his
success, a charge Marlon denied. He wasn't miserable, he said, but
rather "bewildered . . . because success is something we're all inculcated to. You've got to have money. And I've found that since
I've achieved it, by accident, by intention, however it's happened,
that it really doesn't have the fiber."

"Well, let me ask you," Susskind said. "Are you prepared to turn
your back on Hollywood, on films, on fame, on money—and say,

'I'm going to try another pursuit? I'm going to see if I can build up my own new interests and optimism about living.'"

Marlon didn't hesitate. "Yes, I think so," he said.

"Are you going to turn your back on acting in films?"

"Yeah."

"Soon?"

"I feel that's something that has been—something that is coming in my life."

Susskind still couldn't entirely fathom why. He couldn't grasp why Marlon felt exploited. Sure, they all made concessions to the monetary culture, but it was worth it, he felt, to do work that they loved.

That was just it, Marlon said: *Was* it worth it? What were they prioritizing as markers of their success?

"I will go to have dinner someplace," Marlon said. "It will be a crowded restaurant, but as soon as I appear, they'll say, 'Mr. Brando, table right here. You just come down to the front of the line.'" And he'd be glad that he could get a table, but he'd also think, "My God, these people have been waiting here an hour." Another example: he'd call an airline to make a reservation. No, he'd be told, there were no tickets. But when he'd tell them his name, they'd sing a different song: "Let's see what we can do."

"And somebody who has paid good, decent money," Marlon lamented to Susskind, "for a cook's tour vacation for two weeks out of the year gets bumped off a flight."

"Yes, Marlon," Susskind responded. "That's called the American way."

The answer seemed to infuriate Marlon for a moment. "Is it worth it?" he demanded. "What are we pursuing here with our money and success and fame?"

The program concluded soon after that, with that question still hanging in the air, unanswered. Marlon would keep asking it, pretty much for the rest of his life.

**JULY 27, 1963** / Angry faces glared from windows, and men stood defiantly in driveways, as one hundred fifty marchers made their way through the all-white neighborhood singing "We Shall Overcome." The marchers, both black and white, were protesting the exclusionary sales policy of the Southwood Riviera Royale housing development in Torrance, California, a coastal community nineteen miles south of Los Angeles. They walked peacefully and orderly along the sidewalks of the 650-home tract, followed by a nearly equal number of police officers in the street, eleven of them on motorcycles. From their front porches, many homeowners jeered and spat at the marchers. One stuck a sign in his lawn: WE HAVE CIVIL RIGHTS TOO.

Several clergymen walked with the protesters. So did two actors: Pernell Roberts and Marlon Brando.

Wearing a black-and-white-checked sports jacket, black trousers, a white shirt, and a red tie, Marlon was pale and drawn. He'd only recently gotten out of Saint John's Hospital in Santa Monica, where he'd spent five days recovering from a kidney infection. For a couple of blocks, he got by without being recognized by the reporters covering the protest. Then the jig was up and he was deluged. Newsmen trooped alongside him, peppering him with questions. Several times, Marlon stopped and patiently explained the reasons he was walking with the Congress of Racial Equality. "This will communicate to others the truth that discrimination does exist," he said. He still held on to the belief that the problem was largely one of ignorance: if more people knew about the reality of racial discrimination, they wouldn't stand for it. People were too distracted, he said, by silly stories about scandals and movie stars. "Many people are just not aware of what's going on," he told a reporter. "Anyone who believes in civil rights should demonstrate."

Each time he stopped to talk, however, a white-helmeted police officer would get in very close and threaten to arrest him if he didn't start moving. "You are blocking the sidewalk," the officer told Marlon repeatedly.

By now the homeowners had realized that Marlon Brando was coming down their street, and many gathered to get a look at him. Some appeared giddy as he passed, cheering and calling his name. Others booed. One person shouted that if he couldn't make movies, he could at least come here. The message was unclear: was Marlon being taunted for the less-than-satisfactory box office of his latest films—*The Ugly American* had utterly flopped—or was he being welcomed to visit by some hopeful admirers? Up the street, however, there was no mistaking one homeowner's intent. "Communist!" the man yelled at him. Marlon gave no response. "Everyone is entitled to his point of view," he told the reporter walking with him.

Another angry homeowner approached Marlon and pointed to the flowers that were getting trampled, largely by reporters, as the marchers kept to the sidewalk. Marlon nodded sadly. "I'm sure some of the flowers are being stepped on today," he said. "But so are some people's civil rights."

The marchers began to sing again, this time the old Negro gospel tune "(Give Me That) Old-Time Religion," but changing the lyrics to "It was good enough for Medgar Evers / it's good enough for me." Just a month and a half earlier, Evers, an NAACP field secretary, had been murdered in Mississippi.

At one corner, the group turned, and waiting for them were three men in the white robes of the Ku Klux Klan. Several others wore Nazi insignias. One of the neo-Nazis carried a hastily scrawled sign: BRANDO IS A STOOGE FOR COMMUNIST RACE MIXTURE. In response, the marchers kept singing, though this time with new lyrics: "It was good enough for Marlon Brando / it's good enough for me."

When they reached the housing sales office at 23448 Evalyn Avenue, the protestors halted. About fifty of them stepped forward

and sat on the ground, blocking the entrance. Twelve police officers, marching in close formation, immediately moved to the front
of the group and stood over the sitters. "You have been requested
to move," the captain of the officers declared. "You are on private
property. You are trespassing. You people are under arrest."

No one moved. Instead, they sang, "I will go to jail for freedom."
So, the policemen moved in and began to physically lift them, one
by one, and carry them to a nearby paddy wagon. The demonstrators let their bodies go limp. One homeowner who thought the
police were being too gentle shouted, "Drag 'em!" Several officers
made fun of a heavy woman who required four of them to lift her.
Two of the clergymen, the Rev. Morris V. Samuel Jr. of the Episco-
pal parish of East Los Angeles and the Rev. George Killingsworth
of the United Church of Christ of South Los Angeles, were also
hauled away.

Marlon watched in horror. "To see people just carted off in that
way," he'd later recall, unable to finish his statement. It brought
back to mind newsreels he'd seen during his time with the ALFP,
of British soldiers forcibly removing Jewish refugees from a ship
heading to Palestine. Back then, he'd called the world "topsy-
turvy," because America and its allies had just fought and won a
war to safeguard freedom. No doubt he felt the same way now.

After two and a half hours of marching, still weak from his hospital stay, Marlon told a reporter his legs were getting "wobbly"
and departed. The next day, his name was in the headlines about
the demonstration, and his photo was on many front pages. "If I
have to endure publicity," he said, "this is the sort I'll accept."

FOLLOWING THE FINANCIAL disaster of *The Ugly American*, Marlon
seemed liberated. He was no longer answerable to anyone. That
summer, MCA agreed to buy the beleaguered Pennebaker. While
the company had assets of $217,371.15, a good part of that came
from story rights and development deals for such unproduced titles

as *Strike Me Lucky* and *Arabella*, and from Marlon's aborted American Indian and Tahitian projects. Its assets were also diminished by Pennebaker's tax liabilities, which now stood at nearly $100,000. In the sale, MCA acquired all Pennebaker's stock; in exchange, the Pennebaker partners received 22,000 shares of the common stock of MCA. Marlon got 19,800 of them.

There was no fanfare about the sale; Pennebaker continued on under MCA for a time. But Marlon was done with it. The idea to go into production and make films that he felt were important had been an idealistic one. But without the support of a studio infrastructure, and in an industry increasingly dependent on extremely high returns, the risks of independent production were high. Paramount might have absorbed most of the estimated $5.6 million that *One-Eyed Jacks* lost, but $1.7 million of that had been directly deducted from Pennebaker's books. Marlon wasted no tears on his exit from Pennebaker. Being free of it meant freedom from the bottom line—not to mention his father's harangues.

He'd agreed to do one other thing in the deal with MCA: he would star in five films for Universal, which MCA now owned as well. Marlon made clear he wouldn't do any publicity or marketing for them: "Those sorts of things I refused to do," he said, "and there was really no debate about that after a certain point." He also agreed to be paid just $270,000 for each film, a considerable pay cut, given that he'd made $1 million for both *The Fugitive Kind* and *Mutiny on the Bounty*. His former partner at Pennebaker, Walter Seltzer, viewed Marlon's five-picture agreement with Universal as a desperate move on his part. Clearly, Seltzer believed, with the decline in his box office, Marlon had "lost his cachet and he knew it, so he was in no position to be selective."

This is precisely the sort of misreading that would become so common in Marlon's post-*Mutiny* career, with events often viewed through the darkest, most distorted lens possible, and usually by people with clear bias against the star. (Seltzer blamed Marlon for

Pennebaker's failure.) Marlon was far from desperate; his account-
ing books reveal he was still financially solvent at this point. But
he also knew the money he'd made from *Mutiny* wouldn't last forever. As always, his expenses were rising. He had three households
to support (his own, Anna's, and Movita's) plus, soon, a fourth
(Tarita's). He was also hoping to buy Teti'aroa and develop the
atoll as both a residence and a marine laboratory. So he accepted
MCA's rather modest deal, and with apparent sangfroid. True, the
money wasn't tremendous, but here was the point: it was *enough*.
Teti'aroa's owner had agreed to sell the islands for $200,000, which
was less than Marlon would make on just one picture under his
MCA deal. Just one movie, then, would bring him his long-desired
sanctuary.

Seltzer, fired by his own determination to make it as a successful
producer, saw things very differently: accepting a quarter of what
you'd made on a previous picture was a real comedown, a desperate move, a career disaster. Apparently, he hadn't been listening to
Marlon in his recent interviews. Once "you've got enough," he'd
said, making more "doesn't matter." The income guaranteed by
the MCA deal would not make Marlon rich. But it was enough to
support him and his various families and projects. That was what
mattered.

At last Marlon was free to live his life on his terms.


THAT SUMMER, MARLON turned up everywhere in support of "racial
freedom," as activists called it. With Paul Newman, he paid a "freedom visit" to a group of sit-ins at the State Capitol in Sacramento,
calling for a ban on housing discrimination. "It is time now," Marlon declared, "to assist the Negro in doing something we should
have done in the first place." At a meeting at the Beverly Hilton
sponsored by the American Civil Liberties Union, he denounced
the prejudice that existed in the film industry. "I've seen people
refuse to hire Negroes," he said from the podium. Producers told

him they'd "lose forty percent of the market" if they hired black actors. Many Hollywood power brokers, Marlon charged, felt their "moral obligation" was "to the banker." Noting the other actors in attendance (Newman, Charlton Heston, Anthony Franciosa), Marlon said, "All of us are late in joining this movement. We can do something. We must do something. This is not a Negro movement. This is a democratic movement."

He might have been a scoundrel to Hedda Hopper, but in the gossip columns of African American newspapers, Marlon was a hero. "If Marlon Brando succeeds in getting Paul Newman in the rights demonstrations," wrote Lillian Calhoun in the *Chicago Defender*, "he'll make the choice of integration pretty easy for Southern white womanhood. I wouldn't bet on Mrs. Ross Barnett [the wife of the governor of Mississippi] remaining true to the Dixie cause if those two hit Jackson."

But from other corners, the hate mail was once again piling up. The words in these letters were ugly and full of hate: "White traitor." "Nigger lover." One letter writer charged, "Many people know you mouth off for the Jews," but now Marlon was "being with the Negroes against the whites." He was accused of wanting a "race war." One man sent him a newspaper clipping in which Marlon was quoted as saying, "We must change people's hearts and minds." The correspondent had scrawled across the clipping in ink: "Not mine. I'll die first." Many of the letters called Marlon a Communist. "America has been very good to you," one woman wrote. "Why do you hate our nation so?"

Ellen Adler believed such attacks only emboldened Marlon. "It was always so ironic [when Marlon was called anti-American]," she said, "because he was so endemically American." Protesting for rights and democracy was an "American core value." Marlon took the criticism and the hate mail he received for his political activism as "affirmation that he was doing the right thing," Ellen said.

He was in no hurry to return to a soundstage. The previous

spring, as a last commitment to Pennebaker, he'd made the comedy *Bedtime Story*, an experience he found enjoyable because he no longer had to worry about cost overruns or schedules. He had gotten along well with his costars, David Niven and Shirley Jones, playing a version of his Casanova self, bed-hopping his way through the movie. But after that, his political activism and frequent trips to Tahiti became much more important to him than any acting job. Sidney Poitier was eager for Marlon to play Iago to his Othello onstage, willing to work around any scheduling to make that happen. Marlon didn't say no but also didn't say yes. He cabled that he regretted not being able to "be more definite" about the part, because Poitier was "perfect for Othello, perhaps the best." Eventually, the project fizzled. Marlon's ambivalence had nothing to do with Poitier, whom he liked and admired. But if movies disinterested him, the stage held even less appeal.

Marlon had also been frustratingly noncommittal to the producer Ray Stark, who wanted him to play the lead in the film version of Tennessee Williams's *The Night of the Iguana*. At one point, Marlon had apparently expressed some interest, but after that, Stark complained in a letter to him, "I have never been able to arrange a phone call or meeting." The part went to Richard Burton.

Marlon truly didn't care about his acting career. For the first time, he described himself in interviews as "serene." The question was: could he bring that same peace of mind to the conflicted relationships in his life? That would be his real challenge.

ANNA KASHFI WASN'T sure what to make of the flowers that had just been delivered to her front door. The card revealed that they were from Marlon, wishing her well with the part she'd landed on an episode of *Kraft Mystery Theatre*. Their last few interactions hadn't exactly been pleasant ones. Curses and slamming doors had punctuated Marlon's picking up and dropping off Christian on his visitation days. Recently, angered over reports of her ex-husband dating Marie Cui, Anna had called Alice and shouted, "Tell that fat-ass movie actor boss of yours that as soon as Devi gets over his chicken pox we're both leaving the country." Alice reported this to the social worker; it was duly noted in the file.

But now, these flowers. Anna telephoned Marlon and thanked him. He offered to run lines with her. "Marlon very sweet," Anna recorded in her diary. "Sent flowers, went over my lines with me and had lunch with me." Could it be possible that the violent feud, after four long years, had finally come to an end?

By the middle part of 1963, just as his civil rights activism was reaching a peak, Marlon attempted to bring some of that goodwill into his personal life as well. While not explicitly apologizing for any bad behavior, he was, possibly, trying to atone for it. He knew Anna's insecurities ran deep, and how terrified she was to go back to work. "Utter misery," Anna admitted to her diary after her first day on the set. "Very nervous." The day ended in tears: "Felt I had not done my best," she wrote.

Yet, despite Anna's anxieties, Marlon also knew that going back to work was the very best thing for her. Work would boost her self-esteem, and only when Anna felt better about herself, stronger and more independent, would their acrimonious court battles end. Anna's diary, partially preserved in custody court records, reveals a sad, lonely, frightened woman, often ruminating over what she wanted but didn't have: "Marlon brought the baby back in time. Thought about love today, and marriage." She grieved over her failed personal life and longed for redemption professionally. "Help me make a good career, a good and competent actress, not a joke," she wrote in her diary, adding also, "Help where my heart is concerned."

Marlon's compassionate outreach to her, unmentioned in most chronicles of his life, was not done only for Anna. He could also see the toll their battles were taking on Christian. "He is so bright and alert," he told Anna during this period of détente. "He hears everything and what he doesn't hear, he feels." Once, overhearing his parents argue on the phone, the five-year-old called Marlon back and told him not to say such things again because "the operators are listening." The words of one judge had haunted Marlon for years: "I know you want to have a secure, healthy child. You are not going to have one if this bitterness continues."

Accordingly, sometime early that spring, Marlon asked Anna to see a therapist. Psychoanalysis had been beneficial for him, and he hoped it might help her as well. To his surprise, she agreed.

Marlon was overjoyed. He called her decision "the finest moment" of her life. "I mean it with all my heart that I'm proud of you," he wrote to her, "and glad for you that you have decided to stand and fight the *real fight*, the inside one, not the ones on the outside, the ones that really don't count and can never be won." He would cut off his arm, he said, if it helped her, but he can't help "other than to tell you that I've lived through it and I never thought I would have the courage or the strength to stand it, and to assure you that there are people who really, really care about you and want to help and will stand by you."

Despite how angry she could get with him, Anna never doubted the sincerity of Marlon's outreach to her. "The sympathy was genuine," she later wrote. Indeed, Marlon was never sincerer than when he was talking about analysis, one area where he had real experience. "You have to explore the depths of your soul by yourself," he told Anna. "No one can do it for you—you and Dr. McGuire must take, as someone put it, 'the underwater journey through the night sea.'" And although Christian couldn't tell her so, Marlon said, "the baby is proud of you, too. He feels your struggle, Anna, and he would express his gratitude in words if he could."

How long Anna remained in therapy is unknown; she didn't mention it in her diary, or at least not in the portions preserved. But apparently it didn't last long. She was soon angry with Marlon again. Often, when he was kind and solicitous, Anna convinced herself he was coming back to her. Then, when reality hit, she'd lash out. One afternoon, returning Christian to his mother, Marlon was met at the door by a furious Anna, screaming at him that he was late, that he wasn't a fit role model for their son. Christian burst into tears. Marlon left, feeling utterly beaten. There was only one thing left to do.

On May 24, he penned an extraordinary letter to his ex-wife, perhaps the most difficult letter of his life. "I think it is best for all concerned," he wrote, "that I do not see the baby anymore." Writing those words surely broke his heart, but he saw no other way to protect Christian. Anna was constantly "enraged" by the things he did or didn't do, Marlon wrote; no matter how he tried to reach out, she was "filled with loathing and contempt" for him. He could think of no other way to change the dynamic between them except by removing himself from the picture. "I am exhausted emotionally trying to think of some way to assist you with your difficulties," he wrote. "Somehow no matter what I do, the blame is mine, the pain is yours and the curse is on the baby."

Christian was his main concern. "All this conflict has a corrosive and damaging effect on the baby," he told Anna. "The presence of hatred and violent feeling is destructive in the extreme to children." Marlon knew of what he wrote. He would continue to support them, he promised, but he'd no longer attempt to see Christian. "You'll be free of me now, Anna," he wrote. "There'll be no more torments for you." But he asked one thing of her: "I implore you, Anna, not to tell the baby that 'Your Daddy doesn't want to see you.' For God's sake don't say that to him." Marlon planned to write to the boy and tell him that he was away but that he thought of him and loved him. "I can stand my heart breaking," Marlon wrote, "only if I know you are giving him love and peace and happiness."

"This, in writing, is powerful," Anna confided to her diary. "He has signed Devi over to me completely. That means I can go and come as I please or go away completely." That was what she had been asking for, and what she'd been threatening to do if Marlon didn't let her. But now that she had his permission, she went nowhere. In fact, the only place Anna went was Tahiti, after Marlon offered to send her and Christian there on an all-expenses-paid holiday. If he was hoping Anna would return with the same sense of tranquility and equanimity he'd found in the islands, he was disappointed. She found it a "wasteful, vacuous existence." Restless, and suspicious of Marlon's motives, she returned to Los Angeles as unhappy as ever.

What Anna didn't know was, despite his absence from her life, Marlon continued advocating for her behind the scenes. "Anna must have work to gain a little confidence in herself," he wrote to her lawyer, Albert Pearlson. Marlon was pressuring MCA to get Anna a spot in a film or on a television show, but under no circumstances should she learn he was "trying to push this thing."

In the summer of 1963, Marlon still held out hope that Anna and, even more important, their son might be saved. His ex-wife would remain one of the two people whose very name uttered in his presence could transform him into a cyclone of rage. Still, he did all he could for her.

The other person, of course, who could instantly set off Marlon's fury was his father. And it was his father who would provide the real test of whether the peace of mind Marlon had found was solid and enduring.

SINCE THE PENNEBAKER sale, Marlon had barely seen his father. Even before that, he'd avoided crossing paths with the old man whenever possible. The elder Brando had remarried. His new wife (like his son's ex-wife, named Anna) was six years younger than Marlon. Her father, Russian-born film producer Eugene Frenke, lived next door to the elder Brandos. Marlon Junior took a shine

to Frenke, who told stories of Europe before the war. He'd sometimes pass by his father's yard on his way to visit Frenke, without
stopping to say hello to Senior or his wife.

"The one thing I regret," the elder Brando told columnist Art
Buchwald, "is giving Marlon Brando my name. One shouldn't have
that much ego to name his son after himself." Surely, he wasn't
ashamed of the name, Buchwald posited. "It's just too much darn
confusion," Marlon Senior replied. "When I take a plane or check
into a hotel everyone expects to see my son and when I show up,
they look at me as if I were an imposter. Only last week I paid a
hotel bill and I heard the cashier say, 'He's a phony. He's not Marlon
Brando.' It's even tougher on my wife . . . Everyone thinks she's
Marlon's ex-wife, instead of my present one."

The lord and master of Libertyville didn't like being subsumed
by his ne'er-do-well son. Marlon Senior existed now only in service
to his namesake. While he enjoyed the perks (the trips to Paris
on Pennebaker business, the Hollywood parties, the attention), he
was reminded, every day, that his importance was not his own.

In some ways, Senior attempted to do right by his son. He'd
tried to make Pennebaker work. "All his life I knew Marlon never
cared anything about money," he said. "It's never been important
to him. So I figured somebody had to help him." Throughout his
business career, Senior had made a lot of bad choices. But he'd
been right about Pennebaker. To achieve financial success, they
should have made more commercial films. But everything his father suggested, Marlon instinctively resisted. His father was still
a huckster, selling movies now instead of calcium, and Marlon
despised hucksters. Brando Senior was left to impotently dictate
miles of memos that went unread. "On some level," one business
acquaintance mused, "I wonder if Marlon wanted his father to fail,
yet again. I can't imagine he would have enjoyed the experience of
having to be grateful to his father for Pennebaker's success."

Like his son, Marlon Senior was in analysis, where he tried

to sort through his own conflicted emotions. Unlike his son, he would leave no record of his feelings, so what he struggled with can only be conjecture. Whatever his therapy was about, it was difficult work. At one point, Marlon Senior's analyst phoned Marlon Junior, telling him that his father was "very unstable." Might this have been a moment for father and son to come together, facing their demons on common ground? According to his analyst, the elder Brando was "on the brink of a precipice." But his son was unmoved. "When he falls into it," Marlon told the analyst, "call me up and let me know." He shared this story with Janice Mars. "Your voice was hard when you told me this," Mars revealed to him years later. "It shocked me."

For all his newfound equilibrium, Marlon was unable to find any sort of peace with his father, unable to make the sort of gesture he'd made to Anna. He simply could not let the anger go. "That went back so far," Ellen Adler said. Marlon had never forgotten the day he burst into his parents' room after hearing his father strike his mother. "I came close to killing a man once," he told friends. "My father."

In *One-Eyed Jacks*, Rio tells Dad, deceitfully, "A man can't stay angry for five years." Marlon had been angry for thirty years by this point. He burned for revenge against his father in a way not dissimilar to Rio's feelings against Dad. The film's ultimate message, of course, exposes revenge as a hollow, self-defeating emotion. On some level, Marlon understood this. But when it came to his father, he was simply incapable of letting his resentment go.

Thankfully, more uplifting emotion awaited elsewhere.

That summer, Marlon, with Alice Marchak in tow, flew to Tahiti. Tarita had given birth to Marlon's son that past May. She'd named the boy Teihotu. Arriving on the island, Marlon was handed the naked little baby, his dark eyes wide and alert and looking up at his father. Marlon melted. "He fell in love with Teihotu," Alice remembered, "as I did. He was an adorable child." Marlon now had a third chance, a third responsibility, to undo his father's legacy.

**AUGUST 1963** / With mounting outrage, Marlon read the telephone message Alice had taken for him. The past few weeks, he'd been busy coordinating the Hollywood contingent for the up-coming March on Washington for Jobs and Freedom. He'd been on the phone for hours at a time, lining up support, "reduced to practically begging," he said, to get some well-known actors to at-tend, or at least to allow use of their names. He'd assembled quite the impressive list so far—but now, one of the most prominent names was backing out, and for reasons Marlon found cowardly.

Jack Paar, the popular variety show host, was an emotional, high-strung sort of man. He once walked off the set of his live show during a spat with his producers. The press had "heaped vilifica-tion and harm" on him and his family in the past, Paar explained in his message to Marlon. By courting new controversy, Paar said, he was afraid he would be leaving himself open for more abuse.

Furious, Marlon grabbed the typewriter and began banging out a reply. He was "surprised and disappointed" to get Paar's message. "I don't think I need to remind you that the list of people [supporting the March] contains many people, including myself, who have had hostile relations with the press . . . As to the vilifi-cation and harm that has been heaped on you and your family, it is not uncommon or strange to me nor many others who are in support of this action . . . Certainly all of us will suffer to some degree, no matter what we say, from the description of 'publicity seeking personality will stoop to [any] method of gaining atten-tion' to" . . .

Marlon stopped typing. His outrage was getting ahead of him. He never finished the letter. There was no use arguing with people like Paar. Written across the page were the words: NOT SENT.

He'd spent much of the summer organizing for the big event, set for August 28 in Washington, DC. Finally free of movie commitments, he had turned his full energies toward civil rights, helping to organize a Hollywood fund-raiser for the children of the slain Medgar Evers that raised seventeen thousand dollars. He'd also met with NAACP attorney Thomas Neusom to strategize the best ways he could help the cause.

On July 17, he and Neusom had held a joint press conference announcing that Marlon would visit Cambridge, Maryland, where riots had recently broken out over segregated businesses, and Gwynn Oak Park, an amusement park in Baltimore which had also refused to desegregate. Neusom thought Marlon's celebrity might draw attention to the problems there and elsewhere: there was "a need," he said, "for appearances by personalities such as Brando to dramatize the integration movement." Marlon was hoping to make "a simple statement as a private citizen." He was willing to risk arrest, he said, given that the National Guard had issued a ban on protests in Cambridge. If he were attacked, he added, he would "not fight back." He planned to depart on July 21.

But then he was hospitalized with his kidney infection. The NAACP announced that his travel plans were being held "in abeyance" until after he recovered. The usual cynics said Marlon was chickening out, or that he really wasn't all that committed. His response to such talk was to show up for the demonstration in Torrance immediately after his release. Neusom announced that the NAACP was looking into the best place to send him. More than anything, Marlon told friends, he wanted to go into "the deep south" and see the situation there firsthand.

Until then, he concentrated on mobilizing the Hollywood contingent for the march. He hosted the first meeting of the

Hollywood Civil Rights Committee at his bungalow at Universal's Revue Studios on August 4. The purpose of their group, he wrote, was "to support all civil rights legislation now pending before Congress and to improve that legislation; to dramatize the issues for the general public through peaceful demonstration, through meetings with congressmen and senators, through a conference with the president; and to discuss what can be done to follow up after the march."

The first order of business was to raise money to defray the costs for those who wanted to attend but couldn't afford it. Marlon started off the kitty with a thousand dollars. He was matched by Eugene Frenke. Jay Kanter contributed five hundred, as did Charlton Heston, James Garner, and Anthony Franciosa. Carolyn Jones gave two hundred fifty dollars. Those were the original donors, but Marlon rounded up more. It was vital, he believed, for people of all incomes to attend the march. "Without the armies of people who were ragged and poor and angry," he said, "there wouldn't have been a movement." They were "the nameless heroes of the struggle."

On August 7, Marlon and the original committee members held a larger gathering at the Lytton Center for Visual Arts, on Sunset Boulevard. Judy Garland opened the meeting with the Pledge of Allegiance; Charlton Heston read the statement of purpose; and young television actors Peter Brown and Virgil Frye read the Bill of Rights. The proceedings were directed by Billy Wilder. "We're no organization, we have no name," Heston told the press waiting outside the building. "This is all on an individual basis."

Marlon wasn't satisfied with the turnout. He wanted the contingent going to Washington to be absolutely star-studded. That was the best way, he said, to get "average Americans sitting in front of their television sets" to pay attention and grasp "the importance of this cause." He understood the power of celebrity, even if he deplored it. Everyone expected Marlon Brando to show up—and Paul Newman, Shirley MacLaine, and Sammy Davis Jr. So, they needed more than just the usual suspects. Marlon was pressing Billy Wilder to get fellow directors George Sidney and John Sturges to take part. He cabled Doris Day, asking her to come and also to rope in Rock Hudson and Cary Grant. "I have nothing to propose to you," he wrote to Day. "Perhaps as the names come in, you would like to have yours numbered amongst them. At any rate I would very much appreciate five minutes of your time on the telephone." Whether Day granted him those five minutes was not recorded in his notes.

Alice was tasked with compiling lists of the top stars from film, radio, recording, and television. The final catalog of people Marlon reached out to (by letter, cable, or phone) included virtually everyone in the entertainment business, people with whom he'd had limited contact or, in some cases, none at all: Bette Davis, Lana Turner, Rita Hayworth, Red Skelton, Betty Grable, Barbara Stanwyck, Danny Thomas, Milton Berle. As the days went on, he received commitments from Debbie Reynolds, Eartha Kitt, Lena Horne, Burt Lancaster, Sidney Poitier, Gene Kelly, Dean Martin, Gregory Peck, Robert Goulet, and his old friend from New York, Harry Belafonte. Alice was instructed to take over from him on the recruitment efforts because, on August 22, Marlon finally set off on his long-desired mission into the Deep South.

THE PLANE TOUCHED down in Birmingham, Alabama. Here, in this gracious old city, black families were routinely bombed out of their homes. In less than a month's time, there would be another tragic bombing here, this one at the Sixteenth Street Baptist Church. Four little girls would lie dead in the rubble.

The summer had been intense and violent all across the country. Evers had been murdered in Jackson. At Florida A&M, police attacked demonstrators with tear gas. Fannie Lou Hamer, a coordinator for the Student Nonviolent Coordinating Committee, was badly beaten by police in a Mississippi jail. Fights broke out during an NAACP protest of a segregated Philadelphia construction site. In Indiana, the governor was confronted by a burning cross after addressing the local chapter of the NAACP. And in Alabama, where Marlon had just landed, Governor George Wallace had defiantly positioned himself in front of a door at the state university to prevent two black students from entering.

Accompanying Marlon on his trip were Paul Newman, Anthony Franciosa, and the young Virgil Frye. The NAACP had decided that the four actors might do some good in the northern Alabama town of Gadsden, where desegregation demonstrations had led to more than a thousand arrests over the summer. Residents also complained that the town's two main employers, Goodyear and Republic Steel, discriminated in their hiring practices. Gadsden was a stronghold of the Ku Klux Klan; a few years earlier, a Jewish synagogue had been firebombed by American neo-Nazis. Into this "racial hot spot," as the *Chicago Defender* called the town, Marlon and his colleagues hoped to bring some détente. "We are here," Marlon insisted, "as devoted and peaceful representatives of good will, not as agitators, interlopers or interferers." But local officials were already calling them "rabble rousers."

On the bus to Gadsden, Frye was apprehensive. But Marlon, he said, "was cool all the way through." Arriving in the town of fifty-eight thousand, Marlon made a point of speaking with as many black citizens as he could. His intent was to understand the reality of discrimination in a place where it was an everyday fact of life. How did it affect their families? Their children? "He was concerned with how people *felt* about the situation," Frye recalled, "not so much their politics or ideas."

A cheering crowd welcomed them at the Union Methodist Church. Fifteen hundred people packed the pews and spilled out into the street. The four actors were brought up front by Bishop G. W. Garrison, where they took seats on high-backed chairs flanking the pulpit. News crews scrambled for position with their cameras. Just before Garrison opened the rally with a prayer, Marlon leaned over to Frye. "Now remember," he whispered, "don't lick your lips because there are photographers, and they like to catch you with your tongue out."

Each of the actors spoke to the congregation. Marlon promised that the civil rights movement was "a wave that would sweep the nation." The rally was "tumultuous," the *Chicago Defender* reported. People sang and cheered and clapped their hands and stamped their feet. Marlon assured them they'd come to Gadsden to create an "atmosphere for negotiations," pledging to meet with the mayor and the city council, as well as representatives from Goodyear and Republic Steel. "If that fails," he shouted from the pulpit, "we'll try again and we'll try again!" The assembly went wild. The rally ended with the four actors linking hands with the pastor and joining the congregation in a rendition of "We Shall Overcome."

The next day, Marlon and his colleagues were welcomed into the offices of Republic Steel. Promises were made to look into the grievances they presented. Goodyear, however, declined to meet with them, as "company officials were in conference." The actors were also rebuffed by the town's elected leaders. Mayor Leslie Gilliland told a reporter that Marlon and the others were "serving no purpose in Gadsden except to create trouble and chaos." They were just after publicity, the mayor said, drumming up business for their movies. But the minute any one of them stepped out of line, the mayor warned, they would be jailed. Hearing this, Paul Newman told the press that they were willing to go to jail.

Denied meetings with municipal officials, the actors returned to the black community. There, several NAACP field workers displayed an electric cattle prod, the same kind used by some police to break up demonstrations. Marlon took the device into his hands. It was a lightweight stick with electrodes protruding from the end, designed to herd cattle with high-voltage but low-current electric shocks. The cattle prod was the ideal weapon to disable protesters. The electric shocks could be localized to sensitive places on the body, causing fleeting but intense pain—and the process could be repeated many times. Al Lingo, Alabama public safety director, reportedly used a cattle prod to break up antisegregation demonstrations.

Marlon was both fascinated and revolted by the prod. Suddenly he looked up into the faces of the others and suggested they try it on themselves in order to truly understand what it felt like. The actors all submitted to a jolt from the prod. It was some of the worst physical pain Marlon had ever experienced. "When you're stuck with these things," he told a reporter, "you can't control your emotions. What they do down here, Colonel Al Lingo and his state troopers, is to hold you somewhere, in jail or somewhere, and press it into your flesh until the flesh becomes scarified." All this, he alleged, was under the direction of Governor George Wallace.

Marlon was not afraid at this point in his life to call people out by name. When he appeared on *Open End*, he'd told David Susskind that one of the "ugliest Americans," in his opinion, was Louisiana senator Allen Ellender, who'd declared that African Americans had been "incapable of leadership except through the assistance of Europeans." Naming names, Marlon said, was an important tactic in the cause of civil rights: "Some people only respond to public shame." What had been a loathsome act when Kazan and others gave names to Congress was morally justified in this context, Marlon believed; instead of naming the powerless, he was calling out the powerful.

After Gadsden, the group of actors moved on to Washington, DC, where hundreds of thousands were already beginning to gather.

IN THE SUBURBS of the nation's capital, the Pentagon readied nineteen thousand troops in case they were needed to put down an uprising in the city. President Kennedy warned the marchers that violence would not be tolerated. Some white residents were taking no chances, shuttering their windows and double-bolting their doors. Jails in the District were emptied out, with prisoners transported elsewhere to make room for the expected mass arrests. Local hospitals postponed scheduled elective surgeries to leave open beds for riot casualties. The sale of alcoholic beverages was banned throughout the city. And black residents flocked to the Mall, where they were met by people from all over the nation.

The march began at the Washington Monument, where musicians and speakers fired up the crowd. Then the multitudes made their way to the Lincoln Memorial. "That day was frenetic and hot," Marlon would remember. "We were herded here and there and put on the right of Dr. King's people by the Reflecting Pool." In the end, only a few of those celebrities he'd gotten commitments from had actually come. Newman and Franciosa were there, and Charlton Heston, Burt Lancaster, and Joe Mankiewicz. Sidney Poitier, too, and Harry Belafonte—who'd convinced the Los Angeles theater he was appearing at to release him for the day so he could attend. With another old pal, James Baldwin, Marlon enjoyed an emotional reunion.

From their privileged vantage point, the Hollywood group listened to the collection of speakers. Walter Reuther, John Lewis, and Floyd McKissick had the crowd cheering and whistling. There were shorter speeches, too, from Rabbi Joachim Prinz, of the American Jewish Congress, and singer Josephine Baker, the American who'd found fame in Europe. Finally, at the close of the afternoon, just when people's throats were growing sore from cheering, Martin Luther King Jr. took the podium.

Marlon had never been so transfixed by a speech. "The timber in his voice was such that you knew he was speaking from the bottom of his soul," he said of King.

There was little time to bask in the moment, however. Marlon, Heston, Poitier, Mankiewicz, Baldwin, and Belafonte were hustled over to the television studio of the U.S. Information Agency, where they were asked to give their opinions on what the march meant. Marlon was feeling heady and inspired, but not so reverent that he didn't surprise Mankiewicz with a quick jolt from the cattle prod, which he'd brought from Gadsden. "That was what was so great about Marlon's sense of humor," Joe's son Tom Mankiewicz said. "You never knew when it would appear."

When it came time for him to speak, however, Marlon was appropriately serious. "This is a revolution that is sweeping our country," he told moderator David Schoenbrun. Americans, he said, had a chance to transform themselves. It couldn't just be political, Marlon insisted; change had to come from the heart. "The inherent anger that goes on in all men, no matter where you look," he said, "whether in Franco's Spain or Chiang Kai-shek's government, gives evidence to the fact that we are—all human beings— filled with anguish and hatred and fear."

Certainly, Marlon wrestled with his own anguish and fear. Over the past few years, he'd looked some of his devils in the face— not all of them, but more than he'd ever confronted in the past— and experienced some transformations of his own. As he sat there discoursing on the need for Americans to examine their souls, Marlon knew what he was talking about. He'd done at least some of the work he was asking his fellow Americans to do. His remarks came across as rambling at times, that old struggle of his to express exactly what he meant. But even through the cloud of words, his gist was clear enough. Anguish and hatred and fear were what the march was intending to overcome. "I think," Marlon told the television camera, "it is one step closer to trying to understand the human heart."

Cynics be damned: Marlon had no time for them. He was never so earnest or so sincere as he was that day, surrounded by colleagues he respected, celebrating a monumental triumph of the human spirit. He was filled with hope and optimism for the future. The revolution, he said, was inevitable. Racism, he believed, could be vanquished. The buildup to war in Vietnam could be stopped. After all, the number of executions in the country had dropped to less than half what it was a year ago, and pundits were now predicting an end to capital punishment. America was on the right path, Marlon believed. He was filled with optimism. Once people learned the truth, he was convinced, they would do the right thing.

Such confidence Marlon exuded that day.

How different he is as we take our leave of him this time compared to eight years before. Bracketed by James Baldwin and Joseph Mankiewicz, Marlon is calm, determined, and utterly secure in the choices he has made.

# A

# FAMILY

# MAN

**FALL 1970** / Marlon was being obstinate. The book had sat unopened on his desk for months. Alice kept telling him to read it. But the more she pressed, the more he resisted. *The Godfather*, by Mario Puzo, had been a fixture on the *New York Times* bestseller list for more than a year. Alice reminded her boss that the author wanted him to play the lead in a film adaptation. The role might just be Marlon's ticket back to the top.

But the forty-six-year-old wasn't looking for any comeback. While Marlon hadn't turned out a successful film in more than a decade, he despised the idea of making movies more than ever. Bitter and resentful, all the hope and optimism of seven years earlier had drained out of him. He remained steadfast in his refusal to read the book. It was about gangsters, he grumbled to Alice, and he didn't want to glorify criminals.

Besides, the letter from the author had rubbed him the wrong way. "I think you're the only actor who can play the part with that quiet force and irony the part requires," Puzo wrote. "I really think you'd be tremendous. Needless to say I've been an admirer of your art." Marlon had tossed the letter aside. Using flattery and cajolery and talk about his "art" was never the way to win him over.

That fall, it was nearly impossible to get Marlon to do anything. The previous spring and summer had been pretty much the same. Conversations such as the one he was having with Alice about *The*

*Godfather* usually ended with him suddenly and simply going quiet and, in a sulk, wandering off. No more incognito strolls through Los Angeles. Instead, Marlon prowled around his backyard on Mulholland Drive, his head down, his shoulders hunched, pacing the perimeter of his property like a caged lion. From inside, his staff pressed their faces against the glass to watch him.

In Hollywood, Marlon was a pariah. Director John Boorman had wanted him for his film *Deliverance*, but Warner Bros. chairman Ted Ashley had balked: "Brando? Oh, God. He doesn't mean a thing anymore—he's box office poison." The total domestic revenues for Marlon's movies from 1964 to 1967 added up to $9.5 million, which was what *Guys and Dolls* had racked up *all on its own* in its first year of release. "I couldn't get arrested," Marlon said, looking back on this period.

The lack of work wasn't what depressed him, of course. What sunk his spirits by the early 1970s was the state of the world, which had come undone since the high of the March on Washington. Just months after that glorious assembly, President Kennedy had been assassinated. Five years later, Martin Luther King Jr. was himself gunned down, and not long afterward, Robert Kennedy, Marlon's last hope to turn things around, was murdered as well. America, Marlon regretfully concluded, had missed its chance to transform itself. The hate and the fear went far deeper than he had ever imagined. Once upon a time Marlon had thought if people only knew what was happening, understood the injustices, they would come around. But the battle, as he now understood, would be much longer, much harder, and much bloodier than he'd anticipated.

Worst of all, he'd lost the agency to have an impact. Seven years ago, Marlon had been a champion, with the power to take on the culture. Now he was a washed-up movie actor, yesterday's news, without any power at all.

Marlon's fame had only ever been good for one thing, he believed. The platform it gave him to call attention to matters he cared about. He'd never gotten to make his film about Chessman, but he, and others, had made sure the issue of capital punishment remained front and center, and they'd made a difference. But now Marlon's name guaranteed no crowds, no headlines. None of the films he'd made under his MCA-Universal deal had made any money. He'd banked his salary just as he'd planned, but when the deal was done, no one was asking him to renew.

He'd had one chance to reclaim his crown. In 1968, Marlon had agreed to star in Elia Kazan's *The Arrangement*, the most personal project the director had ever undertaken, based on his own novel and script. Despite the personal and political distance between the former collaborators, their mutual respect had endured: Marlon frequently cited Kazan as "the best," and Kazan still considered Marlon "the best actor in the country." But Marlon had gotten off track, Kazan believed; the director had "never admired versatility in acting as a matter of new accents [and] different costumes"—an obvious swipe at *Teahouse, Sayonara, Mutiny*, and most of Marlon's other films since 1954. *The Arrangement*, Kazan hoped, would bring his one-time disciple "back from some bad outings." Discussions of the script got under way, and Marlon was even measured for the hairpieces he'd wear in the film.

Then, suddenly, he backed out. Calling Kazan to his home, Marlon met the director in his driveway. He was distraught, rambling on about the "terrible state the country was in," Kazan remembered. Just days before, King had been assassinated. Marlon told Kazan he couldn't do the movie, not now. "He kissed me and looked so sorry I didn't ask any questions," Kazan said. Driving away, the director watched Marlon through his rearview mirror, slouching back toward his house. "He looked desolate," Kazan said. The two men never saw each other again.

Many people, including Kazan, thought Marlon wasn't entirely sincere. "The depth of emotion he projected came as much from his talent as from his sense of tragedy," Kazan wrote in his memoir. The press also suspected a ruse. BRANDO: A CRUSADE OR A COP-OUT? asked the *Chicago Tribune*: "The scuttlebutt is that he either a) was never offered the role in the first place, or b) was asked to withdraw because of his controversial activities or his waning box office appeal."

The scuttlebutt was wrong. Once again, cynical eyes could not perceive genuine convictions. The murder of the man Marlon had considered the nation's savior was "overwhelming" to him, he said in his official announcement. "There are issues facing us with which I think everyone ought to concern himself first and fore-most." On *The Tonight Show*, he acknowledged that dropping out of Kazan's film was "a tough decision." But as he'd sat glued to the television coverage of King's death, Marlon knew he couldn't con-centrate on making a movie. "As I watched the news reports, they showed [King's] last words the night before, and he said he'd been to the mountain and he'd seen the promised land [but] he said, 'I don't know if I'm going to get there.'" King, Marlon believed, was passing the torch to others to continue his work. "I thought," Marlon said, "somehow this has got to matter. If we don't all, as citizens, do something, person to person, we won't have any place to come home to." From that perspective, his decision to withdraw from Kazan's film was obvious to him. "I couldn't think of any other alternative," Marlon explained, "than to make my time, my energy and my money fully available to do what I can as an indi-vidual to rectify the situation we're in."

For the past two years, Marlon had done just that. On *The To-night Show* he'd made an appeal for all Americans to donate no less than 1 percent of their annual income to the Southern Christian Leadership Conference in order to "further King's philosophy and his good works." He'd succeeded in getting commitments from Barbra Streisand, Merv Griffin, Joey Bishop, Paul Newman, Joanne Woodward, and Johnny Carson. Marlon himself was contributing 10 percent of his income. The effort needed to be extraordinary, he said, because racism was so deeply ingrained in America. "I think all of us," Marlon said, "if we mine the deepest areas of our feelings, will find maybe some trace of that. We've got to find it and root it out."

That hadn't happened. Few others joined Marlon's list of donors; certainly, there was no grassroots groundswell to his cause. In the fall of 1968, Richard Nixon had won the presidency using a strategy of attracting white Democrats in the South who were opposed to full civil rights for black Americans. Meanwhile, the war in Vietnam raged, with American deaths reaching almost seventeen thousand in the year of King's assassination. The U.S. government, Marlon charged, "was burning up villages and children in the name of democracy and Christ."

At the root of Marlon's depression, as he stood there two years later in the darkness of his backyard, was a crippling despair about the world. When finally he snapped out of his fugue and marched back inside the house, he did what he usually did after one of these episodes: he began to rant. It was the same old pattern of depressive episodes followed by manic ones, only now those episodes happened much more quickly, sometimes two or three in the course of a day. Marlon could not bear feeling pessimistic; it seemed congenitally abhorrent to him. When the despair got to be too much, he fought it with anger and with something that approached nihilism: *if we can't change it, let's burn it all down and start over.* That was his worldview by the fall of 1970.

When he'd worked for the American League for a Free Palestine, Marlon had sympathized with the militants in the movement who'd advocated direct action (some called it terrorism) against the British occupiers. Now his politics went similarly radical. After a seventeen-year-old Black Panther by the name of Bobby Hutton was fatally shot in Oakland while surrendering to police, Marlon had spoken at the young man's funeral, charging police with the boy's murder. In response, the Oakland Police Officers Association had sued him for libel for $26 million. (The case rolled on for years, ending finally in a settlement.) Marlon also befriended such radical leaders as Hakim Jamal, spokesman for the Malcolm X Organization of Afro-American Unity, and New Left activist Tariq Ali, to whom he called American involvement in Southeast Asia as "immoral as that of Nazi Germany and Fascist Italy in Spain during the 1930s."

By the fall of 1970, Marlon was both depressed and angry, and utterly convinced that something bad was coming. He'd once predicted civil war if changes weren't made fast enough. Now the streets and campuses of America were on fire. Since 1963, race riots had broken out in New York, Rochester, Philadelphia, and the Watts section of Los Angeles. After King's death, the unrest only grew, tearing apart Detroit, Washington, Chicago, Baltimore, Louisville, and elsewhere. Most recently, students had been shot dead in antiwar protests at Kent State University and Jackson State College. So worried about civil unrest was Marlon that he told Alice to buy "twelve shotguns and twelve revolvers," his friend, the photographer Gordon Parks, remembered. Marlon was ready to go "out in the street," Parks said, if necessary, to defend himself and his home.

No longer was he King's disciple of nonviolence assuring reporters, as he had back in 1963, that if he were attacked, he would not fight back. When he wasn't too depressed to move, Marlon was itching to fight. The Charles Manson murders left him even more convinced of a world gone mad. "Mulholland Drive is full of crazy people," Marlon said. More than once, he'd gone after intruders on his property with his gun, forcing them to lie down so he could frisk them. When asked if he'd had his finger on the trigger at these times, Marlon replied, "Damn right I did." He insisted he would "kill somebody" if they came for him. "I wouldn't hesitate."

"It was a dark period of Marlon's life," said one friend. "Frightened, resentful, angry, deeply paranoid." He was certain he was being watched. Every night around eleven, Marlon noticed a truck from the electric company parked outside his house. Finally he trooped down his driveway and tapped on the truck's window to ask what the problem was. "Oh, just fixing the lines," the man in the truck told him. Marlon decided to smoke him out. "I happen to know something about electricity," he recalled, "so I asked some questions and the guy in charge gave me dumb answers." That cinched it for Marlon. He was being spied on.

Some of his friends thought he was being absurd. But, in fact, as a Freedom of Information Act request proved, the Federal Bureau of Investigation had indeed been keeping tabs on Marlon since at least December 1968, when a joke he'd made while boarding a flight to Colombia ("Is this the flight to Havana?") had gotten him into trouble. Alarmed by recent Cuban hijackings and not recognizing Marlon due to his beard, the airline had bumped him off the plane; after realizing their mistake, they'd tried to get him to reboard, but the offended actor took another flight. From that point on, FBI director J. Edgar Hoover kept an open file on Marlon. "Brando is known to have participated in various anti-war and civil rights protests in the past," Hoover wrote as his reason. "He has publicly supported the Black Panther party."

Sometimes even paranoids have enemies, after all.

MARLON'S DEPRESSION WENT deeper still. Something else more fundamental was tearing at him, something he would do his best to avoid and deflect for as long as he possibly could, for fear of the darkness it portended.

His room was filled with pictures of his children. He sat in there with the lights turned off, "actively thinking," as Alice would describe him, looking at the faces of his children and ruminating on what had gone wrong in his life. How had he come to this place, when a decade earlier everything had seemed so hopeful? Marlon knew he was going to have to do something eventually. Civil war or no civil war, he was going to need money to get by. He was too old to make a different kind of a living now; that ship had sailed. And while he still only wanted "enough" and not a surplus of cash, he had, by now, *two* expensive ex-wives: the marriage to Movita had ended in 1968 with a considerable settlement. He was also sending large sums of money to Tarita. And, significantly, he was still tithing 10 percent of his annual income to the Southern Christian Leadership Conference, even after some of the other donors had backed out. "Just a note to let you know how grateful I am for what you are continuing to do," Coretta Scott King wrote to him. "Friends like you have made [difficult times] less difficult."

He was thinking of his children's educations, Marlon would say, when he agreed late that fall to take a part in a British picture, *The Nightcomers*. A prequel to Henry James's *The Turn of the Screw*, *The Nightcomers* was being marketed for the horror genre, always the port of last call for aging former stars. Marlon knew the picture wasn't going to make him a fortune, but at least he would be paid up front and on time. Soon enough he'd need to start thinking about colleges for Christian.

Finally, sometime during the holidays, Marlon picked up *The Godfather* and started to read.

**DECEMBER 1970** / Marlon watched in the mirror as his old pal Phil Rhodes expertly lined his eyes with kohl. He scowled, making himself look mean. Phil used a charcoal stick to darken Marlon's eyebrows, then slicked his graying blondish hair with black shoe polish. Marlon studied himself in the mirror, turning his head this way and that.

Behind them, Alice Marchak was observing the transformation.

Turning his chair, Marlon spoke to her in an Italian accent. She shrugged. He tried it a different way, attempting to sound more like an Italian from New York. Phil plopped a fedora on his head. They played with it in several different ways before discarding the hat altogether.

Marlon was endeavoring to find the character of Don Vito Corleone, the mighty Godfather of Puzo's novel. He'd read the book, cover to cover, in just a few sittings. Reading novels wasn't Marlon's favorite pastime. Give him a book of science or philosophy or poetry, and he was much happier. But he'd devoured Puzo's tale of an Italian Mafia family living daily with moral quandaries. In Puzo's letter, he found a passage far more compelling than the flattery. *The Godfather*, its author contended, was "an ironical comment on American society." Marlon agreed. "It was a mythology of a man who cares about family values and who was forced into the circumstances," he said of the book. It was also "a comparison between the manner in which big business conducts itself and the manner in which the Mafia conducts itself"—which, to Marlon's mind, wasn't really all that different. This was the stuff of a worthwhile movie.

So, he told Francis Ford Coppola, the film's young director, who also wanted him, that he was on board—so long as Paramount agreed.

That remained doubtful. The whole town shared Ted Ashley's opinion that he was "box-office poison." Moreover, he was a troublemaker. The suits wanted Laurence Olivier, Ernest Borgnine, Edward G. Robinson, or Anthony Quinn (who'd been dogging Marlon's career since *Streetcar*) to play Don Corleone. Or even Danny Thomas, the television host and sitcom star. "Anyone but Brando" was the message delivered loudly and strongly to Coppola and Puzo. WILL NOT FINANCE BRANDO IN TITLE ROLE, Paramount cabled. DO NOT RESPOND. CASE CLOSED.

Marlon resolved to get the part. For the first time in his career, he set out to actively persuade producers to cast him. It wasn't just dollar signs driving him, even though *The Godfather* was being touted as potentially a gigantic moneymaker. Something else was going on with Marlon. For the first time in many years, his creative impulses were fired up. Not since possibly *Waterfront* had the creation of a character so excited him. And as usually happened when his creativity was sparked, his depression lifted. The rants about the state of the world declined; the despair retreated; the darkness was vanquished once more.

Marlon asked Phil to help with makeup. For several days he tried different accents with Alice. He needed to get this right, because he'd agreed to do a screen test. Marlon Brando—onetime box-office champ, Academy Award winner, the "greatest of all time," in the opinion of many—was submitting to being tested as if he'd never made a movie before, as if he were twenty-one years old again and testing for *Rebel Without a Cause*. That was how determined Marlon was to get the part.

Coppola, of course, didn't refer to it as a screen test; the thirty-one-year-old director told Marlon he was just coming by his house to shoot some "experimental footage." George Englund, however, called it for what it was. Marlon just shrugged. "I guess you could call it that," he acknowledged.

The stakes were high for Coppola as well. He'd had a few successes since his directorial debut in 1962, but he hoped *The Godfather* would propel him into the major leagues. The idea of possibly working with Brando was thrilling, despite how far the star had fallen in the industry's favor. Coppola was of the generation who'd grown up with *Streetcar* and *Waterfront*; who'd witnessed, at a young, impressionable age, the power and newness of Marlon Brando. No matter how paunchy Brando had gotten, how slouchy and red-eyed, the director was still in awe. In Coppola's eyes, Marlon was still Terry Malloy in the backseat of that taxi.

So, when the director showed up bright and early at Marlon's house one morning that winter, he was prepared for magic. Coppola would always believe that what he observed that day was an impromptu audition on the star's part, a spontaneous expression of Brando's artistry. Apparently, Coppola did not know about the rehearsals with Phil Rhodes; only many years later did Alice reveal those. Yet, any earlier preparation should not diminish Marlon's exercise that morning with Coppola; it simply underscores how, for the first time in many years, the enterprise of acting actually excited him.

Coppola had brought along a couple of assistants to Mulholland Drive. One lugged a camera and the other a box of props: provolone cheese, cigars, some olives. Coppola had heard Marlon didn't like noise, so he told his assistants as they approached the house to be very quiet. "We'll do hand signals like ninjas to set up the camera and get ready for him," Coppola instructed.

There was a stealthy pause as the three of them waited for Marlon to appear. Finally, he made a star entrance from his bedroom, wearing a Japanese robe, his long hair tied back in a ponytail. Marlon spoke little as he watched Coppola set up his props. Out came the cheese, the olives; the cigars were placed on the table.

"Marlon got the drift of what I was doing," Coppola remembered. Once everything was arranged, Marlon stood and moved around the room. Almost lethargically at first, he began to inhabit the character. Coppola had the presence of mind to switch on his camera.

The first thing Marlon did was untie his ponytail. Then he opened the makeup case Phil Rhodes had given him and slicked his hair back with the shoe polish. Sauntering over to the table, he sampled the provolone and the olives. At last he spoke—in a low, raspy voice that was not his own. "In the book," Marlon told Coppola, "he gets shot in the throat. So I think he should talk like this." In awe, Coppola watched as Marlon took tissue paper and stuffed it into his cheeks, making his voice even more garbled. "He should be like a bulldog," he told the director, turning to face the camera with his jowls. At one point, the phone rang. Marlon answered, still in character. "And I'm amazed," Coppola said, "because this transformation is happening from this handsome guy with a po-nytail into this Italian guy like my Uncle Louie."

At last he told his assistant to switch off the camera. They'd got-ten what they'd come for—even more, perhaps. "So now I have this extraordinary tape," Coppola remembered, "so I figure I'm going to take it to Charlie Bluhdorn," the head of Paramount. He hopped on a plane to New York. One chance in a million, people called the odds that the Paramount chief would agree to hire Brando.

Bluhdorn was a hot-tempered, foul-mouthed Austrian with an accent as thick as concrete. He watched with deep skepticism as Coppola set up his video player. When Marlon appeared in his po-nytail and kimono, Bluhdorn began to bark, "No, no, I told you absolutely—"

And then, suddenly, as Coppola would describe the moment, Bluhdorn fell uncharacteristically quiet, mesmerized by the meta-morphosis he was witnessing on the tape. "That's incredible," he breathed at last.

Marlon Brando would be the Godfather.

**JANUARY 1971** / Marlon's casting, announced on January 27, 1971, topped entertainment columns all over the country. The naysayers didn't wait long to sound off. Columnist Vernon Scott complained that Marlon was a "white, Anglo-Saxon Midwest-erner" and about a decade too young to play Corleone. Would the millions of Puzo's readers accept "mumbling Marlon in the role of the dignified, brutal, scheming godfather?" Scott likened the casting to Audrey Hepburn getting the lead in *My Fair Lady* over Julie Andrews, who'd done the part on Broadway, because she was considered more recognizable at the box office. Except, as Scott pointed out, Marlon's earning power was hardly dependable these days, because his acting had become "stylized" and "predictable." Perhaps, the columnist concluded, "with makeup and talent Brando hasn't tapped yet," he could pull it off.

The critics had once hailed Marlon as the master, in full control of his prodigious talents; now, proving how far he'd fallen in the public estimation, a critic was suggesting there were talents he had yet to tap. Marlon rarely read the columns, but he knew what people were saying about him. He professed not to care, but the old competitive streak was still there. He hoped for a comeback with *The Godfather* not so much to prove his weight as an actor, but to prove the naysayers wrong.

Whatever personal satisfaction he took in his victory, however, was muted. Not long before his casting was announced, Marlon got word that Christian had run away from his boarding school in Ojai, California. No one knew where the boy was until Marlon got a phone call from JoAn Corrales, an old friend who lived in Washington State. Christian had traveled more than one thousand miles, largely by hitchhiking, in order to take refuge with Corrales, who had a son his age and who offered him the sort of safe harbor he'd never known elsewhere.

This was the heaviness Marlon carried around with him, of which he almost never spoke. This was the deepest root of his depression and despair. This wasn't the first time Christian had run away. At twelve years old, the boy was already smoking tobacco and marijuana. Marlon would become furious with his son, apparently not making the connection between the ways Christian was acting out now and the ways he himself had acted out when he was that age, facing similar family troubles: a mother who drank too much and a distant father who couldn't control his anger.

Marlon was now playing Brando Senior to a Brando Junior. His own father had been dead these past six years, taken by heart trouble—some might have said that that was the old man's trouble all along. If Marlon had a playbook for parenting, it was to do the exact opposite of his father, but that lacked much practical application. He never berated Christian the way his father had berated him, and he made sure to praise the boy when he occasionally brought home good grades. But empathy was in short supply. Instead, Marlon just got angry.

When Christian was little, it had been easy to be a good father: putting him up on his shoulders, horsing around with him in the swimming pool, taking him for ice cream and hot dogs. But now Marlon had no idea what to do with him. From the fertile depths of his imagination, he had brought memorable characters to vivid, emotional life. He'd just won over a hardened opponent by acting with brilliance and skill. But father to a troubled adolescent boy? That was one role Marlon had very little conception of how to play.

**MARCH 10** / With his eyes closed, Marlon sat in a chair at Filmways Studios on East 127th Street in Harlem, a barber's cape draped across his chest. Applying latex jowls to his face were the makeup men, Dick Smith and his own Phil Rhodes. Many of Marlon's own innovations were being incorporated into the character. His eyebrows were darkened, his hair clipped and greased. After two hours, Marlon was feeling slightly groggy, but when he finally opened his eyes and looked in the mirror, he'd been transformed (jowls, bags, and Italian eyes) into the Godfather.

Phil removed the cape and helped him out of the chair. Standing in just a tee shirt, Marlon was told to lift his arms. A fake foam stomach was attached to his waist. Pads were secured to round his shoulders and make his neck look squatter. Over that went a gray double-breasted suit. As a last effect, weights were inserted into Marlon's shoes to give him a heavy, ponderous walk.

Finally, he emerged from the makeup room. As he strode onto the set, he took the breath away from the assembled cast and crew. So impressed was producer Al Ruddy that he decided to keep the star's appearance a secret from the public; no photos would be released ahead of time, so that the finished picture would offer a big surprise. Ruddy anticipated all the columnists wondering how the forty-six-year-old Brando would be turned into the sixtyish crime boss. Classic Hollywood hucksterism, of course, but Marlon went along with it.

He was going along with lots of things on this picture that he wouldn't have tolerated on earlier films. For one thing, he was working for no money up front. He'd never done that before, certainly not on *The Nightcomers*, which he'd finished shortly before starting *The Godfather*. He had also, somewhat miraculously, agreed to put up a bond for any overruns he caused. A decade wasn't long enough to dim producers' memories of *One-Eyed Jacks* or *Mutiny on the Bounty*. He did all this because he was counting on *The Godfather*, frankly, to make him solvent for the rest of his life—or at least a good portion of it. He'd finally bought Teti'aroa, and was building a marine sanctuary there; it would be nice to finally get that finished.

Marlon trusted he was making a low-risk investment. Puzo's book was popular; the odds were that the picture would be a hit. George Englund told him that *The Godfather* was "the hottest picture going." He'd gone into other projects, of course, over the past several years that had also been touted as the "hottest thing," only to end up disappointed: *The Chase* and *Reflections in a Golden Eye*. And those two films had boasted well-respected directors, Arthur Penn and John Huston, while *The Godfather* was being helmed by the relatively unknown Coppola. Stomping across the set in his heavy shoes, Marlon had no guarantee that this film wouldn't turn out to be just one more clunker in his long list of them.

Nonetheless, he'd prepared well for the part. The more Marlon studied the script, written by Puzo in collaboration with Coppola, the more he saw parallels to issues that mattered to him. If the Mafia had been "black or socialist," Marlon said, "Corleone would have been dead or in jail." But because the crime bosses patterned themselves so closely on corporate America, "and dealt in a hard-nosed way with money," they prospered.

"The Mafia is so American," Marlon said. A "key phrase" in Puzo's story had resonated for him: "Whenever they wanted to kill somebody," Marlon said, "it was always a matter of policy. Before pulling the trigger, the Godfather's gangsters would say, 'Just business, nothing personal.'" Reading that, Marlon couldn't help but think of Robert McNamara, Lyndon Johnson, and Dean Rusk, whom he considered the architects of the Vietnam War.

Coppola had sent him tapes of organized crime figures being grilled at Senate hearings chaired by Estes Kefauver of Tennessee. But Marlon wasn't interested in doing imitations. He knew people in the Mafia. They'd been moving through his life and across his film sets since *Waterfront*. "I've met Mafia people," he said, "and Mafia people vary as much as the people who run Con Edison." He wanted to create a character out of whole cloth, assembling him from bits of memory, instinct, and imagination, the way he'd done with all his most memorable roles.

The last time Marlon had really thrown himself, body and soul, into creating a character had been with Fletcher Christian in *Mutiny*, and he'd been opposed, thwarted, and mocked in the effort. Without a supportive, trustworthy director, he had learned, the process was nearly impossible. Only Kazan had been able to partner with Marlon in the way he desired, though Joe Mankiewicz had proven valuable on *Julius Caesar*. Marlon had also found "a very close rapport on an artistic level" with Gillo Pontecorvo, the director of his most recent film, *Burn!*, but he'd also considered the Italian a "martinet" and almost came to blows with him. Now it was Coppola's turn at bat. Whether the young whippersnapper would be helpful or obstructionist in Marlon's manufacture of Corleone remained to be seen.

So far, the signs looked promising. The whole bit with the cigars and provolone cheese had gone over well with Marlon; that was how you got the ball rolling. Indeed, Kazan might have done something similar. Coppola provided just enough direction for Marlon to take things to the next level on his own. That was a winning formula. "He gives you space to find what you need to do," Marlon told a friend about Coppola just before shooting began.

Yet much more than latex jowls would be needed to fully flesh out Vito Corleone; the hard work was ahead, and Marlon knew it. Everyone was impressed with how he'd stuffed tissue in his mouth to change his voice, but that was just affectation, Marlon believed. "I don't think that because you put something in your mouth you develop a character," he said. "That's what Charlton Heston does—puts a wig on, or a beard, and he calls that a characterization. It's silly self-delusion." The real process of characterization was interior, and that was what Marlon set out to do that March of 1971 at Filmways Studios. Nearly every director since Kazan had failed him. Would the young Francis Ford Coppola prove a help or a hindrance?

ON AN ECHOING Filmways soundstage, with space heaters to ward off the damp and the cold, Coppola called his cast together. They included James Caan as the Don's eldest son, John Cazale as his middle son, Al Pacino as his youngest, Talia Shire (Coppola's sister) as his daughter, Robert Duvall as his unofficially adopted son and consigliere, and Diane Keaton as his future daughter-in-law. As the actors looked over the latest version of the script, Coppola explained that they'd be building their characters over a two-week period of rehearsals. Two weeks was all the producers were allowing them, the director lamented; he'd wanted more. "A play has six, seven weeks" to develop interior motivations and relationships between characters, Coppola argued. So, they were going to have to learn fast.

In fact, the *Streetcar Named Desire* company had had only three weeks to rehearse, but they'd also had the luxury of previews to get everything perfect before their Broadway debut. In moviemaking, there were few luxuries. In just fourteen days, according to the schedule approved by the top brass at Paramount, Coppola was required to call his first "Action!" and get the cameras rolling. Marlon made no complaints about the lack of rehearsal time. Two weeks was, in fact, more than he'd had on his recent films, so he was glad enough.

Filmways had been MGM's East Coast facility in the 1920s; it was old and drafty and cavernous. The actors wrapped blankets over their shoulders to keep warm. On one of the larger soundstages, Coppola paced back and forth "like a wind-up toy," one observer recalled, describing the entire film, sometimes down to very specific scenes, though not necessarily in the order they would appear in the finished product. "I think more spatially, less linear," Coppola would recall, "so I need to see the whole thing in order to be motivated to go on. I want all of it at once, to bring it up the way a Polaroid picture comes out."

The younger members of the cast clustered around a table, some of them making notes on their scripts. Marlon sat off to the side in an easy chair, his eyes mostly on Coppola. During *Streetcar* rehearsals, he'd been the one to pace. Now, twenty-four years later, he sat "Buddha-like," a press agent thought, watching, listening, and possibly judging them all.

Coppola stopped his pacing and told the cast he had an idea. He wanted them to play some scenes he had in mind, scenes just for the rehearsals—"not in the shooting script," he said—scenes that would give them "memories" to carry with them through their performances. No doubt, from his comfortable repose, the Buddha stirred a little at this. "One thing I often do," Coppola explained, "is have a scene where two characters meet for the first time, even though in the story they've already known each other for a while. I find that giving the cast sensual memories always helps them. As artists, as they're playing a scene, just the fact that they share a memory—it becomes like a little emotional deposit in their bank account that enables them to better know each other."

Now *this* was the sort of direction Marlon could respond to. Indeed, Kazan himself might have suggested such a thing—or Stella, back at the Dramatic Workshop. "When you have really talented actors," Coppola explained, "and they have been properly prepared and properly rehearsed, you never know when something you couldn't have planned, or couldn't have caused, might happen. You keep adding stimuli to invite that kind of accident." If Marlon had harbored any doubts about whether he could work with Coppola, they were alleviated during those first few days of rehearsals.

Coppola had learned his lessons the hard way. As a young director, fresh out of UCLA film school, he'd honed his craft on low-budget shockers such as *The Terror* and *Dementia 13*, eventually earning his stripes on *You're a Big Boy Now*, which he'd also written; Geraldine Page was nominated for a Best Supporting Actress Oscar for her part as a clinging mother. He'd gone on to direct *Finian's Rainbow* and *The Rain People*, but a big box-office hit had so far eluded him. Coppola had founded his own company, American Zoetrope, to subvert the studio structure he felt was stifling him, but he realized he'd also been stifling himself. Looking back at his films, he'd spot "some incredible thing" start to happen, and then "some schmuck" would say, "Cut." The schmuck was himself, he said. "The mere fact that [a scene] felt wrong when you were watching [it] meant that something had *happened*," Coppola recalled—and as a director, he had gotten in the way of it. He wasn't going to allow that to recur on *The Godfather.*

On Wednesday evening, March 17, Saint Patrick's Day, a cool but clear night with a bright moon, Coppola trooped his cast down the block to Patsy's, a neighborhood institution since 1933. According to no less an authority than Frank Sinatra, Patsy's served the finest pizza in the world. The owner, Pasquale "Patsy" Lancieri, welcomed Coppola and the others, turning over his wood-paneled back room to them and whipping up a classic Italian feast: antipasti, spaghetti, meatballs, lasagna. But this wasn't a night off for the *Godfather* company. The restaurant's Italian accents and aromas of oregano and baking crust provided ambience but even more than that: it gave the actors an opportunity to deepen their characterizations. As his cast took their seats around the long dining table, Coppola told them to consider this a real Corleone family dinner. They were to stay in character, improvising, the director said, "for two or three hours, over a meal, that they were a family."

At first, there was some awkwardness at playacting in a restaurant. "We were all new to each other," John Cazale remembered. "We stood there not knowing what to do." It was Marlon, he said, who "broke the ice." This was precisely the kind of exercise that inspired him, that made him remember why, all those years ago, acting had seemed fun and creative. He opened a bottle of wine just as the patriarch of the family would do, and then began pouring glasses for all his children. Sitting at the head of the table, Marlon was served his meal by the women in the cast, the way dutiful Italian wives and daughters were supposed to do. The men, like dutiful sons, responded swiftly and respectfully to everything Marlon said. "Everyone was doing what their roles were," Al Pacino recalled. "You couldn't help it."

In those couple of hours at Patsy's, Marlon became the powerful Don, presiding over the table. "I think we all realized then that he was acting with us the way the Don would have acted with his own family," said Cazale.

Marlon took to the role of paterfamilias as if he had been born to it. It was fortunate how strongly Stella had always emphasized imagination as the bedrock of performance, because in life, Marlon had little experience as a wise, respected patriarch. *The Godfather*, in fact, was the first time in his career he'd ever played a father. It was a role he had yet to master in real life as well. Marlon now had as many children as Don Vito Corleone, but he never knew a family dinner like the one he playacted at Patsy's.

LIKE THE DON, Marlon had three sons, Christian, Miko, and Tei-hotu, who was also sometimes called Simon. Also like the Don, he now had a daughter. A year before, Tarita had given birth to Chey-enne. When Marlon visited Tahiti after the birth, he'd been struck by how much the baby girl resembled his mother.

One of his greatest regrets, he would say, was that he could never hope to have all of his children with him at the same time.

One night around this time, Marlon received a phone call from Alice. In Los Angeles, Anna was acting out, drunk again, and Christian was angry and in tears. For a day, Marlon moped around the set before taking control of himself again. Eight years earlier, he'd offered to stay away from his son if his absence might bene-fit the boy. But Anna had quickly unraveled. Her alcoholism got worse; in 1964, she'd attempted suicide, leaving six-and-a-half-year-old Christian to call the operator when she failed to awaken. Rush-ing to the house, Marlon had found "empty bottles thrown on the floor" and his son hungry from not having eaten since the day be-fore. No doubt the scene sent him back thirty-five years, to when his own mother lay unconscious on the bed. And so the custody battles roared back to life. At one point, Anna kidnapped Christian from Marlon's house and hid out at a motel, drunkenly attacking Marlon in the parking lot when he came to get his son.

Was this what drew Marlon so strongly to the role of the Godfather? "I often wondered if one of the reasons he admired Don Corleone so," said Jack Larson, "was because he was such a successful family man in addition to businessman." There was no way Vito Corleone would have allowed an ex-wife to mistreat his son, or the courts to keep his son away from him. But Marlon's own failure to gain full custody of Christian left him both frustrated and infuriated. Despite the principal of Christian's Montessori school reporting a "marvelous" change in the boy's mood whenever he was living with his father, the court never acted to take him away from Anna, reluctant to remove a child from his mother's care even in the worst of circumstances. Of course, stories of women slapping Marlon with paternity suits (the latest being Marie Cui) hadn't helped his case either.

So, Christian remained with Anna, even as she continued spiraling downward. Neighbors would later testify to hearing physical abuse. One time Anna locked Christian, no more than ten or eleven, out of the house. Asking a neighbor for cab fare, the boy had explained, "I want to go up to my dad's because my mother won't let me in the house." No surprise that Christian turned to marijuana, the only way he seemed able to check out of the daily pressures of his life.

Finally, social workers had prevailed upon the court to enroll the boy at the Ojai Valley School, north of Los Angeles, where he would receive greater round-the-clock attention. Still, he ran away. Still, the problems continued.

Marlon longed for family. Not since the days of the Adlers had he ever really had a family. Perhaps that was why the role of Don Corleone fit him so well; it fulfilled a dream, a fantasy of his. "With all those women he got pregnant," Jack Larson mused, "I wonder how much of it was a subconscious desire to have a family." After all, Marlon always left the birth control up to the woman, quite a risk for someone so ostensibly opposed to becoming attached. "Maybe he was just being self-destructive," said another friend, "going after what he secretly wanted but knew he could never maintain."

When Tarita had expressed a desire to have another child, Marlon, no longer worried about what the public might say about him, agreed. Working with a medical company, he sent his sperm express to Tahiti, where Tarita was artificially inseminated. He was happy for his children in the South Seas; they were safe there, he believed, in ways they wouldn't have been in Los Angeles. "They would be destroyed in the pace of life in the States," he said.

In his own, limited way, he tried to be a good father. Columnist Walter Scott, who knew him, told his readers in 1965 that Marlon was "an excellent father, kind, considerate, and painstaking, well-loved by all three boys." Yet when Christian stayed with him, Marlon became as strict as his old man had been with him. The boy worked for his money, Marlon decreed, or he got nothing. That meant that, when he was staying with his father, Christian, alone among his friends, never had any spending money. Alice took pity on him, slipping him a few dollars for "lunch, snacks and cokes." Once, when Christian was planning to see a movie with some friends, Alice asked Marlon if he could break a hundred-dollar bill so she could give Christian a twenty. He refused. No more than five dollars for the boy, he insisted. Alice was irate. "Marlon had not been to a movie house and paid for his own ticket in twenty years or more," she wrote in her memoir. Defying her boss, she took the twenty from his wallet and gave it to Christian anyway.

The boy made no open protest of his father's rules, but he would often stay in his room for hours at a time smoking cigarettes. Marlon no longer tried to get him to stop smoking. "If you're gonna drink and smoke pot, do it at home," he told his son. "I don't approve, but if you're going to do it, do it in front of me." Brando père and fils would hibernate in their own spaces, licking their wounds, just down the hall from each other, but in fact, a continent away.

Miko Brando, who visited frequently, had an easier relationship with his father. He came to understand that Marlon's own parentage limited him. "He never made us feel the way supposedly his father did him," Miko would remember. Less rebellious than Christian, and better served by his own mother, Miko had fewer conflicts with his father. "He always made us feel number one and happy and cherished and loved."

At various times, Marlon would bring his American children to the South Seas. He desperately wanted to instill in them the message of simplicity and self-sufficiency that he'd found in the islands. He worried that Christian might be targeted for his mixed-race heritage in America, and imagined him being happier in Tahiti. But that wasn't the answer. The only way to find peace, Marlon eventually concluded, was to solve "the emotional algebra" of their lives. He'd never been very good at mathematics, however. Even in his Polynesian sanctuary at Teti'aroa, Marlon found the answers to his life hard to come by: "My first seven years as a child growing up in Illinois always get in the way," he said, "and I meet myself coming around the other side of the island."

He'd thought that by walking away from Hollywood, by playing by his own rules, he had liberated himself, cleared the way for happiness to enter his life. But the old traumas were always there, reflecting back at him from the faces of his children, especially his eldest son. Marlon was back in therapy, with a new analyst. To treat his depressive episodes, and the explosions of anger that inevitably followed, his doctor had prescribed a steady regimen of Valium. Alice worried that her boss was getting addicted to the pills, but Marlon assured her he didn't have an addictive personality like others in his family. His midnight raids of the refrigerator, putting away entire cakes or pies, might dispute that theory.

What no drug and no cake or pie could help him with was the loneliness. Almost forty-seven years old, Marlon had still never found a serious, committed, steady, mature relationship in his life.

His most successful relationship was with Tarita, where there was no expectation of exclusivity. When Marlon was in the South Pacific, he was hers; when he wasn't, he was somebody else's. Tarita, too, took other lovers; she even had children by them. Marlon did ask, however, that when he visited her and Teihotu and Cheyenne, she keep her other men away. In this manner, for a few days, Marlon could indulge the fantasy of presiding over a happy, united family—husband, wife, and children, the Corleones in a grass hut.

Because, on some level, he wanted that—or at least, he wanted the steady companionship and sense of family that a marriage might bring him. Marriage as an institution remained a bourgeois idea. But Alice, who saw him in his private moments more than anyone else, would describe many lonely nights when Marlon sat by himself, lamenting the course his life had taken. Tape recordings he would make toward the end of his life would also reveal his wistfulness about his solitary existence. That might be his fate. He was still unable to tell any woman he loved her. Tarita would recall a moment when she attempted to tell Marlon she loved him. He'd responded angrily, insisting she never speak those words again. And so, Tarita said, "I promised him I wouldn't."

WHEN THE DINNER at Patsy's had finished, it was past midnight. Cast and crew stumbled out of the restaurant, spirits high, voices loud. They piled into cars to head back to their apartments or hotels. Most of them were young people. The actors were all on the edge of fame; *The Godfather* would hopefully take them over the top. Everyone was giddy with excitement. In one car, James Caan rode with Robert Duvall. Caan, a strapping, handsome thirty-year-old, had won some acclaim for his role in *The Glory Guys*, but his more recent *Rabbit, Run*, based on the John Updike novel, had been so bad that it was barely released. Nine years older than Caan, Duvall was still waiting for his big break; he'd scored in the previous year's *M\*A\*S\*H*, but his role had been a small one in the colorful ensemble. If *The Godfather* was the hit everyone expected it to be, it would change all their lives.

On Second Avenue, Caan and Duvall pulled up alongside the car in which Marlon was riding. To them, Brando was the king. "When we were young," Duvall said, "Brando was like the godfather of actors." He and Dustin Hoffman, as struggling young New York actors, would get together to talk about their craft, "and if we mentioned [Brando's] name once, we mentioned it twenty-five times in a day." Duvall had worked with Marlon before, on *The Chase*, but still regarded him with reverence. The first day on the *Godfather* set, Caan said, "Everybody was in awe."

Now they looked over and saw their hero in the car beside theirs. Not long before, he'd been the consummate Don, their revered patriarch, as they'd all embodied their characters over dinner. But Caan and Duvall had also heard the stories about Brando that, by 1971, were already hardening into legend: dropping bags full of water from roofs onto passersby, boxing backstage during *Streetcar* and heading out onstage with a broken nose, pranking Josh Logan with the fake broken arm. Duvall leaned into Caan. "Come on," he said, "moon him!"

"Are you crazy?" Caan asked. But it didn't take much convincing. "So I roll my window down," Caan said, "and I just stick my ass out." Marlon saw, and laughed so hard he was "falling down," Caan remembered. "And we went away crying, laughing. That was the first moon of my life, to *Brando*, and it was on the first day we met."

The camaraderie was officially established. This wasn't going to be *Mutiny on the Bounty*. This was going to be fun. The next day, the actors made a bet as to who'd be named the "mighty moon champion" by the end of the shoot. Marlon would win the contest, Caan said, "after he mooned five hundred extras one day."

For the past two decades, moviemaking had been a chore for Marlon, a necessary evil to keep his family fed and his projects humming. Now, in the spring of 1971, acting before the cameras promised not only to refill his coffers but to reinvigorate him. Marlon's work at Filmways Studios gave him an outlet for his creativity, an escape from the pain of his personal life, and, most significantly, a family. *The Godfather* saved Marlon's life in more ways than one.

**APRIL 1971** / On an unseasonably warm day on Mott Street in New York's Little Italy, lots of people were grumbling, reported the *Daily News*: "the little old ladies who couldn't do their daily pushcart shopping," and "the neighborhood kids who were chased away" by security guards, and "an ambulance driver who was detoured around the block." That was because a Paramount crew had taken over the whole area between Hester and Grand Streets to shoot some scenes of Marlon Brando in full Godfather drag. The movie's publicists still wanted to keep his appearance a secret, but they hadn't counted on *Daily News* photographers, "who know more people in Little Italy than the M ___ does." (*Mafia* was supposedly an unspeakable term at the time, though the paper printed the blanks mostly in jest.) As usual, the *News* got its scoop: a surreptitious shot of Marlon, looking about sixty-five, appeared in the newspaper's April 20 issue.

Marlon found it all very amusing. He was having a ball making the film. The actors scribbled FUCK YOU notes and then stuck them in their mouths, revealing them at crucial moments to crack each other up. Some of their spontaneous laughter made it into the final film. This was a set unlike any Marlon had ever worked on. His costars were pranksters like him. He got along with everyone. "He was like a big kid in a way," Coppola remembered. "Extremely intelligent. Even beyond his talent for film. You can talk to him about all kinds of things and feel you've learned something."

And everywhere, to Marlon's delight, there were gangsters. No longer did he worry about glorifying them. Their presence made the set more interesting. Threatened by boycotts from Italian American organizations (and worse from Mob kingpins), Bluhdorn had hired a number of "family" members as extras and crew: "Half of the people who were behind the camera were in the Mafia," Marlon said, "and I think there were four or five actors in front of the camera attached to Mafioso affairs." Al Martino (Johnny Fontane) would admit to his connections with the Mob, and Lenny Montana (Luca Brasi) had been a bodyguard for several gangland leaders.

On Mott Street, Marlon finished his scene and strolled over to his trailer to remove his makeup. Suddenly there came a knock at his door. When the door was opened, two men stood there with a message in their hands. "One was a rat-faced man with impeccably groomed hair and a camel's-hair coat," Marlon remembered; "the other a less elegantly dressed man who was the size of an elephant." So large was the second man that he nearly tipped the trailer over when he entered. The men announced that Russell Bufalino, head of one of the Mafia's most notorious crime families, wanted to meet the star of *The Godfather*. Marlon braced himself. Was Bufalino happy or unhappy with the film?

Before long, Bufalino himself stepped regally into the trailer. Soft-spoken, with a lazy eye and two missing fingers, he nonetheless exuded authority. He immediately began complaining about government investigations into his business dealings. "I didn't have an answer," Marlon said, "so I didn't say anything." Then, in a whisper, Bufalino added, "The word's out you like calamari." Marlon nodded, not sure where this was going. Bufalino invited him to dinner with him and his wife. Marlon never took him up on the offer, but he did give him a tour of the set.

This sort of stuff just didn't happen on other movies. Not since

*Bedtime Story*, where David Niven's bon mots had kept Marlon in stitches, had he so enjoyed making a film. And part of his delight, despite the myths that would arise, was his fondness for his young director, who looked and dressed like a hippie.

"Marlon liked Francis Coppola," Alice Marchak stated. "I don't believe he tried to frustrate him as he did other directors." Marlon thought Coppola had talent; he'd been a fan of *You're a Big Boy Now*. Coppola might not have been Kazan—who was?—but he was "smart enough," Marlon said, "to get actors that can handle themselves, and then just sort of let them bring it out."

Not in many years had Marlon's talent been allowed to flourish so freely and unimpeded, nurtured by a solid script, an astute director, and equally inspired fellow actors. Marlon's suggestions for his role and for the film as a whole were accepted readily and gratefully. Ten years had passed since his attempts to rewrite *Bounty* were considered the inexpert meddling of a narcissistic star. Now, a young director and hero-worshipping costars were inclined to trust Marlon's instincts and judgment. A comparison of original versus final scripts, covered with Marlon's handwritten revisions, suggests they were wise to do so.

In Marlon's rewrites, there is little ego: everything he changed was done in service to the story. When a scene required it, he pared down his own lines and gave others more to say. He often ignored stage directions calling for him to gesture with his hands; in his view, the Don was as stingy with gestures as he was with words. The Don could not be an expressive, loquacious man; he must be a quiet, coiled snake. That is what makes him feared. That is the manifestation of his power.

Reading one version of the script, Marlon was busy with his pen, crossing out and rewriting whenever something stopped the flow of the action. The opening of the film could move faster, more powerfully, he believed. The first scene has Bonasera the undertaker pleading with the Don to take retribution on two men who assaulted his daughter, despite having disapproved of the Don's methods in the past. The scene sets up everything we need to know about Vito Corleone, his business, and his code of honor. In his revision of the scene, Marlon revealed how keenly he understood the way story and emotion were communicated through the medium of film.

The original, consisting of exactly one hundred words, has Corleone speaking to Bonasera this way: "Why are you so afraid to give your first allegiance to me? You go to the law courts and wait for months. You spend money on lawyers who you know you're to be made a fool of. You take judgment from a judge who sells himself like the worst whore on the street. But, if you had come to me as a friend, those scum who ruined your daughter would be weeping bitter tears this day. If by some misfortune an honest man like yourself made enemies, they would become my enemies, and then believe me, they would fear you." Marlon's rewrite consisted of almost half the number of words, and he made the speech more personal and less overwrought—delivered, it should be noted, as he plays idly with a cat lying in his lap. "Bonasera, Bonasera," the Don says, "what have I ever done to make you treat me so disrespectfully? If you had come to me in friendship, then the scum that ruined your daughter would be suffering this very day. And if by chance an honest man like yourself should make enemies, then they would become my enemies, and then they would fear you."

The rest of the passage—the part suggesting that working with the Mafia was no more compromised than working with a corrupt judicial system—was organically woven into earlier dialogue. The Don's sense of his own honor will not be challenged by Bonasera's judgment of him. He tells Duvall: "We're not murderers, in spite of what this"—he pauses for a fraction of a second that speaks volumes—"*undertaker* says." The scene might have ended there, but then Marlon does something remarkable and unexpected, perfectly emblematic of the character. He lifts his lapel and takes a sniff of the rose he has pinned there. Seven minutes into the film, we know exactly how Don Vito Corleone sees himself and his place in the world.

The Don's unflappable sense of himself defines the character. But it's the small moments where he loses control that reveal the fire raging within. Al Martino, playing the singer Johnny Fontane, whines at one point over the state of his career, crying to the Don that he doesn't know what to do. Suddenly the coiled snake springs. Marlon roars, "You can act like a man!" and slaps Martino across the face. The slap wasn't in the original script; Marlon and Coppola kept it from Martino, who "didn't know whether to laugh or cry," James Caan remembered. Even after repeated viewings, the moment still startles the viewer.

Coppola wasn't lording over his actors, orchestrating their every move; what makes *The Godfather* feel so real is its fluidity of motion and the naturalness of the people passing through the frame. Under such freedom, Marlon thrived. He didn't need a director telling him when or how to do things. Over the course of his career, saddled with directors he disrespected more often than not, he'd learned how to protect the "delicate" membrane of a performance all by himself. "Sometimes it rides on very, very thin tissue," Marlon said; clumsy directors or intrusive cast members, he said, could "break the spell." In between takes, he avoided chit-chat, people "coming over and talking to you and talking about the girl that they had an affair with at lunch, or something like that." So, he mostly stayed away from people, including the director, during a shoot, and instead concentrated on blocking out the scene for himself. Even the best director, Marlon said, "can't get [a performance] out of you" if you don't already have it "in your back pocket."

The best decision Coppola made in his direction of Marlon was to inspire him with rehearsals and then leave him alone. That was why, when the director faced his own crisis on the film, Marlon was ready to fight for him. Those on the set felt the magic happening as the cameras rolled, but the suits in the front office weren't sure what they were watching when they looked over the rushes. Was Marlon just mumbling through his part? Was there a coherent story? Rumors floated that Coppola was about to be fired. He'd remember being in the men's room at Paramount, after production had moved back to Los Angeles, and overhearing two executives talking about the film, calling it "a load of shit" and speculating that the director was in over his head. In a stall, Coppola lifted his feet so the execs wouldn't recognize his shoes. All their work might be lost if he were canned.

But Marlon laid down the law. If Coppola was fired, he was quitting. He was not about to risk another Lewis Milestone coming on board. After Marlon's ultimatum, there was no more talk of firing Coppola. Marlon had found a director he could work with, a rare and wonderful thing. He wasn't about to lose that now, not after enduring those ten "dismal, dank failures," as he referred to his films of the late 1960s—all of which, in varying degrees, at least to his mind, could be blamed on the deficiencies of their directors.

"NO TALENT ASSHOLES," Marlon called the majority of his directors from the 1960s, sparing no words, "who all think they're young Eisenstein, or Orson Welles. And you know fucking well when they say 'print,' that's just a thumbs-up-the-ass place. Those are the guys that are tough to work with."

Which directors was he including in that description? Among those who'd helmed his "dismal, dank failures," Austrian-born Bernhard Wicki, the director of *Morituri* (1965), might be a likely candidate. Wicki had been a student of Max Reinhardt, and Marlon found him pretentious and authoritarian. The story of an undercover agent who attempts to disable the explosive cargo of an enemy freighter during World War II, *Morituri* was plagued with delays that dragged out the film's schedule—though this time the problems were blamed more on the director than the star. Marlon quipped to Bob Thomas, "It's like pushing a prune pit with my nose from here to Cucamonga." No doubt, the best part of the experience for Marlon was working with Wally Cox, for whom he secured a small role in the film. It was the only time the two best friends ever appeared together on the screen.

Other candidates for Marlon's "no talent" list (his judgment, not the judgment of critics) might include Sidney Furie, who directed him in *The Appaloosa* (1966). Furie was a young (thirty-two when he made *The Appaloosa*) Canadian-born filmmaker who'd made a name for himself in the British New Wave (*The Leather Boys, The Ipcress File*). Cineastes considered Furie an "auteur"—precisely the sort of attitude Marlon was mocking when he made his "young Eisenstein" comment. *The Appaloosa*, a Western drama about horse bandits, was marked by tension between star and director. Marlon didn't trust Furie's vision and so, halfway through the shoot, started tuning him out, reading Nietzsche in between takes.

Another possibility for Marlon's "young Eisenstein" included Hubert Cornfield, his director on *The Night of the Following Day* (1969), who was the son of a Twentieth Century–Fox studio executive and an enthusiast of Godard and Truffaut. Virtually all of Marlon's dismal, dank failures were directed by men the star found unbearable.

Indeed, the problems with his films from 1963 to 1969—all of which garnered overwhelmingly negative reviews, with the exception of *Reflections in a Golden Eye* (1967)—can be laid at the feet of their directors. That is true not only for those on Marlon's "no talent" list, but also for such expert filmmakers as John Huston and Arthur Penn, who either failed to gain their star's trust or to fully understand the material they were asking him to interpret. In the case of the great Charlie Chaplin, who directed Marlon in *A Countess from Hong Kong* (1967), he failed utterly at both tasks.

In the public's mind, however, it was Marlon who was to blame for the failure of these films. EIGHT BOMBS IN A ROW—BRANDO WON'T CHANGE, read the headline of Bob Ellison's syndicated column in the *Chicago Sun-Times* in March 1967. "There was a time, a very long time ago," Ellison wrote, "when Marlon's fellow actors defended him and some of the bad movies he made. But that time, like the dime box of popcorn, seems to be gone forever." The problem with Marlon's films, Ellison wrote, was the fact that the star "doesn't take direction." Marlon was the one messing these films up, from Ellison's (and others') point of view; if only he had listened to Chaplin or Penn (or Bernhard Wicki or Sidney Furie), then the films would have turned out brilliant, apparently. It was an absurd argument, yet by 1971, the general consensus was "Marlon Brando no longer knows how to make a good movie."

Yet it was Wicki's inefficiency that Bosley Crowther cited for *Morituri*'s deficits: "[T]he whole thing has pretty well foundered long before the explosives are touched off." Likewise, he blamed Penn and screenwriter Lillian Hellman for the problems of *The Chase* (1966), in which Marlon played a sheriff in a story that tackled racial injustice and small-town bigotry. It was just the sort of project Marlon wanted to be involved with, but everything came out "overheated," Crowther complained, from the direction to the writing to the scenery. Huston wasn't quite as savaged for *Reflections in a Golden Eye*, but his lack of authority over the complex material—Marlon plays an army major struggling with his repressed sexual desire for another man—sometimes left audiences confused, and laughing during serious scenes, as the reviewer for the *Boston Globe* pointed out.

It was Chaplin, however, who received the worst notices. *A Countess from Hong Kong*, in which Marlon took the part of an American who finds a beautiful Russian stowaway (Sophia Loren) in his ship's cabin, failed because the seventy-eight-year-old director simply didn't know how to make a modern comedy. Marlon found him hopeless as a director. "He wasn't a man who could direct anybody," he said. "He probably could when he was young." *Countess*, Bosley Crowther wrote, was a "painfully antique bedroom farce," one that he wished he could "draw the curtain fast on . . . and pretend it never occurred."

If Marlon shared any blame for these disasters, it was because he no longer chose projects for what he might do with them creatively; they were, bottom line, paychecks. At the start of a film, there was usually some hope that he and the director might click, and Marlon often came in with some creative ideas. But never in eight years had such hopes panned out. So, Marlon would finish each film as quickly as possible and hightail it back to Teti'aroa.

Some of his colleagues found his attitude deplorable. The actress Shirley Knight accused him of a lack of "self-respect." His old friend Billy Redfield made his long-simmering resentments public, castigating Marlon in a *New York Times* opinion piece for not fulfilling the American theater's expectations of him. "He is a movie star," Redfield wrote contemptuously. "A little more than kind (Rock Hudson) and less than kin (Spencer Tracy.)" Even more painful was the scolding Marlon took from Budd Schulberg, who considered the actor's current roles to be leagues beneath Terry Malloy. "You're doing pictures they couldn't pay me to write," Schulberg told Marlon in a letter. "You've got stronger convictions than anybody I know out here, but I wish you could find some way to get your ideals and your professional work together." Marlon later told Schulberg that his letter gave him "nightmares."

Yet he made no apology for his position. Marlon had turned his back on the hypocrisy and avarice of Hollywood; if producers were going to continue to pay him good money, he'd take it, but he wasn't about to start trying to repair unfixable projects again, the way he'd done on *Mutiny*. He wasn't about to pour blood, sweat, and tears into a project like *One-Eyed Jacks*, either, only to have it cut up beyond recognition. He was tired of the Hollywood game; the reward, as lucrative as it could be, was simply not worth it, not with the way the spotlight had been turned on Christian every time Anna dragged Marlon into court; or with the wild tales spread about Movita or Tarita; or with the way the industry went on blithely stereotyping and discriminating against Negroes and American Indians even as the civil rights movement moved into its second decade. Marlon made no apologies for his relationship with the film industry, or for what he did or didn't do.

On the one occasion he was roped into doing a publicity press junket (for *Morituri* in 1965), he absolutely refused to play by the rules. His rebellion was captured by filmmaker brothers H. Albert and David Maysles. Playing to the Maysleses' video camera, Marlon was in rare form, cracking jokes, flirting with reporters, and generally upending the parameters of the celebrity interview. "I don't think we ought to sneak around it," Marlon said. "I think we ought to say we're here as hucksters. I'm thumping the tub for a picture named *Morituri*"—and he clearly wasn't happy about it. When Marlon asked about the long fingernails of one interviewer and was told that they were useful for playing classical guitar, his eyes lit up: at last something interesting to talk about! But when the interviewer told him they needed to get back to huckstering, he deflated. "Let's talk about *Morituri*," another reporter suggested. "Let's don't," Marlon replied. The reporter remarked that she'd heard it was great. "We mustn't believe propaganda," Marlon cautioned. "It might be an absolutely terrible film, you don't know." Later he turned sarcastic: "All the pictures they make in Hollywood are really great. Everybody knows that."

People such as Budd Schulberg and Billy Redfield, who'd invested their lives, their very sense of self, in the idea that acting was art, noble and inherently valuable, could never comprehend what Marlon was telling them about real worth and the dangers of self-absorption: it was as if he were speaking Greek.

Others, such as Kazan, grasped the concept at its edges, but kept trying to get Marlon to reconsider it, or temper it. Kazan wrote him another tough letter during this period, when he was trying to convince him to do *The Arrangement*. "You said to me that you'd lost a lot of your feeling for acting, that there were now other things you preferred doing," Kazan wrote. He knew Marlon was "tired of his trade . . . disillusioned . . . wishing he was someone else, not an actor." But if there was some lingering desire for one more great film, one more great performance, Kazan hoped Marlon would go for it: "If you really want to, you can be a blazing actor again. The wanting is the hard part."

What no one seemed able to accept was that Marlon *didn't* want it, and there was absolutely no appeal that could *make* him want it. That didn't mean he couldn't enjoy a project: certainly, in the spring of 1971, he was taking real fulfillment in creating the character of Don Vito Corleone in *The Godfather*. Tapping old creative energy that he hadn't used in a while felt good; it lifted him out of his funk. But *The Godfather* was a rare experience, in which directors, actors, and script were all in alignment. In those circumstances, Marlon could indulge what the rest of the world called his artistry or his genius. He didn't think in those terms, but if others did, let them.

Even in his lesser films, even when he was there just to earn some cash to pay for construction of a turtle farm on Teti'aroa, Marlon managed to make his performances compelling. In *Morituri*, he plays with "evident enjoyment," Bosley Crowther thought, "milking the moments of suspense with all his beautiful skill at holding pauses and letting tense thought churn behind his bland eyes." In *The Chase*, Marjory Adams of the *Boston Globe* found him to be "outstanding [and] authentic," which wasn't the case for anyone else in the cast. Director Arthur Penn agreed that Marlon delivered "a perfectly fine performance" as the sheriff; the problems with the film were not because of him. *The Nightcomers*, which premiered at the Venice Film Festival that August, was "quite bad under any circumstances," Vincent Canby wrote, but Marlon, playing Quint, seemed "to be in another film entirely," offering "small, beautiful moments when [his] intelligence creates a truly complex character." Despite his indifference to the actual productions, Marlon never once walked through a performance.

He himself thought he did some good work in *Burn!* (1969), original title *Queimada*. Playing a nineteenth-century British mercenary who cynically incites a Caribbean slave revolt to boost trade, Marlon felt he was exposing the evils of capitalism. "But nobody saw that film," he lamented, after he'd spent months making it in Colombia, "eleven degrees off the equator, sweating and putting up with terrible circumstances, and a lot of fighting." Most of the fighting was with director Gillo Pontecorvo, whom Marlon called "a complete sadist"; the director carried a gun in his belt while on the set, so Marlon started toting a knife in response. At one point, he confronted Pontecorvo when he learned that black extras were being paid less than whites, and another gigantic fight ensued. Still, he thought the picture was an important one and that Pontecorvo was skilled at directing it: "You have to separate people from their talent," Marlon said. "I did not want to blow the picture. I really felt that it could have been a wonderful movie."

Critics, however, came down hard: "*Burn!* aspires to be a prole epic," Vincent Canby wrote, "but winds up the sort of prole pageant in which characters always seem to be conceptualizing great issues, mostly freedom, as they pass in front of history, as if it were a scenic view, instead of moving in and out of it." Marlon, though, was "worth watching under almost any circumstances"; here he was "a tired and tragic hero whom life has somehow double-crossed." Gerald Peary would call *Burn!* "the most undervalued Brando film of all."

Yet, without question, his best acting in this period came in *Reflections in a Golden Eye*. As the sexually conflicted Major Penderton (a role he'd taken only after Montgomery Clift, originally cast, died in July 1966), Marlon summons the tension between longing and self-loathing. There's a scene in the woods when he cries, where the emotion builds, then gets forced back, then starts to escape, bit by bit, until it seems as if he will go mad and completely disintegrate into nothing right before our eyes. Was this how Marlon himself decompensated, those times when the darkness came and he was unable to get up off the floor? It's a shattering moment, matched by the quiet intensity of another scene, when Penderton stares in a mirror, trying to will himself the courage and fortitude to be the (heterosexual) man he is expected to be. Penderton is, of course, exactly the opposite of Marlon; the open borders of Marlon's sexuality defined who he was, and he took some gratification in that. Yet the very confidence he had in his own sexuality allowed him to imagine what the inverse would be like; certainly he'd encountered many men like Penderton over the years.

John Huston would remember his star being unsure at first whether to take the part. But after a long walk in a thunderstorm, Marlon had announced simply to the director, "I want to do it." Once production began, Huston noticed that Marlon seemed fearful of the horses in the film, so much so that costar Elizabeth Taylor, a legendarily good horsewoman, also began to be frightened. Marlon had, of course, ridden horses in many of his films; he'd spent almost a year on horseback during *One-Eyed Jacks*. Huston was left to wonder "if Marlon got this fear because he had so immersed himself in his role"—Penderton had a pathological fear of horses. Huston recalled, "I remember he once said of acting, 'If you care about it, it's no good.' Meaning you've got to get into a role to the point that you're no longer acting."

Marlon liked Huston, for the same reason he'd later like Coppola: "He gives you twenty-five feet. He's out in the background. He listens. He can tell by the tone of your voice whether you're cracking or not. But he leaves you alone pretty good." After the film was done, Marlon sent Huston a note: "Think of you with very warm feelings. I enjoyed your company very much and the working relationship was the best." Very few directors would have notes like that from Marlon among their papers.

*Reflections* received mixed reviews, but Marlon was invariably praised. Robb Baker of the *Chicago Tribune* called Penderton an "excellent, well-developed characterization," and Marlon's "best since *Waterfront*." The director of *Waterfront* seemed to agree: Kazan told Marlon he was "bold and daring, and made a most difficult part moving and human." It was "tough to do," Kazan suspected, because of Clift's shadow hanging over the part, "so I admired you more."

Only in a few films was Marlon not entirely successful. When *The Night of the Following Day* came out in February 1969, critic Howard Thompson said it was "high time Marlon Brando landed himself a good picture." This wasn't it, however. In this tale of counterculture kidnappers holding a woman for ransom, Marlon looks like "a demobilized storm trooper," in the words of critic Clifford Terry, in his "black turtleneck and Dippity-done blonde hair." He also sounded like "Stanley Kowalski turned hippie." That much was the fault of the script, which Marlon clearly didn't try to rewrite, and which forced him to say such lines as, "Listen, man, if you want to get freaky, don't do it with her."

Yet he fared even worse in *A Countess from Hong Kong*. He'd taken the part because it meant working with Chaplin, whose early films, along with Laurel and Hardy's, Marlon loved watching, tumbling off his couch onto the floor in laughter. "Chaplin is a man whose talent is such that you have to gamble," he said, explaining why he took the chance on working with the old man, who hadn't made a film in ten years. Chaplin made everyone else look "Lilliputian," Marlon believed. Yet it was the legendary director who seemed the more intimidated. He and Marlon had just one row on the set, when he berated the actor for being late; Marlon retreated to his dressing room in protest. After that, Chaplin was obsequious, deferring to Marlon in every way, even when he did things the director didn't like. "I thought I'd only confuse him," Chaplin explained. "We might destroy his personality by doing it my way." To everyone else, however, especially his son Sydney, who was playing a supporting role, Chaplin was "nasty and sadistic and mean," Marlon said. Chaplin degraded his son and others in the cast and crew on a regular basis. "A remarkable talent but a monster of a man," Marlon remembered. "I don't even like to think about it."

For *Countess*, Marlon received the worst reviews so far in his career. "Brando, trying to master light comedy," wrote Clifford Terry of the *Chicago Tribune*, "comes across more like Pinky Lee trying to master King Lear." Even the usually supportive Bosley Crowther could manage only tepid appreciation for how gamely Marlon and costar Sophia Loren try to be "elegant and airy," only to be brought down by "ditch-water dull dialogue." More personal (and brutal) criticism came from Kazan. "You were terribly overweight," he wrote to Marlon, "in fact to the point where you did not seem to be the same fellow." He added: "They were right about your indifference. That's the word I'd use."

Worse than *Countess*, however, in many critics' estimation, was *Candy*, an overblown sex farce Marlon made in 1968 as a favor to Christian Marquand, who was trying his hand at directing. Marlon wasn't singled out for reproach any more than the others in the all-star cast, which included Richard Burton, Charles Aznavour, James Coburn, John Huston, and Walter Matthau. Everyone and everything, adjudged the *Chicago Tribune*, was "tediously rotten." The *Hartford Courant* called the film "a tasteless piece which misses the satire mark by several thousand light years." Yet Marquand had intended the film to be over the top; he'd instructed his actors to ham it up. So, it's hard to call *Candy* worse than *A Countess from Hong Kong* or *The Night of the Following Day*, which were taken seriously by their directors. In *Candy*, Marlon plays a lecherous guru in a black wig, affecting a Hindi accent and presiding over a makeshift ashram in the back of a semi-trailer. Although the *Hartford Courant* thought he "should be ashamed of his participation," Marlon never regretted any of his films, he said, not even those "dismal, dank failures" that had turned him into box-office poison. "I don't regret any movie I ever made except some that I've made in the privacy of my bedroom," he joked. "Very poorly directed and not entirely well acted." Besides, for all its preposterousness, *Candy* introduced him to Jill Banner, an extra in the film—and who, for the past three years, had been his most regular (although not exclusive) girlfriend.

Still, for all his celluloid disasters from this period, Marlon remained the bar by which young actors measured themselves. Studio heads, columnists, even the public may have despaired of Marlon and written him off as finished, but not the new generation of actors coming up, many of whom, like James Caan and Robert Duvall, had first been inspired in their craft by Marlon Brando in *Streetcar* or *Waterfront*—or possibly *Viva Zapata!* or *Julius Caesar* or even *The Wild One*. Jack Nicholson, who'd recently become Marlon's neighbor on Mulholland Drive, eagerly admitted how much the older actor had influenced him. "I am part of the first generation that idolized Marlon Brando," Nicholson recalled. "I was in high school back in the Fifties when he came into the game, and I watched him change the rules. Perhaps he would tell you he saw the same thing in Paul Muni, but the truth is, Brando was always different. For my money, nothing has ever gotten near him."

"Even when Brando mocks himself," wrote Pauline Kael, "the self he mocks is more prodigious than anybody else around."

WHEN COPPOLA CALLED "cut" on Marlon's final scene in *The Godfather*, cast and crew applauded. They'd just filmed the Don's death scene, and as always, Marlon had done things no one could have expected, small, telling moments that left tears in people's eyes when he was finished. He acknowledged the applause with a little smile and a wave. For once, he seemed to appreciate the acclaim.

Altogether, it had been a very satisfying shoot: no conflict, no major schedule problems, no severe budget overruns. "Director Francis Ford Coppola is thumbing his nose at those who said that Marlon Brando would cause problems," one reporter observed. There was every expectation that the film would be an enormous hit. "Brando knows this will bring him back where he should be," producer Al Ruddy said. Marlon's long exile in the wilderness was apparently over.

Even more than the satisfaction of the work, Marlon had been buoyed by the camaraderie he'd found with the younger actors. "He liked that sense of being a hero to these up-and-comers," said one friend who got to know him well during this period. Even more, he seemed to take pleasure in still being "a part of the vanguard." He'd just turned forty-seven. Already getting paunchy before *The Godfather*, he had gained additional weight for the role, pounds he'd find very difficult to lose. He got winded easily. Yet, returning to his house on Mulholland Drive after production wrapped, he felt younger than he had in years, more relevant, more vital.

Spring was in the air. Marlon had plans to go to France, and then to Tahiti. But first, there was something else he needed to do.

**LATE SPRING 1971** / As the mother of Marlon Brando's girlfriend, Muriel Molumby had gotten used to drama. She lived on the second floor of a two-story apartment building on a tree-lined stretch of Irving Avenue in Glendale, California. The place wasn't very big, but Mrs. Molumby always kept a room ready for her twenty-four-year-old daughter, Mary Kathryn, who went by the stage name Jill Banner. Several times a year, Mary Kathryn would show up at her mother's apartment hurt or angered or confused by something Brando had said or done. The last time she'd arrived brokenhearted and disillusioned, Mrs. Molumby had vowed she'd never allow that brute to see her precious daughter again, no matter how rich and famous he was.

Outside the apartment, Marlon pulled up in his car. He turned off the ignition and sat there waiting, hoping Jill would see him.

As Alice Marchak remembered, Mrs. Molumby "wouldn't allow Marlon near" Jill; nor would she let her take his calls. "So he sat out there in the street," said Pat Perez, a friend of Banner's. "It was all pretty high school, very teenage sort of behavior."

Marlon knew how angry Jill's mother was with him and didn't want to cross her. She blamed him for Jill's dependency on downers such as Valium. A free-loving flower child since her early teens, Jill had experimented with drugs long before she met Marlon. But over the past year, her use of Valium had increased; she'd sometimes wander through the halls of Marlon's house like a ghost, Alice would remember. Still, she was "by no means an addict," Alice insisted. Pat Perez, however, tempered that conclusion somewhat: "She might not have been an addict yet, but she was fast moving down that path. And Marlon was the reason for that, Jill's mother believed."

In his memoir, where he disguised Jill as "Weonna" (much the way he also disguised Ellen Adler and Celia Webb), Marlon called her "troubled" and "distrustful." Yet these were not adjectives her friends would have chosen for her. If Jill became troubled and distrustful, they believed, it was only after spending the past three years with the often troubled and distrustful Marlon. And if her use of Valium was increasing, it was only because Marlon's was, too.

Muriel Molumby knew all this. So, she was not pleased when, just as Marlon hoped, Jill spotted him from the window and went outside to sit with him in his car. Since returning with him from England after the *Nightcomers* shoot, Jill had "cleaned up her act,"

Alice said. While Marlon had been off making *The Godfather,* Jill had cut out all the pills. "The only way she was going to go back to him now," Pat Perez said, "was if he would stop using them, too." Marlon, of course, didn't see any problem with his Valium use. But to appease Jill, Perez said, he promised to cut back. He'd "do anything," Marlon told her, "to make things work."

In many ways, Marlon's yo-yo relationship with Jill (pushing her away, pulling her back, making promises he usually broke) resembled the pattern he'd established with Rita Moreno and so many other women. But Jill was different. "She was the one woman," Perez reflected, "who he didn't feel trapped by, who wouldn't come running after him when he walked away. He was the one who went after her, every time. Jill never, ever, went after him. That made him want her more. Jill was strong. Stronger than he was."

Marlon had recognized Jill's strength, her difference from the others, right from the start. She'd made a name for herself in such underground films as *Cannibal Orgy, or the Maddest Story Ever Told,* the tale of three deranged teenaged killers cared for by Lon Chaney Jr. With no acting experience, Jill had played her role (that of a young woman who thinks she's a spider killing bugs in her web) with unself-conscious exuberance. She's sexy and sinister, obviously having a great time running around in a diaphanous dress carrying a butcher knife. When the film was finally released in late 1967, three years after production, the title was changed to *Spider Baby* because everyone recognized Jill as the best thing in the picture.

In a number of films and television shows in the mid- to late 1960s, Jill was a quintessential "swinging chick." In *The President's Analyst* (1967), a comedy starring James Coburn, she plays a hippie by the name of Snow White, who teaches the uptight hero to hang loose: "Let's smell the flowers," she says as she leads Coburn out into a meadow. "Love now. I'm now. Love me." When they walk out of the meadow, she's bare-assed. In episodes of *Dragnet, Ironside,* and

*The Name of the Game,* she plays similar flower girls. Film critic Chuck Stephens, looking back at her career, said Jill "knew how to make a big impression by doing very little at all." She seemed to embody the polarity of sixties screen heroines: vulnerable yet powerful, spiritual while at the same time fiercely carnal. Marlon himself said he was drawn by Jill's mix of "street smarts" and "childlike naïveté." She "sneered as naturally as she exhaled," Stephens wrote. Her characters drove men crazy "just by being there, maybe because, though sexy as hell, you knew that—like a spider, baby—she'd probably fuck you then chew your head clean off."

By the time Jill met Marlon in Rome in 1968, on the set of *Candy,* she was a very seasoned twenty-one-year-old who'd dated Clint Eastwood and was now sleeping with Christian Marquand. Pat Perez said Jill's first encounter with Marlon was a ménage à trois with Marquand. As Marlon told it, he and Marquand made a game of seducing each other's girlfriends, so he made a play for Jill. "Why don't we go upstairs and fuck?" he recalled as his pickup line. Jill had replied, "Why not?"

Jill shared Marlon's free-and-easy approach to sexuality, his rejection of monogamy as a bourgeois construct. What also made her different from Marlon's other women was that she was a Midwesterner like him. He'd spent his life in search of the exotic, but the woman who most shared his unorthodox worldview had been raised in Storm Lake, Iowa, a little more than a hundred miles, depending on the route, from Omaha, Nebraska, where Marlon was born.

Jill looked nothing like his other girlfriends. "An extraordinary piece of construction," Marlon remembered, "with white skin, soft, natural blond hair, freckles, a lot of moles, green eyes." Her eyes were big, intense, not unlike Bette Davis's. Marlon would claim she had the "slightest hint" of an Irish accent, a "hand-me-down from her mother, who was from Ireland." But that was the fictional "Weonna" of his memoir he was describing: Jill's mother was, in fact, Norwegian. Her father had been Irish, however, so maybe Marlon really did remember Jill that way: he called her his "Irish potato." Certainly, she had the gift of gab: "She told great stories," Pat Perez said. "Her laugh went on for days." Her irreverent sense of humor appealed to Marlon. "She made me laugh harder than any woman I've ever known," he said. "She was quick to understand and laughed at me a lot, too." Like his mother, Marlon said, "she had a sense of the absurd . . . no limits on her imagination."

All his life, Marlon had avoided small-boned, delicate, light-eyed, light-haired women, terrified they would snap apart in his arms, the way his mother had snapped. But Jill seemed unbreakable. Nothing Marlon did destroyed her. She knew about his other women and made no complaint, which only made him want to be with her more, and them less. After a few days at his house, she always returned to her own place; she knew not to wear out her welcome. "She was perceptive enough to realize Marlon became restless after a day or two and would go into silences," Alice said, "so she'd gather all her possessions and depart." She also didn't pull the trick of leaving something behind, as many women did, giving themselves an excuse to come back. Not since Ellen Adler had Marlon been involved with a woman this strong, this independent, this resourceful.

And now she sat there beside him in the car telling him she'd given up pills and wanting him to do so, too. She was the one woman, try as he might, Marlon could not destroy. Had all the abuse he'd heaped on other girlfriends been part of some kind of unconscious test, to see if they were strong enough to survive, if they were more resilient than his mother? If so, only Jill had passed.

"You are the apple of my eye," Marlon told her. It became his name for her. "Come here, Apple," Pat Perez remembered him saying, folding his arms around Jill and pulling her down into his lap. She was so tiny and slight, barely five two, while Marlon was getting wider and bulkier by the day. But they seemed to fit.

SITTING ACROSS FROM his therapist, Marlon shifted in his chair. "I was always squirming in analysis sessions," he said. His latest shrink was George L. Harrington, a proponent of what some called "reality therapy," an approach to psychiatric treatment that spent less time dredging up the past than charting paths for the future. Marlon had spent years ruminating over his past. What he'd never been able to figure out was what came next.

Harrington believed there are four basic human psychological needs after the most basic, the survival instinct: to love and to be loved; to achieve and to feel worthwhile; to be free while also being responsible; and to have fun and pleasure. Only when these needs are in balance could a person function effectively, and only through conscious choice could a person make changes in his or her behavior. This was the ideology Marlon now lived by. In the early 1970s, in the aftermath of the happy experience on *The Godfather*, he did not return to the pessimism of the year before but instead actively attempted to make real change in his life.

Harrington was a rugged, masculine type—the sort of man Marlon had always instinctively distrusted, because they reminded him of his father. The psychiatrist walked with a limp, the result of a car accident, a daily reminder of his resilience. On his wall hung citations for bravery during World War II. He spoke in "a low, husky rumble," Marlon recalled, and when he shook his client's hand, he crushed it. "A lot of male hormones," Marlon said. For all that, Harrington was also "one of the funniest, wittiest, most creative, sensitive and insightful people" Marlon had ever met. His then-radical approach (today, the basis for much psychotherapy) was a revelation. On one of his first visits to Harrington's office in Pacific Palisades, Marlon attempted to dump his "wheelbarrow full of analytic misinformation" at the psychiatrist's feet, wanting to itemize his "neurotic dysfunctions." But Harrington waved him off. "We'll get to them when the time comes," he said. They never did.

What Marlon wanted most was to get a handle on his rage. Not long before starting therapy with Harrington, he'd been in several fights with paparazzi; another time, he'd overturned a table in a club when an annoying fan kept pestering him. That wasn't even counting the sort of rage that prompted him to smash his way into Jill's apartment when he thought she was seeing someone else—he could, she couldn't—and sent her running home to her mother. For too long, Marlon had been at the mercy of his rage, and he asked Harrington to help.

"I think I've got a lot of rage because of my father," Marlon told him.

"You're mad at your father?" Harrington asked.

"Yes," Marlon replied.

"Well," the doctor inquired, "you're not mad now, are you?"

By this point, Marlon Senior had been dead for more than five years. "Well, not right this minute," Marlon admitted.

"Okay," Harrington said. And there the discussion ended. Marlon could have gone further. He could have spent the session lamenting how his father had never believed in him, how he'd destroyed his mother, how he'd never told him he loved him—but, for some reason, Marlon said, Harrington's insouciance about the matter seemed to disarm his anger. A great weight suddenly lifted from his shoulders. Eventually, Marlon was even able to summon some compassion for his father. He imagined that as Marlon Senior passed from this world to the next, he'd been "slump-shouldered" like the beleaguered Willy Loman from *Death of a Salesman*. "And he got to the edge of eternity," Marlon said, "and he sort of looked back and said, 'I did the best I could, kid.'" As his father turned away, Marlon imagined him anticipating being with Dodie.

Possibly Harrington's resemblance to his father had helped Marlon finally, after half a century, let go of his rage. Originally, he thought he and his psychiatrist would "end up in fisticuffs." Instead, "he laughed me out of a lot of trouble." By trusting that a man who reminded him of his father could actually care about him, Marlon seemed to heal himself: "Ultimately I realized I would have to forgive my father if I was ever going to be able to get on with my life." Harrington taught him less about how to resolve his problems than simply "how to forgive," Marlon said, "myself and others."

So, when he told Jill that he would do whatever was needed to make things between them work, he meant it. Whether he could deliver on his promise was the big unknown. But no doubt he was genuine when he made it. The task was never going to be easy. There was a curse on him, after all. Marlon often used that word, or words like it. "The curse" was "on the baby," he'd told Anna. The "family curse" had turned everyone in his family into alcoholics, except for him. The "sins of the father" had come back to haunt him and his children. Curses weren't easily lifted, but Marlon promised he would try.

MID-FEBRUARY 1972 / Sunlight streaming in from the tall windows did little to warm up the drafty, sparsely furnished flat. To make this film, the director had chosen an actual Parisian apartment, rather than a soundstage, because everything in this movie was going to be real. Across a bed stretched Marlon Brando, looking awful. A month and a half before his forty-eighth birthday, his eyes were sunken, his gut hung over his pants, and his hair was wild and coarse. A few feet away, the director was perched on the balls of his feet, studying him. The cameraman focused his lens.

Bernardo Bertolucci was just thirty-one years old. At the moment, he was considered Italy's most fearless auteur. His earlier film, *The Conformist*, had been hailed as an Expressionist indictment of fascism. His current film, shooting with Marlon Brando in a cold, empty apartment in Paris, was about his sexual fantasies, the director admitted. Once, he'd dreamed of having sex with a beautiful woman on the street without ever knowing her name. That separation of sex and love fascinated Bertolucci: why did humans do it, what did it mean, was it sustainable? He'd written the screenplay himself, with Franco Arcalli and later, when additional dialogue was needed, Agnès Varda. His cameraman was Vittorio Storaro, the same who had shot *The Conformist*. They were calling the film *Last Tango in Paris*.

Marlon was playing the part of a middle-aged man named Paul, who has an affair with a much younger woman named Jeanne. But this was no romantic rendezvous. The couple meets when they're looking to rent the same flat; drawn to each other, and with minimal words, they have sex standing up, against the wall. Paul takes the apartment, and they continue their anonymous sexual trysts there. Neither of them, on Paul's insistence, shares any personal information; they don't even reveal their names. All social connection and convention is excised; their relationship is purely sex. Bertolucci intended to be more graphic and explicit in showing that sexual relationship than anything yet seen in a nonpornographic film. "I decided that to suggest and allude," the director explained, "instead of saying it outright would create an unhealthy climate for the spectator."

The script was mostly a road map to get from scene to scene. Much of the dialogue was spontaneous. "I did a lot of improvisation in *Last Tango in Paris*," Marlon remembered. "Bertolucci gave me—because he had no sense of what American slang was like—wide latitude to do what I pleased." The director would suggest to Marlon a general idea of the scene and his character's motivation, and then just set him free. To such direction, Marlon always responded eagerly; whenever his imagination was unleashed in this way, he was happy. "Bertolucci is extraordinary in his ability to perceive," Marlon said. "He's a poet." The best directors, he said, "put you in the psychological circumstances so you do all of that stuff and that is . . . that's the essence of reality."

Marlon had agreed to do the film after a couple of meetings with the director, first in Paris and then in Los Angeles. He'd admired *The Conformist*; Bertolucci, a film aficionado, had admired Marlon's entire career. The director was taking a chance on him, however. Advance word on *The Godfather* continued to be positive, but the film still hadn't been released: had Marlon Brando really reclaimed his genius, or was that all hype? From what Bertolucci had seen so far on the *Tango* set, however, rumors of Brando's comeback were on point. What the actor conjured daily on the set was nothing short of "miraculous," he said.

Yet while Bertolucci might be a poet, there was something about him that Marlon never fully trusted. The director had "some cockamamie notion," Marlon said, "of melding the image of the actor, the performer, with the part." In Bertolucci's vision, Paul would become Marlon; he would be built upon Marlon's specific memories and experiences. Bertolucci said, "Give me some reminiscences about your youth." Stretched across a daybed, with Storaro rolling his camera, Marlon gave it a try. He rambled for a while about his father being a drunk and a "whore fucker." His mother, he said, was "poetic and also a drunk." She'd be gone when he came home from school, off at a bar or locked up in jail. He told the story of the time he was dressed for a date and his father forced him to milk the cow. He talked about digging ditches, and how his mother taught him to love nature. "That," Marlon/Paul said, "was the most she could do." He was opening himself up on that daybed just as he would on his psychiatrist's couch. "Wonderful, wonderful," the director said.

More autobiography can be found throughout the film. Paul punches doors and slams his fist down on tables, possessing the same sudden, explosive rage Marlon was trying to make a thing of the past. Like Marlon, Paul is not a man who's been widely loved. When Jeanne suggests she ought to invent a name for him, Paul replies, "I've been called a million names all my life." He also has Marlon's humor. When he teases Jeanne with a dead rat, joking, "I gotta get some mayonnaise for this," it's an echo of the way Marlon once kidded his sisters with dead mice or the staff on Mulholland Drive with dead bugs. ("A little peanut butter would make it a nice snack," he'd joke.) At the dance hall, Paul moons the officious woman who scolds him, just like the "mighty moon champion" playing him. How Marlon would have loved to have mooned some of the scolds of his past, like Hedda Hopper.

He fascinated Bertolucci. "We are usually dominated by space," the director observed, "but Brando strangely dominates space. Even if Brando is absolutely still, say, sitting on a chair [he] has already taken for himself that privileged space. And Brando's attitude toward life is different from that of other people because of this fact." What Bertolucci was observing was the intensity with which Marlon contemplated his place in that world—the same phenomenon Ellen Adler had once observed herself, when she said she could see Marlon *think*.

The director was fortunate to have such an actor because, outside its general theme of sexual exploration, *Tango* has very little story; nuance and meaning were layered in as they went along. The film was really the self-indulgence of a director obsessed with his own sexual interests and conflicts. With lesser actors, *Tango* might have collapsed under its director's narcissism. "I don't think Bertolucci knew what the film was about," Marlon said. "He went around telling everyone it was about his prick. He looks at me one day and says, 'You are the embodiment . . . the symbol of my prick.' I mean what the fuck does that mean?"

Marlon never did quite figure out what the film was about. Not for three years after its release, in fact, did he even see it, and his best conclusion was "It was about a man desperately trying to find

some meaning in life, full of odd symbols. It's a mythological tale."
As such, *Tango* was a reflection of his life: Marlon was, at the moment, in the midst of his own search for meaning.

His despair over the state of the world had caused him to look
inward. If he couldn't change the world, perhaps the salvation he
sought would be something more personal, something closer to
home. He was, after all, trying to commit to a relationship with
Jill. Paul's desire to keep sex nameless and detached was something Marlon understood and, indeed, had lived. Now he was on
the verge of coming to the same conclusion that Paul realizes for
himself by the end of the film: life without connection is meaningless.

So, it wasn't an easy film to shoot. Marlon was exposing himself
in ways he'd never done before. "Forty years of Brando's life experiences went into the film," Christian Marquand observed. "It is
Brando talking about himself, being himself."

Marlon spends most of the film interacting with Maria Schneider, who plays Jeanne. From day one, their chemistry was apparent. Just nineteen when she started shooting and looking even
younger, Schneider embodied a "blithely amoral charm," one
critic thought, that perfectly expressed the "vie de bohème" of
the film—and indeed of the times. Despite the sexuality they'd be
playing out, Schneider felt only a paternal vibe from Marlon. Just
before production began, he gave her some advice. "We're going
to go through quite a lot together," he said. The best way to get
into their characters, he advised, was not to talk about it: "Just look
me in the eye as hard as you can." Schneider considered the advice
sound. The next day, Marlon sent her flowers, almost as if to apologize in advance for the abuse he'd dole out in the film.

Off-screen, Marlon was quite tender with her, Schneider recalled; he could see his two-year-old daughter, Cheyenne, in her
eyes, he told her. From then on, "he was like a daddy," Schneider
said. In the film, "his character takes that girl and teaches her a lot

of things," Schneider said, "makes her stretch, makes her explode. That's what he did to me as an actress."

Yet his advice not to talk about what they were filming, wise perhaps in the abstract, would have repercussions for all of them.

"BERTOLUCCI," MARLON EXPLAINED, "wanted me to screw Maria Schneider on the screen. I told him, 'That's impossible. If that happens our sex organs become the centerpiece of the film.' He never did agree with me."

The most extreme moment in the script called for Paul to rape Jeanne while instructing her to repeat after him a rejection of love, family, and religion. Everyone knew the basics of the scene. Jeanne would come into the apartment looking for Paul. For a moment, she's afraid, thinking he might be hiding behind a sheet; she calls him "monster" almost as a way to bluff through her fear. Then Paul is revealed to be harmlessly lying on the floor eating a bagel. He tells Maria to go to the kitchen and get him some butter. She throws it at him. Then he comes on to her, trying to have sex with her. When she demurs, he anally rapes her.

"The director wanted you to fuck her?" an interviewer later asked Marlon, just to make sure he had the story straight. "Yes," Marlon replied. "But I said, 'No.'"

Denied that bit of authenticity, Bertolucci still wanted something that would make the scene feel real. "I wanted her reaction as a girl, not as an actress," the director said. So, on the day the scene was to be shot, Bertolucci came up with a bit of business that would achieve that result. The stick of butter Jeanne tosses at Paul would be used as lubricant when Paul sodomizes her. "The sequence of the butter is an idea that I had with Marlon in the morning before shooting," Bertolucci said. "To obtain something I think you have to be completely free. I didn't want Maria to act her humiliation, her rage, I wanted Maria to *feel* the rage and humiliation." Bertolucci instructed no one to tell Schneider about the butter.

The scene played out largely as they had discussed. Marlon is very rough with his young costar, flipping her over and pulling down her jeans. This much Schneider would have been prepared for. "[Maria] knew perfectly well what she was doing," said cameraman Vittorio Storaro. "She was an actress and had no problems with this." What Schneider didn't know was that Marlon was going to slather butter on her exposed buttocks. That was the extent of any direct genital contact, however; Marlon only simulated unzipping his own pants, and when he crawled on top of Schneider he remained fully clothed and unexposed.

But the touch of his greasy fingers on her skin had been enough. "I was so angry," Schneider said, looking back. "Even though what Marlon was doing wasn't real, I was crying real tears." She'd remember Marlon whispering to her, "Maria, don't worry, it's just a movie," but she was inconsolable. She was terrified and humiliated—precisely the reaction Bertolucci was hoping to capture on film.

"I should have called my agent," Schneider reflected, "or had my lawyer come to the set because you can't force someone to do something that isn't in the script." But at the time, she said, "I didn't know that." Bertolucci's admission that he'd kept the use of the butter secret from Schneider would fuel outrage over the film for decades. The director maintained that the actress was fully aware of the violence in the script and that "the only novelty was the idea of the butter." Yet, whether he wanted to think so or not, that novelty in and of itself offered plenty of reason to justify Schneider's reaction.

Bertolucci's seeming inability to appreciate his leading lady's sense of violation is perhaps not surprising, given the resolutely male gaze of the film. Jeanne is only a vehicle to tell Paul's— Bertolucci's—story. Her own story doesn't seem to matter as much. When, at the end, Jeanne shoots and kills Paul, Bertolucci surmised she did it because she was either "too bourgeois" to continue with their bohemian existence or, the opposite: she's "better than he is and doesn't want to accept his new conventionality." It didn't seem to occur to him that the reason Jeanne might have shot Paul was *because he raped her.*

Bertolucci's sympathies become even more obvious when one realizes that he cut a nude scene for Marlon because he was sensitive that it might embarrass him. Originally, the verisimilitude the director was going for had included nudity for both his stars. But when Marlon had to take his clothes off, as the star himself remembered, the apartment "was freezing cold, and my prick was the size of a peanut, reduced to nothing, and I was standing there with this peanut prick that you couldn't get a hold of if you had a button hook." The scene was cut to spare Marlon that shame. "I had so identified myself with Brando that I cut it out of shame for myself," Bertolucci said. "To show him naked would have been like showing me naked."

No such sensitivity for Schneider, however, whose body is frequently exposed for the camera. Clearly, Bertolucci was working through his demons on this film; he'd said it was about his "prick," after all. Some critics thought if he'd been braver, he would have cast a young man as Paul's sexual partner, not a young woman. "You have to understand what kind of world Bertolucci is in," Maria Schneider said, many years later. "The part I play was written for a boy! That's why the butter, the sodomization, the gag . . ." Whether or not Bertolucci was exploring repressed homosexuality in *Last Tango in Paris*, he has never acknowledged, though, clearly he felt some discomfort with the idea of same-sex desire: "I've been in Freudian analysis for eight years," he said, not long after the film was released, "and I think 'adult' homosexuality is an impossible contradiction. It can't exist."

Yet the question remains: was it wrong for the director (and Marlon, and everyone else on the set) to withhold the detail of the butter from Schneider until the cameras were rolling? At the time,

Marlon likely didn't think much about it either way: the director had said to keep it secret, so he had. That was commonplace in film-making. Alfred Hitchcock was notorious for not telling his actors something that was about to happen, to catch them by surprise. Directors had in fact been catching their actors off guard since they dangled them out of windows during the silent film days. A year earlier, Al Martino had been blindsided by the slap Marlon, as Don Vito Corleone, delivered across his face; it made for better cinema because his reaction was real. Eighteen years earlier, during *On the Waterfront*, Eva Marie Saint had been utterly unprepared for what Marlon was going to do when, as Terry Malloy, he burst into her apartment. She was terrified, Saint recalled, especially when Marlon started kissing her. But the terror on her face, real terror, was exactly what Kazan wanted for the scene. Saint later called the moment "beautiful."

But just because the practice was commonplace didn't make it right. Today, "consent" means something more specific, more humane, than it did in 1972. What Bertolucci did—with the complicity of Marlon and the cameraman and everyone else on the set—was wrong. Upon the film's release, the National Organization for Women condemned *Tango*'s "male definitions of female sexuality." Grace Glueck, the art news editor for the *New York Times*, slammed the "male fantasy" of the film, the idea that "women may protest, but they really wallow in rough handling." Glueck argued that *Tango*'s real "breakthrough" wasn't about art, but in its exposé of "the real sexual status" of women in the culture: they were little girls for whom rape could sometimes be "good for their souls."

Schneider never blamed Marlon for her trauma. In fact, she said, "the best part" of making the film had been getting to know him. "We stayed friends until the end," she said. She did say at one point that she felt raped by both Marlon and Bertolucci, but her point seemed to be that she felt as violated by the director as her character had felt violated by Paul. Neither did Schneider fault

Marlon for his complicity in the silence on the set; that was the way things were done then; consciousness had yet to be raised. Indeed, she pointed out that Marlon had himself felt violated by Bertolucci's "very manipulative" methods: "And he was Marlon Brando," Schneider said, "so you can imagine how I felt." Yet Marlon had not endured a simulated anal rape, and his body hadn't been exposed for the camera, groped with greasy fingers. The truth was what happened on that set was wrong. Schneider never wavered in that belief for the rest of her life.

ALTHOUGH NOT AS horrifying as Schneider's experience, Marlon's time on *Last Tango in Paris* was nonetheless devastating. When Bertolucci showed him a rough cut, Marlon was speechless. "When he realized what we were doing," Bertolucci said, "that he was delivering so much of his own experience . . . he was very upset with me." The director was unsympathetic. "Listen," he told Marlon, "you are a grown-up. Didn't you realize what you were doing?" Apparently not, for once filming was complete, Marlon did not speak to the director again for many years.

Perhaps embarrassed when rumors of his reaction to the film surfaced, Marlon tried to deny that what audiences were seeing up there on the screen was actually him and that the emotions Paul was expressing were really his own. "There's a certain line you draw," he told Chris Hodenfield from *Rolling Stone*, beyond which he would not exploit memories for "some goddamn check that came in at the end of the week." Hodenfield asked him how he'd managed to deliver such a powerful performance in *Tango*, in that case. "After a while," Marlon replied, "it becomes a technical thing. I was putting things in my eyes to make tears. I was making the right noises, the sound of sobs."

Hodenfield was right to be skeptical. Marlon's work in the film, he argued, "seemed like more than mere technique." Certainly Marlon had the technical expertise and the imagination to do a great many convincing things on film, but his performance in *Last Tango in Paris* is far more than just technique. In private, he admitted the truth: "That was a very, very difficult film," he said in taped recordings for his memoir that he would censor from the finished book. "That's when I decided that I was never going to kill myself again, emotionally. That's what is exhausting about acting. It was very taxing to do that." From then on, he said, any parts that he played would be enacted "in a different manner." He would rely only on technique. "If you have a smooth enough technique," he said, "people can't tell."

Taking Marlon at his word, then, *Last Tango in Paris* was the last time he put himself fully into a character. That didn't mean other credible performances weren't still to come. It did mean, however, that his great ones were over. And despite the fact that *Tango* was in some ways the seedy vanity project of a self-absorbed director obsessed with his own "prick" (or perhaps it was "all about his psychoanalysis," Marlon said elsewhere), there's no question that its two mistreated leads render great, powerful, heartbreaking performances. Everything Marlon had learned in three decades of acting was brought to the part. No matter what Marlon tried to claim after the fact, it is not just technique we see when Paul breaks down and sobs. That is Stella and Kazan; and Stanley Kowalski and Terry Malloy and Sage from *Truckline Café*; and the young man at his mother's deathbed; and the still-younger man bailing her out of jail and saving her from his father's fists; and the young father snatching his son away from a drunken, hysterical ex-wife; and the crusader marching through all-white housing projects; and the lonely older man sitting outside Jill's mother's apartment, hoping Jill will give him another chance.

But that was it. *Finis.* Marlon concluded that he was too old, too weary, too raw from his sessions with Harrington, to "commit harikari," as he called it. When, at the end of *Tango*, Jeanne shoots Paul, Marlon made the choice to have him expire in a fetal position, "in a self-conscious way," he said. Paul dies in his quest to reach consciousness. Marlon, on the same journey, didn't want to have to go that far.

**MARCH 8, 1972** / In El Paso, Texas, a man without any hands answered a ringing telephone with his steel claw. He was Jay J. Armes, a forty-year-old private detective. On the other end of the line was Marlon Brando, world-famous movie star. He was calling from Paris, where he was making a movie. Brando told Armes his son had been kidnapped and he wanted the detective to find him.

On the set of *Last Tango in Paris*, Marlon was distraught and in tears. His lawyer had called to tell him that Anna had taken Christian out of the Ojai Valley School and had not brought him back as promised. The boy had slipped out of his mother's control and made his way to his father's house, but Anna, drunk and abusive, had caught up with him. Police were summoned, but they didn't know how to resolve the situation; Anna was the boy's mother, sharing legal custody with her ex-husband, who was out of the country. Fourteen-year-old Christian eventually acted as the grown-up and told his increasingly hysterical mother that he'd go with her. But first thing in the morning, he insisted, he was returning to his father's house.

He never made it back. Anna hired a friend to drive Christian to Mexico. When Marlon's attorneys learned this, they finally placed a call to him in Paris.

Those on the set recalled how upset Marlon was when he got the news. Shooting was suspended as he dealt with the crisis. The police had no evidence, other than Marlon's attorneys' word, that any kidnapping had occurred. The best approach, they advised, was to wait. But Marlon wasn't about to just sit around, six thousand miles away. He booked a flight to Los Angeles and began searching for someone outside law enforcement to help him. Jill, who was with him in Paris, had an idea. She'd heard about Armes from actor-producer Jack Webb, with whom she'd worked several times on *Dragnet*. (Webb was also Marlon's long-ago costar in *The Men*.) The detective came highly recommended by Webb. Despite his handicap, Armes had a track record of success and was known for taking cases the police either didn't have time to pursue or felt powerless to investigate.

Over the phone, Marlon gave the detective the few details he had. What he'd learned about Armes made him optimistic he was the man for the job. Despite losing his hands in a childhood accident, the detective was muscular, a fitness fanatic, and an expert marksman with both a pistol and a machine gun. He was also a deep-sea diver, and a pilot, not to mention an electronics surveillance expert. And he did "not hesitate to use his hooks in a fight," according to one report. While he might have been the only investigator operating out of that seedy little office on the outskirts of El Paso, Armes boasted that he had more than two thousand contacts across the country he could call on at any time.

Marlon told him he wanted Christian found and returned safely to him in Los Angeles. Armes told him his rate was $25,000 plus all expenses. Marlon agreed.

Hanging up the phone with the detective, Marlon broke down. Christian's kidnapping tapped the fear and paranoia that were constantly roiling just under the surface for him. "Marlon had his gun always ready," said one friend. "He was always so afraid that he or one of his children would be targeted." He'd been told that the friend Anna had hired to drive Christian into Mexico was a decade younger than she was and a "hippie." For all his counterculture credibility, Marlon wasn't above imagining his son's kidnapper "as some stoned-out Manson family groupie," his friend said. Jill calmed him down and got him on the flight back to LA.

Meanwhile, Armes started hunting. He phoned his contacts at the United States–Mexico border control and learned that a red Volkswagen carrying persons matching the descriptions of the suspects had crossed the border the day before, March 7. They were heading south into Baja California. After interviewing friends of Anna, Armes determined that "the abductors were not the types to stay in cities, much less hotels." So, he chartered a jet helicopter and set off into Mexico.

From high above the arid, rocky Mexican terrain, the detective hunted for the telltale red Volkswagen. On his first day of searching, he focused his attention inland, dropping the chopper low over towns to scour streets and parking lots. The Baja peninsula south of Tijuana and Mexicali was sparsely populated, making this needle-in-a-haystack search at least theoretically possible. On the second day of the hunt, operating on a tip that Anna's friend hung out with fishermen, Armes began flying low over the coastline of the Sea of Cortés. Finally, on the third day, he spotted a red Volkswagen parked along the coast, about four hundred miles south of the California border. The encampment, which looked to be made up of fishermen, was remote, far from any towns. Armes radioed federal agents and then landed the chopper some miles away. Meeting up with Mexican police, he rode with them to the encampment. "To be honest," Armes said, "I didn't know what to expect. It might have been a false alarm, or they might have had machine guns waiting for us."

What they found was a bunch of stoned-out "hippie types," Armes said, just what Marlon imagined. At gunpoint, the police lined up the six men and two women. In one vehicle, Armes discovered a stockpile of canned goods, enough to last several months.

He found Christian, shirtless and barefoot, in a tent. The boy was terrified and "didn't appear to be in good health," Armes later reported to a judge. One of the men, James Barry Wooster, revealed that Anna had offered him ten thousand dollars to hide the boy for a few months.

As police took the men into custody, Armes was given permission to drive Christian home. That proved almost as difficult as finding him. The fourteen-year-old remained frightened; he didn't trust that Armes was working for his father. He'd later tell a friend that when the detective found him in the tent, it was like "a bad dream . . . these two hooks [coming] through the flap at him." Twice on their way back to the United States, Christian tried to escape from Armes's rental car; at one point, the detective chased him down across a mesa, where the boy almost fell off a high cliff. Armes then hired a cab to drive them the rest of the way to Los Angeles, so he could sit in the backseat with Christian and watch him.

It wasn't until he saw his father that Christian finally believed that Armes had been trying to help him. The boy was ecstatic to see Marlon, running to him, hanging on to him. An emergency hearing was called in family court in Santa Monica, where Armes described the kidnapping and the conditions in which he'd found the boy. But would this finally be enough to get Christian away from his mother?

That day in court, Anna was not present. She was, in fact, being bailed out of jail. She'd gone off on her own quest to seize Christian, but had gotten into several drunken brawls with her companions along the way. Run out of one town, she was thrown into jail in another. She'd never made it over the Mexican border.

Anna had sunk to her lowest point. When she was finally sober enough, she called the kidnapping charge ludicrous; she insisted to the court that she was simply heading to Mexico to join Christian for a vacation with friends. No one believed her, but kidnapping charges were never filed against her. She was the boy's legal custodian, after all. She wasn't even charged with child endangerment.

Marlon was apoplectic with rage. To the court, he demanded that there be no more indulgence of Anna. He had tried helping her; the court had tried, too, by giving her the benefit of the doubt. But Anna was now as much a hopeless alcoholic as Dodie had been during Marlon's youth, perhaps even worse. Now she had actually placed Christian's life in jeopardy, all because of her obsessive need to see Marlon "lose." He asked the court to grant him sole custody.

A final hearing was called for the following month, at which time the judge would make a decision. In the meantime, Marlon was given permission to take Christian with him back to France so he could finish *Last Tango in Paris*. Boarding the plane, as one friend of Christian's would tell the story, Marlon looked into his son's big, dark eyes and made him a promise: "You will never, ever, have to feel afraid again."

MARCH 14, 1972 / Despite the pouring rain, spotlights swung across Broadway and Forty-Fifth Street and hundreds of fans crowded around Loew's State Theatre in Times Square as *The Godfather* was given its world premiere. Limousines pulled up in front of the theater to discharge famous passengers. From one limo stepped Henry Kissinger, national security advisor for President Nixon. From another came former diplomat Sargent Shriver and his wife, Eunice Kennedy. Movie stars were in abundance, posing for photographs under the theater marquee to keep out of the rain: Raquel Welch, Alan Arkin, James Coburn, Gene Hackman. Ali MacGraw arrived with her husband, producer Robert Evans, one of the men at Paramount who'd financed the picture they were all about to see. Then there was the director of *The Godfather* himself, Francis Ford Coppola, along with his stars: James Caan, Al Pacino, Robert Duvall, Diane Keaton—all of them, in fact, except one.

Marlon Brando had promised to be there. So strongly did he feel about this film that he'd even arranged with Bernardo Bertolucci to get out of filming *Last Tango in Paris* in order to attend the New York premiere. He'd wanted to be there because he liked the film, liked his director, liked his costars, and indeed, liked his performance. But then his son got kidnapped. Even though the situation was resolved happily in time for the premiere, Marlon had decided not to subject Christian to more photographers, and flew straight back to Paris. The show in New York went on without him.

His presence was felt regardless. That first-night crowd was thunderstruck by the power and emotion that flashed before them on the screen, cut through with "a scarlet skein of violence," as Frederick Winship, reviewing for UPI, described it. For Vincent Canby, *The Godfather* was "the gangster melodrama come of age, truly sorrowful and truly exciting, without the false piety of the films that flourished forty years ago, scaring the delighted hell out of us while cautioning that crime doesn't (or shouldn't) pay."

This was a new world, one where sex and violence were being shown in all their complicated truth on the screen. Just as *On the Waterfront* had done two decades earlier, *The Godfather* tapped the public's desire for grittier, more honest, more rule-breaking films. Within days of its premiere, it was the number-one movie in America, far outpacing every single other picture released that year. When the final revenues were tallied at the end of 1972, *The Godfather* would rack up $81.5 million, making it the biggest-grossing picture of all time. The Mafia epic trounced its nearest competitor, *Fiddler on the Roof*, which made $25 million.

And the name at the top of every ad, the one that dominated every review and every public and private conversation about the film, was Marlon Brando.

"The film is affecting for many reasons," Canby wrote, "including the return of Marlon Brando, who has been away only in spirit, as Don Vito Corleone, the magnificent, shrewd, old Corleone patriarch. It's not a large role, but he is the key to the film, and to the contributions of all the other performers." Marlon's presence is so strong, in fact, wrote Foster Hirsch, historian of the Actors Studio, "that he dominates the long film even though in actual screen time he has a supporting role." The Don's "hushed voice rasping out commands in darkened rooms, [his] hand raised in a benediction that looks like a death sentence" were images that left "a potent memory in the minds of the other characters as well as of the audience."

Marlon had taken what could have been a solid, if typical, character part and turned the Don into the centerpiece, the heart, of the film. When Ellen Adler saw the film, she was duly impressed, though she knew it was a "no-no" to congratulate Marlon on a performance. But *The Godfather*, she discovered, was an exception. Marlon was happy to talk about it when she raised the subject; he was very proud of his work in it. He told Ellen how he'd played much of it "with his hands behind his back, so he wouldn't use all the clichés of Italians speaking with their hands."

There's so much that Marlon does in the film, sometimes in milliseconds, that invests an entire script in just one breath, much the same way his simple "wow" conveys so much in *On the Waterfront*. In the garden scene with Al Pacino, where the Don ruefully accepts his youngest, favorite son as his successor in the family business, Marlon proved that his mastery had remained even after eleven flops in a row. "The moment with Pacino, where they're sitting talking," said Tom Oppenheim, Ellen Adler's son and today the director of the Stella Adler Studio of Acting, "Marlon has a wandering thought. He's going to say it, then decides not to say it, and you think, what was that? The question opens up so much mystery. I'm sure it's not in the script." It wasn't: it was Marlon, once again, inhabiting the character and making the audience believe, care, and want more.

Many reviewers also praised the Don's death scene, done mostly in pantomime with a little boy, the first time, in fact, Marlon had ever acted opposite a child. He made sure to play with the boy, four-year-old Anthony Gounaris, ahead of the scene, so there would be familiarity with his on-screen grandchild. Again, no script: just the camera rolling and Marlon, in character, playing with the child in the vegetable garden. There's a sweetness between them, an easy rapport, a glimpse of what Marlon may have been like with his own children when they were that age, before their adolescence left him uncertain and tentative with them.

Marlon was taking a chance with the scene. To make the boy laugh, he slips an orange peel into his mouth to cover his teeth. He growls—but instead of delighting little Anthony, he frightens him. The child's eyes widen, and he emits a little shriek. Marlon hadn't known how the boy would react to his prank, but he was so much in the character that he was ready for anything. If the boy had laughed, Marlon might have growled some more and laughed along with him. But when the child whimpered, Marlon scooped him up in his arms. Little Anthony is reassured. Grandfather consoles grandson. This isn't acting—at least, it's not the acting most actors do. It's *living*.

Marlon always said that the best acting came from just being in the moment; memorizing lines killed any connection to reality. Everyone acts, he said, every day. Nowhere is that vision better manifested than here. The scene of the Don and his grandson is as real as anything ever committed to film, and because of that, it is all the more heartbreaking when the old man, chasing the boy through the tall tomato plants, drops dead of a heart attack. Little Anthony, genuinely frightened a moment earlier, now genuinely laughs at the funny man who has fallen to the ground, just as any little boy, unacquainted with mortality, might do.

The Brando magic lived. Not only were bettors laying odds that Marlon would be nominated for an Academy Award, but a large number of pundits were predicting he would win. If so, it would be the comeback of the decade.

"BRANDO'S BACK!" READ the headline in a film and television fan magazine, declaring that the one-time matinee idol and box-office champ had returned "once more to the pinnacle of stardom." With the success of *The Godfather*, Marlon was offered all sorts of parts, and it seemed every reporter on every payroll (radio, newspapers, magazines, television) was trying to land an interview with him.

Since his previous heyday, however, the entertainment press had changed a great deal. Such old foes as Hedda Hopper, Dorothy Kilgallen, and Mike Connolly were dead. Many of the leading Hollywood scribes were younger, in tune with the changing times. No longer was the most important celebrity news found in fan magazines such as *Photoplay* or *Screenland*, which had either morphed into TV journals or gone out of business. Rather, stories about films and film stars could be found in hip, counterculture-resonant publications such as *Rolling Stone*, the *Village Voice*, and *After Dark*—even *Playboy*. Marlon could say "fuck" in interviews now (which he said a lot) and get it printed, at least in these publications.

At age forty-eight, he wasn't the heartthrob he'd been at twenty-eight, and his part in *The Godfather* made him seem even older than he was. Still, it was remarkable how much cachet his name still carried. In the flush of his post-*Godfather* success, he was on the covers of *Time*, *Life*, and *Newsweek*, and featured prominently in such myriad titles as *Vogue*, *Coronet*, *Rolling Stone*, *After Dark*, *Ladies' Home Journal*, and *Playboy*. Yet, despite the novelty of seeing his "fucks" in black and white (though, not in *Ladies' Home Journal*, of course), much of the coverage Marlon received wasn't all that different from a decade before. He was still asked about whether he'd been in a feud with James Dean or Montgomery Clift, which wife or girlfriend he'd loved best, whether he'd ever had an affair with Marilyn Monroe. It was enough to make him pine for the indifference with which he'd been treated through much of the late 1960s.

"This at a time," he said, looking back, "when what the national conversation should have been about [was] how we were in the midst of a mass disintegration, how every part of society was coming undone." Nine years since he'd launched his lawsuit against *The Saturday Evening Post* (which had finally ended with a small settlement), Marlon was still pointing fingers at the media. "The American public lives in a state of denial," he said. If such comments derailed his comeback, he was blasé. "Somebody has to say these things," he said.

It wasn't that he was against escapist entertainment. Marlon could spend entire days laughing at old Laurel and Hardy movies. His objection was to its ubiquity: serious magazines were going out of business, replaced by the *National Enquirers* and the *People* magazines, and for every editor who assigned a story on race relations, there were a dozen more who sent reporters chasing after celebrity trifles. "There are news items that are worth one hundred dollars," Marlon explained. "There are some that are worth several thousand dollars. Some news items are worth one hundred thousand dollars. People sell news, and unfortunately people in my position, people in the public eye, are sellable commodities. [We're] not any different from Kleenex or Dial soap, or anything else."

The rise of the paparazzi was especially egregious, Marlon felt. The shutterbugs from *Photoplay* who'd chased him around in the 1950s were intrepid, to be sure, but they were nothing compared to this new breed of photographers, turned rabid by the promise of big bucks. Christian's kidnapping had brought the wolves to Marlon's door. The boy, already traumatized by the experience, was further agitated by men with cameras jumping out at him from behind bushes as he headed to court with his father. "Anytime it has to do with the kids," Marlon said, "I just go berserk. I can't stand any kind of invasion of privacy like that." Once, in Italy, when one of his boys was little, a paparazzo jumped at them, and Marlon took after him like a bullet. "I chased him for two fucking blocks," he recalled.

Younger stars being mentioned as potential Oscar nominees might have played nice with the press, been deferential and ingratiating. Not Marlon. All journalists who requested interviews with him, he decreed, would have to adhere to his rules: there would be no more Truman Capote surprises. Writers Marlon didn't know had to prove themselves first. At one point, one of Marlon's staff tried to get him to speak with a reporter, but because Marlon wasn't familiar with him, he said the reporter needed to sign a contract granting him approval of the entire text and nature of the interview. The staffer argued, "Well, this fellow is an established Hollywood correspondent." Marlon shot back, "Then he's probably going to write a standard Hollywood correspondent piece." The staffer backed down, and the reporter signed. It was either Marlon's way or no way.

What interviewers got (those lucky enough to get anything at all) was a very different Brando from the taciturn, enigmatic figure of his early career. This was the garrulous Brando, fully in charge, the Brando who sat back in his chair and expounded on whatever he chose to expound on, often in a rather idiosyncratic stream of consciousness. "He does not take up a point and extrapolate to the far measures," a writer from *Rolling Stone* observed. "He starts on a virgin asteroid and winds his way back to earth, free versing and free associating, leaving behind his poetic blur of images about the Russian troops hovering at the Mongolian border, and what starvation does to a baby's brain, and the time he drove through the African riverbeds during monsoon season." And so on, in that vein.

Marlon might be eccentric. He might come across as arrogant, or stubborn, or exasperating, or provocative, or pretentious. But the one thing he absolutely refused to be was superficial. He didn't have to play the game. He no longer needed anything from Hollywood or the media. He'd collected his final installment on *The Godfather* and was once again solvent. Maybe even rich. After initially working for nothing, he'd walked away with a million and a half for his services. Of course, he could have made more if he'd held out for the back end, as *The Godfather* was making more money than any movie ever. But money hadn't been Marlon's goal. His goal had been the freedom that money bought, the independence, the ability to say, "Fuck you," and get it printed.

IN A SMALL motel in Santa Fe, Marlon was climbing the walls. Jill tried to calm him down, but she had little success. They'd come to this place, "where no one would recognize him," in order for Marlon to go "cold turkey" off the Valium that kept his moods even. It was a promise he'd made to Jill when they got back together. But after a few days, he couldn't stand it. He "was cramping [and] bugs were crawling on him," Alice would report later. "You name it, it was happening to him." Going cold turkey wasn't the way to do it, but Marlon was determined. "He did not want to be a drug addict," Alice said. If Valium was making him one, as both Alice and Jill seemed to think, then he wanted off it.

When they got Marlon back home, doctors prescribed a tapering down of his dosage rather than a complete withdrawal. Valium and drugs like it, if carefully regulated, can be lifesavers for some people, especially those with post-traumatic stress; this was the case for Marlon. Dr. Harrington never advised that he completely stop taking it. Without the moderating influence of the drug, Marlon "couldn't face the world," Alice said; it kept the darkness from taking over the way it had so often done when he was younger.

Yet it had been more than just Valium that had freed him from the darkness. Not in many years had Marlon found himself lying on the floor unable to move or speak. That was due to the very difficult work he did, week after week, year after year, in psychotherapy, confronting issues other people spent lifetimes avoiding.

The attempt to go cold turkey off the Valium may have been misguided, but it speaks to Marlon's determination in these years to wrestle down, once and for all, the demons of his past. He could be a "master manipulator," Alice said, so she never knew if what he told her about his psychotherapy was absolutely true, but even if half of what he told her was accurate, even a third, then he was making progress. Sometimes he had her and other friends speak to Dr. Harrington themselves, to give him their take on his conflicts. He hoped it would give the doctor "a more rounded impression" of him. It was a brave move on Marlon's part, because his friends could expose any of the half-truths he'd told, or tell their sides of the story, or reveal insights of which even Marlon was unaware. But he was that "committed to his psychological healing," another friend said. "He really wanted to get better."

Around this time, as Alice would recall, Marlon arrived home beaming from a session with Harrington. "I'm not crazy," he sang out. He might still need to work on his "explosive anger" and his sometimes "juvenile behavior," but Harrington had assured him, probably in response to a question from Marlon, that that didn't mean he was crazy: he was just "eccentric," the psychiatrist said. Marlon was relieved. "He could live with this type of crazy," Alice said.

That spring of 1972, he was indeed feeling good about himself. The courts had finally awarded him full custody of Christian. Despite Marlon's fears of civil war and government crackdowns— those never entirely went away—he couldn't help but feel some measure of optimism. "We're going to do okay together," he told his son, as one of Christian's friends recalled. "Things are going to be better from here on."

JANUARY 28, 1973 / The audience for the Golden Globe Awards at the Century Plaza Hotel in Century City was getting unruly, heckling the presenters. "That's what happens when you put a lot of booze on the tables of celebrities who haven't yet had dinner," quipped presenter Walter Matthau. The Golden Globe ceremony was not the prestigious event the Oscars were. There'd been no rehearsals, which meant "mix-ups, no shows, and jokes that fell flat," in the words of one reviewer. Gene Hackman's speech was "so muffled you couldn't catch the name of the winner," and oldtimers Robert Young and June Allyson "just messed up everything as a tandem."

Toward the end of the night, Matthau and Carol Burnett presented the award for Best Actor in a Drama. The nominees were Marlon Brando for *The Godfather*, Michael Caine and Laurence Olivier for *Sleuth*, Al Pacino for *The Godfather*, and Jon Voight for *Deliverance*. The winner was Marlon Brando. Several awkward moments followed as the applause died down and no one came forward to accept Brando's award. Thinking fast, Burnett ad-libbed, "This is for Marlon Brando, who's in Tahiti, and I'm going to take it to him right now." That got a laugh, and the ceremony stumbled on, handing the Best Picture prize, as everyone expected, to *The Godfather*.

Marlon's absence wasn't all that remarkable. Other actors had skipped what was, at the time, a distinctly second-rate affair: Liv Ullmann wasn't there to accept her Best Actress award for *The Emigrants*, nor was Jack Lemmon present to pick up his award for Best Actor in a Comedy for *Avanti!* So, Marlon's no-show evoked little public comment—until he sent a telegram to various members of the press.

"There is a singular lack of honor in this country today," Marlon wrote in his cable, "what with the government's change of its citizens into objects of use, its imperialism and warlike intrusion into foreign countries and the killing not only of their inhabitants but also indirectly of our own people, its treatment of the Indians and the blacks, the assault on the press and the rape of the ideals which were the foundations of this country." By "assault on the press," Marlon was referring to ongoing attempts by the Nixon administration to curtail First Amendment rights, especially during the release of the Pentagon Papers, and the president's frequent hostile comments about a free press. Marlon went on: "I respectfully ask you to understand that to accept an honor, however well-intended, is to subtract from the meager amount [of honor] left. Therefore, to simplify things, I hereby decline any nomination and deny anyone representing me."

Marlon's statement was both a retroactive explanation for his absence at the Golden Globes and a proactive message to the Academy of Motion Picture Arts and Sciences, which was preparing to announce its own nominees for that year's Oscars in just a few days: *I hereby decline any nomination*. The language was clear, straightforward, and unambiguous.

Still, some refused to believe it. Marlon's friend at the Associated Press, Bob Thomas, wrote a piece wondering if the star would truly decline a nomination if one were given to him. Yet Marlon had stated, categorically, that he would, indeed. Certainly, there was precedent for turning down an Academy Award: just two years earlier, George C. Scott, whose distaste for acting contests was well known in Hollywood, had refused the Best Actor prize for *Patton*. "The whole thing is a goddamn meat parade," Scott said. "I don't want any part of it."

Marlon shared that belief. The Academy Awards, he insisted, had been founded as a way "for the movie men to capitalize on their profits." Honoring the best was a sham rationale, Marlon argued, because it was impossible to do: how could his performance in *The Godfather* truly be compared against Paul Winfield's in

*Sounder*, for example, or Peter O'Toole's in *The Ruling Class*? Even more absurd, how could he possibly be in competition with Al Pacino, for the same film, for two performances that were so intrinsically tied together?

Marlon's position on the awards went even further than Scott's, however. It was less a critique of the Academy than a declaration on how citizens in the public eye ought to conduct themselves in a time of national crisis, which Marlon genuinely felt the early 1970s to be. His depression might have lifted, but he still felt that bad times were at hand. While a cease-fire in Vietnam had been called, the war could reignite at any moment. Moreover, Nixon's attacks on the press were escalating due to reports that his administration was involved in a cover-up of a burglary at the Democratic National Committee offices at the Watergate complex in Washington, DC. According to several friends, Marlon feared the president might actually start imprisoning journalists and possibly even declare martial law in order to save his own skin.

At what point in a national crisis does business as usual become complicit in the problem? For Marlon, that time had already arrived. The idea of "business as usual" for public figures felt morally wrong. To Marlon, it was not acceptable for a president to attack his own citizens, to subvert the law, and to refuse to meet with aggrieved parties, as Nixon's assistant secretary of the interior, Harrison Loesch, had done after a delegation of American Indians crossed the country, in a well-publicized demonstration, to present their grievances to him. Nixon's landslide reelection the previous November had left him feeling cocky: he believed he could contain the growing scandal. He denounced the Watergate investigations of the *Washington Post*, causing its publisher, Katharine Graham, to express anxiety over the president's threats. This was the context in which Marlon wrote his telegram about award shows, the "singular lack of honor" he so passionately decried.

To proceed normally, Marlon believed, would make him "part

of the problem." Others, even those who shared his political beliefs, might not yet have felt the crisis had reached such a tipping
point. But Marlon had been ready for this sort of public protest ever
since King's assassination and the derailment, in his view, of the
civil rights movement. There was no way he could have blithely
gone on with the show, hawking a movie to pump even more dollars into Paramount's coffers, no matter how highly he thought
of the movie. He could not pretend that such things as Best Actor
awards mattered when, in his view, the Constitution was being
subverted—and young men of color were being routinely singled
out and murdered.

That wasn't just rhetoric. Just days before Marlon sent his telegram, Wesley Bad Heart Bull, twenty years old, a resident of the
Pine Ridge Indian Reservation in South Dakota, had been stabbed
to death by a white man in what witnesses called a race-motivated
attack. The murder led to a riot at the Custer County Courthouse,
ignited when police attempted to suppress a demonstration by two
hundred Indians protesting crimes of hate and discrimination. The
victim's mother was arrested in the melee; she would serve five
months in jail, while her son's killer got no jail time at all. After
this, business as usual was simply inconceivable to Marlon.

Nonetheless, when the nominees were announced on February
12, his name was on the Academy's list. Most members likely voted
to nominate him before his telegram had been made public. But
now that his feelings were clear, would they still vote to give him
the statuette? A flurry of articles followed, speculating on what
might happen at the awards ceremony. Various columnists wondered what it would mean to the Academy if actors started disregarding their awards. "Will we lose that venerable tradition?" one
especially fretful writer asked. The banality of these articles was
made only starker when they were read against the contempora-
neous accounts of Wesley Bad Heart Bull's funeral or his mother
being sent to jail.

Marlon once again became a lightning rod for anger from the right. The editorial board of the *Hattiesburg American* in Hattiesburg, Mississippi, had read Marlon's statement, and decided "to put him up for some sort of award for the most puerile radical-chic snow job of the year." Hattiesburg, of course, had been the site of numerous civil rights demonstrations, and the *American* had run a headline accusing Marlon of "making trouble" during his visit to Gadsden, in neighboring Alabama. "What the world needs least right now," the *American's* editorial board declared, "is a lecture on honor from Marlon Brando," who, they pointed out, had just engaged in "some rather kinky explicit sex in his latest movie, an arty pornography thing called *The* [sic] *Last Tango in Paris*." The editorial asked the question: "Which diminishes honor most, accepting an honorable award for acting or playing the lead role in a pornographic movie?"

At least nine other newspapers took similar positions denouncing Marlon's telegram; none addressed the specific charges of racism in Hollywood, and nearly all used *Tango* as their means of attack. If Marlon thought he'd encountered problems and controversies on the set of that picture, he had no idea what was waiting for him when the film was released.

*LAST TANGO IN PARIS* had been shown for one night during the New York Film Festival in October 1972 in order to generate a buzz. It then premiered in Europe in December. Most American reviewers, therefore, had to wait to see the picture when it opened in the United States in February. Still, its reputation preceded it: the raw sex, the frank dialogue, the rape. For the American market, *Tango* was rated X. In the early days of the rating system, a number of prestige pictures had been given an X: *Midnight Cowboy* started out with an X rating and won the Best Picture Oscar. Three years later, however, major-studio films were rarely tagged with an X; that designation had been happily appropriated by the pornographic film industry, hoping to draw attention to itself. But *Last Tango in Paris* was a major-studio exception. The X loomed large in its ads.

United Artists, therefore, needed to be very shrewd in its marketing of the film. One of the reviewers who'd seen *Tango* at its October screening had been the influential Pauline Kael, and she'd been awestruck. "Bernardo Bertolucci's *Last Tango in Paris* was presented for the first time on the closing night of the New York Film Festival, October 14, 1972," she wrote in *The New Yorker*. "That date should become a landmark in movie history comparable to May 29, 1913—the night *Le Sacre du Printemps* was first performed—in music history. *Last Tango in Paris* has the same kind of hypnotic excitement as the *Sacre*, the same primitive force, and the same thrusting, jabbing eroticism." Bertolucci and Brando, Kael declared, "have altered the face of an art form."

Kael's review generated a sense of heightened expectation for the film, which allowed United Artists to land the covers of both *Time* and *Newsweek* in its advance promotion of *Tango*. "With a propagandist like Miss Kael," William Collins of the *Philadelphia Inquirer* wrote, "United Artists doesn't really need a publicity department." On Christmas Eve, UA bought two facing pages of the *New York Times* and reprinted Kael's review in its entirety—along with an order form to reserve tickets for the film's February 1 premiere. The box office opened at noon the next day, Christmas be damned. Holiday closings were for prudes and squares.

The critics who were allowed in for advance screenings were selected with a sharpshooter's precision. Liz Smith of *Cosmopolitan* reported that UA was keeping magazine reviewers out because they tended to be more conservative than their newspaper colleagues; Smith called the policy "demented." Anyone who UA thought might be repelled by the blatant sexuality in the picture was iced out. Rex Reed was barred because he'd panned the UA film *Man of La Mancha*. Bill Wolf of *Cue* magazine, the New York arts resource since 1932, was also banned.

A rare flower like *Last Tango in Paris* had to be handled carefully. While *The Godfather* had opened at several New York theaters at the same time, hitting other big cities in relatively short order, *Tango* played just one house in New York and did not arrive in other cities until much later in the spring. The strategy was to promote strong advance word from the New York avant-garde to convince provincial audiences that *Tango* was art and, despite its blunt sexual expression, should be taken seriously.

The strategy didn't fully work. While most serious critics did take the movie seriously, defending it against charges of pornography, Kael's superlatives generated somewhat of a backlash. Her chief rival, Andrew Sarris of the *Village Voice*, was much more measured in his reaction: "Bertolucci is suddenly the director of the hour," he wrote just before the film opened, "but who knows what the next few hours will bring?" Everyone was asking Sarris if *Tango* was "as great as 'everybody' says it was," and he answered that "nothing is as great as 'everybody' says it is." Still, "it isn't bad, either," though he cautioned, "let the buyer beware."

*Last Tango in Paris* polarized moviegoers and exposed the fault-line between people who lived with diametrically different world views. In Italy, Bertolucci and the film faced charges of obscenity. In the United States, the *Voice* reported walkouts at screenings and "vomiting by well-dressed wives." In *Newsweek*, conservative columnist William F. Buckley derided the film as "pornography disguised as art." By the time *Tango* finally made it out of New York, the city of Montclair, New Jersey, tried to ban it. When that failed, two hundred people picketed the Bellevue Theater, which was packed nearly to its capacity of eight hundred. The mayor called the picture "absolutely filthy, out-and-out smut"; one little girl carried a sign that read BRING BACK WALT DISNEY. Meanwhile, two young men who hoisted placards championing free speech were taunted by cries of "pervert" and "homo." Once the film began showing, a bomb threat closed the theater for a few minutes, with management asking the audience to check under their seats.

The one thing most critics (if not the mayor of Montclair) agreed on was that Marlon's performance was superlative. *Time*'s reviewer thought it affirmed "the resurgence of one of the great talents of the age," one who had seemed, throughout the 1960s, to be "erratically and sometimes disastrously in decline." Marlon's "emotionally wrenching, coruscating performance as the protagonist of *Tango* fulfills all the promise he gave in [*The Godfather*] of regaining his old dominance, not only as an actor but also as a star and a legend." The two films, Foster Hirsch observed, "define the two poles of Brando's genius: the first is his greatest disguise performance, the second his most unsparing act of self-revelation." Indeed, without his transcendent achievement in *Tango*, Marlon's *Godfather* comeback might have been seen as a fluke. These two back-to-back performances had now secured his position as the greatest American actor, perhaps for all time; it didn't matter, in some ways, what he did from here on out.

Marlon himself, exhausted from the ordeal, was, perhaps not surprisingly, lukewarm about *Tango*. Pauline Kael, he said, "gave much more to the film than was there."

Still, she'd helped ensure its profits: even with its carefully orchestrated release, *Tango* earned $12,625,000 by the end of the year, a sliver of *The Godfather*'s gross, but still enough to make it the sixth-most-popular film of 1973. The boldness of Marlon's performance, in an X-rated film no less, also ensured he would remain a god to that new generation of young American actors who worshipped him. It also enshrined him, at the age of forty-nine, as a leading figure in the youth-led counterculture that was taking on Nixon, the war, race, sexuality, free expression, the "silent majority," and all the tyrannies of the Establishment.

MARLON COULDN'T BELIEVE what he was seeing on television. On the night of February 27, more than two hundred members of the American Indian Movement seized the historic settlement of Wounded Knee, South Dakota, holding ten persons hostage and exchanging gunfire with federal agents. Armed with weapons seized during a takeover of the settlement's trading post, the Indians were demanding that the U.S. Senate begin investigations into the treatment of native peoples and the rampant corruption in the management of tribal affairs. "We will occupy this town until the government sees fit to deal with the Indian people, particularly the Oglala Sioux tribe in South Dakota," read the Indians' demand. "We want a true Indian nation, not one made up of Bureau of Indian Affairs puppets."

Marlon sat riveted to the television screen. He was aware of the symbolic significance of the site that had been taken. In December 1890, U.S. forces had fired on a group of Lakota Sioux at Wounded Knee, killing eighty-four men, forty-four women, and eighteen children and wounding many others. In between news reports, Marlon telephoned people he knew in the Indian movement, including Jack Tanner, an African American lawyer for the NAACP who'd advised Indian leaders on legal matters. No one he spoke with had any idea what would happen at Wounded Knee; the organizers of the protest were incommunicado at this point. Marlon wanted to help but didn't know how.

For the next several days he followed the siege on television and in the newspapers. Hostages were released; heavily fortified federal agents surrounded the camp; an assistant U.S. attorney general was allowed in to negotiate, but had little success. The Indians' demands, Marlon believed, should not have been difficult to meet. "All they were asking for were investigations," he said. "But the government didn't want to investigate because it knew what it would find." Meanwhile, polls showed a majority of Americans in support of the Indians' actions.

Marlon had recognized early on that the fight for Indian rights grew out of the same deep, corrosive racism that refused to extend full civil rights to African Americans. This racism was "eating away at America's soul," he said, "undermining the very foundation of the country." Conversations about what was happening at Wounded Knee were far more urgent to have than those about whether *Last Tango in Paris* was pornography, or whether he should accept an Oscar—but of course, that was all the press wanted to talk to him about. Such superficiality infuriated him. "We are not able to function as a useful and creative society," he argued. "We've lost our leadership in the world. We've lost our credibility."

What fascinated Marlon was society's need for scapegoating. "If Hitler had killed all Jews, black people and Orientals," he mused, "and was left with nothing but pure, blue-eyed, Aryan types, he'd have started killing left-handed people, or people with crooked teeth." This was what was going on in America, he feared. A nation demoralized by assassination, war, and economic woes was looking to place blame, and the targets people chose were those more oppressed than they, not those who enjoyed more privilege. It made no sense to him. "We must change now," he said. "Here. Today. Being willing to change is the essence of it all."

Marlon was well aware that some called him starry-eyed and impractical, believing he was chasing after some impossible utopian dream. Worse, they called him a hypocrite: "Cynics and doubters ask why a Hollywood artist should presume the role of a civil rights worker," journalist Vernon Scott observed, "when his own personal life is anything but exemplary." Marlon was measured in his reply: "People who take that point of view don't know me or what I believe. They read gossip about me and choose to believe it. They really aren't interested in communication."

Indeed, most people didn't know just how long Marlon had been working on various civil and human rights issues behind the scenes. For about a decade, he'd been an ambassador for UNICEF. In 1961, mostly under the radar of the press, he'd participated in a strategy meeting of the National Indian Youth Council in Denver, "one of the few non-Indians working with us," the group's director said. In March 1964, Marlon was arrested for taking part in a "fish-in" at the Puyallup River in Washington State, protesting the denial of treaty rights. "We went to the jail and they just dismissed us," he remembered. "They got a call from the governor's office or something." But the point had been made.

The experience opened his eyes to the raw deal the original Americans had gotten from the Americans who had conquered them. "I always enjoyed watching John Wayne," Marlon said, "but it never occurred to me until I spoke with Indians how corrosive and damaging and destructive his movies were—most Hollywood movies were." Hearing of Wayne's statement that abuses against American Indians were so far in the past that protests were irrelevant, Marlon grew incensed. "According to that point of view," he responded, Wayne would consider Gandhi a "rabble-rouser." The only freedom fighters he would recognize "would be those who were fighting Communists; if they were fighting to get out from under colonial rule, he'd call them terrorists." It was precisely this sort of attitude, Marlon believed, that made the current protests at Wounded Knee so important.

Since late the previous year, Marlon had been meeting with Sacheen Littlefeather, an Indian rights activist based in San Francisco. She'd written to Marlon and such others as Jane Fonda and Sidney Poitier, hoping to enlist their support for the eighteen-month occupation of Alcatraz Island by American Indians. Several times during 1972, Littlefeather had visited Marlon's home, sometimes to meet with invited guests, sometimes simply to educate him on Indian issues. An attractive twenty-six-year-old former model, Littlefeather was treated very respectfully by her host; there was no affair, as many would presume later. Besides, Jill was always around.

Still, the young activist instilled political passion in her host. Marlon had always been fervent in his support of the Indian movement; during the interviews of 1965 that were caught on camera by the Maysles brothers, Marlon had immediately stopped clowning around when someone asked him about discrimination against Indians. "That's something I can't be flippant about," he said. He was frustrated at how little Americans knew about the original peoples of their country: "Nobody knows that the mortality rate for Indian children is five to one compared to any other minority group here in America. I think it would benefit all of us to know what the American Indian is, what his position is." Littlefeather drove that point home for him: despite all the protests, the stereotypes remained, and the real issues were not being addressed. "It is *not* the plight of the American Indian," Marlon insisted. "If anything, it is the plight of the non-Indian, non-Native American person who [*sic*] is in trouble." His argument echoed the one being made by the social historian Lerone Bennett Jr., who wrote, "There is no Negro problem in America. The problem of race in America . . . is a white problem."

With the country ready to go up in flames, this was no time for business as usual. It was with that thought in mind that Marlon woke up on March 27, 1973, the date of the Academy Awards.

**MARCH 27, 1973** / The audience at the Dorothy Chandler Pavilion in Los Angeles braced themselves in their seats. Up on the stage, Roger Moore and Liv Ullmann were preparing to announce the winner of the Best Actor Award. This was the moment many had been wondering about for weeks. What was Marlon Brando going to do?

Both Moore and Ullmann seemed unusually stiff and uncomfortable as they read from the teleprompter. Brando was not in the audience. But word had gotten around that he'd sent someone in his place, someone who'd arrived late. Perhaps Brando had softened. Perhaps his admiration for *The Godfather*, his hugely successful comeback film, had persuaded him to accept the award.

The names of the nominees were read: Brando, Caine, Olivier, O'Toole, Winfield. "The winner is," Ullmann said as Moore opened the envelope. Six long, anticipatory seconds passed as the card was handed over. "Marlon Brando in *The Godfather*," Ullmann announced. The room burst into applause.

The camera swung to a young woman with long black hair and a traditional Indian buckskin dress making her way to the stage. "Accepting the award for Marlon Brando in *The Godfather*," the announcer intoned, "is Miss Sacheen Littlefeather." The camera caught the people in the audience following her with their eyes. As Littlefeather approached the podium, Moore held out the gold statuette to her, but in a gesture that would become an iconic moment in American film history, the young woman held out her right hand, as if to say, "Halt." Moore backed off, exchanging a look with Ullman. The applause sputtered.

Littlefeather took the microphone. "Hello," she said, in a voice that was warm and surprisingly assured for someone so young and so unaccustomed to the spotlight. "My name is Sacheen Littlefeather. I'm Apache, and I am president of the National Native American Affirmative Image Committee. I'm representing Marlon Brando this evening, and he asked me to tell you, in a very long speech—" (she held up several pages in her right hand) "—which I cannot share with you presently because of time, but [which] I will be glad to share with the press afterward, that he very regretfully cannot accept this very generous award, and the reasons for this being are the treatment of American Indians today by the film industry—"

Until this point the audience had been stunned into silence. But now some of those in attendance began to growl. The rising rumble clearly unnerved Littlefeather, who lost her way for a moment. "Excuse me," she said, looking down. A burst of sympathetic applause attempted to drown out the chorus of boos, and Littlefeather found her voice.

"—and on television," she carried on, "and in movie reruns, and also with recent happenings at Wounded Knee. I beg at this time that I have not intruded upon this evening and that we will, in the future, our hearts and understandings, will meet with love and generosity. Thank you on behalf of Marlon Brando." With that, she walked off to renewed, if somewhat halfhearted, applause.

Backstage, Littlefeather spotted a furious John Wayne. For years to come, the diminutive young woman would remember how the big, strapping Wayne had to be physically "restrained by six security guards" from confronting her.

LATER, LOOKING BACK at this moment, Marlon said, "Those people were booing at me. They were booing because they thought, 'This moment is sacrosanct, and you're ruining our fantasy with intrusion of a little reality.' I suppose it was unkind of me to do that, but there's a larger issue, an issue that no one in the motion picture industry had ever addressed themselves to, and this forced [them to do so]."

Backstage, Littlefeather distributed copies of Marlon's statement to the press. If people wondered "what the hell has all this got to do with the Academy Awards," Marlon said, he was ready with an answer: "The motion picture community has been as responsible as any for degrading the Indian and making a mockery of his character."

The Hollywood press, however, wasn't content with just a printed statement. They wanted to hear from Littlefeather herself. The young woman was mobbed as she left the building, and momentarily prevented from getting into a car driven by Marlon's nephew Marty Asinof, Jocelyn's son. Cameras flashed, and fists pounded on the car's windows as Littlefeather managed to slip inside. Asinof maneuvered the car through the crowd and sped off for Mulholland Drive.

Back inside the auditorium, the producers of the show were seething. Howard Koch, producer of the ceremony, had told Littlefeather that if she tried to read that lengthy speech, he'd cut her off and move the camera away. The young woman's arrival had taken everyone by surprise. Expecting Marlon not to show, Paramount president Robert Evans had planned to pick up his award if he won. "I knew Marlon was into this Indian thing," Koch recalled years later, "but I didn't know about the girl."

"This Indian thing" rankled many in the auditorium that night. Immediately, the wagons began circling around the industry and its cherished traditions. When Clint Eastwood strode onstage with the Best Picture envelope, he looked directly into the camera and said: "I don't know if I should present this award on behalf of all the cowboys shot in all the John Ford Westerns over the years." The audience clapped enthusiastically. (The award went to *The Godfather*, and was collected by Al Ruddy, who made no comment about Marlon or the Best Actor award.)

At the very end of the show, out sauntered John Wayne himself. The audience roared its welcome. Wayne's appearance was the industry's response to Marlon's charges: they would apologize for *nothing*. What mattered to the Hollywood establishment wasn't "this Indian thing." What mattered was the integrity and the reputation of the motion picture industry, which was more important than anything else—and, as the show was about to make clear, was selfsame with America. Although Wayne made no direct response to Marlon, his words carried pointed significance: "I know the show is just about over," the cowboy star drawled, "but I wanted to come out here and be a part of this wonderful night, to be with so many talented people who make our industry a great industry." Though he hated to "break a precedent," Wayne said, he thought "all the winners and presenters" should come back out onstage "to take a much-deserved bow." Looking out into the audience, he asked, "Whad'ya say?" The auditorium cheered.

At that point, stars and directors began dutifully trotting out onto the stage, some clutching their awards, most looking bewildered and bemused. At that point, Wayne exhorted them all to sing, "You Oughta Be in Pictures," and looking into the camera, he ordered the television audience—"you people on TV all over the world, you the movie audience that make us possible"—to do so as well. He was "watchin'," Wayne warned, "so you better sing, or *pow!*" He slammed his right fist into his left hand. Falling into line was a global command.

The orchestra began, and the stars obediently began to sing. Clint Eastwood, Liza Minnelli, Joel Grey, Eileen Heckart, Natalie Wood, Robert Wagner, Julie Andrews, Sonny and Cher, Cloris Leachman, Katharine Ross, Billy Dee Williams, John Gavin, Greer Garson, George Cukor, Eddie Albert, an actor dressed as Mickey Mouse—all were made to appear complicit in their industry's defense of the status quo, and all of them white except for Williams. The figures on that Oscar stage were turned into Hollywood's front line of defense, and the message they conveyed was clear: *Unlike that traitor who refused to join us, we're proud to be in pictures.* Because pictures were *America*—and if anyone doubted that, ads for the sponsors of the show were superimposed over the smiling stars. "The forty-fifth annual Academy Awards Show," the announcer said, "has been brought to you by"—and he named StoveTop Stuffing from General Foods, Shell gasoline, Arrow shirts, and Chevrolet, "building a better way to see the U.S.A." Huckstering at its best.

Watching at home, Marlon wouldn't have missed the irony.

WHEN LITTLEFEATHER ARRIVED at Mulholland Drive, Marlon embraced her and told her she had spoken "eloquently." Every television set in the house was on, tuned to different channels, Littlefeather recalled. Both local and national coverage of the awards led off with her statement. On the floor, their chins in their hands, Christian and Miko watched the furor being raised over their father's refusal of "Hollywood's greatest honor," as the announcers were calling it. Christian Marquand arrived to celebrate Marlon's defiance. Jack Nicholson called to cheer Marlon on. But they were among the few filmland figures to offer their support.

In the days and weeks that followed, the attacks against Marlon mounted. "Marlon Brando should never appear in public," one television viewer wrote into a syndicated question-and-answer column. "He's rude, unkempt, and above all, a colossal bore." Another insisted, "As far as Brando being a spokesman for the Indians and their plight, I think they would be better off with John Wayne representing them." One columnist reported that the letters coming in were "unanimous" against the star. Rona Barrett, who'd succeeded Hedda Hopper as the queen of the Hollywood tattlers, implied that Marlon had been a coward for not showing up at the Oscar show himself: if he'd wanted "to tell the world how he felt about the Black Panthers, or the Indians, or whatever," she said on her TV gossip show, why had he sent the message via "an alleged Indian princess?"

If Barrett had bothered to read Marlon's statement, she would have seen his reason for his absence. Part of the problem was the lack of Indian visibility: why speak for them when they could speak for themselves? "I thought it would be an opportunity for an American Indian to speak to sixty million people for the first time in history," Marlon said. And, of course, Littlefeather had never claimed to be a princess, merely an Apache, but that was the way white America thought. When the *National Enquirer* learned that Littlefeather's original surname was "Cruz," the tabloid pronounced her a fraud, as if Native Americans couldn't have Hispanic last names.

Then came the big scoop: it was discovered Littlefeather had been named "Miss American Vampire of 1970" during a promotion for the gothic soap opera *Dark Shadows*, a contest the young woman had entered in an attempt to bring attention to the Alcatraz cause. When she won, she gave Alcatraz as her hometown and declined the prize of a guest spot on the show. Yet, somehow, the mere fact that she had once won a contest meant, in the mind of the public, that she was in this just to become famous, as guilty as Marlon of milking the Indian cause for publicity purposes.

"That's how Hollywood thought," said Marlon's old friend from the Dramatic Workshop, Elaine Stritch. "Everything had a dollar sign attached to it. Nobody does anything because they believe in it. Marlon must be fleecing them somehow."

The experience left Littlefeather disillusioned. "I don't think Mr. Brando meant to exploit me or hurt me in any way," she wrote to the Academy several years later, describing the experience. "I was exploited in a cruel and vicious way by the media. Instant fame and celebrity is a hard thing to deal with."

If John Wayne's rousing finish to the Academy Awards wasn't obvious enough, a week later the industry made its rejection of Marlon's charges utterly plain. On March 31, the American Film Institute paid tribute to, of all people, John Ford, whose classic Westerns epitomized for many the racist treatment of American Indians in Hollywood films. The event had been planned for a while, but the timing proved perfect: they could honor a man whose films they believed had been unfairly maligned by Brando's gambit. Moreover, Ford was being honored at the ceremony by none other than President Nixon himself. "This marks a historical first," columnist Joyce Haber wrote reverentially, "the first time a U.S. President has so honored the art of the film."

The wagons were still circling, and now they'd brought in the high sheriff himself. This was personal for Nixon: his private tapes would reveal that he was still smarting over the fact that *Time* magazine had put Marlon on its cover (for *Last Tango in Paris*) instead of him during the week of his second inauguration.

John Wayne hosted a personal reception for the president at the Beverly Hilton, with Hollywood's elite lining up to shake his hand. At the exact same moment, Nixon's former aide, convicted Watergate burglar James McCord, was revealing to U.S. District Court judge John Sirica the president's deep personal involvement in the Watergate conspiracy. But at the AFI ceremony, Nixon was a hero, introduced by Charlton Heston, who had come a long way from his support of Martin Luther King Jr. "Mr. Ford is a great man," Nixon told the audience. "But I think Mr. Ford would want me to say, we also honor a great profession." No matter that he was, also at that very same period of time, calling for the censorship of motion pictures, Nixon insisted he was "an unabashed fan." The best movies, in his view, entertained while offering "the good picture of America." He presented Ford with the Presidential Medal of Freedom for all those good pictures and dead Indians he'd given the country over the years.

Ford, of course, was one of the great American filmmakers: *The Grapes of Wrath*, *Stagecoach*, *How Green Was My Valley*, *The Quiet Man*, and so many others attest to the truth of his artistry. But Marlon's discomfort while watching Ford's depiction of American Indians, almost always cast as villains or savages or as dependent upon the white man, arose from an equally valid truth. In 1973, Hollywood saw no contradiction, no moral conflict, in honoring John Ford just a week after Marlon had made plain the United States' history of injustice against the American Indian—all while a couple hundred Indians were barricaded at Wounded Knee, their power and water cut off by the government, trying desperately to make their voices heard while fearing for their lives. Indeed, barely two weeks after the John Ford testimonial, the first Indian casualty was reported at Wounded Knee, shot by U.S. Marshals; another man was killed on April 26.

In his complete statement to the press, Marlon had said he intended to go to Wounded Knee himself, to help forestall "in whatever way I can the establishment of a peace which would be dishonorable as long as the rivers shall run and the grass shall grow." The statement contained some of his usual bombast and affectation, but it was also, like most of his statements, utterly sincere. He *did* intend to go—until friends such as Jack Tanner advised him against it. "Wounded Knee was surrounded by federal officers, marshals, state police, deputized ranchers, anybody who wanted to hold a gun and make himself feel good," Marlon later explained. "There were also local Indians representing the administration view who were opposed to [the takeover]. All that was needed to make it a flop was for me to go to Wounded Knee and be arrested by a vigilante group or stopped by a U.S. marshal and turned over to deputized conservative Indians. The headlines would be: INDIANS REPULSE BRANDO AT WOUNDED KNEE. The thing the government would be looking for."

The fact that Marlon didn't go to Wounded Knee left him open, yet again, to charges of hypocrisy. "Don't believe a word Brando says," one columnist wrote, without ever inquiring into the reasons the actor had stayed away. Marlon was experienced enough with the media by now not to have expected anything different. The nationalistic rallying cries, the accusations of hypocrisy, the "revelations" about his "Indian princess"—all were par for the course. But just because he wasn't surprised didn't mean he wasn't disappointed. "You always hope," he said, looking back on this period, "that maybe people will start talking about the things that matter." Instead, most of the coverage was sensationalistic and celebrity-driven: Were Marlon and "his Sacheen" having an affair? Was she pregnant with his "papoose"? Was Marlon feuding with his *Godfather* costars over the Oscar snub?

Yet there were also some journalistic attempts to look into the complaints of the Wounded Knee protesters, some of them using Marlon's Oscar statement as a hook. More reporters turned up at the encampment after March 27 than before. The *New York Times*

published Marlon's entire statement as an op-ed, under the headline
THAT UNFINISHED OSCAR SPEECH. And one of the leading African
American newspapers, the *Chicago Defender*, offered a full-throated
endorsement of Marlon's actions: "He has served as a gadfly stinging America's conscience," the paper editorialized, "reminding the
country of its evil past and urging it to face up to the responsibility to redeem itself. Americans don't like to be criticized for their
racial misdeeds. They falsify their history to bolster their sense of
Nordic superiority. The Indians have been deprived of land and
culture. Their rates of unemployment, suicide and alcoholism are
above the national averages. The family incomes on the reservations are below the accepted poverty levels by nearly half. They
need all the publicity they can get. Brando used the right forum,
the right audience, the right moment to draw attention to a cause
that has been too long neglected."

At Wounded Knee, there was stunned disbelief that evolved
into deep appreciation when word of Marlon's action reached them.
Many years later, at Brando's funeral, the Indian activist Russell
Means, who was serving as spokesman at Wounded Knee, stood
up to offer a eulogy. As Ellen Adler remembered, an emotional
Means told the crowd, "It's not possible for you to understand how
inferior we felt, how we were made to feel. We were the enemies
of the American government. We were drunks. We were ne'er-do-
wells. We were nothing." Then Marlon Brando spoke out, Means
said, and for the first time, those beleaguered men and women at
Wounded Knee thought that maybe, finally, some white man got
it, some white man was willing to say that this was his issue, too,
that it was an American issue. The Indians who watched the Oscar
telecast, Means said, felt unexpected joy. "We never dreamt that
he would turn [the moment] over to us," Means said. "We started
to scream and cry. But in Hollywood, well, they were disgusted."

"Truth lasts forever," said Sacheen Littlefeather, almost fifty
years after the whole brouhaha. "It doesn't go away. It resonates

from one generation to the next. We have become a generation of diversity. That is our truth." And, she added, our culture should reflect that truth.

**JULY 21, 1973** / From the backseat of a taxicab, Marlon gazed out at the granite structure of Field Club Elementary School, in Omaha, Nebraska, at the American flag flapping from the pole out front. He'd gone to kindergarten there, he told the driver, in what must have felt like a very long time ago.

Marlon was in Omaha, where he'd been born, on what the newspapers would later call a "sentimental journey" through the Midwest of his youth. From the school, Marlon asked the driver to head north, past Hanscom Park, to 1026 South Thirty-Second Street. When they arrived, Marlon peered out of the window at the big yellow house with the green roof. He told the driver he'd be right back.

Marlon didn't have many happy memories of his childhood. But, every once in a while, the darkness would lift, and suddenly there was sunlight. This house had been his grandmother's, with its big backyard and its sandbox and its wisteria-covered arbor— "fresh air all day," his sister Fran had recalled. Here there had never been the smell of whisky.

Marlon rapped on the door. The surprise of the owner who looked out to see Marlon Brando standing on his front porch was considerable. The movie star explained that he'd lived in the house as a boy, and asked if he might see the place. The owner agreed to give him a tour. In the backyard, Marlon pointed at the great oaks that lined the property and remembered a tree house he had played in.

That he had time for such a sentimental journey was astonishing, given what his schedule had been like the past few years. But that summer, life for Marlon suddenly skidded to a crawl. The uproar over the Oscars had finally died down. No movies were on the horizon, except for personal projects he hoped to make: a story he was calling *Apache Chronicle* and maybe a documentary about Tahiti. Marlon was tired, depleted. In New York City the week before, he'd appeared on *The Dick Cavett Show* with representatives from various Indian tribes, and they'd managed to talk about substantive issues. But afterward, a paparazzo confronted him on the street, and Marlon slugged him and broke his jaw. He felt bad about it. He'd been working with Dr. Harrington on the rage, but it wasn't yet entirely exorcised.

His sentimental journey to Omaha was part of a larger sojourn through the Midwest, a stop-off on his way back to Los Angeles from New York and before he flew off for Tahiti. Jill was with him, though she'd spent the day seeing friends. When he was finished with his trip down memory lane, he headed to Eppley Airfield to wait for her. They planned to fly out together to Chicago.

Wandering through the terminal, Marlon was not instantly recognized. His hair was streaked with gray, slicked back from his forehead, and curling over his shoulders. He wore a short, stubbly beard that was almost entirely gray. His hips had grown wider than ever. During *Last Tango in Paris*, he'd weighed 175 pounds. Now he certainly topped two hundred. He might have evaded the "family curse" of alcoholism but had simply replaced it with another addiction. He made fewer pretenses of going on a diet. He was, as one reporter would describe him not long after this, "a hero whose vanity had surrendered. Beneath those wide oakstump shoulders was a vast rippling cargo hold, 240 pounds on a 5-foot-10 frame." When he recently ran into his old friend Janice Mars, after not seeing her for a while, she had asked him, "Where is the slim young poet I used to know?" Marlon replied, "He's inside somewhere."

Settling himself at the counter of the airport cafeteria, Marlon ordered a sandwich. By now, a stringer for the UPI had discerned his identity and was keeping tabs. As Marlon consumed his open-faced steak sandwich and large chef's salad, a seven-year-old boy wandered up to the counter and took a seat not far away. Marlon watched the child surreptitiously. The boy ordered a slice of pie. The waitress told him that would cost twenty cents, but the boy had only a nickel and a dime. "Give the boy a piece of pie," Marlon called over, telling the waitress to put it on his tab. "And he's got to have a glass of milk to go with it."

Marlon had been around the boy's age when his family had moved away from Omaha, up to Evanston, Illinois, where his memories got darker and the sunshine disappeared. When the little boy thanked him for the pie, Marlon told him not to mention it: "Just have fun, kid."

Shortly thereafter, the UPI reporter spotted a "mystery woman" wearing a brown velvet pantsuit greeting Marlon with an embrace. Together they headed off to board a plane to Chicago. Inquiring at the desk, the reporter learned that the woman was a "Miss Molumby." The UPI stringer then hurried back to the office to type up the report on "Brando in Omaha" and get it onto the wires.

MARLON AND JILL had wanted to make this trip together for some time. Jill was on her own sentimental journey, and for the previous few days, Marlon had accompanied her. Flying into Kansas City from New York the previous week, they'd rented a car and headed north, driving the five hours to Storm Lake, Iowa, where Jill had been raised. As they drove through the emerald-green grasslands stretching all around them, Marlon and Jill could have been any Midwestern couple out on a lark. "Jill thought Marlon had never been so quiet, or reflective, or content as he was on that trip," Pat Perez recalled.

They stopped at dairy farms and creameries and bought ears of corn at roadside stands. Marlon would later say that he and Jill "spoke the same cultural language," which hadn't been the case with any of his other women. "They talked about the sound tractors made," Perez said, "and bought fruit at farmers' markets." Completely on their own, there were no producers or newspapermen or secretaries to distract them. It was surprising how rarely Marlon was recognized out here in Missouri and Iowa and Nebraska; he just seemed to blend in.

"That trip [to the Midwest] was when it all changed for them," said Pat Perez. "Jill thought Marlon really made a commitment to her at that point, even if he never said the words. And I think she was right. I think he felt the same."

Freud, whom Marlon still read assiduously, wrote that love and affection could be antidotes to the destructive impulses of the libido. No doubt Marlon had discussed the idea with his various analysts over the years. With Harrington, he went the deepest in exploring his own self-destructive tendencies. For a survivor of childhood trauma, overcoming the propensity to self-destruct is a gargantuan feat. By the middle part of the 1970s, however, Marlon was closer to that goal than ever before. He was struggling to control "the impulse to hate and exact vengeance," as he described it. The slug to the paparazzo's jaw had truly bothered him. He was consciously trying to become more empathetic, and not only toward oppressed minorities or starving children. He was also trying, he said, to feel compassion for those he'd long considered his enemies. He'd always believed that Roy Cohn, for example, who'd "spearheaded Joe McCarthy's bloodletting, personified evil more than any other person." Yet even Cohn, Marlon came to realize in his therapy, deserved empathy. "I don't know what forces made him do what he did," Marlon said. If he could find compassion for Roy Cohn, then he could find it for those who'd vilified him after the Oscar scandal, for the federal agents who'd shot the Indian protestors at Wounded Knee, for Richard Nixon. And, quite possibly, he could find it for himself.

"What Marlon was struggling to learn," said one very close friend, "was that he was worth loving."

But to do that, he first had to confront, at long last, how he had treated the women in his life. To his psychiatrist before Harrington, Marlon had recounted the breakup with a woman who'd left him to take a job in England. Marlon had told her that if she left, they were finished. Once again, his needs came first; while his career often took him away from his women, no woman should put her career before him. How many stories like this had Marlon's psychiatrist heard? No doubt exasperated, the doctor told his client, "I don't think I can help you anymore." In his memoir, Marlon would angrily describe this as "abandonment." But underneath his self-pity, he was smart enough to know that he'd been the problem. "I had a real Ford assembly line going throughout much of my life," he said. "If you're rich and famous, getting laid a lot isn't that difficult. I knew what I was doing but I didn't know why I was doing it."

He'd tried, in his own way, to make amends with Rita Moreno. He'd gotten her a part in *The Night of the Following Day* when movie offers dried up after her Oscar win for *West Side Story* (a phenomenon many Best Supporting winners encountered). Moreno had taken a chance and asked Marlon for help. "He didn't just get me the role," Moreno said. "He fought for me and shamed the producers into giving me a decent salary instead of the peanuts they initially offered." Moreno was married now, with a child; Marlon was careful with her, polite, and always gracious to her husband. "We had made a civilized segue into a friendship that preserved our better instincts," Moreno said.

*The Night of the Following Day* had, of course, turned out to be a dud, but it was enlivened by the scene in which Moreno violently throws punches at Marlon, surprising him with her intensity. She surprised herself as well, realizing that the scene had allowed her finally to release "the rage stored somewhere deep within." Off camera, they were gentler with each other. At one point, Marlon lay down beside her on a bed. Moreno told him it wasn't a good idea. "Just let me sleep with you," he pleaded. "That's all I want." Wisely, Moreno moved away, though she wasn't angry at him. She seemed to sense his loneliness.

Of course, Marlon may have just been up to his old tricks, trying to seduce her. But he may also have meant what he said: that all he wanted to do was be close to her, the way he'd once asked Ellen Adler if he could lie next to her on her hospital bed. These were women who had once mattered to him, who had loved him. Maybe he was hoping, even subconsciously, that they might love him again and prove he was still lovable.

Loving Jill had freed him in many ways. "Up to then I had spent my life searching for a woman who would love me unconditionally," Marlon said, "a woman I could trust to never hurt or abandon me." He had, in fact, found several such women in his life; the problem had been his own inability to trust. After years of therapy, however, he had decided to try trusting Jill. Was it because of their shared language and cultural history? Was it the fact that, out of all his women, she was the most like his mother: Midwestern, blonde, delicate, quirky, poetic? Was it time at last to forgive his mother the way he had forgiven his father?

FROM CHICAGO, MARLON and Jill drove the forty-five minutes to Libertyville. Here was the nexus of Marlon's pain. None of his other women had ever seen the place he came from. Marlon took Jill around the farm. He showed her where he'd milked the cows. He took her out to the railroad tracks that had provided the nightly music outside his window. He walked her into the field of wildflowers where Dodie first shared with him her love of nature.

They stood on the sidewalk where Bud once lined up his parents' empty liquor bottles as they quarreled inside.

Marlon introduced Jill to his sister Fran and her husband, and to old local friends such as Bob Hoskins. Everyone loved Jill. But Marlon seemed on edge, as if being so close to these old memories threatened to upend all his progress, and at least once, he phoned Dr. Harrington in California to talk through his feelings. A few days after their arrival, Marlon complained to Jill that he felt dizzy; she got him to lie down, but he became only more distressed, alarmed by what he believed was an irregular heartbeat. "He thought he was having a heart attack," Pat Perez recalled Jill telling her. Marlon was rushed to a nearby hospital, where he submitted to an EKG. Doctors concluded that he was fine, "just overwrought," Perez said, and they sent him home.

This wasn't the first time, nor the last, that Marlon would convince himself he was having a heart attack. Jill was with him the entire time in the hospital. "She kept telling him," Perez said, "'You are strong, Marlon. You can get through this.'"

To outsiders, the two seemed always to be bickering. Jill called Marlon "fatso," and sometimes it infuriated him. Sacheen Littlefeather, during her visits earlier in the year, had observed "storms and clouds, name-calling and turmoil" between them. Alice Marchak, however, who saw them more often than most, remembered as many lighthearted moments as stressful ones. Pat Perez said there was "a lot of kidding around, and that took the edge off their disagreements." Both Marlon and Jill could be "high-strung," Perez said, and "neither backed down immediately from a point of view." That was why Jill had lasted. Marlon couldn't overwhelm her the way he'd overwhelmed others.

When their Midwest trip was over, they flew back to Los Angeles, where Marlon collected Christian and took off for Tahiti. But even as he flew to the other side of the globe, he was likely thinking about Jill and what came next. At some point over the next couple of months, he asked her to marry him.

MARLON HAD SPENT his life not trusting women, ever since his mother falsely told him she was drinking Empirin for her headaches instead of whisky. He'd allowed some women to love him too much and had used others for sex or convenience. Nearly every one of them he'd pushed away when the risk of love became too great.

But "being willing to change," he said, "is the essence of it all." This was his motto in his work with Harrington. Women, Marlon concluded, "were not my enemy. Nor were they archangels whom I could count on to give me a perfect life. If I was ever going to be happy, I realized, it was up to me to achieve it and not to some woman who would enter my life with a holy grail filled with a magic elixir guaranteeing me a full and happy life."

The key to accomplishing that, in fact, was also the key to everything else: "If I were ever to forgive myself for all the things that I had done," Marlon realized, "I had to forgive my mother." But forgiving his mother would be much, much harder than forgiving his father, because Marlon had loved her as much as he'd hated him.

When he popped the question to Jill, he was convinced he could finally allow a woman into his life as an equal. He was fifty-something, overweight, full of aches and pains, and once again without any box-office pull. "What the hell, I'm no prize," his character had said in *Last Tango in Paris*. Despite that, Jill said yes.

She was the first woman Marlon had ever asked to marry him simply because he loved her: Celia, Anna, and Movita had all received their offers because of pregnancies, and Josanne had been part of that anomalous five-year collusion with the power structure of Hollywood, a period almost impossible to recall by the mid-1970s. Instead of an engagement ring, Jill asked for a tiny apple that she could wear around her neck. After all, Marlon called her "the apple of his eye." So, he had one made for her, studded with rubies and emeralds, and she wore it on a gold chain. "She loved that apple," Pat Perez remembered. "She never took it off."

EVEN AS HE made peace on one front of his life, other struggles remained for Marlon to settle. In the spring of 1974, Christian turned sixteen. Not long after that, he dropped out of school. It was just as well, as he couldn't pay attention to his studies and was skipping classes. For a while, Marlon worried that the teenager might suffer from the same dyslexia that had made studying so difficult for him thirty years earlier. Even if so, there was a significant difference. If Marlon's interest was sufficiently sparked by something (the migratory patterns of penguins, for example, or the philosophy of Immanuel Kant), he would spend as much time as he needed reading and rereading the sentences until he'd absorbed their meanings. Christian evinced no similar interest in anything except smoking grass.

His son, Marlon would admit years later, was already "a basket case of emotional disorders" by the time he came to live with him full time. The teen still woke up in cold sweats, terrified of being kidnapped again. Marlon had him see Dr. Harrington, but Christian resisted psychotherapy, convinced the doctor was just going to report back to Marlon everything he said. "He felt like he didn't belong anywhere," said a friend whom Christian met during one of his visits to JoAn Corrales's house in Vancouver, Washington. "Definitely not at his mother's, but even at his father's he felt that wasn't his world. He hated that his father was famous."

Marlon tried to do the right things. "I never said anything bad to Christian about his mother," he recalled. She was ill; she loved him. He did his best to make Christian feel at home. Friends would recall the little notes he left on his son's pillow: "I'm very glad to have you home," one read. "You make the house feel good."

Another time, he surprised Christian with the gift of a woodcarving knife, attaching a note to it that read, "For no reason in particular except I love you." Marlon's strategy was to be the complete antithesis to his own father, for whom such messages of love and support would have been unthinkable. And it's significant that, while he was uncomfortable saying, "I love you," to women—even to Jill, the woman he'd asked to marry him—he said the words freely enough to his son.

Yet, still the anger could erupt. When Christian neglected his chores and loafed in his room, a frustrated Marlon would become a ghost of his father: "What do you think this is, a fucking hotel?" Christian would sass back at him, in the same way Marlon had learned to do with his own father, and just like a generation earlier, the younger Brando proved too swift, too agile, for the older one to catch him. He would shout back at his winded father, "Fuck you, Fats, fuck you!"

The worst part was the press, hounding the boy, waiting to jump him outside the house, pummeling him with questions about his father. When police found some marijuana on Christian in 1974, it took considerable effort on Marlon's part to keep the incident out of the papers. "Any other kid gets busted for some pot, and it's not big news," said Christian's friend, "but this would have been front page in the *Times*." In January of 1976, still learning to drive, Christian stepped too hard on the gas of the Jeep he was steering and struck a car. After the driver of the other vehicle recognized the boy's father sitting next to him, he sued both of them for $50,570—$570 for the damages to his vehicle, $50,000 for "injuries to his nervous system." Christian's friend remembered the seventeen-year-old being mortified: "It wouldn't have happened if his father wasn't who he was."

This was why Marlon hated the media, deplored the fame he had never wanted and never pursued. Somehow, he'd hoped to shield his son from all that, from the harsher realities of his life, much as Don Vito Corleone had tried to protect his favorite son, Michael, from the down-and-dirty business of his. "I never wanted this for you," the Don says to Michael. Producer Al Ruddy called the story of *The Godfather* "a great tragedy of a man and the son he worships, the son who embodied all the hopes he had for his future." Like the Don, Marlon wanted his son to benefit from what he had done, reaping what he could from his father's achievements, but he also wanted him safely removed from the line of fire. Yet, just as it wasn't possible in *The Godfather,* it wasn't possible in real life, either.

So, when Christian started running away again, turning up at JoAn Corrales's, Marlon eventually allowed him to spend long stretches away from home. Christian loved the Northwestern forests, the hiking and the fishing. He learned how to weld, and became quite expert at it. He found a refuge far away from the circus that constantly surrounded his father. "We were a family," JoAn Corrales said simply.

Marlon would visit. Slipping away from the circus was good for him, too. Corrales would remember fondly sitting on the porch as Christian played the guitar and Marlon followed along on harmonica. Bunking in with Christian in the little loft above the Corrales family's rec room, Marlon taught his son and the boy's friends how to build ham radios. Neighbors who spotted the man in a coat and stocking cap up on the Corrales roof installing a radio antenna had no idea it was the Godfather himself. In the spring of 1976, Marlon told a reporter of his son, "I not only love him, I like him. We spend a lot of time together."

One of Christian's friends remembered being on that roof with Brando père and fils, looking up at the night sky, the dome of stars, the moon. Marlon and Christian were scooping leaves from the gutter, the friend recalled, and dropping them over the side, watching them drift and hover in the air, seeing whose leaf reached the ground first. It wasn't all that different from the way another young man had once watched, transfixed, as the pages of a newspaper took flight over Greenwich Village.

So, let's end our story here, even if we know the man on the witness stand, with his tears and regrets, awaits us some years down the road. Let's take our leave of Marlon here, as he sits on this roof, high above the world, not so differently from where we came in on him. Let's fade out on Marlon with his son at his side, as he plans to marry the woman he loves, hoping to be happy at last. Even if it's just for this fragile, fleeting moment in time, let's leave Marlon here, and give him the happy ending he worked so hard to find.

# THE BARD OF THE HOLLYWOOD HILLS

"WHAT'S IN THE FUTURE?" a reporter once asked Marlon. "I don't know," he replied. "I'm not an astrologer. The future is difficult to predict."

Even with the aid of a horoscope, he would have been hard-pressed, at that confident, defiant, hopeful moment, after the success of *The Godfather* and *Last Tango in Paris*, to imagine himself more than two decades later, weighing in at three hundred pounds, sitting in a courtroom tearfully admitting to his failures as a parent while his son faced a long prison term for manslaughter. For nearly fifty years, Marlon had strived to be conscious, responsible, honorable, enlightened. But a combination of bad luck, wrong choices, the woundedness of others (including his children), and the old devils of his own self-destructive impulses had brought him to this place of misery nonetheless.

On that terrible day in February 1991, the judge sentenced Christian to ten years in prison—not as much as the prosecution had been asking for (sixteen years) but considerably more than the defense had been hoping for (three years). This Santa Monica courthouse had ruled Christian's life; he'd been coming through these doors since he was a boy, attending all those custody hearings with his parents. Now, without looking over at his father slumped in the front row, Christian was led through the courtroom doors by sheriff's deputies one last time.

Marlon got to his feet. Even under the best of circumstances, this wouldn't have been easy. During his testimony, he'd actually made a joke about his weight: after saying he'd never been addicted to any substance, he added, "Maybe food." A wan smile followed. "That'll appear in the papers." (It did.) His weight was a ponderous thing, something Marlon both deplored and accepted. "It's the King of Fat," he'd say, leaving a message for Ellen Adler on her answering machine.

Breathing heavily, Marlon left the building through a door normally reserved for defendants in custody. Fitting, perhaps, as ever since Christian's arrest he'd felt that he was the one on trial— or at least that his notoriety had made things so much worse for his son. His predictions of a world consumed by celebrity madness had come true in a terribly personal way: his pain was being merchandized for cable news channels and supermarket tabloids. Outside the building, reporters caught up with him, as they always did. Their questions bounced off his wide back. Trundling toward a black Mercedes-Benz, he stumbled into the backseat and, in moments, was spirited away to his refuge in the Hollywood Hills.

So much pain. Unbearable. His old bogeyman, the darkness, returned to swallow him whole. He'd once promised Christian he'd never have to be afraid again. How terribly he had failed him. In those days after Christian's sentencing, Marlon wallowed in a pit of self-recrimination and despair. "He was blaming himself for everything," said George Englund, who came to see him at his house.

*Everything*—not just his son's calamities, but his own as well. Since 1975, the tragedies had been piling up. In that year, after he broke his promise to be faithful one too many times, Jill had left him. Marlon would remember it as "a grisly conclusion" to their engagement. He'd been carrying on with, among others, Lucy Saroyan, the daughter of the author William Saroyan. He had tried to be faithful; he'd honestly tried. But, in the end, he was unable to stop his tomcatting. Once, Jill had looked the other way;

now it was just too much. Their break came in Hawaii, on a hotel room balcony. When Jill moved in to slap him, Pat Perez said,
Marlon grabbed hold of the ruby apple she wore around her neck
and snapped it off its chain. "As Jill watched," Perez said, "Marlon
threw the apple she loved so much over the balcony and into the
ocean below." And that was the end of that fairy tale.

Not for five years did Marlon see Jill again. Eventually his anger
died down, as it always did. He looked for her, wanting to apologize. He "thought about her often," he admitted, missing her
laughter, the way she knew so much about him. Unbeknownst to
anyone, Jill had moved to Taos, New Mexico, where Marlon's old
pal Janice Mars got her a job as a real estate agent. After Marlon
finally found her, Jill consented to see him again. He asked for
another chance to make things right.

"She symbolized my mother," Marlon said. Both physically
and emotionally, Jill evoked Dodie. And so, just as he had forgiven his mother, he needed to forgive Jill and ask her to forgive
him as well. "We had been cruel to each other out of ignorance
and anguish," Marlon said. To Alice, he confided that he was
going to propose to Jill again. But then on August 6, 1982, Jill
was killed on the Ventura Freeway when an "out-of-control"
truck slammed into her car. She died early the next morning.
"Marlon was inconsolable," Alice said.

In Marlon's memory, Jill became the great love of his life, "the
only woman I ever really loved," he wrote. "He talked about her
a lot," said Avra Douglas, his good friend and assistant toward
the end of his life. But Douglas also thought he might have been
kidding himself if he'd really thought that marriage with Jill, with
anyone, would have been sustainable. "He didn't hold the institution
of marriage in high regard," Douglas said. "He wasn't a big cheerleader when people in his life were getting married." Unless it was
the more flexible Tahitian variety, marriage cut against Marlon's
grain. As much as he may have convinced himself otherwise in

the rush of feelings he had for Jill, marriage almost certainly would not have been a route to happiness for him. He was still carousing, after all, at the age of seventy.

Other tragedies followed. One of Marlon's business managers committed suicide; a car accident claimed the life of Miko's wife. But it was the double cataclysm of Christian and Cheyenne that overwhelmed Marlon with a sense of guilt. In Paris, Cheyenne was still in a hospital, on suicide watch; Marlon flew to be with her. Later, he brought her back to Los Angeles to live with him.

The fear that she'd take her life haunted Marlon not just "every waking hour," he told George Englund, but "every sleeping hour" as well. Englund thought his friend had done "coolie work" in trying to repair the lives of his children, but he counseled Marlon that they needed to take charge of themselves. Marlon argued that it was impossible for Cheyenne to do that, since she'd been incapacitated by mental illness long before Christian shot her lover. While never as disabled as Cheyenne, Marlon understood what emotional powerlessness felt like. When Cheyenne started to exhibit mental instability as a girl, Tarita had complained that Marlon kept his distance. If that was true, he made up for it in the 1990s, when his daughter's safety and wellbeing became "his whole world," according to Avra Douglas.

But, eventually, he couldn't save her, just as he'd been unable to save his mother. His beautiful Cheyenne, in whose face he could see Dodie, hanged herself on April 16, 1995, outside her mother's home in Tahiti. She was just twenty-five.

Marlon had once said he wanted to protect his Tahitian children from the harsh outside world, and he sent his other children to the South Pacific as often as he could. Yet the world in which his children grew up was artificial and illusory no matter its geographic coordinate, contained by the parameters of their father's fame. What if, Ellen Adler wondered, Marlon had raised them in New

York? What if he had abandoned that Southern California lifestyle he once so despised and returned to the city that had given him his first taste of his own true self? What if he had raised his children, all of them, in New York?

"He thought if he took them to an island in the South Pacific they'd be happier," Ellen said. "He didn't get that if they'd lived on Sixty-Third Street, they'd have known all the kids on the block." New York has a realness, an authenticity, that neither Los Angeles nor Tahiti can claim. In Tahiti, celebrity might be a foreign construct, but how had that made it any easier for Cheyenne, pining over a father, whom she revered as some kind of deity, on the other side of the globe? In New York, celebrity was a well-known quantity. "There are lots of famous fathers and famous children in New York," Ellen said. But it also didn't matter as much as it did in Los Angeles. What if Marlon had taken Christian and moved back east after he finally won full custody? What if the boy had grown up there, instead of in Tinseltown?

Marlon had tried so hard to make the lives of his children better than his own; when problems arose, he tried hard to fix them. But the one thing he hadn't done was teach them how to survive in the world, the way he had learned to do for himself; instead, he'd tried to protect them from the world. "If Marlon's children had lived in New York," Ellen firmly believed, "they would have lived in the *world*. Marlon thought that by taking them out of the world he was being good to them. He was trying to protect them from his fame. But he ended up making it worse."

THE LAST THIRTY years of Marlon Brando's life represent a catalog of tragedies that approach the Shakespearean: the sins of the father, whatever society deemed them to be, visited upon the children. Of his loss of Christian (to prison) and Cheyenne (to suicide), Marlon would never speak. Working on his memoir, he'd angrily rebuke his cowriter, Robert Lindsey, if he mentioned Christian's name. To Ellen Adler, he said, "I can't talk about that. That's like putting my hand on a red hot doorknob." The phrase stuck in Ellen's mind, an example of his idiosyncratic way with words.

Yet it is so important to realize the fact that, in the end, Marlon survived. The trauma of his childhood had debilitated him for so long. But all those years in therapy had given him the skills to at last transcend it. Gradually, he got back on his feet. "The tragedies [of Christian and Cheyenne] deeply affected every aspect of his life afterward," said Avra Douglas. "But he'd been through so much his whole life, so much trauma, that he did have some strong coping mechanisms. This was a very psychically strong man. He just got pummeled with one thing after another, and still he came up for air."

Part of it, Douglas added, was his "amazing ability to compartmentalize." These terrible things had happened, but Marlon also had a life to keep living, other children, grandchildren—and ideas for projects that were constantly occurring to him. Those coping mechanisms kicked in, and he survived. Throughout the early and middle part of the 1980s, he had continued to see Dr. Harrington, but then, one day, several years before the crisis with Christian, he told the doctor that he was done, that he could take it from there. Rather than the psychoanalyst's couch, Marlon now relied on meditation for going within, sometimes with the aid of biofeedback. "He was always looking for ways to calm his mind," Avra Douglas said. "The meditation he took very seriously. I don't know if he had a mantra or not, but he would shut the doors and the windows and hibernate in his room, meditating."

He continued to reject the idea of God, but spiritual practice proved to be a very effective survival skill. For hours, in person and on the phone, he'd talk about meditation and spirit with the actor Harry Dean Stanton, whom he'd known since they worked together on *The Missouri Breaks* (1976), but who became a much closer friend later. Marlon was inspired by Stanton's talk of Buddhism and Taoism, a way of seeing the world that didn't require any sort of orthodox dogma; the moment any rules were introduced into his spiritual practice, Marlon lost interest. It's easy to see how Stanton's worldview appealed to Marlon. "Everything just happens," Stanton believed. "Nobody's in charge. It's just a big phantasmagoria. Everything's unfolding perfectly." People might think they're in control of their lives, Stanton said, but they're not. He advised, therefore: "Just go along with the trip."

Marlon told one friend, "I have spent my life trying to become less crazy." He tape-recorded his musings, in essence playing analyst to himself; often he'd use the tapes as a form of self-hypnosis, playing them back and reminding himself of what he believed and was capable of. Stevan Riley, a filmmaker who used the tapes in his powerful documentary *Listen to Me Marlon*, found himself carried away on his subject's journey as he listened to the recordings of nearly three decades earlier. "Brando was inviting me to understand his flaws, taking me on a Freudian journey," Riley wrote. "Do we ever live long enough to take proper heed of life's lessons? Are we doomed by our genetics and upbringing to repeat the mistakes of our parents? He seemed so keen to rectify the wrongs of his past, I found myself rooting for him to find resolution and happiness at the end."

Resolution, perhaps. But was happiness too much to ask? For many artists, such as Tennessee Williams, what sustained them and brought them joy was their work. But work, at least acting work, was never Marlon's fulfillment. The twelve feature films and one television miniseries he made after 1973 were all done for the money, and he hated working on every one. "He might have enjoyed *Don Juan DeMarco* a little bit," Avra Douglas said of his 1994 comedy with Johnny Depp, largely because he liked his costar. The rest were just to pay the bills.

As always, his expenses kept increasing. A hurricane in 1983 destroyed much of the buildings and aquaculture he'd erected on Teti'aroa, and he had to start from scratch. He adopted more children (Tarita's by another lover and the offspring of several friends), which meant continued educational and living expenses. And then came the legal and medical costs for Christian and Cheyenne, which had proven overwhelming. "I think the fact that he *had* to do [these films] took all the fun out of them," Avra Douglas said—if indeed Marlon ever really had fun making a movie, *The Godfather* being the most notable exception.

One thing, however, was profoundly different in his life: after the age of fifty, Marlon had largely triumphed over the rage. "He was really pretty quiet most of the time," Douglas recalled. Only when he was making a film would he still sometimes explode, Douglas said. Asking her to accompany him to Spain, where he was planning to appear in the film *Christopher Columbus* (1992), he qualified his offer: "I should warn you, I am so horrible to be around when I'm making a film that I don't think you'll enjoy yourself." Despite his warning, Douglas ended up liking the experience, because Marlon's ability to bring "humor and levity" to a tense situation made everything bearable. Still, the blowup on the set always came when the phoniness and the mercenariness got to be too much.

He might have felt differently if he'd had a chance to direct his "Indian picture," as he called it. For several years, he'd labored to get it off the ground; Jay Kanter was negotiating with various studios as late as the 1980s. Marlon even flew in Gillo Pontecorvo, with whom he'd almost come to blows on *Burn!*, to discuss directing the film. But as with the Caryl Chessman project, Marlon could never fit his passion into the regimental development process required for a Hollywood film. His message to the studios certainly wasn't productive: "Look," he remembered saying, "you people have done more damage to the American Indian's cause than any other group outside the United States government, and you ought to kick in and do something about it." Not surprisingly, that approach went nowhere. "So I'm scraping my ass to get financing for this film," Marlon said in 1976. He wasn't successful.

Instead, he was consigned to working on other people's films. His second Western with Arthur Penn, *The Missouri Breaks*, shot in Montana, was no more successful than *The Chase*. While Marlon liked working with his friend and neighbor Jack Nicholson, the script was a mess, and he simply didn't care enough this time to try to fix it. Vincent Canby called his performance "out of control." But who had the gravitas to control Marlon Brando by now? He was a world unto himself. "People were embalmed with awe," Chris Hodenfield wrote in *Rolling Stone*. "They'd see him walking in their direction, with that head balled up like a clenched fist, that forehead all knotted and complicated. Beethoven must have had the same air." It was the sort of adulation Marlon loathed.

From the dry, cracking plains of Montana he headed to the dense, muggy jungles of the Philippines, where he shot *Apocalypse Now*, his reunion film with Francis Ford Coppola. In 1971, they'd been collaborative, hungry, and eager; now they butted heads. Marlon arrived on the set overweight (not yet three hundred pounds, but still heavy), and he wanted to "camouflage" that fact. Coppola, however, wanted to use it, imagining Marlon's character, the demented Colonel Kurtz, as "a man eating all the time and overindulging." They were also at odds over the script. "You're making an enormous error," Marlon told Coppola. "This guy Kurtz, don't misuse him." The film, a commentary on the Vietnam War, was inspired by Joseph Conrad's *Heart of Darkness*. Kurtz, Marlon argued, needed to be that terrible, evil beating heart: a justifier of genocide. Eventually, Coppola gave in to Marlon's demands, allowing him to do what he wanted with the character, agreeing that the script was deficient in that regard.

A fascinating, gorgeous, at times brilliant film, *Apocalypse Now* is ultimately unsatisfying: the whole is not as great as its parts, most critics agreed. Vincent Canby called *Apocalypse* an "adventure yarn with delusions of grandeur, a movie that ends . . . not with a bang, but a whimper." The actors, Canby wrote, were all "superlatively right," however, with one notable exception: "Mr. Brando, who has no role to act." The barely glimpsed Kurtz, living in the shadows, is a terrifying creation, but just what is he? No one seemed to know, not even Marlon, who may have shown us, for the first time since threatening it, what a performance made entirely of technique looks like. After the film's release, he came to believe (unfairly) that Coppola blamed him for the problems on the film, and never again had a good word to say about the director. It was another sad, regrettable end to an actor-director partnership that had once produced magic.

At least *Apocalypse Now* was a serious, important film. Those would be few and far between from this point on. Instead, Marlon chose big-budget epics (*Superman*, for which he earned $3.7 million and a large chunk of the back end for just a few minutes of screen time; *Roots: The Next Generation*; and *Columbus*) and middlebrow thrillers and comedies. All he needed to do was show up, display some technique for the camera, collect his paycheck, and go home.

When *Last Tango in Paris* was released, one reviewer for *Time* magazine had lauded Marlon for answering "the imperative of his talent by regenerating it." But in truth Marlon didn't feel that "the imperative of his talent" required an answer. By this point, he *hated* acting. There's no clearer way of stating it. He despised not only the business of acting but also acting itself: it took him away from other things, more important things, such as civil rights advocacy and his aquaculture in Tahiti, but also mindless, trivial things such as playing practical jokes on his friends.

On movie sets, there would invariably be problems, conflicts, and egos; Marlon had absolutely no patience for any of it. He did his best to get through. On the set of *The Island of Dr. Moreau* (1996), he reacted to the fighting going on all around him (involving director

John Frankenheimer, costar Val Kilmer, and others) by gleefully and devilishly adding to the chaos. When Frankenheimer spoke with him, ever so seriously, about what he wanted in a scene, Marlon would reply with "Sid Caesar's double talk," Douglas remembered: unrelated words strung together with gibberish. "And the director would be nodding, 'Uh huh,' agreeing with him," which made Marlon laugh even more. "He was showing how people would agree with him just because he's Marlon Brando," Douglas said, "no matter what he was saying"—or *not* saying, as the case may be.

The genius remained, however. Bursts of it would appear when least expected. His human rights lawyer in *A Dry White Season* (1989), taking on South African apartheid, a subject close to Marlon's heart, becomes a fully fleshed character in the short time Marlon is on-screen; he justly won an Oscar nomination for Best Supporting Actor. In *The Freshman* (1990), Marlon is a delight playing affectionate tribute to Don Corleone, and exhibiting the best comic timing of his career. He's equally likeable in *Don Juan De-Marco* (1994), as the aging psychiatrist who, by the end of the film, comes to believe once more in magic and romance.

The biographer Patricia Bosworth, working on a book about Marlon, visited him on the set of *The Score* (2001), which would turn out to be his final film. His costars were Robert De Niro and Edward Norton. "It's amazing to see three generations of superb actors all in sync, improvising," Bosworth recorded of the shoot. "Their words overlap. It's almost as if they're composing a piece of music. Finally they shoot the scene, and I am able to study Brando's expression. He has the same haunted eyes, the same electrically charged energy, as he had when he played the despairing expatriate Paul in *Last Tango in Paris*. The long pauses are still there, too, the faraway looks, the chuckles, the moment-to-moment behavior so organic and genuine it almost overwhelms the other two actors."

Marlon never lost his skill. Even in his least successful roles, there is *something*. None of his performances is a throwaway. After all, an expert shoemaker who has long since wearied of crafting fancy shoes with bows and patent leather would still, when put to the task, bring forth a product that, even in its simplicity, was far more solidly and ingeniously built than most.

IN 1994, CNN interviewer Larry King showed up with a crew at Mulholland Drive and attempted what many had sought and few had secured: a full hour of Marlon Brando. The star, closing in on those three hundred pounds by now, had done his own makeup, darkening his eyebrows to look like King; he even wore red suspenders, the interviewer's trademark. Marlon claimed he looked like—"who was that guy," he asked, "the famous Italian, not Ramon Novarro, the other guy, the big lover, played the Sheik?" King replied, "Valentino? *That's* the look you have?" Marlon—with his pudgy round face, short gray bangs combed down onto his forehead, and his body as big as a house—smirked. "That's right," he said.

As his assistants stood on the sidelines biting their nails, Marlon proceeded to demolish the very construct of the celebrity interview. He interrupted his usual diatribe against the monetization of journalism to point out that King was sweating; later, he patted the host's face with a cloth. Marlon fed his enormous mastiff dog, Tim, treats from his own mouth, revealed he wasn't wearing any shoes, sang an impromptu duet with King, and finally kissed the interviewer full on the mouth. At one point, when King told viewers they'd be back after a commercial, Marlon stuck his face into the camera and announced, "I'm leaving now, no matter what he says," then laughed impishly, the dimples appearing in his fat face. For a second, he was the young prankster again, the kid from Shattuck pulling pins from door hinges.

"He did not enjoy the interview process, so he had to take charge," Avra Douglas said. With his memoir, *Songs My Mother*

*Taught Me*, just released by Random House, Marlon had been forced, by contract, into his despised role of huckster. The only way to get through it was to play the provocateur. Some people watching the King interview were horrified by Marlon's antics. The actress Anne Jackson found him "monstrous," but her husband, Eli Wallach, who'd known him since before he was famous, countered that when he kissed King on the mouth, "That was his way of saying this whole business of interviewing is such a stupid game."

Marlon's pranks, his sense of humor—these, too, were coping skills. On the set of *The Score*, "no one was in a good mood," Douglas recalled. So, Marlon rigged up a remote-controlled fart machine that went off whenever Robert De Niro sat down on the couch. "That made everybody laugh," Douglas said.

Marlon once said, "If you don't laugh, you might as well just die." For all the tragedies he'd endured, "he retained his joie de vivre, his mischievous sense of humor," Douglas said. It was how he survived.

HE ALSO TOOK sustenance from the big, sprawling family he had created. His kids didn't live with him, but he liked them to visit, to keep in touch with him, to pay him homage, in a way, rather like Vito Corleone, the family man. Miko frequently came by with his children, Shane and Prudence; Movita's daughter, Rebecca, born just before the divorce, was also a big part of Marlon's life. Even Marie Cui, despite the paternity suit she'd once filed, brought her daughter, Maya, around; they remained close to Marlon right up to the end.

It was a wide, expansive view of family that Marlon possessed; his children didn't need to be biologically his for him to accept them. Tarita's other children became his, too; he included them in his will. "He had a tendency to adopt people," officially and unofficially, Douglas said. That same impulse had powered his generosity over the years to so many friends, such as when he paid for Freddie Fiore's rehab and Janice Mars's psychotherapy. The man who'd lacked a sustaining family in his youth was constantly increasing the size of his family as an older man. In 1988, at the age of sixty-four, Marlon took a fancy to his twenty-eight-year-old housekeeper, Guatemalan-born Maria Cristina Ruiz; she was soon pregnant with his child. Two more children followed. One accident might have been believable, but not three in a row. "He was really devoted to the children," said Avra Douglas.

Jack Larson found it "astonishing how virile" Marlon remained, even being "so overweight [and] in his late sixties and seventies." When Ellen visited once during these years, she left a note calling Marlon "sweetheart." His current girlfriend found it and blew her top. "Don't ever leave me a note saying sweetheart," Marlon told Ellen later. "This was war!"

In the wake of Cheyenne's death, he'd also found a new connection with Tarita. They attended grief counseling together, and Tarita finally broke that long-ago promise she'd made not to tell him she loved him. When she finally spoke the words, Marlon told her that he loved her, too. "It was without doubt an impossible love," Tarita remembered, "but it was our love."

When he felt the old rage, the desire for revenge, bubbling up, he wrestled it down. "I realize," he wrote, "that it is a wasted emotion and I have better things to do with the rest of my life." The most useful thing Dr. Harrington had ever taught him, Marlon declared, was "how to forgive"—himself and others. He forgave George Englund after a big blowout. He forgave his sister Jocelyn, after some years of holding a grudge, for speaking to a biographer. He forgave Movita for what he considered her manipulations in getting him to marry her, welcoming her back into the sweeping expanse of his family.

But there was one family member with whom he was, sadly, never fully reconciled. Shortly after midnight on January 10, 1996, Christian was released from prison after serving just under five years of his ten-year sentence. His early release was granted because of good behavior and work credits. While in prison, Christian had earned his general equivalency diploma and continued his vocational education in the machine shop program. Moving back to his beloved Northwest, he found a job as a welder. Marlon was relieved that Christian was free, and hopeful he could start a new life. But for the next eight years, father and son saw each other only rarely.

MARLON'S VISION OF people coming together to renounce aggression, racism, and greed—the dream articulated by Martin Luther King Jr. on that glorious August day in Washington, DC—had evaporated for him by the early 1990s. While his fears of civil war eventually subsided, he'd become, in some ways, one of the cynics he'd always deplored. The only hope for the world now, Marlon argued, was to find a way to alter "the enzymes, the hormones, the testosterone" to eliminate hate and belligerence in people. If scientists could complete "the analysis of the human genome," he said, perhaps the problem of "criminality and aggression" could be solved by biogenetics.

Once, he'd imagined a world where all people were treated fairly, where the hatred in people's hearts could be overcome by compassion and honest dialogue and education. He'd campaigned for UNICEF, donated land to the American Indian Movement, and continued his financial support of civil rights organizations. But the rise of international terrorism in the 1990s and the attacks of September 11, 2001, persuaded him that the world had devolved into "crocodiles" eating their young. "It's odd that our brains would service us so well in some cases, and not at all in others," he said. "Why have our brains not seen that we are destroying ourselves?"

Tired and disillusioned in his last years, he chose to retreat from the world more than engage with it. As always, Teti'aroa remained his sanctuary. "If I've come closer to a sense of peace, it would be there," he said into his ubiquitous tape recorder. The islands were more than just his personal refuge. As one reporter described it, Marlon had turned the atoll into an "ecological test tube for Third World self-sufficiency," consulting with such experts as Stewart Brand (*Whole Earth Catalog*) and Jacques Cousteau on aquaculture, solar energy, and wind power. Various scientists had set up programs for growing fruits and vegetables under environmentally friendly conditions; there was also the farming of fish and crustaceans in underwater cages. In addition, Marlon worked with local schools to bring Tahitian students to Teti'aroa to learn about marine biology. "It was like a living laboratory," his son Teihotu said. Marlon "would put a mask on and spend hours in three inches of water, just watching, releasing. He loved everything about this place."

He wasn't entirely finished, as it turned out, with his warnings to the world about the dangers it faced. His was one of the earliest voices cautioning against climate change; Marlon told Larry King in 1994 that he'd signed on with a company "designed to reduce the $CO_2$ in the earth [in order] to preserve it for your grandchildren and for mine." In that otherwise lighthearted interview, he turned serious long enough to sound an alarm: "Each one of us, everybody here in this room, sound, gaffers, assistants, we all have to do something to reverse the effects of the $CO_2$."

AFTER *THE SCORE* (2001), Marlon made no further films, but "his mind never stopped," said Avra Douglas. "He was always coming up with ideas." He hosted a series of seminars called "Lying for a Living," in which both well-known and up-and-coming actors sat in homage as Marlon lectured. As long as he was considered the "greatest," why not make that image pay for the upkeep of the aquaculture farm? Ultimately, the series was shelved, however, and not released on DVD, as had been intended. Still, the ideas kept coming. Marlon wrote a couple of screenplays: *Jericho*, an action thriller about the CIA running drugs; and *Bullboy*, about saving bulls from bullfighting, which Sean Penn was interested in directing. "You are the greatest actor since Charlton Heston," Marlon teased Penn in one fax, signing himself, "Someone who has no name." But, as always, the hellish process of film development left him frustrated, and the scripts remain unproduced.

The impetus for these ideas wasn't just to make money, but to keep that prodigious imagination occupied and stimulated. During these last years, Marlon became the Benjamin Franklin of Mulholland Drive. "He was quite the inventor," said Avra Douglas. Diagrams and detailed drawings document his marvelous ingenuity. Some of his inventions were drawn precisely to scale with a drafting program: moveable thatched-roof cottages on wooden platforms; a rolling pier that made docking easier for boats; a traveling tree house that could glide between the palms. Another device lulled babies to sleep by mimicking the movement of an automobile. One drawing, of an earthquake-proof house, was rendered with particular care. A twelve-story apartment building with a rounded roof rises up from a protective ball of some kind in the earth. The image looks unmistakably like a giant penis, and knowing Marlon's sense of humor, it was almost certainly intentional. "I'm sure he would have enjoyed showing this to his friends as a great idea," said his estate archivist Austin Wilkin, "and watching how they reacted."

Marlon also dabbled in abstract art, much of it evocative of the female form. In his sketchpads, he drew hundreds of human faces, some comical doodles and others more realistic, with shading and personality. He drew men, women, and children of all ages and races. "He did a lot of drawing the last ten years," Avra Douglas remembered. "He got so much pleasure out of that. He asked me to learn Photoshop so that I could teach him, and he'd sit at the computer spending hours moving the sunset around, creating different realities from photographs."

He also indulged his love of poetry, reading verses out loud as he wandered through his house. Janice Mars often sent him poems, especially by Yeats, whom they'd both loved since the days of the 37 West Fifty-Second Street Regulars. Marlon's favorite, "The Lake Isle of Innisfree," seemed especially resonant these days, as he sought a life beyond the spotlight:

> *I will arise and go now, and go to Innisfree,*
> *And a small cabin build there, of clay and wattles made;*
> *Nine bean rows will I have there, a hive for the honey bee,*
> *And live alone in the bee-loud glade.*

But most of all, Marlon loved reciting Shakespeare. He'd intone lines from *Julius Caesar* and *Twelfth Night* as well as other plays he'd never performed in. He'd phone friends to deliver a soliloquy from *Henry V* or *Macbeth*. "How spectacular was that," said one friend, "to pick up the phone and hear Marlon Brando, 'Is this a dagger which I see before me?'" Avra Douglas was treated to many such renditions. "He truly, truly appreciated Shakespeare," she said.

Finally, Marlon found ways to do what he loved most: observe the world and its people surreptitiously. The rise of the Internet had created a whole new kind of anonymity. He was the first in his house to discover what he called "the information super-highway," and he urged his staff to get on it. With one of the original Apple computers, Marlon spent hours in America Online chatrooms, getting into political arguments that nearly always ended with him telling the other person to fuck off. His account would then get suspended. "So many times, I had to call AOL," Douglas remembered, "and say, 'That was my kid and he'll never do it again.'"

The other technology he embraced enthusiastically was the fax machine. His fax line was always busy, either sending or receiving. In some ways, faxing was the perfect means of communication for him. If he didn't feel like speaking with someone, he could just send a fax; he could also send doodles and cartoons and magazine articles he found interesting. He often *did* want to talk, however, especially with old friends. He'd spend hours on the phone with Ellen Adler, or George Englund, or Janice Mars, or anybody from the old days he could find at home. The conversations would be lengthy and rambling, complete with his trademark long periods of silence. "At the end of his life," Ellen said, "Marlon just talked on the phone. Nobody in to see him, but he'd talk on the phone three hours at a time."

WITH OLD AGE comes an inevitable loneliness as friends and colleagues die off. Perhaps that was why Marlon spent so much time talking on the phone with the ones who were left. Wally Cox's death in 1973 from a heart attack at the age of forty-eight had devastated him. "I'm not sure I will ever forgive Wally for dying," he said. "I felt mystified and could not accept it." Alice Marchak remembered Marlon's "anguish, the wailing and cursing." For a long time afterward, he would curse the "son of a bitch" for leaving him. Wally, after all, "was my brother," Marlon said. Wally remembered Bud, the boy Marlon had been before the fame. He was one of the few who had carte blanche at Mulholland Drive, coming and going as he pleased. When Wally's widow asked Marlon to scatter his ashes, Marlon held on to them instead, intending that they be scattered with his own when the time came.

As the years went by, there were other losses. Celia Webb died in 1981, shortly before her sixty-third birthday, of cancer; Marlon was still helping pay her bills. Sam Gilman died in 1985; Stella Adler passed away in 1992, at the ripe old age of ninety-one; and Marlon's sister Fran died in 1994, at seventy-one. In 2000, the loss of Christian Marquand, friend, lover, fellow carouser, and partner in crime, was particularly hard felt. Elia Kazan died in 2003.

Harder than losing friends through death, however, was losing them through betrayal. A number of old pals sold out and wrote about Marlon. He'd long ago cut off Billy Redfield for doing so, but he'd never expected Freddie Fiore to cash in on him. In 1974, Freddie (under his real name, Carlo Fiore) authored *Bud: The Brando I Knew*, billed as "the untold story of Brando's private life." It was a particularly grievous betrayal; Freddie went all the way back to Sayville with him, and Marlon had propped him up for years, helping him to beat heroin. Bob Thomas, Marlon's faithful cheerleader from the Associated Press, also wrote a book, *Marlon: Portrait of the Rebel as an Artist*. "I considered [Bob] a friend," Marlon said, but after Thomas's book came out, he realized the journalist had "just sort of wormed his way in" to get a scoop.

Still, Marlon approached the end with few regrets. "I think to regret is useless in life," he told Larry King in that memorable interview. "It belongs in the past. The only moment we have is right now sitting here and talking to each other." King pressed him: he'd heard he'd really wanted to be a musician instead of an actor. Didn't he regret not taking that route? "I don't know," Marlon replied. "If the dog hadn't stopped to pee, he might have caught the rabbit. How could I possibly know?"

If there were no regrets, there was one significant mea culpa. "We've all been guilty, most men, of viewing women through prejudice," Marlon said. "I always thought of myself not as a prejudiced person, but I find, as I look over it, I was." Still, guilt was "a useless emotion," he said. "It doesn't do anybody any good." Far more useful, he insisted, was "a healthy sense of conscience."

His 1994 memoir had been carefully circumspect, but as he approached eighty years of age, Marlon wanted a more honest, complete version of his life. He'd been making his tape recordings for some time, and would continue to do so until very close to the end. He envisioned them as background to a film he would narrate, chronicling his eight decades on the planet. "It will be a highly personalized documentary on the life of myself, Marlon Brando," he said on one tape. Facing his mortality, he wanted his story told, with all its fascinating contradictions. Sadly, the film was not made in his lifetime. But *Listen to Me Marlon* was produced from his tape recordings, based largely on his vision, and released in 2015.

"BY THE TIME I get to a certain age," Marlon once told Ellen Adler, "if anything's the matter with my heart, they'll replace it. Modern science will be just ahead of me so that I'll always lick it. I plan to live to be very old."

As his health declined, he spoke to Ellen frequently on the telephone. "I'm not sure if he was afraid of death," she said, "or if he just couldn't conceive of himself not being alive. He said once, 'Isn't it odd to think that we just won't be here?' I don't think he knew he was dying."

During his last months, Marlon was cared for by Angela Borlaza Magaling, his Filipino housekeeper and devoted companion, as well as by her sister, who was a nurse. Behind the scenes, friends, family, and employees wrangled over who was really in charge and who would get what when Marlon died. As executor, he had replaced Alice Marchak, now in her seventies and retired, and brought in younger people: Avra Douglas, his business manager Larry Dressler, and producer Mike Medavoy. Tensions and rivalries were perhaps inevitable, but the absurd stories that were leaked to the press about dead rats in Marlon's house, and about how the dying man was being kept a prisoner, were regrettable. It was exactly the sort of fabricated sensationalism Marlon had railed against for the past forty years.

Thankfully, he was past worrying about that. His body was shutting down, and during the spring of 2004, he slept most of the time. Suffering from pulmonary fibrosis, he found breathing increasingly difficult, and his eyesight was fading from diabetes. That spring, too, doctors had diagnosed liver cancer.

On the night of June 30, 2004, Marlon's breathing became extremely labored. In the morning, he was taken to UCLA Medical Center. Doctors realized there was nothing further to do. At a little before six o'clock on the evening of July 1, Marlon Brando died. He was eighty. He'd lost quite a bit of weight in his last months, shriveling down to just half of what he'd been. And yet he remained a giant.

Despite the lurid stories in the press, Marlon seemed, in his last years, to find a sense of peace, even of closure, to his tumultuous, picaresque life. There was a moment at the Monterey airport just a couple years earlier that Avra Douglas would remember fondly. She'd left him sitting by himself as she went to the counter to collect their tickets. "I was always worried about leaving him alone, as if he were a kid," Douglas said. When she returned, she found him "surrounded by people." Fans had recognized him. "Here's this old man," Douglas said—overweight, balding, and yet "he still had it." Marlon was beaming, she said, "gracious" to these strangers who seemed to sincerely like and appreciate him. That day, there was no railing about the intrusion of celebrity or the immaturity of autograph seekers. For once, Marlon seemed touched by the public's affection.

A couple of months after his death, a memorial was held for him at Mike Medavoy's house, with Jack Nicholson, Warren Beatty, Sean Penn, and others in attendance. Later, some of his ashes were scattered in Death Valley, along with Wally's; the rest were spread over his beloved Teti'aroa.

Four years after his father's death, Christian Brando died of pneumonia, aged only forty-nine. Over the past decade, he'd struggled with drug addiction, but an autopsy showed no drugs in his body at the time of his death. Anna Kashfi lived on until 2015, when she died at age eighty. Their long, sad family story was finally over.

IN 1973, *TIME* magazine had expressed frustration over Marlon's longing "to find something in life that is permanently true" and his need "to lay down his life for it." Like so many others, the writer of the article believed he knew better than his subject: "The pity is," the article went on, "that Brando seems unwilling to accept that he has already found that something: his art." Why, *Time* and so many others asked, couldn't his art, his talent, give him the satisfaction he sought?

It *is* a conundrum: what happens when a great artist doesn't share the world's respect for his art? What if Picasso had considered what he did nothing all that special and the entirety of modern art to be mostly irrelevant to humankind? What if Eugene O'Neill had been indifferent to the American theater? The analogies are not, of course, perfect, as Picasso and O'Neill created their art on their own, and Marlon, like most actors, was an interpretive artist, an intermediary between the true creators (the writers or the directors) and the audience. Perhaps that was part of his disdain for the profession of acting. His one shot at original creation, *One-Eyed Jacks*, was taken away from him and ultimately reshaped by others. So, we never got to see how Marlon might have viewed his work if it had carried his full imprimatur.

His adamant belief that everyone acts, and that the only difference with his acting was that he did it consciously, gave the impression that he didn't value his work. It was an attitude that left Karl Malden, and so many others, frustrated. "He just wouldn't accept that what he did was anything special," Malden lamented. Marlon pointed to the fact that he'd learned the lesson that "everybody acts" from Stella, and who would know better than she? But years later, Stella's grandson challenged him on that belief, suggesting that Stella's point was perhaps more nuanced than that, and Marlon might have drawn the wrong conclusion from his mentor's lesson.

"What if," Tom Oppenheim asked him over the phone, sometime in 2003 or 2004, "you lived in a tribal situation and your role was to come forward at the end of the day and tell great stories around the campfire?" Shrewdly, Oppenheim was presenting a scenario very dear to Marlon's sensibilities; most of the answers to life's questions, Marlon believed, could be found through anthropological studies of primitive societies. "So," Oppenheim asked him, "as the storyteller of the tribe, would you still feel that acting as a vocation had no value?"

"Well, Tommy," Marlon said, "I think you've just asked me a question that requires a five-hour answer, and I just don't have the time for it right now." Remembering the moment, Oppenheim smiled. "I think I cornered him into something," he said. Sadly, it was their last conversation. Marlon died not long afterward. Just how he might have answered Oppenheim's question is unknown.

There are hints that Marlon didn't totally disparage his work. George Englund came into his room once to find him watching *On the Waterfront* on television. "As he lay back looking on himself," Englund remembered, "there was no emotion in him, only the absorption with the details of the times he was recalling." Marlon had once called his work on *Waterfront* "in and out." But over the years, he seemed to recognize the significance of his achievement. The way he watched the film that day, "in no rush to leave" to keep their dinner appointment, as George Englund recalled, suggests that this was the case.

Ellen Adler suspected that, in his later years, Marlon wished he'd done more Shakespeare; his loving recitation of the Bard's work when he was in his seventies, wandering around his house and calling people on the phone, lends credence to her theory. During the making of *Don Juan DeMarco*, Johnny Depp recalled Marlon telling him to play Hamlet while he was still young enough. Depp thought Hamlet was "kind of the cliché thing," but Marlon insisted, "No, man, do it before you're too old to do it. I never got the chance." If only he had tried Lear.

It must be remembered that Marlon didn't so much put acting down as resent others who, he said, "put it up." Avra Douglas, too, thought he was proud of the work he did. "He did appreciate how

films affected people," she said. "But in the end, he would have preferred to have been a great philosopher or a great writer."

His ambivalence, however, cannot dislodge his genius. On the
screen, Marlon was peerless: "no one deeper, truer, more real,
more complex," declared Foster Hirsch. With the work he did for
Kazan, Marlon changed film acting forever, and his Marc Antony, according to Jack Nicholson, "adjusted how most American
actors feel about what [is] possible with Shakespeare." No matter
what Marlon may have thought, or wished, or grumbled about, he
still towers over the history of American film. "His impact in the
movies was bigger than anybody else's, ever," Nicholson wrote.
"Brando will be there forever—that's all there is to it. He might not
like that, but he'll be there forever anyway."

Still, for all that, *Time* was presumptuous to insist that he accept what other people felt should be his life's fulfillment. In fact,
Marlon *did* find something beyond his art to "lay down his life
for." Specifically, it was his fight for civil rights and his relentless
commitment to social justice. More generally, it was his insistence
on authenticity and his demand that society prioritize the good
and the valuable over the mercenary and the superficial. From
the 1960s until his death, Marlon was a voice in the wilderness,
warning about the celebrity culture he spied coming down the
tracks, picking up steam as it prepared to deliver Kardashians and
Real Housewives and a dynasty named Duck and creatures called
Snooki and Honey Boo Boo and, finally, a president of the United
States.

Marlon saw it coming. But he was powerless to stop it.

When a clerk in a hardware store once insisted that she couldn't
call him "Marlon" because she needed to show respect, he asked,
"Show respect for what? For notoriety? For fame?" David Shipman,
with shudders of self-righteousness, had accused Marlon in 1995
of selling out in the roles he took. But Marlon *never* sold out. Except for those few years in the late 1950s, when he was fulfilling

his mother's dying wish, he never played the Hollywood game. He would remain one of the very few stars never to buy his own publicity, never to aggrandize himself or his industry, and never to claim more for himself than what he honestly believed in his heart he deserved.

Marlon simply couldn't have lived any other way. For a while, he had a recurring dream that he was trapped in the midst of war, "freezing and sick . . . no way of getting back." That was what selling out would have been like for him. Unendurable. He wouldn't have survived, which was what the dream was all about.

More than just his great acting, Marlon should be remembered for his unwavering commitment to his own vision, for insisting on excellence but also on authenticity, and for forever being wary of the dehumanizing costs of fame. When Patricia Bosworth was working on her biography of him, she tried in vain to get Marlon to speak with her, sending him letters explaining that she intended "to show how he has influenced three generations of actors with his range, his flamboyance, his nerve" and to prove that he was "as singular an artist as Orson Welles." But that was exactly the wrong approach. Marlon never spoke with her.

I'm not sure I would have had any more luck reaching my subject than Bosworth, who is one of the very best biographers in the business. But during my five years of living with Marlon through this book and digging as deep as I could into his story, I learned a basic fact: Marlon talked about only what he wanted to talk about. And what he wanted to talk about were things that mattered, which didn't include influencing actors or being like Orson Welles. True, he could be cajoled into conversations about less weighty topics than race relations or the military-industrial complex. He could spend hours regaling his listeners with tales of his sexual exploits or the practical jokes he'd played on friends. But, mostly, he wanted to talk about life, and what it meant, and what the hell he was doing on this planet.

Stevan Riley, the director of *Listen to Me Marlon*, remembered listening to the last audiotape Marlon ever recorded. Just months before his death, Marlon reflected on finding peace in the "Jungian collective unconsciousness." He'd never believed in God. He didn't hold out any hope for an afterlife. But there just might be peace. At the end, he was one with everyone and everything around him. After eighty years, he was finally unafraid of the darkness.

Marlon Brando should be remembered as a searcher. He spent his life trying to become ever more conscious—more "woke," as they say today. He didn't always succeed in his goal. Trauma cannot always be completely overcome. What matters, however, is that he tried, accepting the failures, however heartbreaking, and the successes, however big or small. That's the mark of a life well lived. You *try*. You make a difference for yourself and for others the best you can. You're a contender—you fight the good fight, as Marlon did.

He sometimes worried that all his efforts had been in vain, that racism was not only unvanquished but stronger than ever; that the culture was not more enlightened but, in some ways, less; and that while some of his children did well for themselves, he'd failed Christian and Cheyenne. But when one is truly a contender, as Marlon was, what matters is the sincerity and fortitude of the effort. His success was in the trying. How many never try?

"Oh, Marlon," wrote Janice Mars, who knew him longer than most, "you did so want to make a difference for the better, but the evils of the world reach so far back that to repair or restore what has been damaged needs a completely new kind of approach, if that is within the capacity of our genes. We still have not disavowed the politics of imperialism and the self-righteousness of patriotism, even though now the survival of the planet itself is at stake. Our proud assertions of progress have been a delusion. But your heart has been good, and it deserves a place at Innisfree."

# ACKNOWLEDGMENTS

THANKS TO THE MARLON Brando estate for its support and generosity, and for its willingness to have Marlon's story told honestly and completely. In particular, I am grateful to Avra Douglas, Marlon's longtime assistant and friend, for sharing her insights into the man and his mind, and to Austin Wilkin, Brando expert and archivist, who could always find exactly the material I needed. I am also deeply appreciative to Mike Medavoy and Jeffrey Abrams for their trust.

Getting as close to my subject as I did would not have been possible without the valuable contribution of Ellen Adler, Marlon's great friend and the daughter of Stella Adler. I am profoundly grateful for her assistance and wisdom. Thanks go also to Ellen's son, Tom Oppenheim, artistic director and president of the Stella Adler Studio of Acting, for his keen perception on Marlon's life and art.

For insights, memories, context, and connections, I am indebted to Kaye Ballard, Clark Bason, C. A. Carter, Michael Childers, Les Hall, Gahan Hanmer, Foster Hirsch, Jack Larson, Pat Perez, Liz Smith, Sam Staggs, and several others (who, for reasons of their own, requested anonymity; these last include friends of both Marlon and his son Christian). Posthumous credit must go to Dick Clayton, Tom Mankiewicz, Robert Shaw, Maureen Stapleton, Elaine Stritch, Noel Taylor, and Miles White, as I discovered conversations about Marlon in interviews I'd conducted with them as part of earlier projects. I would also like to acknowledge the help and contributions of my research assistants, Collin Berill, David Williams, and Catherine Lindstrom.

My ability to re-create Marlon's world with such detail was due to the extraordinary archival material that exists in various repositories, and which is meticulously maintained by archivists whose work of safeguarding our history too often goes unheralded. My gratitude to Jenny Romero and Kristine Krueger at the Margaret Herrick Library of the Academy of Motion Picture Arts and Sciences; Joan Miller and Andrea McCarty at the Cinema Archives at Wesleyan University; Laura Schieb of the Rauner Special Collections Library at Dartmouth College; Jenny Swadosh at the New School Archives; Lorna Kirwan at the Bancroft Library, University of California, Berkeley; Mary K. Huelsbeck at the Wisconsin Center for Film and Theater Research, at the University of Wisconsin–Madison; Lewis Wyman of the Manuscript Division at the Library of Congress; Aaron M. Lisec at the Morris Library of Southern Illinois University; J. C. Johnson at the Howard Gotlieb Archival Research Center, at Boston University; Judy Solberg at the Shields Library, UC Davis; the staff at the New York Public Library for the Performing Arts; and last, but certainly not least, Ewa Wolynska and Renata Vickrey in Special Collections at the Elihu Burritt Library, at Central Connecticut State University. A full list of collections used is provided in the bibliography.

My editor, Jonathan Jao, conceived this idea and offered encouragement and excellent advice all the way through. My thanks also to Sarah Haugen and Fritz Metsch for the efficient production and elegant design of the book. As always, I could not have undertaken or completed this project without the steady support and nurturance of my agent, Malaga Baldi, and my husband, Tim Huber.

# MARLON BRANDO STAGE AND TELEVISION CREDITS

## *Stage Credits*

### THE MARCH OF DRAMA

*(These are mostly excerpts, not entire plays. The schedule was frequently revised from week to week. This is the best and most accurate account based on New School Bulletins and newspaper reports.)*

Selections from
*Awake and Sing, Hello Out There,*
and *Winterset*                    October 7, 1943          New School Auditorium

*Playwrights*: Clifford Odets, William Saroyan, Maxwell Anderson. *Extra/ unknown role/crew*: Marlon Brando. *Director*: John Gassner/Choteau Dyer.


*Strange Interlude*                 October 15, 1943         New School Auditorium

*Playwright*: Eugene O'Neill. *Extra/unknown role/crew*: Marlon Brando. *Director*: John Gassner/Choteau Dyer. (Note: a selection from *Mourning Becomes Electra* may have been staged as well.)


*Madras House*                      October 22, 1943         New School Auditorium

*Playwright*: Harley Granville-Barker. *Extra/unknown role/crew*: Marlon Brando. *Director*: John Gassner/Choteau Dyer.


*Journey's End*                     October 22, 1943         New School Auditorium

*Playwright*: R. C. Sherriff. *Extra/unknown role/crew*: Marlon Brando. *Director*: John Gassner/Choteau Dyer.

*Saint Joan*     October 29, 1943  New School Auditorium

*Playwright*: George Bernard Shaw. *Brother Martin Ladvenu*: Marlon Brando.
*Director*: John Gassner/Choteau Dyer. (Note: this is Marlon's first known role.)

*Riders to the Sea*    November 5, 1943  New School Auditorium

*Playwright*: John Millington Synge. *Bartley*: Marlon Brando. *Director*: John
Gassner/Choteau Dyer.

*Power*      November 12, 1943  New School Auditorium

*Playwright*: Arthur Arent. *Extra/crew member*: Marlon Brando. *Directors*: John
Gassner/Erwin Piscator/Choteau Dyer.

*War and Peace*    November 12, 1943  New School Auditorium

*Playwright*: Leo Tolstoy. *Prince Anatole Kuragin*: Marlon Brando. *Director*: John
Gassner/Choteau Dyer. (Note: this performance may have been canceled and
*Power* presented alone, or excerpts of both may have been staged.)

*The Insect Comedy*   November 19, 1943  New School Auditorium

*Playwright*: Karel Capek. *Extra/unknown role/crew*: Marlon Brando. *Director*:
John Gassner/Choteau Dyer.

*Gas*       November 19, 1943  New School Auditorium

*Playwright*: Georg Kaiser. *Workman*: Marlon Brando. *Director*: John Gassner/
Choteau Dyer. (Note: this performance may have been canceled and replaced
with *The Insect Comedy*, or excerpts of both may have been staged.)

*On the Eve*     December 3, 1943  New School Auditorium

*Playwright*: Alexander Afinogenov. *Golya, a student*: Marlon Brando. *Director*:
John Gassner/Choteau Dyer.

*The Power of Darkness*  December 10, 1943  New School Auditorium

*Playwright*: Leo Tolstoy. *Nikita*: Marlon Brando. *Director*: John Gassner/
Choteau Dyer.

*Hannele's Way to Heaven*          December 17, 1943          New School Auditorium

*Playwright*: Gerhart Hauptmann. *Hannele*: Priscilla Draghi. *Gottwald/Stranger*: Marlon Brando. *Director*: John Gassner.


### DRAMATIC WORKSHOP PRODUCTIONS

*Bobino*          December 25, 1943–February 27, 1944          Studio Theatre

*Playwright*: Stanley Kauffmann. *Boy*: Priscilla Draghi. *Prince*: Mae Cooper. *Giraffe*: Marlon Brando. *Tiger/Cow*: Elaine Stritch.


### THE MARCH OF DRAMA

*Improv*          January 7, 1944          New School Auditorium

*Extra/unknown role/crew*: Marlon Brando. *Director*: John Gassner.


*Chantecler*          January 14, 1944          New School Auditorium

*Playwright*: Edmond Rostand. *Chicken*: Marlon Brando. *Director*: John Gassner/ Choteau Dyer.


*Hannele's Way to Heaven*          January 21, 1944          New School Auditorium

*Playwright*: Gerhart Hauptmann. *Hannele*: Priscilla Draghi. *Gottwald/Stranger*: Marlon Brando. *Director*: John Gassner/Choteau Dyer.


*The Father*          January 28, 1944          New School Auditorium

*Playwright*: August Strindberg. *Extra/unknown role/crew*: Marlon Brando. *Director*: John Gassner/Choteau Dyer.


Unknown play          February 11, 1944          New School Auditorium

*Playwright*: Johann Wolfgang von Goethe. *Extra/unknown role/crew*: Marlon Brando. *Director*: John Gassner/Choteau Dyer.


Unknown play          February 11, 1944          New School Auditorium

*Playwright*: Friedrich Schiller. *Extra/unknown role/crew*: Marlon Brando. *Director*: John Gassner/Choteau Dyer.

Unknown Restoration comedy    February 18, 1944    New School Auditorium

*Extra/unknown role/crew*: Marlon Brando. *Director*: John Gassner/Choteau Dyer.


*Othello*                        April 2, 1944            New School Auditorium

*Playwright*: William Shakespeare. *Othello*: Canada Lee. *Extra/unknown role/ crew*: Marlon Brando. *Director*: Choteau Dyer.


*Macbeth*                        April 2, 1944            New School Auditorium

*Playwright*: William Shakespeare. *Extra/unknown role/crew*: Marlon Brando. *Director*: Choteau Dyer.


## BROADWAY

*Bobino*                        April 6–15, 1944        Adelphi Theatre

*Produced by*: American Theatre for Young Folks. *Producer*: Henri Leiser. *Playwright*: Stanley Kauffmann. *Boy*: Priscilla Draghi. *Prince*: Mae Cooper. *King*: Jack Bittner. *Scioravante*: Alfred Linder. *Princess*: Margaret Coates. *Tiger/ Cow*: Elaine Stritch. *Unknown cast/crew*: Marlon Brando, Marcia Mann, Joy Thomson, Eugene von Grona. *Director*: Maria Ley-Piscator.


## THE MARCH OF DRAMA

*Twelfth Night*                  April 14, 1944          New School Auditorium

*Playwright*: William Shakespeare. *Viola*: Rosalyn Weiss. *Sebastian*: Marlon Brando. *Malvolio*: Eugene von Grona. *Feste*: Elaine Stritch. *Maria*: Beulah Roth. *Sir Andrew Aguecheek*: Darren Dublin. *Director*: Choteau Dyer.


## DRAMATIC WORKSHOP PRODUCTIONS

*Twelfth Night*                  April 22–23, 1944       Studio Theatre

*Playwright*: William Shakespeare. *Viola*: Rosalyn Weiss. *Sebastian*: Marlon Brando. *Malvolio*: Eugene von Grona. *Feste*: Elaine Stritch. *Maria*: Beulah Roth. *Sir Andrew Aguecheek*: Darren Dublin. *Director*: Choteau Dyer.


*Dr. Sganarelle*                 May 20, 1944            Studio Theatre

*Playwright*: Milton Levene, based on Molière. *Sganarelle*: Jack Bittner. *Argan*:

George Bloostein. *Toinette*: Eleanor Emery. *Angelique*: Mae Cooper. *Dr. Diafoirus*: Marlon Brando. *Thomas*: Darren Dublin. *Director*: Maria Ley-Piscator.

| *Hannele's Way to Heaven* | May 22, 1944 | Studio Theatre |

*Playwright*: Gerhart Hauptmann. *Hannele*: Priscilla Draghi. *Gottwald/Stranger*: Marlon Brando. *Director*: Choteau Dyer.

| *Twelfth Night* | May 24, 1944 | Studio Theatre |

*Playwright*: William Shakespeare. *Viola*: Rosalyn Weiss. *Sebastian*: Marlon Brando. *Malvolio*: Eugene von Grona. *Feste*: Elaine Stritch. *Maria*: Beulah Roth. *Sir Andrew Aguecheek*: Darren Dublin. *Director*: Choteau Dyer.

## DRAMATIC WORKSHOP SUMMER STOCK

| *Claudia* | July 1–4, 1944 | Sayville Playhouse |

*Playwright*: Rose Franken. *Claudia*: Priscilla Draghi. *David Naughton*: Dorman Leonard. *Mrs. Brown*: Suzanne Freeman. *Bertha*: Margaret Bell. *Fritz*: Darren Dublin. *Jerry Seymoure*: Eugene von Grona. *Mme. Darushka*: Helene Morris. *Julia Naughton*: Victoire Fine. *Extra/unknown role/crew*: Marlon Brando. Director: *Choteau Dyer*.

| *Dr. Sganarelle* | July 7–9, 1944 | Sayville Playhouse |

*Playwright*: Milton Levene, based on Molière. *Sganarelle*: Marlon Brando. *Argan*: Eugene von Grona. *Angelique*: Beulah Roth. *Cleante*: Gordon Green. *Toinette*: Rosalyn Weiss. *Dr. Diafoirus*: Frederick Stevens (né Carlo Fiore). *Thomas*: Darren Dublin. *Dancers*: Leni von Grona, Elisabeth Kahn. *Director*: Maria Ley-Piscator.

| *Hannele's Way to Heaven* | July 14–16, 1944 | Sayville Playhouse |

*Playwright*: Gerhart Hauptmann. *Hannele*: Priscilla Draghi. *Gottwald/Stranger*: Marlon Brando. *Sister Martha*: Joan Patricia Basch. *Children*: local Sayville children. *Director*: Choteau Dyer.

| *Twelfth Night* | July 21–23, 1944 | Sayville Playhouse |

*Playwright*: William Shakespeare. *Viola*: Rosalyn Weiss. *Olivia*: Sara Farwell.

*Sebastian*: Marlon Brando. *Malvolio*: Eugene von Grona. *Feste*: Elaine Stritch.
*Sir Toby Belch*: Dorman Leonard. *Maria*: Beulah Roth. *Sir Andrew Aguecheek*:
Darren Dublin. *Director*: Choteau Dyer.

| *Ladies in Retirement* | July 28–30, 1944 | Sayville Playhouse |

*Playwrights*: Reginald Denham, Edward Percy. *Ellen Creed*: Chouteau Dyer.
*Albert Feather*: Marlon Brando. *Lucy*: Rosalyn Weiss. *Leonora Fiske*: Beulah
Roth. *Sisters*: Elaine Stritch, Blossom Plumb. *Unknown role*: Joan Patricia
Basch. *Extra/unknown role/crew*: Marlon Brando. *Director*: Maria Ley-Piscator.

| *Charley's Aunt* | August 4–6, 1944 | Sayville Playhouse |

*Playwright:* Brandon Thomas. *Charley*: Eugene von Grona. *Butler*: Stuart
Becker. *Spettigue*: Fred Stevens (né Carlo Fiore). *Colonel*: Dorman Leonard.
*College Kid*: Darren Dublin. *Unknown roles*: Nancy Strauss, Joan Patricia Basch,
Elisabeth Kahn, Greta Shoobe. *Extra/unknown role/crew*: Marlon Brando.
*Director*: Maria Ley-Piscator. (Sara Farwell had been announced but was not
listed in the final cast.)

| *Cry Havoc* | August 11–13, 1944 | Sayville Playhouse |

*Playwright*: Allan R. Kenward. *Cast*: Sara Farwell, Elaine Stritch, Rosalyn
Weiss, Beulah Roth, Margaret Bell, Blossom Plumb, Alene Hatch, Victoire
Fine, Bunny Holcombe, Esther Nighbert, Greta Shoobe. *Doc*: Dorothy Brando.
*Crew*: Marlon Brando. *Director*: Choteau Dyer.

[Note: Marlon was announced as part of the cast for the next Sayville
Playhouse production, *The Petrified Forest*, but he had left the company by
the time it opened on August 18. It is not known what part he was intended
to play.]

### BROADWAY

| *I Remember Mama* | October 19, 1944–February 7, 1946 | Music Box Theatre |

*Playwright*: John Van Druten. *Mama*: Mady Christians. *Uncle Chris*: Oscar
Homolka. *Katrin*: Joan Tetzel. *Papa*: Richard Bishop. *Nels*: Marlon Brando.
*Christine*: Frances Heflin. *Aunt Jenny*: Ruth Gates. *Aunt Trina*: Adrienne
Gessner. *Aunt Sigrid*: Ellen Mahar. *Dagmar*: Carolyn Hummel. *Stage manager*:
Edward Mendelsohn.

*Truckline Café* February 27–March 9, 1946 Belasco Theatre

*Playwright*: Maxwell Anderson. *Anne*: Virginia Gilmore. *Mort*: Richard Waring. *Tory McRae*: Ann Shepard. *Sage McRae*: Marlon Brando. *Evvie Garrett*: Joann Dolan. *Kip*: Ralph Theadore. *Min*: June Walker. *Stag*: Karl Malden. *Wing Commander Hern*: David Manners. *Director*: Harold Clurman.

*Candida* April 3–May 4, 1946 Cort Theatre

*Playwright*: George Bernard Shaw. *Miss Proserpine Garnett*: Mildred Natwick. *Rev. James Mavor Morrell*: Wesley Addy. *Alexander Mill*: Oliver Cliff. *Mr. Burgess*: Cedric Hardwicke. *Candida*: Katharine Cornell. *Eugene Marchbanks*: Marlon Brando. *Director*: Guthrie McClintic.

*Antigone* Mid-April–May 4, 1946 Cort Theatre

*Playwright*: Sophocles. *Creon*: Cedric Hardwicke. *Haemon*: Wesley Addy. *Nurse*: Bertha Belmore. *Page*: Albert Biondo. *Messenger*: Marlon Brando. *Antigone*: Katharine Cornell. *Eurydice*: Eveline Vaughan. *Ismene*: Ruth Matteson. *Staged by*: Guthrie McClintic.

*A Flag Is Born* September 5–mid-November 1946 Alvin Theatre

*Playwright*: Ben Hecht. *Tevye*: Paul Muni. *Speaker*: Quentin Reynolds. *Zelda*: Celia Adler. *David*: Marlon Brando. *The Singer*: Mario Berini. *Director*: Luther Adler.

### TOURING COMPANY

*Eagle Rampant* November 17, 1946–January 2, 1947 On Tour

*Playwright*: Jean Cocteau. *Edith Le Berg*: Eleanor Wilson. *Duke of Willenstein*: Colin Keith-Johnston. *The Queen*: Tallulah Bankhead. *Stanislas*: Marlon Brando. *Tony*: Cherokee Thornton. *Baron Foehn*: Clarence Derwent. *Staged by*: John C. Wilson.

### BROADWAY

*A Streetcar Named Desire*
December 3, 1947–May 31, 1949 Ethel Barrymore Theatre

*Playwright*: Tennessee Williams. *Blanche DuBois*: Jessica Tandy. *Stanley Kowalski*: Marlon Brando. *Stella*: Kim Hunter. *Mitch*: Karl Malden. *Director*: Elia Kazan.

*Arms and the Man*          July 6–August 1, 1953          New England playhouses

*Playwright*: George Bernard Shaw. *Raina*: Anne Kimball. *Catherine*: Nydia Westman. *Bluntschli*: William Redfield. *Nicola:* Philip Rhodes. *Louka*: Janice Mars. *Major Petkoff*: Sam Gilman. *Sergius*: Marlon Brando. *Settings*: Norman Rock. *Costumes*: Valerie Judd. *Director*: Herbert Ratner.

[Note: Philip Rhodes took ill on July 22 in Ivoryton, Connecticut, and was replaced in the part by Carlo "Freddie" Fiore.]


## Television Dramatic Credits

*Actor's Studio*, Episode 16:
"I'm No Hero"          January 9, 1949          ABC

*Production company*: World Video Inc. *Producer*: Richard Lewine. *Originating station*: WJZ (New York). *Script*: Henry Kane. *Doctor*: Marlon Brando. *Gangster*: Henry Bellaver. (30 minutes)


*Come Out Fighting*          April 18, 1950          NBC

*Production company*: World Video Inc. *Producer*: Louis G. Cowan. *Originating station*: WNBT (New York). *Stick Keenan*: Lee Tracy. *Jimmy Brand*: Marlon Brando. *Champion*: Johnny Britenbruck. *Unknown roles*: J. Edward Bromberg, Richard Boone, Audrey Christie. (30 minutes)

Note: some sources claim Marlon appeared with Jessica Tandy, reprising their roles from *A Streetcar Named Desire*, in an episode of the *Omnibus* anthology series titled "Advice to Bathers," on October 30, 1955. Tandy *did* appear in the episode, although her costar was her husband, Hume Cronyn. According to newspaper accounts, they enacted "a series of famous dramatic courtships," so it's possible she did reprise Blanche, but no contemporary newspaper account lists Marlon as joining her. Correspondence regarding the *Omnibus* appearance in Cronyn's papers at the Library of Congress also fails to make any mention of Marlon. At this point, Marlon's popularity was at its peak; if he had made an appearance on the program, even just a surprise cameo, surely it would have been noted somewhere.

Marlon also appeared in one episode of the television miniseries *Roots: The Next Generation* (1979).

# SOURCES

## Archival Material

AMPAS   Margaret Herrick Library at the Academy of Motion Picture Arts and Sciences: Jane Ardmore Papers; Rudy Behlmer Papers; Marlon Brando Material on *One-Eyed Jacks*; Charles Champlin Collection; George Cukor Papers; Robert DoQui Papers; George Englund Papers; Howard W. Fleming Collection; Sidney Furie Papers; Gladys Hall Papers; Jack Hirshberg Papers; Hedda Hopper Papers (HHP); James Wong Howe Papers; John Huston Papers (JHP); Louis and Irene Kamp Papers; Sacheen Littlefeather Letter; Joseph L. Mankiewicz Papers; Morgan Maree Collection; Lewis Milestone Papers; Paramount Pictures Production Records; Gregory Peck Papers; Frank P. Rosenberg Papers; David Zeitlin Papers; Fred Zinnemann Papers.

Bancroft Library at the University of California, Berkeley: Fang family, *San Francisco Examiner* photograph archive; *San Francisco News–Call Bulletin* photograph archive.

BSC   Budd Schulberg Collection: Rauner Special Collections Library at Dartmouth College.

EKP   Elia Kazan Papers: Cinema Archives at Wesleyan University.

EPC   Erwin Piscator Collection: Morris Library at Southern Illinois University.

Harry Ransom Center at the University of Texas, Austin: Stella Adler and Harold Clurman Papers; Tennessee Williams Collection; Audrey Wood Papers.

ISC   Irene Selznick Collection: Howard Gottlieb Archival Research Center, Boston University.

LC   Library of Congress: Hume Cronyn–Jessica Tandy Papers; Joshua Logan Collection (JLC).

MBEA   Marlon Brando Estate Archives: Material included the original transcript of conversations between Marlon Brando (MB) and Robert Lindsey for *Songs My Mother Taught Me*; tape-recorded observations made by MB on a variety of subjects; production files and contracts on various films, including *Apocalypse Now*, *The Appaloosa*, *A Countess from Hong Kong*, *The Godfather*, *Missouri Breaks*, *Morituri*, *Mutiny on the Bounty*, *Superman*, and *The Ugly American*;

production and business records for Pennebaker Inc.; MB's personal files on Caryl Chessman and various Native American civil rights issues; MB's files on Los Angeles planning for the March on Washington, 1963; MB's files on Tahiti and Tahitian culture; MB's inventions and patents; legal files on Anna Kashfi, Movita Castaneda, and the Oakland Police Department; various correspondence with family and friends; various transcripts of other interviews; unpublished essays by MB; and fan (and hate) mail.

NSA  New School for Social Research Archive: Dramatic Workshop Collection.

NYPL  New York Public Library for the Performing Arts: Luther Adler Papers; Stella Adler Collection; Montgomery Clift Papers; Katharine Cornell Papers; Leland Hayward Papers; Martin Kalmanoff Papers; Jack Kerouac Papers; Beatrice Lillie Collection; John Van Druten Papers; various clippings and essays in the Marlon Brando file.

Wisconsin Center for Film and Television Research: David Brinkley Papers; John Patrick Papers; David Susskind Collection.

## Secondary Sources

Books, films, newsreels, and magazine and newspaper articles are cited in the notes.

# NOTES

In quoting from interviews both published and in-person, I have fixed punctuation and spelling and largely dispensed with using ellipses, unless doing so would change the meaning of the quote.

## PROLOGUE: THE MAN ON THE WITNESS STAND

1 The large old man: My description of Christian Brando's arrest and sentencing comes from the *Los Angeles Times*, May 17 and 18, 1990; January 4 and 5, 1991; and March 1, 1991, as well as from transcripts of testimony, Los Angeles Superior Court, Marlon Brando archives, courtesy the Brando estate, hereafter MBEA.

3 "I can't convey": Marlon made the comment in a tape recording he made himself, MBEA; it was used in the documentary *Listen to Me Marlon* [hereafter "MB tape recordings"].

4 "We act every single day": Original transcript of conversations between Marlon Brando (MB) and Robert Lindsey for *Songs My Mother Taught Me*, MBEA [hereafter "*Songs*, original transcript"].

5 "What a life": MB tape recordings.

6 "a genius who fought": Foster Hirsch interview with William J. Mann [hereafter "WJM"].

7 "not give a damn": *The David Letterman Show*, March 1, 1982, NBC.

7 "Brando is certainly": *The Independent*, April 18, 1995.

8 "the Congressman with his hand": Marlon Brando interview, *Playboy*, January 1979 [hereafter "MB *Playboy* interview"].

9 "After you've got enough": *Los Angeles Times*, November 3, 1961.

9 "like Kleenex or Dial soap": MB on *The Dick Cavett Show*, June 12, 1973, ABC [hereafter "MB on *Dick Cavett*"].

10 "When I was young": *Songs*, original transcript.

10 "It might be an absolutely": *Meet Marlon Brando*, a twenty-seven-minute 1966 documentary made by H. Albert and David Maysles, available on YouTube [hereafter *Meet Marlon Brando*].

11 "They're about making": Notes from New York *Daily News* interview, Marlon Brando file, NYPL [hereafter "MB file, NYPL"].

11 "If you smoke the grime": MB on *Dick Cavett*.

11 "the rich getting richer": *Songs*, original transcript.

11 "bullshit is all that's": Notes for memoir, [nd], [1991], MBEA.

13 "said more about him": Harold Brodkey, "Translating Brando," *The New Yorker*, October 24, 1994.

13 "that is permanently true": *Time*, January 22, 1973.

13 "You can say the same": *Meet Marlon Brando*.

13 "Acting comes easily": *Larry King Live*, October 7, 1994, CNN [hereafter "MB on *Larry King Live*"].

13 "a fundamentally childish": *Life*, May 4, 1960.

14 "He felt very protective": Avra Douglas interview, WJM.

14 "the mark of maturity": *Life, May 4, 1960*.

14 "In your heart," "I don't put": MB *Playboy* interview.

16 "The common perception": *Songs*, original transcript.

17 "Whenever anyone would": Avra Douglas interview, WJM.

18 "I only mean about forty": Truman Capote, "The Duke in His Domain," *The New Yorker*, November 9, 1957.

18 "Seldom do I say": MB to Jessica Tandy, [nd] "Friday night" [Fall 1947], Hume Cronyn and Jessica Tandy Papers, LC.

18 "Marlon did not tell": Alice Marchak, *Me and Marlon: A Memoir* (Self-published, 2008).


### AN IMAGINATIVE YOUNG MAN

23 an open window: This first section comes from the transcripts of Brando's conversations with Robert Lindsey for *Songs My Mother Taught Me* (*Songs*, original transcript), which often deviate significantly from the final published version. "Quick temper" comes from MB on *Larry King Live*, in which he recalls the young man he was.

24 The morning was cool: My description of New York City comes from various articles in the *New York Times* and the New York *Daily News*, as well as from various interviews given by Brando: *Songs*, original transcript; MB *Playboy* interview; others. Although September 27 was the first official day of the fall semester in 1943, classes did not begin until October 4 (*New York Times*, September 5, 1943).

25 "Somebody tells me": *Songs*, original transcript.

26 registration had "boomed": *New York Times*, November 7, 1943. Also see the "Comparative Statement of Dramatic Workshop," March 1, 1945, NSA.

27 "for want of something": *New York Times*, July 23, 1950.

27  "I did a little manual labor": *Meet Marlon Brando.*

27  "when bought with my own": Marlon Brando with Robert Lindsey, *Songs My Mother Taught Me* (New York: Random House, 1994).

27  five hundred dollars for the first year: Dramatic Workshop course catalog, 1943–1944, NSA.

27  "propper-upper": Quoted in Peter Manso, *Brando: The Biography* (New York: Hyperion, 1994). Although Manso and I have differing interpretations of Brando's character, I am indebted to the exhaustive interviews he undertook, getting many people on the record who have since passed on.

27  "old-looking" face: Liz Schofield interview with Jocelyn Brando, July 22, 1981, Jane Ardmore Papers, AMPAS [hereafter "Schofield interview with JB"].

28  He "couldn't imagine": *Songs*, original transcript.

28  "Perform while you learn!": *New York Times*, January 16, 1944.

28  "very, very busy": Manso, *Brando.*

29  Bud stood in front: I am indebted to a Workshop participant who was a second-year student the year Brando was there and who recalled certain wonderful details like this, but who has asked to remain anonymous. Hereafter in the notes I source this person as XY.

29  The curriculum featured: Dramatic Workshop press release, July 15, 1940, NSA.

29  There were also readings: Course of study, fall term, 1943, NSA.

29  "the most fascinating town": Brando and Lindsey, *Songs.*

30  "A great feeling of inadequacy": *Songs*, original transcript.

30  "Students must have had at least": Course catalog, 1943–1944, NSA.

30  "Since it is in the interest": *New School Bulletin*, Fall 1943, NSA.

31  taught very few classes: John Willett, "Erwin Piscator: New York and the Dramatic Workshop, 1939–1951," *Performing Arts Journal* 2, no. 3 (Winter 1978).

31  "The Dramatic Workshop serves": Piscator gave an address based on the description he'd written for the *New School Bulletin*, September 11, 1944, NSA.

31  "a more interesting life": *New York Post*, September 24, 1943.

32  "A haven for hounded": *New York Times*, May 31, 1943.

32  "This is not a war": Course catalog, 1943–1944, NSA.

33  "not art, but life": Quoted in Maria Ley-Piscator, *The Piscator Experiment: The Political Theatre* (Urbana: Southern Illinois University Press, 1970).

33  Bud was struck by a "clear sense": *Songs*, original transcript.

33  "rather superficial": Manso, *Brando.*

33  "I don't understand life": Marlon Brando [MB] to Marlon and Dorothy Brando, Fall 1943, MBEA.

33  "a naïve kid trying hard": Brando and Lindsey, *Songs.*

33  "argued a lot": *Songs*, original transcript.

34  Much of his time: Background on Celia comes from her Petition for Naturalization, February 8, 1943; 1940 Census; *New York Times*, June 12, 1937. Thomas R. Webb's rental of an apartment at 16 Washington Mews was recorded in the *New York Times*, January 19, 1942. Also see Carlo Fiore, *Bud: The Brando I Knew* (New York: Delacorte Press, 1974), in which Celia is described under a pseudonym, "Maria Lorca." In Brando and Lindsey, *Songs*, Marlon calls her "Estrelita," and claims she was ten to fifteen years older than he—perhaps to help disguise her true identity.

34  Her husband, Thomas R. Webb: Webb had been in the service since at least June 2, 1943, Register of Commissioned and Warrant Officers of the U.S. Naval Reserve, July 1, 1944.

34  "I lost my virginity": Brando and Lindsey, *Songs.*

35  "screwed her dog-fashion": Fiore, *Bud.*

35  Celia confided to friends: See Budd Schulberg interview with Ellen Adler, BSC [hereafter "Ellen Adler interview, BSC"].

36  "She *presented* herself": "Stella Adler: Awake and Dream!," *American Masters*, July 10, 1989, PBS.

37  "Who's the vagabond?": Possibly apocryphal. See Patricia Bosworth, *Marlon Brando* (New York: Viking, 2001); Stefan Kanfer, *Somebody: The Reckless Life and Remarkable Career of Marlon Brando* (New York: Knopf, 2008); and others.

37  "listening closely": XY.

38  "Acting didn't grate on me": *Songs*, original transcript.

38  Originally open only: *Brooklyn Daily Eagle*, April 2, 1943.

38  "An audience of surprised playgoers": Ley-Piscator, *Piscator Experiment.*

39  "distant" and "prickly": *Songs*, original transcript.

39  "An actress does not excuse": Manso, *Brando.*

39  Studio Theatre: See Ley-Piscator, *Piscator Experiment*; also *Variety*, October 13, 1943.

39  In the early days: Dramatic Workshop press release, January 15, 1940, NSA; also Ellen Adler interview with WJM. The press noted how the New School agreed to leaves of absence for Stella whenever she had other commitments. In the fall of 1942, she had just returned from a year's leave and "will again head the acting department" (*Staten Island Advance*, September 1, 1942).

40  "no particular theories": *New School Bulletin*, September 11, 1944, NSA.

40  "sugared realism": Hirsch interview, WJM.

40  "anything that didn't make": XY.

41  "an aversion to theater people": Manso, *Brando.*

41  "Our lives are strange dark interludes,": XY.

41  "I was an anomaly": *Songs*, original transcript.

41  Most of his classmates: Information on these students comes from the U.S. Census of New York, 1920, 1930, 1940; New York State censuses 1915 and 1925; from *New York Times*, January 21, 1952; October 11, 1965; and June 17, 1984. Also, from interviews with XY.

42  "I could hardly speak": *Songs*, original transcript.

42  When one of his new friends: Ellen Adler interview, BSC.

42  "He was laughing": Manso, *Brando*.

43  "I could'a been a drummer": *Meet Marlon Brando*.

43  "I started banging": Brando and Lindsey, *Songs*.

43  "I would turn the radio up": *Songs*, original transcript.

43  "He'd just sit there": Manso, *Brando*.

44  "Keg Brando and his Kegliners": *Songs*, original transcript.

44  "Some people": *The Ed Sullivan Show*, October 9, 1955, CBS.

44  "about a third of a bag on": *Songs*, original transcript.

45  "one of the few times": Ibid.

45  "stop that infernal noise": Ellen Adler interview, WJM.

45  "musically gifted," "far more structure": Ibid.

45  "I had some notion": *Songs*, original transcript.

45  "I remember his putting": Brando and Lindsey, *Songs*.

46  "It was yellow and very spiffy": Frances Brando recollections, transcript, MBEA.

47  "Make an actor improvise": "Stella Adler: Awake and Dream!"

48  "There wasn't much crime": *Songs*, original transcript.

49  "Just before Thanksgiving" said one classmate: XY.

49  "I mean, who wouldn't be?": *New York Observer*, July 12, 2004.

49  "I was a reasonably attractive": *Songs*, original transcript.

50  "This is how he got into things": Elaine Stritch interview, WJM.

50  "Do you know how": Capote, "The Duke in His Domain."

51  "clean-fingernailed city people": XY.

51  "The smell of hay": *Songs*, original transcript.

52  "fresh air all day": Frances Brando recollections, transcript, MBEA.

53  At school, he set the record: William Crary to MB, March 3, 1965, MBEA. Crary was a fellow student at Julia Lathrop.

53  "he'd miss the bucket": MB interview with Edward R. Murrow, *Person to Person*, April 1, 1955, CBS [hereafter "MB interview with Murrow"].

53  "and all the barn cats": *Songs*, original transcript.

53  His sense of humor: Manso, *Brando*.

54  "a little red costume": MB interview with Murrow.

54  "a sense of closeness": *Songs*, original transcript.

55  "Quite a character": Schofield interview with JB.

55  "broke apart like a piece": Capote, "The Duke in His Domain."

55  Snow came early that year: *New York Times*, November 12, 14, 15, 22, and 25, 1943.

56  "He was so beautiful": Elaine Stritch interview, WJM.

56  "awkward silences": XY.

56  "I am by nature": MB to Jessica Tandy, [nd] "Friday night" [Fall 1947], Hume Cronyn and Jessica Tandy Papers, LC.

57  "it was probably a relief": Manso, *Brando*.

57  "no different": Capote, "The Duke in His Domain."

57  "he went out and fucked": Elaine Stritch interview, WJM.

57  "It made me dizzy": *Songs*, original transcript.

58  "I'd never met any black people": *Songs*, original transcript.

59  "Got to make a hole": Manso, *Brando*.

59  "she probably would not": Ellen Adler interview, BSC.

59  "tolerance of others": *New York Times*, July 25, 1954.

60  "It used to bother me": Transcript, MB interview with Gladys Hall, circa 1951, Gladys Hall Collection, AMPAS [hereafter "MB interview with Gladys Hall"].

60  "behaving like everybody": Manso, *Brando*.

61  "because she couldn't face the day": Ibid.

61  "took her home": *Songs*, original transcript. Jocelyn remembered the anecdote slightly differently, believing that her parents were away when Bud brought the woman home (Manso, *Brando*). But Marlon recalled them both standing on the porch as he stood there with the woman.

62  Gassner's Friday night lecture: March of Drama schedule, cast lists, NSA.

62  "very intense": Manso, *Brando*.

63  "The Epic Theatre": Erwin Piscator, "Theatre of the Future," *Tomorrow*, February 1942.

63  "We refuse to admit": *Songs*, original transcript.

63  "a naïve kid": Brando and Lindsey, *Songs*.

64  In this country: *New York Times*, November 8, 9, 10, 11, and 12, 1943. The second Communist elected was Peter Cacchione, for Brooklyn; Davis represented Manhattan.

64  "bitterness and fear": MB to Marlon and Dorothy Brando, Fall 1943, quoted in Brando and Lindsey, *Songs*.

65  "My father," Bud said, "was a miser": *Songs*, original transcript.

65  "He was a card-carrying": Brando and Lindsey, *Songs*.

66  "would get louder and louder": Manso, *Brando*.

66  "All dressed up": Frances Brando recollections, transcript, MBEA.

66 "You have to milk the cow": This is how Marlon described the experience in the film *Last Tango in Paris*, in a scene that he later revealed was ad-libbed on the spot using his own memories [hereafter "MB ad-libbed recollections *Last Tango*"].

67 "not smiling, eyes cast down": Gahan Hanmer interview, WJM.

67 "Very extreme in his inaccessibility": Ibid.

67 "everybody outside the family": Manso, *Brando*.

68 "black moods and thunderous silences": Frances Brando recollections, transcript, MBEA.

68 Dodie had hated leaving her friends: In addition to Frances Brando's recollections, transcript, MBEA, I've based my description of Dodie's troubles on Jocelyn Brando's interview in Manso, *Brando*, and on Schofield interview with MB. Finally, Marlon paints his own picture in *Songs*, original transcript.

68 "Whore fucker": MB ad-libbed recollections *Last Tango*.

68 "It was an era": Brando and Lindsey, *Songs*.

68 "At least you could get": Fiore, *Bud*.

69 at the time, AA membership was largely male: *Chicago Tribune*, June 9, 1943. At the time, there were about five hundred members of AA in the Chicago area.

69 "there was this grinding": *Songs*, original transcript.

69 Her letters reveal intimate: Manso, *Brando*.

70 "She'd put liquor in": *Songs*, original transcript.

70 "I used to come home": Capote, "The Duke in His Domain."

70 One time, however, as he'd confide: Fiore, *Bud*.

71 "She was all mine": Brando and Lindsey, *Songs*. Stories that Irmy "sexually initiated" Marlon at the age of three or four are gross misreadings of what he actually said, though he probably didn't mind the perception of being sexually precocious and may even have encouraged the stories.

71 If Irmy had Indonesian blood: U.S. Census, 1920 and 1930.

71 Irmy's photograph in her high school: Central High School, Omaha, Nebraska, 1928. Available online at Ancestry.com.

72 "You're just going to leave": Manso, *Brando*.

72 "Bud was upset by it": Ibid.

72 "that was the most": Marlon's ad-libbed recollections *Last Tango*.

72 "I drank half a quart": Dorothy Pennebaker to Marlon Brando Sr., quoted in Brando and Lindsey, *Songs*.

73 "My mother was everything": Capote, "The Duke in His Domain."

73 "Releasing inhibitions": XY.

73 "I used to love the smell": *Songs*, original transcript.

74 "Whose detail is whose": Frances Brando recollections, transcript, MBEA.

74  "We were all bruised": *Songs*, original transcript.

74  he became "a delinquent": Ibid.

74  "He always put on a tough": Manso, *Brando*.

74  "emotionally resembl[ing]": Ibid.

75  "I remember stealing money": *Songs*, original transcript.

75  "I think that when things": Ibid.

75  "The golem that stomped": Ibid.

76  "If you touch her again": Ibid. Carlo Fiore reported the story in a very similar way in Fiore, *Bud*, having been told it by Marlon.

76  "He hit me!": The incident with the man making the pass at Marlon is based on three sources: an interview with XY; Manso; and *Songs*. Manso wrote that the incident happened during rehearsals for *Saint Joan*; XY disputes this, pointing out that Piscator was directing that night, and he did not direct *Saint Joan*. Marlon wrote that it happened "during rehearsals for a play," but does not say which play. Since this clearly occurred before Piscator's directorial duties that summer at Sayville, it must have happened the only other time Piscator was directing the students, which was on the night when epic theatre was the focus.

76  "Planting my foot": *Songs*.

77  The Dramatic Workshop: Course schedule, 1943–1944, NSA.

78  "tended to disregard": XY.

78  "He was so exciting": Manso, *Brando*.

78  "They just weren't serious": XY.

78  "There but for the grace": Manso, *Brando*. Marlon told this story as well to Robert Lindsey for his memoir, though he didn't mention Dublin. "That would be the worst thing . . ." comes from *Songs*, original transcript.

79  "They were always looking": Manso, *Brando*.

79  "many of the artists": *Songs*, original transcript.

79  "You talk about a femme fatale": *New York Observer*, November 12, 2004.

80  Earle M. Wagner: Background on Duke Wagner comes from the U.S. Census, 1900–1940; World War I draft registration records; U.S. passenger lists; *Stars and Stripes*, August 12, 1949; and October 29, 1949.

80  "I had never received accolades": *Songs*, original transcript.

80  "I can't even remember": He thought the teacher's name might have been Wilkinson. The only Wilkinson (of all variant spellings, including Wilkerson) recorded as a teacher in the Orange County–Los Angeles area in 1930 or 1940 was a Morris Wilkinson, born in 1889. He taught at various public and private schools, although I could not specifically place him at Julia Lathrop. Lathrop Intermediate, the current name of the school, reported that it did not have records to identify a shop teacher from the 1930s, and Santa Ana city directories also do not list local faculty. Morris

Wilkinson lived in Los Angeles in both 1930 and 1940, but he could have commuted to teach a shop class in Santa Ana. For now, the identity of the first person to offer Bud encouragement remains uncertain.

81 a world traveler: U.S. ship passenger lists document several international trips taken by Duke over the years. His argument over Mansfield was printed in the January 27, 1929, issue of the *Chicago Tribune*.

81 "He wore his coat": *Songs*, original transcript.

81 "He seems to be taking hold": Earle Wagner to Marlon Brando Sr., October 23, 1941, Shattuck Military Academy Archives, Faribault, MN, quoted in Manso, *Brando*. A Shattuck representative told me the records were not currently available.

82 "I feel that he must be": Marlon Brando Sr. to H. R. Drummond, November 29, 1941, Shattuck Military Academy Archives, Faribault, MN, quoted in Manso, *Brando*.

82 "The mind of the military": *Songs*, original transcript.

83 "All my life": MB to parents, [nd] 1942, MBEA.

83 "I feel as though I were": MB to Mrs. E. G. Meyers, February 5, 1942, MBEA.

84 "had gone against the grain": *Songs*, original transcript.

84 "We have been studying men": MB to parents, [nd] 1942, MBEA.

84 "an eager, lonely child": Brando and Lindsey, *Songs*.

85 "To see people regimented": *Songs*, original transcript.

85 At one point, an army colonel: This is how Marlon told the story in *Songs*, original transcript. A slightly different version appears in Brando and Lindsey, *Songs*.

85 "The Greatest Family": MB to parents, October 6, 1941, MBEA.

86 "having an affair": Shattuck recollections, William Peverill Papers, Amherst College, Amherst, MA.

86 "During the night": Manso, *Brando*. According to *Stars and Stripes*, August 12, 1949, Duke first came overseas in January 1949, and he left Shattuck sometime in 1948.

86 "He was, after 26 years": Shattuck recollections, William Peverill Papers.

86 "enthusiasm and loyalty": Ibid.

87 "For me, sex is something": *Ciné-Revue*, January 22, 1976.

87 "soft, sweet, moony": The quote comes from former cadet William Burford, in Manso, *Brando*.

87 "homosexual experiences": See *Ciné-Revue*, January 22, 1976, for the full quote in the original French (Marlon was fluent in French).

88 "For a second, I was worried": XY.

88 "depression he got into": Elaine Stritch interview, WJM.

88 "hated anybody prying": Manso, *Brando*.

89  "A major swing from October to December": XY.

89  "I came to New York": MB to Donald Henning, January 29, 1944, Shat-tuck Military Academy Archives, Faribault, MN, quoted in Manso, *Brando* [hereafter "MB to Henning"].

89  "great feeling of inadequacy": *Songs*, original transcript.

90  "best . . . to tear the school": Ibid.

90  "I was always sensitive": Ibid.

92  "an asshole": Manso, *Brando*.

92  "a case of the straw": *Faribault Daily News*, July 3, 2004.

92  But another story circulated: See Manso, *Brando*. The story was heard by several other cadets.

92  "a vicarious thrill": *Songs*, original transcript.

92  "didn't keep to the rules": Harry Drummond to Marlon Brando Sr., May 22, 1943, Shattuck Military Academy Archives, Faribault, MN, quoted in Manso, *Brando*.

92  "I was bored": *Songs*, original transcript.

92  "something *did* happen," "They were very close," "there was never": Manso, *Brando*.

93  "He put his hands": *Songs*, original transcript.

93  "Memories," Bud said, "get fuzzed over": Ibid.

93  One interviewer, many years later: Ibid.

93  After his own dismissal: Duke's later life was documented in *Stars and Stripes*, August 12, 1949; and October 29, 1949; Social Security Death Index, available at Ancestry.com.

94  "mad as hell": Manso, *Brando*.

94  "nogoodnik": MB *Playboy* interview. In *Songs*, original transcript, Marlon described his father's reaction to the expulsion as rather indifferent— "[H]e said he didn't care what I did as long as I did my best"—although this seems like more sandpapering over a rough spot, much as he did with his memories of Duke Wagner.

95  "I had the fear that everyone": *Songs*, original transcript.

96  Bud entered, stage right: According to the *New School Bulletin*, December 13, 1943, NSA, *Hannele's* first performance was at 8:30 on Friday night, December 17, and not in January, as has previously been stated. A repeat presentation of *Hannele* was given on January 21, 1944, according to the *New School Bulletin*, January 17, 1944, NSA.

96  "There weren't a lot": XY.

97  "was almost rendered ridiculous": See *New York Times*, April 19 and 21, 1910.

97  "Stilted" and "quaintly": See *New York Times*, February 15, 16, 19, and 26, 1924.

98 Stella Adler had taught him: See *Songs*, original transcript; and Ellen Adler interview, BSC.

99 The story of a boy: For details on *Bobino*, see *New York Times*, December 12, 19, and 21, 1943; and *New York Times*, January 6, 1944; also, *Brooklyn Daily Eagle*, February 7, 1944.

99 "why the animals": *New York Times*, April 7, 1944.

99 "There are happy shouts": *New York Times*, April 9, 1944.

100 "already part of the Brando": Judith Malina, *The Piscator Notebook* (New York: Routledge, 2012).

100 After that January 21 show: It is unclear when the offer for a screen test was made to Marlon, or who made it. Most sources agree that it was after *Hannele*, and it's the January performance that most people seem to remember. Judith Malina, in *The Piscator Notebook*, says it happened at that point, and that Maynard Morris was the agent who encouraged Marlon. She might be confusing the fact that Marlon signed up with Morris after he left the Workshop in the summer of 1944.

103 "It must have been": Manso, *Brando*.

103 "Found that I had an unusual": MB to Henning, quoted in Manso, *Brando*.

104 "You must listen": "Stella Adler: Awake and Dream!"

104 "It's either life or the theatre": For descriptions of Stella's classes and, methodology, see Foster Hirsch, *A Method to Their Madness: The History of the Actors Studio* (New York: Da Capo Press, 1984); and Sheana Ochoa, *Stella! The Mother of Modern Acting* (Milwaukee, WI: Applause Theatre and Cinema Books, 2014).

104 "He just loved": Manso, *Brando*.

104 His impersonation of a chicken: This story has been told many times. Ellen Adler confirmed its essential authenticity, even if the various versions told of it may be somewhat fanciful.

105 "She got to know him": Ellen Adler interview, WJM.

105 "Stop coughing": "Stella Adler: Awake and Dream!"

105 "When you were wrong": *Songs*, original transcript.

105 "In the course of one exercise": XY.

105 "Let's do it again": Manso, *Brando*.

106 "Actors bow to their audiences": *The Villager*, November 3–9, 2004.

106 "was always about uplifting": Tom Oppenheim interview, WJM.

107 "My mother is a queen": Ellen Adler interview, BSC.

107 In Tiffany's one time, "I'm not a playgirl": "Stella Adler: Awake and Dream!"

107 "they didn't have anything": Ellen Adler interview, WJM.

107 "She had this image": XY.

108 "to uplift, to be a part": *The Villager*, November 3–9, 2004.

108 "An Adler could never," "Stella Adler: Awake and Dream!"

109 "If I can pronounce it": Ibid.

109 "If you like a man": Ibid.

109 a sort of "shidduch": Ellen Adler interview, BSC.

110 "She was, I think": *Songs*, original transcript.

110 Bud frequently missed class: According to attendance sheets, he missed five voice classes, four acting classes, four dance movement classes, three theater research classes, and one makeup class. He wasn't the only one; most of the *Bobino* cast was missing from those classes as well. Piscator was apparently indulgent for only so long; after April 10, they were no longer excused but simply marked as absent (EPC).

110 "I am studying the part": MB to Marlon and Dorothy Brando, quoted in *Songs*.

111 Not content with: For more on *Nathan the Wise*, see *Variety*, February 9, 1944; *New York Times*, February 22, 1944; and *New York Post*, February 5, 1944.

111 "That's not theatre": XY.

111 "I didn't want to think about": "Stella Adler: Awake and Dream!"

111 "He wanted to take the actor," "A great disservice": Quoted in Hirsch, *A Method to Their Madness*.

112 "Oh, sweetheart": "Stella Adler: Awake and Dream!"

112 "I think if he hadn't run": Ellen Adler interview, WJM.

112 "Your life is one-millionth": "Stella Adler: Awake and Dream!"

113 "the way he moved": Interview with Les Hall, friend of Chouteau Dyer, WJM.

114 The Bryn Mawr graduate: Background on Dyer comes from Les Hall, WJM; Dramatic Workshop catalogs 1943–1944 and New School Curricula 1943–1944, NSA; and Malina, *Piscator Experiment*.

114 "Wait till you meet": Manso, *Brando*.

114 "not permitted to ask": *New School Bulletin*, September 11, 1944, NSA.

115 "helping a lost young man": Ellen Adler interview, WJM.

115 "a very kind woman": MB *Playboy* interview.

115 "put Bud in touch with himself": Manso, *Brando*.

115 "the actor confidence in himself": "Stella Adler: Awake and Dream!"

116 "just did it. He didn't think": Ellen Adler interview, WJM.

116 "You don't feel anything": *Songs*, original transcript: Marlon spoke to interviewer Lindsey of getting his mother out of jail; in MB ad-libbed recollections *Last Tango*, he described her being "arrested nude." Ellen Adler remembered his telling her, when recounting that anecdote, that his mother was "wrapped in a blanket." I used the 1942 Libertyville telephone directory to re-create Bud's drive into town.

117 "sensed he had never said": Ellen Adler interview, WJM.

117 "He found some of me": Told to Mel Gordon, April 1986, quoted in Manso, *Brando*.

117 "She was very helpful": MB *Playboy* interview.

118 "Stella and Harold and Luther and the rest": Ellen Adler interview, WJM.

118 "He came into that world,": Tom Oppenheim interview, WJM.

119 "asking questions, arguing": Brando and Lindsey, *Songs*.

119 "a Jewish smartness": MB to parents, May 10, 1944, MBEA.

119 "I was never educated": *Songs*, original transcript.

120 "She walked sideways": Ellen Adler interview, BSC.

120 "Omaha, Nebraska": Ellen Adler interview, WJM.

120 "I have to read": Manso, *Brando*.

120 "She taught me to read": Ibid.

120 "He felt badly": Ellen Adler interview, BSC.

120 "His intellectual appetite": *Forward*, July 9, 2004.

120 "He read about science": Ellen Adler interview, BSC.

120 "But he read everything else": Ellen Adler interview, WJM.

121 "the feelings were shown": Ellen Adler interview, BSC.

121 "If I said, 'That's incredible'": Ellen Adler interview, WJM.

121 "just thinking": Ellen Adler interview, BSC.

121 "You could see the ideas": Ellen Adler interview, WJM.

122 "and stockings with a seam": Ellen Adler interview, BSC.

122 "But you're not American": Ellen Adler interview, WJM.

123 "one thing led to another": *Songs*, original transcript.

123 "What we had was special": Ellen Adler interview, WJM.

123 "There is so much talk": Ellen Adler interview, BSC.

124 "all over the stage": *New York Times*, April 18, 1944.

124 Out-of-town critics: See, for example, *Boston Globe*, March 29, 1944.

124 "Stinks. Terrible acting": MB to parents, May 10, 1944, MBEA.

124 panned by New York critics: See, for example, *Brooklyn Daily Eagle*, April 18, 1944.

124 "She made it as good": XY.

125 "He'd come in from riding": Ibid.

125 "That's what they talk about": *New York Observer*, July 17, 2004.

125 He'd also scored his Broadway debut: Although his name is not mentioned in newspaper reviews of the show, the evidence that Marlon Brando's Broadway debut was *Bobino*, and not *I Remember Mama*, is found in the lists of absences sent daily to Piscator, which indicate that MB was in the cast of *Bobino* from March 28 to April 15 (EPC).

125 "one of the funniest things": *New York Observer*, July 17, 2004.

126 "I found I can't pay": MB to parents, May 10, 1944, MBEA.

126 The elevator of the New School: Ley-Piscator, *Piscator Experiment*.

127 The pressure was on: *New School Bulletin*, May 22, 1944, NSA.

127 "well with two": (New York) *Morning Telegraph*, May 21, 1944.

127 "Easily the best acting": (New York) *Morning Telegraph*, May 23, 1944.

128 "Marlon Brando handled": (New York) *Morning Telegraph*, May 25, 1944.

128 "I would have been better off": *Songs*, original transcript.

128 "My name is Marlon": Fiore, *Bud*.

128 "He was Bud when we first": XY.

129 "We're radical": *Collier's*, August 19, 1944.

129 Piscator had brought his company: *Patchogue Advance*, June 29, 1944; Manso, *Brando*. See also *New York Times*, March 25, 1942.

130 "He was carrying two leather bags": Fiore, *Bud*.

131 "as amusing, attractive": *Los Angeles Times*, October 22, 1989.

131 "spoke in poetic metaphor": Ellen Burstyn, *Lessons in Becoming Myself*
(New York: Riverhead Books, 2006).

131 "everybody was to sleep": Manso, *Brando*.

132 "He wanted her": Ibid.

132 the best-looking girl: *Bridgeport Post*, June 4, 1941.

132 "it was like looking": Manso, *Brando*.

132 Blossom's late father had been: Norwalk and Darien (Connecticut)
city directories; *Westport Town Crier*, December 7, 1958; *Westport News*, June
10, 1981.

132 Marlon preferred to spend: Ellen Adler interview, WJM.

133 "They live on stardust": *Collier's*, August 19, 1944.

133 "Life was pleasant": Fiore, *Bud*.

133 "Here we are in the sun": Manso, *Brando*.

133 "We had to do something": MB interview, [nd], MBEA.

134 The cast was populated: *Suffolk County News*, July 21, 1944.

135 "When I think I will go": *Collier's*, August 19, 1944.

135 "I don't think Piscator": XY.

136 He would direct a melodrama: *New York Times*, June 21, 1944.

137 The Libertyville house was vacated: There are listings for Marlon Brando
on Townline Road in the Libertyville phone directories for 1943 and 1944,
which actually record the previous year, but no listing for him in 1945.

138 "make a family": Ellen Adler interview, WJM.

138 "There was nothing there": Manso, *Brando*.

138 "Dodie's pad was really hip": XY.

138 "She was divine," "one of the gang": Manso, *Brando*.

138 "off-color jokes": XY.

138 "She was very dainty": Ellen Adler interview, WJM.

139 "She was a true beauty": Fiore, *Bud*.

139 "That took courage": MB interview transcript [nd], MBEA.

140 "for what she had done for Marlon": Ellen Adler interview, WJM.

140 "a la Walt Disney": *Bay Shore Sentinel*, July 27, 1944.

141 "heroic story of valiant women": *Patchogue Advance*, August 10, 1944.

141 "fiery, swaggering Irish girl": *Suffolk County News*, August 18, 1944.

142 "Katharine Hepburn-ish": Manso, *Brando*.

142 "I'm sorry about your having": Fiore, *Bud*.

143 "You're like Rumpelstiltskin": Ellen Adler interview, BSC.

144 "I suppose that kind of anger": Ellen Adler interview, WJM.

144 "moving and thought-provoking": *Suffolk County News*, August 18, 1944.

144 "While [Marlon] was humping": Fiore, *Bud*.

144 "There was a lot of fucking": *Songs*, original transcript.

144 *Last Stop* was already tagged: *New York Times*, September 4, 1944.

145 At some point midweek: I have pinpointed Marlon's dismissal from the Sayville players to sometime during this week, and most likely midweek, perhaps the fifteenth, sixteenth, or seventeenth. He was announced for *The Petrified Forest* in the *Suffolk County News* on August 17, but as this was a weekly paper, it may have been too late to retract the announcement. By the time *The Petrified Forest* was performed on August 18, Marlon was no longer with the company. He was not kicked out before *Cry Havoc*, however, as Manso (*Brando*) writes, as Blossom Plumb was kicked out with him and she was in *Cry Havoc* through August 13, as reviews indicate. Press releases for the next show routinely went out early in the week, so it seems clear that the expulsion took place midweek.

145 Hauling another ladder: Carlo Fiore (Freddie Stevens) wrote in *Bud* that the ladder was there, but Joy Thomson specifically remembered in her interview with Manso (*Brando*) that Piscator had gotten a different ladder. Because Marlon routinely pulled the ladder up, and because Thomson's memory is specific, I have gone with the second scenario. The story told by Judith Malina, who was not there, in *The Piscator Experiment*, is less reliable.

145 "this face appeared": Manso, *Brando*, quotes Joy Thomson repeating what Marlon told her.

145 "You can't fire me": Manso, *Brando*.

146 "This lady": *Songs*, original transcript.

146 "in very *deutsche* fashion": Stella told this to David Diamond, quoted in Manso, *Brando*.

146 "It wasn't so much": *Songs*, original transcript.

146 "We all felt shock": Manso, *Brando*.

147 "I saw him toss his bags": Fiore, *Bud*.

147 "What's this I hear?": Manso, *Brando*.

147  "I just blew with the wind": *Songs*, original transcript.

147  "an also-ran": *Boston Globe*, August 22, 1944.

148  "little horror": *New York Times*, September 6, 1944.


## THE HOODLUM ARISTOCRAT

151  Heat and humidity choked the city: See the *New York Times*, August 9, 10, 13, 14, 15, 16, and 17, 1947.

151  The agency was abuzz: The account of Liebling's sponsorship of Brando for the part of Stanley Kowalski comes from a letter written by Audrey Wood to Elia Kazan, August 14, 1978, Elia Kazan Papers, Cinema Archives, Wesleyan University (hereafter "EKP"). Wood was correcting Kazan's inaccurate account of Brando's hiring, which he'd given to *The Hollywood Reporter*. Kazan claimed he'd considered Brando all along, having remembered him from *Truckline Café*. However, in his memoir (Elia Kazan, *A Life* [New York: Knopf, 1988]), he said Brando was a student in Bobby Lewis's class at the Actors Studio when he went looking for him for *Streetcar*, which is not true; Brando visited the Actors Studio only a few times, and that was a couple of years later. Brando himself said that it was Harold Clurman, the director of *Truckline*, who recommended him to Kazan for Stanley. Probably all these claims have some truth. Brando may well have been in Kazan's mind; Clurman very likely would have echoed that idea. But Wood's account is so specific that it seems to have been the clincher: when Liebling walked into the theater with Brando, it all came together. The account is also backed up by a telegram sent to Irene Selznick from her business manager, Irving Schneider, on August 15, 1947, urging her to bring in the Lieblings, among others, "to make the vital decision of . . . finding another good Stanley" should the deal with Garfield fall through, which, two days later, it did (Irene Selznick Collection, Howard Gottlieb Archival Research Center, Boston University (hereafter "ISC").

151  Brando, apparently, didn't want to be found: Marlon's complete removal from the theater and New York dramatic scene for the first eight months of 1947 has gone unnoticed by most chroniclers. But after several mentions in *Variety* and the *New York Times* throughout 1945 and 1946, he is completely absent from press coverage from the time he last appears in *Eagle Rampant* in December 1946 and when he is mentioned for *Streetcar* in September 1947. In fact, Marlon completely removed himself from the world of theater during this period; the only mention found for him in a digitized search of hundreds of newspapers wasn't anything theatrical, but rather, his appearance in support of the American League for a Free Palestine in Kenosha, Wisconsin, at Beth Hillel Temple in June 1947.

153 he'd gone "on the road": Ellen Adler interview, WJM.

154 "I am now an active": MB to Marlon and Dorothy Brando, [nd], MBEA.

154 "trampled" on the Jews: *Songs*, original transcript.

155 At Beth Hillel Temple: Ellen Adler interview, WJM. See also *Kenosha* (Wisconsin) *Evening News*, June 8, 1947.

155 "the bitterness, fear, hate": MB to Marlon and Dorothy Brando, Fall 1943, quoted in Brando and Lindsey, *Songs*.

156 "The work that we'll be doing": MB to Marlon and Dorothy Brando, [nd], MBEA.

156 "terrorism and military action": Brando and Lindsey, *Songs*.

156 "I had a sense that though": Ibid.

157 "working for something": Ellen Adler interview, WJM.

157 "stimulated more than": MB to Marlon and Dorothy Brando, [nd], MBEA.

157 "I knew what it was like": *Songs*, original transcript. Also Ellen Adler interview, WJM.

157 "To see the British soldiers": *Songs*, original transcript.

158 "The best acting I ever": Ibid.

158 "an obvious bit of propaganda": *Variety*, September 11, 1946.

158 "emotional intensity": *Variety*, November 27, 1946.

159 "constantly drinking and sloshed": *Songs*, original transcript.

159 For the rest of his life: Ibid.; see also *New York Times*, July 23, 1950.

159 "to impress as a revolutionary": *Variety*, December 4, 1946.

159 "not equal to his role": *Boston Globe*, December 11, 1946.

160 "ineffectual as assassin": *Hartford Courant*, December 27, 1946.

160 "with holes in my socks": *Songs*, original transcript.

160 "I must learn how to handle": MB to Marlon Brando Sr., [nd, 1946–47], MBEA.

161 Bill Liebling kept grabbing: I have deduced that this was on August 20, as we know Liebling began looking for Marlon on August 18, the day that the collapse of the Garfield deal became known; it probably took a day or two to reach him through "the grapevine." Kazan made his first notes regarding Marlon as Stanley on August 21, which suggests he had seen him the day before. It is, of course, possible that he made the notes the same day he saw Marlon.

162 "There are no 'good'": Quoted in Kazan, *A Life*.

162 "She was especially": Brando and Lindsey, *Songs*.

163 So, it was decided: Kazan, *A Life*; Ellen Adler interview, WJM.

163 Marlon was game: The reporter Bob Thomas writes in *Marlon: Portrait of the Rebel as an Artist* (New York: Random House, 1973), that Marlon called Kazan back the day after the audition, preparing to turn down the

part because it was "a size too large." He was thwarted in his attempt, however, when he got a busy signal. When he called back a second time, Kazan answered with so much enthusiasm for his casting that Marlon "gulped and said 'yes.'" The anecdote has been repeated in many subsequent books and articles. Thomas, however, does not source the story. Presumably, it was something Brando had once told him; Thomas was one of the few journalists whom Marlon liked and trusted (until Thomas wrote his book about him). A digital newspaper search did not, however, reveal that phrase in any of Thomas's newspaper stories. "A size too large" does not sound at all like Marlon, and he never told the story himself in his conversations with Robert Lindsey for his memoir; indeed, Kazan does not tell the story in his memoir, either. I'm inclined to think that this is an example of Marlon's fanciful storytelling with reporters.

164 "A few people would get together": Kaye Ballard interview, WJM.

164 "I never liked the idea": Interview transcript, [nd, circa 1975], MBEA.

165 "So I just stepped": *Songs*, original transcript.

165 "I was swept up in acting": *Newsweek*, November 19, 1962.

165 "very nasty": *Songs*, original transcript.

165 "a torture chamber": Ibid.

165 just sixty-five dollars a week: Irving "Swifty" Lazar wrote about helping Marlon get a raise from just sixty-five dollars a week in his memoir, *Swifty: My Life and Good Times* (New York: Simon and Schuster, 1995).

165 "going nine to five": MB *Playboy* interview.

166 "Maureen Stapleton had": *New York Observer*, July 12, 2004.

166 "We'd make a big pot": Kaye Ballard interview, WJM.

167 "the most artistic soul": Undated commentary, MBEA.

167 "I had never met any white man": James Campbell, *Talking at the Gates: A Life of James Baldwin* (New York: Viking, 1991).

167 "was dominated": MB on *Larry King Live*.

167 "A family of waifs": Brando and Lindsey, *Songs*.

168 "Bud was a charter member": Maureen Stapleton, *A Hell of a Life: An Autobiography* (New York: Simon and Schuster, 1995).

168 "commit the act of aggression": Janice Mars note to Marlon, MBEA.

168 "never got serious": Kaye Ballard interview, WJM. See also Ballard's memoir, *How I Lost 10 Pounds in 53 Years* (New York: Backstage Books, 2006).

169 "Hello, Bud," Wally had said: *Coronet*, April 1955.

169 "Wally Cox wasn't really": *Songs*, original transcript.

169 "Marlon was kind of a rough": *Los Angeles Times*, October 17, 2004.

169 "They were both intellectuals": Ibid.

169 "came closer than anyone": Brando and Lindsey, *Songs*.

169 "Marlon was fascinated": *Los Angeles Times*, October 17, 2004.

170 Once, Marlon found some magazines: Undated transcripts, MBEA.

170 "He had a wild-kid kind": Capote, "The Duke in His Domain."

171 "very anxious to see": Tennessee Williams to Audrey Wood, August 25, 1947, in Albert J. Devlin ed., *The Selected Letters of Tennessee Williams*, vol. 2 (Sewannee, Tennessee: New Directions Publishing, 2004). Kazan gives the impression in *A Life* that Williams was unaware that Marlon was coming to see him; Williams's letters clearly disprove that.

172 Somewhere east of Manhattan: The Merritt Parkway was given as the starting point of Marlon's hitchhiking route to Cape Cod by columnist J. P. Shanley in *New York Times*, July 6, 1953, information he likely got from the star himself. At some point, however, the fastest route to the Cape would have been to cut down to what was then Route 134, along the coast.

173 "She wasn't to blame": Ellen Adler interview, WJM.

174 "some shit Broadway show": Manso, *Brando*.

174 "He liked that Clayton": Interview with Provincetown resident, name withheld by request, WJM; also see Manso, *Brando*.

174 During his third sojourn: My account of this incident is drawn from *Provincetown Advocate*, July 18, 1946. Manso (*Brando*) places the arrest in September, but the newspaper is clear that it occurred in July.

175 "The spectators were convulsed": Beata Cook, *Provincetown Banner*, June 18, 2015.

175 "to counteract the grey weather": Tennessee Williams to Elia Kazan, [nd] 1947, EKP.

176 "there was considerable consumption": Tennessee Williams, *Memoirs* (Sewannee, Tennessee: New Directions Publishing, 2006).

176 "we had to go out": Tennessee Williams to Audrey Wood, August 29, 1947, quoted in Devlin, ed., *Selected Letters of Tennessee Williams*.

176 "He was just about": Williams, *Memoirs*.

176 "That way," Ellen said, "he didn't have": Ellen Adler interview, WJM.

177 "He wasn't happy in that world": Ibid.

177 "I believe they behaved": Quoted in John Lahr, *Tennessee Williams: Mad Pilgrimage of the Flesh* (New York: W. W. Norton & Company, 2014).

177 "And so we did": Williams, *Memoirs*.

178 which was announced: *New York Times*, September 3, 1947. Word had leaked before this; on September 1, the *Times* had reported Brando "may" get the part.

178 he'd had to commit: Contract between Irene Selznick and Marlon Brando, August 29, 1947, ISC.

179 "all three women had a place": Ellen Adler interview, BSC.

179 "As long as we lived": Ellen Adler interview, WJM.

179 "She was very important to me": Brando and Lindsey, *Songs*. (Celia is referred to by a pseudonym in *Songs*.)

179 "looking for a substitute mother": Janice Mars to Marlon, quoted in Brando and Lindsey, *Songs*.

180 "She was worried that": Ellen Adler interview, WJM.

180 "a big shock": Interview with WJM, source choosing anonymity for this particular discussion.

181 Parkway Hotel, a resort: Contemporary ads in the *Reno Evening Gazette* and *Nevada State Journal*.

181 "and he would come along": Ellen Adler interview, WJM.

181 On Tuesday, January 16: Certificate of Stillbirth, January 16, 1945, Nevada State Department of Health.

182 "extreme cruelty of a mental": Decree of Divorce, Case No. 87887, January 24, 1945, Second Judicial District, State of Nevada.

183 "Volcanic, explosive": *Songs*, original transcript.

183 "I had kind of a nervous": Ibid.

183 "I was there, fending for myself": *Songs*, original transcript.

184 "I felt as if I were being": Brando and Lindsey, *Songs*.

184 "severe for several months": Ibid.

184 "There would be thirty": Kaye Ballard interview, WJM.

184 "For him, sex was like": Manso, *Brando*.

184 "What the hell": *Songs*, original transcript.

185 "You had a perverse need": Janice Mars to Marlon, quoted in Brando and Lindsey, *Songs*.

185 "I was killing myself": *Songs*, original transcript.

186 "Hysteria," he said: MB to his parents, February 1946, quoted in Brando and Lindsey, *Songs*.

186 His last performance: *Billboard*, February 9, 1946.

186 "If not for Harold": Ellen Adler interview, BSC.

187 "I don't know how": Ellen Adler interview, WJM. She also described Clurman's approach to getting Marlon to project.

187 "The show looks good": Quoted in Brando and Lindsey, *Songs*.

187 "Anderson has written": (New York) *Daily News*, February 28, 1946.

187 "Rarely in the theatre": H. I. Phillips syndicated column, as in the *Marion* (Ohio) *Star*, March 5, 1946.

188 "never been onstage": Ellen Adler interview, BSC.

188 "curling up in": Anne Jackson interview, BSC.

189 *The actor has in him*: "Stella Adler: Awake and Dream!"

189 "the single memorable": Associated Press (AP) review, as in the *Zanesville* (Ohio) *Signal*, March 2, 1946.

190 For his performance: *Variety*, May 29, 1946.

190 "She saw him in *Truckline*": Ellen Adler interview, WJM.

191 "a brawny young man stretched out": Capote, "The Duke in His Domain."

192 "You're so ugly": Ellen Adler interview, BSC.

193 "the favorite director": *New York Times*, November 9, 1947.

193 "hit the audience": Ibid.

193 "It's a strong, violent": MB to Marlon Brando Senior, [nd] 1947, MBEA.

193 "an extraordinary writer": *Songs*, original transcript.

194 "He was smart enough": Ibid.

194 "For Marlon to really": Elaine Stritch interview, WJM.

194 "adept at striking up": *New York Times*, November 9, 1947.

196 "scientific approach": Ibid.

196 "Now, listen," he said. "You go off": MB interview with David Susskind, *Open End*, April 21, 1963, WNEW-TV [hereafter "MB interview with Susskind"].

196 "Kazan will not tell": *New York Times*, November 9, 1947.

197 "As you know, no villains": Note listed under heading "General Talk" in front of bound script, EKP.

197 "day and night": All quotes from Kazan's notebooks come from the *A Streetcar Named Desire* folders, EKP.

198 "I never met Kowalski": *Songs*, original transcript.

199 "The only way to understand": Kazan notebooks, EKP.

200 "How can I keep taking": Rita Moreno, *A Memoir* (New York: Celebra, 2014).

200 "the physical, immediate": Kazan notebooks, EKP.

201 "listened experientially": Jeff Young, *Kazan: The Master Director Discusses His Films* (New York: Newmarket Press, 2001).

202 "the brooding sadness in it": *New York Times*, July 25, 1954.

202 "social intuitions": MB to Jessica Tandy, [nd] "Friday night" [Fall 1947], Hume Cronyn and Jessica Tandy Papers, LC.

202 "an impossible, psychopathic": *The Independent*, September 12, 1994.

203 "Perhaps you are not": Jessica Tandy to MB, January 30, 1948, LC.

204 "Perhaps Hume meant": Kazan, *A Life*.

205 Marlon's gripes about Tandy: Bob Thomas, *Marlon: Portrait of the Rebel as an Artist*.

205 "Blanche, at the beginning": Kazan notebooks, EKP.

206 "lady of culture": *New Haven Register*, October 31, 1947.

207 The young playwright Robert Anderson: Philip C. Kolin, "*A Streetcar Named Desire*: A Playwrights Forum," *Michigan Quarterly Review* (Spring 1990).

208 "a papal audience": Williams, *Memoirs*. Williams was right about Wilder.

Deeply repressed and guilt-ridden over his homosexuality, Wilder engaged in sexual encounters "so hurried and reticent," his biographer wrote, "so barren of embrace, tenderness or passion that [they] might never have happened" (Gilbert A. Harrison, *The Enthusiast: A Life of Thornton Wilder* [New York: Fromm, 1986]).

208 "richer" than *The Glass Menagerie*: *Hartford Courant*, November 1, 1947.

208 "a mixture of seduction": *Variety*, November 5, 1947.

208 That was encouraging: Audrey Wood, *Represented By* (New York: Doubleday, 1991).

209 "shrewd" and "properly resentful": *New Haven Register*, October 31, 1947.

209 Williams took pencil to script: That Williams rewrote parts of *Streetcar* on the road was attested to by several sources. See Philip C. Kolin, "The First Critical Assessments of *A Streetcar Named Desire*, *Dramatic Theory and Criticism* 6, no. 1 (Fall 1991); Albert J. Devlin, ed., *Selected Letters of Elia Kazan* (New York: Knopf, 2014); and Lahr, *Tennessee Williams*.

209 The Boston censors were not happy: *New York Times*, November 23, 1947; Kolin, "The First Critical Assessments."

209 "wizardry with lighting": *Boston Traveler*, November 2, 1947.

209 "very violent [with] a smidge": *Boston Globe*, November 2, 1947.

209 He was reassured by a carpenter backstage: *Boston Globe*, November 6, 1947.

210 "The remarkably responsive": (Boston) *Evening American*, November 4, 1947.

210 "This smells like a hit": Wood, *Represented By*.

210 "Last week I heard it called": *Boston Globe*, November 9, 1947.

210 "There seem no words": *Boston Herald*, November 2, 1947.

210 "only be described as magnificent": *Boston Globe*, November 2, 1947.

211 "one cubit to her professional": *Boston Post*, November 2, 1947.

211 "an absolute dead eye": Joshua Logan, *Josh: My Up and Down, In and Out Life* (New York: Delacorte, 1976).

211 "Colossally proud and vain": *Boston Post*, November 9, 1947.

211 "to talk to Tennessee himself": Kazan to Irene Selznick, November 11, 1947, Devlin, ed., *Selected Letters of Elia Kazan*.

212 "settled and pleased": Jocelyn Brando Hanmer to parents, November 13, 1947, MBEA.

212 "the former almost insupportably": *Philadelphia Inquirer*, November 23, 1947.

213 "*Streetcar* travels from the gutter": *Philadelphia Inquirer*, November 18, 1947.

213 "inspired company of actors": (Philadelphia) *Evening Bulletin*, November 18, 1947.

213 "on the strength": Williams, *Memoirs*.

214 "Marlon called me the night": Ellen Adler interview, WJM, supplemented with Ellen Adler interview, BSC.

215 "Packed house": Tennessee Williams to James Laughlin, December 4, 1947, in Devlin, ed., *Selected Letters of Tennessee Williams*.

215 "Marlon's father had this little": Ellen Adler interview, WJM.

216 "I was always a ne'er-do-well": *Songs*, original transcript.

216 "You can't imagine": Capote, "The Duke in His Domain."

216 "Everybody being phony": Undated transcript, MBEA.

217 "high quality," "insight": *New York Times*, December 4, 1947.

217 "The door was never locked": Ellen Adler interview, WJM, supplemented with Ellen Adler interview, BSC.

218 "he seemed to shrug": *Screenland*, June 1954.

219 "It is difficult to talk": Brodkey, "Translating Brando."

219 New York Drama Critics': *Variety*, May 26, 1948. Marlon lost Best Actor in a Play, however, to Paul Kelly in *Command Decision*. Jessica Tandy also lost Best Actress, to Judith Anderson for *Medea*.

219 "He was very restless": Dwight King interview, BSC.

220 "This is child's play": Karl Malden interview, BSC. Malden said he began making these comments six months into the play's run.

220 "This huge crown": Ellen Adler interview, WJM.

### THE AMERICAN HAMLET

223 "Everybody looked ten pounds": Karl Malden interview, BSC.

223 "The bite of the wind": Kazan, *A Life*.

224 "fighter's eyes": Elia Kazan interview with Charlie Maguire, December 9, 1985, EKP.

224 "was reversed": Ellen Adler interview, WJM.

225 "the brooding quality": MB interview with Gladys Hall.

225 They'd come out to Hoboken: Details from Fiore, *Bud*; Eva Marie Saint and Karl Malden interviews, BSC.

226 "couldn't understand how": *Songs*, original transcript.

226 "the bottom of everything": Ellen Adler interview, WJM.

227 "I had a strong sense": *Songs*, original transcript.

227 "could take virtually any form": Manso, *Brando*.

227 "Do you take inspiration": Ed Sullivan column, [nd], 1954, NYPL.

228 "pretty much formula": *Chicago Tribune*, February 23, 1954.

228 "The morality of Clift's characters": Brodkey, "Translating Brando."

229 "I think," Marlon said, "I was enjoying": *Songs*, original transcript.

230 "It's over": Ellen Adler interview, BSC.

230  "I became an actor": MB interview with Gladys Hall.

230  "There isn't anything": MB on *Larry King Live.*

230  "able to speak to any girl": *The Telegraph,* December 2, 2000.

230  Marlon and Marquand became lovers: Marlon's first wife, Anna Kashfi, wrote that the two men shared "an affection towards each other that far overreached the usual expressions of friendship" (*Brando for Breakfast*). Josanne Mariani, who was engaged to Marlon for a time, also reportedly believed the friendship with Marquand was sexual. Friends today concur that a sexual relationship was likely.

231  "Poor Farley": Ellen Adler interview, WJM.

232  "he found it so difficult": Maureen Stapleton interview, WJM.

232  "In the old days": Jack Larson interview, WJM.

233  "one of the best roles": *Chicago Tribune,* November 27, 1953.

233  "This was not a project": Unsourced clip, April 3, 1954, MB file, NYPL.

234  "This is the fifth time": *New Haven Register,* January 4, 1954.

234  "I don't know why all the fuss": *Hartford Courant,* February 13, 1954.

234  "too little promotional": *New York Times,* February 15, 1951.

235  how Marlon compared to other actors: Interview transcript, Hedda Hopper Papers, January 21, 1952, AMPAS [hereafter "HHP"].

235  "you had to work maybe," "You can imagine": *Songs,* original transcript.

235  "theater in a jar": Jack Larson interview, WJM.

236  "competent" in the role, "but imparted": *Variety,* January 12, 1949.

236  In the half-hour drama: Although no contemporary listing could be found that named Marlon as a costar with Lee Tracy in *Come Out Fighting,* the television critic John Crosby recalled the match between Brando and Britenbruck a couple of years later in the *Boston Globe,* March 8, 1952.

236  "looking in the mirror": *Modern Screen,* April 1955.

236  Marlon was now collecting $150,000: Salary notes, EKP.

236  "Most who were successful": *Songs,* original transcript.

236  "a greater potential": Capote, "The Duke in His Domain."

237  "working out of a wheelchair": Manso, *Brando.*

237  "quiet and distant": Interview with Richard Erdman, February 6, 2010, EightMillionStories.com.

237  He spent a couple of days: "Brando and I went out to Birmingham General Hospital in Van Nuys, where all the war paraplegics were still being treated, and we stayed there a few days, learning how to use wheelchairs, and how to get in and out of bed without using our legs." Erdman, EightMillionStories.com. Pat Grissom, one of the vets, told Manso (*Brando*) that Marlon stayed at the hospital for two days.

237  "the Method" school of acting: Foster Hirsch points out that the Method

was not exclusively about an actor's memory; this may have been Stella Adler's framing of it. Hirsch quotes Eva Marie Saint: "The Method is not playing yourself—that's one of the misunderstandings people have about the Studio. The Method helps you to observe, to see life, to look outside yourself" (Hirsch, *A Method to Their Madness*).

237 "I went through": *Songs*, original transcript.

238 "a place to go": Ibid.

238 "He managed to mock": Anthony Quinn with Daniel Paisner, *One Man Tango* (New York: HarperCollins, 1995).

238 In membership lists: See, for example, *New York Times*, April 29, 1951; and July 1, 1952.

238 "They did such PR": Ellen Adler interview, WJM.

238 "took credit for everything": *Songs*, original transcript.

239 "Spencer Tracy is the kind": Capote, "The Duke in His Domain."

239 "style of luminous": Hirsch, *A Method to Their Madness*.

239 "So vividly real": *New York Times*, July 21, 1950.

239 "dried up completely": *Songs*, original transcript.

239 "There was a good deal": Unsourced transcript, MBEA.

240 "the world's greatest actor": Stanley Kramer, *A Mad Mad Mad Mad World: A Life in Hollywood* (New York: Harcourt Brace, 1997).

241 "preferred Brando to anybody": Kazan, *A Life*.

241 "be hungry and anxious": Elia Kazan to Budd Schulberg, [nd] July– August 1953, BSC.

242 "unenthusiastic" about the film: Elia Kazan to MB, July 12, 1967, EKP. The passage reads, "I remembered *On the Waterfront* where you told me repeatedly while we were shooting the picture that you weren't enthusiastic about it and were only making the picture 'because your psychoanalyst was in New York' and that you wanted to make enough to pay his bills while still remaining in that city."

242 "the slightly rolling deck": *New York Times*, December 20, 1953; December 10, 1961. According to Kazan's notes, they returned to the freighter for some final location shots in January. He mentions they "will be coming back" in the December 20, 1953, article.

243 "I like Hoboken": *New York Times*, December 20, 1953.

243 "a character study," "Why am I doing": Ibid.

244 "When Brando at the end": Kazan, *A Life*.

244 "was going to tell": Karl Malden interview, BSC.

245 "revolting, injurious, hurtful": *New York Times*, September 2, 1992.

245 "As long as you live": Ellen Adler interview, WJM.

245 "I'd been snubbed": Kazan, *A Life*.

246 "I can't pretend": Elia Kazan to MB, [nd, but shortly before August 12, 1953]. This exact letter was possibly never sent; the draft was sent to Schulberg for review, and remained in his papers, BSC.

246 "its orders from the Kremlin": *New York Times*, April 12, 1952.

246 "I can never work with him": Ellen Adler interview, WJM.

247 "He squealed on a lot": *Songs*, original transcript.

247 Shortly after learning: Marlon sailed on the *Queen Mary*, departing from Cherbourg on April 24, 1952, and arriving in New York on April 29.

247 "What do I do when": Manso, *Brando*. Mankiewicz told Manso that Marlon learned of Kazan's testimony while making *Julius Caesar*; that was impossible, because the film wasn't made until the summer of 1952, some four months after Kazan's appearance before the congressional commit-tee. Manso incorrectly places the filming of *Julius Caesar* in the summer of 1951. Mankiewicz was clearly recalling Marlon's turmoil in the aftermath of Kazan's testimony.

247 "The moral problem [the film] treats": Elia Kazan to MB, [nd, but shortly before August 12, 1953], BSC.

247 "What I didn't realize": *Songs*, original transcript.

248 "He hates the gang": Elia Kazan notes, *On the Waterfront*, EKP.

248 "What I am especially anxious": Elia Kazan to Budd Schulberg, [nd] July–August 1953, BSC.

249 "he was working through": Ellen Adler interview, WJM.

249 "It's so easy to judge": *Songs*, original transcript.

249 Marlon was getting: Steiger's attitude is described by Karl Malden in his interview with Budd Schulberg, BSC; Steiger himself talked about Marlon in a number of documentary interviews.

250 Karl Malden thought Kazan: Karl Malden interview, BSC.

250 "I remember on *Waterfront*": Elia Kazan to MB, July 12, 1967, EKP.

250 "In movies," Kazan explained, "much more than": *New York Times*, November 9, 1947.

251 "I've always thought": Brando and Lindsey, *Songs*.

251 "what he's going": Kazan, *A Life*.

251 "throbs with passion": *New York Times*, September 20, 1951.

252 five months: *New York Times*, September 7, 1950; March 15, 1951.

252 "The theme of this movie": Kazan notebooks, *Viva Zapata!*, EKP.

252 "Here again we mention": Darryl Zanuck to Elia Kazan, October 2, 1951, EKP.

252 "no Communist has ever": Elia Kazan to Darryl Zanuck, January 29, 1952, EKP.

253 "The gist of the thing": Elia Kazan to "Max," February 14, 1952, EKP.

253 "Truth has become anti-American": *Sunday Worker*, March 16, 1952.

254 "very sinister or noble": Cheryl Crawford to Elia Kazan, [nd] 1951, EKP.

254 "We want to turn on": Darryl Zanuck to Elia Kazan, April 18, 1951, EKP.

254 "It is about a man": Kazan notebooks, *Viva Zapata!*, EKP.

255 "only half as good": Maureen Stapleton interview, WJM.

255 "the realities of revolution": *New York Times*, February 17, 1952.

255 "occasional lapses": *Chicago Tribune*, April 10, 1952.

255 "sensitive, cruelly honest": *Boston Globe*, February 22, 1952.

255 "violent and smoldering": *Chicago Tribune*, April 10, 1952.

255 "something besides a lively," "artistic stature": *Hartford Courant*, March 8, 1952.

255 "Some other guy": Jack Larson interview, WJM.

257 "make his 57th Street": Syndicated, as in the *Lowell* (Massachusetts) *Sun*, October 29, 1953.

258 Marlon had finished: *Variety* reported that Marlon had finished early from *Waterfront*, so he could start *The Egyptian*; he left for "the Coast" on Sunday, January 17. Kazan continued filming *Waterfront* that following week (*Variety*, January 20, 1954). The "wrap party" that friends recalled must have taken place that weekend before Marlon departed.

258 "Actually, no": Tape-recorded interview with Walter Pidgeon, 1955, available on YouTube.

259 "I am indebted to him": Brando and Lindsey, *Songs*.

259 "very creative fights": *Songs*, original transcript.

259 "It comes alive better": MB interview with Susskind.

259 "regular, nice guy": Elia Kazan notes, *On the Waterfront*, EKP.

260 "Terry is lonely, by himself": Elia Kazan to MB, November 1, 1953, EKP.

260 "As a kid," Kazan wrote: Elia Kazan to MB, November 2, 1953, EKP.

261 "There was something": Karl Malden interview, BSC.

261 acting "a survival": MB on *Dick Cavett*.

261 "[Marlon's] whole idea was": Karl Malden interview, BSC.

261 "I was so nervous": Eva Marie Saint, BSC.

262 As drafts of the script reveal: In the Elia Kazan collection at Wesleyan, the earliest script for what would become *On the Waterfront* was called *Crime on the Waterfront* and was dated April 14, 1951. This is a very different story from what eventually emerged. The next script is titled *The Golden Warriors* and is dated April 1, 1953. This is more recognizable, although Terry doesn't appear until page 17, and while there is a taxi scene between him and Charley, there is no "I could have been a contender" speech. This famous moment was written sometime between April and June of 1953, as the next version of the script, dated June 1, contains it. Still called *The Golden Warriors*, this is the script that was most likely sent to Marlon when Kazan approached him for the part.

262 "It was *you*, Charley!": The dialogue varies among versions of the script and even between the final shooting script and what is on-screen.

263 Schulberg didn't know: See Ellen Adler interview, BSC; Budd Schulberg, "The King Who Would Be Man," *Vanity Fair*, March 2005.

263 "That's absolutely absurd": *Songs*, original transcript. The published version of this anecdote includes a whole section that Marlon did not actually say in the interview, at least not at that particular point. This is about the scene being "actor-proof," which reads very much like what he said in the 1979 *Playboy* interview.

263 "Nobody," Schulberg remembered Marlon insisting: Schulberg discussed the scene and his objection to Marlon's account of it in his interview with Ellen Adler, BSC.

264 "If you're just waiting": MB *Playboy* interview.

264 "I could've been a contender": Final bound script, *On the Waterfront*, Kazan collection. Martin Scorsese revealed on *The David Letterman Show* that Marlon had told him that he used cue cards in the taxi scene of *On the Waterfront*. Nowhere in Schulberg's transcripts, however, is there any mention of such a thing; given Schulberg's obsessiveness on the subject, about whether Marlon said the lines he'd written or not, I think if Marlon had used cue cards, it would have been mentioned.

265 "He's one of those actors": Capote, "The Duke in His Domain."

265 "Acting is basically reacting": Rod Steiger interview with Robert Osborne, *Private Screenings*, September 6, 2000, Turner Classic Movies; also *Scene by Scene*, BBC television program, 2000. Budd Schulberg said that Kazan, not the stage manager, filled in for Marlon during Steiger's close-up (Eva Marie Saint interview, BSC).

265 Steiger would carry a grudge: Eva Marie Saint interview, BSC.

265 "If I knew what made him tick": Karl Malden interview, BSC.

266 Marlon pulled the blinds: My description comes from interviews with Kaye Ballard and Ellen Adler, WJM. *Variety* (January 20, 1964) reported the date of his departure for "the Coast"; *Modern Screen*, August 1954, reported the day of his return to New York.

267 "intervals of anxiety": Brando and Lindsey, *Songs*.

267 "My life [was] a mess": Capote, "The Duke in His Domain."

268 "to work for a period": *New York Times*, February 5, 1954.

268 "instituting a suit": *Variety*, February 10, 1954.

268 "working with another man": Darryl Zanuck to Elia Kazan, July 15, 1954, BSC. Zanuck described Marlon's objection as "of a personal nature that went way back to the time when [Marlon] was a young boy." A perusal of the full cast and crew list turned up no obvious possibilities. Might the objection have been to Curtiz? Marlon's mother knew Curtiz's wife, but it's

unclear how Marlon might have known the director in his youth. Zanuck wrote that the man in question was "assigned to" the production. That sounds like a rank-and-file studio employee, and if so, he could easily have been removed if the star had objected. Would Zanuck really have allowed the presence of an extra or a second-unit director to jeopardize the film?

269 "by Jade Snow Wong": MB to James Wong Howe, November 9, 1953, James Wong Howe Collection, AMPAS.

269 "isolated and a little alone": MB on *Larry King Live*.

269 "woman troubles": *Songs*, original transcript.

269 "emotionally upset": *Modern Screen*, May 1954.

269 "Marlon Brando will wed": Syndicated, as in the *Brownsville* (Texas) *Herald*, March 15, 1948.

269 "People here would have you": Syndicated, as in *Rocky Mount* (North Carolina) *Evening Telegram*, May 10, 1950.

270 "in-between love affairs": Shelley Winters interview, 1980, available on YouTube.

270 "I really couldn't compete": Shelley Winters, *Shelley: Also Known as Shirley* (New York: Morrow, 1980).

270 she left Marlon's employ: Celia first left for Paris on the SS *America* on April 14, 1951. She would make several trips back and forth over the next few years. Her former husband, Thomas Webb, worked for the law firm of Coudert Frères, and later for the Paris office of the New York law firm of White and Case.

270 "The romance twixt": Syndicated, as in *Nevada State Journal*, April 20, 1951.

270 "pop the $64 question": Syndicated, as in the *Lowell* (Massachusetts) *Sun*, October 16, 1951.

270 "It wasn't that he couldn't": Kaye Ballard interview, WJM.

270 "He was mythologized": Ellen Adler interview, WJM.

271 "We would try something": Ibid., and Ellen Adler interview, BSC.

272 A theater aficionado: *New York Times*, January 10, 1952.

272 "I recognized him": Interview with Josanne Mariani by Lanie Goodman, 2016, posted at DuJour.com [hereafter "Josanne interview with Goodman"].

273 "in a trance over": Syndicated, as in the *Pottstown* (Pennsylvania) *Mercury*, December 18, 1953.

273 "Don't have anything": Ellen Adler interviews, WJM and BSC.

274 "long periods of silence": Moreno, *A Memoir*.

274 "She was not only physically": Brando and Lindsey, *Songs*.

275 "Colder than ice": *Songs*, original transcript.

275 "I think Marlon found," "He probably realized": Manso, *Brando*.

276 "very important to somebody": Jack Larson interview, WJM.

276 "When something would": Manso, *Brando*.

276 "I don't think he ever imbibed": Jack Larson interview, WJM.

276 "I was afraid of it": Capote, "The Duke in His Domain."

277 "emotional disorders": *Songs*, original transcript.

277 "I knew I had to find": MB on *Larry King Live*.

277 "What difference does": Untitled transcript, MBEA.

277 Mittelman had led a study: *New York Times*, September 5, 1940. Background on Mittelman comes from U.S. Census records; ship passenger records; U.S. naturalization papers, January 2, 1929; the American Medical Association deceased physician file; *New York Times* obituary, October 5, 1959.

278 Mittelman also lectured: *New York Times*, May 15, 1950; April 3, 1951.

278 Summoned before the draft: Marlon told the story of his draft board interview in Brando and Lindsey, *Songs*, though it seems a little fanciful. I have used here *Songs*, original transcript.

279 "What you're saying": *Songs*, original transcript.

279 "in stride, no questions": Josanne interview with Goodman.

279 "sick-making": Manso, *Brando*.

279 "It was really frightening": Ellen Adler interview, WJM. *Modern Screen* carried a story (August 1954) saying that the subpoena server got Marlon to open his door by claiming to have news about his Oscar nomination for *Julius Casear*, which sounds unlikely. See also (New York) *Daily News*, April 2, 1954.

279 "to perform under his current": *New York Times*, February 17, 1954.

280 "unfairness of a business": *Songs*, original transcript.

280 "self-conscious and modest": John Gielgud, *An Actor and His Time* (New York: Sidgwick and Jackson, 1979).

281 "the delight and surprise": *New York Times*, June 6, 1953.

281 "the only American actor": *New York Times*, January 15, 1967. See also William Redfield, *Letters from an Actor* (New York: Viking, 1967).

282 a 3-D film of *Richard III*: Morgan Maree to John Huston, May 26, 1953, Morgan Maree Collecton, AMPAS.

282 "Cannot fathom Brando's": John Huston to Paul Kohner, May 22, 1953, John Huston Papers, AMPAS [hereafter "JHP"].

282 "In spite of the fact": MB to John Huston, May 22, 1953, JHP.

283 "would only prove": Paul Kohner to John Huston, May 28, 1953, JHP.

283 "I think you would make": John Huston to MB, June 7, 1953, JHP.

284 "falls short": *New York Times*, December 31, 1953.

285 "You would have had": Ellen Adler interview, BSC.

285 "he'd been more serious": Ellen Adler interview, WJM.

285 "brilliant once or twice": *New York Times*, January 15, 1967.

285 "to the size of a blown-up cartoon": Janice Mars to MB, letters in preparation for *Songs*, MBEA.

286 "a tour de force": *Hartford Courant*, July 22, 1953.

286 "Brando was handsome": *Boston Globe*, July 15, 1953.

286 "Marlon Brando opened here": *Boston Post*, July 27, 1953.

286 Norton's review infuriated: Manso, *Brando*.

287 his photograph was routinely slapped: See, for example, *Boston Globe*, July 26, 1953.

287 "the audience lost interest": *Boston Globe*, July 15, 1953.

287 "is the measure": MB to parents, July 28, 1953, MBEA, quoted in Brando and Lindsey, *Songs*.

287 "Man, don't you get it": *New York Times*, January 15, 1967.

288 "I hated with every fiber": Untitled transcript, MBEA.

288 "He scoffs at our films": *Hartford Courant*, January 24, 1954.

288 "He reminds me of a fellow": *Chicago Tribune*, March 30, 1952.

288 "Can you picture": *Altoona Mirror*, June 1, 1951.

288 And he might even be a Communist: During the Broadway run of *Streetcar*, Hopper had received an anonymous letter from someone "well known in the amusement field." The letter writer claimed to possess evidence that Marlon was a Communist—a charge, Hopper's correspondent insisted, Marlon "never denied" when supposedly confronted with it. The letter, dated November 25, 1949, claimed Ed Sullivan made the charge in his column; however, an exhaustive search of those Sullivan columns that have been digitized did not turn this up. Had Sullivan made such a direct claim, it would likely have been reported on elsewhere, and there was no corresponding mention anywhere else. The correspondent's signature was "Yours for justice, an American" (HHP).

289 "with a grunt": *Chicago Tribune*, March 30, 1952.

289 "nincompoop": Jack Larson interview, WJM.

289 "Hedda Hawker": *Meet Marlon Brando*.

289 "getting out of the business": Jack Larson interview, WJM.

290 "speak with people": MB interview with Susskind.

290 "people with pencils": Capote, "The Duke in His Domain."

290 "a cardinal sin": MB interview with Susskind.

290 "I needed to feel I was doing": *Songs*, original transcript.

290 "bitterness and fear": MB to Marlon and Dorothy Brando, Fall 1943, quoted in Brando and Lindsey, *Songs*.

290 "He really hated the fame": Budd Schulberg discussing Marlon in his interview with Eva Marie Saint, BSC.

291 "a normal person": MB tape recordings.

291 "just scribbled something": *Songs*, original transcript.

291 "contemptuous of people": Ellen Adler interview, WJM.

291 "terminated one part": *New York Times*, November 30, 1947.

292  "They had similar attitudes": *Los Angeles Times*, October 17, 2004.

292  "the vacuity of life": Ibid.

292  "half beast and half human": Darryl Zanuck interview with Hedda Hopper, January 21, 1952, HHP.

293  "the Beat preference": Lyall Bush, "Doing Brando," *Film Comment*, January 1996.

293  "a reaction against the postwar": Pauline Kael, "Marlon Brando: An American Hero," *The Atlantic*, March 1966.

293  "dressed like Brando": Proceedings of the U.S. Senate Subcommittee on Juvenile Delinquency, June 16–18, 1955, quoted in *Film Bulletin*, July 11, 1955.

294  "The public Somebody": *New York Times*, November 30, 1947.

294  There Dodie had suffered: Details of Dodie's illness come from her death certificate, March 31, 1954, State of California.

294  Dodie's embarrassment: Ellen Adler interview, WJM. Hedda Hopper also called Mrs. Curtiz "a great friend of Marlon Brando's mother" (*Chicago Tribune,* April 3, 1954).

295  "My mother didn't like": Ellen Adler interview, BSC.

295  Darryl Zanuck suggested: See Hedda Hopper's column, *Chicago Tribune*, March 22, 1954; for *Désirée*, see Hopper, *Chicago Tribune*, August 5, 1953.

296  At just past midnight: Description of the hospital comes from various issues of the *Pasadena Independent*, 1945-1955.

297  Rushing her to the hospital: Details of Dodie's illness are from her death certificate, March 31, 1954, State of California.

297  "beautifully, very calmly": Manso, *Brando*.

298  "family curse": *Songs*, original transcript.

298  "the merest courtesy sip": Capote, "The Duke in His Domain."

298  "your little boy": Several letters in MBEA contain this closing.

298  "There was a time": Manso, *Brando*.

299  "She had a happy time": *Songs*, original transcript.

299  "on dangerous ground": Kay Phillips Bennett to Manso, *Brando*. This is backed up by Ellen Adler's memory of Dodie being upset about the Fox lawsuit.

299  "Be sensible with your life": Maila Nurmi to Manso, *Brando*.

300  "Demolished," "He didn't say much": Manso, *Brando*.

300  He would pay half the costs caused: AP report, April 2, 1954; *Motion Picture Daily*, April 5, 1954.

300  "It was half a victory": *Songs*, original transcript.

300  "She made him promise": Manso, *Brando*.

301  In the orchestra: Background on Weiler comes from an interview with a *Times* source, WJM; Weiler's obituary, *New York Times*, February 8,

2002; U.S. Census. Weiler may have seen *Waterfront* in a "sneak preview" before July 28, as we know the film was screened privately ahead of time for a few people in New York (*Variety*, July 14, 1954). But reviewers were still required to see the film upon its release as well, in case any changes were made to the picture in the interim.

301 "A small but obviously dedicated": *New York Times*, July 29, 1954.

302 "It is Brando's portrayal": *New York Times*, August 1, 1954.

302 "Marlon Brando puts on": *Variety*, July 14, 1954.

302 "the fascinating spectacle": *Brooklyn Daily Eagle*, July 29, 1954.

302 "moving with the speed": *New York Times*, August 1, 1954.

303 "being hailed as the best": *Oakland Tribune*, August 10, 1954.

303 "If there is a better": Kazan, *A Life*.

303 "the finest performance": Hirsch, *A Method to Their Madness*.

303 "Okay, we'll say it": *New York Times*, July 25, 1954.

303 "glorified readings": Brodkey, "Translating Brando."

303 "He doesn't think": *New York Times*, July 25, 1954.

303 "great respect for Tennessee's play": MB interview with Murrow.

303 "in and out": Karl Malden interview, BSC.

304 "I took a look": MB interview with Susskind.

304 "actor proof": MB *Playboy* interview.

304 "roaring along": *Variety*, September 22, October 6, 1954.

304 "immaculate in pale": *New York Times*, July 25, 1954.

305 "a new man": *Modern Screen*, November 1954.

305 "Up until a while ago": *Modern Screen*, July 1955.

305 "Throughout the many months": *Screenland*, June 1954.

306 Downing's *Screenland* article: *Screenland*, June 1954; *Variety*, May 5, 1954.

306 "Where do you come off": *Modern Screen*, November 1954.

306 "Marlon wearing a spit curl": *Screenland*, July 1954.

307 "I had a very satisfactory": George Cukor to Harry Cohn, May 2, 1954, George Cukor Papers [hereafter "GCP"], AMPAS.

307 Marlon never did sign on: Marlon stood Cukor up for their meeting. Two weeks passed before he offered the director an apology, and then a very bizarre one. The errors and misspelling are all his: "I was unpleasantly surprised to find this morning amongst a pile of as yet unanswered correspondence, a letter which I had written to you a considerable length of time aho, in which, I oppoligized at perhaps too much length for not appearing at your hotel on the day we had agreed to meet . . . In explanation I have only to ofcer the fact that there was lidigemate confrsion (I might as well go back to bed and get up again) . . . as to time, telephone, tea and tardiness. If you were inconveinienced on

thay fatefull afternoon I hope you will give me a opportunity to adjust the loss." (MB to George Cukor, May 20, 1954, GCP.)

Marlon did sometimes misspell words, but never to this extent; the hand-written notes he sent to Jessica Tandy confirm that fact. Was he dictating the note to a particularly sloppy, illiterate associate? Or, perhaps, was he trying to sway Cukor against approaching him again in the future?

307 "only the greatest": *New York Times*, July 25, 1954.

307 "which can only mean": *Chicago Tribune*, July 20, 1954.

307 "a bathtub singer": *Motion Picture Daily*, August 14, 1954.

307 "Marlon Brando gets the plum": *Hartford Courant*, August 4, 1954.

308 "the stereotypical Latina": *Miami Herald*, September 14, 2008.

308 "chewing gum": *Chicago Tribune*, June 15, 1954.

309 "swaggeringly irresistible": Moreno, *A Memoir*.

310 "very naïve": Josanne interview with Goodman.

310 "charming, beautiful": *Songs*, original transcript.

311 The night was warm: This account comes from a letter Marlon wrote to a friend, who shared it with me but allowed only paraphrasing. Jack Larson also recalled Marlon's wanderings in disguise, and Josanne Mariani remem-bered Phil Rhodes making him up (Josanne interview with Goodman).

311 "his own pals": Louella Parsons syndicated column, November 2, 1954. See also her column from March 29, 1962.

312 "I was very hurt": Manso, *Brando*. The falling out between the friends was also noted in syndicated gossip columns, as in the *Nevada State Journal*, September 7, 1954.

313 Twelve months earlier: MB to parents, July 28, 1953, MBEA.

313 "It's a daytime town": MB interview with Murrow.

313 "*Ils sont là!*": My account comes from UPI and AP accounts that appeared in various newspapers, including the *Boston Globe* and the *Hartford Courant*, on October 30, 1954. Also *Modern Screen*, February 1955.

315 "a beautiful silver": Josanne interview with Goodman.

315 "I want to get to know": *Modern Screen*, February 1955.

316 "I cried at first": United Press report, as in the *Hartford Courant*, October 31, 1954.

316 "smoldering with something": Tennessee Williams to Elia Kazan, November 1954, in Devlin, ed., *Selected Letters of Tennessee Williams*.

316 "At first I didn't believe": United Press story, as in the *Long Beach* (Cal-ifornia) *Press Telegram*, November 2, 1954.

316 "It is difficult": *Modern Screen*, February 1955.

317 "cut short his idyll": United Press report, as in the *Hartford Courant*, October 31, 1954. See also the Reuters report, *Chicago Tribune*, October 31, 1954, as well as various AP reports that appeared on November 8 and 9, 1954.

317 "the year's low in taste": *Modern Screen*, February 1955.

317 "The movie star meekly": *New York Times*, October 7, 1954.

318 "He would need a very tolerant wife": Kaye Ballard interview, WJM.

319 "He needed to have control": Ellen Adler interview, BSC.

319 "He never wanted to hurt": Kaye Ballard interview, WJM.

319 During the fall: *Modern Screen*, February 1955.

320 "That was part": Manso, *Brando*.

320 "I went after women": *Songs*, original transcript.

320 "I don't believe he ever meant": Moreno, *A Memoir*.

320 "Whatever damage was done": Ibid.

320 "I lived with value systems": *Songs*, original transcript.

320 they were being "hysterical": Jack Larson interview, WJM.

320 "Marlon could perceive": Manso, *Brando*.

321 "I think, essentially": MB *Playboy* interview.

321 "He avoided having": Molly Haskell, "Marlon the Misogynist?" *The Guardian*, July 8, 2004.

321 He was intimidated: This becomes very clear reading his letters to Williams, who was trying to get him to appear opposite Magnani in *Orpheus Descending*, a play he'd written for both of them. (See, for example, MB to Tennessee Williams, [nd], Tennessee Williams Papers, Columbia University, quoted in Devlin, ed., *Selected Letters of Tennessee Williams*). George Englund also writes about Marlon's intimidation in *Marlon Brando: The Way It's Never Been Done Before* (New York: Harper, 2004). See also Haskell, "Marlon the Misogynist?"

321 "Who's the blonde?": My account is taken from several news reports from the United Press and Reuters, all dated November 1, 1954. There are several different UP stories, published in various newspapers, including the *Hartford Courant* and the *Hayward* (California) *Daily Review*.

323 "The Motion Picture Export": *Variety*, August 29, 1954.

323 "A ruffled but grinning": *New York Times*, November 10, 1954. See also *Variety*, November 30, 1954; *Motion Picture Daily*, November 10, 1954.

324 "next month": AP report, as in the *Chicago Tribune*, November 26, 1954.

324 "In France, it is different": AP report, as in the *Hartford Courant*, November 7, 1954.

324 More photographers were waiting: AP report, as in the *Hartford Courant*, November 9, 1954; AP newsreel, available on YouTube.

324 "She did little more": AP report, as in the *Racine* (Wisconsin) *Journal Times*, December 26, 1954. Josanne's appearance took place on the night of Sunday, November 14.

325 "Four months ago": *Modern Screen*, February 1955.

325 "Whenever he'd come": Ellen Adler interview, WJM.

326 "I spend my time": Leonard Lyons syndicated column, as in the *Chicago Defender*, April 17, 1957.

326 Clurman had penned: *New York Times*, September 26, 1954.

326 Marlon had brought Stella a gift: The story of the Lhasa Apso was reported in *Variety*, October 24, 1954.

328 "He's supposed to sing": Manso, *Brando*.

328 "offers nothing but variations": See Samuel Goldwyn cable to Joseph Mankiewicz, July 23, 1954; and Mankiewicz to MB, [nd] 1954, both from Joseph L. Mankiewicz Papers, AMPAS.

328 "The contest fixes": *Motion Picture Daily*, March 19, 1955.

328 "dislikes Hollywood turf": *Motion Picture Herald*, April 9, 1955.

329 twenty-four princes: *Motion Picture Daily*, October 27, 1954; *Variety*, November 17, November 24, 1954.

329 "Whether this break": *Film Bulletin*, November 29, 1954.

329 "stylish knee pants": *Variety*, October 13, 1954.

329 On his train trip across: *Motion Picture Herald*, January 22, 1955.

329 "Marlon had never done": Manso, *Brando*.

329 In just its first week: *Variety*, November 17, November 24, 1954.

329 "No one ever lost money": *Songs*, original transcript.

330 "ponderous panorama": *New York Times*, November 21, 1954.

330 "a fancy façade": *New York Times*, November 18, 1954.

330 "leap from commercial nowhere": *Motion Picture Daily*, December 30, 1954.

330 "ridiculous [and] nonsensical": *Songs*, original transcript. See also Eli Wallach interview, BSC. Brando gave variations on this idea in many other places.

330 "Marlon was sounding off": *Vanity Fair*, January 22, 2007.

330 Marlon sat in the Goldwyn: Schulberg told this story to Eli Wallach while interviewing him, BSC.

331 "Screw that": Manso, *Brando*.

332 "They tried to record": *Meet Marlon Brando*.

332 "Masterson didn't fit him": *Newsweek*, July 20, 1959.

333 "It's not so important": Tape-recorded interview with Walter Pidgeon, 1955, available on YouTube.

334 "Marlon could get very angry": Jack Larson interview, WJM.

334 "Wrap up all the Oscars": *Variety*, July 14, 1954. Although Bogart gave this praise before knowing he would be nominated alongside Marlon, he had to have been expecting the competition.

335 "Wouldn't it be fascinating": Hopper column, as in the *Hartford Courant*, March 30, 1955.

335 "especially on warm nights": MB interview with Murrow.

335 "after a couple of hours of this": Dick Clayton interview, WJM.

336 "a thick, red-rubber schlong": Jeff Brown to MB, [nd], 1990s, MBEA. Marlon would remember his costume as consisting of a sock worn over his "sexual parts" (*Songs*, original transcript).

336 "Who stole my bike?": Jeff Brown to MB, [nd], 1990s, MBEA.

337 "They were utter bohemians": Ellen Adler interview, WJM.

337 "pined for him": Manso, *Brando*. Maila Nurmi's observation also comes from the same source.

337 "I've reversed my views": *Modern Screen*, July 1955.

337 "Like most misers": *Songs*, original transcript.

338 "I don't remember why": Ibid.

338 if Marlon's personal income: This particular argument was made by Marlon Senior on October 25, 1957, in a Pennebaker memo (MBEA). He made a more general argument using the same ideas many, many times.

338 The deal was this: Marlon's longtime trusted assistant, Caroline Barrett, told this story to Robert Lindsey when Lindsey was working with Marlon on his memoir (*Songs*, original transcript). When Lindsey brought it up, Marlon denied it, evidently unwilling to give his father credit for anything. "After my father lost all my money," he said, "I don't think I would be disposed to believing that he could handle money." Lindsey told Marlon he didn't think Barrett would make the story up; Lindsey believed it to be true and that Marlon didn't remember. The story did not make it into Brando and Lindsey, *Songs*. Still, it fits similar stories told by Ellen Adler and Jack Larson, and makes sense of Marlon's uncharacteristic willingness to play cooperative movie star for as long as he did.

339 "my father bought tailings": *Songs*, original transcript.

339 "As soon as I could": Undated notes for memoir, MBEA.

340 "biggest shots on the lot": Robert Dorff recollections, [nd] MBEA.

340 *To Tame a Land*: *Independent Film Journal*, October 15, 1955.

340 *Man on Spikes*: *Motion Picture Herald*, May 14, 1955.

340 "a British officer": *Songs*, original transcript.

340 "spoke in a hypnotic": Englund, *The Way It's Never Been Done*.

341 A guard stopped him: *Life*, April 11, 1955. The clip of the Oscar show reveals a young, dark-haired woman seated beside Marlon. Could this be Celia Webb? One source reported that his secretary also accompanied him, and Celia often worked as his secretary.

344 "slumped in his seat": Sidney Skolsky, *Don't Get Me Wrong—I Love Hollywood* (New York: G.P. Putnam's Sons, 1975).

344 "He felt, boy": Karl Malden interview, BSC.

345 "An error in judgment": MB *Playboy* interview.

345 "Not much is left": *Screenland*, September 1955.

346 "a likeable, decent": *The Ed Sullivan Show*, October 9, 1955, CBS.

346 "Brando was Dean's hero": Kazan, *A Life*.

346 the actress Arlene Martel: Interview with Avra Douglas, Martel's daughter, WJM.

346 "on the person he thought": Brando and Lindsey, *Songs*.

346 "Mr. Dean appears": Manso, *Brando*.

### THE RABBLE-ROUSER

353 The prison sat at the tip: My description of Marlon's visit to San Quentin and his feelings toward the Chessman case is drawn from several sources, notably letters from Eugene "Bud" Burdick, from May 1960, located at MBEA. Also, many newspapers gave colorful accounts of the day: *San Francisco Chronicle*, May 2 and 3, 1960; *Stanford Daily*, May 2 and 3, 1960; *Boston Globe*, May 3, 1960; *Chicago Tribune*, May 3, 1960; *Chicago Defender*, May 2 and 3, 1960; and *New York Times*, May 2 and 3, 1960.

355 "in the fight to abolish": *Chicago Defender*, May 3, 1960.

355 "I am powerless to act": *San Francisco Chronicle*, May 2, 1960.

356 "He was embarrassed": Joshua Logan, "Answers to Questions about Marlon Brando," transcribed interview, Joshua Logan Collection [hereafter "JLC"], LC.

356 "Food was always a friend": *Songs*, original transcript.

357 "Everybody, male and female": Karl Malden interview, BSC.

357 He'd dominated the box office: What's significant is that while Marlon had no new films in release during 1959, he remained in the annual compilation of top box-office stars (coming in as the eighth-most-profitable male star) because earlier films continued to do good business throughout the year. *The Fugitive Kind* had just been released at this point, and was a box-office flop, but that didn't register yet in the annual rankings. See *Box Office Barometer*, February 1960.

357 "to do something": MB to Marlon and Dorothy Brando, Fall 1943, quoted in Brando and Lindsey, *Songs*.

357 That his father had failed him: Marlon recalled that his father "hid all his money, everywhere, in different banks, and so when he finally died, he left his wife only about $3,000 in [an] insurance policy—and the rest of the money was hidden. So nobody ever found that money. It's probably floating around here in some bank account." In 1992, Marlon estimated that the investments would be worth "millions and millions of dollars" (*Songs*, original transcript).

357 "was in a profession": Marchak, *Me and Marlon*.

357 "balding [and] middle-aged": Kazan, *A Life*. In the late 1950s, Kazan wanted

to do another film with him; he suggested *Young Joshua*, about Moses and his protégé. Marlon seemed interested in doing the picture; Hedda Hopper mentioned it in her column of September 6, 1956. But nothing ultimately came of it (MB to Elia Kazan, December 9, 1957, MBEA).

358 "With so much prejudice": Brando and Lindsey, *Songs*.

359 "idea of a divine father": Englund, *The Way It's Never Been Done*.

360 "To devote one's life": Undated essay by MB, MBEA.

360 "I often get terribly discouraged": MB to Edward R. Murrow, January 28, 1958, MBEA; other letters in Murrow correspondence folder, MBEA.

361 "thinking" actors "in vogue": *New York Times*, May 5, 1960.

361 "I think people who are looking": *Meet Marlon Brando*.

362 "That's how I trapped Marlon": Gerald Clarke, *Capote: A Biography* (New York: Simon and Schuster, 1988).

362 "I thought if she loved": Capote, "The Duke in His Domain."

362 "To be an actor": Bob Colacello and Andy Warhol, "New Again: Truman Capote," *Interview*, January 1979.

362 The publication of his *New Yorker* article: For a thoughtful analysis of the Brando-Capote episode, see Douglas McCollam, "In Cold Type," *Columbia Journalism Review* (November–December 2012). McCollam points out that "The Duke in His Domain" changed celebrity journalism and "heralded the arrival of the invasive, full-immersion pop culture of today." The veracity of Capote's quotes, given the fact that he used no tape recorder nor took any notes during the interview, has sometimes been questioned. But, in fact, Marlon never disputed the content of the piece, merely the appropriateness of its publication. In the 1979 *Playboy* interview, Marlon said Capote was "too good a writer just to write sensational claptrap." To Anna Kashfi, he admitted Capote had the gift of "total recall."

363 "It required fifty": *New York Times*, November 4, 1955.

363 "He was extremely vigilant": Gahan Hanmer interview, WJM.

363 "the highest crime rate": United Press syndicated article by Vernon Scott, as in the *Brownsville* (Texas) *Herald*, January 7, 1958.

364 "To try may be to die": *New York Times*, January 15, 1967.

365 "expiated his guilt": *L'Osservatore Romano*, February 1960.

365 "He had an incurably": Clinton T. Duffy, *88 Men and 2 Women* (New York: Doubleday and Co., 1962).

365 "I could have been him": Jack Larson interview, WJM.

366 "an act of vengeance": MB to Eugene Burdick, [nd] May 1960, MBEA.

366 "Your visit here did": Eugene Burdick to MB, May 11, 1960, MBEA.

366 "Those of us outside": Burton H. Wolfe to MB, May 11, 1960, MBEA.

366 "None of us felt like": Alex Hoffman to MB, May 4, 1960, MBEA.

367 "It would take a derrick": *Hartford Courant*, May 7, 1960.

367  "*Now* it comes out": *Chicago Tribune*, May 12, 1960.

367  "publicity or fanfare": *San Francisco Chronicle*, June 5, 1960.

368  "What is your interest": Marlon's hate mail is preserved in several Chessman folders in MB's personal file on Chessman, MBEA. There is also considerable hate mail in response to his work on behalf of civil rights. He told *Playboy* in 1979 that he did not get a lot of hate mail; these folders disprove that statement.

369  "big, profitable Hollywood": Memo from Marlon Brando Sr. to MB, George Glass, and Walter Seltzer, October 25, 1957, MBEA. Financial records for Pennebaker are kept in several company files and ledgers at MBEA.

369  "conservative estimate": *Chicago Defender*, November 11, 1957.

370  "conspiracy, mismanagement": *Chicago Tribune*, November 11, 1955.

370  "it was the only way": *Songs*, original transcript.

371  "didn't matter to Marlon": Dick Clayton interview, WJM.

371  He read John Laurence's: For an in-depth consideration of Marlon's library and how what he read influenced his thoughts and actions, see Susan L. Mizruchi, *Brando's Smile: His Life, Thought, and Work* (New York: W. W. Norton, 2014).

371  "a cultural sacrifice": *Partisan Review*, June 1960.

372  "# He was in mortal combat": MB's personal file on Chessman, 1960–1961, MBEA.

372  "a piece of reportage": Elia Kazan to MB, January 29, 1958, MBEA.

372  "not just cowboys": Capote, "The Duke in His Domain."

373  "underwritten in terms": Englund, *The Way It's Never Been Done*. Reading through Marlon's notes on the project (held at AMPAS) leaves the impression that Englund was correct in his evaluation.

373  "Alice, I want you": Marchak, *Me and Marlon*.

374  Yet Movita had continued to show up: Rumors would persist, reported by Manso and others, that it was actually the actress France Nuyen, whom Marlon dated for a time, who gave birth to his child. These stories seem to have emerged as part of the mystery over Movita and her baby. Given the somewhat suspicious circumstances (Movita being perhaps too old to get pregnant and the fact that she and Marlon hadn't been seeing each other), the idea that Nuyen was the actual mother seemed to make more sense: to cover it up, the stories went, Marlon asked his old flame Movita to claim to be the mother. Anna Kashfi alleged Marlon called her and told her Nuyen had just had his baby. But Anna admitted that she was asleep when he called, and groggy while she spoke to him; given that she was also often drunk during this period, her testimony isn't very reliable. The truth of the matter, in any event, is very different, and is spelled out in detail in the

divorce files between Marlon and Movita (*Marlon Brando v. Movita Brando*, August 1967).

375 "someone took a pickaxe": MB to Albert Pearlson, [nd], legal file on Anna Kashfi, MBEA.

375 "We refuse to admit": *Songs*, original transcript.

375 "felt responsible": No record of the marriage could be found in Xochimilco, but that doesn't mean it's not there. Some have expressed skepticism that Marlon and Movita were actually married, but if that were the case, he would never have had to take her to court for a divorce some years later. The date of the marriage is given in their divorce case. In *Songs*, original transcript, Marlon said he'd "only been legally married twice," and describes Movita as "a woman I was married to."

375 Marlon didn't know: He arrived into Los Angeles on July 6, 1960, from Paris, on board Air France. See also Hedda Hopper's column, July 12, 1960; *Motion Picture Daily*, July 12, 1960; and *Songs*, original transcript.

376 The plan was to return: *Motion Picture Daily*, August 17, 1960.

376 He was pleased: Burdick's travel to Tahiti and Marlon's plans to see him are discussed in various letters from May 1960 in MB's personal file on Chessman, MBEA.

376 "the Hollywood hamster wheel": United Press story, as in the *Syracuse Post Herald*, June 3, 1957.

376 "take her call because": Marchak, *Me and Marlon*.

377 "Everybody loved Alice": Ellen Adler interview, BSC.

377 A native of Minooka: For Marchak's background, see *Orange County Times*, November 26, 2008; also U.S. Census, 1920, 1930, and 1940.

379 "I feel Brando": United Press International (UPI) report, as in the *Chicago Defender*, May 10, 1960.

380 "unregistered alliance": Kashfi, *Brando for Breakfast*.

381 When Anna was hospitalized: Ibid.

381 "It is far more creative": Anna Kashfi to MB, postmarked June 20, 1957, MBEA. He was in Paris making *The Young Lions*.

382 "incredibly beautiful East Indian": Janice Mars to MB, [nd], MBEA.

382 "I'm experiencing loneliness": Englund, *The Way It's Never Been Done*.

382 "He wrote lengthy": Kashfi, *Brando for Breakfast*.

382 "Little did I know": Marchak, *Me and Marlon*.

383 "Do you know what love is": Kashfi, *Brando for Breakfast*.

383 "to find someone": Ellen Adler interview, WJM.

383 "Who'd have you?": Marchak, *Me and Marlon*.

383 "You can still back out," "he entertained us": Kashfi, *Brando for Breakfast*.

384 "Most people here shrug": Hedda Hopper to Jack Podell, December 13, 1957, HHP.

384 "He hadn't given up": Marchak, *Me and Marlon*.

384 "To me he's always played": Hedda Hopper notes, September 30, 1958, HHP.

384 "very sweet little girl": Hedda Hopper to Podell, December 13, 1957, HHP.

385 Friends reported finding: Englund, *The Way It's Never Been Done*.

385 "a wide, swinging personality": AP, as in the *Hartford Courant*, February 17, 1965.

385 When they divorced: The details were given in Marchak, *Me and Marlon*. Marlon later went to court to have the age on Christian's trust raised to thirty. When he reached that age, Christian signed the money over to his father so he could buy a house for him.

385 "I can teach him so much": George Englund note [nd], MBEA; Englund, *The Way It's Never Been Done*; *The Guardian*, April 28, 2008.

385 "emotionally disturbed": Kashfi, *Brando for Breakfast*.

385 And so it went: Just some of the coverage of the "Battling Brandos": *Boston Globe*, March 17 and July 2, 1959; *Boston Globe*, January 14, 1960; *Chicago Defender*, November 3, 1958; *Chicago Defender*, November 19, 1959; *Chicago Defender*, January 12, 1960; *Chicago Tribune*, April 27 and November 19, 1959; *Hartford Courant*, March 7, April 25, August 9, and October 31, 1959; *New York Times*, October 1, 1958; *New York Times*, March 17, 1959; and *New York Times*, January 14, 1960.

386 "What I brought to Tahiti": Unsourced article, circa 1977, MB file, NYPL.

387 "the ancient score": Englund, *The Way It's Never Been Done*.

387 "like an obscene trophy": Kashfi, *Brando for Breakfast*.

387 *sex addict*: Marchak, *Me and Marlon*.

388 "It's collusion": *Wall Street Journal* online video interview, available on YouTube.

388 "Those Beverly Hills ladies": *Songs*, original transcript.

389 "He comes in": *Los Angeles Times*, October 17, 2004.

389 "I'd heard that he'd": Ellen Adler interview, BSC.

390 "Each particle of water": Eugene Burdick, *The Blue of Capricorn* (New York: Houghton Mifflin, 1961).

390 "I love it down here": According to Ridgeway Callow, quoted in Manso, *Brando*.

391 "There are more laughing": *Songs*, original transcript.

392 "Lean was a very good": Brando and Lindsey, *Songs*.

393 *First Train to Babylon*: The film's title would be changed to *The Naked Edge*; it turned out to be Cooper's last film, released a month after his death.

393 "Marlon had no interest": Englund, *The Way It's Never Been Done*.

393 "lost interest in moviemaking": Marchak, *Me and Marlon*.

393 A pessimist by nature: Englund, *The Way It's Never Been Done*.

393 At the moment, *Ben-Hur*: For Gore Vidal's "junk" comment, see the film *The Celluloid Closet*.

395 His psychiatrist was Gerald Aronson: Background comes from *Los Angeles Magazine*, November 1996; Fred Charles Iklé, *Annihilation from Within: The Ultimate Threat to Nations* (New York: Columbia University Press, 2006); California Licensure Registration, 1955; U.S. Census 1930 and 1940.

395 For some time: Marlon's withdrawal of his personal finances from his father's control is described in Marchak, *Me and Marlon*. She seemed to suggest that it occurred in 1959, but a study of the Pennebaker financial files suggests that it was a more gradual process, and was finally completed sometime in the early fall of 1960 (Pennebaker files, MBEA).

396 "Things are moving along": Hedda Hopper column, as in the *Chicago Tribune*, January 4, 1961.

397 "The Tahitians have withstood": MB interview with Susskind.

399 "He was really floating": Manso, *Brando*.

400 "always completely sincere": Bengt Danielsson, *The Truth About the Film on Bounty* (Madrid: Europa-Press, 1963). Danielsson was a Swedish anthropologist hired by MGM as a technical consultant on the film.

401 "There seemed to be": *New York Times*, May 21, 1962.

401 "Do this, do that": An insider reported this to Hedda Hopper, who printed it in her column on February 18, 1962.

401 "An actor always needs": *The Tonight Show*, May 15, 1963, NBC.

403 "the warmth and candor": *New York Times*, November 30, 1956.

403 "Acting is such a tenuous": Capote, "The Duke in His Domain."

403 "felt he couldn't trust": Karl Malden interview, BSC.

404 "Most of the time": Chris Hodenfield, "Mondo Brando: The Method of His Madness," *Rolling Stone*, May 20, 1976.

404 "the magic of the play": *Songs*, original transcript.

405 "stricken with depression": Ibid.

405 "He simply didn't trust me": Logan, "Answers to Questions," JLC.

405 "the greatest actor": "Am I Directing Marlon Brando" essay by Josh Logan, JLC.

405 try an "experiment": Capote, "The Duke in His Domain."

406 "Josh was a sitting duck": *Songs*, original transcript.

406 "I have received a lot": MB to Joshua Logan, January 24, 1958, MBEA.

406 "dominates" the picture: *Chicago Tribune*, December 25, 1957.

406 "His offbeat acting": *New York Times*, December 6, 1957.

407 "all the Germans were bad": *Songs*, original transcript.

407   "scared to death": Manso, *Brando*.

407   "It's my character": See *Los Angeles Times*, March 30, 1958. Manso, *Brando*, writes of a televised debate between Brando and Shaw on the topic, but I could find no such program in searches of digitized television listings.

407   "Marlon felt terrible": Jack Larson interview, WJM.

408   "positively uncanny": *Film Comment* (May–June 1974).

409   "a much better way": *Songs*, original transcript.

409   "sort of kid gloves": Manso, *Brando*.

410   "Lightning will strike": Various issues, *Motion Picture Daily*.

410   "She's like a vacuum": Manso, *Brando*.

410   "soaring poetry": *Motion Picture Daily*, April 13, 1960.

411   "the film as a whole": *Chicago Tribune*, April 22, 1960.

411   "weird": Herb Lyon's column, as in the *Chicago Tribune*, May 5, 1960. How much audiences were turned away from the picture by its flaws and how much was a result of Marlon's controversial stand on Caryl Chessman's execution, which occurred just as the picture was being released, is impossible to determine.

411   About one-third of the picture: *New York Times*, April 3, 1961.

412   "He would sleep": Manso, *Brando*.

412   "We've gone pretty far": Leonard Lyons's column, as in the *Chicago Defender*, February 20, 1961.

413   "We'd leave one place": *Boston Globe*, March 26, 1961.

413   "Come early and bring": *Boston Globe*, March 21, 1961.

413   Marlon trimmed: Both Herb Lyon's column, as in the *Chicago Tribune*, October 17, 1960, and Leonard Lyons's column, as in the *Chicago Defender*, October 27, 1960, refer to a two-hour, forty-minute version.

414   "a masterpiece": Manso, *Brando*.

414   "It's as brilliant": Hedda Hopper's column, as in the *Hartford Courant*, December 1, 1960. The implication in some previous accounts has been that Paramount came in and took the film from Marlon before he was ready to give it away. Manso, *Brando*, wrote that he had only cut it down to three hours. But a careful consideration of the Pennebaker account books, as well as newspaper coverage of the late 1960 to early 1961 period, indicates that Marlon cut a two-hour-forty-minute version that he was satisfied with. This is what he gave to the studio.

414   "This was going to be": Manso, *Brando*.

415   "walked away from": Thomas, *Marlon*.

415   "It took the same amount": Leonard Lyons's column, as in the *Chicago Defender*, December 14, 1960.

415   "arrived on another world": Various UPI reports, February 21–23, 1960.

416 "He attracted me": Tarita Teriipaia, *Marlon, Mon Amour, Ma Déchirure* (XO edition, 2005).

416 "a longterm contract": Various UPI reports, April 10–11, 1961.

416 "I've been very impressed": *Los Angeles Times*, April 2, 1961.

416 a troop of reporters tagging along: *Brazil* (Indiana) *Daily Times*, February 21, 1961.

416 she made another appearance: *Los Angeles Times*, April 2, 1961.

416 "Tahiti is going to see": Louella Parsons column, as in *San Antonio Light*, April 18, 1961.

416 "exploitation purposes": Leonard Lyons's column, as in the *Chicago Defender*, May 17, 1961.

417 "An interview with Tarita": *Pacific Stars and Stripes*, March 7, 1961.

417 "That," Moreno said, "along with the sheer": Moreno, *A Memoir*.

418 she issued an ultimatum: Rita Moreno to MB, December 19, 1960, MBEA.

418 "He was deeply hurt": Karl Malden interview, BSC.

419 "Paramount is banking": *Film Bulletin*, February 20, 1961.

419 the script, by Sam Peckinpah: The script is dated November 11, 1957. An earlier title had been "Guns Up!"

419 "Waiting for Brando": *New York Times*, March 26, 1961.

419 "I want to make a frontal": *Boston Globe*, October 9, 1955.

420 "The new forty pages": Frank Rosenberg to MB, July 11, 1958, MB AMPAS.

421 "Everyone was calm": *New York Times*, March 26, 1961.

421 "We never got the story": Frederic Raphael, *Eyes Wide Open: A Memoir of Stanley Kubrick* (New York: Ballantine Books, 1999).

422 "Omigod, what next?": Daniel Taradash to Frank Rosenberg, [nd], Frank P. Rosenberg Papers, AMPAS.

422 "You direct yourself": MB *Playboy* interview.

422 "It was [an] ass-breaker": Ibid.

423 "deep personal satisfaction": *Life*, April 4, 1960.

423 "Karl, I've got a film": Karl Malden interview, BSC.

423 "# What do you do for fun": *One-Eyed Jacks* notebooks, MB AMPAS.

425 "two weeks behind": *New York Times*, March 26, 1961.

426 "fervently in love": Marchak, *Me and Marlon*.

426 "Think of the horrible": *Life*, April 4, 1960.

426 "Too prolonged": Luigi Luraschi to Frank Rosenberg and MB, March 10, 1959, MB AMPAS.

426 Rosenberg recalled a day: *New York Times*, February 20, 1961.

427 "That's what you": Scorsese made the remark speaking before a screening of *One-Eyed Jacks* at the Fifty-Fourth New York Film Festival, 2016.

428 "Half a buck": *New York Times*, March 26, 1961.

428 "Wildly enthusiastic": MB interview with Susskind.

428 "over length": Jacob H. Karp to MB, November 10, 1959, Paramount production records, AMPAS.

429 "One of the most awful": MB *Playboy* interview.

429 "he had cut it to the bone": *New York Times*, March 26, 1961.

429 thirty-four suggestions: Jacob H. Karp to MB, November 10, 1959, Paramount production records, AMPAS.

430 On January 27, 1960, he shot: MB AMPAS.

430 "I kept fiddling round": MB *Playboy* interview.

431 "find a way to forget it": MB to Jacob Karp, April 12, 1960, MB AMPAS.

431 "I have every reason": MB to D. A. Doran, April 27, 1960, MB AMPAS.

432 "The original ending": Sheilah Graham's column, as in the *Bluefield* (West Virginia) *Daily Telegraph*, November 15, 1960.

432 "I think it might": Harrison Carroll's column, as in the *Brazil* (Indiana) *Times*, November 21, 1960.

432 "The audience storms": Paramount production records, AMPAS.

432 The print that Paramount: It's possible that the version Marlon saw was actually two hours and *seventeen* minutes. An AP report on October 25, 1960, reported 137 minutes as the length of the upcoming *One-Eyed Jacks*. Either that report was wrong or four minutes were added back in before the release the following March. (*Film Bulletin* reported a length of 141 minutes on release.) It's tempting to wonder if possibly, after Marlon saw the film in February and was disappointed, Paramount restored four minutes, hoping to placate him. If so, it didn't work.

433 "In slimming the picture": *New York Times*, March 26, 1961.

433 "In my film, everybody": Thomas, *Marlon*.

433 "The scissoring reportedly": *Film Bulletin*, February 20, 1961.

433 "It's a potboiler now": Erskine Johnson's column, as in the *Rhinelander* (Wisconsin) *Daily News*, March 28, 1961.

433 "I took a long time": *Songs*, original transcript.

435 "Marlon Brando's first try": *The Hollywood Reporter*, March 15, 1961.

435 "There's a lot of jack": *Variety*, March 15, 1961.

435 "more worlds to conquer": *New York Times*, March 30, 1961.

435 "a self-centered": *The Hollywood Reporter*, July 31, 1961.

435 "two-hour-and-twenty": *Film Bulletin*, March 20, 1961.

436 Budgeted at $2.3 million: Figures come from Paramount production records, AMPAS.

436 "I'm a captain of industry": *Newsweek*, April 10, 1961.

437 "terribly unhappy": Dorothy Kilgallen's column, as in *Salt Lake Tribune*, March 11, 1961.

437 "to end the humiliation": Moreno, *A Memoir.*

437 "The sound of the blow": *Chicago Tribune,* December 29, 1961. Also, AP report and UPI reports; *Los Angeles Times,* December 29, 1961.

439 "That was a period": Jack Larson interview, WJM.

440 "Keening": Moreno, *A Memoir.*

441 One girlfriend recorded: These are the diaries of Saira Ahmed, who sent some of them to Marlon when he was working on his memoir. MBEA.

441 "a few choice epithets": Kashfi, *Brando for Breakfast.*

441 "Give me a child": This was the observation of Stevan Riley, director of *Listen to Me Marlon,* in the *Guardian,* October 2, 2015.

441 "I was here at nine": *Los Angeles Times,* November 3, 1961.

442 His contract gave him: *Saturday Evening Post,* June 16, 1962.

443 "Milly is so exhausted": Kendall (Mrs. Lewis) Milestone to Harry Kleiner, May 10, 1961, Lewis Milestone Papers, AMPAS.

443 "He was directing himself": *Saturday Evening Post,* June 16, 1962.

444 "was really out of control": Arthur Penn interview, BSC.

445 "I was snapping": *Los Angeles Times,* November 3, 1961.

445 "rotten film": Marlon kept Fulbright's press release, dated September 6, 1959, in his *Ugly American* files, MBEA.

445 "attempting to do an honest": *New York Times,* April 24, 1959.

446 "He never said": C. A. Carter interview, WJM.

446 "Anytime they have": See *New York Times,* December 3, 1961.

447 sign a demand: See *Chicago Defender,* April 13, 1960.

447 "Racism is as much": *Songs,* original transcript.

447 "Negroes in Los Angeles": *Los Angeles Times,* February 17, 1962.

447 "libelous and provocative.": *Los Angeles Times,* March 8, 1962.

448 "A dozen varieties": Brando and Lindsey, *Songs.* A notice in Earl Wilson's column in the *Los Angeles Times,* May 5, 1962, reported that Marlon was "dickering for two uninhabited Tahiti islands."

449 "I don't suppose": AP report, as in the *Bridgeport Post,* March 20, 1963.

449 seemed "content": Marchak, *Me and Marlon.*

453 "at a tremendous": *Songs,* original transcript.

453 "I have kids growing up": *Los Angeles Times,* April 30, 1963.

453 "ephemera": This paragraph comes from several sources: *Songs,* original transcript; MB interview with Susskind; and *Meet Marlon Brando.*

455 "If I didn't": AP report, as in the *Bridgeport Post,* March 30, 1963.

455 "a Dead End Kid playing": Kael, "Marlon Brando: An American Hero."

455 "a trifle too arch": (Rochester, New York) *Democrat and Chronicle,* November 9, 1962.

455 "extremely disconcerting": *New York Times,* November 9, 1962.

457 "Look who's turned": AP, as in the *Bridgeport Post,* March 20, 1963.

458 "I didn't want to live": Teriipaia, *Marlon, Mon Amour.*

458 "false and libelous": *New York Times,* January 10, 1963.

459 "he must have even less": Essay on Marlon Brando, Jack Hirshberg Papers, AMPAS.

459 "I'm going after": *Los Angeles Times,* April 30, 1963.

459 "Good evening and welcome": The transcript of Marlon's appearance on *Open End* was provided by the Wisconsin Center for Film and Theater Research. All quotes in this section, unless otherwise cited, are from this transcript.

459 discoursed with Johnny Carson: Marlon appeared on the show on May 15, 1963. It was during Carson's first visit to Los Angeles as host. The tape appears to be lost; Carson would refer to the show during Marlon's later appearance in April 1968. Marlon recalled drinking champagne backstage while waiting to be called onto the set, and getting a little tipsy. "Not being a habitual tippler," he told Carson, "I would listen [to the show] and jabber with people and take a drink and talk, and first thing you're over the abyss, and you haven't realized it, and they say, 'Now, on the stage.'" He said he "almost fell down" as he made his entrance. Carson said he wasn't all that bad, though when he came in, he grunted like Stanley Kowalski: "Those lights are kind of bright, aren't they?" Given his state, it's unclear how eloquent or effective Marlon was in his condemnation of an irresponsible media (1968 videotape courtesy of MBEA).

460 "I was concerned": *Songs,* original transcript.

461 "multimillion dollar": *Today,* April 19, 1963.

464 Angry faces glared: My description comes from *Los Angeles Times,* July 28, 1963, as well as AP and UPI reports from the same day.

466 "To see people just carted": *Songs,* original transcript.

466 "If I have to endure": AP report, July 31, 1963.

466 While the company had assets: Figures from Pennebaker financial and sale records, production and business records for Pennebaker Inc., MBEA. The final balance sheet was made on September 30, 1963. The closing took place on October 25, 1963.

467 Paramount might have absorbed: Figures from Paramount production records, AMPAS.

467 "Those sorts of things": *Songs,* original transcript.

467 "lost his cachet": Manso, *Brando.*

468 "you've got enough": *Los Angeles Times,* November 3, 1961.

468 "It is time now": UPI report, June 12, 1963.

468 "I've seen people refuse": *Los Angeles Times,* July 13, 1963.

469 "If Marlon Brando succeeds": *Chicago Defender,* July 18, 1963.

469 "White traitor": These have been culled from various fan (and hate) mail folders in MBEA.

469 "It was always": Ellen Adler interview, WJM.

470 Sidney Poitier was eager: Telegram, Martin Baum, General Artists Corp., to MB, January 24, 1963; and MB to Martin Baum, March 13, 1963, both at MBEA.

470 "I have never been": Ray Stark to MB, June 7, 1962, MBEA.

471 "Tell that fat-ass": Kashfi diary, MBEA.

471 "Marlon very sweet": Kashfi diary, May 21, 1963, partial transcripts in Kashfi files, MBEA.

471 "Marlon brought the baby": Kashfi diary, January 5, 1963, MBEA.

471 "Help me make": Kashfi diary, March 1963, MBEA.

471 "He is so bright": MB to Anna Kashfi, April 25, 1963, MB legal file on Anna Kashfi, MBEA.

472 "I know you want": *Los Angeles Times*, October 21, 1960.

472 "the finest moment": MB to Anna Kashfi, April 25, 1963, legal file on Anna Kashfi, MBEA. Kashfi would also quote parts of this letter in her memoir, *Brando for Breakfast*.

472 "The sympathy was genuine": Kashfi, *Brando for Breakfast*.

473 "I think it is best": MB to Anna Kashfi, May 24, 1963, legal file on Anna Kashfi, MBEA.

474 "wasteful, vacuous": Kashfi, *Brando for Breakfast*.

474 "Anna must have work": [nd] Summer 1963, legal file on Anna Kashfi, MBEA. Pearlson followed up with Jay Kanter: "[Marlon] asked me to keep after you to keep Anna active. There is no doubt that activity is the best therapy in the world for anyone." Albert Pearlson to Jay Kanter, September 26, 1963, legal file on Anna Kashfi file, MBEA.

475 He'd sometimes pass: Manso, *Brando*.

475 "The one thing": Art Buchwald's column, as in the *Boston Globe*, October 30, 1960.

476 "very unstable": Janice Mars to MB, October 17, 1991, MBEA.

476 "He fell in love": Marchak, *Me and Marlon*.

477 "surprised and disappointed": MB to Jack Paar, [nd] summer 1963 [not sent], MBEA.

478 there was "a need": *Chicago Defender*, July 17 and 18, 1963.

478 "in abeyance": UPI report, July 20, 1963.

479 "to support all civil rights": Hollywood civil rights meeting, March on Washington file, MBEA.

479 "Without the armies": *Good Morning America*, April 4, 1983, ABC, the fifteenth anniversary of Martin Luther King Jr.'s assassination.

479 "We're no organization": *Los Angeles Times*, August 8, 1963.

481 "racial hot spot": *Chicago Defender*, August 26, 1963.

481 "We are here": *New York Times*, August 24, 1963.

481 "was cool all the way": Manso, *Brando*.

482 "company officials were": *New York Times*, August 24, 1963.

482 "serving no purpose": *Chicago Defender*, August 25, 1963.

483 "When you're stuck": *New York Post*, August 23, 1963.

484 "That day was frenetic": *Good Morning America*, April 4, 1983, ABC.

## A FAMILY MAN

489 "I think you're the only": Mario Puzo to MB, January 23, 1970, MBEA (original sold at auction).

490 Director John Boorman: *Garden and Gun*, August–September, 2015.

490 The total domestic revenues: *Variety*, May 15, 1968. Some later historians would suggest that Marlon's films from 1963 to 1971 hadn't actually done all that badly at the box office, but that's a bit of revisionism that doesn't hold up. The exact definition of earnings can get murky, with some films making back their costs years later through foreign bookings or other revenues. But, at the time, the film industry recorded a string of flops for Marlon. In 1967, Lloyd Shearer in *Parade* categorized Marlon's last six pictures—from *Bedtime Story* to *Reflections in a Golden Eye*—as "box-office disappointments" (*Parade*, September 16, 1967). In their first year of release, *Bedtime Story* and *The Chase* both made less than $3.4 million, and *The Appaloosa* made under $4 million; in each case, their production costs were higher. *Morituri* cost $6.2 million to make; it earned back just $3 million. Even a last-minute revision of its name didn't help: the change to *Saboteur: Code Name Morituri* was supposed to boost sales, but didn't (*Pasadena Independent Star News*, October 17, 1965). *A Countess from Hong Kong* cost about $3 million to make and took in a third of that. Even the better-reviewed *Reflections* brought in less than $5 million after costing $4.5 million; if it made back its costs, it was only marginally. In any event, columnist George Anderson labeled it "a flop" (*News Record* [North Hills, PA], December 4, 1968). The films after *Reflections* were barely released. I've drawn these figures from *Variety*'s annual box-office reports, which are based on film rental revenues, but I also used, wherever possible, production records held at AMPAS, NYPL, and MBEA for costs and actual box-office ticket receipts.

490 "I couldn't get arrested": *Rolling Stone*, May 20, 1976.

491 "the best actor," "back from some bad": Kazan, *A Life*.

491 "never admired versatility": Elia Kazan to MB, December 16, 1957, EKP.

492 BRANDO: A CRUSADE: *Chicago Tribune*, June 26, 1968.

492 "overwhelming," "There are issues": *New York Times*, April 17, 1968; *Los Angeles Times*, April 17, 1968.

492 "a tough decision": *The Tonight Show*, April 19, 1968.

493 "was burning up": *Songs*, original transcript.

493 Bobby Hutton: See *Los Angeles Times*, April 17, 1968. For the police lawsuit, see *Los Angeles Times*, June 21, 1968; *Santa Cruz Sentinel*, September 19, 1968; *San Mateo Times*, September 19, 1968; UPI report, May 4, 1969. Marlon appealed it all the way to the Supreme Court, which rejected his appeal (AP report, June 14, 1971).

494 Hakim Jamal: See letter from Jamal to MB, [nd] 1968, MBEA.

494 "immoral as that": Tariq Ali, *Street Fighting Years: An Autobiography of the Sixties* (New York: Citadel Press, 1987).

494 "twelve shotguns": *Vanity Fair*, January 22, 2007.

494 "Mulholland Drive is full": MB *Playboy* interview.

495 "Oh, just fixing": Ibid. Marlon specifically placed this story in "the Sixties."

495 "Brando is known": J. Edgar Hoover memo, December 13, 1968, FBI file on MB, acquired under the Freedom of Information Act.

496 the marriage to Movita: The settlement was finalized in July 1968, after many hours of agonizing testimony. (*Marlon Brando v. Movita Brando*, August 24 and 25, 1967).

496 "Just a note to let you": Coretta Scott King to MB, September 9, 1969, MBEA.

496 Marlon watched in the mirror: Marchak, *Me and Marlon*; also notes from Marchak and others, MBEA.

497 "It was a mythology": *Songs*, original transcript.

497 WILL NOT FINANCE BRANDO: Robert Evans, *The Kid Stays in the Picture* (New York: Hyperion, 1994).

498 "I guess you could call": Englund, *The Way It's Never Been Done*.

498 So, when the director showed up: Coppola's morning visit to Marlon's home has been vaguely dated, with sometimes a December 1970 date being suggested. In her memoir, *Me and Marlon*, Alice Marchak recalled that it took place after a January 7 meeting between Marlon, Coppola, and producer Al Ruddy, apparently when Marlon was given the terms of Paramount's agreement to work with him. This would have been right before he left for London to shoot *The Nightcomers*.

499 "We'll do hand signals": Francis Ford Coppola interview at the 92nd Street Y, New York, June 9, 2015, available on YouTube.

499 "Marlon got the drift": Coppola interview at the Actors Studio, available on YouTube. Also see his interview at the 2017 Tribeca Film Festival, also available on YouTube.

500 "white, Anglo-Saxon": Vernon Scott's syndicated UPI column, as in the *Detroit Free Press*, January 30, 1971.

502 With his eyes closed: My descriptions of the early days and rehearsals on *The Godfather* set come from *Songs*, original transcript; production files, *The Godfather*, AMPAS; original outlines and first, second, and final draft scripts of *The Godfather*, Paramount scripts, AMPAS; production budgets March-July 1971, Paramount scripts, AMPAS; Harlan Lebo, *The Godfather Legacy: The Untold Story of the Making of the Classic Godfather Trilogy* (New York: Touchstone, 2005).

503 "the hottest picture going": Englund, *The Way It's Never Been Done*.

504 "black or socialist": *Life*, March 10, 1972.

504 "I've met Mafia people," "a very close rapport": *Songs*, original transcript.

505 "I don't think that because": Ibid.

506 "like a wind-up toy," "Buddha-like": Draft of press release, *The Godfather*, Paramount, [nd], NYPL.

506 "I think more spatially": David Breskin, *Inner Views: Filmmakers in Conversation* (New York: Da Capo Press, 1997), originally published in *Rolling Stone*, February 7, 1991.

509 One of his greatest regrets: Alex Freeman's column, as in the *Hartford Courant*, October 19, 1965.

509 "empty bottles thrown": For the renewed custody battle of 1964, see the *Los Angeles Times*, December 9, 10, 11, 12, 17, and 24, 1964.

510 Despite the principal: For the 1965 custody battles, see the *Los Angeles Times*, February 18 and 19, 1965.

510 "I want to go up": Testimony of Virginia Harding in Christian Brando's sentencing hearing, quoted in Manso, *Brando*.

510 "With all those women": Jack Larson interview, WJM.

511 "They would be destroyed": *Time*, May 24, 1976.

511 "an excellent father": Walter Scott, *Parade*, March 28, 1965.

511 "lunch, snacks and cokes": Marchak, *Me and Marlon*.

511 "If you're gonna drink": *USA Today*, March 1, 1991.

512 "He never made us feel": Publicity for the film *Listen To Me Marlon*, MBEA.

512 "the emotional algebra," "My first seven years": *Songs*, original transcript.

514 "When we were young": *Vanity Fair*, March 2009.

515 "the little old ladies": (New York) *Daily News*, April 20, 1971.

516 "He was like a big kid": *The David Letterman Show*, February 8, 1982.

516 "One was a rat-faced": *Songs*, original transcript.

516 "I didn't have an answer": Brando and Lindsey, *Songs*. Marlon referred to Bufalino as "Joe," but his name was Russell; Al Martino called him "Russ." As there were no sons or junior members of the Bufalino crime family, "Joe" is clearly an error.

517 "smart enough": *Songs*, original transcript.

518 "Why are you so afraid": For the comparison of the scripts, which are held by a private collector, I am indebted to Susan Mizruchi, *Brando's Smile*.

519 "didn't know whether": *Vanity Fair*, March 2009.

519 "Sometimes it rides": *Songs*, original transcript.

520 "a load of shit": Lebo, *The Godfather Legacy*.

520 "No talent assholes," "dismal, dank failures": *Songs*, original transcript.

521 "It's like pushing": AP report, as in the *St. Louis Post-Dispatch*, December 13, 1964.

521 Marlon didn't trust: For more background, see Manso, *Brando*.

522 "There was a time": *Chicago Sun-Times*, March 26, 1967.

522 "Marlon Brando no longer": UPI report, February 11, 1971.

522 "[T]he whole thing": *New York Times*, August 26, 1965.

522 Huston wasn't quite: *Boston Globe*, October 12, 1967.

522 "He wasn't a man": MB *Playboy* interview.

523 "draw the curtain fast": *New York Times*, March 17, 1967.

523 lack of "self-respect": *Chicago Sun-Times*, March 26, 1967.

523 "He is a movie star": *New York Times*, January 15, 1967.

523 "You're doing pictures": *Vanity Fair*, January 22, 2007.

524 "I don't think we ought": *Meet Marlon Brando*.

525 "You said to me": Elia Kazan to MB, July 12, 1967, EKP.

525 "evident enjoyment": *New York Times*, August 26, 1965.

525 "outstanding [and] authentic": *Boston Globe*, February 18, 1966.

525 "a perfectly fine": Arthur Penn interview, BSC.

525 "quite bad under any": *New York Times*, February 16, 1972.

526 "But nobody saw": *Songs*, original transcript.

526 "a complete sadist": MB *Playboy* interview.

526 "*Burn!* aspires to be": *New York Times*, October 22, 1970.

526 "the most undervalued": *American Film*, June 1986.

527 "I want to do it": John Huston, *An Open Book* (New York: Alfred A. Knopf, 1980).

527 "He gives you twenty-five": *Rolling Stone*, May 26, 1976.

527 "Think of you": MB to John Huston, August 3, 1967, JHP.

528 "excellent, well-developed": *Chicago Tribune*, October 13, 1967.

528 "bold and daring": Elia Kazan to MB, July 12, 1967, EKP.

528 "high time Marlon Brando": *New York Times*, February 3, 1969.

528 "a demobilized storm": *Chicago Tribune*, February 3, 1969.

528 "Chaplin is a man": *Rolling Stone*, May 26, 1976.

528 "Lilliputian": *Songs*, original transcript.

529 "I thought I'd only": Chaplin interview, AMPAS.

529 "nasty and sadistic": *Rolling Stone*, May 26, 1976.

529 "A remarkable talent": MB *Playboy* interview.

529   "Brando, trying to master": *Chicago Tribune*, May 27, 1967.

529   "elegant and airy": *New York Times*, March 17, 1967.

529   "You were terribly": Elia Kazan to MB, July 12, 1967, EKP.

529   "tediously rotten": *Chicago Tribune*, December 23, 1968.

529   "a tasteless piece": *Hartford Courant*, December 20, 1968.

530   "I don't regret any movie": *Songs*, original transcript. In *Listen to Me Marlon*, Marlon is heard asking how he could ever have done such a bad movie as *Candy*. But Avra Douglas said that quote didn't really reflect how he felt about the film. "I don't think he actually took the *Candy* film all that seriously," Douglas said.

530   "I am part of the first": Jack Nicholson, "Remembering Marlon Brando," *Rolling Stone*, August 19, 2004.

530   "Even when Brando": Kael, "Marlon Brando: An American Hero."

531   "Director Francis Ford": *Chicago Tribune*, June 3, 1971.

531   "Brando knows this": Earl Wilson's column, as in the *Hartford Courant*, March 2, 1971.

532   Outside the apartment: Pat Perez interview, WJM. "So he sat out there in the street, hoping Jill would see him from the window."

532   "wouldn't allow Marlon near": Marchak, *Me and Marlon*.

532   "So he sat out there": Pat Perez interview, WJM.

533   "The only way she was": Ibid.

534   "knew how to make": *Film Comment*, January–February, 2015.

534   "street smarts": Brando and Lindsey, *Songs*.

534   "Why don't we go": Ibid.

535   "She was perceptive": Marchak, *Me and Marlon*.

536   "I was always squirming": *Songs*, original transcript.

536   "reality therapy": Background of Harrington comes from the U.S. Census 1940; William Glasser, *Reality Therapy* (New York: Harper and Row, 1965); *Palasadian Post*, September 8, 1988. Harrington's approach was detailed in Glasser's book, which made him very popular with many artists, among them the librettist George Furth, who dedicated his musical play *Company*, written with Stephen Sondheim, to the psychiatrist.

536   "a low, husky rumble": *Songs*, original transcript.

537   "end up in fisticuffs": MB on *Larry King Live*.

537   "laughed me out of a lot of trouble": Brando and Lindsey, *Songs*.

539   "I decided that": *Time*, January 22, 1973.

539   "I did a lot": *Songs*, original transcript.

539   "Bertolocci is extraordinary": *Rolling Stone*, May 20, 1976.

541   "We are usually": *Rolling Stone*, June 21, 1973.

541   "I don't think Bertolucci": *Rolling Stone*, May 20, 1976.

542   "Forty years of Brando's life": *Time*, January 22, 1973.

542 "blithely amoral charm": Ibid.

542 Marlon was quite tender: *Daily Mail*, July 19, 2007.

542 "his character takes": *Time*, January 22, 1973.

543 "Bertolucci," Marlon explained, "wanted me," "The director wanted": *Songs*, original transcript.

543 "I wanted her reaction": Bernardo Bertolucci interview at an event for Cinémathèque Française, 2013, available on YouTube. It is this interview that revived the controversy in 2016 over the film, leading to angry tweets from the likes of Ava DuVernay, Anna Kendrick, Jessica Chastain, and Chris Evans. While the treatment Schneider endured during *Last Tango in Paris* was reprehensible, some of the comments on social media seemed to assume an actual rape had taken place. Comments that Brando could never be looked at the same way again after this incident seem unfair, given what actually happened and the fact that Schneider herself never blamed him.

544 "[Maria] knew perfectly well": *Guardian*, December 7, 2016.

544 "I was so angry": *Daily Mail*, July 19, 2007.

544 "the only novelty": *Washington Post*, December 16, 2016.

545 "was freezing cold": *Songs*, original transcript.

545 "I had so identified": *Newsweek*, February 12, 1973.

545 "You have to understand": *Premiere*, October 2000.

545 "I've been in Freudian": Interview with Gerald Peary, *The Real Paper* (Boston), October 29, 1977.

546 "male definitions": *New York Times*, August 24, 1973.

546 "male fantasy": *New York Times*, March 18, 1973.

546 "the best part": *Daily Mail*, July 19, 2007.

547 "When he realized": *Huffington Post*, January 2, 2011.

547 "There's a certain line": *Rolling Stone*, May 20, 1976.

548 "all about his psychoanalysis": MB *Playboy* interview.

549 In El Paso, Texas: My description of Armes and his investigation comes from *Los Angeles Times*, March 13, 1972; *Los Angeles Times*, May 6, 1973; a long profile in the *Chicago Tribune*, June 11, 1972; an interview with KLAQ, available on YouTube; and other online interviews.

552 "a bad dream": Manso, *Brando*.

554 "the gangster melodrama": *New York Times*, March 16, 1972.

555 "that he dominates": Hirsch, *A Method to Their Madness*.

555 "with his hands behind": Ellen Adler interview, WJM.

558 "Anytime it has to do": MB *Playboy* interview.

559 "Well, this fellow": *Rolling Stone*, May 20, 1976.

560 "where no one would": Marchak, *Me and Marlon*. Also notes from Marchak, MBEA.

562 "a lot of booze": *Boston Globe*, January 30, 1973; also AP reports, January 30 and 31, 1973.

562 "There is a singular lack": Marlon's statement was published in many outlets at the time, including an AP report, February 8, 1973.

563 "The whole thing": *Time*, March 8, 1971.

563 "for the movie men": *Songs*, original transcript.

566 "What the world needs": *Hattiesburg* (Mississippi) *American*, February 13, 1973.

567 she'd been awestruck: Kael's review was published in *The New Yorker* on October 28, 1972.

567 "With a propagandist": *Philadelphia Inquirer*, February 18, 1973.

567 "Meanwhile, two men": For the full story of UA's publicity around *Tango*, see *Village Voice*, February 8, 1973.

568 "Bertolucci is suddenly": *Village Voice*, January 25, 1973.

568 "pornography disguised": *Newsweek*, February 12, 1973.

568 "absolutely filthy": *New York Times*, April 26, 1973.

569 "the resurgence of one": *Time*, January 22, 1973.

569 "define the two poles": Hirsch, *A Method to Their Madness*.

569 "gave much more": MB *Playboy* interview.

570 "We will occupy": *New York Times*, March 1, 1973.

570 "All they were asking": Transcription of unsourced interview, [nd], MBEA.

571 "eating away at America's": UPI report, May 2, 1973.

571 "We are not able," "If Hitler," "Cynics and doubters": UPI report, July 11, 1968.

572 "one of the few non-Indians": *San Bernardino County Sun*, December 31, 1963.

572 "We went to the jail," "I always enjoyed": MB *Playboy* interview.

573 "That's something I can't": *Meet Marlon Brando*.

573 "It is *not* the plight": *Songs*, original transcript.

573 "There is no Negro problem": *Ebony*, August 1965.

574 "My name is Sacheen": Littlefeather's speech is taken directly from the video of her appearance at the Academy Awards, available on YouTube. She did *not* conclude her statement with a promise that Marlon would head to Wounded Knee, as Manso (*Brando*) writes.

575 "restrained by six security": Dexter Thomas, "Meet the Woman Who Refused Marlon Brando's Oscar and Inspired Jada Pinkett Smith's Boycott," *Los Angeles Times*, February 5, 2016.

575 "Those people were booing": MB on *Dick Cavett*.

575 "what the hell": The full text of Marlon's statement was published in *New York Times*, March 30, 1973.

576 "I knew Marlon was into": Manso, *Brando*.

577 When Littlefeather arrived: Littlefeather's account of her Academy Awards appearance and its aftermath come from a letter she wrote to the Academy, dated May 25 and 26, 1986, AMPAS; and from the interview she gave to Dexter Thomas, "Meet the Woman Who Refused Brando's Oscar," in reaction to the #OscarsSoWhite movement; Manso, *Brando*.

578 "I thought it would be": MB on *Dick Cavett*.

579 "That's how Hollywood": Elaine Stritch interview, WJM.

579 "I don't think Mr. Brando": Letter from Sacheen Littlefeather to the Academy of Motion Picture Arts and Sciences, May 25 and 26, 1973, AMPAS.

580 "Mr. Ford is a great man": *Los Angeles Times*, April 1, 3, 1973.

580 "in whatever way": *New York Times*, March 30, 1973.

581 "Wounded Knee was surrounded": MB on *Dick Cavett*.

582 "He has served as": *Chicago Defender*, April 5, 1973.

582 "It's not possible": Ellen Adler interview, BSC.

582 "Truth lasts forever": Thomas, "Meet the Woman Who Refused Brando's Oscar."

583 From the backseat: Marlon's Midwest journey is detailed in *Lincoln* (Nebraska) *Journal Star*, July 25, 1973; *Press and Sun-Bulletin* (Binghamton, New York), July 31, 1973; various UPI reports, July 26 and 27, 1973; *Omaha World-Herald*, June 8, 2013.

583 "fresh air all day": Frances Brando recollections, transcript, MBEA.

584 "a hero whose vanity": *Rolling Stone*, May 20, 1976.

584 "Where is the slim": Janice Mars to MB, [nd] August 1991, MBEA.

585 "Jill thought Marlon": Pat Perez interview, WJM. Perez recalled many details of this trip taken by Jill and Marlon to explore their Midwestern roots.

586 "spoke the same cultural": Brando and Lindsey, *Songs*.

586 "They talked about the sound": Pat Perez interview, WJM.

587 "I had a real Ford assembly": *Time*, May 24, 1976.

587 "We had made a civilized": Moreno, *A Memoir*.

588 "Up to then": Brando and Lindsey, *Songs*.

589 "storms and clouds": Manso, *Brando*.

589 "a lot of kidding around": Pat Perez interview, WJM.

590 "being willing to change": UPI report, July 11, 1968.

591 "a basket case of emotional": *Los Angeles Times*, March 1, 1991.

591 "I never said anything bad": Ibid.

591 "I'm very glad": Manso, *Brando*.

592 "injuries to his nervous": UPI report, January 6, 1976.

593 "a great tragedy": *Vanity Fair*, March 2009.

593 "I not only love him": *Time*, May 24, 1976.

### EPILOGUE: THE BARD OF THE HOLLYWOOD HILLS

596 "Maybe food": *Los Angeles Times*, March 1, 1991.

596 "It's the King of Fat": Ellen Adler interview, BSC.

596 "a grisly conclusion": Brando and Lindsey, *Songs*.

596 He'd been carrying on: A note from Saroyan in Marlon's papers shows he hadn't changed much from the 1960s. "Something's not as it should be," Saroyan wrote. "There's an odd separation, a coldness . . . Maybe I pushed a little too far, maybe it's the moon [but] I kept thinking: Marlon's never really been vulnerable with me, told me his secrets, his fears, shared his soul—but I have. And that scares me. I feel like a fool." (Lucy Saroyan to MB, March 25, 1974, MBEA). Rita Moreno could have written the exact same note a decade earlier.

597 Their break came in Hawaii: Marchak, *Me and Marlon*; Pat Perez interview.

597 "As Jill watched": Pat Perez interview, WJM. Writing in his memoir, disguising Jill as "Weonna," Marlon says his former fiancée then seduced one of his sons in retaliation. (He left it vague as to which one.) Pat Perez disputed this: "Jill and Christian were very close, and had been since he was young. She may have cried in his arms as she said good-bye." Christian was eighteen years old at that point; as far as Perez knew, nothing more occurred. "But perhaps that in itself was inappropriate," she conceded. Marlon certainly thought so. He didn't blame "his boy," however: Jill had done this to get back at him, he said.

597 "symbolized my mother": Brando and Lindsey, *Songs*.

597 But then on August 6: Jill Banner (Mary Kathryn Molumby) death certificate, August 7, 1982.

597 "Marlon was inconsolable": Marchak, *Me and Marlon*.

597 "He talked about her": Avra Douglas interview, WJM.

598 "every waking hour": Englund, *The Way It's Never Been Done*.

599 "He thought if he took": Ellen Adler interview, WJM.

599 "Working on his memoir": Lindsey, *Ghost Scribbler*.

600 "I can't talk about that": Ellen Adler interview, BSC.

601 "Everything just happens": AP video interview, September 4, 2013.

601 "I have spent my life": He told this to Pat Quinn, quoted in Manso, *Brando*.

601 "Brando was inviting me": *Telegraph*, October 16, 2015.

601 "He might have enjoyed": Avra Douglas interview, WJM.

602 "Look, you people have done": *Rolling Stone*, May 20, 1976.

603  "out of control": *New York Times*, May 20, 1976.

603  "People were embalmed": *Rolling Stone*, May 20, 1976.

603  "a man eating all": Eleanor Coppola, *Notes on the Making of "Apocalypse Now"* (New York: Limelight Editions, 1979).

603  "You're making an enormous": MB tape recordings. Also see the film *Listen to Me Marlon*.

604  "adventure yarn with delusions": *New York Times*, August 15, 1979.

604  After the film's release: An article in *Life* magazine pinned most of the film's problems on Marlon; it seemed to be *The Saturday Evening Post* all over again. Although Coppola was not quoted as a source, Marlon was convinced, without much evidence, the director had sold him out. "Francis Coppola, he's a prick," he raged. "How could he do that to me? I saved his fucking ass and he shows his appreciation by dumping on me" (MB tape recordings). Also see the film *Listen to Me Marlon*.

604  "the imperative of his talent": *Time*, January 22, 1973.

605  "Sid Caesar's double talk": Avra Douglas interview, WJM.

605  "It's amazing to see": *New York Times*, July 8, 2001.

606  "He did not enjoy": Avra Douglas interview, WJM.

607  "monstrous": Anne Jackson and Eli Wallach interview, BSC.

608  "so overweight": Jack Larson interview, WJM.

608  "Don't ever leave me": Ellen Adler interview, WJM.

608  "It was without doubt": Teriipaia, *Marlon, Mon Amour*.

608  "I realize": Brando and Lindsey, *Songs*.

609  "the analysis of the human genome": *Songs*, original transcript.

609  "If I've come closer": MB tape recordings.

610  "ecological test tube": *Rolling Stone*, May 20, 1976.

610  "It was like a living": Video of Teihotu Brando, available on YouTube.

611  "You are the greatest actor": MB to Sean Penn, July 4, 2001, MBEA.

611  "I'm sure he would have": Austin Wilkin interview, WJM.

611  "He did a lot": Avra Douglas interview, WJM.

613  "At the end": Ellen Adler interview, WJM.

613  "I'm not sure I will ever": *Songs*, original transcript.

613  "anguish, the wailing": Marchak, *Me and Marlon*.

614  "I considered [Bob]": *Songs*, original transcript.

614  "We've all been guilty": MB *Playboy* interview.

615  "By the time I get": Ellen Adler interview, BSC.

616  "to find something": *Time*, January 22, 1973.

618  "As he lay back looking": Englund, *The Way It's Never Been Done*.

618  "kind of the cliché thing": Johnny Depp interview, available on YouTube.

618  "He did appreciate": Avra Douglas interview, WJM.

619 "no one deeper, truer": Foster Hirsch interview, WJM.

619 "adjusted how most": Nicholson, "Remembering Marlon Brando."

619 "Show respect for what": *Songs*, original transcript.

620 "freezing and sick": MB *Playboy* interview.

621 "Oh, Marlon": Janice Mars to MB, [nd] August 1991, MBEA.

# INDEX

# ABOUT THE AUTHOR

WILLIAM J. MANN is the author of several books on film, popular culture, and politics, including *Tinseltown: Murder, Morphine, and Madness at the Dawn of Hollywood*, winner of the Edgar Award for Best Fact Crime; *The Wars of the Roosevelts: The Ruthless Rise of America's Greatest Political Family; Kate: The Woman Who Was Hepburn*, a *New York Times* Notable Book; and *Wisecracker: The Life and Times of William Haines*, winner of the Lambda Literary Award for Best Biography. He is an assistant professor of history at Central Connecticut State University.